BUSINESS LAW

Foundations for the 21st Century

Terrence P. Dwyer, J.D. | **Thomas A. Miller, J.D.**

Western Connecticut State University

Kendall Hunt
publishing company

Kendall Hunt
p u b l i s h i n g   c o m p a n y

www.kendallhunt.com
Send all inquiries to:
4050 Westmark Drive
Dubuque, IA 52004-1840

Dedication

To the loving memory of my parents, Terrence J. and Anne M. Dwyer, who taught me the value of education, and to the loving memory of my mother-in-law Agnes B. Cagney, who inspired me to write.

    And, as always, to Joan, who continues to encourage, edit, and endure my writing projects.

T.P.D.

To my wife, Stacey, who has loved and supported me in equally immeasurable measure, and to all of the people, of which there are far too many to list in such a short space, who have taught me to love to learn the law.

T.A.M.

Special Dedication

To Professor Emeritus Dr. Harold B. Schramm whose guidance and example has assisted each of us in our respective journeys in academia. In and out of the classroom your concern for the welfare of your students, as well as that of your colleagues, served as a reminder that the privilege of teaching is so much more than just the application of rote lecture and the extrication of memorized facts. Teaching is a creative activity that calls upon our humanity. Thank you for that enduring lesson.

T.P.D. & T.A.M.

Contents

Preface

This textbook, like so many projects and undertakings in life, began with a conversation. The conversation turned into an idea. Fortunately, the idea did not fade nor was it shelved under the weight of other tasks and responsibilities. Rather, it gained momentum as we discussed teaching philosophies and student learning outcomes. Invariably it led to our discussion about the teaching of a common course at our university, Commercial Law, and the need to find a suitable resource for our students. Our conversation and the problems we expressed to each other was further guided by our different approaches to the same course. One was the approach of the younger academic who regularly taught the 16-week course, the other of the older academic who taught the shortened six week summer online version of the course. An additional novelty to our discussions was that they were held in my office where only a few years earlier Tom entered as an undergraduate student to discuss some legal issue. Fast forward and Tom is back entering my office to discuss a legal issue but this time as a colleague. As a cum laude law school graduate and former law review editor Tom returned to his alma mater, Western Connecticut State University, as a professor after a few years in private law practice. Not too far removed from the classroom he brought the perspective of scholar and student to the project. Together we agreed that we could design and write a textbook to serve our teaching needs and the learning needs of our students. From that simple desire we also endeavored to create a textbook useful to faculty and students at other universities.

To begin with we had to come up with an outline and decide how we wanted to structure the book. We each reviewed other business law texts and found as many disparities as commonalities. While you could review a criminal law or criminal procedure law textbook and find slight organizational variations you would be hard pressed to see any major difference in the coverage of certain substantive areas of law. This was not the case in our review of business law texts. One business law textbook might have a substantial chapter on bankruptcy law while another included no mention yet provided a comprehensive coverage of internet sales and goods transfers. A third text might have included bankruptcy but in a brief chapter, though it was quite extensive in its explanation of employment law. And, what of employment law? Does such a chapter include labor law, which arguably is related but really is a separate substantive area? Or should a chapter more properly be about labor and employment law? As you see, our problem was not going to be a shortage of substantive material for the text, it was to be our choice of what substantive areas we thought appropriate to include in the text. To this discussion we brought our own biases and interests which quickly gave way to a common understanding of what we felt were the core student learning outcomes that should result from a business law course. What resulted is the basic outline of our text that you find in the Table of Contents.

As a university professor you have one concern each day and that is the learning outcome of your students. At the end of every semester you want the students, individually and collectively, to take a body of knowledge from the course that they did not previously possess. Each semester is about the student's growth and the job of the professor is to figure out how to enhance that growth and bring value to the learning experience. Too often textbooks are not written with the student in mind. They are either too formulaic in approach and do not properly convey the necessary material or are too scholarly and incomprehensible. A text should be challenging but readable. It should also be a resource to be referenced when needed. While we do not profess to be experts at this, nor desire to be overly critical of the multitude of text authors who have toiled to produce their works (and we can attest to the fact that it is no easy task), we simply want to provide something new in the field that we know has worked for us. Our material has evolved from our experiences teaching the subject matter as well as our practical experience in many of these areas as legal practitioners.

Justice Oliver Wendell Holmes wrote in *The Common Law*, "The life of the law has not been logic; it has been experience."[1] With that being said, the challenge for us as professors was to teach Commercial Law to students who may have limited experience as far as business or legal involvement is concerned. We set out to do so, as we have in many other law courses we teach, by immersing them in the law, for this is part of the experience Holmes referred to. Thus, we have them read case law, past and present, and put the case law in the context of a particular situation, or perhaps a particular time, since law evolves over time. This is the follow through to Holmes' famous legal maxim, best expressed in the remaining paragraph to his opening chapter of *The Common Law*:

> *"The felt necessities of the time, the prevalent moral and political theories, intuitions of public policy, avowed or unconscious, even the prejudices which judges share with their fellow-men, have had a good deal more to do than the syllogism in determining the rules by which men should be governed. The law embodies the story of a nation's development through many centuries, and it cannot be dealt with as if it contained only the axioms and corollaries of a book of mathematics. In order to know what it is, we must know what it has been, and what it tends to become. We must alternately consult history and existing theories of legislation. But the most difficult labor will be to understand the combination of the two into new products at every stage. The substance of the law at any given time pretty nearly corresponds, so far as it goes, with what is then understood to be convenient; but its form and machinery, and the degree to which it is able to work out desired results, depend very much upon its past."*

The law is not stagnant, nor does it atrophy over time. It is vibrant, progressive, responsive, and yet, reliable. We did not want to lose that in our text. We wanted to make the law accessible and relatable to the student. Because if it is not then it becomes something foreign, remote, and dangerous.

The law guides our relations—those personal, professional and international. It is a constant in our lives; whether or not we actually realize its reach, the law surrounds us in our daily social interplay. It civilizes us and defines us as a society. The world of business is so immersed in the law that every business curriculum requires at least one full semester on the subject. Our undertaking is therefore not taken lightly. We owe a debt of service to those legal scholars and practitioners who came before us as well as a responsibility to ensure the law remains a guiding light in our collective lives. It is with this humble goal that we have written this text for business students who will carry on the noble aims of commerce and business transactions which are methods for improvement of all society.

Terrence P. Dwyer, J.D.

---

[1] Holmes, Oliver Wendell Jr. (1881). *The Common Law*, Boston: Little, Brown and Company.

About The Authors

Terrence P. Dwyer, J.D.   Terry Dwyer is a tenured Professor in the Division of Justice & Law Administration at Western Connecticut State University in Danbury, CT where he teaches within the Legal Studies curriculum. He received his undergraduate degree from Fordham University in 1985 and his law degree from Pace University School of Law in 1991. He subsequently earned a post-graduate certificate in Labor Studies from Cornell University. He is admitted to practice law in Connecticut and New York, as well as before the Southern and Eastern Districts of New York and the United States Supreme Court. His law practice has included several general practice areas over the years, including real estate; criminal; civil and commercial litigation; business formation; estate planning and administration; and public sector labor law. Professor Dwyer's representation of clients has included litigation before the National Labor Relations Board, NYC Office of Administrative Trials & Hearings, NYC Office of Collective Bargaining, NYS Public Employees Relations Board, NYS Division of Human Rights, trial matters in state and federal court, and client appeals to the New York State Appellate Term, 9th Judicial District and the New York State Appellate Division, 2nd and 3rd Departments.

Professor Dwyer has authored over 50 articles, including several peer-reviewed academic articles and is the author of the textbook *Legal Issues in Homeland Security: U.S. Supreme Court Cases, Commentary & Questions.* Professor Dwyer's publications have been cited in criminal justice textbooks, academic articles and case briefs before the U.S. Supreme Court.

Professor Dwyer has been a three-time recipient of the Ancell School of Business "Outstanding Faculty Member" award and in 2016 was recognized by the National Society of Leadership & Success, WCSU Sigma Alpha Pi Chapter, with the Excellence in Teaching Award. In 2017 Professor Dwyer was honored with the title of Connecticut State University Professor.

Thomas Miller, J.D.   After several semesters as an adjunct instructor Tom Miller joined the faculty of Western Connecticut State University as a one-year special appointment professor in 2016, just seven years removed from his own graduation from Western Connecticut with a degree in Justice & Law Administration. In January 2018 he was awarded a full-time tenure track position as an Assistant Professor. He graduated summa cum laude from Western Connecticut State University in 2009 and in 2012 he graduated cum laude from the Regent University School of Law. While attending Regent, Professor Miller had the honor to serve on the editorial board of the Regent University Law Review. During law school he also served as a law clerk for the United States Senate Committee on the Judiciary.

Prior to establishing the Law Offices of Thomas Miller LLC, Professor Miller served as a temporary assistant clerk for Stamford Superior Court. While working for the court Professor Miller played a hands-on role in the management of more than a thousand cases in addition to editing and reviewing judicial decisions.

Professor Miller teaches a variety of courses including Commercial Law, Legal Writing, Constitutional Law, and Moot Court. Professor Miller also serves as the Director of the University's Moot Court Program. In 2015, he received the "Outstanding Faculty Member" Award for WCSU's Ancell School of Business, and is the only adjunct professor in any discipline at WCSU to earn this designation.

Professor Miller is admitted to practice in both state and federal courts in Connecticut where he has been extensively engaged in civil and commercial litigation matters, business formation, contract review, property transactions and tort litigation. He also serves as a State of Connecticut Justice of the Peace.

INTRODUCTION TO THE LEGAL SYSTEM AND LEGAL REASONING

LEARNING OUTCOMES

Upon completion of this chapter the student will be able to:

1 Understand the connection between business and the law.
2 Be familiar with legal citation and terminology.
3 Discuss the concept of judicial review and the different methods of judicial interpretation.
4 Identify the different schools of legal philosophy.
5 Brief a case and know how to do legal research.

KEY TERMS

binding authority	mootness
dictum	persuasive authority
interlocutory appeal	ripeness
judicial review	standing
justiciability	stare decisis

I. Business and the Law

The business world is essentially about relationships and business law is concerned with the respective rights and liabilities among those within the business relationship. There are simply no areas of the business world that the law does not touch. Whether it be the relationship between sellers and buyers of goods, employers and employees, owners and tenants of property under a commercial lease, or third-party beneficiaries to an agreement, the law outlines and defines the respective obligations among the parties. It is for this reason that a core requirement in any business school curriculum is Business Law, also known as Commercial Law. Further, it is the reason law students endure two semesters of Contract Law in addition to a semester each of Torts and Property Law among the many first year, 1L, courses they will encounter. Of course, Civil Procedure is another required course as is Constitutional Law and the Federal Courts. As the law student advances through the law school curriculum he or she may enroll in a Remedies course or spend a semester studying the finer points of Secured Transactions. Add to the curriculum Securities, Corporations, Real Estate Financing, Negotiable Instruments, and you get the idea that the law is primarily concerned with the regulation, transfer, and protection of property and property rights. The separate realms of Criminal Law and Criminal Procedure seem almost a world away in content and practicality. Though we do find that in the business world crimes are committed and the offenders, who we generally and genteelly refer to as white collar criminals, are punished and subjected to the harsh realities of the American criminal justice system, it still remains an anomaly in the greater scheme of American and international business relations.

What then is this area of the law we have condensed into this text and labelled Business Law? Well to answer that question is not so simple a task and the actual answer may vary among legal scholars and practitioners alike. We may be best served by first seeking to define what we mean when we say "business," what exactly do we mean by the term? The U.S. Supreme Court, in a 1911 case concerned with the constitutionality of an act of Congress known as "The Corporation Tax" law, defined business as *". . . a very comprehensive term and embraces everything about which a person can be employed. Black's Law Dict., 158, citing People v. Commissioners of Taxes, 23 N.Y. 242, 244. "That which occupies the time, attention and labor of men for the purpose of a livelihood or profit." Bouvier's Law Dictionary, Vol. I, p. 273.*[1] An even earlier definition can be found in the Massachusetts case of *Goddard v. Chaffee, 2 Allen 395, 75 Am. Dec. 796,* which held that "business" is *"a word of large signification, and denotes the employment or occupation in which a person is engaged to procure a living."* Subsequent Massachusetts cases citing *Goddard* further elaborated on the court's definition of business as not being restricted to a single act pertaining to a business but included a series of acts for that same purpose as engaging in business.[2] However, these are older, much antiquated and long forgotten cases, replaced with a more intricate statutory framework and well-developed body of post-colonial, modern case law. Add to this the regulatory edifices of government and the extensive administrative state that has been created. The definition of "business" has thus evolved beyond its more simplistic iterations in cases like *Goddard* to reflect the realities of modern society and its progress from industrial muscle to digital intelligence. Similarly, what we substantively refer to as "business law" has evolved as well.

For a definition of "business law" we can turn to an online source which defines it as follows: *"Business law encompasses the law governing contracts, sales, commercial paper, agency and employment law, business organizations, property, and bailments. Other popular areas include insurance, wills and estate planning, and consumer and creditor protection."*[3] Another online source defines it under the term Commercial Law and describes it as: *"A broad concept that describes the substantive law that governs transaction between business entities . . . Commercial law includes all aspects of business, including advertising and marketing, collections and bankruptcy, banking contracts, negotiable instruments, secured transactions, and trade in general. It covers both domestic and foreign trade; it also regulates trade between the states."*[4] The clearest sense of any definition that you will find is that business law is many things and covers many core areas of commercial relationships and transactions. The substantive area of law is so broad and comprehensive that a single textbook could easily resemble the monolithic United States tax code and consume thousands of pages. However, there is general agreement on several substantive areas

---

[1] *Flint v. Stone Tracy Co.,* 220 U.S. at 171 (1911)

[2] See e.g., *Baker v. Willis,* 123 Mass. 194 (1877); *Allen v. Commonwealth,* 188 Mass. 59 (1905)

[3] U.S. Legal.com, *Business and Legal Definition* (December 20, 2016), http://definitions.uslegal.com/b/business/

[4] Farlex Inc., The Free Dictionary, *Commercial Law* (December 20, 2016), http://Legal-dictionary.thefreedictionary.com/Business+law

of law that a student must encounter in order to have a firm foundation in business law. These substantive areas include administrative law, contracts, torts, property, business entities, employment law, civil procedure, the court systems and alternative dispute resolution, and the Uniform Commercial Code (U.C.C.). This textbook will cover many of those substantive areas as an introduction into the multitudinous entanglements between business and the law.

II. Legal Citation and the Language of the Law

The law, like any profession, has its own language and terms of art. Additionally, legal references and citations are different than those the average student may be familiar with. Let's begin with legal citations. Rather than follow the MLA (Modern Language Association) or APA (American Psychological Association) formats legal writing conforms to *The Blue Book: A Uniform System of Citation*. *The Blue Book* is so named because since 1939 its cover has been blue. Originally the creation of Karl Llewellyn at Yale Law School, *The Blue Book* has been the standard for law schools in teaching students how to properly cite statutes, law reviews, case law, and other reference sources. It is the source most commonly known and remembered by practicing attorneys, though it is not the exclusive source of legal citation style. Alternate citation manuals are the *ALWD Citation Manual* published by the Association of Legal Writing Directors and *The Maroon Book*, an alternate citation manual created by the University of Chicago School of Law and *The Indigo Book*, a free content version of the 10th edition of *The Blue Book*. Lastly, there is the *The Supreme Court's Style Guide*, a heretofore closely held national secret until made available on Amazon.com in 2016. More of a secret treasure trove of stylistic idiosyncrasies and Supreme Court preferences it nonetheless now has a place among citation authorities. Below are some examples of citation format and style:

U.S. Supreme Court

Pennoyer v. Neff, 95 U.S. 714 (1877)

Kelo v. City of New London, 545 U.S. 469, 125 S. Ct. 2655, 162 L. Ed. 2d 439 (2005)

Federal Courts of Appeals

United Technologies Corp. v. Federal Aviation Administration, 102 F.3d 688 (2d Cir., 1996)

Raven Services Corp. v. National Labor Relations Board, 315 F.3d 491 (5th Cir., 2002)

Federal District Courts

King v. Charleston Cnty. Sch. Dist., 664 F. Supp. 2d 571 (D.S.C. 2009)

Haghighi v. Russian-Am. Broad. Co., 945 F. Supp. 1233 (D. Minn. 1996).

Court Rules

Fed. R. Civ. P. 12(b)(6)

N.Y. CPLR 3211(a)(5)

Constitutions

U.S. Const. art. I, § 3

Conn. Const. art. IV, § 4

Art V, 3(b)(3), Fla. Const.3

Federal and State Statutes

18 U.S.C. § 1001

735 ILCS 5/2-615, 2-619 (West 2010) (Note: ILCS is Illinois Compiled Statutes)

Further guidance on proper legal citation can be found online at The Legal Information Institute of Cornell University, https://www.law.cornell.edu/citation/ or *The Indigo Book* at https://law.resource.org/pub/us/code/blue/IndigoBook.pdf or at the many official state reporter sites found on the internet.

There is a distinct etymology to many legal words and phrases. To attempt a broad survey of the development of what is referred to as legal English in the narrow space we devote here to legal language and usage would be impossible. A better comprehensive source for students interested in word origins and historical development would be *The Language of the Law* by David Mellinkoff. Another good source is *Legal Language* by Peter M. Tiersma. Additional useful primers on avoiding the arcane and cloudy language too often found in legal writing are *Plain English for Lawyers* by Richard C. Wydick and *Legal Writing in Plain English* by Bryan A. Garner. However, we are able to provide a short outline of the development of legal terms in the English language and the reason for students to know what certain legal phrases mean.

The language of the law contains many words of French and Latin origin. It is not necessary to know either language in order to understand and use these words or phrases since they have attained a separate life of their own by steady usage. In a sense they have become professional jargon, or what some would refer to as "legalese," a verbal shorthand easily understood among working professionals. It is a language and usage not too dissimilar from what may be found in other professions. However, the law, because of its Latin roots, retains a sense of aloofness and seeming inaccessibility. Terms like res ipsa loquitur, which translated means the "thing speaks for itself," refers to a common law tort doctrine wherein negligence is inferred from the nature of the accident or incident without any direct evidence of an individual's conduct. Attorneys may refer to a client's claim as being "res ipsa" which means little to the client, yet another attorney involved in the same conversation would know exactly what was being said. The same confusion and inability to comprehend can come from reading legalese in a court's decision or an article in a law review. While an overextended use of this language form is not a good sign of clear and comprehensive legal writing, and is actually pedantic, such writing exists and the reader must be able to wade through it. In his 1987 book *Cultural Literacy: What Every American Needs to Know*, the literary critic and academic E.D. Hirsch wrote that in order for an individual to be truly culturally literate he or she had to have a certain base of knowledge and awareness of past events, idioms, places, symbols, and people. It was only with this base of knowledge that the individual could be truly culturally acclimated and literate as a reader. Our similar argument pertaining to understanding the law and being literate within the law's cultural milieu is that the student must know and understand legal terms and their specific meanings in order to fully comprehend what they read and discuss. To that end we provide below a short list of significant legal terms and phrases every student should know in their reading and study of the law:

Latin origin:

Ad hoc – for this

Ad valorem – according to value

Amicus curiae – friend of the court

Certiorari – to be apprised, a writ of review

Caveat emptor – buyer beware

De jure – according to the law

De novo – anew, as in trial de novo, a new trial when a verdict is not reached in the first trial

Ergo – therefore

Erratum – having been made in error

Ex ante – of before, or before the event

Forum non conveniens – a disagreeable judicial forum

Habeas corpus – you have the body, a writ used to challenge the legality of detention

Ibid – in the same place, abbreviation of ibedem, used when citing sources to signify the same prior identical source

Idem – the same, used in citation to indicate the material came from the same cited source as the prior though not the same page or location

Inter alia – among others, used to indicate a cited source has been gathered from another larger, list of sources

Inter vivos – among or between the living, as in a gift between living parties

In forma pauperis – in the manner of a pauper or a poor person, refers to an individual unable to afford the costs of a legal proceeding

In limine – at the threshold, as in a motion in limine, made prior to the resolution of a case

Lis pendens – suit pending

Mandamus – we command, a writ issued by a higher court to a lower court or government officials to compel them to perform some administrative act

Mens rea – guilty mind

Modus operandi – method of operation

Nisi prius – unless first, refers to a court of original jurisdiction

Nolle prosecui – not to prosecute

Nolo contendere – I do not wish to dispute

Nunc pro tunc – now for then, an act by a court to correct a prior clerical or procedural error

Obiter dictum – a thing said in passing

Pendente lite – when the litigation is pending

Per curiam – through the court, a decision rendered by a multi-judge panel

Prima facie – at first face or glance, a matter sufficiently based in the evidence to be regarded as true

Pro hac vice – for this turn, refers to a lawyer who is allowed by a court to appear in a case and represent a client though not admitted to the jurisdiction

Pro se – for himself, representing oneself without counsel

Pro tanto – for so much, a partial payment of an award or claim based on the judgment debtor's ability to pay

Quantum meruit – as much as was earned or is deserved, a quasi-contractual remedy that allows payment for incomplete work

Quid pro quo – this for that, refers to an exchange of services, also refers to a form of sexual harassment based on an individual's submission to an employer's or supervisor's sexual advances in return for an employment benefit such as a raise or promotion

Quoad hoc – as to this, used to refer to some named thing

Ratio decedendi – reason for the decision

Res judicata – a thing decided

Res ipsa loquitur – the thing speaks for itself

Respondeat superior – let the master answer

Scienter – knowledge or knowingly

Seriatim – in a series

Stare decisis – to stand by things decided

Sua sponte – of its own accord

Sui generis – of its own kind or genus

Supra – above, used in citation to refer to previously cited source

Ultra vires – beyond the powers

French origin:

Cestui que trust – the beneficiary of a trust

Chattel – personal property or goods

Chose – thing, as in chose in action or chose in possession

Cy-pres doctrine – the power of the court to transfer one charitable trust to another charitable trust when the first trust may no longer exist or be able to operate

Escheats – a reversion of property, normally used when it reverts back to the state

Estoppel – prevention of a party from contradicting a position previously taken in a matter

Force majeure – superior force, clause in certain contracts, usually insurance contracts, that frees a party from liability or performance based on acts of God

Laches – laxity, a common law doctrine that disallows an action to be brought after the passage of time

Mortgage – dead pledge, refers to security interests in property

Oyer et terminer – to hear and determine, reference to jurisdiction of law courts

Parol evidence – oral or spoken evidence, rule of law that disallows the introduction of extrinsic evidence to contradict or prove the elements of an unambiguous fully executed contract

Profit a prendre – individual's right to take the "fruits" of the property of another, e.g., mining and mineral rights, crops and planting rights

Per autre vie – during the term of another's life

Replevin – a civil suit to recover unlawfully taken personal property

Voir dire – to say the truth, process used to challenge evidence submitted at trial or to determine the suitability of jurors in a case

While the above list is not exhaustive it covers the more common words and phrases a student may encounter. Those that the student may come across that are not on the list can easily be found in a secondary source like Black's Law Dictionary or Oran's Law Dictionary.

Still, the question remains—where did the Latinate base come from and why do we find many French phrases and French derivative words in the legal lexicon? To answer that question we must go far back in history. In the 11th century, specifically the year 1066, the Duke of Normandy, William the Conqueror, crossed the English Channel and invaded England. Seeking to gain what he deemed to be his rightful inheritance, William defeated the forces of King Harold at the Battle of Hastings. What followed was an influx of French words into the English vocabulary as Norman-French became the official language of the English court. There are an estimated 10,000 words that entered the English lexicon with more than one-third of them surviving in the present-day English language. Of those, several have remained in use in legal language. After the Norman Conquest the division between an Anglo-Norman speaking aristocracy and an English speaking lower class led to the use of Anglo-Norman in government and the courts. Latin had already established its place in the Roman Empire and its influence would spread through Germanic tribes but mainly survived in the texts, transcriptions and teachings of Catholic monks. Even with the loss of Norman territories by 1204 and a transition wholly to English, Latin was still used in the church and it was the lingua franca of Europe. Latin, as it was used in antiquity, occupied a place among the educated, was taught in universities and remained an international language. Its influence in ecclesiastical courts carried over into government courts. The fact that we still find Latin being used in our American legal system today—albeit with less frequency than in the 19th and early 20th century, though not totally removed from modern use—attests to the purely definitional aspects of many words and phrases we find in the law.[5]

III. The Common Law

The common law is an area of law not derived from statutes or constitutions, but directly from case law. Judicial decisions and opinions of judges form the body of common law. The term is also used to refer in general to those principles of law inherited in our legal tradition from England. Since the common law is not codified it is based on the precedent of prior court decisions. This places a lot of power to shape law in the hands of judges in the American and English systems of justice. Unlike a civil law system in which a judge's role is limited due to codes and statutes aimed at covering every eventuality a judge may encounter, common law judges rely more actively on past court decisions as a guide for their determinations. Statutes are no less prevalent in a common law system but they are informed by common law principles. For instance, in defining the crime of larceny every state will have a statute defining it as taking the property of another without permission. Severity of the offense is determined by the monetary amount of the property or the type of property. However, the common law adds more to the requisites of proof by providing for the elements of trespassory taking (caption) and asportation (removal) of the property. While many state statutes define the act of larceny as the taking and deprivation of another's property, common law principles aid in the interpretation of the law as applied to different factual situations.

The common law tradition dates back to after the Norman Conquest when the king's courts were used to unify the country and the law. Customs in place across England and prior rulings by the king were the basis of a developing common law. Today the 80 common law countries are countries that were either former British colonies or influenced by Anglo-Saxon traditions.[6] A main feature of

---

[5] Peter R. MacLeod, *Latin in Legal Writing: An Inquiry in to the Use of Latin in the Modern Legal World*, Boston College Law Review (1998)
[6] The Economist, *What is the difference between common and civil law?* (July 17, 2013), http://www.economist.com/blogs/economist-explains/2013/07/economist-explains

common law is the doctrine of stare decisis which relies on the binding authority of prior cases, or precedent, to give permanency and predictability to the common law (see discussion in section IV to follow.) Civil law countries, which number 150 worldwide, have a foundation in Roman law and the Justinian Code. The Justinian Code, known as the Body of Civil Law (Latin: Corpus Juris Civilis) is a collection of laws and legal interpretations created during the time of the Byzantine emperor Justinian.

One of the most influential treatises on the common law is the *Commentaries on the Laws of England* by William Blackstone. This is a four volume work dividing coverage on the laws of property, persons, private wrongs, and public wrongs. The author, Sir William Blackstone, was an English jurist whose *Commentaries* had a tremendous impact upon the legal development of the common law in the colonies. Many colonial lawyers during the Revolutionary Period, including those among the Founding Fathers who were trained lawyers, had read Blackstone's *Commentaries* as part of their legal education.[7] Even though the treatise had its detractors over time and contained legal errors regarding English law, it served as a reliable source of early American common law theory after independence, especially as a body of case law was being built in America.[8] The relevancy of Blackstone's *Commentaries* to our common law tradition is still prevalent today in Supreme Court decisions. In *Shaw v. United States*, 137 S.Ct. 462 (2016), Justice Stephen Breyer cited the *Commentaries* early in his majority opinion while discussing bailments and property rights. Justice Samuel Alito, in a 2017 dissent in *Pena-Rodriguez v. Colorado*, 137 S.Ct. 855 (2017), cited Blackstone when discussing Sixth Amendment rights and impartiality. A Lexis search from June 2017 yielded 382 U.S. Supreme Court case citations to Blackstone's *Commentaries* since 1793, with another 274 cases citing the treatise in the federal circuit courts of appeal since 2000.

IV. Judicial Review and Interpretation of the Law

The 1803 U.S. Supreme Court case of *Marbury v. Madison*, 5 U.S. 137 (1803), stands at the apex of American constitutional law because it is from this case that Chief Justice John Marshall set the foundation for the concept of judicial review. Furthermore, Chief Justice Marshall's decision emphatically set the boundary between the competing branches of government. Separation of powers case law would continue to develop throughout the long history of the Supreme Court, but the uniquely crafted *Marbury v. Madison* decision was the initial case to place the role of the judiciary as the political body that was to interpret what the law was and to apply the law to a specific situation. In his *Marbury* decision Marshall also established the Supreme Court as the final arbiter of the Constitution's meaning. He did so by ruling a portion of a law, the Judiciary Act of 1789, was unconstitutional. The Supreme Court had previously considered the constitutionality of an act of Congress in the 1796 case of *Hylon v. United States*, 3 U.S. 171 (1796) but it ruled the law constitutional. The *Marbury* decision was a first for the Court to declare a law unconstitutional. This was important because prior to *Marbury* the Supreme Court was a relatively weak branch of government not given much consideration by the executive or legislative branch. Elected officials at the time did not regard the Court as a co-equal branch to Congress or the Presidency. Over time, in the post-*Marbury* years, the Supreme Court would be at the center of disputes between these same two branches concerning the reach of their power. For instance, in *Youngstown Sheet & Tube Co. v. Sawyer*[9] the Supreme Court in 1952 clearly outlined the limits of executive power and did

---

[7] Lawrence Friedman, A History of American Law (1985)
[8] Id.
[9] 349 U.S. 579 (1952)

the same 43 years later in *United States v. Lopez*[10] wherein it limited Congressional power under the Commerce Clause. These two cases are examples of the growth of the Supreme Court's influence as a co-equal branch of government since *Marbury v. Madison.*

Still, it is with the *Marbury* case that our American concept of judicial review begins and the background facts of the case are instructive in assessing its impact. In the presidential election of 1800 John Adams was defeated by his friend, vice-president, and political nemesis Thomas Jefferson, a Democrat-Republican. Adams decided he would increase the presence of federalist judges in the judiciary by appointing a number of federal circuit court judges to the recently expanded federal courts, as well as a number of local justices of the peace. William Marbury was a loyal federalist who was one of 42 justices of the peace appointed by Adams. His justice of the peace position was for the District of Columbia. Prior to the end of his presidency Adams signed the federal judicial appointments, which became known as the "midnight judges," and gave them, along with the justice of the peace appointments, to his Secretary of State John Marshall to deliver. Marshall had recently been appointed Chief Justice of the Supreme Court but remained on as Secretary of State until the end of Adams' term. Many of the appointments were delivered but not all. Marbury's commission as justice of the peace was one of those that went undelivered and Jefferson, upon taking office, refused to have his new Secretary of State, James Madison, deliver them. Marbury brought a writ of mandamus in the Supreme Court to compel the delivery of his commission. It is at this juncture that Chief Justice Marshall found himself in a precarious position since it is he who as the prior Secretary of State left the commission in dispute undelivered and now as a federalist judge had to preside over a controversy involving a Democrat–Republican president who was also his cousin. Marshall's subsequent decision held that Marbury was entitled to his commission since it was duly signed and delivery was a mere formality. He further held that Marbury had a remedy which he could pursue to enforce the delivery of his commission. However, because the writ of mandamus was brought directly to the Supreme Court under the Judiciary Act of 1789 which granted the Supreme Court original jurisdiction over petitions for writs of mandamus, Marbury's claim failed since the section of the Judiciary Act granting this original jurisdiction was unconstitutional. Marshall reasoned that the original jurisdiction of the Supreme Court was firmly set in the Constitution, limited to cases between the states and involving ambassadors, ministers and consuls. All other cases before the Supreme Court were appellate in review. In establishing the judicial review power of the Supreme Court and its ability to rule Acts of Congress as unconstitutional Chief Justice Marshall wrote the following in *Marbury*:

> *"It is emphatically the province and duty of the judicial department to say what the law is. Those who apply the rule to particular cases, must of necessity expound and interpret that rule. If two laws conflict with each other, the courts must decide on the operation of each. So if a law be in opposition to the constitution: if both the law and the constitution apply to a particular case, so that the court must either decide that case conformably to the law, disregarding the constitution; or conformably to the constitution, disregarding the law: the court must determine which of these conflicting rules governs the case. This is of the very essence of judicial duty . . . The judicial power of the United States is extended to all cases arising under the constitution."*[11]

The Supreme Court's decision in *Marbury v. Madison* was not its final word on its powers of judicial review. As noted in the above cases of *Youngstown Sheet & Tube Co.* and *Lopez*, both

---

[10] 514 U.S. 549 (1995)
[11] *Marbury* at 177, 178

decided over 150 years since *Marbury*, the Supreme Court was still exerting its power of judicial review over the executive and legislative branches.[12]

The case of Martin v. Hunter's Lessee, decided just 13 years after *Marbury v. Madison* with Marshall still presiding as Chief Justice, is another significant decision focusing on the Supreme Court's power of judicial review. The dispute here though is much different as is the central question regarding the Supreme Court's power of review.

❖❖

Martin v. Hunter's Lessee
14 U.S. 304 (1816)

Justice Story delivered the opinion of the Court.

This is a writ of error from the Court of Appeals of Virginia founded upon the refusal of that Court to obey the mandate of this Court requiring the judgment rendered in this very cause, at February Term, 1813, to be carried into due execution. The following is the judgment of the Court of Appeals rendered on the mandate:

The Court is unanimously of opinion, that the appellate power of the Supreme Court of the United States does not extend to this Court, under a sound construction of the Constitution of the United States; that so much of the 25th section of the act of Congress to establish the judicial courts of the United States, as extends the appellate jurisdiction of the Supreme Court to this Court, is not in pursuance of the Constitution of the United States; that the writ of error in this cause was improvidently allowed under the authority of that act; that the proceedings thereon in the Supreme Court were coram non judice in relation to this Court, and that obedience to its mandate be declined by the Court.

The questions involved in this judgment are of great importance and delicacy. Perhaps it is not too much to affirm that, upon their right decision rest some of the most solid principles which have hitherto been supposed to sustain and protect the Constitution itself. The great respectability, too, of the Court whose decisions we are called upon to review, and the entire deference which we entertain for the learning and ability of that Court, add much to the difficulty of the task which has so unwelcomely fallen upon us. It is, however, a source of consolation, that we have had the assistance of most able and learned arguments to aid our inquiries; and that the opinion which is now to be pronounced has been weighed with every solicitude to come to a correct result, and matured after solemn deliberation.

***

The Constitution of the United States was ordained and established not by the States in their sovereign capacities, but emphatically, as the preamble of the Constitution declares, by "the people of the United States." There can be no doubt that it was competent to the people to invest the general government with all the powers which they might deem proper and necessary, to extend or restrain these powers according to their own good pleasure, and to give them a paramount and supreme authority. As little doubt can there be that the people had a right to prohibit to the States the exercise of any powers which were, in their judgment, incompatible with the objects of the general compact, to make the powers of the State governments, in given cases, subordinate to those of the nation, or to reserve to themselves those sovereign authorities which they might not choose to delegate to either.

---

[12] See also, *United States v. Texas*, 579 U.S. ___ (2016) for a more recent example of the Supreme Court limiting executive action, in this instance siding with 26 states that sued the Obama Administration over its immigration policy in the Deferred Action for Parents of Americans (DAPA) legislation.

The Constitution was not, therefore, necessarily carved out of existing State sovereignties, nor a surrender of powers already existing in State institutions, for the powers of the States depend upon their own Constitutions, and the people of every State had the right to modify and restrain them according to their own views of the policy or principle.

***

It must therefore be conceded that the Constitution not only contemplated, but meant to provide for, cases within the scope of the judicial power of the United States which might yet depend before State tribunals. It was foreseen that, in the exercise of their ordinary jurisdiction, State courts would incidentally take cognizance of cases arising under the Constitution, the laws, and treaties of the United States. Yet to all these cases the judicial power, by the very terms of the Constitution, is to extend. It cannot extend by original jurisdiction if that was already rightfully and exclusively attached in the State courts, which (as has been already shown) may occur; it must therefore extend by appellate jurisdiction, or not at all. It would seem to follow that the appellate power of the United States must, in such cases, extend to State tribunals; and if in such cases, there is no reason why it should not equally attach upon all others within the purview of the Constitution.

***

It has been argued that such an appellate jurisdiction over State courts is inconsistent with the genius of our Governments, and the spirit of the Constitution. That the latter was never designed to act upon State sovereignties, but only upon the people, and that, if the power exists, it will materially impair the sovereignty of the States, and the independence of their courts. We cannot yield to the force of this reasoning; it assumes principles which we cannot admit, and draws conclusions to which we do not yield our assent.

It is a mistake that the Constitution was not designed to operate upon States in their corporate capacities. It is crowded with provisions which restrain or annul the sovereignty of the States in some of the highest branches of their prerogatives. The tenth section of the first article contains a long list of disabilities and prohibitions imposed upon the States. Surely, when such essential portions of State sovereignty are taken away or prohibited to be exercised, it cannot be correctly asserted that the Constitution does not act upon the States. The language of the Constitution is also imperative upon the States as to the performance of many duties. It is imperative upon the State legislatures to make laws prescribing the time, places, and manner of holding elections for senators and representatives, and for electors of President and Vice-President. And in these as well as some other cases, Congress have a right to revise, amend, or supersede the laws which may be passed by State legislatures. When therefore the States are stripped of some of the highest attributes of sovereignty, and the same are given to the United States; when the legislatures of the States are, in some respects, under the control of Congress, and in every case are, under the Constitution, bound by the paramount authority of the United States, it is certainly difficult to support the argument that the appellate power over the decisions of State courts is contrary to the genius of our institutions. The courts of the United States can, without question, revise the proceedings of the executive and legislative authorities of the States, and if they are found to be contrary to the Constitution, may declare them to be of no legal validity. Surely the exercise of the same right over judicial tribunals is not a higher or more dangerous act of sovereign power.

***

There is an additional consideration, which is entitled to great weight. The Constitution of the United States was designed for the common and equal benefit of all the people of the United States.

The judicial power was granted for the same benign and salutary purposes. It was not to be exercised exclusively for the benefit of parties who might be plaintiffs, and would elect the national forum, but also for the protection of defendants who might be entitled to try their rights, or assert their privileges, before the same forum.

***

We have thus gone over all the principal questions in the cause, and we deliver our judgment with entire confidence that it is consistent with the Constitution and laws of the land . . . It is the opinion of the whole Court that the judgment of the Court of Appeals of Virginia, rendered on the mandate in this cause, be reversed, and the judgment of the District Court, held at Winchester, be, and the same is hereby, affirmed.

Questions Presented

1)   What is the issue in the case confronting the U.S. Supreme Court?
2)   How did Justice Story's opinion interpret the Constitution's grant of judicial review when it involves state courts?
3)   Does judicial review extend to the executive and legislative branches of state governments as well?

❖❖

When confronting questions of federal judicial review, there are two questions that must be asked. First, does the court have jurisdiction. Both *Marbury* and *Martin* were cases dealing with the jurisdiction of the Supreme Court. Second, is the case suitable for court review? This is referred to as justiciability. Federal courts (and lower state courts as well) are limited to hearing only those cases that meet a set of procedural requirements in order to be properly before the court.[13] Article III limits the power of the courts to "cases or controversies." If a case is determined to be nonjusticiable then a court cannot preside over the case. The factors a court considers for justiciability are: standing, ripeness, mootness, whether a political question is involved, and is the party seeking an advisory opinion. Federal and state courts will not consider cases that seek the determination of a political question since if it were to do so the court would be violating the separation of powers and invading the territory of another branch of government. This leaves the Supreme Court without jurisdiction to review.[14] The advisory opinion restriction, linked in theory to the political question doctrine, on judicial review is slightly different on the federal level than it is at the state level. Advisory opinions, the Supreme Court has held, do not meet the "case or controversy" requirement of Article III.[15] Some states alter this doctrine by allowing their state supreme courts, either by constitutional grant or statute, to give advisory opinions to their governors. Eight state constitutions—Colorado, Florida, Maine, Massachusetts, Michigan, New Hampshire, Rhode Island, and South Dakota—allow their supreme courts to give advisory opinions to the governor, while three—Alabama, Delaware and Oklahoma—permit it by statute.[16]

---

[13] Procedural aspects are discussed more fully in Chapter 2, section IV.

[14] See e.g., *Schlesinger v. Holtzman*, 414 U.S. 1321 (1973) in which the U.S. Supreme Court said that military decisions are vested in the executive and legislative branches, thereby the decision whether or not to bomb another country was a political question outside of its jurisdiction; see also, *El-Shifa Pharmaceutical Industries Co. v. United States*, 607 F.3d 836 (D.C. Cir., 2010).

[15] See, *Muskrat v. United States*, 219 U.S. 346 (1911); *Ashwander v. Tennessee Valley Authority*, 297 U.S. 288 (1936).

[16] M.L. Buenger, P.J. DeMuniz, American Judicial Power: The State Court Perspective (2015)

Questions of ripeness and mootness also go to the "case or controversy" analysis. A case is not ripe if it has not become sufficiently concrete to be adjudicated. The U.S. Supreme Court has defined this policy as follows: "*. . . its basic rationale is to prevent the courts, through avoidance of premature adjudication . . . The problem is best seen in a twofold aspect, requiring us to evaluate both the fitness of the issues for judicial decision and the hardship to the parties of withholding court consideration.*"[17] Ripeness is a problem of prematurity, while mootness is a question of staleness or no longer having an effect upon the plaintiff. A case is not justiciable and moot if events that occur after it was filed deprive the plaintiff's stake in the claim. Once again, a case or controversy is lacking. An example of mootness is the case of *DeFunis v. Odegaard*, 416 U.S. 312 (1974), in which the plaintiff was originally denied admission to the University of Washington School of Law, but was subsequently provisionally admitted during the pendency of his lawsuit. By the time his discrimination case reached the U.S. Supreme Court he was months away from graduating. The Supreme Court said it could not reach a decision on the substantive issues raised by the case because DeFunis "*will complete his law school studies at the end of the term for which he has now registered regardless of any decision this Court might reach on the merits of this litigation*"[18] Further, the Court noted, "*DeFunis did not cast his suit as a class action, and the only remedy he requested was an injunction commanding his admission to the Law School. He was not only accorded that remedy, but he now has also been irrevocably admitted to the final term of the final year of the Law School course. The controversy between the parties has thus clearly ceased to be "definite and concrete" and no longer "touch[es] the legal relations of parties having adverse legal interests.*"[19] The mootness doctrine can be overcome if the issue before a court is one "capable of repetition yet evading review."[20]

The concept of standing, often viewed as a third prong to a court's power of judicial review, is part of the justiciability prong. Standing, more fully explained in Chapter 2, section IV, refers to an individual's personal stake in a claim. There has to be an injury in fact to the individual, thereby preventing a person from asserting the rights of a third-party (jus tertii). In limited circumstances an individual can assert standing for a third-party but this has been limited to cases where the third-party is unable to assert their own rights.

Even though the Supreme Court asserted its right of judicial review over state court decisions involving questions of federal law or those impacting Constitutional interpretation, it did not mean that the Court would always exercise that right. The Supreme Court created its own policy of constitutional avoidance, thereby limiting its power of review, if the case before it can be decided on independent and adequate state law grounds. If there are federal laws or constitutional issues present in a case they will be reviewed by the Supreme Court; however, if the Court can find a resolution of the case on independent and adequate non-federal grounds to support the state court decision it will pass on its authority to review. This comes from a policy of judicial self-restraint. The principle is mostly taken in its modern formulation from Justice Louis Brandeis' concurrence in *Ashwander v. Tennessee Valley Authority: "The Court will not pass upon a constitutional question although properly presented by the record, if there is also present some other ground upon which the case may be disposed of."*[21]

---

[17] *Abbott Laboratories v. Gardner*, 387 U.S. 136, 148–9 (1967)

[18] *DeFunis* at 319.

[19] *Id.* at 317.

[20] See, *Roe v. Wade*, 410 U.S. 113 (1973)

[21] *Ashwander* at 397.

Once the Supreme Court decides it is within its power to review a case, how do the justices go about interpreting the law? That is a question that has had profound philosophical as well as political impact. No modern judiciary confirmation proceeding before the Senate has culminated without a searing inquiry into the judicial interpretive philosophy of the Supreme Court nominee. A justice's method of constitutional interpretation may be tied to that particular justice's politics, though in an ideal world and fictional view of the Supreme Court, the Court and the justices are supposed to be above politics. In a more realistic and practical sense we have to acknowledge that personal philosophies and political views impact a justice's decision-making process. While an individual justice will take an objective view toward a case and its facts, it is the justice's interpretive philosophy that will drive his or her decision and impact the outcome of the case. Table 1.1 summarizes some of the different methods of constitutional interpretation and some of the main judicial practitioners of a particular method.

In Federalist No. 78—part of a series of essays, written alternatively by Alexander Hamilton, John Jay and James Madison under the pseudonym Publius, arguing for ratification of the Constitution—Hamilton wrote about the judicial branch and the concept of judicial review:

> *"To avoid an arbitrary discretion in the courts, it is indispensable that they should be bound down by strict rules and precedents, which serve to define and point out their duty in every particular case that comes before them and it will readily be conceived from the variety of controversies which grow out of the folly and wickedness of mankind, that the records of those precedents must unavoidably swell to a very considerable bulk, and must demand long and laborious study to acquire a competent knowledge of them."*

This passage from the essay highlights the importance of precedent in evaluating cases that come before a court on appeal. A court's adherence to precedent, or stare decisis (Latin for "to stand by things"), gives the law regularity and permanence. Courts are reluctant to overturn precedent unless

TABLE 1.1 Methods of Constitutional Interpretation

Constitutional Interpretation Method	Definition of Method	Main Proponent or Practitioner of Interpretive Method
Originalism	Views the Constitution's meaning as fixed as of the time of enactment	Justice Hugo Black, Justice Antonin Scalia, Justice Clarence Thomas
Textualism	The plain text of a statute is used to determine the meaning of a statute	Justice Antonin Scalia, Judge Frank Easterbrook
Structuralism	Constitutional interpretation should be consistent with the structures of government, i.e., federalism, separation of powers, democracy	Chief Justice John Marshall, Chief Justice William Rehnquist
Pragmatism	Focuses on a more evolving interpretation when originalism is unacceptable as a policy consideration	Justice Oliver Wendell Holmes, Judge Richard Posner
Polling Jurisdictions	Examines the practices of other U.S. courts, early English traditions, state practices or foreign courts to arrive at a decision	Justice Steven Breyer, Justice Anthony Kennedy

there has been a clear error in a prior decision. However, one of the main strengths of our common law legal system is the ability of a court to overturn itself and correct a prior decision's holding. In the 1896 case of *Plessy v. Ferguson* the U.S. Supreme Court upheld racial segregation under a doctrine of "separate but equal." Fifty-eight years later in *Brown v. Board of Education*[22] the Supreme Court overturned its awful decision in *Plessy* when it held that segregated public school districts in Topeka, Kansas were unconstitutional. This is one classic example of a court overturning a prior decision and not abiding by precedent. But, for the most part, absent some egregious ruling or mistake of law a court will be bound by precedent. A recent Supreme Court decision on stare decisis, *Kimble v. Marvel Entertainment*, points to the importance of it as a limiting concept in judicial review.

❖❖

Kimble v. Marvel Entertainment
135 S.Ct. 2401 (2015)

Justice Kagan delivered the opinion of the Court.

In *Brulotte v. Thys Co.*, 379 U. S. 29 (1964), this Court held that a patent holder cannot charge royalties for the use of his invention after its patent term has expired. The sole question presented here is whether we should overrule *Brulotte*. Adhering to principles of *stare decisis*, we decline to do so. Critics of the *Brulotte* rule must seek relief not from this Court but from Congress.

I

In 1990, petitioner Stephen Kimble obtained a patent on a toy that allows children (and young-at-heart adults) to role-play as "a spider person" by shooting webs—really, pressurized foam string—"from the palm of [the] hand." U. S. Patent No. 5,072,856, Abstract (filed May 25, 1990). Respondent Marvel Entertainment, LLC (Marvel) makes and markets products featuring Spider-Man, among other comic-book characters. Seeking to sell or license his patent, Kimble met with the president of Marvel's corporate predecessor to discuss his idea for web-slinging fun. Soon afterward, but without remunerating Kimble, that company began marketing the "Web Blaster"—a toy that, like Kimble's patented invention, enables would-be action heroes to mimic Spider-Man through the use of a polyester glove and a canister of foam.

Kimble sued Marvel in 1997 alleging, among other things, patent infringement. The parties ultimately settled that litigation. Their agreement provided that Marvel would purchase Kimble's patent in exchange for a lump sum (of about a half-million dollars) and a 3% royalty on Marvel's future sales of the Web Blaster and similar products. The parties set no end date for royalties, apparently contemplating that they would continue for as long as kids want to imitate Spider-Man (by doing whatever a spider can).

And then Marvel stumbled across *Brulotte*, the case at the heart of this dispute. In negotiating the settlement, neither side was aware of *Brulotte*. But Marvel must have been pleased to learn of it. *Brulotte* had read the patent laws to prevent a patentee from receiving royalties for sales made after his patent's expiration. So the decision's effect was to sunset the settlement's royalty clause. On making that discovery, Marvel sought a declaratory judgment in federal district court confirming that the company could cease paying royalties come 2010—the end of Kimble's patent term. The court approved that relief, holding that *Brulotte* made "the royalty provision . . .

---

[22] 347 U.S. 483 (1954)

unenforceable after the expiration of the Kimble patent." 692 F. Supp. 2d 1156, 1161 (Ariz. 2010). The Court of Appeals for the Ninth Circuit affirmed, though making clear that it was none too happy about doing so. "[T]he *Brulotte* rule," the court complained, "is counterintuitive and its rationale is arguably unconvincing." 727 F. 3d 856, 857 (2013).

We granted certiorari, 574 U. S. ___ (2014), to decide whether, as some courts and commentators have suggested, we should overrule *Brulotte*. For reasons of *stare decisis*, we demur.

***

Overruling precedent is never a small matter. *Stare decisis*—in English, the idea that today's Court should stand by yesterday's decisions—is "a foundation stone of the rule of law." *Michigan v. Bay Mills Indian Community*, 572 U. S. ___, ___ (2014) (slip op., at 15). Application of that doctrine, although "not an inexorable command," is the "preferred course because it promotes the evenhanded, predictable, and consistent development of legal principles, fosters reliance on judicial decisions, and contributes to the actual and perceived integrity of the judicial process." *Payne v. Tennessee*, 501 U. S. 808–828 (1991). It also reduces incentives for challenging settled precedents, saving parties and courts the expense of endless re-litigation.

Respecting *stare decisis* means sticking to some wrong decisions. The doctrine rests on the idea, as Justice Brandeis famously wrote, that it is usually "more important that the applicable rule of law be settled than that it be settled right." *Burnet v. Coronado Oil & Gas Co.*, 285 U. S. 393, 406 (1932) (dissenting opinion). Indeed, *stare decisis* has consequence only to the extent it sustains incorrect decisions; correct judgments have no need for that principle to prop them up. Accordingly, an argument that we got something wrong—even a good argument to that effect—cannot by itself justify scrapping settled precedent. Or otherwise said, it is not alone sufficient that we would decide a case differently now than we did then. To reverse course, we require as well what we have termed a "special justification"—over and above the belief "that the precedent was wrongly decided." *Halliburton Co. v. Erica P. John Fund, Inc.*, 573 U. S. ___, ___ (2014) (slip op., at 4).

What is more, *stare decisis* carries enhanced force when a decision, like *Brulotte*, interprets a statute. Then, unlike in a constitutional case, critics of our ruling can take their objections across the street, and Congress can correct any mistake it sees. See, e.g., *Patterson v. McLean Credit Union*, 491 U. S. 164 –173 (1989). That is true, contrary to the dissent's view, see *post*, at 6–7 (opinion of Alito, J.), regardless whether our decision focused only on statutory text or also relied, as *Brulotte* did, on the policies and purposes animating the law. See, e.g., *Bilski v. Kappos*, 561 U. S. 593–602 (2010). Indeed, we apply statutory *stare decisis* even when a decision has announced a "judicially created doctrine" designed to implement a federal statute. *Halliburton*, 573 U. S., at ___ (slip op., at 12). All our interpretive decisions, in whatever way reasoned, effectively become part of the statutory scheme, subject (just like the rest) to congressional change. Absent special justification, they are balls tossed into Congress's court, for acceptance or not as that branch elects.

And Congress has spurned multiple opportunities to reverse *Brulotte*—openings as frequent and clear as this Court ever sees. *Brulotte* has governed licensing agreements for more than half a century. See *Watson v. United States*, 552 U. S. 74–83 (2007) (stating that "long congressional acquiescence," there totaling just 14 years, "enhance[s] even the usual precedential force we accord to our interpretations of statutes" (internal quotation marks omitted)). During that time, Congress has repeatedly amended the patent laws, including the specific provision (35 U. S. C. § 154) on which *Brulotte* rested. See, *e.g.*, Uruguay Round Agreements Act, § 532(a), 108Stat. 4983 (1994) (increasing the length of the patent term); Act of Nov. 19, 1988, § 201, 102Stat. 4676 (limiting patent-misuse claims). *Brulotte* survived every such change. Indeed, Congress has rebuffed bills that would have replaced *Brulotte's per se* rule with the same antitrust-style analysis Kimble now urges. See, e.g., S. 1200, 100th Cong., 1st Sess., Tit. II (1987) (providing that no patent owner would be guilty of "illegal extension of the patent right by reason of his or her licensing practices . . . unless such practices . . . violate the antitrust laws"); S. 438, 100th Cong., 2d Sess., § 201(3) (1988). Congress's continual reworking of the patent laws—but never of the *Brulotte* rule—further supports leaving the decision in place.

Nor yet are we done, for the subject matter of *Brulotte* adds to the case for adhering to precedent. *Brulotte* lies at the intersection of two areas of law: property (patents) and contracts (licensing agreements). And we have often recognized that in just those contexts—"cases involving property and contract rights"—considerations favoring *stare decisis* are "at their acme." E.g., *Payne*, 501 U. S., at 828; *Khan*, 522 U. S., at 20. That is because parties are especially likely to rely on such precedents when ordering their affairs. To be sure, Marvel and Kimble disagree about whether *Brulotte* has actually generated reliance. Marvel says yes: Some parties, it claims, do not specify an end date for royalties in their licensing agreements, instead relying on *Brulotte* as a default rule. Brief for Respondent 32–33; see 1 D. Epstein, Eckstrom's Licensing in Foreign and Domestic Operations § 3.13, p. 3–13, and n. 2 (2014) (noting that it is not "necessary to specify the term . . . of the license" when a decision like *Brulotte* limits it "by law"). Overturning *Brulotte* would thus upset expectations, most so when long-dormant licenses for long-expired patents spring back to life. Not true, says Kimble: Unfair surprise is unlikely, because no "meaningful number of [such] license agreements . . . actually exist." Reply Brief 18. To be honest, we do not know (nor, we suspect, do Marvel and Kimble). But even uncertainty on this score cuts in Marvel's direction. So long as we see a reasonable possibility that parties have structured their business transactions in light of *Brulotte*, we have one more reason to let it stand.

As against this super-powered form of *stare decisis*, we would need a superspecial justification to warrant reversing *Brulotte*. But the kinds of reasons we have most often held sufficient in the past do not help Kimble here. If anything, they reinforce our unwillingness to do what he asks.

***

What we can decide, we can undecide. But *stare decisis* teaches that we should exercise that authority sparingly. Cf. S. Lee and S. Ditko, Amazing Fantasy No. 15: "Spider-Man," p. 13 (1962) ("[I]n this world, with great power there must also come—great responsibility"). Finding many reasons for staying the *stare decisis* course and no "special justification" for departing from it, we decline Kimble's invitation to overrule *Brulotte*.

For the reasons stated, the judgment of the Court of Appeals is affirmed.

It is so ordered.

Questions Presented

1) What was the dilemma Justice Kagan felt was faced in deciding whether to overturn *Brulotte*?

2) What did Justice Kagan mean when she wrote that the relief from the precedent of *Brulotte* had to come not from the Court but from Congress?

3) What did Justice Kagan say was the power of stare decisis, especially in this case?

❖❖

V. Schools of Legal Philosophy

The preceding section outlined the different methods of judicial interpretation, which is distinct from legal philosophy, yet potentially impacted by it. Philosophy itself is defined as a pursuit of wisdom, a search for the general understanding of values and reality by speculative rather than observational means.[23] It is also defined as a theory underlying or regarding a sphere of activity or thought.[24] Legal philosophy then would be the study of the nature of law and legal systems. Particular interests in the area focus on the law and morality as well as the legitimacy and justification of legal systems. An individual judge's legal philosophy could have a significant impact on his or her method of interpreting the law. For example, consider the moral and legal issues surrounding the abortion debate in the United States. A natural law theorist would find abortion laws and the Supreme Court decision in *Roe v. Wade* anathema to his or her belief. Yet, where does that legal philosophy place the individual judge in considering an abortion issue when that same judge espouses a more conservative judicial interpretive process of Textualism or Originalism? The textualist and originalist would be more bound to the value of precedent. Would the precedent of *Roe v. Wade* control the decision-making process or would the judge's natural law philosophy control? These are not just hypothetical questions, but in fact are real issues confronted when trying to reconcile potentially competing interpretive schools and dogmas of legal philosophy. It is a process of inquiry engaged in by appellate level judges, particularly U.S. Supreme Court Justices, as well as those who closely follow and analyze the impactful decisions made by these men and women. A consideration of legal philosophy then is not a benign or esoteric exercise in the law, it has meaning and impact.

There is no less impact either when considering the actions of a legislature and its individual members. Is the law guided by certain immutable natural law principles, like the sanctity of life or is it able to be categorized by way of a positivist law? Is positive law necessarily moral law? The German legislature in the 1930s passed a series of laws, known as the Nuremburg Laws, which eventually led to the mass murders of people based on race, ethnicity and religion. Even though these were laws passed by a sitting legislative body it does not mean they are lawful in any real sense. As a separate matter, how far should or could law go in legislating morality? Are certain behaviors, like homosexuality, able to be outlawed based on a community standard? Once again the answer is seemingly apparent but the debates open an often incongruous relationship between the different schools of legal philosophy. A review of the different legal schools of philosophy and their main tenets in Table 1.2 highlights how these philosophical inquiries are shaped. The law is ever evolving as is our understanding of the nature, use and reach of the law in our lives. Even in the realm of business these considerations have an impact. The lassez-faire economic philosophy of the Supreme Court in the early 20th century rejected the progressive push toward reform in labor and business practices. Eventual judicial policy moved toward a more paternalistic approach favored by progressives, thereby creating a shift in the legal philosophy employed by a majority of judges. This in turn affected businesses operating within the United States.[25]

Legal philosophies fall into one of three different jurisprudential categories: analytical, critical, and normative. Analytical jurisprudence looks at the essence of the law and considers the relationship between law and morality. Natural law and positive law theory fall into this category. Analytical legal theorists included Jeremy Bentham and H.L.A. Hart. Critical jurisprudence challenges the traditional norms of legal philosophy and views the law as an extension of politics and existing

---

[23] "philosophy." Merriam-Webster Online Dictionary. 2017. http://www.merriam-webster.com (June 14, 2017).
[24] Id.
[25] See discussion in Chapter 3 on Business Law and the Constitution.

TABLE 1.2 Schools of Legal Philosophy

School of Legal Philosophy	Basic Philosophical Tenet	Main Theoretical Proponent
Natural Law	Natural law principles are inherent in nature and exist whether or not government recognizes or enforces them.	Thomas Aquinas, Sir William Blackstone, Lon L. Fuller
Legal Positivism	The only legitimate sources of law are those legal principles which have been expressly adopted or enacted by a government entity.	John Austin, H.L.A. Hart
Legal Realism	Rejects the view of law as the logical application of objective rules and principles and instead posits that the law is an inconsistent and unreliable application of the social, political and moral biases of judges.	Justice Oliver Wendell Holmes, Roscoe Pound, Karl Llewellyn, Jerome Frank, Justice Benjamin Cardozo
Legal Interpretivism	This is a doctrine of constitutional interpretation in which judges must follow norms or values that expressly states or implies the language of the Constitution.	Ronald Dworkin
Legal Paternalism	The state has a legitimate interest legislating in areas where individuals could do physical or mental harm to themselves. The interference with individual liberties is sanctioned by the protection of individual welfare, happiness, needs and interests.	Gerald Dworkin
Legal Moralism	The law can legitimately be used to prohibit behaviors that conflict with society's collective moral judgments, even if those behaviors do not result in physical or psychological harm to others.	Patrick Devlin
Critical Legal Studies	Borrowed from legal realism's more radical aspects with an aim to challenge and change existing social structures and give power to otherwise marginalized sectors of the social strata. Grew out of the social unrest of the 1960s in the U.S. but its roots go back further to 19th century social theorists such as Karl Marx and Friedrich Engels.	Duncan Kennedy, Karl Klare, Mark Kelman
Law and Economics	Considers economic analysis as a valuable way of interpreting the law. The law is viewed as a means of maximizing the wealth of a society and this should be the norm in judging the efficient application of the law.	Richard Posner

power structures in society. As a result critical legal theory does not see the law as neutral. Legal realism and critical legal studies form this category of jurisprudence. Normative jurisprudence is concerned with the goal or purpose of the law. It evaluates the law. Legal moralism and legal paternalism are examples of normative jurisprudence.

VI. Sources of Law

An important part of studying, researching or practicing the law is knowing where to find it. Judges, lawyers, legislators, researchers, and students are all dependent upon primary and secondary sources of the law. Primary sources of law are the actual law itself. These include: the U.S. Constitution, state constitutions, statutory law, administrative agency regulations, case law, and common law doctrines. Of these primary sources case law and common law come from the judiciary; statutes, including constitutions, are products of the legislature; and administrative regulations come from the executive and the administrative agencies that function under the executive branch. Secondary sources are those that discuss, interpret, explain, or analyze the law. They can discuss what the law is, what the law should be, how the law is or should be applied, and historical explanations of the law. Some examples of secondary sources are: legal treatises; restatements of the laws, for example the Restatement of Torts; legal encyclopedias; and law review articles. These sources will cite primary law sources as well as other secondary law sources.

It is easy to discern the different primary sources, these are the best sources for what the law is, but secondary sources can be trickier to navigate and to understand their importance in research or citation in court documents. Therefore it is best to discuss some of these sources and their relative value.

Legal encyclopedias are comprehensive sets of brief articles on legal topics.[26] However, they are not authoritative and should not be used in case briefs and legal memoranda. But, it is not uncommon to include citations to legal encyclopedias as a closing authority in a string of references to primary authorities. The most popular of these legal encyclopedias are the *Corpus Juris Secundum* (C.J.S.) and *American Jurisprudence 2d* (Am. Jur. 2d). Topics are arranged in alphabetical order and there is separately bound index included with each volume. Legal encyclopedias are useful in providing a general introduction to an area of law and for finding citations to relevant case law on a subject.

Legal treatises are book length expositions on a legal subject.[27] Treatises can be a scholarly presentation on an area of law, for example *Corbin on Contracts*, or sources more geared toward the legal practitioner, such as *Wright's Federal Practice & Procedure*. Treatises can also be legal hornbooks used as teaching tools for law students. Hornbooks contain detailed treatments of a particular area of the law along with summaries of important cases.[28]

Law review articles are scholarly articles published by law school law review boards, which are managed by law students with faculty oversight. There is an editorial process of article selection. The articles are usually an analysis or critique of a development in the law. These articles, written by law school faculty or practicing attorneys, are quite lengthy and scholarly in tone. Shorter student written articles, referred to as Notes, also appear in the law reviews. Caution has to be taken when citing to law review Notes since these are not given the same gravitas and precedential weight as other law review articles. Law reviews can be general in their focus or restricted to a particular area of law, like environmental law or national security law. When conducting research there are several sources of law review articles that can be accessed online. The HeinOnline Law Journal Library, LexisNexis, and WestLaw are a few of the main sources of law review articles and indexes.

A Restatement is a form of treatise "published by the American Law Institute, describing the law in a particular area and guiding its development."[29] The ALI is an organization headquartered

---

[26] Legal Encyclopedias Research Guide, Georgetown University Law Library, 02/28/17, http://guides.ll.georgetown.edu/encyclopedias
[27] Secondary Sources: ALRs, Encyclopedias, Law Reviews, Restatements, & Treatises, Harvard University School of Law, 02/09/17, http://guides.library.harvard.edu/
[28] Id.
[29] Black's Law Dictionary, (19th ed., 2010).

in Philadelphia, Pennsylvania which was founded in 1923 after a group of lawyers, judges, law professors and legal scholars decided there was a need to establish a unified core of the common law and improve administration of the law. Early members and incorporators of the ALI included two of the preeminent judicial administrators in the history of the Supreme Court—former President and then present Chief Justice William Howard Taft, former Associate Justice and future Chief Justice Charles Evans Hughes—as well as two of most brilliant jurists in the country, Benjamin Cardozo and Learned Hand.

The Restatements can be found in diverse legal topics, covering areas spanning contracts, property, torts, conflicts of law, foreign relations, to trusts. The Restatements explain the meaning of the common law in a particular area and its development. "Black letter law", which is settled and fundamental legal principles, is highlighted and distilled in a set of principles and rules.[30] Even though the Restatements are not primary law they are often treated as persuasive authority due to their influence and their scholarly completion. Copies of individual Restatements can be purchased from the ALI or found in any law school or courthouse library. Online copies can be obtained through commercial legal research websites like WestLaw.

VII. Case Briefing and Legal Research

The practice of law is often about remedying the different issues that a client brings to their attorney. Thus, it is important for the practitioner to be able to understand the issues presented in a particular case and to provide a plan for meeting the client's needs. The ability to problem solve requires the development of critical thinking skills. By having students read case law and answer theoretical scenarios based on their reading of the cases, law professors teach students to work their way through complex, multi-layered problems. The ability to read a judicial opinion and understand it is learned by case briefing. The case brief becomes a standardized way for students to approach case law and develop their critical thinking skills. Using classroom discussion and the application of legal concepts and principles established in the cases read, students learn to "think like lawyers" and effectively present oral arguments advocating their position. This time-worn method of training lawyers, also used in undergraduate and graduate university lectures, is known as the Socratic method of instruction. However, there has been a shift in law school teaching methods over the last few years as the Socratic Method came under criticism within the legal profession. Law school faculty have shifted to a teaching method that relies less on lectures and theoretical problem solving and more on legal rules, statutory analysis, policy discussion and practical training in clinic settings.[31] No matter what method of instruction is used the ability to read a judicial opinion, understand it, and apply its holding to real world problems is a key skill of the legal professional. While those employed in the legal profession obviously need to know how to read and understand case law, so too do those employed in business, since the law impacts so many areas of the business world. Another benefit of reading cases and writing out case briefs is that it attunes students to the language of the law and develops their ability to apply legal reasoning.

---

[30] http://guides.library.harvard.edu/, Harvard University School of Law, 02/09/17, Secondary Sources: ALRs, Encyclopedias, Law Reviews, Restatements, & Treatises.

[31] W. David Slawson, *Changing How We Teach: A Critique of the Case Method.* Southern California Law Review, Vol 7:43, (2000).

> ### *Legal Definitions*
>
> **Persuasive authority** – these are sources of law, such as other court cases, law review arti-
> cles, or legal treatises, which a court may consult or consider in deciding a case, however, the
> court will not rely on it in reaching its decision. Unlike binding authority these sources of law are
> merely advisory in nature to the court's decision-making process.
>
> **Binding authority** – these are sources of law which a reviewing court must consider in reach-
> ing its decision in a case. Sources of binding authority includes higher court cases within the
> state, and relevant state statutes.

In order to properly read a judicial opinion, whether it is a trial court determination on a motion or
an appellate decision, it is necessary to know what to look for and how to dissect the decision down to
five key sections: the Facts, the Procedural History, the Issue, the Holding, and the Rationale. These five
sections when fully briefed will provide a summary of the whole case. The idea behind a case brief is
to take a judicial opinion that may run several pages in length and synopsize it into a concise 1-1½ page
case brief. This is an exercise in summarizing and simplifying complex legal issues that over time trains
the student to quickly "spot" the key issues in a case and analyze a court's legal solution.

Formats for case briefs will vary depending upon a particular professor's preference. However,
the goal of every case brief is to be able to outline the Issue, the Rule, the court's Analysis, and the
court's Conclusion. This IRAC method of case briefing is best discerned by formatting the case brief
into the five sections stated above preceded by the case name and citation. The case citation is an
indispensable part of the case brief since this indicates the official (and possibly the unofficial
reporter) where the case can be found. For example, the citation for the well-known tort case of
Palsgraf v. Long Island Railroad is 248 N.Y. 339, 16 N.E. 99 (1928). If a student were to look for
the above case in a library the student would go to where the New York court volumes are kept. The
number preceding the reporter designation is the bound volume in which the case can be found and
the second number after the reporter designation is the page number on which the case begins. It is
important to be able to distinguish between different state case reporters. The "N.Y." designation in
the above citation indicates the case is from the New York State Court of Appeals, which is the highest appellate court in New York. New York has three different case reporters, unlike many states
which have no official case reporter and rely on unofficial reporters or West Publishing regional
reporters. In addition to the "N.Y." designation for the New York Reporter, a "Misc." designation
indicates the New York state Miscellaneous reports which carries published lower court decisions.
An "A.D." designation indicates state Appellate Division decisions (this is New York's intermediate
appellate level court). Due to the size of the state New York has four Appellate Departments and
two Appellate Terms, so a case citation may look something like this: *Rudd v. Magee, 51 A.D. 624,
65 N.Y.S. 65 (2d Dept., 1900).* Note that in the citation just before the case year is the designation
of the specific appellate department the case was decided in. This is an important designation for
legal researchers since if they are looking for case precedent from the New York Appellate Division,
Second Department the designation would key them in that the decision was from the same department. Likewise, a designation from the Third Department would indicate the case may not have the
same binding authority within the Second Department, though it may have persuasive authority.

Note that in the *Magee* citation is another reporter citation, 65 N.Y.S. 65, which indicates the reporter as the New York Supplements. This is one of two special reporters (the other being for California) printed by West Publishing Company, which carries New York appellate court decisions. West also publishes seven regional reporters, an example of one which can be found in the *Palsgraf* citation above: 16 N.E. 99. This is the North Eastern Reporter and it covers appellate cases from courts located in the Northeast region of the United States. The regional reporters and their designations are as follows:

Atlantic Reporter – A., A.2d, A.3d

North Eastern Reporter – N.E., N.E.2d

North Western Reporter – N.W., N.W.2d

Pacific Reporter – P., P.2d, P.3d

South Eastern Reporter – S.E., S.E.2d

South Western Reporter – S.W., S.W.2d, S.W.3d

Southern Reporter – So., So.2d, So.3d

In this example, *West Coast Hotel v. Parrish,* 300 U.S. 379 (1937) the student would be directed to where the U.S. Supreme Court volumes are kept (there are three reported volumes for the U.S. Supreme Court—the official reporter for U.S. Supreme Court decisions is the *United States Reports* (designated by *U.S.* after the volume number and preceding the page number.) Unofficial reporters are the *Lawyers' Edition of the Supreme Court Reports* (*L.Ed.*) and the *Supreme Court Reporter* (*S.Ct.*). In a law library the above *West Coast Hotel* decision would be found in volume 300 of the *United States Reports* at page 379. If a student were to look for the case online through Lexis or WestLaw the citation would provide direct access to the case.

In addition to the U.S. Supreme Court reporters discussed above, other federal court decisions are published in unofficial reporters. There are no official reporters for federal decisions other than the United States Reports for U.S. Supreme Court decisions. Federal Circuit Courts of Appeal decisions are published in unofficial reporters by West Publishing Company. These are found under the designation Federal Reporter - "F.", Federal Reporter Second Series - "F.2d" and Federal Reporter Third Series - "F.3d". Federal District Court opinions are published by West in unofficial case reporters known as the Federal Supplement and found under the designations "F. Supp." and Federal Supplement Second Series - "F. Supp.2d".

Now that you are familiar with the various federal and state case reporters and case citations we can begin to take a look at each separate part of the case brief:

Facts – a court's decision can go on for a number of pages, a few the length of a novel (the full decision in *Furman v. Georgia*, a death penalty case, was over 200 pages), and much of it may contain an extensive recitation of the background facts to the case. It is not necessary in the case brief to include all the facts, only the relevant facts pertinent to the legal analysis should be included. These are the key facts which are essential to forming a legal conclusion and which aid in establishing elements of the rule of law to be applied.

Procedural History – many judicial opinions read by students are appellate court cases, which means that the case began somewhere else in either a federal or state court of general jurisdiction.

The Procedural History provides a synopsis of the route a case took to its present appellate destination. The following is an example of a Procedural History from a civil case based on an employment termination case: *"Petitioner appeals from a circuit court decision which reversed a district court order dismissing the complaint for failure to state a claim upon which relief can be granted. The district court dismissed the complaint based on a failure to specifically plead a cause of action for constructive discharge. The circuit court of appeals reversed after finding that the petitioner's complaint, while narrowly meeting the requirements, did state an arguable claim for relief based on a constructive discharge of the petitioner from his employment."* This recitation of the Procedural History is the "road map" of where the case has been and what occurred along the way as it progressed through the courts.

Issue – every case involves a problem or issue for resolution that is presented to the court. What is the question before the court seeking resolution? This is the Issue in any case and in the case brief it is posed as a question. The following is an example of how the Issue should be presented in a case brief: *"Whether the plaintiff was able to obtain personal jurisdiction over the defendant based on his one week stay within the state while on business?"* The Issue is simply an inquiry into what the court is being asked to decide.

Holding – this is the court's response to the question presented by the Issue. The Holding begins with a "yes" or "no" response to the question posed in the Issue. This simple response is then followed by a one to two sentence statement of the rule applied by the court. It is the rule decided on by the court that resolves the problem framed by the Issue.

Rationale – this section is the most important part of the brief and, aside from the Facts, should be the case brief's lengthiest section. The Rationale explains the legal reasoning the court used to arrive at its decision. It is the interpretive part of the case brief that outlines the important facts relied on and the ultimate legal rule established by the court.

Legal Definitions

Interlocutory appeal – this is an interim appeal taken to an appellate court to settle a question of law prior to trial. It does not result in a final decision in the case but merely decides an issue in the case that must be resolved so as not to cause irreparable harm in the prosecution of the case against the parties. It is a limited type of appeal that courts are reluctant to give so as to avoid what is termed "piece-meal" litigation.

Dictum – these are ancillary or collateral remarks made by a judge in an opinion which has no binding authority in a case and cannot be cited as precedential authority in a subsequent case. It is judicial commentary made in a case as a suggestion or analogy or extended argument. The singular Latin form is dicta.

After assembling all the above components the student's finished product will be a case brief. The student will also, after reading several cases and writing out case briefs, have a better understanding of the language of the law and how to apply legal reasoning. The case brief that follows in Figure 1.1 is of one of the cases you will later read in Chapter 3, *McCulloch v. Maryland*. Take some time to jump ahead a bit, read the case and then see how it is briefed in the sample.

The foregoing illustrates the proper format and content of a case brief. By mastering this process you will eventually be able to read court decisions more critically and become more

FIGURE 1.1 Sample Case Brief

McCulloch v. Maryland
17 U.S. 316, 4 Wheat 316, 4 L.Ed. 579 (1819)

Facts: In 1816 Congress chartered the Second Bank of the United States. Branches were established in many states, including one in Baltimore, Maryland. In response, the Maryland legislature in 1818 adopted an Act imposing a tax on all banks in the state not chartered by the state legislature. James McCulloch, a cashier for the Baltimore branch of the United States Bank, refused to pay the tax and claimed the state could not properly tax the federal bank. He was subsequently sued for violating the state Act.

Procedural History: The case was initiated in the Baltimore County Court where McCulloch lost. He appealed to the Maryland Court of Appeals which affirmed the lower court decision. The case was then brought to the U.S. Supreme Court on a writ of error. The Supreme Court reversed and annulled the lower courts' decisions and held that judgment should be entered in favor of McCulloch.

Issue: Does Congress have the authority to establish a Bank of the United States under the Constitution? And, if so, did the Maryland law unconstitutionally interfere with Congressional powers?

Holding: Yes, in a unanimous decision the Court held that Congress had the power to establish the bank and that the State of Maryland acted unconstitutionally in taxing the federal bank.

Rationale: The Court held that the State of Maryland could not tax instruments of the national government employed in the execution of constitutional powers. Congress possesses unenumerated powers, in addition to its enumerated powers, not explicitly outlined in the Constitution. Chief Justice Marshall, writing for the unanimous court, held that even though the individual states retain the power of taxation, "the Constitution and the laws made in pursuance thereof are supreme." The unenumerated powers of Congress can be found in the wording of the "necessary and proper clause" to the Constitution, i.e., that Congress is given the right to pass "all laws which shall be necessary and proper for carrying into execution the foregoing powers . . ." This means that Congress is given the discretion to implement ways that it believes are most efficient in carrying out the powers granted to it by the Constitution. Further, the necessary and proper clause is among the powers of Congress and not its limitations, as such it was not included in the Constitution to limit the power of the Congress but rather to enhance those powers already enumerated to it.

immediately aware of the important points in a case. This in turns enhances your legal reasoning skills, which is part of the overall critical thinking ability you want to cultivate as a business or law student.

When it comes to legal reasoning there are a few basic skills required. First, you need to be able to find the key facts in a case. This is the initial process of selecting from the mass of facts presented in a written opinion those particular facts which have the most legal significance. Key facts are those facts which raise an issue of law. Next, you need to spot the issues. This is similar to finding key facts. A legal issue is simply the question or questions raised by key facts concerning their legal significance. Issue spotting connects key facts with the rule to be applied. But, in order to apply a rule you need to know its elements and to be able to precisely specify every element of the rule. Once you have the rules and the elements you need to apply them by the correlation of key facts with the elements of the rule(s). This shows that the rule selected is applicable because there are sufficient facts to prove each element of the rule. When you have arrived at this stage of your reasoning you are able to discern the basis of the court's decision and perhaps the individual judge's interpretive arguments for his or her decision. This in turn may lead to a broader analysis of competing schools of judicial interpretation and legal philosophies. Finally, you need to be able to communicate your reasoning. This requires you to write in an organized, clear, concise, logical and persuasive manner. Here is where you argue facts, rules and legal principles which rest on the foundation of your research and briefing skills.

SUMMARY

This chapter has provided an introduction to the study of business law by first defining business law as a substantive area of law covering diverse topics like contracts, sales, negotiable instruments, torts, property, secured transactions, business entities, collections and bankruptcy. It is a broad legal subject with many sub-specialties in which attorney practitioners often limit their areas of specialization. However, it is useful and practical for the legal practitioner as well as the business person to be familiar with all of the different areas of business law because they are often related. Before any study of the law can be undertaken it is necessary for the student to know how cases are referenced, or cited, as the term is used by lawyers, in primary and secondary sources. Additionally, the law has its own language, just like other professions, with terms that are French or Latin in their origin. Often legal practitioners use these terms as a type of short-hand in making written or oral argument or using it as a point of reference. The law even utilizes its own style of citation format based on *The Blue Book: A Uniform System of Citation*, which is much different than other more popular citation forms, such as MLA or APA.

Since the United States is a common law country wherein judge-made rules and the legal precedent resulting from it form the basis for other judges to follow, the concept of stare decisis ("to let a decision stand") is a key interpretive aspect of judicial decision-making. When it comes to the interpretation of the Constitution or other laws there are a broad array of judicial interpretive methods. These methods include originalism, textualism, pragmatism, structuralism, and polling jurisdictions. A Justice's or a judge's method of interpretation may be closely tied to his or her embrace of a certain philosophy of law. Legal philosophy is the study of the nature of the law and its legal systems. Different legal schools of philosophy see the purpose and aim of the law quite differently and it is through this lens that judges may interpret the law if they favor one philosophical view of the law over another.

Interpretations of the law, legal arguments made in court or within motion papers, and the study of law within and outside the classroom all have no impact if one does not know where to find the law and how to critically analyze the law. Primary sources of the law are constitutions, statutes and administrative rules. Secondary sources are legal encyclopedias, treatises and hornbooks which explain, interpret and criticize different aspects of the law. One of the more important skills in studying the law is being able to critically analyze case law. The case briefing method—which is organizing a case into its component parts of Facts, Procedural History, Issue, Holding and Rationale—enables law students to learn to critically read and understand case law and apply it to different situations.

THE COURTS, LEGAL PROCESS AND PROCEDURE

LEARNING OUTCOMES

Upon completion of this chapter the student will be able to:

1 Discuss the foundations of the American legal system.
2 Explain the differences between state and federal court systems.
3 Explain the difference between jurisdiction and venue.
4 Understand the basics of civil procedure and the litigation process.
5 Understand and explain the basics of alternative dispute resolution.

KEY TERMS

arbitration	in personam	quasi-in-rem
bill of particulars	in rem	retainer
complaint	interrogatory	standing
contingent fee	jurisdiction	summary judgment
counterclaim	mediation	venue
cross-claim	minimum contacts	voir dire
default judgment	motion	
deposition	preponderance of evidence	

I. A Brief History of Early American Law

Where do we begin in crafting an early history of American law? Do we start in colonial America or do we venture further back? Clearly, the law, like so many other customs and traditions brought over to America from foreign shores had its origin elsewhere, yet in time developed into its own uniquely American creation. Our American legal tradition has its roots in English common law. This is a natural progression since prior to the colonists' bold pronouncements in the Declaration of Independence and the subsequent war for independence our country was thirteen disparate colonies of England. These colonies were bound to England not only in loyalty but in trade and economics. Interestingly enough, if we look at the root causes of the revolution, the colonists' belief that England was engaging in unfair commercial trade practices and excessive taxation were a catalytic cause of the American Revolution. We do not intend to trivialize the more complex issues behind the Revolutionary War, which clearly were the result of grievances fomenting for many years among the colonies, yet it is not inaccurate to point out that some basic business disputes between colonial merchants and their English counterparts as well as the unfair treatment of colonial merchants and colonial taxpayers by the English government contributed to the eventual support for independence. But, if we are to discuss the roots of American law and provide a brief overview of our complex system of American law we must begin further back in U.S. history to earlier colonial times and the first organized settlement on North American shores. This occurred at Jamestown, Virginia in 1607 when the Virginia Company of London created the first English settlement in the America. The Virginia Company's 1606 charter said that all settlers to the colony *"shall have and enjoy all the liberties, franchises and immunities . . . to all intents and purposes, as if they had been abiding and born within this realm of England."*[1] But the colony operated more or less under military control and the laws that govern the military.[2] Furthermore, the inhabitants were under the "free laws which his Majesty's subjects live under in England."[3] Therefore, for the actual genesis of American law we begin with the arrival in 1620 of a scattered group of 102 settlers aboard the Mayflower onto the shores of Cape Cod. The majority of the group was comprised of Separatists, a Puritan sect, who split from the Church of England. They sought self-government in church as well as in civil affairs.[4] Shortly after their arrival 42 men entered into and signed a contract, known as the Mayflower Compact, which set out their unified goals to *"covenant and combine our selves together into a civil Body Politick, for our better Ordering and Preservation and Furtherance of the Ends aforesaid; And by Virtue hereof to enact, constitute, and frame such just and equal Laws, Ordinances, Acts, Constitutions and Offices, from time to time, as shall be thought most meet and convenient for the general Good of the Colony."*[5] This was the first apparent legislative enactment in the new settlement, an example of John Locke's social contract theory at work, an idea that would more fully express itself in the Declaration of Independence 156 years later. Yet, the settlement of what was to become the Massachusetts Bay Colony was chiefly administered by a commercial venture, the Massachusetts Bay Company, whose charter from the King of England gave this joint-stock corporation a license to inhabit and settle the New England area. The charter was typically that of a business corporation but with modifications made by the members who had it operating more like an English town.[6] What was evident from a study of this early form of government is a system separated by class or status within the community, as well as a deeply theocratic foundation.[7] Religious tolerance, which is an embedded tenet of our First Amendment to the Bills of Rights, was not openly respected then as it is today. One need only look back to the Salem Witch Trials in 1692–1693 in Massachusetts to understand the hold that religious doctrine and belief had in early colonial law. Also, not to be overlooked in discussing the Salem Witch Trials, is the impact of community status and class upon those who were singled out for prosecution. It is from this background that our early legal system began to develop. English common law and custom provided the foundation, but a uniquely

---

[1] William F. Swindler. *Common Law at Jamestown Celebration.* (1959).

[2] Id.

[3] Id.

[4] Rene A. Wormser. *The Story of the Law and the Men Who Made It—From the Earliest Times to the Present.* (1962).

[5] Yale University Law School. (2017 12-May). *Mayflower Compact: 1620.* From The Avalon Project: Documents in Law, History and Diplomacy: http://avalon.law.yale.edu/17th_century/mayflower.asp

[6] Lawrence M. Friedman. *A History of American Law.* (1985).

[7] Wormser at 309.

American system of law and understanding of the basic functions of government and its legal system within an ordered society would take root. This sentiment was stated by Justice Story in *Van Ness v. Pacard*, 27 U.S. 137 (1829), when he wrote: *"The common law of England is not to be taken in all respects to be that of America. Our ancestors brought with them its general principles, and claimed it as their birthright; but they brought with them and adopted only that portion which was applicable to their situation."* Two years later this incorporation of the English common law and statutes was noted by Chief Justice John Marshall in *Cathcart v. Robinson*, 30 U.S. 264 (1831): *"By adopting them, they became our own as entirely as if they had been enacted by the legislature of the State. The received construction in England at the time they are admitted to operate in this country, indeed, to the time of our separation from the British Empire may very well properly be considered as accompanying the statutes themselves, and forming integral parts of them. But, however we may respect the subsequent decisions, we do not admit their absolute authority."* However, the English influence, as reflected by Story and Marshall, was not without limits. The colonists made the law their own invention and innovation—many as improvements upon the English common law, some as retrogression. An example of the latter was the overly theocratic nature of the criminal law and subsequent punishments being public spectacles of shame and humiliation coupled with some severe forms of physical punishment.

The colonial court system grew out of the Massachusetts Bay Company's charter, initially providing for disputes and the handling of the affairs of the corporation.[8] Over time the Company would expand these courts to include general jurisdiction county courts, which additionally had an appellate function, and specialty courts to handle certain specified types of cases.[9] While mirroring the courts and procedures of England the colonial courts did not defer to the appellate control of English courts, though they did follow the rule that any laws not allowed in England would similarly be void in the colonies.[10] As the colonies settled and more areas developed along the east coast, different regions would establish their own unique court systems. From Virginia to the northern parts of New England the colonies slowly developed their legal infrastructure.

One of the more frequent areas of court claims in the colonies centered on land disputes, and a body of law and codification followed. This has been part of the historical record when it comes to understanding the nature of the law in general and public interest in the law.[11] Land in the colonies was abundant and viewed differently than in England which measured wealth and social standing in terms of estates in land and distribution rights to that land. Still, most rights to land in the colonies came through grants from the king. Conveyances were an intricate and mostly undocumented occurrence. Rare was the paper conveyance, a more primitive feudal practice known as livery of seisin was the practice. This entailed a symbolic transfer of "turf and twig" whereby a grantor turned over a piece of tree branch and soil to the grantee.[12] Eventually a uniquely American system of conveyance and recording would develop in the colonies whereby a written instrument was used to transfer property and it was recorded. This system and the reliance on recorded land titles to prove ownership developed in New England and pre-dated the system used in England.[13]

---

[8] Friedman at 38.
[9] Friedman at 37–40.
[10] Friedman at 46.
[11] E. Washburn (1860). *A Treatise on the American Law of Real Property: Volume 1.* (1860).
[12] Friedman at 236.
[13] Friedman at 237.

Other areas of the law developed as well, including inheritance law, criminal law and the law of commerce. The English standard of land inheritance of primogeniture, where the eldest son is entitled to succession, was not followed in the northern colonies. The southern colonies of Maryland, Virginia, North Carolina, and South Carolina, would follow the practice until the Revolutionary War, but the northern colonies followed a pattern of succession that was split among the children.[14] Surviving spouses were also given a portion of the estate and the making of formal written wills came into practice.[15]

The criminal law was initially very harsh and draconian.[16] As the colonies developed the more severe aspects of the criminal common law became less cruel, though public, corrective punishments were still in use. The intertwining of community well-being, social order and the religious observances of the colonists ensured that public punishments—flogging, the use of pillory and stocks—were maintained to ensure public opinion and shame as deterrents and correctives to bad and immoral behaviors.[17] Massachusetts established an early penal code in 1648 and was part of a movement toward codification of the criminal laws. Serious felonies, like murder, arson, burglary, rape, robbery and larceny, were punishable by death.[18] However, the majority of crimes involved social disorder offenses—fighting, drunkenness, lewd sexual acts, and assault.[19] The most significant colonial improvement over the common law was in the area of criminal procedure.[20] Jury trials become more prevalent and the accusatorial system was gradually replaced with an adversarial system.[21]

Commercial law in the early colonies was uniquely tied to English law and was, in nature and practice, truly international law. European markets in the latter part of the 17th century were tied to the concentration of financial capital and credit in England.[22] This fact plus the natural tie the colonists still had to English customs, particularly English law, was part of the colonists' commitment to abide by a set of legal rules and, in doing so, borrow from their English legal heritage.[23] However, as in other areas of the law, the colonies were more innovative in recognizing certain rights, particularly in the area of intangible property. The English common law was not as diligent in protecting the rights of an individual who received an intangible transfer of property, such as a note for payment.[24] Beginning in the early part of the 18th century the colonies would experience an influx of commercial cases in which plaintiff-creditors sought relief against defendant-debtors.[25] The recognition in colonial courts of the enforceability of secured credit agreements soon followed.[26]

---

[14] Friedman at 238–9.

[15] Stoebuck, W. B. (1968). Reception of English Common Law in the American Colonies. *William & Mary Law Review*, 393–426.

[16] Friedman at 68–70.

[17] Id.

[18] W.R. Miller. *The Social History of Crime and Punishment in America: An Encyclopedia.* (2012)

[19] Id.

[20] Id.

[21] Id.

[22] Benton, L. &. (2014). Law for the Empire: The Common Law in Colonial America and the Problem of Legal Diversity. *Chicago-Kent Law Review*, 937–956.

[23] Id.

[24] Friedman at 234–6.

[25] Priest, C. (1999). Colonial Courts and Secured Credit: Early American Commercial Litigation and Shay's Rebellion. *The Yale Law Journal*, 2413–2450.

[26] Id.

A most unfortunate and despicable aspect of colonial law relating to commerce was the propagation of the slave trade in the colonies. While indentured servitude was one means of securing labor in the north and south, slavery was prevalent in the southern tobacco, rice, and sugar colonies.[27] In these areas they would eventually replace white and captured Indian servants. The regulation of slaves as property became part of the law in the colonies. Despite there being free blacks in the colonies their treatment was not much improved over that of the slave. The law discriminated against them and they had a quasi-slave status, even as free persons. Ironically, it would be the innovative legal argument and use of the Commerce Clause to the U.S. Constitution (discussed more fully in Chapter 3) that would end the "separate but equal doctrine" and application of Jim Crow Laws in the south.

The 18th century in the colonies would bring about a more complete codification of the law and the emergence of the legal profession. While lawyers were still viewed with the same contempt and suspicion as they had been in the 17th century, they were becoming more of a "necessary evil."[28] Eventually, during the latter part of the 18th century the winds of revolution would blow, with many prominent legal minds of the time—John Adams, Thomas Jefferson, James Monroe, Alexander Hamilton, among many others—at the center of the controversy. Beginning with the Declaration of Independence in 1776 and followed by the Constitution in 1788, a complex legal system would evolve into the modern system presently in place. While it is often easy to mark our American legal traditions with all that occurred after the Revolutionary War and the Constitutional Convention, it is apparent from the foregoing that the seeds were sown much earlier.

II. The State and Federal Court Systems

The American court system is basically a dual, three-tiered system. It is dual in the fact that we have a separate federal court system and each state has a separate court system independent of the federal courts. The court systems at both the federal and state levels are three-tiered because each has a trial level, an intermediate appellate level court, and then a final appellate level court or Supreme Court. Each system acts independent of the other, though state law cases can find their ultimate way to the U.S. Supreme Court if a federal question or constitutional issue is involved.

At the federal level the general jurisdiction trial courts are known as the district courts. Federal district courts are divided geographically throughout the 50 states. Depending on the size of the state there may be multiple federal districts within the state. California, New York and Texas each have four federal districts within their borders. Smaller states like Connecticut, Delaware and Rhode Island have only one federal district. The intermediate appellate courts in the federal system are known as the U.S. Courts of Appeals. These are limited jurisdiction courts that are also divided geographically across the United States. There are 13 federal circuit courts of appeals numbered 1–11 with the twelfth circuit encompassing the District of Columbia Circuit Court of Appeals and the thirteenth covering the Court of Appeals for the Federal Circuit, which has jurisdiction to hear appeals in specialized cases such as patent cases or those emanating from the Court of International Trade or Federal Court of Claims.[29] Figure 2.2 shows the geographical distribution of the different federal circuit courts across the country.

---

[27] Friedman at 85–9.

[28] Id

[29] Administrative Office of the United States Courts. (2017 12-May). *U.S. Courts*. From Court Role and Structure: http://www.uscourts.gov/about-federal-courts/court-role-and-structure

FIGURE 2.1   Basic U.S. Court System

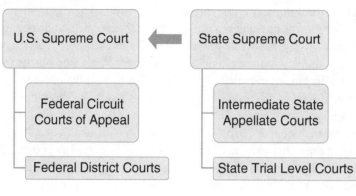

FIGURE 2.2   Federal Court System Geographical Organization

Source: http://www.uscourts.gov/uscourts/images/CircuitMap.pdf

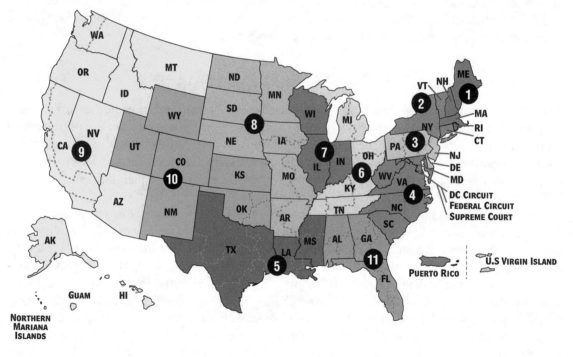

As can be seen from the map in Figure 2.2, many of the circuit courts' jurisdictions extend over multiple states. Finally, the last level in the federal system is the U.S. Supreme Court, the court of last resort for cases at both the federal and state level. The Supreme Court is also a court of limited jurisdiction which generally has only appellate jurisdiction in most cases and original jurisdiction only in those ". . . cases affecting ambassadors, other public ministers and consuls, and those in which a state shall be a party."[30] The Supreme Court derives its powers from Article III, section 1 of the United States Constitution:

"The judicial power of the United States, shall be vested in one Supreme Court, and in such inferior courts as the Congress may from time to time ordain and establish. The judges, both of the supreme and inferior courts, shall hold their offices during good behavior, and shall, at stated times, receive for their services, a compensation, which shall not be diminished during their continuance in office."

The specific powers of the Supreme Court are further outlined in section 2 of Article III:

"The judicial power shall extend to all cases, in law and equity, arising under this Constitution, the laws of the United States, and treaties made, or which shall be made, under their authority;—to all cases affecting ambassadors, other public ministers and consuls;—to all cases of admiralty and maritime jurisdiction;—to controversies to which the United States shall be a party;—to controversies between two or more states;—between a state and citizens of another state;—between citizens of different states;—between citizens of the same state claiming lands under grants of different states, and between a state, or the citizens thereof, and foreign states, citizens or subjects.

In all cases affecting ambassadors, other public ministers and consuls, and those in which a state shall be party, the Supreme Court shall have original jurisdiction. In all the other cases before mentioned, the Supreme Court shall have appellate jurisdiction, both as to law and fact, with such exceptions, and under such regulations as the Congress shall make.

The trial of all crimes, except in cases of impeachment, shall be by jury; and such trial shall be held in the state where the said crimes shall have been committed; but when not committed within any state, the trial shall be at such place or places as the Congress may by law have directed."

When reading Article III an obvious question comes to mind regarding the "inferior courts" referenced in section 1—where is the explanation of the powers of these courts and, more importantly, from what authority, besides a brief reference in section 1, do these courts emanate from? The answer came during the First United States Congress with the passage of the Judiciary Act of 1789, also more formally known as "An Act to establish the Judicial Courts of the United States." The Judiciary Act of 1789 established the beginning framework for the federal district and circuit court system we find in place today, as well as further outlining the jurisdiction of the Supreme Court. Additionally, the Act contained two other important provisions: (1) it created the Office of the Attorney General, which is the chief law enforcement title within the federal government; and (2) it created the Alien Tort Statute (28 USC 1350), which provides federal district court jurisdiction for aliens seeking to bring a civil lawsuit against the United States for violations of international law or treaties between the United States and other nations. The Judiciary Act of 1789 was authored and sponsored by Senators Oliver Ellsworth from Connecticut, and William Paterson from New Jersey. Both senators were original framers and signers of the U.S. Constitution and each would eventually serve on the U.S. Supreme Court, Ellsworth as Chief Justice from 1796 to 1800 and Paterson as an Associate Justice from 1793–1806.

---

[30] Article III, section 2 U.S. Const.

However, despite the significance of the Judiciary Act of 1789 it would be the Judiciary Act of 1891 (the Circuit Courts of Appeals Act), also known as the Evarts Act so named after its primary sponsor Senator William M. Evarts of New York, which would create the present U.S. Court of Appeals system. Since the passage of the Judiciary Act of 1789, in addition to having appellate jurisdiction over the district courts and requiring U.S. Supreme Court justices to "ride the circuit" by traveling to assigned circuit courts to preside over pending cases, the circuit courts retained original jurisdiction over cases involving serious federal crimes and disputes between citizens of different states (referred to as diversity jurisdiction). The Judiciary Act of 1891 established nine original U.S. Circuit Courts of Appeal and limited the courts' jurisdiction to appellate jurisdiction over the federal district courts. Although the circuit courts originally established by the Judiciary Act of 1789 still continued to exist they were eventually abolished by the Judicial Code of 1911.

Before concluding this discussion of the federal court system and moving onto the state courts system it is necessary to provide a definition of some terms already referenced. The concepts of general jurisdiction and limited jurisdiction may seem self-explanatory and simple at first but this is an assumption that has led many a litigant to file a lawsuit only to have it dismissed for lack of jurisdiction. When it is said that a court has general jurisdiction the reference is to a trial level court that has the ability to adjudicate a number of claims. These general jurisdiction courts have the ability to consider cases involving substantial sums of money in dispute or to adjudicate criminal cases involving felony offenses. However, at the trial level there are still courts which retain only a limited general jurisdiction and those that retain a specific general jurisdiction. Courts with limited general jurisdiction include small claims courts that can consider only contract matters up to a certain statutory amount (for example, $5,000.00 in New York and Connecticut) or local municipal courts that can adjudicate low level criminal offenses. Courts of specific general jurisdiction include courts that hear family offenses or family related matters, probate courts that deal only with decedent estates and trust matters, and state chancery courts (which exist in Delaware, New Jersey, Mississippi, South Carolina and Tennessee) that deal only with equitable claims. Courts of limited jurisdiction are those courts that do not have any general jurisdiction powers (or if they do they are like the U.S. Supreme Court and extremely narrow.) These courts have appellate jurisdiction over lower level courts of general jurisdiction or courts of limited general jurisdiction and specific general jurisdiction. The authority of these courts is often defined by statute. An example would be the jurisdiction of the federal appellate courts which is defined in Title 28 of the United States Code section 1291 (*"The courts of appeals (other than the United States Court of Appeals for the Federal Circuit) shall have jurisdiction of appeals from all final decisions of the district courts of the United States, the United States District Court for the District of the Canal Zone, the District Court of Guam, and the District Court of the Virgin Islands, except where a direct review may be had in the Supreme Court."*)

Legal Definitions

General jurisdiction – jurisdiction of a court to preside over a broad range of cases, including both criminal and civil, within the geographic area it is located.

Limited jurisdiction – jurisdiction of a court limited to a particular area of the law, such as probate matters, whose jurisdiction is set by statute.

The statutory power of appellate jurisdiction is critically important since it dictates whether or not an appeal may be taken by a party. The U.S. Supreme Court has held that with regard to federal appellate jurisdiction an appeal is not a constitutional guarantee in either a criminal or civil case. Beginning with *Durousseau v. United States*, 10 U.S. 307 (1810), the Court held that its constitutional powers of review, given by the Constitution, are still limited and regulated by the Judiciary Act of 1789 and other Congressional acts.[31] In a much later case, *Abney v. United States*, 431 U.S. 651 (1977), the Court said the ability to appeal a criminal case was dependent upon an authorizing statute. In *Abney* the Court also referenced civil cases as being similarly limited by statute. State statutes are also important in defining appellate jurisdiction in the state courts. For instance, the North Carolina Constitution in Article IV § 12(2) succinctly states that, *"The Court of Appeals shall have such appellate jurisdiction as the General Assembly may prescribe."* The statute thereby limits appellate jurisdiction to that which has been granted by the legislature. A good example of the limiting aspect of appellate jurisdiction at the state level is seen in the decision of the Kansas Supreme Court in *Wiechman v. Huddleston*, 304 Kan. 80, 370 P.3d 1194 (2016) wherein the court decided to overturn a 1978 court precedent granting a judicially created right of appeal. In doing so the court wrote that it was going to *"adhere to our jurisprudence that limits appellate jurisdiction in civil cases to that provided by statute."*[32] A broader discussion of jurisdiction will follow in the next section.

State courts arguably are busier than federal courts in that they are the broader venue in terms of jurisdiction but also, they are the most local and familiar. These courts handle the majority of civil and criminal cases heard within the United States. While their structure is generally similar to the three-tiered federal courts system there are some variances among the states. For instance, two states, Maryland and New York do not refer to their final state level appellate court as the Supreme Court, as other states do; rather these two states refer to their top court as the Court of Appeals. New York further confuses the court nomenclature by referring to its general trial level state courts as the Supreme Court. Also, nine states (Delaware, Maine, Montana, New Hampshire, Rhode Island, South Dakota, Vermont, West Virginia and Wyoming) do not have an intermediate level appellate court. These courts permit an appeal directly to their state supreme court. The District of Columbia also has no intermediate appellate court and like Maryland and New York has a Court of Appeals as its court of last resort.

While each state court system runs independent of each other and is guided by a state office of court administration there is a National Center for State Courts, located in Williamsburg, Virginia, whose mission is to "improve the administration of justice" among state courts.[33] Founded in 1971, the National Center for State Courts has provided guidance on court management, technology, and performance standards. It has also produced a yearly resource for court professionals, in a joint project with the Conference of State Court Administrators, through its Court Statistics Project (www.courtstatistics.org). In a yearly report caseload data is published from the 50 state courts, District of Columbia and Puerto Rico. A recent poll by the National Center for Courts indicated that public trust in the state courts is at its highest level in a number of years.[34] Included in the report

---

[31] Easley, D. (2015 6-March). *Federal Appellate Jurisdiction Still Has Its Limits*. From American Bar Association: http://apps.americanbar.org/litigation/committees/appellate/articles/winter2015-0315-federal-appellate-jurisdiction-still-has-its-limits.html

[32] *Wiechman* at 88

[33] National Center for State Courts. (2017 12-May). *National Center for State Courts*. From Mission and History: http://www.ncsc.org/About-us/Mission-and-history.aspx

[34] National Center for State Courts. (2016). *Annual Report* . Williamsburg: National Center for State Courts.

was a 78% satisfaction rating in procedural fairness among those who had direct interaction with the state courts.[35] However, a negative result from the same report was that those who are more knowledgeable about the courts reported less confidence in the court system.

III. Jurisdiction and Venue

Jurisdiction was already briefly covered in the prior section by distinguishing courts with general and limited jurisdiction. When discussing the jurisdiction of a court we are referring to its power to decide a case or to issue a decree.[36] It is quite different from venue which refers to the proper place for the trial of a case; it is an issue of locality. Why the concern with venue? A historical concern in the United States emanates from early grievances against England outlined in a 1774 Petition to the King from the First Continental Congress. Among a list of grievances the Congress took exception to a recent Act of Parliament that provided for colonists to be tried in England for crimes committed in America.[37] This outrage, along with the fact that a colonist could be subject to indictment and tried in any "shire or county within the realm" thereby depriving them of a jury of their peers[38], influenced the subsequent drafting of the U.S. Constitution several years later. Article 3, Section 2 of the U.S. Constitution states:

"Trial of all Crimes . . . shall be held in the State where the said Crimes shall have been committed; but when not committed within any State, the Trial shall be at such Place or Places as the Congress may by Law have directed." Generally, and in its simplest explanation, venue is a matter of the most convenient forum for a case to be tried by the parties. While jurisdiction refers to a court's inherent power, venue is based on some connection with the parties or the place where the event(s) at issue occurred. An attorney can file a case and be in a court with the appropriate jurisdiction but the wrong venue. Similarly, a case can be filed in the proper venue but in a court without the proper jurisdiction. Here is an example of each:

1)   Betty Jensen contracts with a company, Handy Home Contractors, located in County X, State Z to perform work where she lives in County Y, State Z. Betty enters into the contract in County X at the company's office. The company accepts Betty's payment in full and begins to do the contracted for work which consists of building an addition to her home. The company fails to complete the work as scheduled. She wants to initiate a lawsuit against Handy Home Contractors. Her options are to sue in a trial court of general jurisdiction located in either County X or County Y. Since she contracted for the work to be done with the company in County X that would be a proper venue and convenient since the company has offices in County X. But Betty could also sue in County Y since that is where she lives and the location of where the contracted for work was performed. However, let us assume for this scenario that Betty hears that a judge in County W is more favorable to consumers and penalizes businesses that do not adhere to contracts. If she were to file in a trial court located in County W the defendant Handy Home Contractors could make a motion to have to the case moved to a more convenient venue, in this instance likely to County X, since there is no connection in the case to County W. This would be a situation where the case

---

[35] Id.

[36] Black's Law Dictionary (19th ed., 2010)

[37] National Humanities Center. (2017 17-May). *Petition to King George III*. From America in Class: http://americainclass.org/sources/makingrevolution/crisis/text7/petitionkinggeorge3.pdf

[38] Id.

would be in a court with jurisdiction to hear such a case but one which could not exercise its jurisdiction because the case was in the wrong forum.

2)   In this scenario we have a situation wherein Charlie Mathers is struck by a car while crossing the street in a municipality located in County X, State Z. He suffers injuries that require a brief hospitalization and loss of two weeks work. The operator of the motor vehicle that struck Charlie is also a resident of County X, State Z. The proper venue in this scenario is obviously a trial court in County X. Charlie is not too familiar with the court system but knows there is a lot of information on the internet and decides to act as his own attorney. Charlie knows there is a court a few streets away from his apartment and he goes to the court and files his lawsuit for negligence against the motor vehicle operator. The only problem is that the court Charlie files in the County Probate Court which is limited in its jurisdiction to presiding over cases involving decedents' estates and trusts. A court clerk advises him of this and directs Charlie down the street to the state superior court for the County of X. This is a situation wherein Charlie has filed in the right county but the wrong court. The County Probate Court has no jurisdiction over negligence cases.

In neither of the scenarios above is there a detriment to the improper filings, provided there are no time limitations for filing which have passed as a result of the wrong venue and jurisdiction filings. Of course, if a case remains in a court in which it does not belong there may be a problem if the relevant statute of limitations has passed. But, in general these are matters resolved early in a case.

Venue is guided in civil cases by each state's civil procedural rules. A plaintiff bringing a lawsuit can base venue on the following:

i)   county where the plaintiff resides when the action is commenced;
ii)   county where the defendant resides when the action is commenced;
iii)   county where the dispute or incident arose;
iv)   county where the business is located if a business defendant.

Separate venue rules apply in criminal cases and these are covered separately in state criminal procedure codes. There are less venue options since venue in criminal cases is restricted to those locations where a crime occurred. Because of the nature of some criminal offenses venue may be proper in one of two places, where a crime emanated from and where it had an end result.

In both criminal and civil cases a party can request a change of venue, thereby taking the case out of the locality which has a connection to the occurrence at the center of the case. The ability to change venue is grounded in the guarantee contained in the 6th Amendment to the U.S. Constitution which provides the right of an individual to a fair and impartial trial. Grounds for a change of venue are based on state statute but judges are left to their discretion in whether or not to grant a change of venue. Only an abuse of the discretion exercised by a judge will overturn a change of venue decision.[39] A party moving for a change of venue has to show some prejudice or predisposition on the part of a potential pool of jurors that would create a lack of impartiality. Other causes for a change may relate to convenience of witnesses or to further the interests of justice. An available option to a change of venue when there is a concern about juror impartiality due to pre-trial publicity involves retaining the venue but bringing in a jury pool from another location.[40]

---

[39] See eg., State ex rel. Dunbar v. Ham, 45 Ohio St.2d 112, 341 N.E.2d 594 (1976)
[40] See eg., California Penal Code section 1036.7

Jurisdiction has already been broadly defined above and distinguished in the prior section between courts of general and limited jurisdiction. However, there are several more terms and definitions to be explained before a more comprehensive understanding of jurisdiction can be gained. A court can only act if it has the necessary jurisdiction, which has already been defined as the power or authority to carry out some process, such as to issue a decision or judgment in case. There are two basic types of jurisdiction that a court can have—subject matter jurisdiction and personal jurisdiction. The prior segment on courts of general and limited jurisdiction dealt with subject matter jurisdiction, the general power of a court to hear a case. In the second scenario above involving Charles Mathers the probate court lacked subject matter jurisdiction to preside over his case. Subject matter jurisdiction can never be waived by the parties to litigation. It is a defense that is available to litigants through litigation.[41]

Personal jurisdiction is the second type of jurisdiction a court can exercise. This is the court's "power to bring persons into its adjudicative process."[42] It is also referred to as in personam jurisdiction. Similar to in personam jurisdiction is in rem jurisdiction which is limited to a court's jurisdiction over property. A court may not be able to assert in personam jurisdiction over an individual but may be able to assert in rem jurisdiction over their property. Even though there is no personal jurisdiction over the individual an in rem proceeding still gives the court some control over the individual by way of the property. The parties to litigation can waive personal jurisdiction, however, lack of personal jurisdiction can also be asserted as a defense. There are four means by which personal jurisdiction can be obtained over a defendant:

i)   presence in the forum state (this includes even temporary presence);
ii) a domicile or residence in the forum state, including the operation of a business;
iii) consent to personal jurisdiction in the forum state;
iv) minimum contacts with the forum state.

This latter category of minimum contacts requires some additional explanation. Also referred to as minimal contacts, this requires that a nonresident have some connection with the forum state in order for a plaintiff to establish court jurisdiction over a nonresident defendant. Typically this concept is used to obtain jurisdiction over out-of-state businesses.

The U.S. Supreme Court has established a four-part test for minimum contacts:

i)   continuous, systematic contact in the forum state and the lawsuit is related to that activity or contact—personal jurisdiction can be obtained;
ii) continuous, systematic contact in the forum state and the lawsuit is not related to that activity or contact—there can still be personal jurisdiction due to the continuity and volume of the contacts, even though the activity or contact is not related;
iii) sporadic or casual activity in the state that is related to the lawsuit—personal jurisdiction can still be maintained because of the nexus between the activity or contact and the lawsuit;
iv) sporadic or casual activity in the state that is not related to the lawsuit—in this instance there will not be personal jurisdiction because of the tenuous nature of the contact.

---

[41] See eg., Fed. R. Civ. Pro. 12(b)6; NY CPLR § 3211(a)(2)
[42] Black's Law Dictionary (19th ed., 2010)

Legal Definitions

In personam jurisdiction – the power of a court to assert jurisdiction over an individual and personal rights; it is a broader assertion of jurisdiction than in rem.

In rem jurisdiction – the power of a court to assert jurisdiction over property and determine an individual's rights to that property; it includes the authority to seize the property.

Minimum contacts – these are the activities of a nonresident defendant, such as business activities, in a forum state that permit a plaintiff to assert a forum state's court's jurisdiction over that individual in a civil suit.

A landmark U.S. Supreme Court case establishing the concept of minimum contacts is *International Shoe Company v. Washington*. As you read the following text of the case focus on what the Court established as the grounds for finding jurisdiction over the company by the State of Washington.

❖❖❖

International Shoe Co. v. Washington
326 U.S. 310 (1945)

Mr. Chief Justice Stone delivered the opinion of the Court.

The questions for decision are (1) whether, within the limitations of the due process clause of the Fourteenth Amendment, appellant, a Delaware corporation, has by its activities in the State of Washington rendered itself amenable to proceedings in the courts of that state to recover unpaid contributions to the state unemployment compensation fund exacted by state statutes, Washington Unemployment Compensation Act, Washington Revised Statutes, 9998-103a through 9998-123a, 1941 Supp., and (2) whether the state can exact those contributions consistently with the due process clause of the Fourteenth Amendment.

The statutes in question set up a comprehensive scheme of unemployment compensation, the costs of which are defrayed by contributions required to be made by employers to a state unemployment compensation fund. The contributions are a specified percentage of the wages payable annually by each employer for his employees' services in the state. The assessment and collection of the contributions and the fund are administered by respondents. . . .

***

In this case notice of assessment for the years in question was personally served upon a sales solicitor employed by appellant in the State of Washington, and a copy of the notice was mailed by registered mail to appellant at its address in St. Louis, Missouri. Appellant appeared specially before the office of unemployment and moved to set aside the order and notice of assessment on the ground that the service upon appellant's salesman was not proper service upon appellant; that appellant was not a corporation of the State of Washington and was not doing business within the state; that it had no agent within the state upon whom service could be made; and that appellant is not an employer and does not furnish employment within the meaning of the statute.

The motion was heard on evidence and a stipulation of facts by the appeal tribunal which denied the motion and ruled that respondent Commissioner was entitled to recover the unpaid contributions. That action was affirmed by the Commissioner; both the Superior Court and the Supreme

Court affirmed. Appellant in each of these courts assailed the statute as applied, as a violation of the due process clause of the Fourteenth Amendment, and as imposing a constitutionally prohibited burden on interstate commerce. The cause comes here on appeal under 237(a) of the Judicial Code, 28 U.S.C. 344(a), 28 U.S.C.A. 344(a), appellant assigning as error that the challenged statutes as applied infringe the due process clause of the Fourteenth Amendment and the commerce clause.

The facts as found by the appeal tribunal and accepted by the state Superior Court and Supreme Court, are not in dispute. Appellant is a Delaware corporation, having its principal place of business in St. Louis, Missouri, and is engaged in the manufacture and sale of shoes and other footwear. It maintains places of business in several states, other than Washington, at which its manufacturing is carried on and from which its merchandise is distributed interstate through several sales units or branches located outside the State of Washington.

Appellant has no office in Washington and makes no contracts either for sale or purchase of merchandise there. It maintains no stock of merchandise in that state and makes there no deliveries of goods in intrastate commerce. During the years from 1937 to 1940, now in question, appellant employed eleven to thirteen salesmen under direct supervision and control of sales managers located in St. Louis. These salesmen resided in Washington; their principal activities were confined to that state; and they were compensated by commissions based upon the amount of their sales. The commissions for each year totaled more than $31,000. Appellant supplies its salesmen with a line of samples, each consisting of one shoe of a pair, which they display to prospective purchasers. On occasion they rent permanent sample rooms, for exhibiting samples, in business buildings, or rent rooms in hotels or business buildings temporarily for that purpose. The cost of such rentals is reimbursed by appellant.

The authority of the salesmen is limited to exhibiting their samples and soliciting orders from prospective buyers, at prices and on terms fixed by appellant. The salesmen transmit the orders to appellant's office in St. Louis for acceptance or rejection, and when accepted the merchandise for filling the orders is shipped f.o.b. from points outside Washington to the purchasers within the state. All the merchandise shipped into Washington is invoiced at the place of shipment from which collections are made. No salesman has authority to enter into contracts or to make collections.

The Supreme Court of Washington was of opinion that the regular and systematic solicitation of orders in the state by appellant's salesmen, resulting in a continuous flow of appellant's product into the state, was sufficient to constitute doing business in the state so as to make appellant amenable to suit in its courts. But it was also of opinion that there were sufficient additional activities shown to bring the case within the rule, frequently stated, that solicitation within a state by the agents of a foreign corporation plus some additional activities there are sufficient to render the corporation amenable to suit brought in the courts of the state to enforce an obligation arising out of its activities there. *International Harvester Co. v. Kentucky,* 234 U.S. 579, 234 U.S. 587; *People's Tobacco Co. v. American Tobacco Co.,* 246 U.S. 79, 246 U.S. 87; *Frene v. Louisville Cement Co.,* 77 U.S. App.D.C. 129, 134 F.2d 511, 516. The court found such additional activities in the salesmen's display of samples sometimes in permanent display rooms, and the salesmen's residence within the state, continued over a period of years, all resulting in asubstantial volume of merchandise regularly shipped by appellant to purchasers within the state. The court also held that the statute, as applied, did not invade the constitutional power of Congress to regulate interstate commerce, and did not impose a prohibited burden on such commerce.

Appellant's argument, renewed here, that the statute imposes an unconstitutional burden on interstate commerce need not detain us. For 53 Stat. 1391, 26 U.S.C. § 1606(a) provides that

"No person required under a State law to make payments to an unemployment fund shall be relieved from compliance therewith on the ground that he is engaged in interstate or foreign commerce, or that the State law does not distinguish between employees engaged in interstate or foreign commerce and those engaged in intrastate commerce."

It is no longer debatable that Congress, in the exercise of the commerce power, may authorize the states, in specified ways, to regulate interstate commerce or impose burdens upon it. *Kentucky Whip & Collar Co. v. Illinois Central R. Co.*, 299 U.S. 334; *Perkins v. Pennsylvania*, 314 U.S. 586; *Standard Dredging Corp. v. Murphy*, 319 U.S. 306, 319 U.S. 308; *Hooven & Allison Co. v. Evatt*, 324 U.S. 652, 324 U.S. 679; *Southern Pacific Co. v. Arizona*, 325 U.S. 761, 325 U.S. 769.

Appellant also insists that its activities within the state were not sufficient to manifest its "presence" there, and that, in its absence, the state courts were without jurisdiction, that, consequently, it was a denial of due process for the state to subject appellant to suit. It refers to those cases in which it was said that the mere solicitation of orders for the purchase of goods within a state, to be accepted without the state and filled by shipment of the purchased goods interstate, does not render the corporation seller amenable to suit within the state. See *Green v. Chicago, B. & Q. R. Co.*, 205 U.S. 530, 205 U.S. 533; *International Harvester Co. v. Kentucky, supra*, 234 U.S. 586–587; *Philadelphia & Reading R. Co. v. McKibbin*, 243 U.S. 264, 243 U.S. 268; *People's Tobacco Co. v. American Tobacco Co., supra*, 246 U.S. 87. And appellant further argues that, since it was not present within the state, it is a denial of due process to subject it to taxation or other money exaction. It thus denies the power of the state to lay the tax or to subject appellant to a suit for its collection.

Historically the jurisdiction of courts to render judgment in personam is grounded on their de facto power over the defendant's person. Hence his presence within the territorial jurisdiction of court was prerequisite to its rendition of a judgment personally binding him. *Pennoyer v. Neff*, 95 U.S. 714, 733. But now that the capias ad respondendum has given way to personal service of summons or other form of notice, due process requires only that in order to subject a defendant to a judgment in personam, if he be not present within the territory of the forum, he have certain minimum contacts with it such that the maintenance of the suit does not offend 'traditional notions of fair play and substantial justice.'

Since the corporate personality is a fiction, although a fiction intended to be acted upon as though it were a fact, *Klein v. Board of Tax Supervisors*, 282 U.S. 19, 24, 51 S.Ct. 15, 16, 73 A.L.R. 679, it is clear that unlike an individual its 'presence' without, as well as within, the state of its origin can be manifested only by activities carried on in its behalf by those who are authorized to act for it. To say that the corporation is so far 'present' there as to satisfy due process requirements, for purposes of taxation or the maintenance of suits against it in the courts of the state, is to beg the question to be decided. For the terms 'present' or 'presence' are used merely to symbolize those activities of the corporation's agent within the state which courts will deem to be sufficient to satisfy the demands of due process. L. Hand, J., in *Hutchinson v. Chase & Gilbert*, 2 Cir., 45 F.2d 139, 141. Those demands may be met by such contacts of the corporation with the state of the forum as make it reasonable, in the context of our federal system of government, to require the corporation to defend the particular suit which is brought there. An 'estimate of the inconveniences' which would result to the corporation from a trial away from its 'home' or principal place of business is relevant in this connection. *Hutchinson v. Chase & Gilbert, supra*, 45 F.2d 141.

'Presence' in the state in this sense has never been doubted when the activities of the corporation there have not only been continuous and systematic, but also give rise to the liabilities sued on, even though no consent to be sued or authorization to an agent to accept service of process has been given. Conversely it has been generally recognized that the casual presence of the corporate agent or even his conduct of single or isolated items of activities in a state in the corporation's behalf are not enough to subject it to suit on causes of action unconnected with the activities there. To require the corporation in such circumstances to defend the suit away from its home or other jurisdiction where it carries on more substantial activities has been thought to lay too great and unreasonable a burden on the corporation to comport with due process. While it has been held in cases on which appellant relies that continuous activity of some sorts within a state is not enough to support the demand that the corporation be amenable to suits unrelated to that activity, there have been instances in which the continuous corporate operations within a state were thought so substantial and of such a nature as to justify suit against it on causes of action arising from dealings entirely distinct from those activities.

Finally, although the commission of some single or occasional acts of the corporate agent in a state sufficient to impose an obligation or liability on the corporation has not been thought to confer upon the state authority to enforce it, other such acts, because of their nature and quality and the circumstances of their commission, may be deemed sufficient to render the corporation liable to suit.

***

Whether due process is satisfied must depend rather upon the quality and nature of the activity in relation to the fair and orderly administration of the laws which it was the purpose of the due process clause to insure. That clause does not contemplate that a state may make binding a judgment in personam against an individual or corporate defendant with which the state has no contacts, ties, or relations. Cf. *Pennoyer v. Neff*, supra; *Minnesota Commercial Men's Ass'n v. Benn*, 261 U.S. 140, 43 S.Ct. 293.

But to the extent that a corporation exercises the privilege of conducting activities within a state, it enjoys the benefits and protection of the laws of that state. The exercise of that privilege may give rise to obligations; and, so far as those obligations arise out of or are connected with the activities within the state, a procedure which requires the corporation to respond to a suit brought to enforce them can, in most instances, hardly be said to be undue. Applying these standards, the activities carried on in behalf of appellant in the State of Washington were neither irregular nor casual. They were systematic and continuous throughout the years in question. They resulted in a large volume of interstate business, in the course of which appellant received the benefits and protection of the laws of the state, including the right to resort to the courts for the enforcement of its rights. The obligation which is here sued upon arose out of those very activities. It is evident that these operations establish sufficient contacts or ties with the state of the forum to make it reasonable and just according to our traditional conception of fair play and substantial justice to permit the state to enforce the obligations which appellant has incurred there. Hence we cannot say that the maintenance of the present suit in the State of Washington involves an unreasonable or undue procedure.

We are likewise unable to conclude that the service of the process within the state upon an agent whose activities establish appellant's 'presence' there was not sufficient notice of the suit, or that the suit was so unrelated to those activities as to make the agent an inappropriate vehicle for communicating the notice. It is enough that appellant has established such contacts with the state that the particular form of substituted service adopted there gives reasonable assurance that the notice will be actual. Nor can we say that the mailing of the notice of suit to appellant by registered mail at its home office was not reasonably calculated to apprise appellant of the suit.

***

Appellant having rendered itself amenable to suit upon obligations arising out of the activities of its salesmen in Washington, the state may maintain the present suit in personam to collect the tax laid upon the exercise of the privilege of employing appellant's salesmen within the state. For Washington has made one of those activities, which taken together establish appellant's 'presence' there for purposes of suit, the taxable event by which the state brings appellant within the reach of its taxing power. The state thus has constitutional power to lay the tax and to subject appellant to a suit to recover it. The activities which establish its 'presence' subject it alike to taxation by the state and to suit to recover the tax.

Affirmed.

Questions Presented

1) Why is the 14th Amendment implicated in this case and what is the due process issue before the Court?
2) What did the Court indicate was the prior test for in personam jurisdiction over a corporation?
3) What did the Court say about the appellant's commerce clause argument?
4) What was the extent of the "minimum contacts" the Court found in order to establish personal jurisdiction over the International Shoe Corporation?

❖❖

The *International Shoe* opinion cites an earlier case, *Pennoyer v. Neff*, 95 U.S. 714 (1878), in which the Supreme Court held that a state court could not exercise personal jurisdiction over a nonresident unless that individual was personally served while in the state or had property attached in the state. In that case Neff was sued by his former attorney for legal fees owed. The attorney, Mitchell, sued Neff in Oregon state court. Neff was not personally served. According to Oregon state law Mitchell published a notice of the lawsuit in a local paper and this constituted constructive notice of service of the lawsuit upon Neff. When Neff did not answer the lawsuit in court Mitchell obtained a default judgment against Neff. Mitchell obtained an attachment of the land and subsequently, pursuant to a sheriff's sale, sold the land to Pennoyer. Neff later sued Pennoyer in federal court to recover his land. In an opinion by Justice Stephen J. Field the Supreme Court ruled in favor of Neff, citing the need for a court to obtain personal jurisdiction over a defendant:

> ". . . *in an action for money or damages where a defendant does not appear in the court, and is not found within the State, and is not a resident thereof, but has property therein, the jurisdiction of the court extends only over such property, the declaration expresses a principle of general, if not universal, law. The authority of every tribunal is necessarily restricted by the territorial limits of the State in which it is established. Any attempt to exercise authority beyond those limits would be deemed in every other forum, as has been said by this Court, an illegitimate assumption of power, and be resisted as mere abuse. In the case against the plaintiff, the property here in controversy sold under the judgment rendered was not attached, nor in any way brought under the jurisdiction of the court. Its first connection with the case was caused by a levy of the execution. It was not, therefore, disposed of pursuant to any*

adjudication, but only in enforcement of a personal judgment, having no relation to the property, rendered against a nonresident without service of process upon him in the action or his appearance therein . . . If, without personal service, judgments in personam, obtained ex parte against nonresidents and absent parties, upon mere publication of process, which, in the great majority of cases, would never be seen by the parties interested, could be upheld and enforced, they would be the constant instruments of fraud and oppression. Judgments for all sorts of claims upon contracts and for torts, real or pretended, would be thus obtained, under which property would be seized, when the evidence of the transactions upon which they were founded, if they ever had any existence, had perished."[43]

Pennoyer v. Neff established a territorial theory of personal jurisdiction that is still viable—if an individual is within the state there is jurisdiction over that individual. However, *International Shoe Co. v. Washington* made the consideration of whether a party-defendant has "minimum contacts" within the forum state a necessary element when determining in personam jurisdiction. *Pennoyer's* quasi in rem jurisdictional basis, that is the use of land or property unrelated to the claim as a substitute for in-state personal service, was overturned in the case of *Shaffer v. Heitner*.

Legal Definition

Quasi in rem – a court's jurisdiction over an individual based on an interest in property located within the forum state.

❖❖

Shaffer v. Heitner
433 U.S. 186 (1977)

Mr. Justice Marshall delivered the opinion of the Court.

The controversy in this case concerns the constitutionality of a Delaware statute that allows a court of that State to take jurisdiction of a lawsuit by sequestering any property of the defendant that happens to be located in Delaware. Appellants contend that the sequestration statute as applied in this case violates the Due Process Clause of the Fourteenth Amendment both because it permits the state courts to exercise jurisdiction despite the absence of sufficient contacts among the defendants, the litigation, and the State of Delaware and because it authorizes the deprivation of defendants' property without providing adequate procedural safeguards. We find it necessary to consider only the first of these contentions.

I

Appellee Heitner, a nonresident of Delaware, is the owner of one share of stock in the Greyhound Corp., a business incorporated under the laws of Delaware with its principal place of business in Phoenix, Ariz. On May 22, 1974, he filed a shareholder's derivative suit in the Court of Chancery for New Castle Country, Del., in which he named as defendants Greyhound, its wholly owned subsidiary Greyhound Lines, Inc., and 28 present or former officers or directors of one or both of the corporations. In essence, Heitner alleged that the individual defendants had violated their duties to Greyhound by causing it and its subsidiary to engage in actions that resulted in the corporations

---

[43] *Pennoyer* at 720, 726.

being held liable for substantial damages in a private antitrust suit and a large fine in a criminal contempt action. The activities which led to these penalties took place in Oregon.

Simultaneously with his complaint, Heitner filed a motion for an order of sequestration of the Delaware property of the individual defendants pursuant to Del. Code Ann., Tit. 10, 366 (1975). This motion was accompanied by a supporting affidavit of counsel which stated that the individual defendants were nonresidents of Delaware. The affidavit identified the property to be sequestered as "common stock, 3% Second Cumulative Preferenced Stock and stock unit credits of the Defendant Greyhound Corporation, a Delaware corporation, as well as all options and all warrants to purchase said stock issued to said individual Defendants and all contractural [sic] obligations, all rights, debts or credits due or accrued to or for the benefit of any of the said Defendants under any type of written agreement, contract or other legal instrument of any kind whatever between any of the individual Defendants and said corporation."

The requested sequestration order was signed the day the motion was filed. Pursuant to that order, the sequestrator "seized" approximately 82,000 shares of Greyhound common stock belonging to 19 of the defendants, and options belonging to another 2 defendants. These seizures were accomplished by placing "stop transfer" orders or their equivalents on the books of the Greyhound Corp. So far as the record shows, none of the certificates representing the seized property was physically present in Delaware. The stock was considered to be in Delaware, and so subject to seizure, by virtue of Del. Code Ann., Tit. 8, 169 (1975), which makes Delaware the situs of ownership of all stock in Delaware corporations.

All 28 defendants were notified of the initiation of the suit by certified mail directed to their last known addresses and by publication in a New Castle County newspaper. The 21 defendants whose property was seized (hereafter referred to as appellants) responded by entering a special appearance for the purpose of moving to quash service of process and to vacate the sequestration order. They contended that the ex parte sequestration procedure did not accord them due process of law and that the property seized was not capable of attachment in Delaware. In addition, appellants asserted that under the rule of *International Shoe Co. v. Washington*, 326 U.S. 310 (1945), they did not have sufficient contacts with Delaware to sustain the jurisdiction of that State's courts.

The Court of Chancery rejected these arguments in a letter opinion . . . the court held that the statutory Delaware situs of the stock provided a sufficient basis for the exercise of quasi in rem jurisdiction by a Delaware court.

On appeal, the Delaware Supreme Court affirmed the judgment of the Court of Chancery. *Greyhound Corp. v. Heitner*, 361 A. 2d 225 (1976).

We noted probable jurisdiction. We reverse.

II

The Delaware courts rejected appellants' jurisdictional challenge by noting that this suit was brought as a quasi in rem proceeding. Since quasi in rem jurisdiction is traditionally based on attachment or seizure of property present in the jurisdiction, not on contacts between the defendant and the State, the courts considered appellants' claimed lack of contacts with Delaware to be unimportant. This categorical analysis assumes the continued soundness of the conceptual structure founded on the century-old case of *Pennoyer v. Neff*, 95 U.S. 714 (1878).

***

By concluding that "[t]he authority of every tribunal is necessarily restricted by the territorial limits of the State in which it is established," *Pennoyer* sharply limited the availability of in personam jurisdiction over defendants not resident in the forum State. If a nonresident defendant could not be found in a State, he could not be sued there. On the other hand, since the State in which property was located was considered to have exclusive sovereignty over that property, in rem actions could proceed regardless of the owner's location. Indeed, since a State's process could not reach beyond its borders, this Court held after *Pennoyer* that due process did not require any effort to give a property owner personal notice that his property was involved in an in rem proceeding.

The *Pennoyer* rules generally favored nonresident defendants by making them harder to sue. This advantage was reduced, however, by the ability of a resident plaintiff to satisfy a claim against a nonresident defendant by bringing into court any property of the defendant located in the plaintiff's State.

The advent of automobiles, with the concomitant increase in the incidence of individuals causing injury in States where they were not subject to in personam actions under *Pennoyer*, required further moderation of the territorial limits on jurisdictional power. This modification, like the accommodation to the realities of interstate corporate activities, was accomplished by use of a legal fiction that left the conceptual structure established in *Pennoyer* theoretically unaltered. Cf. *Olberding v. Illinois Central R. Co.*, 346 U.S. 338, 340–341 (1953). The fiction used was that the out-of-state motorist, who it was assumed could be excluded altogether from the State's highways, had by using those highways appointed a designated state official as his agent to accept process. See *Hess v. Pawloski*, 274 U.S. 352 (1927). Since the motorist's "agent" could be personally served within the State, the state courts could obtain in personam jurisdiction over the nonresident driver.

The motorists' consent theory was easy to administer since it required only a finding that the out-of-state driver had used the State's roads. By contrast, both the fictions of implied consent to service on the part of a foreign corporation and of corporate presence required a finding that the corporation was "doing business" in the forum State. Defining the criteria for making that finding and deciding whether they were met absorbed much judicial energy. See, e. g., *International Shoe Co. v. Washington*, 326 U.S., at 317–319. While the essentially quantitative tests which emerged from these cases purported simply to identify circumstances under which presence or consent could be attributed to the corporation, it became clear that they were in fact attempting to ascertain "what dealings make it just to subject a foreign corporation to local suit." *Hutchinson v. Chase & Gilbert*, 45 F.2d 139, 141 (CA2 1930) (L. Hand, J.). In *International Shoe*, we acknowledged that fact.

The question in *International Shoe* was whether the corporation was subject to the judicial and taxing jurisdiction of Washington. Mr. Chief Justice Stone's opinion for the Court began its analysis of that question by noting that the historical basis of in personam jurisdiction was a court's power over the defendant's person. That power, however, was no longer the central concern . . . Thus, the relationship among the defendant, the forum, and the litigation, rather than the mutually exclusive sovereignty of the States on which the rules of *Pennoyer* rest, became the central concern of the inquiry into personal jurisdiction. The immediate effect of this departure from *Pennoyer's* conceptual apparatus was to increase the ability of the state courts to obtain personal jurisdiction over nonresident defendants.

No equally dramatic change has occurred in the law governing jurisdiction in rem. There have, however, been intimations that the collapse of the in personam wing of *Pennoyer* has not left that decision unweakened as a foundation for in rem jurisdiction. Well-reasoned lower court opinions have questioned the proposition that the presence of property in a State gives that State jurisdiction to adjudicate rights to the property regardless of the relationship of the underlying dispute and the property owner to the forum . . . The overwhelming majority of commentators have also rejected *Pennoyer's* premise that a proceeding "against" property is not a proceeding against the owners of that property. Accordingly, they urge that the "traditional notions of fair play and substantial justice" that govern a State's power to adjudicate in personam should also govern its power to adjudicate personal rights to property located in the State.

Although this Court has not addressed this argument directly, we have held that property cannot be subjected to a court's judgment unless reasonable and appropriate efforts have been made to give the property owners actual notice of the action. *Schroeder v. City of New York*, 371 U.S. 208 (1962); *Walker v. City of Hutchinson*, 352 U.S. 112 (1956); *Mullane v. Central Hanover Bank & Trust Co.*, 339 U.S. 306 (1950). This conclusion recognizes, contrary to *Pennoyer*, that an adverse judgment in rem directly affects the property owner by divesting him of his rights in the property before the court . . . We think that the time is ripe to consider whether the standard of fairness and substantial justice set forth in *International Shoe* should be held to govern actions in rem as well as in personam.

III

The case for applying to jurisdiction in rem the same test of "fair play and substantial justice" as governs assertions of jurisdiction in personam is simple and straightforward. It is premised on recognition that "[t]he phrase, 'judicial jurisdiction over a thing,' is a customary elliptical way of referring to jurisdiction over the interests of persons in a thing." Restatement (Second) of Conflict of Laws 56, Introductory Note (1971) (hereafter Restatement). This recognition leads to the conclusion that in order to justify an exercise of jurisdiction in rem, the basis for jurisdiction must be sufficient to justify exercising "jurisdiction over the interests of persons in a thing." The standard for determining whether an exercise of jurisdiction over the interests of persons is consistent with the Due Process Clause is the minimum-contacts standard elucidated in *International Shoe* . . .

We therefore conclude that all assertions of state-court jurisdiction must be evaluated according to the standards set forth in *International Shoe* and its progeny.

IV

The Delaware courts based their assertion of jurisdiction in this case solely on the statutory presence of appellants' property in Delaware. Yet that property is not the subject matter of this litigation, nor is the underlying cause of action related to the property. Appellants' holdings in Greyhound do not, therefore, provide contacts with Delaware sufficient to support the jurisdiction of that State's courts over appellants. If it exists, that jurisdiction must have some other foundation.

Appellee Heitner did not allege and does not now claim that appellants have ever set foot in Delaware. Nor does he identify any act related to his cause of action as having taken place in Delaware. Nevertheless, he contends that appellants' positions as directors and officers of a corporation chartered in Delaware provide sufficient "contacts, ties, or relations," *International Shoe Co. v. Washington*, 326 U.S., at 319, with that State to give its court's jurisdiction over appellants in this stockholder's derivative action. This argument is based primarily on what Heitner asserts to be the strong interest of Delaware in supervising the management of a Delaware corporation. That interest is said to derive from the role of Delaware law in establishing the corporation and defining the obligations owed to it by its officers and directors. In order to protect this interest, appellee concludes, Delaware's courts must have jurisdiction over corporate fiduciaries such as appellants.

This argument is undercut by the failure of the Delaware Legislature to assert the state interest appellee finds so compelling. Delaware law bases jurisdiction, not on appellants' status as corporate fiduciaries, but rather on the presence of their property in the State . . .

The Due Process Clause "does not contemplate that a state may make binding a judgment . . . against an individual or corporate defendant with which the state has no contacts, ties, or relations." *International Shoe Co. v. Washington*, 326 U.S., at 319.

Delaware's assertion of jurisdiction over appellants in this case is inconsistent with that constitutional limitation on state power. The judgment of the Delaware Supreme Court must, therefore, be reversed.

It is so ordered.

Questions Presented

1) What was the holding of the Delaware Chancery Court that was affirmed by the Delaware Supreme Court?
2) On what basis did the U.S. Supreme Court reverse the judgment of the lower courts?
3) What was the Supreme Court's analysis of its prior holding in *Pennoyer v. Neff* with regard to in rem and quasi in rem jurisdiction?
4) How did the Supreme Court address the appellees' contention that the state had jurisdiction over the officers and directors of the corporation?

❖❖

Before closing out the discussion on jurisdiction there are four additional terms to know in this area: appellate jurisdiction, concurrent jurisdiction, diversity jurisdiction, and pendent jurisdiction. Appellate jurisdiction is simply the power of a court to hear appeals from a lower court, to review the decision below and to revise it. This power is granted by statute in each state and, as mentioned in Section II above, the U.S. Supreme Court derives its appellate jurisdiction from Article III, section 2 of the U.S. Constitution while the lower federal courts of appeals obtain theirs from 28 U.S. § 1291. Concurrent jurisdiction refers to the ability of two different courts to exercise jurisdiction over the same subject matter within the same geographical area. An example would be the New York State Family Court, a court of limited jurisdiction that has concurrent jurisdiction with the New York State Supreme Court, the general trial level court in the state, over proceedings involving the right of minors to marry. Additionally, the Family Court has concurrent jurisdiction with the state criminal courts over family offenses and domestic violence, and with the New York State Surrogate's Court over adoption and guardianship proceedings. Diversity jurisdiction occurs at the federal level when you have litigating parties from different states and the amount in controversy is over $75,000.00. For example, a plaintiff in Oklahoma is injured by a defendant in Louisiana; the Oklahoma litigant can bring a diversity action in federal district court in Oklahoma, assuming there are no minimum contacts the Louisiana defendant has with Oklahoma that would entitle the plaintiff to file the case in Oklahoma state court. Federal diversity jurisdiction is a form of subject-matter jurisdiction and is provided for by federal statute, 28 U.S.C. § 1332.

28 U.S.C. § 1332(a) provides the following:

The district courts shall have original jurisdiction of all civil actions where the matter in controversy exceeds the sum or value of $75,000, exclusive of interest and costs, and is between—

(1) *citizens of different States;*

(2) *citizens of a State and citizens or subjects of a foreign state, except that the district courts shall not have original jurisdiction under this subsection of an action between citizens of a State and citizens or subjects of a foreign state who are lawfully admitted for permanent residence in the United States and are domiciled in the same State;*

(3) *citizens of different States and in which citizens or subjects of a foreign state are additional parties; and*

(4) *a foreign state, defined in section 1603(a) of this title, as plaintiff and citizens of a State or of different States.*

The next case of *Erie Railroad Co. v. Tompkins* is a diversity case but the question in the case centers on the authority of the federal courts to disregard state law in diversity cases. The issue, highlighted by Justice Brandeis in the opening sentence of the case, is whether the Court should follow its own precedent in *Swift v. Tyson*, an 1842 diversity case in which the Court held that § 34 of the Judiciary Act of 1789 did not prevent federal courts from applying their own common law in diversity cases.

❖❖

Erie Railroad Co. v. Tompkins
304 U.S. 64 (1938)

Mr. Justice Brandeis delivered the opinion of the Court.

The question for decision is whether the oft-challenged doctrine of *Swift v. Tyson* shall now be disapproved.

Tompkins, a citizen of Pennsylvania, was injured on a dark night by a passing freight train of the Erie Railroad Company while walking along its right of way at Hughestown in that State. He claimed that the accident occurred through negligence in the operation, or maintenance, of the train; that he was rightfully on the premises as licensee because on a commonly used beaten footpath which ran for a short distance alongside the tracks, and that he was struck by something which looked like a door projecting from one of the moving cars. To enforce that claim, he brought an action in the federal court for southern New York, which had jurisdiction because the company is a corporation of that State. It denied liability, and the case was tried by a jury.

The Erie insisted that its duty to Tompkins was no greater than that owed to a trespasser. It contended, among other things, that its duty to Tompkins, and hence its liability, should be determined in accordance with the Pennsylvania law; that, under the law of Pennsylvania, as declared by its highest court, persons who use pathways along the railroad right of way—that is, a longitudinal pathway, as distinguished from a crossing—are to be deemed trespassers, and that the railroad is not liable for injuries to undiscovered trespassers resulting from its negligence unless it be wanton or willful. Tompkins denied that any such rule had been established by the decisions of the Pennsylvania courts, and contended that, since there was no statute of the State on the subject, the railroad's duty and liability is to be determined in federal courts as a matter of general law.

The trial judge refused to rule that the applicable law precluded recovery. The jury brought in a verdict of $30,000, and the judgment entered thereon was affirmed by the Circuit Court of Appeals, which held, that it was unnecessary to consider whether the law of Pennsylvania was as contended, because the question was one not of local, but of general, law, and that, "upon questions of general law, the federal courts are free, in the absence of a local statute, to exercise their independent judgment as to what the law is, and it is well settled that the question of the responsibility of a railroad for injuries caused by its servants is one of general law. . . . Where the public has made open and notorious use of a railroad right of way for a long period of time and without objection, the company owes to persons on such permissive pathway a duty of care in the operation of its trains. . . . It is likewise generally recognized law that a jury may find that negligence exists toward a pedestrian using a permissive path on the railroad right of way if he is hit by some object projecting from the side of the train."

The Erie had contended that application of the Pennsylvania rule was required, among other things, by § 34 of the Federal Judiciary Act of September 24, 1789, c. 20, 28 U.S.C. § 725, which provides: "The laws of the several States, except where the Constitution, treaties, or statutes of the United States otherwise require or provide, shall be regarded as rules of decision in trials at common law, in the courts of the United States, in cases where they apply."

Because of the importance of the question whether the federal court was free to disregard the alleged rule of the Pennsylvania common law, we granted certiorari.

First. Swift v. Tyson, 16 Pet. 1, 41 U.S. 18, held that federal courts exercising jurisdiction on the ground of diversity of citizenship need not, in matters of general jurisprudence, apply the unwritten law of the State as declared by its highest court; that they are free to exercise an independent judgment as to what the common law of the State is—or should be, and that, as there stated by Mr. Justice Story: "the true interpretation of the thirty-fourth section limited its application to state laws strictly local, that is to say, to the positive statutes of the state, and the construction thereof adopted by the local tribunals, and to rights and titles to things having a permanent locality, such as the rights and titles to real estate, and other matters immovable and intraterritorial in their nature and character. It never has been supposed by us that the section did apply, or was intended to apply, to questions of a more general nature, not at all dependent upon local statutes or local usages of a fixed and permanent operation, as, for example, to the construction of ordinary contracts or other written instruments, and especially to questions of general commercial law, where the state tribunals are called upon to perform the like functions as ourselves, that is, to ascertain upon general reasoning and legal analogies what is the true exposition of the contract or instrument, or what is the just rule furnished by the principles of commercial law to govern the case."

. . . The federal courts assumed, in the broad field of "general law," the power to declare rules of decision which Congress was confessedly without power to enact as statutes. Doubt was repeatedly expressed as to the correctness of the construction given § 34, and as to the soundness of the rule which it introduced. But it was the more recent research of a competent scholar, who examined the original document, which established that the construction given to it by the Court was erroneous, and that the purpose of the section was merely to make certain that, in all matters except those in which some federal law is controlling, the federal courts exercising jurisdiction in diversity of citizenship cases would apply as their rules of decision the law of the State, unwritten as well as written.

Second. Experience in applying the doctrine of *Swift v. Tyson* had revealed it defects, political and social, and the benefits expected to flow from the rule did not accrue. Persistence of state courts in their own opinions on questions of common law prevented uniformity; and the impossibility of discovering a satisfactory line of demarcation between the province of general law and that of local law developed a new well of uncertainties.

. . . The injustice and confusion incident to the doctrine of *Swift v. Tyson* have been repeatedly urged as reasons for abolishing or limiting diversity of citizenship jurisdiction. Other legislative relief has been proposed. If only a question of statutory construction were involved, we should not be prepared to abandon a doctrine so widely applied throughout nearly a century. But the unconstitutionality of the course pursued has now been made clear, and compels us to do so.

Third. Except in matters governed by the Federal Constitution or by Acts of Congress, the law to be applied in any case is the law of the State. And whether the law of the State shall be declared by its Legislature in a statute or by its highest court in a decision is not a matter of federal concern. There is no federal general common law. Congress has no power to declare substantive rules of common law applicable in a State, whether they be local in their nature or "general," be they commercial law or a part of the law of torts. And no clause in the Constitution purports to confer such a power upon the federal courts.

The fallacy underlying the rule declared in *Swift v. Tyson* is made clear by Mr. Justice Holmes . . . The doctrine rests upon the assumption that there is "a transcendental body of law outside of any particular State but obligatory within it unless and until changed by statute," that federal courts have the power to use their judgment as to what the rules of common law are, and that, in the federal courts, "the parties are entitled to an independent judgment on matters of general law" . . .

Thus, the doctrine of *Swift v. Tyson* is, as Mr. Justice Holmes said, "an unconstitutional assumption of powers by courts of the United States which no lapse of time or respectable array of opinion should make us hesitate to correct."

In disapproving that doctrine, we do not hold unconstitutional §34 of the Federal Judiciary Act of 1789 or any other Act of Congress. We merely declare that, in applying the doctrine, this Court and the lower courts have invaded rights which, in our opinion, are reserved by the Constitution to the several States.

Fourth. The defendant contended that, by the common law of Pennsylvania as declared by its highest court in *Falchetti v. Pennsylvania R. Co.,* 307 Pa. 203; 160 A. 859, the only duty owed to the plaintiff was to refrain from willful or wanton injury. The plaintiff denied that such is the Pennsylvania law. In support of their respective contentions the parties discussed and cited many decisions of the Supreme Court of the State. The Circuit Court of Appeals ruled that the question of liability is one of general law, and on that ground declined to decide the issue of state law. As we hold this was error, the judgment is reversed and the case remanded to it for further proceedings in conformity with our opinion.

Reversed.

Questions Presented

1) What was the trial court result on appeal in the case before the U.S. Supreme Court?
2) What prompted the Supreme Court to grant review?
3) What did Justice Brandeis, writing for the majority in *Erie*, say in the opinion about the lower court's interpretation of § 34 of the Judiciary Act?
4) What was the criticism of the *Swift v. Tyson* doctrine expressed in the *Erie* decision?
5) In diversity cases which law controls, federal common law or state law? Explain.

❖❖❖

Federal courts are generally not fond of diversity cases because they often bring into the federal courts certain types of negligence cases not normally handled in the federal courts and which many judges feel are better suited to the state courts. Nonetheless, without minimum contacts to rely on, a plaintiff's only means to get an out-of-state defendant in state court is through diversity jurisdiction.

Lastly, the concept of pendent jurisdiction involves a federal court exercising jurisdiction over state law claims that are closely related to federal claims before the court. The state law claims are allowed because they are usually intertwined with the federal law claims and it is better that they are decided together.

IV. Civil Procedure

Civil procedure as an undergraduate legal studies course is a semester long. First year law students endure two semesters of it. Lengthy treatises have been written about federal civil procedure[44] and each state has comparable treatments from noted state authorities.[45] This signifies how important civil procedure is as a subject. It is an area in which failure to follow the rules can lead to a disastrous result for a client's case and a malpractice claim against an attorney.

Even though this is a business law text it is important for students to know the "nuts and bolts" of civil procedure since litigation is bound to occur in the course of doing business. Most cases filed do not even get to the trial stage. Court statistics indicate that 95% of all cases filed result in some adjudication prior to trial. Whether the case is settled or dismissed on motion prior to trial, the occurrence of a trial is a rarity. This is not a recent or new phenomenon. There has been a downward trend since the dawn of the millennium.[46] However, every case still has to be prepared with an ultimate trial in mind.

Our American system of law follows an adversarial process wherein competing parties present their case before an independent decision-maker or judge. The rules of procedure ensure a fair process, more commonly referred to as due process of law. A basic element of procedural due process is notice and an opportunity to be heard. Despite the guarantees of due process and the seemingly labyrinthine rules which must be followed to successfully litigate a case many litigants in the civil system find the process frustrating. A statement from the famed French writer Voltaire uttered over two centuries ago probably best sums up many peoples' experience with the civil litigation process: *"I have never been ruined but twice: once when I won a lawsuit and once when I lost."* Voltaire's statement reflects the attitude of many attorneys who know that going to trial is always a risk and not necessarily the best outcome for a case. Trials can be expensive and the process of getting to the actual trial can take months if not years. Litigants also experience the heavy toll, emotionally and financially, that going to trial can bring. Nonetheless, we live in a litigious society and even though the percentage of cases going to trial has decreased over the years the number of lawsuits filed each year has increased. A familiarity with the basic structure of a lawsuit enables non-lawyers to better understand the litigation process.

If you were to do a review of the table of contents for the Federal Rules of Civil Procedure (FRCP) or the various state codes of civil procedure you would find a striking similarity between them. There is a steady and unwavering progression from the commencement of the action, through to pleadings, motions and orders, to disclosure, trial, and judgment, followed by provisional remedies and special proceedings. This is the essential track of a lawsuit when it is filed—from

---

[44] See eg., Moore's Federal Practice; Wright & Miller's Federal Practice & Civil Procedure

[45] See eg., Modern Maryland Civil Procedure by Richard W. Bourne and John A. Lynch, Jr.; Oklahoma Civil Procedure Forms & Practice by Clyde A. Muchmore and Harvey D. Ellis; New York Practice by David Siegel

[46] Refo, P. L. (2017, May 18). *Opening Statement: The Vanishing Trial.* Retrieved from Litigation Online: http://www.americanbar.org/content/dam/aba/publishing/litigation_journal/04winter_openingstatement.authcheckdam.pdf

filing to judgment—with the added procedural devices of provisional remedies (such as an injunction or receivership) and special proceedings (such as writs of attachment or mandamus) added. Figure 2.3 provides an explanatory flow chart of the basic litigation process and its various stages.

Prior to initiating a lawsuit an aggrieved or injured party will likely seek to meet with an attorney for a consultation. The attorney will assess the individual's case based on the information provided as well as any evidentiary documents the individual may possess. If there is a legally cognizable claim which the attorney believes the individual may be able to pursue the next

FIGURE 2.3 Civil Litigation Process

PLEADINGS STAGE
- Plaintiff files a summons & complaint with the court
- Defendant(s) served with pleadings according to federal or state rules
- Defendant either answers complaint or moves to dismiss based on lack of jurisdiction (personal or subject matter), failure to state a claim, statute of limitations

DISCOVERY STAGE
- Defendant(s) have answered & issue is joined; parties attend a preliminary conference with the assigned judge enter into a scheduling order that outlines the various deadlines to complete discovery
- Bill of Particulars, Requests for Admissions, Interrogatories, Requests for Discovery & Inspection of Documents, etc., Depositions

PRE-TRIAL STAGE
- Dispositive motions are made – motion to dismiss, summary judgment
- Court rules on party's motion(s)
- Settlement Conference – assuming the court's ruling does not dispose of the case
- If a settlement is reached the case is closed and no further proceedings take place

TRIAL STAGE
- Jury selection
- Once jury is selected trial judge may make another attempt to settle the case—if case is settled it is closed and no trial occurs, if not, the parties proceed to trial
- Plaintiff presents case, calls witnesses, introduces evidence; Defense is able to cross-examine witnesses and challenge the introduction of evidence
- Defense, at the close of Plaintiff's case, can move for a directed verdict if Defense believes Plaintiff did not prove a prima facie case—a directed verdict by the judge will end the case in Defendant's favor, otherwise trial proceeds.
- Defendant is able to put on its defense case
- Trial concludes and goes to verdict

APPEAL STAGE
- Losing party has the opportunity to appeal the verdict
- Issues of law are considered de novo on appeal
- Issues of fact are only considered as to clear error

step is to make sure that the potential client has standing to sue. Standing refers to a determination of whether the individual has a sufficient stake in the matter. An individual has to show an act caused him harm or injury in fact and that the interest sought to be protected is within a "zone of interest" meant to be protected or regulated by the relevant statute at issue. A lack of standing to sue will lead to dismissal of a case. Standing goes to a person's capacity to sue and is guided by state statute.

Legal Definitions

Standing – an individual's right to make a legal claim or seek enforcement of a legal claim of a duty or right.

Retainer – a client's authorization for a lawyer to act in a case; a fee paid to a lawyer to secure legal representation.

Contingent fee – a legal fee charged by an attorney for professional services only if the lawsuit is successful or favorably settled out of court.

If the attorney decides to accept the case and initiate a lawsuit on behalf of a client a retainer agreement, drafted by the attorney, will be signed by the attorney and the new client. The retainer agreement not only provides the attorney authorization to act on behalf of the client but it details the terms of the newly entered attorney–client relationship. Depending on the type of case involved the retainer agreement may call for the client to give the attorney a sum of money (the retainer fee) in order to secure the attorney's services. The retainer is applied toward the overall fee charged to the client. Some fee arrangements may involve a flat fee of a set amount for legal work to be performed while others may have an hourly rate with monthly billing cycles. Cases that involve a claim of negligence against another individual are handled on a contingency fee basis which means the attorney only gets paid if the case outcome is successful. This can be either by way of a trial or an out of court settlement. Contingent fees are recovered from the amount awarded to the client. This can range from 25% to 33% of the amount awarded.

Once representation is secured by the client and the attorney has a signed retainer agreement the process of preparing the case for court begins.

A. Complaint and Answer

The case begins with the filing of a complaint accompanied by a summons which is served upon the opposing party (the defendant). The complaint outlines in paragraph form the factual and legal reasons for the plaintiff's belief that the defendant is liable for damages (see Figure 2.5). The complaint also contains a demand for damages and other relief that may be sought from the court. A summons is the actual notice of the lawsuit and it is filed in the court and served on the defendant along with the complaint. Figure 2.4 provides an example of a summons with notice. The summons is served by the attorney filing the complaint who does so by employing a licensed process server, or it is served by the clerk of the court, or by a sheriff's officer. State statute will dictate the means of service. Once service is completed on the defendant proof of service has to be filed with the court.

FIGURE 2.4 Example of a Summons with Notice

SUPREME COURT OF THE STATE OF NEW YORK
COUNTY OF WESTCHESTER
--X

JOHN DOE,

                              Plaintiff(s)
          -against-

XYZ CORPORATION,
                              Defendant(s).

--X

Index No. 16-2247

**Plaintiff(s) designate
Westchester County as the place
of trial.**

**The basis of the venue is
the residence of plaintiff**

SUMMONS WITH NOTICE

**Plaintiff(s) reside at: County of
Westchester**

TO THE ABOVE NAMED DEFENDANT(S)

   YOU ARE HEREBY SUMMONED to answer the complaint in this action and to serve a copy of your answer, or, if the complaint is not served with this summons, to serve a notice of appearance, on the Plaintiff's Attorney(s) within 20 days after the service of this summons, exclusive of the day of service (or within 30 days after service is complete if the summons is not delivered personally to you within the State of New York); and in case of your failure to appear or answer, judgment will be taken against you by default for the relief demanded herein.

Dated: May 18, 2017

Kroeger & Gwynn, P.C.

By:_____
Attorneys for Plaintiff
123 Main Street
Pleasantville, NY 10570
(845) 123-4567

Defendant(s) Address:

The nature of the action is one for contractual damages resulting from a breach of contract for the failure of XYZ Corporation to fulfill its obligation to make required repairs.
The relief sought is money damages in the amount of $25,000.00.
Upon your failure to appear, judgment will be taken against you by default for the sum of $25,000.00 with interest from June 9, 2017 and the costs of this action.

   Once the defendant is served with the complaint there is a set statutory time within which the complaint must be formally answered. This period ranges anywhere from 20–45 days depending on state procedural law. If a defendant fails to answer a complaint the plaintiff can file for a default judgment. However, after a default judgment is filed and entered, the defendant, upon a showing of good cause or some justifiable excuse, can petition the court to vacate the default judgment. This is accomplished by way of a motion. It is within the discretion of the court as to whether or not it will vacate the default judgment.

FIGURE 2.5 Example of a Complaint

SUPREME COURT OF THE STATE OF NEW YORK
COUNTY OF ALBANY
--X
JOSEPH SMITH,

                      Plaintiff,

                                                   Index No.: 2016-00157

- against -

                                                   COMPLAINT

ALLEN GREGORY,

                      Defendant.
--X
TO THE SUPREME COURT OF THE STATE OF NEW YORK:

The Complaint of the Plaintiff, Joseph Smith, respectfully shows and alleges as follows:

1. The Plaintiff herein, Joseph Smith, is a resident of the State of New York. Mr. Jones resides at 17 Pine Street, Guilderland, New York.
2. The Defendant herein, Allen Gregory, has a principal place of business at 437 State Street, Albany, New York. Defendant is engaged in the business of building mahogany desks and bookcases.
3. Plaintiff Smith desired to have a two (2) large office desks and six (6) barrister bookcases built pursuant to a design prepared by him. Plaintiff and Defendant discussed Plaintiffs needs and specifications for this project.
4. On September 23, 2015, Plaintiff and Defendant entered into a written agreement. Pursuant thereto, Plaintiff agreed to pay the sum of $50,000.00 for the desks and bookcases. Plaintiff was obligated to make a down payment of $15,000.00 on or before October 15, 2015, with the balance to be due upon delivery of the mahogany desks and bookcases. The Defendant agreed to build the mahogany desks and bookcases in accordance with Plaintiff's design for the aforesaid price and to complete the work and deliver the desks and bookcases to Plaintiff's Guilderland office on or before November 10, 2015.
5. On October 15, 2015, Plaintiff delivered to Defendant a certified check in the sum of $15,000.00, which Defendant cashed.
6. Defendant failed to deliver the desks and bookcases on or before November 10, 2015, as agreed. Plaintiff made numerous phone calls and sent several letters to Defendant about the contract, but received no response.
7. By reason of the facts and circumstances stated above, Defendant has breached the contract.
8. By reason of the facts and circumstances stated above, Plaintiff has been damaged by Defendant in the sum of $15,000.00.

    WHEREFORE, Plaintiff demands judgment against Defendant in the sum of $15,000.00, plus interest from October 15, 2015, costs and disbursements, together with any other relief the Court finds to be just and proper.

Dated: February 4, 2016

                                                       _____

                                                    JOSEPH SMITH – Plaintiff

Legal Definitions

Default judgment – a judgment entered against a litigant who has either failed to comply with a court order or who has failed to appear in the litigation as scheduled.

Motion – a litigant's written or oral application to the court requesting it to enter a requested ruling or order.

The answer submitted by the defendant will address each of the claims asserted in the plaintiff's complaint either by specifically denying them or admitting to them. There may be factual recitations in the complaint which the defendant agrees to, such as the date of an incident or the defendant's address, but there will be many more that are disputed or denied in the formal answer. The answer will also contain any defenses asserted by the defendant as well as any counterclaims or cross-claims the defendant wants to bring.

Legal Definitions

Counterclaim – a defendant's claim in opposition to the plaintiff's claim.

Cross-claim – a claim made between co-defendants or co-plaintiffs in a case and that relates to the subject of the original claim or counterclaim.

Summary judgment – a court disposition on a claim that renders judgment on behalf of a party who makes a motion for relief when there is no genuine issue of material fact and the movant can be granted relief as a matter of law.

B. Pre-discovery Motions

Once the complaint and answer are filed the parties have the opportunity to submit motions. At this stage the motions filed are either for dismissal or summary judgment. Early grounds for dismissal can be based on several statutory reasons, such as a lack of subject matter jurisdiction, a statute of limitations defense, lack of personal jurisdiction, improper venue, insufficient service of process, and failure to state a claim for which relief can be granted. The relevant statute in the Federal Rules of Civil Procedure is Rule 12(b). A motion for summary judgment is brought when the parties agree on the facts in a case and absent a factual dispute one or both parties move the court for a summary judgment. This is a severe disposition at the early stage of a case since it is rendered without any disclosure and further inquiry into the case. It is a rare situation where summary judgment is rendered by a court so early in the litigation process. Usually summary judgment motions are made after discovery has been completed.

C. Discovery and Pre-trial Proceedings

Discovery, otherwise known as disclosure, is the process by which the parties exchange documents and information pertaining to the claims and defenses made in the lawsuit. The process begins after the parties enter into a formal discovery schedule with the court. The discovery schedule, which will be entered as a court order after a preliminary conference, puts the case under the supervision of the court with set timetables for the completion of the different discovery devices. Some common discovery devices include bills of particulars, document demands, depositions, mental and/or medical examinations, and interrogatories. A bill of particulars is issued by a party upon the request of their opposition to more specifically explain their claim. This is usually submitted by the plaintiff upon the request of a defendant; however, a defendant can be requested by a plaintiff to submit a bill of particulars as to any counterclaims, cross-claims or specific defenses. A bill of particulars submitted by a party to litigation becomes part of the pleadings in a case. The document demands are made by both sides and are simply an exchange of relevant documents made upon demand by a party. If the mental or physical capacity of a litigant is in question or a subject of the complaint a discovery demand can be made by a requesting party for an independent medical/psychological examination of an opposing party. This is done at the expense of the requesting party by a medical professional retained by them. Interrogatories are formal written questions that are submitted by an opposing party to its adversary which seek sworn to responses to the questions. This discovery device is sometimes limited by statute. Depending on state procedural rules it is not permitted if a deposition is scheduled or has taken place. The most well-known and common of all discovery devices is the deposition. This is the out-of-court taking of sworn testimony, before a stenographer, which is made into a deposition transcript for possible use later in court or in motion papers for dismissal or summary judgment.

Legal Definitions

Bill of particulars – this is a more detailed statement of a party's pleadings provided at the request of an opposing party; it is an amplification of the pleadings and with the verified complaint constitutes the core of a litigant's claim against the opposing party.

Deposition – also, referred to as an examination before trial (or EBT) it is the stenographically recorded testimony of either a witness or a party to the litigation that is made out of court as part of the pre-trial discovery/disclosure process.

Interrogatory – a numbered list of written questions submitted to an opposing party as part of the formal disclosure/discovery process.

During the course of discovery attorneys are often scheduled to appear before presiding judges for preliminary conferences during which time the judge is advised of the progress of the case and may address any disputes arising during the discovery process. If a party fails to comply with discovery demands their opponent can seek remedies before the court by way of a motion. Some remedies may include the striking of a claim or a defense if a party has not complied.

Once discovery is complete a scheduling order will have a time frame established for dispositive motions. These are the motion to dismiss and the motion for summary judgment. Many of the grounds for a motion to dismiss are waived in some jurisdictions if they are not made at the beginning of the case (for instance, the lack of personal jurisdiction is waived if not raised and the party submits to the jurisdiction of the court) or are not preserved in the answer. A dismissal at this stage of the litigation may not be fatal to a claim since, if the statute of limitations has not passed, the case can be re-filed, assuming the grounds for dismissal can be corrected. However, a summary judgment motion is final and is granted with prejudice, meaning that the plaintiff cannot re-file the case. If the case is not resolved at this stage, either by a dispositive motion or a negotiated settlement, it is scheduled for trial. However, prior to the scheduling for trial the judge will likely schedule a settlement conference to see if the case can be settled between the parties. This is a session wherein the judge informally listens to the merits of each side's case and discusses the strengths and weaknesses confronting each side's position. At some point in the litigation a plaintiff's attorney may submit a demand letter to the defendant. A demand letter may be required by state statute in some

FIGURE 2.6   Sample Demand Letter

Dewey & Jones

Attorneys at Law
2318 Insurance Avenue
Hartford, Connecticut 06156
(203) 123-4567
October 18, 2014

Mr. Ralph Hampton
1414 Debtor Way
Hartford, Connecticut 06156

Dear Mr. Hampton:

On March 4, 2014 you hired my client, Affordable Building Designs, LLC, to design and build an addition to your home. My client contracted with you for his professional services in the amount of $75,000.00 with a down payment in the amount of $25,000.00 due upon signing and a second payment of $15,000.00 due upon framing of the addition and installation of the plumbing and electrical. According to the contract you entered with my client the balance of the payment was due upon completion of the addition to your home and the issuance of a final certificate of occupancy by the city. The addition was completed on July 11, 2014 and the City of Hartford issued a final certificate of occupancy on August 18, 2014. On August 20, 2014 my client's business manager, Pat Jones, sent you a final bill for payment. While you made the first two contract payments as agreed, you have refused to make the final $35,000.00 payment which was due after the issuance of the certificate of occupancy. My client has made repeated attempts to collect, but you have not come forward with the payment. I am requesting that you make the payment in full by November 2, 2014, or make specific arrangements with my client to pay the balance.

   I will expect a response to this letter no later than November 2, 2014. If this matter is not resolved by the time specified above, my client reserves the right to commence legal proceedings to recover the debt without further notice to you and this letter may be tendered in court as evidence of your failure to pay.

Very truly yours,

Harold Dewey
Harold Dewey

jurisdictions as a prerequisite to filing a lawsuit.[47] However, it is often used more informally by attorneys as a precursor to filing a lawsuit or during the disclosure phase of the litigation to generate a settlement offer. Figure 2.6 provides a sample pre-litigation demand letter in a contract dispute.

D. Trial

This is the formal presentation of evidence by the plaintiff before the court. The trial may be conducted before a jury chosen during voir dire by the opposing attorneys, or it may be a bench trial wherein the judge serves as the trier of fact and law. The civil evidentiary burden upon a plaintiff is a preponderance of the evidence, unlike the more stringent criminal standard by which a prosecutor must convict which is proof beyond a reasonable doubt. After trial a decision is entered in the form of a verdict and relief is granted. This typically involves a money judgment. An order of judgment entered by the judge in the case concludes the trial.

---

[47] See eg., Florida General Statutes § 501.98 requiring a demand letter as a condition precedent to filing a lawsuit against a motor vehicle dealer prior to filing a lawsuit under Florida's Deceptive and Unfair Trade Practices Act; Massachusetts General Law Chapter 93A requiring a demand letter from a consumer to a business prior to filing a claim under the state's Consumer Protection Act.

Legal Definitions

Voir dire – refers to either the process of an attorney's questioning of prospective jurors from a panel to see who is qualified and acceptable to serve on the jury, or to the preliminary examination to test the competence of an item of evidence or a witness.

Preponderance of the evidence – the civil evidentiary standard and the lowest trial level burden of proof; it is evidence that tends to weigh in favor of one party over the other.

E. Appeal

After trial there is likely one party not happy with the result. The appeal process is typically governed by a separate and distinct set of procedural rules. Appellate jurisdiction is essentially limited to legal mistakes the appealing party believes occurred during the course of the case. An example would be evidence or testimony that was wrongly admitted at the trial. Issues of fact are not considered unless there was a clear error at the trial level. Oftentimes an appeal can be used strategically by a losing defendant to force a winning plaintiff to settle for a lesser sum than awarded at trial. Since appeals, like trials, are expensive and time consuming, a winning party may compromise their judgment award and settle for a lesser amount in lieu of the defendant withdrawing the appeal. This is but one of the factors that can make litigation the losing proposition that Voltaire encountered in victory and defeat.

V. Alternative Dispute Resolution

We conclude this chapter with a brief discussion of the alternative dispute resolution (ADR) process. In the previous section we covered the litigation process but omitted this important aspect of litigation which provides an alternate method for resolving disputes among litigants. The ADR process involves several different mechanisms for adjudicating disputes. These include the three main methods employed: arbitration, mediation, and negotiation. Collectively the term alternative dispute resolution refers to any device used for settling a dispute by a means other than litigation.[48] The ADR process can be entered into through an agreement between the parties pursuant to a contract whereby it is agreed all disputes will be subject to arbitration rather than a lawsuit. Or, it may be a process the parties are referred to by the court once a case is filed. This latter court referral to ADR is also at the agreement of the parties since it involves a waiver of the right to trial.

The advantage of ADR is that it is less costly and less time consuming than the regular litigation process. Because of its advantage to litigants as well as its time saving aspect, ADR has been integrated into most state court systems to stem the increasing caseload and move cases through the courthouse toward resolution.

Arbitration and mediation are the two most well-known ADR methods. Both methods involve the parties presenting their case before a neutral third-party arbitrator or mediator. The difference with each lies in the method of the presentation and the end result. In mediation the parties may both appear initially before the mediator but the sessions are quickly divided with the mediator talking to one side and then the other with a view toward helping them come to a mutually

---

[48] Black's Law Dictionary (19th ed., 2010)

agreeable solution. However, the decision of the mediator is not binding. An arbitrator acts more like a judge and hears evidence presented by both sides in a trial-like setting. The rules of evidence are more relaxed (for instance certain hearsay testimony is allowed) and the procedural rules are set by the arbitrating body. JAMS (Judicial Arbitration and Mediation Service) is the world's largest private ADR provider and publishes its own comprehensive arbitration rules.[49] Unlike mediation, the decision of the arbitrator is binding upon the parties. Courts are not involved with arbitration unless a party needs to go to court to enforce an arbitration clause in a contract or to enforce an arbitration award.

Negotiation is an often overlooked element of ADR but it is the most common. This is the informal or formal discussion that takes place between disputing parties, either with or without attorneys present, in which the parties try to come to a meeting of the minds in order to resolve their dispute. A successful negotiation can save years of time and expense that would otherwise be wrapped up in litigation. Negotiation is the most rational of all approaches to a dispute but unfortunately not all litigants or their attorneys follow the Aristotelian maxim of "the law is reason unaffected by desire." Too often reasonable negotiated settlements are eschewed out of emotion. A good negotiation begins and ends with the facts of the case and the relevant law. These are the strong positions with which a good negotiator will operate. Negotiation is a back and forth parry between the litigants or their attorneys in which either side attempts to leverage the relative strength of their position in order to obtain a settlement they can accept without giving up too much. For plaintiffs this may entail accepting less in a settlement offer than they believe the case is worth, realizing that dragging the case out can lead to costs that would minimize any recovery after trial. Also, a plaintiff may realize in a negotiation session that the defendant has some defenses which, if successful, could adversely impact the case. For defendants the negotiation session may be a matter of resolving a case for much less than anticipated or being able to quietly settle a case without any negative publicity that could hurt future business.

SUMMARY

American law is derived from the common law and the legal traditions of England. However, upon the first colonial settlement in America the process of developing a uniquely American system of law began to emerge from the corporate rules and regulations of English company charters like those of the Virginia Company of London and the Massachusetts Bay Company. Eventually the colonies began to codify their own laws and court systems developed. Entering the 18th century the practice of law, while still suspect among colonists, became a needed profession. By the latter part of the 18th century, when the colonies were asserting their freedom from England, it was the work of colonial attorneys that produced the Declaration of Independence and our eventual Constitution.

The development of the American court system grew out of Article III of the Constitution and its provision for a separate judicial branch of government. A Supreme Court with appellate jurisdiction and limited general jurisdiction was created, as well as a provision for lower federal courts as

---

[49] JAMS. (2017, May 19). *JAMS Comprehensive Arbitration Rules & Procedures.* Retrieved from JAMS: https://www.jamsadr.com/rules-comprehensive-arbitration/

the Congress deemed to be required. The Judiciary Act of 1789 created the original federal district and circuit courts. Over time the federal and state judiciaries would develop into the dual three-tiered systems they are today with general jurisdiction trial courts, limited jurisdiction intermediate appellate courts and final review appellate courts at both federal and state levels.

Courts, whether at the state or federal level, can only exercise the jurisdiction that is granted to them by statute. There are courts of general jurisdiction which are full trial courts able to preside over civil and criminal cases, and courts of limited jurisdiction, such as probate courts, which are limited presiding over specialized areas of the law. Appellate courts which hear cases on appeal after a determination at the trial level are also courts of limited jurisdiction. While jurisdiction refers to a court's power to hear a case venue is the proper geographical court to hear the case.

The American legal system is an adversarial process in which opposing parties, represented by attorneys or by themselves if they decide to appear pro se, are permitted to present evidence to a neutral fact finder (either a jury or a judge) in support or in defense of their case. The civil litigation process follows a formal set of rules that guide a case through the pre-trial, trial, and post-trial phases of a court case. The rules of civil procedure are found at the federal level in the Federal Rules of Civil Procedure (FRCP) and at the state level in the different state civil procedure codes. Civil litigation generally follows a process wherein a plaintiff files a summons and complaint with the court and the defendant(s) is (are) given a statutory time to answer (anywhere from 20 to 30 days is usual.) Once issue is joined between the parties a conference is held before the presiding judge and a discovery schedule is set. The parties then complete the pre-trial discovery or disclosure process under the court's supervision. In doing so they may utilize a number of disclosure devices available to them, such as interrogatories, depositions, bills of particulars, requests for admissions, and document requests. Few civil cases go to actual trial and many are either settled prior to trial or are dismissed. If after trial or dismissal of a case a losing party does not agree with the results they can file an appeal, but the appeal is limited to a review of alleged legal errors made in a case. A reviewing court on appeal cannot reconsider the facts of the case except in the limited circumstance where it is alleged that the judge or jury's decision was not in line with the facts presented at trial.

Since litigation is so expensive and time consuming many individuals and businesses opt to use alternative dispute resolution also referred to as ADR. There are three main methods of ADR—arbitration, mediation, and negotiation. Each of these methods provide less costly and quicker resolution to civil claims than actual court litigation and they have been a favored method within business agreements and contracts of ensuring that any disagreements are resolved through the ADR process.

CHAPTER 3

BUSINESS LAW AND THE U.S. CONSTITUTION

LEARNING OUTCOMES

Upon completion of this chapter the student will be able to:

1 Explain the concept of separation of powers and the organization and powers of the different branches of government.
2 Explain the impact of the U.S. Constitution upon the transaction of business and commerce within the United States.
3 Discuss the reach and limits of the federal and state governments' regulatory powers.
4 Understand the limits of the First Amendment upon commercial speech.

KEY TERMS

checks and balances
Commerce Clause
commercial speech
Dormant Commerce Clause
federalism
Privileges and Immunities Clause

procedural due process
regulatory powers
separation of powers
substantive due process
Supremacy Clause

I. The Separation of Powers

The word constitution comes from the Latin "constituo" which means to stand or set up, to establish. A constitution performs the function of establishing an entity like a corporation, or governmental body, most notably the United States of America which was formally established with the ratification of the Constitution in 1788. The Constitution of the United States serves as a blueprint for how our government functions. Similarly, each state has its own state constitution which likewise outlines the structure of state government. The genius of the U.S. Constitution is that it is a document that has survived intact for over two centuries (aside from some amendments along the way) and still forms the basis of government structure and individual rights. Further, the Constitution and our form of government survived the most trying crisis in any government's history, a civil war. Today, the Constitution is held in the same regard as England's Magna Carta as a symbol of limited government and rights for the people.

The most important part of the Constitution is found within Articles I, II, and III which establish and define the powers and duties of the respective branches of government—the legislative (the Congress), the executive (the President), and the judicial (the Supreme Court.) They exist as co-equal branches of government, with the ability to challenge the power of the other. This is what is referred to as our constitutional system of checks and balances. Although we may like to credit the Founding Fathers with the brilliant conception of our government, it was not accomplished without some earlier influence. In 1748 Baron de Montesquieu, a French political philosopher, published a widely read political treatise titled *The Spirit of the Laws*. Montesquieu argued, among many other political topics, that the best form of government was one in which power did not reside in one person or one political body. He suggested a tripartite system of governing in which three branches would share in their separate forms of governance. In Book XI, section 6 of *The Spirit of the Laws* Montesquieu explains his formulation:

"In every government there are three sorts of power: the legislative; the executive in respect to things dependent on the law of nations; and the executive in regard to matters that depend on the civil law.

By virtue of the first, the prince or magistrate enacts temporary or perpetual laws, and amends or abrogates those that have been already enacted. By the second, he makes peace or war, sends or receives embassies, establishes the public security, and provides against invasions. By the third, he punishes criminals, or determines the disputes that arise between individuals. The latter we shall call the judiciary power, and the other simply the executive power of the state.

The political liberty of the subject is a tranquility of mind arising from the opinion each person has of his safety. In order to have this liberty, it is requisite the government be so constituted as one man need not be afraid of another.

When the legislative and executive powers are united in the same person, or in the same body of magistrates, there can be no liberty; because apprehensions may arise, lest the same monarch or senate should enact tyrannical laws, to execute them in a tyrannical manner.

Again, there is no liberty, if the judiciary power be not separated from the legislative and executive. Were it joined with the legislative, the life and liberty of the subject would be exposed to arbitrary control; for the judge would be then the legislator. Were it joined to the executive power, the judge might behave with violence and oppression."

It is chiefly from this influence that our government was constructed. As a result it is no accident that we see a progression in the organization of government beginning with the legislative in Article I and moving sequentially to the executive and the judicial. However, there are several questions for you to consider before continuing your reading of this chapter:

How does Montesquieu's vision of the executive resemble the structure of the executive as laid out in Article II of the Constitution?

Why does Montesquieu tie individual liberty so strongly to this tripartite form of government?

What is the chief evil Montesquieu warns of if the judiciary is not its own branch of government?

If you have given the preceding questions serious thought or discussed them in class then the answers to them are quite obvious. In fact they should be somewhat intuitive for those familiar with the wording of the Constitution and our form of government. Article II vests in the executive branch the foreign relations mission as well as the national defense power, what Montesquieu would place in the law of nations category. Also, the executive branch carries out the civil laws of the nation. In the legislative is the power to make the laws and in the judiciary the power to adjudicate disputes between individuals. The diffusion of government power ensures that no one individual will be able to muster it for his own use to the exclusion of others. It is the ideal form of government espoused by Alexander Hamilton in Federalist No. 78: "*there is no liberty, if the power of judging be not separated from the legislative and executive powers*." Hamilton was quoting Montesquieu in No. 78 and borrowed from *The Spirit of the Laws* when arguing for ratification of the Constitution and a particular form of representative government.

Legal Definition

Checks and balances – in terms of a constitutional republic such as the United States it is a system of countermeasures between coordinate branches of government so that one branch cannot exceed its lawful authority or usurp power from another coordinate branch of government.

The danger of the judicial being blended with the legislative is that it would be able to make decisions about the legality of the laws it passed, an obvious conflict. Montesquieu did not develop the concept of the judicial branch much beyond what is written above, in fact, further along in section 6 of *The Spirit of the Laws* he wrote that the judicial was "[O]*f the three powers above mentioned, the judiciary is in some measure next to nothing: there remain, therefore, only two . . .*" This statement was paraphrased by Hamilton in Federalist No. 78 when he wrote: "*the judiciary is beyond comparison the weakest of the three departments of power.*" As already discussed in Chapter 1, section IV, the Supreme Court of the United States was not considered to have much power until Chief Justice Marshall's opinion in *Marbury v. Madison* established the Court's power of judicial review. In the opinion, Chief Justice Marshall also provided a detailed explanation of the constitutional power of the Court to declare a law by the legislature unconstitutional under our structure of government:

> "*This original and supreme will organizes the government, and assigns to different departments their respective powers. It may either stop here; or establish certain limits not to be transcended by those departments.*
>
> *The government of the United States is of the latter description. The powers of the legislature are defined and limited; and that those limits may not be mistaken or forgotten, the constitution is written. To what purpose are powers limited, and to what purpose is that limitation committed to writing; if these limits may, at any time, be passed by those intended to be restrained? The distinction between a government with limited and unlimited powers is abolished, if those limits do not confine the persons on whom they are imposed, and if acts prohibited and acts allowed are of equal obligation. It is a proposition too plain to be contested, that the constitution controls any legislative act repugnant to it; or, that the legislature may alter the constitution by an ordinary act.*
>
> *Between these alternatives there is no middle ground. The constitution is either a superior, paramount law, unchangeable by ordinary means, or it is on a level with ordinary legislative acts, and like other acts, is alterable when the legislature shall please to alter it.*
>
> *If the former part of the alternative be true, then a legislative act contrary to the constitution is not law: if the latter part be true, then written constitutions are absurd attempts, on the part of the people, to limit a power in its own nature illimitable.*"

The Supreme Court continued to place limits on executive power in subsequent historic cases centered on battles between the legislative and executive branches. Justice Robert Jackson, in an often cited concurring opinion in *Youngstown Sheet & Tube Co., v. Sawyer*, 343 U.S. 579 (1952), established the best exposition of executive power when he wrote that this power is at its highest when "*the President acts pursuant to an express or implied authorization of Congress, his authority is at its maximum, for it includes all that he possesses in his own right plus all that Congress can delegate.*" Jackson went on to state that when "*the President takes measures incompatible with the expressed or implied will of Congress, his power is at its lowest ebb, for then he can rely only upon his own constitutional powers minus any constitutional powers of Congress over the matter.*" As expressed by Justice Jackson, the government works best and at its highest constitutional form when the respective branches work within their defined limits. Otherwise, their individual power, as evidenced in the *Youngstown Sheet & Tube* case—wherein President Truman's executive order seizing steel mills during the Korean War was held to be illegal—is not authorized.

These coordinate powers (outlined in Figure 3.1) exist today as they did in 1788 with Congress possessing the law-making function of government and holding the power of the purse as well as the power to regulate commerce. It also has the ability to raise an army and navy, approve treaties, declare war, and confirm presidential appointments. The executive, which is the office of the President, is the branch tasked with carrying out the laws. Toward that end the President has veto power over legislation. The President is also responsible for foreign relations and as commander-in-chief of the armed forces is responsible for homeland security. Congress' powers are enumerated in section 8 of Article I, and while the President's powers are enumerated in Article II they are not as expressly stated. As a result much of the President's power is implied. Lastly, the judiciary acts as the branch that has ultimate say over what the Constitution means and it interprets legislative acts. The judiciary is formed so that there are general trial courts, which are subordinate to an intermediate appellate court system and a court of final review (the Supreme Court at the federal level.) These courts of review only have appellate jurisdiction (see Chapter 2) over the decisions of the trial courts.

Legal Definition

Federalism – a system of government in which two levels of government control; in the United States there is the federal government which has limited, enumerated rights and the individual state governments that have more plenary powers to govern under their general police powers to ensure the health, safety and general welfare of state residents.

Despite conflicts over the years between the executive and legislative branches, which had to be resolved by the Supreme Court, our system functions as it was designed to function. The daily machinations of government, though not immune from criticism, do accomplish the incredibly complex task of governing a country as large, diverse and complicated as the United States. This is the legacy of our federalist system of government—three federal branches of limited, enumerated powers co-existing not only with each other but with the respective governments of each state. While the federal government has limited powers the states retain inherent general police powers of their own charged with protecting the health, safety and general welfare of state residents.

FIGURE 3.1   Separation of Powers

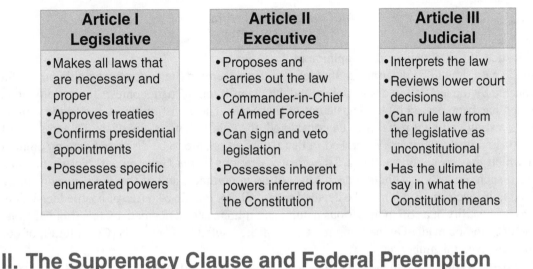

Article I Legislative	Article II Executive	Article III Judicial
• Makes all laws that are necessary and proper • Approves treaties • Confirms presidential appointments • Possesses specific enumerated powers	• Proposes and carries out the law • Commander-in-Chief of Armed Forces • Can sign and veto legislation • Possesses inherent powers inferred from the Constitution	• Interprets the law • Reviews lower court decisions • Can rule law from the legislative as unconstitutional • Has the ultimate say in what the Constitution means

II. The Supremacy Clause and Federal Preemption

It has already been noted that the Constitution is the blueprint for our government and outlines the form of government in Articles I, II, and III. But the Constitution extends beyond these opening articles and provides further instruction for how the government operates. Article IV provides for the relations between the states and the federal government. Article V explains the method of amending the Constitution. This is a difficult process requiring either a two-thirds vote of the House and Senate to amend or two-thirds of the states calling for a constitutional convention to approve amendments. Once an amendment is proposed a three-fourths vote of the states is necessary for amendment. Since the ratification of the Constitution in 1788, which included the original 10 amendments, there have only been an additional seventeen ratified and made a part of the Constitution.

Article VI covers the national debt and its consolidation into the newly formed federal government, the supremacy of the national government and oaths of office. Lastly, Article VII provides for the original ratification process to make the Constitution law.

In this section the focus will be on Article VI and the supremacy language contained within it. The text of Article VI is straightforward and not subject to much interpretation – "the laws of the United States . . . and all treaties . . . shall be the supreme law of the land." This was a critical part of the Constitution since the predecessor Articles of Confederation only provided for a national Congress and the states were still considered autonomous units. James Madison, writing under the pseudonym of Publius, authored Federalist No. 44 wherein he made his argument for the necessity of the states to be limited in power under the terms of the Constitution and for the Constitution to be the supreme law of the land. Anti-federalists were opposed to this and supported states rights. They were concerned about state subservience to an all-powerful federal government. Even though the ratification of the Constitution by the necessary 9 out of 13 states in 1788 gave supremacy to the Constitution the states rights versus centralized government arguments, criticisms and litigation continues to present time.

An early case to address state rights concerns and firmly establish the supremacy of the Constitution was *McCulloch v. Maryland*. Authored by Chief Justice Marshall the case is a fulfillment of Marshall's opinion in *Marbury v. Madison* that the Supreme Court is the final arbiter of the Constitution's meaning. The case is considered one of Marshall's more brilliant written opinions. If the Supreme Court was a weaker constituted branch the outcome in *McCulloch* could have been much different, as could the ability of the federal government to finance its activities.

❖❖

McCulloch v. Maryland
17 U.S. 316 (1819)

Chief Justice Marshall delivered the opinion of the Court.

In the case now to be determined, the defendant, a sovereign State, denies the obligation of a law enacted by the legislature of the Union, and the plaintiff, on his part, contests the validity of an act which has been passed by the legislature of that State. The Constitution of our country, in its most interesting and vital parts, is to be considered, the conflicting powers of the Government of the Union and of its members, as marked in that Constitution, are to be discussed, and an opinion given which may essentially influence the great operations of the Government. No tribunal can approach such a question without a deep sense of its importance, and of the awful responsibility involved in its decision. But it must be decided peacefully, or remain a source of hostile legislation, perhaps, of hostility of a still more serious nature; and if it is to be so decided, by this tribunal alone can the decision be made. On the Supreme Court of the United States has the Constitution of our country devolved this important duty.

The first question made in the cause is—has Congress power to incorporate a bank? It has been truly said that this can scarcely be considered as an open question entirely unprejudiced by the former proceedings of the Nation respecting it. The principle now contested was introduced at a very early period of our history, has been recognized by many successive legislatures, and has been acted upon by the Judicial Department, in cases of peculiar delicacy, as a law of undoubted obligation.

***

The power now contested was exercised by the first Congress elected under the present Constitution. The bill for incorporating the Bank of the United States did not steal upon an unsuspecting legislature and pass unobserved. Its principle was completely understood, and was opposed with equal zeal and ability . . . In discussing this question, the counsel for the State of Maryland have deemed it of some importance, in the construction of the Constitution, to consider that instrument not as emanating from the people, but as the act of sovereign and independent States. The powers of the General Government, it has been said, are delegated by the States, who alone are truly sovereign, and must be exercised in subordination to the States, who alone possess supreme dominion.

It would be difficult to sustain this proposition. The convention which framed the Constitution was indeed elected by the State legislatures. But the instrument, when it came from their hands, was a mere proposal, without obligation or pretensions to it. It was reported to the then existing Congress of the United States with a request that it might be submitted to a convention of delegates, chosen in each State by the people thereof, under the recommendation of its legislature, for their assent and ratification.

This mode of proceeding was adopted, and by the convention, by Congress, and by the State legislatures, the instrument was submitted to the people. They acted upon it in the only manner in which they can act safely, effectively and wisely, on such a subject—by assembling in convention . . .

From these conventions the Constitution derives its whole authority. The government proceeds directly from the people; is "ordained and established" in the name of the people, and is declared to be ordained, in order to form a more perfect union, establish justice, insure domestic tranquility, and secure the blessings of liberty to themselves and to their posterity.

The assent of the States in their sovereign capacity is implied in calling a convention, and thus submitting that instrument to the people. But the people were at perfect liberty to accept or reject it, and their act was final. It required not the affirmance, and could not be negatived, by the State Governments. The Constitution, when thus adopted, was of complete obligation, and bound the State sovereignties.

***

If any one proposition could command the universal assent of mankind, we might expect it would be this—that the Government of the Union, though limited in its powers, is supreme within its sphere of action. This would seem to result necessarily from its nature. It is the Government of all; its powers are delegated by all; it represents all, and acts for all. Though any one State may be willing to control its operations, no State is willing to allow others to control them. The nation, on those subjects on which it can act, must necessarily bind its component parts. But this question is not left to mere reason; the people have, in express terms, decided it by saying, "this Constitution, and the laws of the United States, which shall be made in pursuance thereof," "shall be the supreme law of the land," and by requiring that the members of the State legislatures and the officers of the executive and judicial departments of the States shall take the oath of fidelity to it. The Government of the United States, then, though limited in its powers, is supreme, and its laws, when made in pursuance of the Constitution, form the supreme law of the land, "anything in the Constitution or laws of any State to the contrary notwithstanding."

Among the enumerated powers, we do not find that of establishing a bank or creating a corporation. But there is no phrase in the instrument which, like the Articles of Confederation, excludes incidental or implied powers and which requires that everything granted shall be expressly and minutely described. Even the 10th Amendment, which was framed for the purpose of quieting the excessive jealousies which had been excited, omits the word "expressly," and declares only that the powers "not delegated to the United States, nor prohibited to the States, are reserved to the States or to the people," thus leaving the question whether the particular power which may become the subject of contest has been delegated to the one Government, or prohibited to the other, to depend on a fair construction of the whole instrument . . . A Constitution, to contain an accurate detail of all the subdivisions of which its great powers will admit, and of all the means by which they may be carried into execution, would partake of the prolixity of a legal code, and could scarcely be embraced by the human mind. It would probably never be understood by the public. Its nature, therefore, requires that only its great outlines should be marked, its important objects designated, and the minor ingredients which compose those objects be deduced from the nature of the objects themselves. That this idea was entertained by the framers of the American Constitution is not only to be inferred from the nature of the instrument, but from the language. Why else were some of the limitations found in the 9th section of the 1st article introduced? It is also in some degree warranted by their having omitted to use any restrictive term which might prevent its receiving a fair and just interpretation. In considering this question, then, we must never forget that it is *a Constitution* we are expounding.

Although, among the enumerated powers of Government, we do not find the word "bank" or "incorporation," we find the great powers, to lay and collect taxes; to borrow money; to regulate commerce; to declare and conduct a war; and to raise and support armies and navies. The sword and the purse, all the external relations, and no inconsiderable portion of the industry of the nation are intrusted to its Government. It can never be pretended that these vast powers draw after them others of inferior importance merely because they are inferior. Such an idea can never be advanced. But it may with great reason be contended that a Government intrusted with such ample powers, on the due execution of which the happiness and prosperity of the Nation so vitally depends, must also be intrusted with ample means for their execution. The power being given, it is the interest of the Nation to facilitate its execution. It can never be their interest, and cannot be presumed to have been their intention, to clog and embarrass its execution by withholding the most appropriate means.

***

But the Constitution of the United States has not left the right of Congress to employ the necessary means for the execution of the powers conferred on the Government to general reasoning. To its enumeration of powers is added that of making all laws which shall be necessary and proper for carrying into execution the foregoing powers, and all other powers vested by this Constitution in the Government of the United States or in any department thereof.

***

In ascertaining the sense in which the word "necessary" is used in this clause of the Constitution, we may derive some aid from that with which it is associated. Congress shall have power "to make all laws which shall be necessary and proper to carry into execution" the powers of the Government. If the word "necessary" was used in that strict and rigorous sense for which the counsel for the State of Maryland contend, it would be an extraordinary departure from the usual course of the human mind, as exhibited in composition, to add a word the only possible effect of which is to qualify that strict and rigorous meaning, to present to the mind the idea of some choice of means of legislation not strained and compressed within the narrow limits for which gentlemen contend.

But the argument which most conclusively demonstrates the error of the construction contended for by the counsel for the State of Maryland is founded on the intention of the convention as manifested in the whole clause. To waste time and argument in proving that, without it, Congress might carry its powers into execution would be not much less idle than to hold a lighted taper to the sun. As little can it be required to prove that, in the absence of this clause, Congress would have some choice of means. That it might employ those which, in its judgment, would most advantageously effect the object to be accomplished. That any means adapted to the end, any means which tended directly to the execution of the Constitutional powers of the Government, were in themselves Constitutional. This clause, as construed by the State of Maryland, would abridge, and almost annihilate, this useful and necessary right of the legislature to select its means. That this could not be intended is, we should think, had it not been already controverted, too apparent for controversy.

***

We admit, as all must admit, that the powers of the Government are limited, and that its limits are not to be transcended. But we think the sound construction of the Constitution must allow to the national legislature that discretion with respect to the means by which the powers it confers are to be carried into execution which will enable that body to perform the high duties assigned to it in the manner most beneficial to the people. Let the end be legitimate, let it be within the scope of the Constitution, and all means which are appropriate, which are plainly adapted to that end, which are not prohibited, but consist with the letter and spirit of the Constitution, are Constitutional.

***

This great principle is that the Constitution and the laws made in pursuance thereof are supreme; that they control the Constitution and laws of the respective States, and cannot be controlled by them.

***

The Court has bestowed on this subject its most deliberate consideration. The result is a conviction that the States have no power, by taxation or otherwise, to retard, impede, burden, or in any manner control the operations of the constitutional laws enacted by Congress to carry into execution the powers vested in the General Government. This is, we think, the unavoidable consequence of that supremacy which the Constitution has declared.

We are unanimously of opinion that the law passed by the Legislature of Maryland, imposing a tax on the Bank of the United States is unconstitutional and void.

This opinion does not deprive the States of any resources which they originally possessed. It does not extend to a tax paid by the real property of the bank, in common with the other real property within the State, nor to a tax imposed on the interest which the citizens of Maryland may hold in this institution, in common with other property of the same description throughout the State. But this is a tax on the operations of the bank, and is, consequently, a tax on the operation of an instrument employed by the Government of the Union to carry its powers into execution. Such a tax must be unconstitutional.

JUDGMENT. This cause came on to be heard, on the transcript of the record of the Court of Appeals of the State of Maryland, and was argued by counsel; on consideration whereof, it is the opinion of this Court that the act of the Legislature of Maryland is contrary to the Constitution of the United States, and void, and therefore that the said Court of Appeals of the State of Maryland erred, in affirming the judgment of the Baltimore County Court, in which judgment was rendered against James W. McCulloch; but that the said Court of Appeals of Maryland ought to have reversed the said judgment of the said Baltimore County Court, and ought to have given judgment for the said appellant, McCulloch. It is, therefore, adjudged and ordered that the said judgment of the said Court of Appeals of the State of Maryland in this case be, and the same hereby is, reversed and annulled. And this Court, proceeding to render such judgment as the said Court of Appeals should have rendered, it is further adjudged and ordered that the judgment of the said Baltimore County Court be reversed and annulled, and that judgment be entered in the said Baltimore County Court for the said James W. McCulloch.

Questions Presented

1) What is the conflict in the case?
2) What was the state of Maryland's position with regard to the Act of Congress?
3) How did Chief Justice Marshall answer Maryland's argument?
4) What did Chief Justice Marshall have to say about powers not specifically enumerated in the Constitution?

❖❖❖

Article VI not only placed the Constitution as the supreme law of the land but also any federal laws established by Congress pursuant to Article I. This included treaties made by the federal government, which have the effect of law and thereby bind the states to them. Once the federal government enters into a treaty with another sovereignty the states are bound with the federal government to the terms of the treaty. As an example scenario consider the Webster-Ashburton Treaty from 1842 which set certain geographical boundaries between the United States and Canada. Part of this treaty established a border line between Canada and the U.S. states of New York and Vermont. Suppose the state of Vermont's legislature suddenly decided it was entitled to land originally made part of Canada under the terms of the treaty and as a result sent property tax notices to Canadian residents living in that particular section of Canada? In this scenario you could expect that the Canadian residents would ignore these notices and not pay them. The Vermont State Department of Taxation would in theory then file default notices and attempt to collect the taxes due and in so doing seek enforcement in the state courts. This would be a complete violation of the terms of the treaty and would not be sustained in court since no matter how compelling an argument Vermont could make for its ownership of the land it would be preempted by the treaty made by the federal government. Perhaps this may seem like a ridiculous scenario but it is instructive as to the type of issues that can be involved, and, as compared to some actual cases involving the supremacy clause, it is not so far-fetched. For instance, in Pennsylvania during the early part of the Cold War a sedition law was passed that made it a state crime to advocate the forceful overthrow of the federal government. The U.S. Supreme Court in *Pennsylvania v. Nelson*, 350 U.S. 497 (1956), held that this was an impermissible encroachment of state law into an area of dominant federal interest. In *Cooper v. Aaron*, 358 U.S. 1 (1958), the Supreme Court similarly struck down Arkansas laws aimed at nullifying the Court's prior school desegregation decision in *Brown v. Board of Education*, 347 U.S. 483 (1954). The Arkansas laws, which included a change in the state constitution formally rejecting desegregation, were held to be unconstitutional since *Brown* was the supreme law of the land. The Court's decision in Cooper was based on the Article VI Supremacy Clause as well as the *Marbury v. Madison* holding that the Supreme Court has the ultimate final word on what the Constitution means. State level courts have also invoked the Supremacy Clause to nullify state laws or acts in contravention of federal law. One area of exclusive federal jurisdiction is immigration. This is an enumerated power of Congress under Article I, section 8 of the Constitution. In New Hampshire the state trespass laws were used to arrest several undocumented illegal aliens and prosecute them under the state statute. The theory was that under the definition of trespass an illegal alien within the state of New Hampshire was entering or remaining in a place with knowledge he was not permitted to so enter or remain. The state district court judge in the case of *New Hampshire v. Barros-Batistele*, 05-CR-1474 (Nashua D. Ct., 2005) held that use of the state law as an immigration enforcement method was preempted by federal law under the Supremacy Clause since this was an area pervasively regulated by federal law and exclusive to the federal government. A prior U.S. Supreme Court decision in *Hines v. Davidowitz*, 312 U.S. 52 (1941), a case involving a state's alien registration system which conflicted with the federal Alien Registration Act, said preemption of state laws is permitted when they are an obstacle to the purpose and objectives of Congress. In the area of immigration regulation these different types of preemption were more recently noted in *Arizona v. United States*, 567 U.S. 387 (2012), where state laws aimed at immigration enforcement were partially struck down based on the interference with federal law and being involved in an area exclusively reserved for the federal government.

The U.S. Supreme Court used the Supremacy Clause to strike down state laws as early as 1796 in *Ware v. Hylon*, 3 U.S. 199 (1796), when it ruled that a Virginia state statute nullifying debts between state residents and English creditors violated the Treaty of Paris. Since that time the court has actively enforced the supremacy of federal law. However, just because the federal government is involved in a particular area of interest it cannot be assumed that any state law in that area will be preempted. In the case of *DeCanas v. Bica*, 424 U.S. 351 (1976), Justice Brennan's majority opinion reversed a lower court finding that a California labor law was unconstitutional since it prevented employers from hiring aliens not authorized to work in the United States if it would have an adverse impact on lawful resident workers. Justice Brennan wrote that just because the legislation dealt with aliens it did not make it a regulation of immigration, there was no per se preemption.

As noted in the discussion above, there are two types of preemption under the Supremacy Clause—express and implied. Express preemption occurs when a statute enacted by Congress expressly states that it is intended to supersede or preempt an area of state or local law.[1] An example is the 1969 Federal Cigarette Labeling and Advertising Act, which the Supreme Court in *Cipollone v. Liggett Group, Inc.* ruled expressly preempted state common law claims for failure to warn.[2] Another example is the federal Employee Retirement Income Security Act (ERISA) which has been the subject of a number of preemption cases in the Supreme Court. Since the ERISA statute specifically states that it supersedes state law relating to employee benefit plans the Supreme Court has preempted state statutes trying to alter pension plan benefits.[3] Implied preemption, which is more common, occurs when Congress has not expressly stated it intends to preempt state law but where the purpose of its action implies it intended to supersede state law. There are two types of implied preemption—(1) field preemption, where federal regulation is pervasive and seemingly exclusive, as in the area of immigration and naturalization; (2) conflict preemption, where state law operates in a way that blocks the accomplishment of the aims of federal law.

FIGURE 3.2   The Supremacy Clause

U.S. Constitution, Article VI

This Constitution, and the laws of the United States which shall be made in pursuance thereof; and all treaties made, or which shall be made, under the authority of the United States, shall be the supreme law of the land; and the judges in every state shall be bound thereby, anything in the Constitution or laws of any State to the contrary notwithstanding.

III. The Commerce Clause and the Dormant Commerce Clause

One of the specifically enumerated powers of Congress contained in Article I, clause 8 is the power to regulate commerce with foreign nations, among the states, and among Indian Tribes. The use of the Commerce Clause to regulate commerce among the states (the Interstate Commerce Clause) has been a historically contentious battle between Congress and the states. This battle has made its way to the Supreme Court on a number of occasions.

---

[1] *English v. General Electric Co.*, 496 U.S. 72 (1990)
[2] 505 U.S. 504 (1991)
[3] See 29 U.S.C. section 1144 (a); see also, *Dist. of Columbia v. Greater Wash. Bd. Of Trade*, 506 U.S. 125 (1992); *Boggs v. Boggs*, 520 U.S. 833 (1997); *Egelhoff v. Egelhoff*, 532 U.S. 141 (2001)

FIGURE 3.3   The Commerce Clause

U.S. Constitution, Article I, section 8

The Congress shall have power to . . . To regulate commerce with foreign nations, and among the several states, and with the Indian tribes . . .

An initial Supreme Court case dealing with the commerce clause, *Gibbons v. Ogden*, 22 U.S. 1 (1824), held that intrastate activity that was part of a larger interstate commercial scheme could be regulated under the Commerce Clause. This classic case centered on New York State's licensing of Robert Fulton's and Robert Livingstone's steamboats to navigate state waterways between New York and New Jersey. The Supreme Court found this violated a 1793 Act of Congress aimed at regulating ships and vessels involved in coastal trade and fishing. A 1905 Supreme Court case, *Swift & Company v. United States*, resulted in a unanimous opinion authored by Justice Oliver Wendell Holmes declaring that the Commerce Clause allowed the federal government to regulate monopolies.[4] The decision spoke of the overall effects of monopoly activity upon interstate commerce, even though allegations of Sherman Anti-Trust Act of 1890 violations were only local. This language focusing on the "effects upon interstate commerce" had the potential to expand the Supreme Court's deference to Commerce Clause limitations on the states but it occurred during a time when the Court was taking an opposite course of action. The Supreme Court was still taking a narrow view of what constituted interstate commerce.[5] This narrow interpretation occurred during a period of "economic laissez-faire" on the part of the Supreme Court during the Lochner Era. Named after the 1905 case of *Lochner v. New York*[6] the period saw the Supreme Court take a limiting approach to economic regulation over businesses by the states[7]. In *Lochner* the Court held that a state law limiting the working hours of bakers violated the Fourteenth Amendment due process clause. It was a violation of the liberty of contract that the Court said was implicit in the due process clause. Although the *Lochner* opinion was released in 1905 the era is viewed as beginning in 1897 with the Supreme Court decision in *Allgeyer v. Louisiana*[8] and ending in 1937 with *West Coast Hotel v. Parrish*,[9] a case wherein the Court upheld state minimum wage laws.[10] A parallel expansion of the Supreme Court's Commerce Clause jurisprudence occurred the same year with the Supreme Court's decision in *National Labor Relations Board v. Jones & Laughlin Steel Co.*[11] The Supreme Court took a more expansive view of what constituted interstate commerce in the *NLRB* case. It was an important case due to the fact it upheld the constitutionality of the National Labor Relations Act of 1935, a part of President Franklin D. Roosevelt's New Deal legislation. As the country slowly began to emerge from the Great Depression in the 1930s the Supreme Court shifted its view toward

---

[4] 196 U.S. 375 (1905)

[5] See e.g., *Kidd v. Pearson*, 128 U.S. 1 (1888); *Slight v. Kirkwood*, 237 U.S. 52 (1915); *Hammer v. Dagenhart*, 247 U.S. 251 (1918)

[6] 198 U.S. 45 (1905)

[7] Stephen Siegel. *Lochner Era Jurisprudence and the American Constitutional Tradition*, North Carolina Law Review, 70 N.C.L. Rev. 1 (1991), http://scholarshiplaw.unc.edu/nclr/vol70/iss1/9

[8] 165 U.S. 578 (1897)

[9] 300 U.S. 379 (1937)

[10] Michael J. Phillips. How Many Times Was Lochner-Era Substantive Due Process Effective? *Mercer Law Review*, Vol. 48, 1049–1090 (1997).

[11] 301 U.S. 1 (1937)

noninvolvement in economic regulation and started to expand its Commerce Clause jurisprudence.[12] The issue in the case centered on the authority of the National Labor Relations Board to order back to work several employees who were fired from a local steel company for trying to organize a union. The majority opinion, written by Chief Justice Charles Evans Hughes, found that the "*close and intimate effect which brings the subject within the reach of federal power may be due to activities in relation to productive industry although the industry, when separately viewed, is local.*"[13] The decision resulted in the "*direct and substantial effect*" test for impact of state regulation or action upon interstate commerce.[14]

The Supreme Court expanded on its language in *National Labor Relations Board* a few years later in *Wickard v. Filburn*, 317 U.S. 111 (1942). The test in this case was whether there was a substantial economic effect upon interstate commerce.[15] *Wickard* is considered an important case for the expansion of federal regulatory power over the states. As you read the case pay attention to Justice Jackson's reference to earlier Supreme Court decisions, particularly *Gibbons v. Ogden*, as he develops his reasoning in support of the federal quota on farmers like Filburn.

❖❖

Wickard v. Filburn
317 U.S. 111 (1942)

Mr. Justice Jackson delivered the opinion of the Court.

The appellee filed his complaint against the Secretary of Agriculture of the United States, three members of the County Agricultural Conservation Committee for Montgomery County, Ohio, and a member of the State Agricultural Conservation Committee for Ohio. He sought to enjoin enforcement against himself of the marketing penalty imposed by the amendment of May 26, 1941, to the Agricultural Adjustment Act of 1938, upon that part of his 1941 wheat crop which was available for marketing in excess of the marketing quota established for his farm. He also sought a declaratory judgment that the wheat marketing quota provisions of the Act, as amended and applicable to him, were unconstitutional because not sustainable under the Commerce Clause or consistent with the Due Process Clause of the Fifth Amendment.

***

The appellee for many years past has owned and operated a small farm in Montgomery County, Ohio, maintaining a herd of dairy cattle, selling milk, raising poultry, and selling poultry and eggs. It has been his practice to raise a small acreage of winter wheat, sown in the Fall and harvested in the following July; to sell a portion of the crop; to feed part to poultry and livestock on the farm, some of which is sold; to use some in making flour for home consumption, and to keep the rest for the following seeding. The intended disposition of the crop here involved has not been expressly stated.

In July of 1940, pursuant to the Agricultural Adjustment Act of 1938, as then amended, there were established for the appellee's 1941 crop a wheat acreage allotment of 11.1 acres and a normal yield of 20.1 bushels of wheat an acre. He was given notice of such allotment in July of 1940,

---

[12] J.B. Barnes. The Font of Federal Power: *Wickard v. Filburn* and the Aggregation Principle. *Journal of Supreme Court History*, 42: 49–66 (2017).

[13] Id at 38.

[14] Id at 55.

[15] *Wickard* at 125.

before the Fall planting of his 1941 crop of wheat, and again in July of 1941, before it was harvested. He sowed, however, 23 acres, and harvested from his 11.9 acres of excess acreage 239 bushels, which, under the terms of the Act as amended on May 26, 1941, constituted farm marketing excess, subject to a penalty of 49 cents a bushel, or $117.11 in all. The appellee has not paid the penalty, and he has not postponed or avoided it by storing the excess under regulations of the Secretary of Agriculture, or by delivering it up to the Secretary. The Committee, therefore, refused him a marketing card, which was, under the terms of Regulations promulgated by the Secretary, necessary to protect a buyer from liability to the penalty and upon its protecting lien.

The general scheme of the Agricultural Adjustment Act of 1938 as related to wheat is to control the volume moving in interstate and foreign commerce in order to avoid surpluses and shortages and the consequent abnormally low or high wheat prices and obstructions to commerce. Within prescribed limits and by prescribed standards, the Secretary of Agriculture is directed to ascertain and proclaim each year a national acreage allotment for the next crop of wheat, which is then apportioned to the states and their counties, and is eventually broken up into allotments for individual farms. Loans and payments to wheat farmers are authorized in stated circumstances.

The Act further provides that, whenever it appears that the total supply of wheat as of the beginning of any marketing year, beginning July 1, will exceed a normal year's domestic consumption and export by more than 35 percent the Secretary shall so proclaim not later than May 15 prior to the beginning of such marketing year, and that, during the marketing year, a compulsory national marketing quota shall be in effect with respect to the marketing of wheat. Between the issuance of the proclamation and June 10, the Secretary must, however, conduct a referendum of farmers who will be subject to the quota, to determine whether they favor or oppose it; and, if more than one-third of the farmers voting in the referendum do oppose, the Secretary must, prior to the effective date of the quota, by proclamation suspend its operation.

On May 19, 1941, the Secretary of Agriculture made a radio address to the wheat farmers of the United States in which he advocated approval of the quotas and called attention to the pendency of the amendment of May 26, 1941, which had at the time been sent by Congress to the White House, and pointed out its provision for an increase in the loans on wheat to 85 percent of parity.

***

The court below held, with one judge dissenting, that the speech of the Secretary invalidated the referendum, and that the amendment of May 26, 1941 . . . should not be applied to the appellee because, as so applied, it was retroactive, and in violation of the Fifth Amendment, and, alternatively, because the equities of the case so required. Its Judgment permanently enjoined appellants from collecting a marketing penalty of more than 15 cents a bushel on the farm marketing excess of appellee's 1941 wheat crop, from subjecting appellee's entire 1941 crop to a lien for the payment of the penalty, and from collecting a 15-cent penalty except in accordance with the provisions of § 339 of the Act as that section stood prior to the amendment of May 26, 1941. The Secretary and his codefendants have appealed.

*****

II

It is urged that, under the Commerce Clause of the Constitution, Article I, § 8, clause 3, Congress does not possess the power it has in this instance sought to exercise. The question would merit little consideration, since our decision in *United States v. Darby*, 312 U.S. 100, sustaining the federal power to regulate production of goods for commerce, except for the fact that this Act extends federal regulation to production not intended in any part for commerce, but wholly for consumption on the farm. The Act includes a definition of "market" and its derivatives, so that, as related to wheat, in addition to its conventional meaning, it also means to dispose of "by feeding (in any form) to poultry or livestock which, or the products of which, are sold, bartered, or exchanged, or to be so disposed of."

Hence, marketing quotas not only embrace all that may be sold without penalty, but also what may be consumed on the premises. Wheat produced on excess acreage is designated as "available for marketing" as so defined, and the penalty is imposed thereon. Penalties do not depend upon whether any part of the wheat, either within or without the quota, is sold or intended to be sold. The sum of this is that the Federal Government fixes a quota including all that the farmer may harvest for sale or for his own farm needs, and declares that wheat produced on excess acreage may neither be disposed of nor used except upon payment of the penalty, or except it is stored as required by the Act or delivered to the Secretary of Agriculture.

Appellee says that this is a regulation of production and consumption of wheat. Such activities are, he urges, beyond the reach of Congressional power under the Commerce Clause, since they are local in character, and their effects upon interstate commerce are, at most, "indirect." In answer, the Government argues that the statute regulates neither production nor consumption, but only marketing, and, in the alternative, that, if the Act does go beyond the regulation of marketing, it is sustainable as a "necessary and proper" implementation of the power of Congress over interstate commerce.

***

At the beginning, Chief Justice Marshall described the federal commerce power with a breadth never yet exceeded. *Gibbons v. Ogden*, 9 Wheat. 1, 22 U.S. 194–195. He made emphatic the embracing and penetrating nature of this power by warning that effective restraints on its exercise must proceed from political, rather than from judicial, processes. *Id.* at 22 U.S. 197. For nearly a century, however, decisions of this Court under the Commerce Clause dealt rarely with questions of what Congress might do in the exercise of its granted power under the Clause, and almost entirely with the permissibility of state activity which it was claimed discriminated against or burdened interstate commerce. During this period, there was perhaps little occasion for the affirmative exercise of the commerce power, and the influence of the Clause on American life and law was a negative one, resulting almost wholly from its operation as a restraint upon the powers of the states. In discussion and decision, the point of reference, instead of being what was "necessary and proper" to the exercise by Congress of its granted power, was often some concept of sovereignty thought to be implicit in the status of statehood. Certain activities such as "production," "manufacturing," and "mining" were occasionally said to be within the province of state governments and beyond the power of Congress under the Commerce Clause.

It was not until 1887, with the enactment of the Interstate Commerce Act, that the interstate commerce power began to exert positive influence in American law and life. This first important federal resort to the commerce power was followed in 1890 by the Sherman Anti-Trust Act and, thereafter, mainly after 1903, by many others. These statutes ushered in new phases of adjudication, which required the Court to approach the interpretation of the Commerce Clause in the light of an actual exercise by Congress of its power thereunder.

***

Whether the subject of the regulation in question was "production," "consumption," or "marketing" is, therefore, not material for purposes of deciding the question of federal power before us. That an activity is of local character may help in a doubtful case to determine whether Congress intended to reach it. The same consideration might help in determining whether, in the absence of Congressional action, it would be permissible for the state to exert its power on the subject matter, even though, in so doing, it to some degree affected interstate commerce. But even if appellee's activity be local, and though it may not be regarded as commerce, it may still, whatever its nature, be reached by Congress if it exerts a substantial economic effect on interstate commerce, and this irrespective of whether such effect is what might at some earlier time have been defined as "direct" or "indirect."

The parties have stipulated a summary of the economics of the wheat industry. Commerce among the states in wheat is large and important. Although wheat is raised in every state but one, production in most states is not equal to consumption. Sixteen states, on average, have had a surplus of wheat above their own requirements for feed, seed, and food. Thirty-two states and the District of Columbia, where production has been below consumption, have looked to these surplus-producing states for their supply, as well as for wheat for export and carry-over.

***

Differences in farming conditions, however, make these benefits mean different things to different wheat growers. There are several large areas of specialization in wheat, and the concentration on this crop reaches 27 percent of the crop land, and the average harvest runs as high as 155 acres. Except for some use of wheat as stock feed and for seed, the practice is to sell the crop for cash. Wheat from such areas constitutes the bulk of the interstate commerce therein.

On the other hand, in some New England states, less than one percent of the crop land is devoted to wheat, and the average harvest is less than five acres per farm. In 1940, the average percentage of the total wheat production that was sold in each state, as measured by value ranged from 29 percent thereof in Wisconsin to 90 percent in Washington. Except in regions of large-scale production, wheat is usually grown in rotation with other crops; for a nurse crop for grass seeding, and as a cover crop to prevent soil erosion and leaching. Some is sold, some kept for seed, and a percentage of the total production much larger than in areas of specialization is consumed on the farm and grown for such purpose. Such farmers, while growing some wheat, may even find the balance of their interest on the consumer's side.

The effect of consumption of home-grown wheat on interstate commerce is due to the fact that it constitutes the most variable factor in the disappearance of the wheat crop. Consumption on the farm where grown appears to vary in an amount greater than 20 percent of average production. The total amount of wheat consumed as food varies but relatively little, and use as seed is relatively constant.

The maintenance by government regulation of a price for wheat undoubtedly can be accomplished as effectively by sustaining or increasing the demand as by limiting the supply. The effect of the statute before us is to restrict the amount which may be produced for market and the extent, as well, to which one may forestall resort to the market by producing to meet his own needs. That appellee's own contribution to the demand for wheat may be trivial by itself is not enough to remove him from the scope of federal regulation where, as here, his contribution, taken together with that of many others similarly situated, is far from trivial. *Labor Board v. Fairblatt*, 306 U.S. 601, 306 U.S. 606 *et seq.; United States v. Darby, supra* at 312 U.S. 123.

It is well established by decisions of this Court that the power to regulate commerce includes the power to regulate the prices at which commodities in that commerce are dealt in and practices affecting such prices. One of the primary purposes of the Act in question was to increase the market price of wheat, and, to that end, to limit the volume thereof that could affect the market. It can hardly be denied that a factor of such volume and variability as home-consumed wheat would have a substantial influence on price and market conditions. This may arise because being in marketable condition such wheat overhangs the market, and, if induced by rising prices, tends to flow into the market and check price increases. But if we assume that it is never marketed, it supplies a need of the man who grew it which would otherwise be reflected by purchases in the open market. Home-grown wheat in this sense competes with wheat in commerce. The stimulation of commerce is a use of the regulatory function quite as definitely as prohibitions or restrictions thereon. This record leaves us in no doubt that Congress may properly have considered that wheat consumed on the farm where grown, if wholly outside the scheme of regulation, would have a substantial effect in defeating and obstructing its purpose to stimulate trade therein at increased prices.

It is said, however, that this Act, forcing some farmers into the market to buy what they could provide for themselves, is an unfair promotion of the markets and prices of specializing wheat growers. It is of the essence of regulation that it lays a restraining hand on the self-interest of the regulated, and that advantages from the regulation commonly fall to others. The conflicts of economic interest between the regulated and those who advantage by it are wisely left under our system to resolution by the Congress under its more flexible and responsible legislative process. Such conflicts rarely lend themselves to judicial determination. And with the wisdom, workability, or fairness, of the plan of regulation, we have nothing to do.

*****

Reversed.

Questions Presented

1) What was the purpose of the Agricultural Adjustment Act of 1938?
2) How does Justice Jackson justify the federal government's regulation of Filburn's wheat production as being within the regulatory power of Congress under the Commerce Clause?
3) Why is the growth of wheat for personal use also within the boundaries of Congressional control over commerce?

❖❖

The extent of Congress' power to regulate commerce has rarely been challenged by the Supreme Court. Whether or not an activity comes within Congress' power is measured under a two-part test:

1. does the activity being regulated substantially effect commerce?
2. has the means of regulation chosen by congress been rationally related to its objective in regulating the activity?

Wickard v. Filburn added a "cumulative effects" test to the consideration of whether or not commerce is impacted. This was an expansion of Commerce Clause power during a time when the country was engulfed in World War II and regulation of wheat products was essential.[16] The new test increased the regulatory power of Congress since the Supreme Court said individual acts alone are not the sole criteria of impact but an entire class of acts if they have a substantial economic impact. This applies even if an act may have no interstate impact.

---

[16] Barnes at 59.

During this same period the Supreme Court added to Congress' regulatory power under the Commerce Clause by reversing prior restrictions upon the government's general welfare and police powers and expanding federal involvement into areas previously viewed as local.[17] Commentators have referred to 1937 as a time of "Constitutional Revolution" at the Supreme Court.[18] In *United States v. Darby*[19] the Court was confronted with the issue of whether the Fair Labor and Standards Act of 1938 was a legitimate exercise of Congress' power to regulate commerce. Justice Harlan Fiske Stone, writing for a unanimous majority of the Court, upheld the law, citing the *Gibbons v. Ogden* statement that the power of Congress over interstate commerce "is complete in itself, may be exercised to its utmost extent, and acknowledges no limitations other than are prescribed in the Constitution."[20] Once again the Supreme Court looked at the activity's substantial effect upon interstate commerce, this time considering whether the activity had a prohibition on the interstate transport of goods or people.

Thus, the three theories of Commerce Clause regulation are:

1. the substantial economic effect test;
2. the cumulative effects test;
3. the prohibition of commerce test.

One of the more significant uses of the Commerce Clause came in the area of civil rights enforcement. Discrimination denying individuals "the full and equal enjoyment of the goods, services, facilities, privileges, advantages, and accommodations of any place of public accommodation" based on race, color or national origin was banned by Title II of the Civil Rights Act of 1964.[21] Immediate challenges to Title II were mounted and two cases from 1964 upheld the Civil Rights Act and its reach to local business activities. In *Heart of Atlanta Motel v. United States* the Supreme Court used out of state traveler occupancy rates to find against a hotel that refused to rent rooms to blacks.[22] In a second case, *Katzenbach v. McClung*,[23] argued the same day and subsequently decided the same day as *Heart of Atlanta*, the Supreme Court applied the Act to a restaurant that only provided take-out food service to blacks. Unlike the hotel that did an extensive business with out-of-state travelers the business of the restaurant was in-state. However, the Supreme Court found that a large portion of the food supplied to the restaurant came from an out-of-state supplier and this was enough to invoke the regulatory power of Congress under the Commerce Clause. In both cases the Supreme Court cited its precedents in *Gibbons*, *Wickard* and *Darby* to affirm the constitutionality of Title II.

The Supreme Court continued on a pattern of general deference to Congress' power under the Commerce Clause until 1995 when *United States v. Lopez*[24] invalidated the Gun-Free School Zones Act of 1990. In a narrow 5–4 majority the Supreme Court held that Congress' powers under the

---

[17] William E. Leuchtenburg. *The Supreme Court Reborn: The Constitutional Revolution in the Age of Roosevelt*, (1995).
[18] Id at 228.
[19] 312 U.S. 100 (1941)
[20] *Darby* at 114.
[21] Steven Schwinn. *Civil Rights Act of 1964: Enduring and Revolutionary*, American Bar Association, Insights on Law & Society, Winter 2014.
[22] 379 U.S. 241 (1964)
[23] 379 U.S. 294 (1964)
[24] 514 U.S. 549 (1995)

Commerce Clause were not absolute, there were limits restricting the power. Congress can regulate economic activity tending to have a substantial impact upon commerce, but the Supreme Court said criminal statutes had no connection with commerce or economic activity. Five years later in *United States v. Morrison*, 529 U.S. 598 (2000), the Supreme Court similarly struck down a Congressional statute aimed at curbing violence against women (Violence Against Women Act of 1994).[25] By the same 5–4 majority split, the majority (Chief Justice Rehnquist, Justices O'Connor, Scalia, Kennedy, and Thomas) held that the historical expansion of the commerce power did not undo the outer limits of that power.[26] Referencing its prior *Lopez* opinion the Court outlined the "three broad categories that Congress may regulate under its commerce power":[27]

1. it may regulate the use of the channels of commerce;
2. it is empowered to regulate and protect the instrumentalities of interstate commerce, or persons or things in interstate commerce, even though the threat may come only from intrastate activities;
3. it includes the power to regulate those activities having a substantial relation to interstate commerce, i.e., those activities that substantially affect interstate commerce.

The *Morrison* decision, striking down the Violence Against Women Act, said "[G]ender-motivated crimes of violence are not, in any sense of the phrase, economic activity."[28] But these two decisions by the Supreme Court did not stymie the overall effectiveness of Congress' regulation in legitimate areas of commercial activity. The Court returned to its approval of broad congressional regulation in areas of economic activity. The activity involved in the 2005 case of *Gonzales v. Raich* involved the intrastate, noncommercial cultivation of medical marijuana. In reaching its decision the *Raich* court relied on its prior wheat farming decision in *Wickard v. Filburn*.

❖❖

Gonzales v. Raich
545 U.S. 1 (2005)

Justice Stevens delivered the opinion of the Court.

California is one of at least nine States that authorize the use of marijuana for medicinal purposes. The question presented in this case is whether the power vested in Congress by Article I, § 8, of the Constitution "[t]o make all Laws which shall be necessary and proper for carrying into Execution" its authority to "regulate Commerce with foreign Nations, and among the several States" includes the power to prohibit the local cultivation and use of marijuana in compliance with California law.

California has been a pioneer in the regulation of marijuana. In 1913, California was one of the first States to prohibit the sale and possession of marijuana, and at the end of the century, California became the first State to authorize limited use of the drug for medicinal purposes. In 1996, California voters passed Proposition 215, now codified as the Compassionate Use Act of 1996. The proposition was designed to ensure that "seriously ill" residents of the State have access to marijuana for medical purposes, and to encourage Federal and State Governments to take steps towards ensuring

---

[25] 42 U.S.C. section 13981
[26] *Morrison* at 608.
[27] Id at 608–9.
[28] Id at 613.

the safe and affordable distribution of the drug to patients in need. The Act creates an exemption from criminal prosecution for physicians, as well as for patients and primary caregivers who possess or cultivate marijuana for medicinal purposes with the recommendation or approval of a physician. A "primary caregiver" is a person who has consistently assumed responsibility for the housing, health, or safety of the patient.

Respondents Angel Raich and Diane Monson are California residents who suffer from a variety of serious medical conditions and have sought to avail themselves of medical marijuana pursuant to the terms of the Compassionate Use Act. They are being treated by licensed, board-certified family practitioners, who have concluded, after prescribing a host of conventional medicines to treat respondents' conditions and to alleviate their associated symptoms, that marijuana is the only drug available that provides effective treatment. Both women have been using marijuana as a medication for several years pursuant to their doctors' recommendation, and both rely heavily on cannabis to function on a daily basis. Indeed, Raich's physician believes that forgoing cannabis treatments would certainly cause Raich excruciating pain and could very well prove fatal.

Respondent Monson cultivates her own marijuana, and ingests the drug in a variety of ways including smoking and using a vaporizer. Respondent Raich, by contrast, is unable to cultivate her own, and thus relies on two caregivers, litigating as "John Does," to provide her with locally grown marijuana at no charge. These caregivers also process the cannabis into hashish or keif, and Raich herself processes some of the marijuana into oils, balms, and foods for consumption.

On August 15, 2002, county deputy sheriffs and agents from the federal Drug Enforcement Administration (DEA) came to Monson's home. After a thorough investigation, the county officials concluded that her use of marijuana was entirely lawful as a matter of California law. Nevertheless, after a 3-hour standoff, the federal agents seized and destroyed all six of her cannabis plants.

Respondents thereafter brought this action against the Attorney General of the United States and the head of the DEA seeking injunctive and declaratory relief prohibiting the enforcement of the federal Controlled Substances Act (CSA), 84 Stat. 1242, 21 U.S.C. § 801 *et seq.*, to the extent it prevents them from possessing, obtaining, or manufacturing cannabis for their personal medical use. In their complaint and supporting affidavits, Raich and Monson described the severity of their afflictions, their repeatedly futile attempts to obtain relief with conventional medications, and the opinions of their doctors concerning their need to use marijuana. Respondents claimed that enforcing the CSA against them would violate the Commerce Clause, the Due Process Clause of the Fifth Amendment, the Ninth and Tenth Amendments of the Constitution, and the doctrine of medical necessity.

The District Court denied respondents' motion for a preliminary injunction. *Raich v. Ashcroft*, 248 F. Supp. 2d 918 (ND Cal. 2003). Although the court found that the federal enforcement interests "wane[d]" when compared to the harm that California residents would suffer if denied access to medically necessary marijuana, it concluded that respondents could not demonstrate a likelihood of success on the merits of their legal claims. *Id.*, at 931.

A divided panel of the Court of Appeals for the Ninth Circuit reversed and ordered the District Court to enter a preliminary injunction. *Raich v. Ashcroft*, 352 F. 3d 1222 (2003). The court found that respondents had "demonstrated a strong likelihood of success on their claim that, as applied to them, the CSA is an unconstitutional exercise of Congress' Commerce Clause authority." *Id.*, at 1227. The Court of Appeals distinguished prior Circuit cases upholding the CSA in the face of Commerce Clause challenges by focusing on what it deemed to be the "*separate and distinct class of activities*" at issue in this case: "the intrastate, noncommercial cultivation and possession of cannabis for personal medical purposes as recommended by a patient's physician pursuant to valid California state law." *Id.*, at 1228. The court found the latter class of activities "different in kind from drug trafficking" because interposing a physician's recommendation raises different health and safety concerns, and because "this limited use is clearly distinct from the broader illicit drug market—as well as any broader commercial market for medicinal marijuana—insofar as the medicinal marijuana at issue in this case is not intended for, nor does it enter, the stream of commerce." *Ibid.*

The majority placed heavy reliance on our decisions in *United States v. Lopez*, 514 U.S. 549 (1995), and *United States v. Morrison*, 529 U.S. 598 (2000), as interpreted by recent Circuit precedent, to hold that this separate class of purely local activities was beyond the reach of federal power. In contrast, the dissenting judge concluded that the CSA, as applied to respondents, was clearly valid under *Lopez* and *Morrison;* moreover, he thought it "simply impossible to distinguish the relevant conduct surrounding the cultivation and use of the marijuana crop at issue in this case from the cultivation and use of the wheat crop that affected interstate commerce in *Wickard v. Filburn.*" 352 F. 3d, at 1235 (Beam, J., dissenting) (citation omitted).

The obvious importance of the case prompted our grant of certiorari. 542 U.S. 936 (2004). The case is made difficult by respondents' strong arguments that they will suffer irreparable harm because, despite a congressional finding to the contrary, marijuana does have valid therapeutic purposes. The question before us, however, is not whether it is wise to enforce the statute in these circumstances; rather, it is whether Congress' power to regulate interstate markets for medicinal substances encompasses the portions of those markets that are supplied with drugs produced and consumed locally. Well-settled law controls our answer. The CSA is a valid exercise of federal power, even as applied to the troubling facts of this case. We accordingly vacate the judgment of the Court of Appeals.

Respondents in this case do not dispute that passage of the CSA, as part of the Comprehensive Drug Abuse Prevention and Control Act, was well within Congress' commerce power. Nor do they contend that any provision or section of the CSA amounts to an unconstitutional exercise of congressional authority. Rather, respondents' challenge is actually quite limited; they argue that the CSA's categorical prohibition of the manufacture and possession of marijuana as applied to the intrastate manufacture and possession of marijuana for medical purposes pursuant to California law exceeds Congress' authority under the Commerce Clause.

In assessing the validity of congressional regulation, none of our Commerce Clause cases can be viewed in isolation. As charted in considerable detail in *United States v. Lopez*, our understanding of the reach of the Commerce Clause, as well as Congress' assertion of authority thereunder, has evolved over time. The Commerce Clause emerged as the Framers' response to the central problem giving rise to the Constitution itself: the absence of any federal commerce power under the Articles of Confederation. For the first century of our history, the primary use of the Clause was to preclude the kind of discriminatory state legislation that had once been permissible. Then, in response to rapid industrial development and an increasingly interdependent national economy, Congress "ushered in a new era of federal regulation under the commerce power," beginning with the enactment of the Interstate Commerce Act in 1887, 24 Stat. 379, and the Sherman Antitrust Act in 1890, 26 Stat. 209, as amended, 15 U.S.C. § 2 *et seq.*

Cases decided during that "new era," which now spans more than a century, have identified three general categories of regulation in which Congress is authorized to engage under its commerce power. First, Congress can regulate the channels of interstate commerce. *Perez v. United States*,

402 U.S. 146, 150 (1971). Second, Congress has authority to regulate and protect the instrumentalities of interstate commerce, and persons or things in interstate commerce. *Ibid.* Third, Congress has the power to regulate activities that substantially affect interstate commerce. *Ibid.; NLRB v. Jones & Laughlin Steel Corp.*, 301 U.S. 1, 37 (1937). Only the third category is implicated in the case at hand.

Our case law firmly establishes Congress' power to regulate purely local activities that are part of an economic "class of activities" that have a substantial effect on interstate commerce. See, *e.g., Perez*, 317 U.S. 111, 128–129 (1942). As we stated in *Wickard*, "even if appellee's activity be local and though it may not be regarded as commerce, it may still, whatever its nature, be reached by Congress if it exerts a substantial economic effect on interstate commerce." *Id.*, at 125. We have never required Congress to legislate with scientific exactitude. When Congress decides that the "'total incidence'" of a practice poses a threat to a national market, it may regulate the entire class. See *Perez*, 274 U.S. 256, 259 (1927) ("[W]hen it is necessary in order to prevent an evil to make the law embrace more than the precise thing to be prevented it may do so")). In this vein, we have reiterated that when "'a general regulatory statute bears a substantial relation to commerce, the *de minimis* character of individual instances arising under that statute is of no consequence.'" *E.g., Lopez*, 392 U.S. 183, 196, n. 27 (1968)).

Our decision in *Wickard*, 317 U.S. 111, is of particular relevance. In *Wickard*, we upheld the application of regulations promulgated under the Agricultural Adjustment Act of 1938, 52 Stat. 31, which were designed to control the volume of wheat moving in interstate and foreign commerce in order to avoid surpluses and consequent abnormally low prices. The regulations established an allotment of 11.1 acres for Filburn's 1941 wheat crop, but he sowed 23 acres, intending to use the excess by consuming it on his own farm. Filburn argued that even though we had sustained Congress' power to regulate the production of goods for commerce, that power did not authorize "federal regulation [of] production not intended in any part for commerce but wholly for consumption on the farm." *Wickard*, 317 U.S., at 118. Justice Jackson's opinion for a unanimous Court rejected this submission. He wrote:

> *"The effect of the statute before us is to restrict the amount which may be produced for market and the extent as well to which one may forestall resort to the market by producing to meet his own needs. That appellee's own contribution to the demand for wheat may be trivial by itself is not enough to remove him from the scope of federal regulation where, as here, his contribution, taken together with that of many others similarly situated, is far from trivial." Id.*, at 127–128.

Wickard thus establishes that Congress can regulate purely intrastate activity that is not itself "commercial," in that it is not produced for sale, if it concludes that failure to regulate that class of activity would undercut the regulation of the interstate market in that commodity.

The similarities between this case and *Wickard* are striking. Like the farmer in *Wickard*, respondents are cultivating, for home consumption, a fungible commodity for which there is an established, albeit illegal, interstate market. Just as the Agricultural Adjustment Act was designed "to control the volume [of wheat] moving in interstate and foreign commerce in order to avoid surpluses . . ." and consequently control the market price, *id.*, at 115, a primary purpose of the CSA is to control the supply and demand of controlled substances in both lawful and unlawful drug markets. See nn. 20–21, *supra*. In *Wickard*, we had no difficulty concluding that Congress had a rational basis for believing that, when viewed in the aggregate, leaving home-consumed wheat outside the regulatory scheme would have a substantial influence on price and market conditions. Here too, Congress had a rational basis for concluding that leaving home-consumed marijuana outside federal control would similarly affect price and market conditions.

More concretely, one concern prompting inclusion of wheat grown for home consumption in the 1938 Act was that rising market prices could draw such wheat into the interstate market, resulting in lower market prices. *Wickard*, 317 U.S., at 128. The parallel concern making it appropriate to include marijuana grown for home consumption in the CSA is the likelihood that the high demand in the interstate market will draw such marijuana into that market. While the diversion of homegrown wheat tended to frustrate the federal interest in stabilizing prices by regulating the volume of commercial transactions in the interstate market, the diversion of homegrown marijuana tends to frustrate the federal interest in eliminating commercial transactions in the interstate market in their entirety. In both cases, the regulation is squarely within Congress' commerce power because production of the commodity meant for home consumption, be it wheat or marijuana, has a substantial effect on supply and demand in the national market for that commodity.

***

Under the present state of the law . . . the judgment of the Court of Appeals must be vacated. The case is remanded for further proceedings consistent with this opinion.

It is so ordered.

Questions Presented

1)   Why was the prior decision in *Wickard v. Filburn* so relevant to this case?
2)   What was the Supreme Court's rationale for holding that Congress can regulate a local intrastate activity like marijuana cultivation for personal medical use?

❖❖

So far the discussion has focused on the explicit text of Article I, section 8, the expressed power over commerce provided to Congress. Since this express power is placed in the federal government there is an implied limit on the states. This limit is referred to as the "dormant" Commerce Clause. Every Commerce Clause case discussed to this point has involved federal law and its impact on state activity. What happens when a state law, not in conflict with any previously enacted federal statute, has an impact upon interstate commerce? Does Congress' power under the Commerce Clause extend to this activity? The general answer is that Congress still has the power to regulate. This implied preemption, i.e., the "dormant" Commerce Clause, operates to restrict the states from passing legislation that would negatively impact interstate commerce. This is a concept developed by the Supreme Court. The first case to consider this negative implication on state power contained in the Commerce Clause was *Reading Railroad v. Pennsylvania*, also known as the "State Freight Tax Case."[29] The facts centered on a tonnage tax imposed by state statute on all tonnage shipped within the state as well as out of and into the state. This was determined by the Court to be an unconstitutional burden on interstate commerce.

---

[29] 82 U.S. 232 (1872)

In order to avoid a conflict with federal commerce power the state law must:

1. be rationally related to a legitimate state concern; and
2. the burden on interstate commerce must be outweighed by the benefit to the state's interest. The reviewing criteria here is whether the state objective can be accomplished by less restrictive means on interstate commerce.

Dormant Commerce Clause cases have become increasingly prevalent among Supreme Court cases interpreting the scope of the Commerce Clause since the early 1980s.[30] This is an area of Commerce Clause jurisprudence that has been particularly litigious over the years. Supreme Court review of these cases looks to see if the state law has a discriminatory impact on out-of-state persons or goods, or if in-state economic interests are preferred or favored over out-of-state economic interests. The next case involves a state statute limiting the length of trucks on the highway. When reading the case below, balance the state statute's requirements and the alleged impact on interstate commerce.

❖❖

Kassel v. Consolidated Freightways Corp. of Delaware
450 U.S. 662 (1981)

The question is whether an Iowa statute that prohibits the use of certain large trucks within the State unconstitutionally burdens interstate commerce.

I

Appellee Consolidated Freightways Corporation of Delaware (Consolidated) is one of the largest common carriers in the country: it offers service in 48 States under a certificate of public convenience and necessity issued by the Interstate Commerce Commission. Among other routes, Consolidated carries commodities through Iowa on Interstate 80, the principal east-west route linking New York, Chicago, and the west coast, and on Interstate 35, a major north-south route.

Consolidated mainly uses two kinds of trucks. One consists of a three-axle tractor pulling a 40-foot two-axle trailer. This unit, commonly called a single, or "semi," is 55 feet in length overall. Such trucks have long been used on the Nation's highways. Consolidated also uses a two-axle tractor pulling a single-axle trailer which, in turn, pulls a single-axle dolly and a second single-axle trailer. This combination, known as a double, or twin, is 65 feet long overall. Many trucking companies, including Consolidated, increasingly prefer to use doubles to ship certain kinds of commodities. Doubles have larger capacities, and the trailers can be detached and routed separately if necessary. Consolidated would like to use 65-foot doubles on many of its trips through Iowa.

The State of Iowa, however, by statute, restricts the length of vehicles that may use its highways. Unlike all other States in the West and Midwest, Iowa generally prohibits the use of 65-foot doubles within its borders. Instead, most truck combinations are restricted to 55 feet in length. Doubles, mobile homes, trucks carrying vehicles such as tractors and other farm equipment, and singles hauling livestock, are permitted to be as long as 60 feet. Notwithstanding these restrictions, Iowa's statute permits cities abutting the state line by local ordinance to adopt the length limitations of the adjoining State. Iowa Code § 321.457(7) (1979). Where a city has exercised this option, otherwise oversized trucks are permitted within the city limits and in nearby commercial zones. *Ibid.*

---

[30] See e.g., Martin H. Redish, and Shane V. Nugent. *The Dormant Commerce Clause and the Constitutional Balance of Federalism*, Duke Law Journal, Vol. 1987, September, No. 4.

Iowa also provides for two other relevant exemptions. An Iowa truck manufacturer may obtain a permit to ship trucks that are as large as 70 feet. Iowa Code § 321E.10 (1979). Permits also are available to move oversized mobile homes, provided that the unit is to be moved from a point within Iowa or delivered for an Iowa resident. § 321E.28(5).

Because of Iowa's statutory scheme, Consolidated cannot use its 65-foot doubles to move commodities through the State. Instead, the company must do one of four things: (i) use 55-foot singles; (ii) use 60-foot doubles; (iii) detach the trailers of a 65-foot double and shuttle each through the State separately; or (iv) divert 65-foot doubles around Iowa.

Dissatisfied with these options, Consolidated filed this suit in the District Court averring that Iowa's statutory scheme unconstitutionally burdens interstate commerce. Iowa defended the law as a reasonable safety measure enacted pursuant to its police power. The State asserted that 65-foot doubles are more dangerous than 55-foot singles and, in any event, that the law promotes safety and reduces road wear within the State by diverting much truck traffic to other states.

In a 14-day trial, both sides adduced evidence on safety and on the burden on interstate commerce imposed by Iowa's law. On the question of safety, the District Court found that the "evidence clearly establishes that the twin is as safe as the semi." 475 F.Supp. 544, 549 (SD Iowa 1979). For that reason, there is no valid safety reason for barring twins from Iowa's highways because of their configuration.

The evidence convincingly, if not overwhelmingly, establishes that the 65-foot twin is as safe as, if not safer than, the 60-foot twin and the 55-foot semi. . . .

***

Twins and semis have different characteristics. Twins are more maneuverable, are less sensitive to wind, and create less splash and spray. However, they are more likely than semis to jackknife or upset. They can be backed only for a short distance. The negative characteristics are not such that they render the twin less safe than semis overall. Semis are more stable, but are more likely to "rear-end" another vehicle. *Id.* at 548–549.

In light of these findings, the District Court applied the standard we enunciated in *Raymond Motor Transportation, Inc. v. Rice*, 434 U.S. 429 (1978), and concluded that the state law impermissibly burdened interstate commerce:

[T]he balance here must be struck in favor of the federal interests. The total effect of the law as a safety measure in reducing accidents and casualties is so slight and problematical that it does not outweigh the national interest in keeping interstate commerce free from interferences that seriously impede it. 475 F.Supp. at 551 (emphasis in original).

The Court of Appeals for the Eighth Circuit affirmed. 612 F.2d 1064 (1979). It accepted the District Court's finding that 65-foot doubles were as safe as 55-foot singles. *Id.* at 1069. Thus, the only apparent safety benefit to Iowa was that resulting from forcing large trucks to detour around the State, thereby reducing overall truck traffic on Iowa's highways. The Court of Appeals noted that this was not a constitutionally permissible interest. *Id.* at 1070. It also commented that the several statutory exemptions identified above, such as those applicable to border cities and the shipment of livestock, suggested that the law, in effect, benefited Iowa residents at the expense of interstate traffic. *Id.* at 1070–1071. The combination of these exemptions weakened the presumption of validity normally accorded a state safety regulation. For these reasons, the Court of Appeals agreed with the District Court that the Iowa statute unconstitutionally burdened interstate commerce.

Iowa appealed, and we noted probable jurisdiction. We now affirm.

II

It is unnecessary to review in detail the evolution of the principles of Commerce Clause adjudication. The Clause is both a "prolific of national power and an equally prolific source of conflict with legislation of the state[s]." *H. P. Hood & Sons, Inc. v. Du Mond*, 336 U.S. 525, 534 (1949). The Clause permits Congress to legislate when it perceives that the national welfare is not furthered by the independent actions of the States. It is now well established, also, that the Clause itself is "a limitation upon state power even without congressional implementation." *Hunt v. Washington Apple Advertising Comm'n*, 432 U.S. 333, 350 (1977). The Clause requires that some aspects of trade generally must remain free from interference by the States. When a State ventures excessively into the regulation of these aspects of commerce, it "trespasses upon national interests," *Great A&P Tea Co. v. Cottrell*, 424 U.S. 366, 373 (1976), and the courts will hold the state regulation invalid under the Clause alone.

The Commerce Clause does not, of course, invalidate all state restrictions on commerce. It has long been recognized that, in the absence of conflicting legislation by Congress, there is a residuum of power in the state to make laws governing matters of local concern which nevertheless in some measure affect interstate commerce or even, to some extent, regulate it. *Southern Pacific Co. v. Arizona*, 325 U.S. 761, 767 (1945). The extent of permissible state regulation is not always easy to measure. It may be said with confidence, however, that a State's power to regulate commerce is never greater than in matters traditionally of local concern. *Washington Apple Advertising Comm'n, supra* at 350. For example, regulations that touch upon safety—especially highway safety—are those that "the Court has been most reluctant to invalidate." *Raymond, supra* at 443; *accord, Railway Express Agency, Inc. v. New York*, 336 U.S. 106, 109 (1949); *South Carolina State Highway Dept. v. Barnwell Brothers, Inc.*, 303 U.S. 177, 187 (1938); *Sproles v. Binford*, 286 U.S. 374, 390 (1932); *Hendrick v. Maryland*, 235 U.S. 610, 622 (1915). Indeed, if safety justifications are not illusory, the Court will not second-guess legislative judgment about their importance in comparison with related burdens on interstate commerce. *Raymond, supra* at 449 (Blackmun, J., concurring). Those who would challenge such bona fide safety regulations must overcome a "strong presumption of validity." *Bibb v. Navajo Freight Lines, Inc.*, 359 U.S. 520, 524 (1959).

But the incantation of a purpose to promote the public health or safety does not insulate a state law from Commerce Clause attack. Regulations designed for that salutary purpose nevertheless may further the purpose so marginally, and interfere with commerce so substantially, as to be invalid under the Commerce Clause. In the Court's recent unanimous decision in *Raymond*, we declined to accept the State's contention that the inquiry under the Commerce Clause is ended without a weighing of the asserted safety purpose against the degree of interference with interstate commerce. 434 U.S. at 443. This "weighing" by a court requires—and indeed the constitutionality of the state regulation depends on—a sensitive consideration of the weight and nature of the state regulatory concern in light of the extent of the burden imposed on the course of interstate commerce. *Id.* at 441; *accord, Pike v. Bruce Church, Inc.*, 397 U.S. 137, 142 (1970); *Bibb, supra*, at 525–530; *Southern Pacific, supra*, at 770.

III

Applying these general principles, we conclude that the Iowa truck length limitations unconstitutionally burden interstate commerce.

***

In the absence of congressional action to set uniform standards, some burdens associated with state safety regulations must be tolerated. But where, as here, the State's safety interest has been found to be illusory, and its regulations impair significantly the federal interest in efficient and safe interstate transportation, the state law cannot be harmonized with the Commerce Clause.

***

IV

Perhaps recognizing the weakness of the evidence supporting its safety argument, and the substantial burden on commerce that its regulations create, Iowa urges the Court simply to "defer" to the safety judgment of the State. It argues that the length of trucks is generally, although perhaps imprecisely, related to safety. The task of drawing a line is one that Iowa contends should be left to its legislature.

The Court normally does accord "special deference" to state highway safety regulations. *Raymond*, 434 U.S. at 444, n. 18. This traditional deference derives in part from the assumption that, where such regulations do not discriminate on their face against interstate commerce, their burden usually falls on local economic interests as well as other States' economic interests, thus insuring that a State's own political processes will serve as a check against unduly burdensome regulations. *Ibid.* Less deference to the legislative judgment is due, however, where the local regulation bears disproportionately on out-of-state residents and businesses. Such a disproportionate burden is apparent here . . .

. . . Iowa seems to have hoped to limit the use of its highways by deflecting some through traffic . . . The Court of Appeals correctly concluded that a State cannot constitutionally promote its own parochial interests by requiring safe vehicles to detour around it. 612 F.2d at 1070.

V

In sum, the statutory exemptions, their history, and the arguments Iowa has advanced in support of its law in this litigation all suggest that the deference traditionally accorded a State's safety judgment is not warranted. *See Raymond, supra* at 444, and n. 18, 446–447. The controlling factors thus are the findings of the District Court, accepted by the Court of Appeals, with respect to the relative safety of the types of trucks at issue, and the substantiality of the burden on interstate commerce.

Because Iowa has imposed this burden without any significant countervailing safety interest, its statute violates the Commerce Clause. The judgment of the Court of Appeals is affirmed.

It is so ordered.

Questions Presented

1) How was the Iowa statute impacting interstate commerce?
2) What did the Supreme Court say with regard to Iowa's public health and safety arguments?
3) What is the concept of "weighing" required by a court when considering public safety concerns and impact on interstate commerce and how did this impact the present case?

❖❖

IV. The Privileges and Immunities Clause

The first clause of the Fourteenth Amendment to the U.S. Constitution contains a Privileges or Immunities Clause that is narrowly interpreted as a protection of an individual from state interference with rights of national citizenship. This essentially protects the individual's right to vote in national elections and to travel from state to state. This was part of the post-Civil War amendments (13th, 14th, and 15th) as a partial remedy for the evils of slavery in the United States. The Privileges and Immunities Clause found in Article IV, section 2, clause 1 of the Constitution, also known alternately as the Comity Clause or the Interstate Privileges and Immunities Clause, protects non-citizens of one state from being treated differently in another state. The function and purpose of the Article IV clause is much different than its subsequent Fourteenth Amendment cousin. Recall from section II above that under the Articles of Confederation the states were operating as autonomous sovereigns with little national cohesion. The Privileges and Immunities Clause is considered to be directly descended from Article IV of the Articles of Confederation.[31] The original purpose of the clause in the Articles was one of comity between the states.[32] This was not a goal achieved through the Articles of Confederation. One of the main aims of the Constitution was centralization of a strong, national government and unification of the different states under the new national government. The Supremacy Clause, the Commerce Clause, and the Privileges and Immunities Clause were written with this goal of national unity in mind. The Privileges and Immunities Clause was chief among these constitutional clauses in shaping national unity.[33]

FIGURE 3.4   The Privileges and Immunities Clause

> ### U.S. Constitution, Article IV, section 2
>
> ". . . the citizens of each state shall be entitled to all privileges and immunities of citizens in the several states."

Of course, each of the sections of the Constitution were subject to eventual interpretation by the courts. One of the earliest judicial interpretations of the Privileges and Immunities Clause came in a circuit court case *Corfield v. Coryell*[34] in which Supreme Court Justice Bushrod Washington, sitting as a circuit court judge, had to consider whether a New Jersey law restricting the harvesting of oysters in New Jersey by out-of-state residents violated the Privileges and Immunities Clause. Washington wrote that this included those rights *"which are, in their nature, fundamental; which belong, of right, to the citizens of all free governments."*[35] He went on to list these specific rights: *"The right of a citizen of one State to pass through, or to reside in any other State, for purposes of trade, agriculture, professional pursuits, or otherwise; to claim the benefits of the writ of habeas corpus; to institute and maintain actions of any kind in the courts of the State; to take, hold and dispose of property, either*

---

[31] William A. Knox. *Prospective Applications of the Article IV Privileges and Immunities Clause of the United States Constitution*, 43 Mo. L. Rev. 1 (1978)

[32] Id at 6.

[33] See e.g., *McBurney v. Young*, 133 S.Ct. 1709 (2013)

[34] 6 Fed. Cas. 546 (C.C.E.D. Pa., 1823)

[35] Id at 551–2.

real or personal; and an exemption from higher taxes or impositions than are paid by the other citizens of the State . . . to which may be added, the elective franchise, as regulated and established by the laws or constitution of the state in which it is to be exercised."[36] However, Justice Washington found that not all rights belonging to a citizen of one state transfer over to a citizen of another state and he held that oysters, as a natural resource of New Jersey, could be restricted to harvesting by state residents. The result of Justice Washington's opinion finding a natural resources right exclusive to the state would be rejected in subsequent cases[37] but the impact of his dicta in *Corfield* that outlined the rights protected was to last for many years and serve as the major interpretation of the Privileges and Immunities Clause.[38] Even though some subsequent Supreme Court cases[39] did not embrace the *Corfield* Privileges and Immunities rights found in Justice Washington's dicta, it was followed in a number of later cases.[40]

The Privileges and Immunities Clause, as presently interpreted, applies to rights fundamental to national unity. These rights are invariably tied to commerce, hence the close connection between the Commerce Clause and the Privileges and Immunities Clause. Some of these rights have included the right to engage in a profession, the right not to be subject to a different tax on foods or other goods when coming from another state, the right to engage the court services of another state if there is standing to bring a claim in that forum. Each of these are fundamental national rights as enumerated by Justice Washington in *Corfield*. In order to sustain a violation of the Privileges and Immunities Clause the Supreme Court considers a two-part test: first, is a fundamental right or interest involved?; second, is the distinction between residents and nonresidents justified? For this second part of the test the analysis is further reduced to a consideration of whether the nonresidents were a particular source of the evil the state statute was aimed at and if the discrimination bore a substantial relation to the particular evil the nonresidents are said to represent.[41] For this latter part of the test the state statute has to be narrowly tailored to achieve the perceived problem. The Privileges and Immunities Clause does not therefore exclude all discrimination against nonresidents of a state. Certain preferences have been found to be constitutional if there is a substantial reason for the difference in treatment.[42]

Corporations have historically been excluded from Privileges and Immunities Clause protections since they are not "citizens" under the law. In *Paul v. Virginia*, 75 U.S. 168 (1869) the Supreme Court held that corporations were the "*mere creation of local law, [and] can have no legal existence beyond the limits of the sovereignty where created.*"[43] This interpretation has remained consistent over the years, though the overriding premise of *Paul* has been diminished.[44] *Paul* was argued

---

[36] Id at 552.

[37] See e.g., *Toomer v. Witsell*, 334 U.S. 385 (1948) (where the Supreme Court did not apply the *Corfield* rule to free-swimming fish caught off of the South Carolina coast); see also *Mullaney v. Anderson*, 342 U.S. 415 (1952) (fees set by statute for fishing licenses which charged more for a non-resident license ruled unconstitutional)

[38] See, Douglas G. Smith, *A Lockean Analysis of Section One of the Fourteenth Amendment*, 25 Harv. J.L. & Pub. Policy 1095, 1158 (2002)

[39] See e.g., *McKane v. Thurston*, 153 U.S. 684 (1894)

[40] See, *Austin v. New Hampshire*, 420 U.S. 656 (1975); *Baldwin v. Fish & Game Commission*, 436 U.S. 371 (1978); *Supreme Court of New Hampshire v. Piper*, 470 U.S. 274 (1985); *Saenz v. Roe*, 526 U.S. 489 (1999); *McBurney v. Young*, 133 S.Ct. 1709 (2013)

[41] See e.g., *Hicklin v. Orbeck*, 437 U.S. 518 (1978); *Supreme Court of Virginia v. Friedman*, 487 U.S. 59 (1988)

[42] See, *United Building Trades Council v. Camden*, 465 U.S. 208 (1984)

[43] *Paul* at 181.

[44] The holding of *Paul v. Virginia* was overturned in *United States v. South-Eastern Underwriters Assn.*, 322 U.S. 533 (1944), regarding the regulation of insurance contracts under the Commerce Clause; however, as noted above, and in the case cited in the following endnote, while the exclusion of corporations and other artificial entities from Privileges and Immunities Clause protections continues the overall impact of *Paul* has eroded.

during the December 1868 term and decided on November 1, 1869. The Fourteenth Amendment, containing the Equal Protection Clause, was adopted on July 9, 1868. The equal protection language of the Fourteenth Amendment and subsequent Supreme Court interpretations regarding the extent of protection coupled with general state statutes on incorporation served to undermine the privileges and immunities application of *Paul*.[45]

The exclusion of corporations from Privileges and Immunities Clause protections is unique since corporations have been treated as citizens and persons in other contexts. As early as 1809 the Supreme Court said corporations were citizens for purposes of diversity jurisdiction.[46] In a later case the Supreme Court also said corporations were persons under the Fourteenth Amendment and the Equal Protection Clause applied to them.[47] More recently in *Citizens United v. Federal Election Commission* the Court held that corporations had the same rights as a person to fund a political campaign.[48] A year later in *FCC v. AT&T, Inc.* the Court said the term "person" includes artificial entities.[49] Yet, the extension of the legal fiction of the corporation as a "person" or a "citizen" in other constitutional contexts has not been equally applied to the Privileges and Immunities Clause. This is a curious historical development in the application of Article IV that has been applied to other artificial entities such as investment trusts, partnerships, and associations.[50] The viability of this exclusion extends to present court treatments under the weight of precedent.[51] However, as Justice Blackmun noted in *Baldwin v. Fish & Game Commission* the "*contours of Art. IV, § 2, cl. 1, are not well developed.*"[52]

V. The Regulatory Power of Federal and State Government

It is best to begin our coverage of the regulatory power of the federal and state government with a discussion of due process since it is a concept with which many are familiar but few truly understand. At its most basic level and understanding due process is about fairness. It applies any time we are looking at some deprivation from the government or a governmental entity. The issue in discerning the quality of that fairness is by whose standard are we to judge?

Legal Definition

Due process – a guarantee of fairness within a judicial system, or any governmental quasi-judicial body, such as an administrative tribunal, that ensures fair treatment through standardized procedures and clearly expressed laws or rules.

---

[45] *W. & S. Life Ins. Co. v. State Board of Equalization*, 451 U.S. 648 (1981)

[46] *Bank of the United States v. Deveaux*, 9 U.S. 1 (1809)

[47] *Santa Clara County v. Southern Pacific Railroad*, 118 U.S. 394 (1886)

[48] 558 U.S. 310 (2010)

[49] 562 U.S. 397 (2011)

[50] See *Hemphill v. Orloff*, 277 U.S. 537 (1928)

[51] See e.g., *Utility Contractors Assn. of New England v. City of Worcester*, 236 F. Supp. 2d 13 (D. Mass., 2002); *Metropolitan Washington Chapter, Associated Builders and Contractors, Inc. v. Dist. of Columbia*, 57 F.Supp. 3d 1 (D.D.C., 2014); *Wal-Mart Stores, Inc. v. Texas Alcoholic Beverage Commission*, 170 F.Supp.3d 719 (W.D. Tex., 2015)

[52] 436 U.S. 371, 380 (1978)

Certainly when the British Parliament passed the Tea Act in 1773 there was likely a sense among British politicians that the tax was fair. However, the colonists, who were still considered English subjects, did not have a say in the matter and the famous rallying cry of "No taxation without representation!" became a basis of protest. If the colonists had no representation in Parliament was it really a fair process by which they were taxed? History has provided us with many instances in which due process was a concern for a burgeoning America. It was so important that it was identified as a separate clause within the Fifth Amendment to the Constitution—the requirement of due process of law before subjecting an individual to a denial of life, liberty or property. What we have come to know and understand about government is that it is a monolith, a large impersonal bureaucracy in which the rights and concerns of the individual can be easily disregarded or smothered. This is the precise reason certain delegates to the Constitutional Convention of 1787, during the subsequent ratification process, pushed for the inclusion of a bill of individual rights. Eventually ratified in 1791 were the first 10 amendments to the Constitution, which we know as the Bill of Rights. These were the guarantees of individual liberty and limits upon the federal government, one of the chief concerns among the Anti-Federalist members of the Convention. However, as two Maryland businessmen were to learn a few decades later, these protections did not extend to state action. In the 1833 case of *Barron v. Mayor and City Council of Baltimore*,[53] Chief Justice Marshall held that the Bill of Rights did not apply to state governments; they were only a limit upon federal power. The case involved two wharf owners, John Barron and John Craig, who sued the City of Baltimore over road construction that resulted in mounds of sand and dirt being placed in the adjoining harbor. This caused the deep waters around Barron and Craig's wharf to become shallow, thereby disrupting their lucrative business. In an action under the Fifth Amendment just compensation clause they sought payment from the city of Baltimore for the taking of their property. Marshall's decision denied them the relief they sought.

Despite the lack of recourse under the U.S. Constitution for governmental injuries at the state and local levels, many litigants and their attorneys, subsequent to *Barron,* proceeded to assert protections under separate state constitutions that contained their own due process clauses.[54] However, fifty-five years after *Barron* the Fourteenth Amendment was ratified and it contained a second, separate due process clause, this time specifically applying to the states. The resulting constitutional debate from this new amendment centered on the question of which rights contained within the Bill of Rights would apply to the states. While the theory endorsed by the Supreme Court has been one of selective incorporation—those rights that are fundamental and "implicit in a concept of ordered liberty"[55] are to be incorporated from the Bill of Rights and made binding upon the states—only a handful of rights have not been incorporated.[56] Thus, we have two due process clauses contained in the Constitution not to mention separate state constitutions which also guarantee us due process protections. These separate state due process protections can actually grant broader protections than those provided under the U.S. Constitution. While the Supreme Court

---

[53] 32 U.S. 243 (1833)

[54] William B. Lockhart, Yale Kamisar, Jesse H. Chopper, Steven H. Shiffrin, *The American Constitution: Cases, Comments, Questions*, 6th Ed., 1986.

[55] *Palko v. Connecticut*, 302 U.S. 319, 325 (1937)

[56] The only unincorporated rights are: 3rd Amendment—No Quartering of Soldiers; 5th Amendment—Right to Grand Jury Indictment; 6th Amendment—Right to be informed of the nature and cause of the accusation (held to be implied in due process); 6th Amendment—Right to vicinage and venue (held to be implied in due process); 7th Amendment—Right to a jury trial in a civil case; 8th Amendment—No excessive fines.

establishes the base-line of constitutional protections under the federal constitution which the states cannot narrow, states are able to expand upon those protections under their own state constitutions and due process clauses.

This brings us back to where our discussion began by attempting to define due process, and already stated to mean basic fairness. This fairness is judged at two levels—one that is procedural, the other that is substantive. What does it mean to provide procedural due process? There are two essential components: (1) notice and (2) an opportunity to be heard. Prior to a denial of an individual's right to life, liberty or property the minimal constitutional requirements are that the individual be apprised of the reason for the denial and an opportunity to a pre-deprivation hearing. Our most obvious constitutional example resides within our criminal justice system. Assume an employee is accused of stealing funds from his employer. The employer initiates an internal investigation, gathers evidence, contacts law enforcement with the results of the internal investigation which is followed up by a separate law enforcement investigation that ends with the arrest of the employee. The employee is charged and arraigned before the court. This is the first formal notice of the accusation and the employee's first chance to be heard on the matter with the entry of a plea. Eventually, pursuant to formal state rules of criminal procedure the case will continue and the employee will ultimately have a chance to go to trial. This is procedural due process in a nutshell using a setting we are culturally attuned to through television and the news. However, let's take a different turn in the scenario and this time the employee is not accused of stealing but instead is charged with violating the employer's policy pertaining to sexual harassment. In this scenario the employee is a county worker hired under state civil service law that provides he can only be disciplined upon a showing of just cause. His procedural due process rights would be satisfied by the employer providing him with the sections of the policy he is accused of violating as well as the specifics relating to dates, times, and accusers. He would then be entitled to answer the charges before his supervisors and defend against them. A more formal type of hearing is available if the matter is not resolved between the employer and employee (more on this process is covered in chapter 13 on Labor and Employment Law.)

Legal Definitions

Procedural due process – ensures fairness in the process of a deprivation of a life, liberty or property right by the government by guaranteeing an individual the dual protections of notice and an opportunity to be heard.

Substantive due process – a requirement that legislation or administrative rules be clear and understandable to the average person and not contain any ambiguity or vagueness in their attempt to further a governmental need or objective.

The other half of our due process protections reside in the concept of substantive due process. This protection requires that a law, rule or regulation be clear and understandable to the average person, that it not contain any ambiguity or be vague in its construction. In essence, the act or forbearance required by the law must be obvious.

However, even with these basic protections in place, the regulatory power of the government can result in deprivations to property rights that were not likely envisioned by the Founding Fathers. While the federal government does not have the general police powers of the states to protect the overall safety, health and welfare it does contain many enumerated powers as well as powers that have been implied in constitutional interpretation. The Commerce Clause has proven to be an incredible source of governmental power to regulate that in instances, such as in *Wickard v. Filburn*, resulted in a denial of property rights. The initial concept of limited government as expressed by James Madison in Federalist No. 45 ("*powers delegated by the proposed Constitution to the federal government are few and defined*"[57]) has been discarded for the increased growth of the federal government over time. Many critics—politicians, commentators, attorneys and lay people among them—have said the government has morphed into a regulatory state.[58] The federal government and its vast array of administrative agencies, each with its own regulatory mandate and power as arms of the Executive branch, has become a vast, monolithic bureaucracy that seemingly invades every facet of our lives. The actual number of federal agencies in existence remains a mystery with estimations running from 115 to 430.[59] Yet, the rule-making powers these agencies possess allow them to dictate certain aspects of our lives in a way that many civil libertarians view as being beyond the reach of government. An example would be the Environmental Protection Agency's Waters of the United States rule allowing the agency to regulate bodies of water not previously under its control, for example private ponds on residential property.[60] Despite agency assurances that the new rule is limited and will not impact homeowners or existing agricultural regulations the rule has been viewed as another overreach of federal rulemaking authority.[61] This is a far cry from the limited federal government espoused by Madison: "*The operations of the federal government will be most extensive and important in times of war and danger; those of the State governments, in times of peace and security . . . The more adequate, indeed, the federal powers may be rendered to the national defense, the less frequent will be those scenes of danger which might favor their ascendancy over the governments of the particular States.*"[62]

Much of this federal power has emanated from the reserved powers of Congress contained in Article 1, section 8 of the Constitution under the Necessary and Proper Clause. Also known as the Elastic Clause or the Sweeping Clause, the Necessary and Proper Clause has been the source of most federal laws.[63] It was in *McCulloch v. Maryland* that Chief Justice Marshall first interpreted

FIGURE 3.5 Necessary and Proper Clause

U.S. Constitution, Article I, section 8, clause 18

"The Congress shall have power to . . . make all Laws which shall be necessary and proper for carrying into Execution the foregoing Powers, and all other Powers vested by this Constitution in the Government of the United States, or any Department or Officer thereof".

---

[57] Federalist No. 45

[58] See e.g., Christopher DeMuth, *The Regulatory State*, National Affairs, No. 31, Spring 2017, Edward L. Glaeser & Andrei Shleifer, *The Rise of the Regulatory State*, Journal of Economic Literature, Vol. XLI, June 2003.

[59] Claude Wayne Crews, *Nobody Knows How Many Federal Agencies Exist*, Competitive Enterprise Institute, (August 26, 2015).

[60] Michael Bastasch, *EPA Grants Itself Power to Regulate Ponds, Ditches, Puddles*, The Daily Caller, 05/27/15, http://dailycaller.com/2015/05/27/epa-grants-itself-power-to-regulate-ponds-ditches-puddles/

[61] Id.

[62] Federalist No. 45

[63] Gary Lawson and Neil S. Siegel, *Necessary and Proper Clause*, National Constitution Center, https://constitutioncenter.org/interactive-constitution/interpretations/necessary-and-proper-clause

the Necessary and Proper Clause as giving Congress the authority to create a federal bank. The clause has remained a powerful means for Congress to pass legislation it deems to be necessary to governing. Interpretation is always a matter for the courts and the meaning of what is "necessary" and what is "proper" under Congress' power have been argued. An accepted reading of the clause is one limiting the "necessary and proper" element to the execution of "the foregoing powers", that is the previously enumerated powers in section 8.[64] This is an interpretation that establishes the power as incidental to the already enumerated powers. In the exercise of its "necessary and proper" powers the Supreme Court has given much deference to the "necessary" element while restraining Congress on whether or not the exercise of power is a "proper" one.[65]

One of the more contentious aspects of government power has been over the regulatory taking of private property. A regulatory taking occurs when either the federal or state government's regulation limits or deprives an individual of the beneficial use of their property. The taking does not usually involve actual physical possession or occupation of the property by the government, though these cases are more obvious when there is a permanent physical possession by the government.[66] A taking generally occurs when a government act, though not depriving the individual to title in their property, operates to limit the beneficial use of the property.[67] An example is the situation encountered by the wharf owners in *Barron v. Baltimore* where government construction debris entering the harbor created a shallow area around the wharves of Barron and Craig adversely affecting their business because ships could no longer dock at their wharves. Despite the fact Barron and Craig were at the time denied relief due to the interpretation of the Bill of Rights as applying only to the actions of the federal government, the present reality is that a similar situation encountered today would be compensable since the specific protections were incorporated under the Fourteenth Amendment due process clause and applied to the states.[68] Under the Takings Clause of the Fifth Amendment a property owner in that situation is entitled to "just compensation" from the government.

FIGURE 3.6   Takings Clause

U.S. Constitution, Article V
No person shall be . . . deprived of . . . property, without due process of law, nor shall private property be taken for public use, without just compensation.

The award of "just compensation" has been interpreted by the courts as fair market value;[69] however this is not always in line with what may be either the true value of the property or the value to the owner or the claimed value.[70]

---

[64] See e.g., *National Federation of Independent Business v. Sebelius*, 567 U.S. 1, 29 (2012) where Chief Justice Roberts' majority opinion on the constitutionality of the individual mandate for insurance purchase under the Affordable Care Act (ACA) was outside the power of the Necessary and Proper Clause since "*that Clause involved exercises of authority derivative of, and in service to, a granted power.*"

[65] Id. at 28.

[66] See e.g., *Loretto v. Teleprompter Manhattan CATV Corp.*, 458 U.S. 419 (1982) (municipal government running wires across a small portion of a landowner's property was compensable.)

[67] See e.g., *Lucas v. South Carolina Coastal Council*, 505 U.S. 1003 (1992) (change in state regulations regarding beachfront construction passed subsequent to the plaintiff purchasing the property with the intent to build beachfront condominiums was held to be a taking.)

[68] See, *Chicago Burlington & Quincy Railroad Co. v. Chicago*, 166 U.S. 266 (1897)

[69] *Olson v. United States*, 292 U.S. 246 (1932)

[70] See e.g., *United States v. PeeWee Coal Co., Inc.*, 341 U.S. 114 (1951)

One of the major constitutional cases on the subject of regulatory taking is *Penn Central Transportation Co. v. New York City*. The Supreme Court had to determine what constituted a taking for Fifth Amendment purposes. Is historical preservation a legitimate governmental regulation upon which the beneficial use of one's property can be restricted? As you read the case pay attention to what Justice Brennan writes regarding the owner's use of the property in light of the municipal regulation.

❖❖❖

Penn Central Transportation Co. v. New York City
438 U.S. 104 (1978)

Mr. Justice Brennan delivered the opinion of the Court.

The question presented is whether a city may, as part of a comprehensive program to preserve historic landmarks and historic districts, place restrictions on the development of individual historic landmarks—in addition to those imposed by applicable zoning ordinances—without effecting a "taking" requiring the payment of "just compensation." Specifically, we must decide whether the application of New York City's Landmarks Preservation Law to the parcel of land occupied by Grand Central Terminal has "taken" its owners' property in violation of the Fifth and Fourteenth Amendments.

I

A

Over the past 50 years, all 50 States and over 500 municipalities have enacted laws to encourage or require the preservation of buildings and areas with historic or aesthetic importance. These nationwide legislative efforts have been precipitated by two concerns. The first is recognition that, in recent years, large numbers of historic structures, landmarks, and areas have been destroyed without adequate consideration of either the values represented therein or the possibility of preserving the destroyed properties for use in economically productive ways. The second is a widely shared belief that structures with special historic, cultural, or architectural significance enhance the quality of life for all. Not only do these buildings and their workmanship represent the lessons of the past and embody precious features of our heritage, they serve as examples of quality for today.

[H]istoric conservation is but one aspect of the much larger problem, basically an environmental one, of enhancing—or perhaps developing for the first time—the quality of life for people.

New York City, responding to similar concerns and acting pursuant to a New York State enabling Act, adopted its Landmarks Preservation Law in 1965. *See* N.Y.C.Admin.Code, ch. 8-A, § 201.0 *et seq.* (1976). The city acted from the conviction that "the standing of [New York City] as a world-wide tourist center and world capital of business, culture and government" would be threatened if legislation were not enacted to protect historic landmarks and neighborhoods from precipitate decisions to destroy or fundamentally alter their character. § 201.0(a). The city believed that comprehensive measures to safeguard desirable features of the existing urban fabric would benefit its citizens in a variety of ways: *e.g.*, fostering "civic pride in the beauty and noble accomplishments of the past"; protecting and enhancing "the city's attractions to tourists and visitors"; "support[ing] and stimul[ating] business and industry"; "strengthen[ing] the economy of the city"; and promoting "the use of historic districts, landmarks, interior landmarks and scenic landmarks for the education, pleasure and welfare of the people of the city." § 201.0(b).

The New York City law is typical of many urban landmark laws in that its primary method of achieving its goals is not by acquisitions of historic properties, rather by involving public entities in land use decisions affecting these properties and providing services, standards, controls, and incentives that will encourage preservation by private owners and users. While the law does place special restrictions on landmark properties as a necessary feature to the attainment of its larger objectives, the major theme of the law is to ensure the owners of any such properties both a "reasonable return" on their investments and maximum latitude to use their parcels for purposes not inconsistent with the preservation goals.

***

Although the designation of a landmark and landmark site restricts the owner's control over the parcel, designation also enhances the economic position of the landmark owner in one significant respect. Under New York City's zoning laws, owners of real property who have not developed their property to the full extent permitted by the applicable zoning laws are allowed to transfer development rights to contiguous parcels on the same city block. *See* New York City, Zoning Resolution Art. I, ch. 2, § 12-10(1978) (definition of "zoning lot"). A 1968 ordinance gave the owners of landmark sites additional opportunities to transfer development rights to other parcels.

***

B

This case involves the application of New York City's Landmarks Preservation Law to Grand Central Terminal (Terminal). The Terminal, which is owned by the Penn Central Transportation Co. and its affiliates (Penn Central), is one of New York City's most famous buildings. Opened in 1913, it is regarded not only as providing an ingenious engineering solution to the problems presented by urban railroad stations, but also as a magnificent example of the French beaux-arts style.

***

On August 2, 1967, following a public hearing, the Commission designated the Terminal a "landmark" and designated the "city tax block" it occupies a "landmark site." The Board of Estimate confirmed this action on September 21, 1967. Although appellant Penn Central had opposed the designation before the Commission, it did not seek judicial review of the final designation decision.

On January 22, 1968, appellant Penn Central, to increase its income, entered into a renewable 50-year lease and sublease agreement with appellant UGP Properties, Inc. (UGP), a wholly owned subsidiary of Union General Properties, Ltd., a United Kingdom corporation. Under the terms of the agreement, UGP was to construct a multistory office building above the Terminal. UGP promised to pay Penn Central $1 million annually during construction and at least $3 million annually thereafter. The rentals would be offset in part by a loss of some $700,000 to $1 million in net rentals presently received from concessionaires displaced by the new building.

Appellants UGP and Penn Central then applied to the Commission for permission to construct an office building atop the Terminal. Two separate plans, both designed by architect Marcel Breuer and both apparently satisfying the terms of the applicable zoning ordinance, were submitted to the Commission for approval. The first, Breuer I, provided for the construction of a 55-story office building, to be cantilevered above the existing facade and to rest on the roof of the Terminal. The second, Breuer II Revised, called for tearing down a portion of the Terminal that included the 42d Street facade, stripping off some of the remaining features of the Terminal's facade, and constructing a 53-story office building. The Commission denied a certificate of no exterior effect on

September 20, 1968. Appellants then applied for a certificate of "appropriateness" as to both proposals. After four days of hearings at which over 80 witnesses testified, the Commission denied this application as to both proposals.

***

[A]ppellants filed suit in New York Supreme Court, Trial Term, claiming, *inter alia*, that the application of the Landmarks Preservation Law had "taken" their property without just compensation in violation of the Fifth and Fourteenth Amendments and arbitrarily deprived them of their property without due process of law in violation of the Fourteenth Amendment. Appellants sought a declaratory judgment, injunctive relief barring the city from using the Landmarks Law to impede the construction of any structure that might otherwise lawfully be constructed on the Terminal site, and damages for the "temporary taking" that occurred between August 2, 1967, the designation date, and the date when the restrictions arising from the Landmarks Law would be lifted. The trial court granted the injunctive and declaratory relief, but severed the question of damages for a "temporary taking."

Appellees appealed, and the New York Supreme Court, Appellate Division, reversed. The Appellate Division held that the restrictions on the development of the Terminal site were necessary to promote the legitimate public purpose of protecting landmarks, and therefore that appellants could sustain their constitutional claims only by proof that the regulation deprived them of all reasonable beneficial use of the property. The Appellate Division held that the evidence appellants introduced at trial—"Statements of Revenues and Costs," purporting to show a net operating loss for the years 1969 and 1971, which were prepared for the instant litigation—had not satisfied their burden. First, the court rejected the claim that these statements showed that the Terminal was operating at a loss, for, in the court's view, appellants had improperly attributed some railroad operating expenses and taxes to their real estate operations, and compounded that error by failing to impute any rental value to the vast space in the Terminal devoted to railroad purposes. Further, the Appellate Division concluded that appellants had failed to establish either that they were unable to increase the Terminal's commercial income by transforming vacant or underutilized space to revenue-producing use or that the unused development rights over the Terminal could not have been profitably transferred to one or more nearby sites. The Appellate Division concluded that all appellants had succeeded in showing was that they had been deprived of the property's most profitable use, and that this showing did not establish that appellants had been unconstitutionally deprived of their property.

The New York Court of Appeals affirmed. That court summarily rejected any claim that the Landmarks Law had "taken" property without "just compensation," indicating that there could be no "taking," since the law had not transferred control of the property to the city, but only restricted appellants' exploitation of it. In that circumstance, the Court of Appeals held that appellants' attack on the law could prevail only if the law deprived appellants of their property in violation of the Due Process Clause of the Fourteenth Amendment.

***

We affirm.

II

The issues presented by appellants are (1) whether the restrictions imposed by New York City's law upon appellants' exploitation of the Terminal site effect a "taking" of appellants' property for a public use within the meaning of the Fifth Amendment, which, of course, is made applicable to the States through the Fourteenth Amendment, *see Chicago, B. & Q. R. Co. v. Chicago*, 166 U.S. 226,

239 (1807), and, (2), if so, whether the transferable development rights afforded appellants constitute "just compensation" within the meaning of the Fifth Amendment. We need only address the question whether a "taking" has occurred.

A

Before considering appellants' specific contentions, it will be useful to review the factors that have shaped the jurisprudence of the Fifth Amendment injunction "nor shall private property be taken for public use, without just compensation." The question of what constitutes a "taking" for purposes of the Fifth Amendment has proved to be a problem of considerable difficulty. While this Court has recognized that the Fifth Amendment's guarantee . . . [is] designed to bar Government from forcing some people alone to bear public burdens which, in all fairness and justice, should be borne by the public as a whole, *Armstrong v. United States*, 364 U.S. 40, 49 (1960), this Court, quite simply, has been unable to develop any "set formula" for determining when "justice and fairness" require that economic injuries caused by public action be compensated by the government, rather than remain disproportionately concentrated on a few persons. *See Goldblatt v. Hempstead*, 369 U.S. 590, 594 (1962). Indeed, we have frequently observed that whether a particular restriction will be rendered invalid by the government's failure to pay for any losses proximately caused by it depends largely "upon the particular circumstances [in that] case." *United States v. Central Eureka Mining Co.*, 357 U.S. 155, 168 (1958); *see United States v. Caltex, Inc.*, 344 U.S. 149, 156 (1952).

In engaging in these essentially *ad hoc*, factual inquiries, the Court's decisions have identified several factors that have particular significance. The economic impact of the regulation on the claimant and, particularly, the extent to which the regulation has interfered with distinct investment-backed expectations are, of course, relevant considerations. *See Goldblatt v. Hempstead, supra* at 594. So, too, is the character of the governmental action. A "taking" may more readily be found when the interference with property can be characterized as a physical invasion by government, *see, e.g., United States v. Causby*, 328 U.S. 256 (1946), than when interference arises from some public program adjusting the benefits and burdens of economic life to promote the common good.

Government hardly could go on if, to some extent, values incident to property could not be diminished without paying for every such change in the general law, *Pennsylvania Coal Co. v. Mahon*, 260 U.S. 393, 413 (1922), and this Court has accordingly recognized, in a wide variety of contexts, that government may execute laws or programs that adversely affect recognized economic values. Exercises of the taxing power are one obvious example. A second are the decisions in which this Court has dismissed "taking" challenges on the ground that, while the challenged government action caused economic harm, it did not interfere with interests that were sufficiently bound up with the reasonable expectations of the claimant to constitute "property" for Fifth Amendment purposes.

More importantly for the present case, in instances in which a state tribunal reasonably concluded that "the health, safety, morals, or general welfare" would be promoted by prohibiting particular contemplated uses of land, this Court has upheld land use regulations that destroyed or adversely affected recognized real property interests. *See Nectow v. Cambridge*, 277 U.S. 183, 188 (1928). Zoning laws are, of course, the classic example, which have been viewed as permissible governmental action even when prohibiting the most beneficial use of the property.

***

Finally, government actions that may be characterized as acquisitions of resources to permit or facilitate uniquely public functions have often been held to constitute "takings." *United States v. Causby*, 328 U.S. 256 (1946), is illustrative. In holding that direct over flights above the claimant's land, that destroyed the present use of the land as a chicken farm, constituted a "taking," *Causby* emphasized that Government had not "merely destroyed property [but was] using a part of it for the flight of its planes." *Id.* at 262–263, n. 7. *See also Griggs v. Allegheny County*, 369 U.S. 84 (1962) (over flights held a taking); *Portsmouth Co. v. United States*, 260 U.S. 327 (1922) (United States military installations' repeated firing of guns over claimant's land is a taking); *United States v. Cress*, 243 U.S. 316 (1917) (repeated floodings of land caused by water project is a taking); *but see YMCA v. United States*, 395 U.S. 85 (1969) (damage caused to building when federal officers who were seeking to protect building were attacked by rioters held not a taking).

B

In contending that the New York City law has "taken" their property in violation of the Fifth and Fourteenth Amendments, appellants make a series of arguments, which, while tailored to the facts of this case, essentially urge that any substantial restriction imposed pursuant to a landmark law must be accompanied by just compensation if it is to be constitutional.

***

They first observe that the airspace above the Terminal is a valuable property interest, citing *United States v. Causby, supra.* They urge that the Landmarks Law has deprived them of any gainful use of their "air rights" above the Terminal and that, irrespective of the value of the remainder of their parcel, the city has "taken" their right to this superjacent airspace, thus entitling them to "just compensation" measured by the fair market value of these air rights.

Apart from our own disagreement with appellants' characterization of the effect of the New York City law, *see infra* at 134–135, the submission that appellants may establish a "taking" simply by showing that they have been denied the ability to exploit a property interest that they heretofore had believed was available for development is quite simply untenable. Were this the rule, this Court would have erred not only in upholding laws restricting the development of air rights, but also in approving those prohibiting both the subjacent, *see Goldblatt v. Hempstead*, 369 U.S. 590 (1962), and the lateral, *see Gorieb v. Fox*, 274 U.S. 603 (1927), development of particular parcels. "Taking" jurisprudence does not divide a single parcel into discrete segments and attempt to determine whether rights in a particular segment have been entirely abrogated. In deciding whether a particular governmental action ha effected a taking, this Court focuses rather both on the character of the action and on the nature and extent of the interference with rights in the parcel as a whole—here, the city tax block designated as the "landmark site."

Secondly, appellants, focusing on the character and impact of the New York City law, argue that it effects a "taking" because its operation has significantly diminished the value of the Terminal site. Appellants concede that the decisions sustaining other land use regulations, which, like the New York City law, are reasonably related to the promotion of the general welfare, uniformly reject the proposition that diminution in property value, standing alone, can establish a "taking," and that the "taking" issue in these contexts is resolved by focusing on the uses the regulations permit. Appellants, moreover, also do not dispute that a showing of diminution in property value would not establish a "taking" if the restriction had been imposed as a result of historic district legislation, *see generally Maher v. New Orleans*, 516 F.2d 1051 (CA5 1975), but appellants argue that New York City's regulation of individual landmarks is fundamentally different from zoning or from historic district legislation because the controls imposed by New York City's law apply only to individuals who own selected properties.

Stated baldly, appellants' position appears to be that the only means of ensuring that selected owners are not singled out to endure financial hardship for no reason is to hold that any restriction imposed on individual landmarks pursuant to the New York City scheme is a "taking" requiring the payment of "just compensation." Agreement with this argument would, of course, invalidate not just New York City's law, but all comparable landmark legislation in the Nation. We find no merit in it.

***

Appellants' final broad-based attack would have us treat the law as an instance, like that in *United States v. Causby*, in which government, acting in an enterprise capacity, has appropriated part of their property for some strictly governmental purpose. Apart from the fact that *Causby* was a case of invasion of airspace that destroyed the use of the farm beneath, and this New York City law has in nowise impaired the present use of the Terminal, the Landmarks Law neither exploits appellants' parcel for city purposes nor facilitates nor arises from any entrepreneurial operations of the city. The situation is not remotely like that in *Causby*, where the airspace above the property was in the flight pattern for military aircraft. The Landmarks Law's effect is simply to prohibit appellants or anyone else from occupying portions of the airspace above the Terminal, while permitting appellants to use the remainder of the parcel in a gainful fashion. This is no more an appropriation of property by government for its own uses than is a zoning law prohibiting, for "aesthetic" reasons, two or more adult theaters within a specified area or a safety regulation prohibiting excavations below a certain level.

C

Rejection of appellants' broad arguments is not, however, the end of our inquiry, for all we thus far have established is that the New York City law is not rendered invalid by its failure to provide "just compensation" whenever a landmark owner is restricted in the exploitation of property interests, such as air rights, to a greater extent than provided for under applicable zoning laws. We now must consider whether the interference with appellant' property is of such a magnitude that "there must be an exercise of eminent domain and compensation to sustain [it]." *Pennsylvania Coal Co. v. Mahon*, 260 U.S. at 413. That inquiry may be narrowed to the question of the severity of the impact of the law on appellants' parcel, and its resolution, in turn, requires a careful assessment of the impact of the regulation on the Terminal site.

. . . the New York City law does not interfere in any way with the present uses of the Terminal. Its designation as a landmark not only permits, but contemplates, that appellants may continue to use the property precisely as it has been used for the past 65 years: as a railroad terminal containing office space and concessions. So the law does not interfere with what must be regarded as Penn Central's primary expectation concerning the use of the parcel. More importantly, on this record, we must regard the New York City law as permitting Penn Central not only to profit from the Terminal but also to obtain a "reasonable return" on its investment. Appellants, moreover, exaggerate the effect of the law on their ability to make use of the air rights above the Terminal in two respects. First, it simply cannot be maintained, on this record, that appellants have been prohibited from occupying any portion of the airspace above the Terminal . . . Since appellants have not sought approval for the construction of a smaller structure, we do not know that appellants will be denied any use of any portion of the airspace above the Terminal.

Second, to the extent appellants have been denied the right to build above the Terminal, it is not literally accurate to say that they have been denied all use of even those preexisting air rights. Their ability to use these rights has not been abrogated; they are made transferable to at least eight parcels in the vicinity of the Terminal, one or two of which have been found suitable for the construction of new office buildings.

***

On this record, we conclude that the application of New York City's Landmarks Law has not effected a "taking" of appellants' property. The restrictions imposed are substantially related to the promotion of the general welfare, and not only permit reasonable beneficial use of the landmark site, but also afford appellants opportunities further to enhance not only the Terminal site proper but also other properties.

Affirmed.

Questions Presented

1) What was the governmental interest being asserted by the City of New York?
2) What was the argument of the property owner with regard to the Landmarks Preservation Law in the City of New York?
3) Why did the Supreme Court find that the Landmarks Preservation Law did not constitute a "taking" of the property?

❖❖❖

The states and their subdivisions are not without their own regulatory powers, as witnessed in the preceding case. Even though there is supremacy to federal law and any law passed by a state or one of its subdivisions that encroach on an area of exclusive federal control will be preempted, the states have their own reserved powers. The Tenth Amendment to the U.S. Constitution contains the following: *The powers not delegated to the United States by the Constitution, nor prohibited by it to the states, are reserved to the states respectively, or to the people.* This amendment reserves to the state's and to the people any powers not explicitly delegated to the federal government. The states possess general police powers over the health, safety and general welfare of their residents. In many ways this is a much broader grant of authority to regulate than provided to the federal government under the Constitution. However, whether the government's police power is general or limited in nature it is exercised by the executive and legislative branches. In the wings sits the judicial branch to act as the check on unbridled power by either of these other two branches of government. Constitutional limits on government authority and power are determined under three standards of constitutional judicial review:

1. a mere rationality test, also referred to as rational basis review;
2. strict-scrutiny review; and
3. intermediate scrutiny or middle-level review.

The most stringent form of review over government action is strict-scrutiny review. This type of review seeks to determine if the law, rule or regulation implemented is necessary to achieve a compelling governmental interest. If not then the law, rule or regulation will be unconstitutional. Strict-scrutiny review is applied when a fundamental right is involved or the law is aimed at a suspect classification (race, national origin, religion, alienage). The burden of proof at this level of review is on the government. The lowest level of review, the mere rationality test, simply considers whether the law, rule or regulation is rationally related to a legitimate government interest.[71] Unless the law is clearly outrageous it will be upheld. The initial burden is on the plaintiff to show that

---

[71] See, *Nebbia v. New York*, 291 U.S. 501, 525 (1934) regarding the state of New York regulating milk prices Justice Owen Roberts wrote the requirements of due process were that "*the law shall not be unreasonable, arbitrary, or capricious, and that the means selected shall have a real and substantial relation to the object sought to be attained.*"

there is no rational relation between the law and a legitimate government interest. Intermediate scrutiny, or middle level review, requires that the law, rule or regulation furthers an important government interest and that it is substantially related to the government interest. It is used in quasi-suspect classifications (gender, age, sexual orientation) and in some First Amendment review. The *Penn Central* case was an example of the Supreme Court's use of intermediate scrutiny to sustain the validity of a government regulation.

VI. Commercial Speech

One of the main protections of the First Amendment to the U.S. Constitution is freedom of speech. The text reads as follows: "*Congress shall make no law . . . abridging the freedom of speech.*" Interpretations of the meaning have varied within the Supreme Court. Justice Hugo Black, who sat on the Supreme Court from 1937 to 1971, took an absolutist view of the First Amendment. Black's approach was very literal, understanding the words "no law" to be a complete restriction.[72] However, this was not the interpretation eventually given to the First Amendment. In *Brandenburg v. Ohio*, 395 U.S. 444 (1969), the Supreme Court said inflammatory speech could not be suppressed unless it was directed to inciting or producing imminent lawless action and likely to incite or produce the action. This did not mean that speech could not be regulated by the government. State governments and their subdivisions can enforce reasonable time, place, and manner restrictions on speech.[73] Such reasonable restrictions include requiring permits for parades on public streets, limiting the decibel level and restricting the hours for the use of loudspeakers at events, limiting the location of where a protest can be held. The Supreme Court said time, place and manner restrictions are constitutional if they are (1) neutral in content; (2) they are narrowly tailored to achieve a governmental interest; (3) they leave open an alternative channel or means of communication.[74] These restrictions are within the state's general police power and are geared toward maintaining public order and convenience. Constitutional review of governmental restrictions of time, place and manner is subject to intermediate scrutiny by the courts.

Commercial speech, which is defined as speech relating to business or commercial interests, also has First Amendment protection, though not as extensive as noncommercial speech. The concept of "commercial speech" was first recognized by the Supreme Court in *Valentine v. Chrestensen*, a case in which the owner of an old Navy submarine displayed for profit was prevented by New York City police from distributing handbills advertising the submarine and soliciting visitors for an admission fee.[75] The distribution of handbills was restricted under the city's sanitary code to only those handbills devoted to information or a public protest.[76] While the Supreme Court did not protect the businessman's right to advertise, the majority opinion of Justice Owen Roberts recognized the nature of the speech as commercial by linking it to "advertising matter" and "private profit" and clearly distinguished it from noncommercial speech.[77] *Valentine v. Chrestensen* was overruled in 1976 by

---

[72] See, *Tinker v. Des Moines School District*, 395 U.S. 504, 517 (1969)—dissenting opinion of Justice Black at 517: "*I have always believed that under the First and Fourteenth Amendments neither the State nor the Federal Government has any authority to regulate or censor the content of speech..*"

[73] See e.g., *Grayned v. City of Rockford*, 408 U.S. 104 (1972)

[74] *Ward v. Rock Against Racism*, 491 U.S. 781 (1989)

[75] 316 U.S. 52 (1942)

[76] Id.

[77] Id. at 55.

Virginia State Board of Pharmacy v. Virginia Citizen's Consumer Council, Inc..[78] In that case Justice Blackmun said the commercial speech exception to First Amendment protection was no longer viable, "*concluding that commercial speech, like other varieties, is protected.*"[79] The process of moving away from the *Valentine* exception of commercial speech's First Amendment protection began a year earlier in *Bigelow v. Virginia* when Justice Blackmun likened the outcome in *Valentine* to a manner restriction, but warned of the limited continuing viability of *Valentine*.[80] *Bigelow* was the opening for commercial speech's recognition as being protected under the First Amendment. The Supreme Court later defined commercial speech in *Ohralik v. Ohio State Bar Association* as speech "*proposing a commercial transaction.*"[81] Justice Lewis Powell, a former corporate attorney, was the author of the majority opinion in *Ohralik* and noted that while commercial speech had First Amendment protection it was not on an equal footing with noncommercial speech. Powell wrote that in the past the Supreme Court "*afforded commercial speech a limited measure of protection, commensurate with its subordinate position in the scale of First Amendment values, while allowing modes of regulation that might be impermissible in the realm of noncommercial expression.*"[82] In another opinion by Justice Powell, just two years after *Ohralik*, the Supreme Court considered the constitutionality of a state agency's restrictions on advertising by a utility company. As you read the case pay attention to how Justice Powell analyzes the four-part analysis used in determining if commercial speech is being properly restricted and his eventual holding in the case with regard to the action of the state Public Service Commission. Does it meet the goal of balancing the free flow of information to the public with the government's interest in regulating business?

❖❖

Central Hudson Gas & Electric Corp. v. Public Service Commission
447 U.S. 557 (1980)

Mr. Justice Powell delivered the opinion of the Court.

This case presents the question whether a regulation of the Public Service Commission of the State of New York violates the First and Fourteenth Amendments because it completely bans promotional advertising by an electrical utility.

I

In December, 1973, the Commission, appellee here, ordered electric utilities in New York State to cease all advertising that "promot[es] the use of electricity." App. to Juris.Statement 31a. The order was based on the Commission's finding that "the interconnected utility system in New York State does not have sufficient fuel stocks or sources of supply to continue furnishing all customer demands for the 1973–1974 winter." *Id.* at 26a.

Three years later, when the fuel shortage had eased, the Commission requested comments from the public on its proposal to continue the ban on promotional advertising. Central Hudson Gas & Electric Corp., the appellant in this case, opposed the ban on First Amendment grounds. App. A10. After reviewing the public comments, the Commission extended the prohibition in a Policy Statement issued on February 25, 1977.

---

[78] 425 U.S. 728 (1976)

[79] 428 U.S. 748, 770 (1976)

[80] 421 U.S. 409, 419–420 (1975)

[81] 436 U.S. 447, 456 (1978)

[82] Id.

The Policy Statement divided advertising expenses into two broad categories: promotional—advertising intended to stimulate the purchase of utility services—and institutional and informational, a broad category inclusive of all advertising not clearly intended to promote sales.

***

The Commission's order explicitly permitted "informational" advertising designed to encourage "*shifts* of consumption" from peak demand times to periods of low electricity demand. *Ibid.* (emphasis in original). Informational advertising would not seek to increase aggregate consumption, but would invite a leveling of demand throughout any given 24-hour period. The agency offered to review "specific proposals by the companies for specifically described [advertising] programs that meet these criteria." *Id.* at 38a.

When it rejected requests for rehearing on the Policy Statement, the Commission supplemented its rationale for the advertising ban. The agency observed that additional electricity probably would be more expensive to produce than existing output. Because electricity rates in New York were not then based on marginal cost, the Commission feared that additional power would be priced below the actual cost of generation. The additional electricity would be subsidized by all consumers through generally higher rates. *Id.* at 57a–58a. The state agency also thought that promotional advertising would give "misleading signals" to the public by appearing to encourage energy consumption at a time when conservation is needed. *Id.* at 59a.

Appellant challenged the order in state court, arguing that the Commission had restrained commercial speech in violation of the First and Fourteenth Amendments. The Commission's order was upheld by the trial court and at the intermediate appellate level. The New York Court of Appeals affirmed. It found little value to advertising in "the noncompetitive market in which electric corporations operate." *Consolidated Edison Co. v. Public Service Comm'n*, 47 N.Y.2d 94, 110, 390 N.E.2d 749, 757 (1979). Since consumers "have no choice regarding the source of their electric power," the court denied that "promotional advertising of electricity might contribute to society's interest in 'informed and reliable' economic decision-making." *Ibid.* The court also observed that, by encouraging consumption, promotional advertising would only exacerbate the current energy situation. *Id.* at 110, 390 N.E.2d at 758. The court concluded that the governmental interest in the prohibition outweighed the limited constitutional value of the commercial speech at issue. We noted probable jurisdiction, 111 U.S. 962 (1979), and now reverse.

II

The Commission's order restricts only commercial speech, that is, expression related solely to the economic interests of the speaker and its audience. *Virginia Pharmacy Board v. Virginia Citizens Consumer Council*, 425 U.S. 748, 762 (1976); *Bates v. State Bar of Arizona*, 433 U.S. 350, 363–364 (1977); *Friedman v. Rogers*, 440 U.S. 1, 11 (1979). The First Amendment, as applied to the States through the Fourteenth Amendment, protects commercial speech from unwarranted governmental regulation. *Virginia Pharmacy Board*, 425 U.S. at 761–762. Commercial expression not only serves the economic interest of the speaker, but also assists consumers and furthers the societal interest in the fullest possible dissemination of information. In applying the First Amendment to this area, we have rejected the "highly paternalistic" view that government has complete power to suppress or regulate commercial speech.

[P]eople will perceive their own best interests if only they are well enough informed, and . . . the best means to that end is to open the channels of communication, rather than to close them. . . .

Id. at 770; *see Linmark Associates, Inc. v. Willingboro*, 431 U.S. 85, 92 (1977). Even when advertising communicates only an incomplete version of the relevant facts, the First Amendment presumes that some accurate information is better than no information at all. *Bates v. State Bar of Arizona, supra* at 374.

Nevertheless, our decisions have recognized the "common sense" distinction between speech proposing a commercial transaction, which occurs in an area traditionally subject to government regulation, and other varieties of speech. *Ohralik v. Ohio State Bar Assn.*, 436 U.S. 447, 455–456 (1978); *see Bates v. State Bar of Arizona, supra* at 381; *see also* Jackson & Jeffries, Commercial Speech: Economic Due Process and the First Amendment, 65 Va.L.Rev. 1, 38–39 (1979). The Constitution therefore accords a lesser protection to commercial speech than to other constitutionally guaranteed expression. 436 U.S. at 456, 457. The protection available for particular commercial expression turns on the nature both of the expression and of the governmental interests served by its regulation.

The First Amendment's concern for commercial speech is based on the informational function of advertising. *See First National Bank of Boston v. Bellotti*, 435 U.S. 765, 783 (1978). Consequently, there can be no constitutional objection to the suppression of commercial messages that do not accurately inform the public about lawful activity. The government may ban forms of communication more likely to deceive the public than to inform it, *Friedman v. Rogers, supra* at 13, 15–16; *Ohralik v. Ohio State Bar Assn., supra* at 464–465, or commercial speech related to illegal activity, *Pittsburgh Press Co. v. Human Relations Comm'n*, 413 U.S. 376, 388 (1973).

If the communication is neither misleading nor related to unlawful activity, the government's power is more circumscribed. The State must assert a substantial interest to be achieved by restrictions on commercial speech. Moreover, the regulatory technique must be in proportion to that interest. The limitation on expression must be designed carefully to achieve the State's goal. Compliance with this requirement may be measured by two criteria. First, the restriction must directly advance the state interest involved; the regulation may not be sustained if it provides only ineffective or remote support for the government's purpose. Second, if the governmental interest could be served as well by a more limited restriction on commercial speech, the excessive restrictions cannot survive.

Under the first criterion, the Court has declined to uphold regulations that only indirectly advance the state interest involved. In both *Bates* and *Virginia Pharmacy Board*, the Court concluded that an advertising ban could not be imposed to protect the ethical or performance standards of a profession.

***

The second criterion recognizes that the First Amendment mandates that speech restrictions be "narrowly drawn." *In re Primus*, 436 U.S. 412, 438 (1978). The regulatory technique may extend only as far as the interest it serves. The State cannot regulate speech that poses no danger to the asserted state interest, *see First National Bank of Boston v. Bellotti, supra* at 794–795, nor can it completely suppress information when narrower restrictions on expression would serve its interest as well.

***

In commercial speech cases, then, a four-part analysis has developed. At the outset, we must determine whether the expression is protected by the First Amendment. For commercial speech to come within that provision, it at least must concern lawful activity and not be misleading. Next, we ask whether the asserted governmental interest is substantial. If both inquiries yield positive answers, we must determine whether the regulation directly advances the governmental interest asserted, and whether it is not more extensive than is necessary to serve that interest.

III

We now apply this four-step analysis for commercial speech to the Commission's arguments in support of its ban on promotional advertising.

A

The Commission does not claim that the expression at issue either is inaccurate or relates to unlawful activity. Yet the New York Court of Appeals questioned whether Central Hudson's advertising is protected commercial speech. Because appellant holds a monopoly over the sale of electricity in its service area, the state court suggested that the Commission's order restricts no commercial speech of any worth. The court stated that advertising in a "noncompetitive market" could not improve the decision-making of consumers. The court saw no constitutional problem with barring commercial speech that it viewed as conveying little useful information.

This reasoning falls short of establishing that appellant's advertising is not commercial speech protected by the First Amendment. Monopoly over the supply of a product provides no protection from competition with substitutes for that product. Electric utilities compete with suppliers of fuel oil and natural gas in several markets, such as those for home heating and industrial power. This Court noted the existence of interfuel competition 45 years ago, *see West Ohio as Co. v. Public Utilities Comm'n*, 294 U.S. 63, 72 (1935). Each energy source continues to offer peculiar advantages and disadvantages that may influence consumer choice. For consumers in those competitive markets, advertising by utilities is just as valuable as advertising by unregulated firms.

Even in monopoly markets, the suppression of advertising reduces the information available for consumer decisions, and thereby defeats the purpose of the First Amendment. The New York court's argument appears to assume that the providers of a monopoly service or product are willing to pay for wholly ineffective advertising. Most businesses—even regulated monopolies—are unlikely to underwrite promotional advertising that is of no interest or use to consumers. Indeed, a monopoly enterprise legitimately may wish to inform the public that it has developed new services or terms of doing business. A consumer may need information to aid his decision whether or not to use the monopoly service at all, or how much of the service he should purchase. In the absence of factors that would distort the decision to advertise, we may assume that the willingness of a business to promote its products reflects a belief that consumers are interested in the advertising. Since no such extraordinary conditions have been identified in this case, appellant's monopoly position does not alter the First Amendment's protection for its commercial speech.

B

The Commission offers two state interests as justifications for the ban on promotional advertising. The first concerns energy conservation. Any increase in demand for electricity—during peak or off-peak periods—means greater consumption of energy. The Commission argues, and the New York court agreed, that the State's interest in conserving energy is sufficient to support suppression of advertising designed to increase consumption of electricity. In view of our country's dependence on energy resources beyond our control, no one can doubt the importance of energy conservation. Plainly, therefore, the state interest asserted is substantial. The Commission also argues that promotional advertising will aggravate inequities caused by the failure to base the utilities' rates on marginal cost. The utilities argued to the Commission that, if they could promote the use of electricity in periods of low demand, they would improve their utilization of generating capacity. The Commission responded that promotion of off-peak consumption also would increase consumption during peak periods. If peak demand were to rise, the absence of marginal cost rates would mean that the rates charged for the additional power would not reflect the true costs of expanding production. Instead, the extra costs would be borne by all consumers through higher overall rates. Without promotional advertising, the Commission stated, this inequitable turn of events would be less likely to occur. The choice among rate structures involves difficult and important questions of economic supply and distributional fairness. The State's concern that rates be fair and efficient represents a clear and substantial governmental interest.

C

Next, we focus on the relationship between the State's interests and the advertising ban. Under this criterion, the Commission's laudable concern over the equity and efficiency of appellant's rates does not provide a constitutionally adequate reason for restricting protected speech. The link between the advertising prohibition and appellant's rate structure is, at most, tenuous. The impact of promotional advertising on the equity of appellant's rates is highly speculative. Advertising to increase off-peak usage would have to increase peak usage, while other factors that directly affect the fairness and efficiency of appellant's rates remained constant. Such conditional and remote eventualities simply cannot justify silencing appellant's promotional advertising.

In contrast, the State's interest in energy conservation is directly advanced by the Commission order at issue here. There is an immediate connection between advertising and demand for electricity. Central Hudson would not contest the advertising ban unless it believed that promotion would increase its sales. Thus, we find a direct link between the state interest in conservation and the Commission's order.

D

We come finally to the critical inquiry in this case: whether the Commission's complete suppression of speech ordinarily protected by the First Amendment is no more extensive than necessary to further the State's interest in energy conservation. The Commission's order reaches all promotional advertising, regardless of the impact of the touted service on overall energy use. But the energy conservation rationale, as important as it is, cannot justify suppressing information about electric devices or services that would cause no net increase in total energy use. In addition, no showing has been made that a more limited restriction on the content of promotional advertising would not serve adequately the State's interests.

Appellant insists that, but for the ban, it would advertise products and services that use energy efficiently. These include the "heat pump," which both parties acknowledge to be a major improvement in electric heating, and the use of electric heat as a "backup" to solar and other heat sources. Although the Commission has questioned the efficiency of electric heating before this Court, neither the Commission's Policy Statement nor its order denying rehearing made findings on this issue. In the absence of authoritative findings to the contrary, we must credit as within the realm of possibility the claim that electric heat can be an efficient alternative in some circumstances.

The Commission's order prevents appellant from promoting electric services that would reduce energy use by diverting demand from less efficient sources, or that would consume roughly the same amount of energy as do alternative sources. In neither situation would the utility's advertising endanger conservation or mislead the public. To the extent that the Commission's order suppresses speech that in no way impairs the State's interest in energy conservation, the Commission's order violates the First and Fourteenth Amendments, and must be invalidated. *See First National Bank of Boston v. Bellotti*, 435 U.S. 765 (1978).

The Commission also has not demonstrated that its interest in conservation cannot be protected adequately by more limited regulation of appellant's commercial expression. To further its policy of conservation, the Commission could attempt to restrict the format and content of Central Hudson's advertising. It might, for example, require that the advertisements include information about the relative efficiency and expense of the offered service, both under current conditions and for the foreseeable future. *Cf. Banzhaf v. FCC*, 132 U.S.App.D.C. 14, 405 F.2d 1082 (1968), *cert. denied sub nom. Tobacco Institute, Inc. v. FCC*, 396 U.S. 842 (1969). In the absence of a showing that more limited speech regulation would be ineffective, we cannot approve the complete suppression of Central Hudson's advertising.

IV

Our decision today in no way disparages the national interest in energy conservation. We accept without reservation the argument that conservation, as well as the development of alternative energy sources, is an imperative national goal. Administrative bodies empowered to regulate electric utilities have the authority—and indeed the duty—to take appropriate action to further this goal. When, however, such action involves the suppression of speech, the First and Fourteenth Amendments require that the restriction be no more extensive than is necessary to serve the state interest. In this case, the record before us fails to show that the total ban on promotional advertising meets this requirement. Accordingly, the judgment of the New York Court of Appeals is reversed.

Reversed.

Questions Presented

1) According to the Supreme Court, why is commercial speech not entitled to the same protection as noncommercial speech?
2) What is the four-part analysis used by the Supreme Court to determine the constitutionality of the Public Service Commission's limit on Central Hudson's advertising?
3) Does this test put commercial speech on the same level as noncommercial speech or are there still distinctions to be made?
4) What was the outcome of the Supreme Court's balancing of the state's interest against the need for the advertising ban?

❖❖

FIGURE 3.7   What is Commercial Speech?

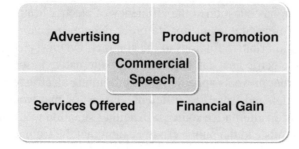

While there is no specific test for determining if speech is commercial, in *Bolger v. Youngs Drug Products Corp.* Justice Thurgood Marshall considered several factors in the aggregate to label speech as commercial. These factors were: (1) is the speech meant to be an advertisement?; (2) does it reference a single product?; and (3) is it for financial gain?[83] Once again he reiterated the Court's position that commercial speech is entitled to a "*qualified but nonetheless substantial protection under the First Amendment.*"[84] Commercial speech that is outside of First Amendment protection is false or deceptive advertising or advertising for illegal goods or services.

The Supreme Court has distinguished commercial speech from noncommercial speech based on a number of factors which contribute to its subordinate level of constitutional protection. One of these factors is the fact that noncommercial speech involves public discourse in the marketplace of ideas necessary to a free democracy.[85] Another factor is that commercial speech is essentially one-sided with no exchange of ideas since it is restricted to profit with the consumer possessing only a First Amendment right to receive the information.[86]

FIGURE 3.8   The *Central Hudson* Four-part Commercial Speech Test

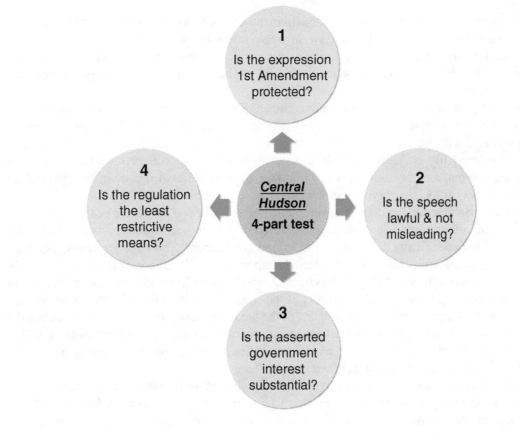

---

[83] 463 U.S. 60, 66 (1983)

[84] Id. at 68.

[85] See e.g., *Hustler Magazine, Inc. v. Falwell*, 485 U.S. 46, 55 (1988); *Rosenberger v. Rector and Visitors of the University of Virginia*, 515 U.S. 819, 831 (1995)

[86] See e.g., *Virginia State Board of Pharmacy* at 757.

The four-part test used in *Central Hudson* relied on a least restrictive means for government regulation. This test was criticized in a dissent to *Central Hudson* by Justice Rehnquist who said it *"elevates the protection accorded commercial speech that falls within the scope of the First Amendment to a level that is virtually indistinguishable from that of commercial speech."*[87] The Supreme Court later chose not to employ the least restrictive means test in *Board of Trustees of the State University of New York v. Fox.*[88] Instead the Court said commercial speech regulation can extend beyond the least restrictive means test in order to advance the government's interest.[89] While this later case indicated that court dicta in other cases suggested the least restrictive means was the required test in the four-part *Central Hudson* analysis the Supreme Court said the inquiry need not be that narrowly drawn in assessing government regulation. Despite the different view expressed by the Court in *Board of Trustees* the *Central Hudson* test is viable and employed in commercial speech cases analyzing government regulations.

SUMMARY

Business corporations do not operate in a vacuum in the United States. They are part of our political and social structure and impacted by the government in much the same way as any individual. Concerns about government overreach and limits on governmental power are not exclusive to noncorporate actors. Governmental regulation can both benefit and harm individual business people and corporate entities.

Our political structure ensures that no one branch of our three separate but co-equal branches of government can usurp the power of the other. Articles I, II and III of the U.S. Constitution establish and enumerate the powers of the respective legislative, executive and judicial branches of government. The legislative is charged with the lawmaking function, the executive with ensuring those laws are carried out, and the judicial with the power of constitutional review of the law and the legality of the acts of its other two coordinate branches of government.

Since we are a federalist system of government, power is divided between a centralized federal government and subordinate state governments. Through the Tenth Amendment state governments retain powers not specifically assigned to the federal government. The state governments have a general police power to provide for the safety, health and overall welfare of their residents. The federal police power is more limited but has been expanded under its enumerated power to regulate commerce. Despite the general police powers of the states reserved to them by the Tenth Amendment the Constitution remains the supreme law of the land. Any state law or regulation that invades an area exclusively reserved by the federal government under the Constitution is preempted. A classic example is in the area of immigration and naturalization which has been enumerated in Article I, clause 8 of the Constitution as an area of exclusive federal control.

The Commerce Clause powers of Congress have resulted in the expansion of federal regulatory control over the states. Through the Commerce Clause the federal government has been able to regulate commerce between the states as long as there is some connection between a state law and interstate commerce. However, even if the activity regulated by the state is strictly intrastate it can

---

[87] *Central Hudson Gas & Electric Corp.*, 447 U.S. at 591.
[88] 492 U.S. 469 (1989)
[89] Id. at 477–8

be regulated by Congress if it has an effect upon interstate commerce. The Supreme Court has historically been highly deferential to Congress' Commerce Clause powers, except when federal legislation attempts to regulate in an area completely outside the definition of interstate commerce. While the Commerce Clause is an affirmative grant of power for Congress to regulate commerce between the states, the dormant Commerce Clause acts as an implied restriction upon the states from creating legislation that would adversely impact interstate commerce.

The Privileges and Immunities Clause of Article IV, also known as the Comity Clause, ensures that citizens of one state are accorded the same fundamental rights and privileges when they enter another state. The aim of this Article IV provision was national unity, a sense of country lacking under the former Article of Confederation. Despite other constitutional protections the Privileges and Immunities Clause has been interpreted by the Supreme Court as not applying to corporations or other artificial entities because they are not persons and cannot be "citizens" as expressed in the clause.

The regulatory powers of both federal and state governments and their subordinate entities are broad but they must be exercised within the limits of their respective lawful powers. Due process ensures basic fairness for those impacted by government action that may adversely impact individual property rights. Procedural due process provides for the minimum protection of notice and an opportunity to be heard. Substantive due process requires that any law or regulation be clear and understandable. Ambiguous and vague laws or regulations will be voided for not meeting constitutional due process demands. The Commerce Clause has been a consistent source of federal regulatory power but other provisions of the Constitution have served as sources of regulation. The Necessary and Proper Clause in Article I gives Congress the incidental power to do what is "necessary and proper" to execute its enumerated powers under section 8 of Article I. The Takings Clause contained in the Fifth Amendment requires "just compensation" anytime the government deprives an owner of the beneficial use of private property. This may result from an occupation of the property but usually involves some government action that impacts the owner's use of the property. Even though the law provides for "just compensation" and this has been interpreted as "fair market value," the reality has been that actual compensation may fall short of owner expectations.

Commercial speech is any speech the purpose of which is primarily to propose a commercial or business transaction. It was originally excluded from First Amendment protection by the Supreme Court but was later granted qualified protection subordinate to noncommercial speech. Despite its subordinate status commercial speech is still entitled to substantial First Amendment protection. However, commercial speech that is false or deceptive will not be protected.

BUSINESS LAW AND ETHICS

LEARNING OUTCOMES

Upon completion of this chapter the student will be able to:

1   Identify the ethical decision making process in business.
2   Discuss the difference between ethics and morals.
3   Discuss the impact of ethical behavior in business on corporate liability.
4   Define the three different schools of ethics.
5   Explain the purpose and benefit of a code of ethics for business.

KEY TERMS

applied ethics
categorical imperative
code of ethics
corporate social responsibility
ethics
meta-ethics
morals

moral philosophy
moral relativism
normative ethics
social norms
Utilitarianism
triple bottom-line
whistleblowing

I. The Importance of Ethics in Business

Hollywood often presents us with an accurate window into the realities encountered in our world. Movies reach a wide audience and have the ability to tell fictional stories loosely based on actual events or to take real-life events and bring them to a cultural consciousness. One of Hollywood's favorite themes has always been the David versus Goliath battle between the lone, righteous individual battling a large, evil entity. A number of past movies, featuring some of the biggest box office draws at the time, have dealt with corporate greed and malfeasance in this manner. Some of these movies have been based on the exploits of real people. *Silkwood*, a 1983 film starring Meryl Streep in the title role, told the story of Karen Silkwood, a plutonium plant worker and nuclear whistleblower, who died in a mysterious car accident. The real life Silkwood was also a union activist who, after being subjected to radiation exposure, sought to hold her employer accountable for the health risks and illnesses from radiation encountered by company employees. A civil suit after her death led to a multi-million dollar verdict against her employer, the Kerr-McGee Nuclear Corporation. The case was settled post-verdict for less than the awarded amount. In another popular film of the time, *Erin Brockovich*, starring Julia Roberts, the poisoning of local groundwater from a chemical solution used at a nearby Pacific Gas & Electric Company plant caused a cancer cluster in a local residential area. Through the efforts of Brockovich, a single mother law clerk working at a local law firm, the complicity of the company is uncovered when she locates records indicating that the company lied about the type of chemicals it was using at its plant. Instead of using one benign form of chromium, a carcinogenic chemical, hexavalent chromium, was being used. The actual case which served as the focal point of the movie resulted in a $333 million settlement against the corporate polluters in 1996. A similar true story played out on the big screen in *A Civil Action*, starring John Travolta as attorney Jan Schlictmann. Based on the nonfictional book of the same name by Jonathan Harr, the movie tells the story about a cancer cluster in a Woburn, Massachusetts neighborhood caused by chemicals used in a local tannery. The chemicals seep into and contaminate the local water supply. The corporate litigants deny responsibility and make efforts in the off-hours to clean up the offending dump sites in order to thwart discovery. The actual case, *Anderson v. Cryovac*, resulted in a multi-million dollar settlement and a substantial chemical cleanup expense for the corporations as a result of a separate Environmental Protection Agency lawsuit. Two other movies featuring Hollywood heavyweights focused on the stories of actual corporate whistleblowers and the risks and potential dangers encountered when exposing corporate fraud and corruption. In *The Insider* Russell Crowe portrays Jeff Wigand, who in a nationally broadcast *60 Minutes* interview, discussed the health dangers from cigarette smoking and the tobacco industry's suppression of the health risks caused by smoking. Matt Damon played a corporate whistleblower, Mark Whitacre, in the 2009 film *The Informant!* who assists the F.B.I. in a price-fixing investigation against his employer, Archer Daniels Midland. The actual investigation resulted in criminal convictions against Whitacre and other company executives, as well as a total anti-trust fine of $100 million against Archer Daniels Midland.

Legal Definition

Whistleblowing – public disclosure by an employee of a private corporation or government agency of fraud, corruption, illegal activity, or mismanagement.

In a lesser known but equally compelling film from 1991, *Class Action*, Gene Hackman and Mary Elizabeth Mastrantonio play father-daughter lawyers who are on opposite sides in a lawsuit against an automobile manufacturer. Hackman represents the underdog victims; Mastrantonio is the lawyer for the corporate auto manufacturer. Liability against the auto manufacturer is based on a corporate decision that it was more cost-efficient to pay out possible future liability claims than to repair a defect in their automobiles that caused them to explode when crashed into while making left turns. The movie's plot, aside from the familial tension between the two main characters, is loosely based on the Ford Pinto cases from the late 1970s involving the vehicle's gas tank design. The Pinto had a tendency to explode in flames when struck from behind. Ford decided the recall and redesign was too costly and went forward with selling the car on the open market. Lawsuits and indictments against the Ford Motor Company ensued with resulting settlements in the multi-millions of dollars and a criminal indictment against the company for reckless homicide. Though the company was found not guilty, the damage to its reputation and the monetary settlement amounts were staggering.

> ### *Legal Definition*
>
> **Ethics** – rules of right and wrong conduct governing personal or organizational behavior and conduct.

Each of the aforementioned movies make for great drama and bring to social prominence and awareness instances of corporate greed, malfeasance, corruption, and ethical compromise. The fact that Hollywood producers had so many actual events as storyline material points to a sad fact about the past ethical health of some corporate cultures. Yet, as much as big business has learned from the sins of others, there are still many instances of the same behaviors being repeated over and over again. We can ask ourselves why this is so when the examples from other companies that lost major revenue and had to pay massive settlement amounts and fund toxic cleanups are there to remind corporations of the downfall that results from unethical conduct. We may be puzzled but we should not be since the situation is no different in individual situations. Our criminal justice system is an obvious sample of daily examples of bad behaviors which should serve as notice for others not to engage in the same behavior. For the majority of the population there is compliance with the law, but there remain those who still do not conform their behavior to societal standards. But, what makes the rest of us conform? Is it a fear of getting caught and punished that acts as a deterrent? Or is the punishment of others simply of no consequence since there is no individual desire to engage in the behaviors shunned by society and punished by the law? People choose to do good acts and be good persons for reasons that go beyond a fear of punishment or retribution. People act as they do because they are guided by their morals. These morals are deep-seated beliefs on how to act, a distinction between right and wrong behavior. While it is true that the law also guides behavior, there are many laws that have no ethical foundation. Speed limits are laws put in place to control traffic flow and safety on the roadways. Driving above the speed limit, though a traffic offense, will not lead even the most righteous to believe that it is moral flaw of character. Now, if the individual motorist was to consistently flout the speed limit that conduct may express more of the individual's moral code than a single offense. However, the point of the matter is that many laws are not based on any moral precept. Still, many others are, such as crimes against the individual—assault, rape, robbery, theft, murder. So the law is also somewhat of an ethical guide for us. Then there are social norms which are a baseline of societal behavior. Social norms exist within smaller groups and larger social structures. They are informal attitudes and standards of behavior adopted over time. Norms, or mores, become fixed over time within a culture or society. The business world is a type of culture that has established mores of its own. Each of these elements—morals, the law, social norms – contribute to the overall individual internal guidance system we call "ethics." Just like a rocket set to be launched into space, if we have a flawed guidance system we will not successfully travel along our intended path. Think of our ethics in another way—we have a mix of morals, law, and social norms which are blended and poured into a funnel, the product of that mix is our ethics, the means by which each of those ingredients is implemented into a final product, as illustrated below in Figure 4.1.

If you remember back to when you were a child playing games with your friends, maybe it was a game of cards, a board game, or a sports competition, and one of your friends cheated or changed the rules mid-game, you would be upset and the oft repeated refrain of "cheaters never prosper" crossed your lips. Where did this come from? Probably a lesson learned from a parent when you were caught not following the rules. It may sound trite but as a lesson it has value. Certainly for companies like Ford, Pacific Gas & Electric and Kerr McGee, as depicted in the movies and experienced in real life, these childhood lessons came to life.

FIGURE 4.1   The Ethical Funnel

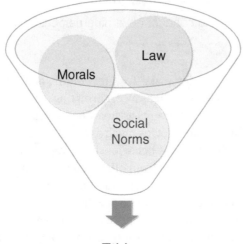

Ethics

Ethics have a place in our lives and are part of our socialization system as we grow and mature into adulthood. For some that socialization part of their lives does not develop properly, for others it gets corrupted along the way. If you consider some of the chief villains in the major business scandals of the past you would likely be hard pressed to identify many who started out with the ambition of becoming an ethically compromised individual. But for many of them that is just what happened, a compromise of their learned behavior. They knew what the correct moral choice was but chose another path. Why the divergence? That is a question better left to psychologists and personality disorder experts but it is likely that greed, ambition, blind competitive desires, each had a role in the process. A win at all costs attitude. Recall those childhood lessons and the cheaters you confronted—what was the motive? Somebody wanted to win and took a shortcut or saw a means to get ahead at the expense of others.

CASE STUDY 4.1

Mountain Goat Vehicles, Inc. is a North American all-terrain vehicle (ATV) manufacturer based in Boise, Idaho. It was formed in 1985 as an affiliate company of All Sports Motors, a Denver, Colorado recreational vehicle manufacturer of sport boats, snowmobiles, and dirt bikes. All Sports Motors owns 40% of Mountain Goat Vehicles' stock. Mountain Goat Vehicles (MGV) was slow to find its place in the U.S. all-terrain vehicle market during its first eight years in business, with its sales mostly occurring regionally, but eventually it gained a foothold and in the year 2000 experienced its largest sale of ATVs across the United States. This led to expansion over the next few years into Canadian, Mexican and Central American markets. In 2010 MGV was poised to expand its sales overseas into European and South American markets. Much of the impetus for expansion was the design of its 2008 model "Mud Dawg" ATV which had a sleeker body design than prior MGV models and boasted a top end speed of 75 mph and a tighter turning radius. This was being aggressively marketed by MGV to its established markets as well as its burgeoning European and South American markets. Meanwhile, All Sports Motors continued with its line of recreational vehicle manufacturing and sales independent of MGV's line but MGV's sales were a part of All Sports Motors annual financial reports. MGV management operates independently of All Sports Motors though All Sport has appointed individuals to serves on MGV's board of directors.

In early 2009 MGV learned from one of its authorized repair shops, Henderson's Motorcycle Repair in Sparks, Nevada, of a problem with the steering system in the new "Mud Dawg" design. Sam Henderson, the owner of the repair shop with over 35 years in the business, reported to MGV's engineering department a problem he began noticing in the "Mug Dawg" ATVs being brought to his shop. Several customers were encountering steering shaft breakages. While none of Henderson's customers were injured because their steering shaft breakage was discovered at lower speeds and they were able to control the ATV enough to stop it, he saw the potential for greater harm to riders at higher speeds. In his letter to MGV's Engineering Department Henderson outlined the problem and the design flaw he detected which he believed leads to the steering shaft breaking. When he did not hear from MGV after two months Henderson followed up with a letter to MGV's CEO, Adam Alsap. In the meantime Henderson advised his close friend, Sandy Hilt, owner of Sparks Recreational Outlet, of the problem with the "Mud Dawg" steering shafts and the potential for serious injury if not death from the shaft breaking at high speeds. Hilt was the largest recreational vehicle retailer in Nevada and 25% of his sales were from ATVs with the new MGV "Mud Dawg" accounting for a majority of those sales. Hilt listened to what Henderson had to say but told him that until MGV issued a recall he would continue to sell the "Mud Dawg". Henderson said that there was a simple design flaw in the steering shaft that was causing it to break and if Hilt wanted to ensure his customers were safe he could easily correct the problem prior to sale of individual units. Hilt said that solution posed two problems for him: 1) it was an added expense he was not willing to either incur on his own or pass on to the customer; and 2) it caused a material change in the product he was selling and voided any warranty of the vehicle by MGV and also exposed him to potential liability if an accident occurred after his store's mechanics corrected the problem.

Back at MGV Henderson's letters to the Engineering Department and CEO Alsap did not go unnoticed. Meetings were held over the course of several weeks between the Engineering Department, Sales Department and Corporate Legal Department. The consensus from the meetings was that the design flaw was real but subsequent testing had shown a probability of failure that was within tolerable ranges of 10–15% of the time. A recall of the "Mud Dawg" line of ATVs, which were now doubled in production due to European and South American market expansion, would be costly and impact projected sales revenues from the expanded market sales, as well as affect potential future sales revenues. It was viewed as a public relations nightmare just as they were on the cusp of securing a stronghold in the ATV world sales market. The legal department surmised that the potential injuries and claims that resulted would be relatively minor and less costly in comparison to a recall and its adverse impact on future sales. A decision was made by management to proceed with the manufacture of the "Mud Dawg" as scheduled and in the next year's production cycle to correct the design defect. A little over 750,000 "Mud Dawg" ATVs were sold worldwide in 2010 by MGV. The total of 2008–2010 "Mud Dawg" ATVs with steering shaft design flaws sold on the market totaled 1.4 million. In 2009, 17 deaths related to steering shaft breakages on "Mud Dawg" ATVs occurred in the United States and there were over 100 reported injuries. Those numbers increased in 2010 to 30 deaths and over 150 injuries in the United States while 11 deaths and 60 injuries were reported in South America and eight deaths and 71 injuries were reported in Europe. The year 2011 began with MGV facing several wrongful death lawsuits in the United States and similar legal actions in Europe.

The ethical compromise made by Mountain Goat Vehicles, Inc. is quite obvious. It is easy to discern the wrong conduct MGV embarked on, but discuss some of the reasons why such decisions would be made by corporate managers, advisors, and the board of directors.

What would be the relative ethical positions of the other involved businesses and corporations? Did they have an ethical duty to act? Did they meet accepted ethical standards? Discuss the ethics exhibited by the principals of All Sports Motors, Henderson Motorcycle Repair, and Sparks Recreational Vehicles.

In business the gold standard of winning is profit margins. Investors want to be part of a company that makes money and produces dividends on its shares. A company needs to be showing steady profits in order to draw investors. Enron Corporation, a Houston based energy company that showed explosive growth in the 1980s and 1990s, was the subject of a major scandal when it was discovered that business liabilities were being reported as assets on company balance sheets. Its cash reserves were exaggerated. The company eventually declared bankruptcy and stock prices plummeted from a high of $90.56 a share to $0.26 a share. The subsequent fall from grace for the company, its executives and ancillary service providers was precipitous. Chief Financial Officer Andrew Fastow served prison time for wire fraud and securities fraud and Chief Executive Officer Jeffrey Skilling received 14 years in prison for conspiracy, fraud, and insider trading. Skilling, as part of a plea negotiation, was also required to reimburse tens of millions of dollars to the victims of the company's fraud. Arthur Anderson LLP, the accounting firm for Enron, was indicted for obstruction of justice and though eventually its conviction was overturned on appeal, the firm suffered a public relations nightmare from which it has struggled to recover. Arthur Anderson was one of the Big Five accounting firms in the United States but had to forfeit its license to practice after it was convicted. Despite the success of its criminal appeal the firm has not been able to retrieve its past reputation and is still subject to investor lawsuits.

The Enron scandal is one of several major business scandals to make headlines in the opening years of the 21st century. Adelphia Communications Corporation, a telecommunications company in Pennsylvania, went bankrupt and two of its corporate officers received extensive federal prison sentences for corrupt practices which included theft of company finances. Worldcom, formerly a large long distance phone service provider, was the subject of a massive accounting scandal that improperly listed billions of dollars of operating expenses as capital investments and overstated its assets while under-reporting its losses. Bernard Ebbers, the Worldcom CEO, was sentenced to 25 years in federal prison for conspiracy and securities fraud. The Worldcom accounting scandal was the largest in the United States until the revelations of Bernard Madoff's fraud in 2008. Madoff, a former NASDAQ chairman and head of his own investment firm, was sentenced to 150 years in federal prison for his elaborate financial frauds involving years of deceiving his investors. His court ordered restitution was in the amount of $170 billion. The extent of his unethical and criminal behavior was not limited to Madoff but extended to other businesses and individuals. Several suicides, including Madoff's son Mark, were linked to the scandal as were other criminal prosecutions.

The lesson to be learned is that individual unethical conduct is not isolated. There can be extensive, reverberating effects from it. The preceding examples from some of the biggest business scandals to occur at the opening of the century underscore the tornado-like destruction resulting from an ethical failure. These cases were highlighted in the news as financial scandals, but they were more pointedly ethical scandals—a complete failure of those involved to gauge their internal guidance systems to steer them on the correct course of action, not the altered and dishonest paths that were taken.

As a result of the Enron Corporation scandal Congress sought to implement measures to protect against corporate fraud. Two legislators, Senator Paul Sarbanes and Representative Michael Oxley, sponsored the Sarbanes-Oxley Act of 2002 (also referred to as "SOX" or "the SOX Act") which sought to place greater oversight on corporate finances and establish punishment for noncompliance. With the passage of the Act Congress instituted several key preventive controls from corporate malfeasance. One of the first was to require the Securities and Exchange Commission (SEC) to promulgate rules to address the prior oversight failure exemplified by the Enron scandal.[1] The rules subsequently established by the SEC had several controls including requiring corporate executives to certify the accuracy of company financial statements. Violations of this provision could lead to jail time. Independent auditors to review accounting practices had to be hired by publicly traded companies and whistleblower protections were implemented for employees who report company fraud. The protection of whistleblowers was an important addition to corporate oversight enhancements since it aimed to eliminate the insidious practice of retaliation against honest employees. A whistleblower is any individual, usually an employee, who informs on a person or organization believed to be engaging in illegal or immoral activity.[2] In 1989 Congress passed the Whistleblower Protection Act to protect federal public sector employees from workplace retaliation connected to the reporting of government agency misconduct. Several other whistleblower protection statutes exist at the federal level, for example section 11(c) of the Occupational Safety and Health Administration Act (OSHA) which protects an employee from employer retaliation based on the employee's assertion of rights under the Act[3] and section 215(a)(3) of the Fair Labor Standards Act (FLSA) protecting employees who file a complaint or testify under the terms of the FLSA.[4] Thirty-nine states have their own whistleblower protection statutes but of those only fourteen protect both private and public sector employees. Rhode Island's Whistleblower Protection Act is unique in the amount of time it allows an aggrieved employee to file a claim—up to three years after the alleged act.[5] Most state whistleblower statutes only allow for filing within 30 to 90 days of the employer's retaliatory act.

Sarbanes-Oxley's whistleblower protection section provides a procedure for employees to file claims through the Secretary of Labor. If successful an aggrieved employee can receive reinstatement if terminated as well as adjusted seniority status, back pay with interest, attorney fees and costs, and any other rights they may have under an employment agreement.[6] The importance of the SOX Act's whistleblower protection provision to corporate oversight is tremendous since it enlists honest employees to expose corporate wrongdoing by assuring job protection. However, the ever-present reality is that despite the law's protections whistleblowers often undertake complicated roles in corporate oversight when they step forward to report wrongdoing and have experienced lengthy ordeals in order to vindicate their claims. The Wells Fargo & Company banking fraud scandal in 2012, when its employees were accused of opening millions of fraudulent accounts to meet sales goals, is a good example of the dark side of whistleblowers coming forward. Many former Wells Fargo employees reported widespread harassment, bullying and retaliation for taking an

---

[1] Erica Beecher-Monas, *Corporate Governance in the Wake of Enron: An Examination of the Audit Committee Solution to Corporate Fraud*, 55 Admin. L. Rev. 357 (ABA Administrative Law Review), Spring 2003.

[2] Oxford University Press, 2017, https://en.oxforddictionaries.com/definition/whistle-blower

[3] U.S. Dept. of Labor, Occupational Safety & Health Administration, *The Whistleblower Protection Programs*, https://www.whistleblowers. gov/

[4] 29 U.S.C. § 215(a)(3).

[5] Gen. Laws Ann. § 28-50-4.

[6] 18 U.S.C. § 1514A(c), (d).

FIGURE 4.2   State Whistleblower Protection Law

Rhode Island Whistleblower Protection Act

Gen. Laws Ann. § 28-50-3

An employer shall not discharge, threaten, or otherwise discriminate against an employee regarding the employee's compensation, terms, conditions, location, or privileges of employment:

Because the employee, or a person acting on behalf of the employee, reports or is about to report to a public body, verbally or in writing, a violation which the employee knows or reasonably believes has occurred or is about to occur, of a law or regulation or rule promulgated under the law of this state, a political subdivision of this state, or the United States, unless the employee knows or has reason to know that the report is false, or Because an employee is requested by a public body to participate in an investigation, hearing, or inquiry held by that public body, or a court action, or Because an employee refuses to violate or assist in violating federal, state or local law, rule or regulation, or Because the employee reports verbally or in writing to the employer or to the employee's supervisor a violation, which the employee knows or reasonably believes has occurred or is about to occur, of a law or regulation or rule promulgated under the laws of this state, a political subdivision of this state, or the United States, unless the employee knows or has reason to know that the report is false. Provided, that if the report is verbally made, the employee must establish by clear and convincing evidence that the report was made.

---

ethical stand against company directives to engage in fraudulent activity.[7] Despite CEO John Stumpf's testimony before a Senate Banking Committee that all employees are encouraged to call the ethics hotline and report wrongdoing, the experiences of the Wells Fargo employees contradicted his claims.[8] The retaliation encountered by the Wells Fargo employees is typical of the continuing unethical practices undertaken by complicit employers who seek to cover-up their misdeeds. It is also a violation of the law as a plain reading of the Sarbanes-Oxley Act indicates. However, interpretations of a statute can vary and the Sarbanes-Oxley Act was also subject to court challenges.

❖❖

Lawson v. FMR, LLC
134 S.Ct. 1158 (2014)

Justice Ginsburg delivered the opinion of the Court.

To safeguard investors in public companies and restore trust in the financial markets following the collapse of Enron Corporation, Congress enacted the Sarbanes-Oxley Act of 2002, 116Stat. 745. See S. Rep. No. 107–146, pp. 2–11 (2002). A provision of the Act, 18 U. S. C. § 1514A, protects whistleblowers. Section 1514A, at the time here relevant, instructed:

"No [public] company . . . , or any officer, employee, contractor, subcontractor, or agent of such company, may discharge, demote, suspend, threaten, harass, or in any other manner discriminate against an employee in the terms and conditions of employment because of [whistleblowing or other protected activity]." § 1514A(a) (2006 ed.).

---

[7] Matt Egan, *I called the Wells Fargo ethics line and I was fired,* CNN Money, September 21, 2016, http://money.cnn.com/2016/09/21/investing/wells-fargo-fired-workers-retaliation-fake-accounts/index.html

[8] Id.

This case concerns the definition of the protected class: Does § 1514A shield only those employed by the public company itself, or does it shield as well employees of privately held contractors and subcontractors—for example, investment advisers, law firms, accounting enterprises—who perform work for the public company?

We hold, based on the text of § 1514A, the mischief to which Congress was responding, and earlier legislation Congress drew upon, that the provision shelters employees of private contractors and subcontractors, just as it shelters employees of the public company served by the contractors and subcontractors. We first summarize our principal reasons, then describe this controversy and explain our decision more comprehensively.

Plaintiffs below, petitioners here, are former employees of private companies that contract to advise or manage mutual funds. The mutual funds themselves are public companies that have no employees. Hence, if the whistle is to be blown on fraud detrimental to mutual fund investors, the whistleblowing employee must be on another company's payroll, most likely, the payroll of the mutual fund's investment adviser or manager.

Taking the allegations of the complaint as true, both plaintiffs blew the whistle on putative fraud relating to the mutual funds and, as a consequence, suffered adverse action by their employers.

***

In the Enron scandal that prompted the Sarbanes-Oxley Act, contractors and subcontractors, including the accounting firm Arthur Andersen, participated in Enron's fraud and its cover up. When employees of those contractors attempted to bring misconduct to light, they encountered retaliation by their employers. The Sarbanes-Oxley Act contains numerous provisions aimed at controlling the conduct of accountants, auditors, and lawyers who work with public companies. Given Congress' concern about contractor conduct of the kind that contributed to Enron's collapse, we regard with suspicion construction of § 1514A to protect whistleblowers only when they are employed by a public company, and not when they work for the public company's contractor.

***

The Sarbanes-Oxley Act of 2002 (Sarbanes-Oxley or Act) aims to "prevent and punish corporate and criminal fraud, protect the victims of such fraud, preserve evidence of such fraud, and hold wrong-doers accountable for their actions." S. Rep. No. 107–146, p. 2 (2002) (hereinafter S. Rep.). Of particular concern to Congress was abundant evidence that Enron had succeeded in perpetuating its massive shareholder fraud in large part due to a "corporate code of silence"; that code, Congress found, "discourage[d] employees from reporting fraudulent behavior not only to the proper authorities, such as the FBI and the SEC, but even internally." When employees of Enron and its accounting firm, Arthur Andersen, attempted to report corporate misconduct, Congress learned, they faced retaliation, including discharge. As outside counsel advised company officials at the time, Enron's efforts to "quiet" whistleblowers generally were not proscribed under then-existing law. Congress identified the lack of whistleblower protection as "a significant deficiency" in the law, for in complex securities fraud investigations, employees "are [often] the only firsthand witnesses to the fraud." *Id.,* at 10.

Section 806 of Sarbanes-Oxley addresses this concern. Titled "Protection for Employees of Publicly Traded Companies Who Provide Evidence of Fraud," § 806 added a new provision to Title 18 of the United States Code, 18 U. S. C. § 1514A, which reads in relevant part:

"Civil action to protect against retaliation in fraud cases

"(a) Whistleblower Protection for Employees of Publicly Traded Companies.—No company with a class of securities registered under section 12 of the Securities Exchange Act of 1934

(15 U. S. C. § 78 *l*), or that is required to file reports under section 15(d) of the Securities Exchange Act of 1934 (15 U. S. C. § 78 *o*(d)), or any officer, employee, contractor, subcontractor, or agent of such company, may discharge, demote, suspend, threaten, harass, or in any other manner discriminate against an employee in the terms and conditions of employment because of any lawful act done by the employee—

"(1) to provide information, cause information to be provided, or otherwise assist in an investigation regarding any conduct which the employee reasonably believes constitutes a violation of section 1341 [mail fraud], 1343 [wire fraud], 1344 [bank fraud], or 1348 [securities or commodities fraud], any rule or regulation of the Securities and Exchange Commission, or any provision of Federal law relating to fraud against shareholders, when the information or assistance is provided to or the investigation is conducted by [a federal agency, Congress, or supervisor]. . . ." § 806, 116Stat. 802.

***

Congress has assigned whistleblower protection largely to the Department of Labor (DOL), which administers some 20 United States Code incorporated whistleblower protection provisions. The Secretary has delegated investigatory and initial adjudicatory responsibility over claims under a number of these provisions, including § 1514A, to DOL's Occupational Safety and Health Administration (OSHA). OSHA's order may be appealed to an administrative law judge, and then to DOL's Administrative Review Board (ARB). 29 CFR § § 1980.104 to 1980.110 (2011).

***

Petitioners Jackie Hosang Lawson and Jonathan M. Zang (plaintiffs) separately initiated proceedings under § 1514A against their former employers, privately held companies that provide advisory and management services to the Fidelity family of mutual funds. The Fidelity funds are not parties to either case; as is common in the mutual fund industry, the Fidelity funds themselves have no employees. Instead, they contract with investment advisers like respondents to handle their day-to-day operations, which include making investment decisions, preparing reports for shareholders, and filing reports with the Securities and Exchange Commission (SEC). Lawson was employed by Fidelity Brokerage Services, LLC, a subsidiary of FMR Corp., which was succeeded by FMR LLC. Zang was employed by a different FMR LLC subsidiary, Fidelity Management & Research Co., and later by one of that company's subsidiaries, FMR Co., Inc. For convenience, we refer to respondents collectively as FMR.

Lawson worked for FMR for 14 years, eventually serving as a Senior Director of Finance. She alleges that, after she raised concerns about certain cost accounting methodologies, believing that they overstated expenses associated with operating the mutual funds, she suffered a series of adverse actions, ultimately amounting to constructive discharge. Zang was employed by FMR for eight years, most recently as a portfolio manager for several of the funds. He alleges that he was fired in retaliation for raising concerns about inaccuracies in a draft SEC registration statement concerning certain Fidelity funds. Lawson and Zang separately filed administrative complaints alleging retaliation proscribed by § 1514A. After expiration of the 180-day period specified in § 1514A(b)(1), Lawson and Zang each filed suit in the U. S. District Court for the District of Massachusetts.

FMR moved to dismiss the suits, arguing, as relevant, that neither plaintiff has a claim for relief under § 1514A. FMR is privately held, and maintained that § 1514A protects only employees of public companies—i.e., companies that either have "a class of securities registered under section 12 of the Securities Exchange Act of 1934," or that are "required to file reports under section 15(d)" of that Act. § 1514A(a). In a joint order, the District Court rejected FMR's interpretation of § 1514A and denied the dismissal motions in both suits.

On interlocutory appeal, a divided panel of the First Circuit reversed. The Court of Appeals majority acknowledged that FMR is a "contractor" within the meaning of § 1514A(a), and thus among the actors prohibited from retaliating against "an employee" who engages in protected activity. The majority agreed with FMR, however, that "an employee" refers only to employees of public companies and does not cover a contractor's own employees.

Several months later, the ARB issued a decision in an unrelated case, *Spinner v. David Landau & Assoc., LLC*, No. 10–111, etc., ALJ No. 2010–SOX–029 (May 31, 2012), disagreeing with the Court of Appeals' interpretation of § 1514A. In a comprehensive opinion, the ARB explained its position that § 1514A affords whistleblower protection to employees of privately held contractors that render services to public companies. We granted certiorari to resolve the division of opinion on whether § 1514A extends whistleblower protection to employees of privately held contractors who perform work for public companies.

***

In determining the meaning of a statutory provision, "we look first to its language, giving the words used their ordinary meaning." *Moskal v. United States*, 498 U. S. 103, 108 (1990) (citation and internal quotation marks omitted). As Judge Thompson observed in her dissent from the Court of Appeals' judgment, "boiling [§ 1514A(a)] down to its relevant syntactic elements, it provides that 'no . . . contractor . . . may discharge . . . an employee.'" 670 F. 3d, at 84 (quoting § 1514A(a)). The ordinary meaning of "an employee" in this proscription is the contractor's own employee.

***

Section 1514A's application to contractor employees is confirmed when we enlarge our view from the term "an employee" to the provision as a whole. The prohibited retaliatory measures enumerated in § 1514A(a)—discharge, demotion, suspension, threats, harassment, or discrimination in the terms and conditions of employment—are commonly actions an employer takes against its own employees. Contractors are not ordinarily positioned to take adverse actions against employees of the public company with whom they contract.

***

Moving further through § 1514A to the protected activity described in subsection (a)(1), we find further reason to believe that Congress presumed an employer-employee relationship between the retaliator and the whistleblower. Employees gain protection for furnishing information to a federal agency, Congress, or "a person with supervisory authority over *the employee* (or such other person working for *the employer* who has the authority to investigate, discover, or terminate misconduct)." § 1514A(a)(1) (emphasis added). And under § 1514A(a)(2), employees are protected from retaliation for assisting "in a proceeding filed or about to be filed (*with any knowledge of the employer*) relating to an alleged violation" of any of the enumerated fraud provisions, securities regulations, or other federal law relating to shareholder fraud. § 1514A(a)(2) (emphasis added). The reference to employer knowledge is an additional indicator of Congress' expectation that the retaliator typically will be the employee's employer, not another entity less likely to know of whistleblower complaints filed or about to be filed.

Section 1514A's enforcement procedures and remedies similarly contemplate that the whistleblower is an employee of the retaliator.

***

Our textual analysis of § 1514A fits the provision's purpose. It is common ground that Congress installed whistleblower protection in the Sarbanes-Oxley Act as one means to ward off another Enron debacle. And, as the ARB observed in *Spinner*, "Congress plainly recognized that outside professionals—accountants, law firms, contractors, agents, and the like—were complicit in, if not integral to, the shareholder fraud and subsequent cover-up [Enron] officers . . . perpetrated." ALJ No. 2010–SOX–029, pp. 12–13. Indeed, the Senate Report demonstrates that Congress was as focused on the role of Enron's outside contractors in facilitating the fraud as it was on the actions of Enron's own officers . . .

Also clear from the legislative record is Congress' understanding that outside professionals bear significant responsibility for reporting fraud by the public companies with whom they contract, and that fear of retaliation was the primary deterrent to such reporting by the employees of Enron's contractors. Congressional investigators discovered ample evidence of contractors demoting or discharging employees they have engaged who jeopardized the contractor's business relationship with Enron by objecting to Enron's financial practices . . .

In the same vein, two of the four examples of whistleblower retaliation recounted in the Senate Report involved outside professionals retaliated against by their own employers . . . From this legislative history, one can safely conclude that Congress enacted § 1514A aiming to encourage whistleblowing by contractor employees who suspect fraud involving the public companies with whom they work.

***

Our reading of § 1514A avoids insulating the entire mutual fund industry from § 1514A, as FMR's and the dissent's "narrower construction" would do. As companies "required to file reports under section 15(d) of the Securities Exchange Act of 1934," 18 U. S. C. § 1514A(a), mutual funds unquestionably are governed by § 1514A. Because mutual funds figure prominently among such report-filing companies, Congress presumably had them in mind when it added to "publicly traded companies" the discrete category of companies "required to file reports under section 15(d)."

Virtually all mutual funds are structured so that they have no employees of their own; they are managed, instead, by independent investment advisers. The United States investment advising industry manages $14.7 trillion on behalf of nearly 94 million investors. These investment advisers, under our reading of § 1514A, are contractors prohibited from retaliating against their own employees for engaging in whistleblowing activity. This construction protects the "insiders [who] are the only firsthand witnesses to the [shareholder] fraud." S. Rep., at 10. Under FMR's and the dissent's reading, in contrast, § 1514A has no application to mutual funds, for all of the potential whistleblowers are employed by the privately held investment management companies, not by the mutual funds themselves.

. . . affording whistleblower protection to mutual fund investment advisers is crucial to Sarbanes-Oxley's endeavor to "protect investors by improving the accuracy and reliability of corporate disclosures made pursuant to the securities laws." 116 Stat. 745.

For the reasons stated, we hold that 18 U. S. C. § 1514A whistleblower protection extends to employees of contractors and subcontractors. The judgment of the U. S. Court of Appeals for the First Circuit is therefore reversed, and the case is remanded for further proceedings consistent with this opinion.

It is so ordered.

Questions Presented

1) What is the issue with regard to § 1514A that is before the U.S. Supreme Court?
2) What would have been the impact of a narrower reading of § 1514A by the Supreme Court on the effectiveness of the Sarbanes-Oxley Act?

3)   What did Justice Ginsberg say was a significant influence upon the implementation of the Sarbanes-Oxley Act and why?

4)   Why is it important for whistleblowers to have protection in the workplace?

❖❖

Supreme Court Justice Louis Brandeis once wrote: "*Publicity is justly commended as a remedy for social and industrial diseases. Sunlight is said to be the best of disinfectants; electric light the most efficient policeman.*"[9] Whistleblowers expose corrupt business practices to the sunlight. They are also in the best position to uncover unethical conduct because they are already on the inside as live witnesses to these practices, unlike audits and other oversight methods which work from a historical perspective and have to uncover and reconstruct fraudulent accounting practices. The analogy is that of the police detective who, when investigating a crime, is reconstructing an event from the past in order to solve the crime. If the detective has an informant or someone who witnessed the crime his task becomes less of a mystery and the crime gets closer to being solved.

The Supreme Court's decision in *Lawson v. FMR, LLC* was its first to address a whistleblower claim under the Sarbanes-Oxley Act. The *Lawson* Court extended whistleblower protections to the employees of contractors and sub-contractors employed by a publicly traded company. As other cases work their way through the federal district and circuit courts they may also come before the Supreme Court on different issues related to the Sarbanes-Oxley Act. It will be important for the Supreme Court to keep the needed sunlight, as Justice Brandeis suggested, shining through the protections extended to corporate whistleblowers.

II. Moral Theory and Business Ethics

The trend toward the study of business ethics as a separate course in business schools has been traced to the mid-1970s and the work of early academic pioneers in the field.[10] Much like courses in legal and medical ethics in professional academic programs, the rise of business ethics was tied to ensuring a standard of professional competence and moral expectations. Moral philosophy, the philosophical field of study covering ethics, became as integral a part of business school curricula as economics and management. Today there are a number of universities with institutes dedicated to education and research in the area of business ethics (see list below). The field of business ethics is a form of professional ethics, otherwise referred to as applied ethics. Applied ethics is one of three core fields of ethical study, with the other two being normative ethics and meta-ethics. Normative ethics focuses on the question of how one should act in a given situation. What is the acceptable norm or standard of conduct? This is the broad question that is asked when attempting to form a general theory of ethical conduct. However, for normative ethics the actor is not viewed in isolation, moral consideration has to be given to the act and to the consequences of the act as well. The field of normative ethics is thus further broken down into virtue theory, deontological theory, and consequentialism. Virtue theory looks at the moral character of the actor. According to virtue theory there are certain character traits we should possess such as fidelity, bravery, honesty, generosity, kindness, which guide our behavior. All action is therefore guided by the virtue regardless of outcome. Deontology, however, focuses on the act and labels certain acts as either morally good or morally bad.

---

[9] Louis D. Brandeis, *Other People's Money and How the Bankers Use It*, (2009).

[10] Richard T. DeGeorge, *A History of Business Ethics*, Markkula Center for Applied Ethics, Santa Clara University, https://www.scu.edu/ethics/focus-areas/business-ethics/resources/a-history-of-business-ethics/, (last visited June 15, 2017.)

University Ethics Resource Centers

Bentley University Hoffman Center for Business Ethics

http://www.bentley.edu/centers/center-for-business-ethics

Georgetown University Business Ethics Institute

https://bioethics.georgetown.edu/library-materials/bioethics-research-library-databases/ethxweb/bibliographies-bioethics-topics/

Harvard University Safra Center for Ethics

https://ethics.harvard.edu/

Santa Clara University Markkula Center for Applied Ethics

https://www.scu.edu/ethics/focus-areas/business-ethics/

St. Louis University Emerson Center for Business Ethics

http://business.slu.edu/centers-of-distinction/emerson-leadership-institute

University of Denver Institute for Enterprise Ethics

http://www.enterpriseethics.org/

University of Pennsylvania Zicklin Center for Business Ethics

https://www.zicklincenter.org/

Depending on how the individual acts are labeled determines whether or not they are performed without any dependency on the consequences. So if an act is deemed to be inherently bad but may have a valid and beneficial purpose, the deontologist view is that the act cannot be performed. This view is linked to Immanuel Kant's categorical imperative which ascribes to an absolute or universal law for all ethical actors. Kant expressed his categorical imperative, which is something that needs to be done at all times, in a basic formulation: "*act only in accordance with that maxim through which you can at the same time will that it become a universal law.*"[11] Kant focused his theory on moral maxims which needed to pass the categorical imperative test. It assumes a rationality of conduct not necessarily a morality of conduct, though moral conduct is at the heart of his philosophy. Immoral or unethical actions are viewed as self-defeating and not proper courses of action.

Finally, consequentialist theory states that individuals should act in a way that brings about the best consequences. This is more of an end justifies the means approach. Thus the morality of an action is judged by its outcome or consequence. The character of the outcome is the key factor with this approach, unlike virtue ethics in which it is the character of the actor and deontology where it is the character of the act that matters. Utilitarianism is a consequentialist theory. According to utilitarian theory ethical principles are judged by whether they bring the greatest good to the greatest number of people. This theory expands on consequentialist theory by seeking not only the greatest good but that good for the greatest number. The two main proponents of utilitarianism were Jeremy Bentham, the theory's founder, and John Stuart Mill, who expanded upon the theory by distinguishing between higher and lower pleasures in the order of things.

---

[11] Robert Johnson, Stanford Encyclopedia of Philosophy, *Kant's Moral Philosophy*, https://plato.stanford.edu/entries/kant-moral/#CatHypImp, Feb. 23, 2004, (last visited June 15, 2017.)

FIGURE 4.3   The Ethical Schools

The Three Schools of Ethics		
Normative Ethics	Applied Ethics	Meta-Ethics
Is the behavior proper?	How is it put into practice?	What does it mean?

Applied ethics studies the moral acceptance of acts and practices. As a field of study it assumes the existence of moral principles in the world and endeavors to determine how to put those principles into practice.[12] In the business world this would entail a consideration of how a corporation is going to define itself as an ethical entity. An assessment of existing business practices would be evaluated to determine if they comply with a standard of moral conduct. A corporate code of conduct and a corporate compliance program to ensure the company and employees follow laws, regulations, standards and ethical practices are two examples of applied ethics in the business world.

Legal Definition

Utilitarianism – a philosophical doctrine that conduct should be directed toward promoting the greatest possible good for the greatest number of people.

Metaethics is focused on the overall definition of moral conduct, the origin and meaning of ethical principles.[13] Unlike the focus of applied and normative ethics on what is moral, metaethics focuses on the existence of morality and what morality itself is.[14] This is more of an esoteric philosophical debate. Metaethics asks questions like, what does it mean to be good or bad? What does it mean to say something is right or wrong? These questions have to first begin with whether there is a state of being we can define as moral, is there a universal ethic? Normative and applied ethics presuppose the existence of a moral good. The next level of metaethical inquiry is whether these morals are universal rules or are they relative. Moral relativism views ethical decision-making as dependent upon personal opinions and beliefs of what constitutes moral and immoral behavior. For instance, a moral absolute would be that theft of another individual's property under any circumstance is wrong. A morally relativist view of someone who is hungry and broke with a family to feed and steals money from a person's wallet would be that the theft was not wrong under the circumstances. This is just one example of a morally relativist view. Other relativist views may extend to moral issues like pre-marital and extra-marital sexual relationships with the relativist holding the belief that personal freedom gives that person the right to choose what to do with their body. The moral absolutist would simply view the action as immoral. The final inquiry for the metaethicist is, once the moral is defined to exist and determined to be either absolute or relative, what is the basis for determining an act to be right or wrong?

---

[12] James Fieser, Internet Encyclopedia of Philosophy, *Applied Ethics*, University of Tennessee at Martin, http://www.iep.utm.edu/ethics/#H1, (last visited June 15, 2017.)

[13] James Fieser, Internet Encyclopedia of Philosophy, *Ethics*, University of Tennessee at Martin, http://www.iep.utm.edu/ethics/#H1, (last visited June 15, 2017.)

[14] Id.

> ### *Legal Definition*
>
> **Moral relativism** – the idea that right and wrong are personalized values based on circum-stances or cultural background; it does not view right and wrong as absolute values.

The foregoing are not easy questions to resolve. Philosophers, religious scholars, and ethicists have spent centuries trying to expound upon the definitions and explanations for ethical conduct. No matter how concrete a theory seems to be in explaining a course of ethical action the complexities of life will present issues that may not be so clear in their resolution. The business decision made by Hobby Lobby, Inc. featured in the following case study illustrates the complexity of ethical deci-sion-making in business. As you read case study 4.2 ask yourself whether or not the company CEO's decision not to follow the requirements of federal law was ethical. How might the actions of CEO David Green be viewed from a perspective of normative ethics? What about applied ethics?

CASE STUDY 4.2

Hobby Lobby, Inc. is a major U.S. based craft retailer with 500 stores and 13,000 full-time employees across the country. It operates as a closely held family business organized as an S-corporation and its revenue is over $3 billion a year. The owners of the company are David and Barbara Green and their three children. All are devout Christians and run the company on the foundation of their Christian beliefs. By all accounts Hobby Lobby, Inc. is an excellent employer, a responsible corporate citizen, and a leader in the retail craft market.

A regulation of the 2010 Patient Protection and Affordable Care Act required the Greens to provide certain contraceptive services to their employees as part of the their employer-sponsored health care plan. The federal government began enforcement of this provision in 2012. A tenet of the Green's faith is the belief that life begins once sperm fertilizes an egg and that it is immoral "to facili-tate any act that causes the death of a human embryo."[15] They challenged the government's mandate that they provide certain contraceptive services to their employees and this challenge eventually made its way to the U.S. Supreme Court in Hobby Lobby, Inc. v. Sebelius, 134 S.Ct. 2751 (2014).

The Green family's challenge to the Affordable Care Act's contraception provision require-ment for employers with over 50 employees was prompted by the government's threat of a fine in the amount of $1.3 million a day for the Green family's refusal to comply with the law. Even though Hobby Lobby was never required to pay any fines the company took the position that it would not violate its religious beliefs and would not provide the contraception coverage. The U.S. Supreme Court decision in the *Hobby Lobby* case sided with the Greens and allowed their religious objection to serve as an exemption for their company as a closely held for-profit corporation.

The *Hobby Lobby* case has been a subject of controversy during its pendency and post-decision. Aside from the legal implications of the case it is an interesting study for a discussion about busi-ness ethics and moral choices. An initial question to consider is whether the family's individual moral choice in this instance, which they have imputed to the company, is the ethical business choice in terms of shareholder interests? What impact would a daily $1.3 million government fine have on corporate finances and shareholder investments? Would the denial of contraception

---

[15] Hobby Lobby Stores, Inc. v. Sebelius, 723 F.3d 1114, 1122 (10th Cir. 2013)

services under a mandated health care plan be fair to employees? Can a religious belief be imputed to a for-profit corporation? Can the family owners reconcile personal religious and moral beliefs with the requirements of the law and ethical commitments to its employees and shareholders?

The government revised its contraception mandate as a result of the *Hobby Lobby* case and this has benefitted other corporations that had religious and moral objections to the mandate. However, the compromise resolution worked out by the government does not foreclose the issue of whether a corporation's moral beliefs will always lead to an ethical business decision. Similarly the *Hobby Lobby* case highlights the distinction between a legal result and an ethical result.

III. The Ethical Company and Codes of Conduct

Thus far the discussion has been about moral theory, individual ethics, social norms and internal personal moral tenets. It is important to identify these concepts and their influence upon our daily interactions but we also need to apply them to the corporate persona. What does the ethical company look like? How do we measure the ethics of an artificial entity like a corporation? If the law is to give corporations, partnerships, and LLCs an equivalent legal status to persons there is no reason not to equally expect the entity to be an ethical actor. Just as we cannot quantitatively measure a person's ethics by a gauge other than how that person behaves and interacts in society, the business entity is ethically judged by its behavior in the community it serves. It may be a small company interacting on a more local level or a major corporation that has a worldwide presence; in either situation there is a cadre of potential evaluators of how that company is perceived as a corporate citizen. These measurements are more qualitative in nature.

Businesses may exist as artificial entities under the law but are brought to life by the people who work for them. Businesses also impact people in their communities, directly and indirectly. Direct interactions can be simply through commercial dealings with customers on a one-on-one basis. Indirect impact, for example, occurs through the taxes a corporation or partnership pays into the local municipal and state treasury. A major corporation operating in a municipal area can bring a large tax break to homeowners who might otherwise have to pay more if the corporation was not present to ease individual tax burdens. If that company were to move its operations from the community to another locale the direct and indirect impact would be substantial. By way of this example it is evident that many companies operating in our midst are more involved as community co-partners with a vested interest than we may acknowledge them to be. How a company treats people on a micro level (within the company itself and its customers) and a macro level (the broader world community) is the obvious measure for evaluating its ethical standards. One organization, Ethisphere, has established a proprietary metric to determine the ethical ratings of different companies.[16] This metric is based on self-reporting by the companies in six different rating categories. The report is then evaluated by Ethisphere and a final score is established. A company's self-reported data is compared against other companies identified as business ethics leaders and then subjected to an independent third-party review. The methodology used by Ethisphere is reviewed annually by its advisory panel. The concept of rating the ethical values of major companies is relatively new. Ethisphere has only been operating since 2006. Two other organizations operating for a comparable amount of time as Ethisphere and located in the United Kingdom, The Ethical Corporation and The Ethical Company Organisation, do not provide a

---

[16] https://ethisphere.com/ethics-data/

ratings system but they do provide major world companies with ethical research information. The Ethics Resource Center in Washington, D.C. and the Ethics & Compliance Initiative in Arlington, Virginia are two U.S. based organizations that are focused on providing best practices in ethics and compliance programs for public and private institutions. Both of these organizations date back to the early part of the 20th century but their focus on corporate business ethics has been more recent. As noted on Ethics Resource Center's website: *"Since the global economic recession began in 2008, ERC has been particularly focused on ethical issues in the financial restructuring and economic policy of the United States, as well as the study of values and ethics in the corporate workplace."*[17]

The great ethics awareness in big business has only been a factor in corporate culture for a decade or so. At some point during the major corporate scandals that greeted the new millennium companies realized that corporate culture had to change. A new mindset that good ethics leads to good business started to take hold. Corporations began to review their performance in several areas: treatment of their employees, environmental impact, compliance with regulations. The code of conduct for Hershey Corporation is an excellent example of a comprehensive ethical statement. It provides a company *"commitment to operate ethically and to lead with integrity."*[18] This commitment is spread among five groups that the company interacts with: (1) fellow employees; (2) consumers: (3) the marketplace; (4) stockholders; and (5) the global community. The expectations and ethical standards for employees, from the CEO on down, among each group interaction is explained in the 44 page Hershey Code of Conduct. Not surprisingly, Hershey Corporation has been recognized as one of America's '100 Best Corporate Citizens.'[19]

Codes of conduct started to develop within corporate policy and procedure manuals in the early 2000s. Based on the private sector corporate model the public sector soon followed. A code of conduct establishes an ethical framework for the company and its employees. It is an expected standard of behavior, the violation of which can lead to discipline of an employee if not outright termination.[20] The Sarbanes-Oxley Act (SOX) required that publicly traded companies had to disclose in their annual reports whether or not they adopted a code of ethics *"that applies to the company's principal executive officer, principal financial officer, principal accounting officer or controller, or persons performing similar functions."*[21] If a company does not have a code of ethics for these financial officers it has to disclose this fact and explain why it has not adopted one. The Federal Acquisition Regulations (FAR) require government contractors to have a code of ethics in place within 30 days of the award of a government contract.[22] Additionally, the company must also have a business ethics awareness compliance program and internal control system in place within 90 days after the award.[23] Excluded from this latter requirement are small business concerns, identified as independently owned and operated companies that are not dominant in the field in which they are bidding and meet federal definitions of a small business. SOX and FAR are just two examples of the increased regulatory requirements placed on businesses to have an established code of ethics in place. The code of ethics, however, is more than a regulatory prerequisite for companies. Even if a company is not affected by the Sarbanes-Oxley Act,

---

[17] Georgetown University, Berkley Center, Ethics Resource Center, *Resources on Faith, Ethics and Public Life,* https://berkleycenter. georgetown.edu/organizations/ethics-resource-center

[18] https://www.thehersheycompany.com/content/dam/corporate-us/docments/investorscode-of-conduct.pdf

[19] http://www.businesswire.com/news/home/20130412005450/en/Hershey-Company-Recognized-America%E2%80%99s-%E2%80%98100-Corporate-Citizens%E2%80%99

[20] See e.g., *Parker v. Verizon PA., Inc.*, 309 Fed. Appx. 551 (3d Cir., 2008)

[21] https://www.sec.gov/rules/final/33-8177.htm

[22] 48 CFR 52.203-13

[23] Id.

Federal Acquisition Regulations or any other of a number of federal or state regulations mandating a code of ethics, having one in place is good business practice.

The ethical company communicates its core values to its employees and its third-party affiliates.[24] If company A operates ethically but it does business or uses the services of a third-party, company B, that does not, the negative attributes of company B may be held against company A potentially causing it a loss of business. Questions may also arise as to the actual ethics of company A if it is doing business with company B. This is the reason it is now imperative for companies to know the background and reputation of any third parties with whom they transact business. This recalls another lesson from childhood that is equally applicable in adulthood—you are judged by the people with whom you associate. The ethical company will hold third-party businesses equally accountable for their actions.[25]

Triple Bottom Line	Economic prosperity
	Environmental quality
	Social justice

It is also valuable for companies to communicate their ethical values directly to their clients. In certain industries, like financial services, this is vital since clients are relying on the provider's integrity, advice and trust.[26] But it is also important for the company to establish its "ethical brand" to consumers, clients, and the general business community. By doing so the company reinforces its ethical credos and their significance to the company's status as a good corporate citizen. This idea of being a good corporate citizen though has also grown to represent more than operating in an ethical manner, just as the consideration of what entails good ethics in business has grown. Business ethics now means more than not stealing clients' money or not falsely inflating company profit margins to attract investors. Broader social interests are involved in a company's ethical decision-making process. Today more companies are focused on what Sustainability co-founder John Elkington in 1994 referred to as the "triple-bottom line" of people, planet, and profit.[27] This business model entails operating with a bottom-line focus not only on economic prosperity or profit, but also on environmental quality and social justice. Good corporate citizenship is now measured in terms of corporate social responsibility (CSR). While profit is still important to a company's economic prosperity the single fact that the company is making money is no longer an isolated criterion. How did the company make its money? Were profits made at the expense of damage to the environment? Did the company do business with corporate polluters? Was slave labor in another country used somewhere in the supply-chain? Are employees subject to a work climate of harassment and intimidation? These are all questions that extend beyond financial performance as the sole indicator of corporate accountability. While corporate shareholders remain an important constituency companies are responsible to, other stakeholders, such as employees and community members, require that the corporation be equally accountable to them.

ISO26000: Seven Principles for an Organization's Socially Responsible Behavior

1) Accountability
2) Transparency
3) Ethical behavior
4) Respect for stakeholder interests
5) Respect for the rule of law
6) Respect for the international norms of behavior
7) Respect for human rights

---

[24] Bob Barker, The Avon Way: Creating and sustaining a culture of compliance, Corporate Counsel, https://www.law.com/insidecounsel/2014/11/18/the-avon-way-creating-and-sustaining-a-culture-of/ (last visited June 14, 2017)

[25] Id.

[26] Sherry Christie, Aiding and Abetting, The Investment Advisor, March 2, 2015, http://www.investmentadvisordigital.com/investmentadvisor/march_2015?pg=36#pg36 (last visited June 14, 2017)

[27] John Elkington, *Cannibals with Forks: The Triple Bottom-Line of 21st Century Business*, 311–13 (1998)

Corporate social responsibility is part of a corporation's *"initiative to assess and take responsibility for the company's effects on environmental and social well-being."*[28] It is a self-directed effort that is not reliant on regulatory directives or legal compliance, but instead on the company's overall goal of maximizing profit while remaining a good corporate citizen. The CSR model operates on the belief that profit and social and environmental responsibility are not mutually exclusive. Surveys indicate that a majority of modern consumers will not support a company that does not support social or environmental issues.[29] Since social responsibility is important to consumers, companies are more focused on their philanthropy, labor practices, community volunteering, and environmental impact.[30] The importance of CSR to a company's overall performance is reflected in the fact that in 2010 the International Organization for Standards established ISO26000 Guidance on Social Responsibility, a voluntary social responsibility standard for implementing a corporate social responsibility program.[31] The International Organization for Standards is an international

FIGURE 4.4   Ethical Decision-Making Process

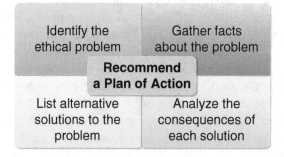

FIGURE 4.5   The Corporate Social Responsibility Model

---

[28] Investopedia, *Corporate Social Responsibility,* http://www.investopedia.com/terms/c/corp-social-responsibility.asp
[29] Cone Communications, Global CSR Study 2015, http://www.conecomm.com/2015-cone-communications-ebiquity-global-csr-study-pdf
[30] Jennifer Post, *What is Corporate Social Responsibility?,* Business News Daily, April 3, 2017, http://www.businessnewsdaily.com/4679-corporate-social-responsibility.html
[31] See, International Organization for Standards, https://www.iso.org/iso-26000-social-responsibility.html

CASE STUDY 4.3

On December 2, 2015 two terrorists killed 14 people and wounded 22 during a mass shooting incident in San Bernardino, California. The suspects were killed in a shootout with responding police officers. The law enforcement investigation that ensued in the aftermath of this tragic and deadly encounter between innocent victims and terrorist criminals involved the Federal Bureau of Investigation among many responding agencies. At the crime scene the cell phone of one of the suspects was recovered but because of encryption the FBI was unable to access the data on the phone. The FBI contacted the phone's manufacturer, Apple, Inc., for assistance in the decryption of the cell phone. Apple refused to assist in the decryption of the iPhone. This led to a legal and media war with Apple over the decryption of the dead suspect's phone. The FBI obtained a court order under the All Writs Act of 1789 in an attempt to compel Apple to assist in the decryption. Apple responded with a motion in opposition to the court order. Apple expressed concern that its customers would be exposed to potential security risks if it created a decryption method for the government to access the dead suspect's cell phone. In a public letter to customers Apple CEO Tim Cook explained the company's position which included protecting customers from privacy breaches, general threats to data security, and avoiding the company's involvement in a dangerous government precedent which sought to expand its powers.

Public opinion polls recorded a clear split with some slight support for the government position versus Apple's in the decryption controversy.

The FBI eventually withdrew its motion to compel Apple to decrypt the suspect's iPhone once it had unlocked the phone's data on its own.

The San Bernardino shooting was a horrific crime leading to loss of life and serious injury. In addition, the looming threat of other planned terrorist attacks and potential accomplices still at large created urgency to the law enforcement investigation. Apple, a major technology company, was quickly drawn into the investigation and took a stand which was unpopular among many Americans. However, the impact of Tim Cook's decision had the potential to extend beyond San Bernardino. As a multinational corporation Apple is in worldwide markets subject to different government regulations. One of the larger international consumer bases for Apple is China. The government of China is communist and has professed it will never be a democracy and follow Western government systems. It is a single party government that exercises widespread control over its population. The creation of decryption software by Apple could be sought by China for mass government surveillance of its residents. It could be used in any number of ways by government and nongovernment entities to access personal information and communications of users. This is part of the concern expressed by Cook in his letter: "Some would argue that building a backdoor for just one iPhone is a simple, clean-cut solution. But it ignores both the basics of digital security and the significance of what the government is demanding in this case . . . The government suggests this tool could only be used once, on one phone. But that's simply not true. Once created the technique could be used over and over again, on any number of devices."

What are the ethical issues that confronted Apple and its CEO Tim Cook?

Did Apple's stance fulfill an ethical duty to its customers while violating a broader ethical duty? Are the ethical duties separable or are they one in the same?

organization of 163 member countries, represented through their own national standards bodies, that uses a team of experts to establish voluntary industrial standards.[32] The representative body for the United States is the American National Standards Institute (ANSI). ISO26000 is built on seven principles of social responsibility, one of them being ethical behavior. Corporate social responsibility and business ethics are now inextricably combined.

IV. The Legal Implications of Ethical Standards in Business

Legal liability equates with responsibility for a harm caused by behavior on the part of the individual or entity charged with causing or creating the harm. Under civil law the evidentiary standard for a plaintiff to prove a defendant's liability is a preponderance of the evidence. In chapter 2 this standard was defined as evidence that weighs in favor of the plaintiff, however slight that may be, in the proof of a case. A failure of the evidence to preponderate in the plaintiff's favor yields a verdict for the defendant. Liability may be based on a contractual claim or on a theory of tort liability for either negligent conduct or intentional conduct that results in harm to the plaintiff. In our discussion of business ethics we have already explained the parameters for ethical conduct but we now focus on the potential legal pitfalls that are sure to result from unethical behavior. It is easy to identify an unethical act like theft and the resulting legal consequence. Steal someone's property and you are bound to not only be arrested as part of the criminal sanction sought by society (and the criminal justice system as the proxy for societal retribution), but you will also be subject to civil remedies sought by the victim resulting from the theft. Restitution as well as further monetary damages in the form of punitive damages and interest are all potential consequences for the thief. Some of the examples of corporate theft highlighted in section 1 above point to such results. However, you must remember that while not all laws are based on moral concepts, (like the example of speed limit laws in section 1 above), neither can all legal outcomes be considered to be ethical outcomes. Here is an example: a client comes to you as an attorney and tells you that he owes a friend $5,000.00 under the terms of a loan agreement executed over 6½ years ago but that he only paid $1,000.00 of it and had to stop payment when he ran into some financial trouble. The client tells you that his friend never filed a lawsuit but that the money still owed caused a break in their friendship and bad feelings among other acquaintances of his. Your client now has his life in order, a new job, and some extra money available. He is able to start payments on the loan but interest has been accruing at a rate of 6%. He asks you how to proceed since he also knows the statute of limitations for his friend to have sued him under the terms of the contractual loan agreement is six years. You tell your client that he should not re-pay the loan because he is no longer under a legal obligation. Any payments made by him would have the effect under state law of resurrecting the lapsed statute of limitations and subject him to liability for the balance of the loan should he not be able to make subsequent payments. Your client says he has the full $4,000.00 to pay his friend but he does not want to pay the interest on what he owes which is over $1,500.00. Your legal advice is still for your client not to pay the loan balance. Now your client tells you that he feels morally obligated to pay back the money. Here is where the split between a valid legal

---

[32] See, International Organization for Standards, https://www.iso.org/about-us.html

solution is in conflict with an ethical decision. There are three options you as the lawyer can give your client:

1. Do not make any payments on the loan because the statute of limitations has passed and your client no longer has any legal liability.
2. Negotiate with the friend to pay the $4,000.00 in a lump sum in full satisfaction of the loan with the friend waiving any interest due.
3. Pay back the full balance owed of $4,000.00 plus the accrued interest of over $1,500.00.

Which of these would you as the lawyer urge your client to follow? Which of these is the more correct ethical choice? Does the friend bear any responsibility in terms of ethical choices in not more vigorously pursuing his money from your client?

This scenario is one that can be argued from a few different perspectives and one which will likely elicit some varied responses. Yet, it is instructive for exhibiting that not all ethical issues are easily divided into a clear good choice over a bad choice. The above scenario could have just as easily involved two corporations and a dispute over payments on goods received. Should the nonpaying corporation pay out on a debt that is no longer a legally viable obligation just out of a sense of fair play? Has the corporation that neglected to timely pursue the money owed to it violated its ethical duty to its shareholders and its employees? Legal, moral, and philosophical arguments aside, the bottom line is that liability is implicated from an ethical choice—whether it is the corporate loan-promisee who can be sued within the applicable statute of limitations for the money owed, or the corporate loan-promissor who may be liable to shareholders for failure to secure a timely claim against the loan-promisee. Actions and choices have consequences and in the context of ethical decision-making this is no less true.

Section 1 explained how the Sarbanes-Oxely Act of 2002 resulted from the corporate scandals that preceded passage of the Act. Historically the government has responded to corporate malfeasance in the form of regulatory legislation intended to police business behavior. The Sherman Antitrust Act of 1890[33] was passed so as to open up competition within business industries and end monopolistic control by small groups of businessmen. The passage of the Antitrust Act coincided with a period of industrial growth within the United States and the rise of unscrupulous businessman whose practices earned them the pejorative nickname of "Robber Barons." Subsequent revisions of the Sherman Act—including the Clayton Antitrust Act of 1914, the Robinson-Patman Act of 1936, and the Celler-Kefauver Act of 1950—responded to loopholes in the original. The Securities and Exchange Act of 1934 regulating security transactions on the secondary market resulted from the belief that unscrupulous and irresponsible financial practices led to the 1929 stock market crash. The U.S. Supreme Court has long held that the Securities and Exchange Act of 1934 was intended to "*substitute a philosophy of full disclosure for the philosophy of caveat emptor, and thus to achieve a high standard of business ethics in the securities industry.*"[34]

Business scandal from the 1970s involving U.S. businessmen paying bribes and other illegal payment to politicians and foreign government officials in order to be granted favorable trade contracts led to the passage by Congress of the Foreign Corrupt Practices Act of 1977 (FCPA).[35] The FCPA criminalizes these payments by U.S. corporations and their representatives. The Dodd-Frank Wall Street Reform and Consumer Protection Act of 2010 (Dodd-Frank Act) was the product of the

---

[33] 15 USC § 1-7
[34] *Affiliated Ute Citizens of Utah v. United States*, 406 U.S. 128, 151 (1972)
[35] 15 USC § 78dd-1, et seq.

financial crisis of 2008 that saw worldwide markets crash to a level not witnessed since the Great Depression. In the United States a key contributor was the sub-prime mortgage lending bubble and the ensuing banking crisis. Much of this was fueled by questionable lending and investment practices by some of the most well-known and respected financial firms in the world. This was an ethical business failure once again captured by Hollywood in *The Big Short,* based on the Michael Lewis book. The Dodd-Frank Act required greater accountability and transparency among financial firms, improved investor protections, more government regulation of the banking and finance industry, and expansion of whistleblower protections under the Sarbanes-Oxley Act.

Aside from major business scandals and the regulating legislation ensuing from it, a company's failure to adhere to an ethical standard and maintain a corporate compliance program can impact the outcome in lawsuits against the company. Whether or not the company followed recognized standards of business ethics can be a pertinent factor in a jury's determination of liability in certain cases.[36] It can be a factor in the awarding of government contracts and subsequent judicial review of those contracts.[37] The presence of a compliance program and a code of ethics can also be a factor in criminal sentencing decisions upon corporate defendants. The 1991 Organizational Sentencing Guidelines[38] to the Sentencing Reform Act of 1984[39] set forth a structure for the sentencing of organizations found in violation of federal law. These guidelines, as one court noted, "*offer powerful incentives for corporations today to have in place compliance programs to detect violations of law, promptly to report violations to appropriate public officials when discovered, and to take prompt, voluntary remedial efforts.*"[40]

Different state courts over the years have recognized a continuing development of modern business ethics and applied it to contractual interpretation.[41] These judicial interpretations have moved away from the strict limitations of caveat emptor and due diligence placed upon a contracting party to one of disclosure when good faith and fair dealing require it.[42] This is similar to the U.S. Supreme Court's holding regarding the Securities and Exchange Act of 1934, thus reflecting the evolving nature of ethical behavior in transactional business relationships. However, one of the more devastating claims that can be lodged against a modern corporation is that it violated its larger ethical obligation as a responsible corporate citizen. The impact in terms of overall liability can be significant. A case on point is *Blanks v. Fluor Corporation* which resulted in a $38 million overall compensatory damages award and a $42 million and $32 million punitive damages award against two corporate defendants.[43] The case involved 16 plaintiffs who, as children from 1986 to 1994, were subjected to lead exposure from a corporate partnership's lead smelter in their town. The Missouri Court of Appeals decision noted that the plaintiffs' attorneys framed the case as "*the age-old conflict of business profits versus human safety.*"[44] Allegations of the children and their parents centered on the claim that the partnership between three companies unified in the ownership and operation of the nearby lead smelter was negligent by exposing them to lead in the air, the streets, and in their homes. At the trial one of the

---

[36] See e.g., Tube City IMS, LLC v. Severstal US Holdings U, LLC, 2014 U.S. Dist. LEXIS 124629 (N.D., WV, 2014)

[37] See e.g., Federal Acquisition Regulations, Part 3, Section 3.10, available at https://www.acquisition.gov/far/html/Subpart%203_10.html

[38] See, United States Sentencing Commission, Guidelines Manuel, Chapter 8 (U.S. Government Printing Office November 1994).

[39] See, Sentencing Reform Act of 1984, Pub.L. 98-473, Title II, § 212 (a)(2) (1984); 18 USCA §§ 3331-4120.

[40] See, *In re Caremark International*, 698 A.2d 952, 969 (Del. Ch. Ct., 1996)

[41] See e.g., *Molokoa Village Dev. Co. v. Kauai Elec. Co.*, 60 Haw. 582; 593 P.2d 375 (1979); *Quashnock v. Frost*, 299 Pa. Super. 9; 445 A.2d 121 (1982); *Richey v. Patrick*, 904 P.2d 798 (1995); *Lerner v. DMB Realty, LLC*, 234 Ariz. 397; 322 P.3d 909 (2014)

[42] See, *Lerner* at 405.

[43] 450 S.W. 3d 308 (MO Ct App., 2014)

[44] Id at 323.

experts for the plaintiffs testified about business ethics and responsibility. The expert testimony emphasized that the company was focused on profit and misled the community about the danger and exposure to lead while trying to appear as "a good corporate citizen."[45] The ethical expert's testimony at trial also explained how the company should have acted if it was actually operating for the community's best interests.[46] The Missouri Court of Appeals upheld the punitive damages award against two of the three companies that formed the partnership and in doing so cited their actions as reprehensible. One of these companies A.T. Massey Coal Company, who was liable for $42 million in punitive damages, was renamed Massey Energy Company in 2000 and was a named defendant in the next case. Here there was a different allegation of corporate malfeasance but one which eventually led to a similar result of liability against the corporation. The issue the court first had to address was whether the plaintiffs' allegations could withstand Massey Energy's motion to dismiss.

❖❖

In re Massey Energy Co. Securities Litigation
883 F.Supp.2d 597 (S.D.,WV, 2012)

Irene C. Berger, District Judge.

Lead Plaintiff, Commonwealth of Massachusetts Pension Reserves Investment Trust ("Massachusetts PRIT") and Plaintiff David Wagner, on behalf of the putative class, allege that the price of Massey Energy Company ("Massey") stock was artificially inflated, between February 1, 2008, and July 27, 2010, because Massey and several of its senior executives and directors misled the market about its safety and compliance record and its disregard for safety regulatory compliance. The Defendants move for dismissal of Plaintiffs' Consolidated Amended Class Action Complaint for Violations of the Federal Securities Laws ("CAC"). The Joint Motion to Dismiss is supported by the Declaration of Julie A. North and various exhibits regarding "screenshots" of webpages from the United States Mine Safety and Health Administration's ("MSHA") website. Plaintiffs move to strike these exhibits. After careful review of the motions and appropriate submissions relative thereto and for the reasons that follow, the Court grants the Plaintiffs' motion to strike and denies the Defendants' motions to dismiss.

***

This civil action, filed on April 29, 2010, arises out of the alleged securities fraud committed by Massey and several of its officers and directors. Massey, a Delaware Corporation with its headquarters in Richmond, Virginia, is the fourth largest coal producer in the United States and the largest coal producer in the regions of West Virginia, Kentucky and Virginia. Massey produces, processes and sells bituminous coal. On January 31, 2010, through its operating subsidiary A.T. Massey, Massey operated fifty-six (56) mines (forty-two (42) underground mines and fourteen (14) surface mines) and twenty-three (23) processing and shipping centers. The company is a publicly owned corporation traded on the New York Stock Exchange.

***

Lead Plaintiff, Massachusetts PRIT, a pooled investment fund with more than $41 billion in total assets under management, including assets managed for the benefit of the Massachusetts State Teachers' and Employees' Retirement Systems and participating county, authority, district and municipal retirement systems, and David Wagner purchased Massey common stock on the open

---

[45] Id at 391.
[46] Id at 357.

market between February 1, 2008, and July 27, 2010. Plaintiffs filed this suit as a class action under Federal Rules of Civil Procedure 23(a) and (b)(3), to represent a class of those who purchased common stock from Massey during the class period and who were damaged as a result. The Court has reviewed the entirety of the one hundred seventy (170) page CAC, but will only briefly detail the facts giving rise to this litigation, viewing them as true, as the Court must in its consideration of the pending Rule 12(b)(6) motions to dismiss.

On January 19, 2006, a fire claimed the lives of two miners at Alma No. 1 mine in West Virginia. At the time, Alma No. 1 mine was operated by Massey subsidiary Aracoma Coal Company. As a result, investigations were conducted by MSHA and the FBI. Plaintiffs aver that the miners died of "carbon monoxide poisoning because monitors were improperly installed and a permanent ventilation control was removed from an emergency escape passage." Following criminal and civil litigation, which included a derivative shareholder action, Massey pled guilty to ten criminal charges and entered into a $4.2 million settlement ($2.5 million in criminal penalties and $1.7 million in civil penalties). The settlement required, among other things, "changes to the corporation's governance policies and procedures relating to director oversight and conduct regarding environmental compliance and mine worker safety"; the Safety, Environmental and Public Policy Committee's ("SEPPC") development of "goals for implementing enhancements to the Company-wide process utilized to monitor, count and report mine safety incidents and complaints (a "mine safety incident" is a lost-time injury suffered in connection with the Company's mining activities) and near misses with high potential for injury"; reports by the Safety, Environmental and Public Policy Committee ("SEPPC") to the Board of Directors "regarding the Company's compliance with all applicable mine safety laws and regulations[,]" including "(a) the number of mine safety incidents overall and by type (b) findings by third-party auditors, and (c) an analysis of any causal factors contributing to safety incidents"; enhancements to the safety and environmental procedures and reporting, including shareholder reporting; and annual shareholder reporting from the Board in its Corporate Social Responsibility reporting "environmental and worker safety compliance."

Following the 2006 miner deaths and the litigation that followed, Defendant Massey sought to restore the Company's reputation and image by announcing that it had a strong company commitment to the safety of its miners and that it had begun "safety improvement initiatives." Massey began to focus on building investor confidence and goodwill with regulators by stating its commitment to safety and affirming that its organization put the safety of its miners before its production, in its SEC quarterly and annual filings, press releases, and investor presentations. For instance, in its 2007 Annual Report, Massey declared that "a safe mine is a productive mine" and explained its "formula for success [as] S-1 + P-2 + M-3 = shareholder value." The Annual Report detailed the meaning of the equation as "safety first, production second and measurement third."

In a 2008 press release, Massey emphasized that "safety first" was "not just a slogan" in its organization and, in its 2009 Corporate Social Responsibility Report, stated that "no coal company can succeed over the long term without a total commitment to safety." Throughout the class period, Massey affirmed and restated its commitment to safety and reported to investors that a key safety measurement rate, the NFDL rate (Non-Fatal, Days Lost), was decreasing year after year for the company. In 2007 through 2010, Massey and its Directors signed SEC filings and made statements in various press releases and presentations to investors that indicated that it had a commitment to safety, that safety of its miners and the successfulness of its company were linked and that it was leading the industry in safety performance.

***

However, on April 5, 2010, twenty-nine (29) miners died in an explosion and fire at Massey's Upper Big Branch Mine ("UBBM") at Montcoal in Raleigh County, West Virginia. The explosion, one of the deadliest United States coal mining accidents in forty years, led to various news reports regarding Massey's safety violations and investigations. Plaintiffs aver that according to MSHA, the cause of the explosion largely involved basic mine safety practices that were not adhered to; namely, inadequate water sprays, dull cutting bits, and extraordinary levels of float coal dust due to inadequate rock dusting. Plaintiffs further aver that the investigations into the explosion and Massey revealed that despite Massey's public statements that it was an "industry leader in safety" and that production was secondary to safety, Massey, with the acquiescence of the Board of Directors, had continued to make production a priority over safety.

MSHA began to release data that showed the number and severity of violations at the UBBM increased drastically in 2009 and 2010 as production increased.

***

Contrary to Massey's asserted claims of safety, during the class period, Massey: (1) had the worst fatality rate in the nation (fifty-four (54) deaths, which includes twenty-three fatalities before the UBBM explosion, and two since); (2) performed worse than the national average when defined by MSHA issued S & S citations, at its large mines, with at least 100 employees and (3) performed worse than the national average in terms of elevated enforcement actions. Plaintiffs allege that these violations at UBBM and other Massey mines were "red flags" to the Company about their safety compliance. However, they were ignored when measuring and reporting Massey's safety performance to investors during the class period.

After the tragic UBBM explosion on April 5, 2010, investors began to learn the truth about "Massey's duplicitous and deceptive schemes." Several current and former Massey miners began to offer insight regarding the Company's commitment to production over safety.

***

In their CAC, Plaintiffs assert claims for securities fraud based on the "fraud on the market" theory of reliance. Plaintiffs contend that the price of Massey common stock was inflated by their false and misleading statements and omissions about the safety of, and risks to, its mining operations.

***

Plaintiffs further allege that Massey and its Directors were positioned to receive reports and other information about its compliance record and MSHA violations, but either ignored the reports or recklessly disregarded the reports in their pursuit to increase coal production. In light of the foregoing, Plaintiffs allege that Massey's stock price was artificially inflated by Massey's fraud and they suffered economic loss as a result.

***

Plaintiffs assert two causes of action: (1) a claim under Section 10(b) of the Securities Exchange Act of 1934 and Rule 10b-5 of the Securities and Exchange Commission, against the Defendants collectively, and (2) a claim under Section 20(a) of the Act, against Officer Defendants Blankenship, Phillips, Tolbert and Adkins. Defendants argue that Plaintiffs have filed a consolidated amended class action complaint that is void of any substantive facts to support a claim under Section 10(b) and Rule 10b-5, and because the cause of action in count one is deficient, Plaintiffs' second claim is also fatally flawed.

A. SECTION 10(B)

Section 10(b) of the Securities Exchange Act of 1934 makes it unlawful for any person, directly or indirectly "[t]o use or employ, in connection with the purchase or sale of any security . . . , [of] any manipulative or deceptive device or contrivance in contravention of such rules and regulations as the [SEC] may prescribe as necessary or appropriate in the public interest or for the protection of investors." The implementing regulation, SEC Rule 10b-5, declares it unlawful:

(a) To employ any device, scheme, or artifice to defraud, (b) To make any untrue statement of a material fact or to omit to state a material fact necessary in order to make the statements made, in the light of the circumstances under which they were made, not misleading, or (c) To engage in any act, practice, or course of business which operates or would operate as a fraud or deceit upon any person, in connection with the purchase or sale of any security. 17 C.F.R. § 240.10b-5 . . . The elements of a private securities fraud claim, based on violations of § 10(b) and Rule 10b-5, are: "(1) a material misrepresentation or omission by the defendant; (2) scienter; (3) a connection between the misrepresentation or omission and the purchase or sale of a security; (4) reliance upon the misrepresentation or omission; (5) economic loss; and (6) loss causation.'"

Collectively, Defendants argue that Plaintiffs have filed a 165-page pleading that is void of any substantive facts to support a claim under Section 10(b) and Rule 10b-5 and assert that Plaintiffs' CAC fails as a matter of law for the following reasons: (1) The alleged misleading statements made by the Company about its safety compliance record, even if presumed to be true, lacked the requisite specificity to perpetrate a fraud on the market, given that accurate information about the Company's safety compliance record was available to the market throughout the class period on the MSHA website; (2) Plaintiffs have failed to plead scienter adequately; (3) Plaintiffs are not entitled to the presumption of reliance; and (4) Plaintiffs have failed to state a coherent theory of loss causation. The Court will consider each of these challenges.

(1) A MATERIAL MISREPRESENTATION OR OMISSION BY THE DEFENDANT

Plaintiffs, in forty-seven (47) pages of their CAC, allege statements made by Massey and Defendant Directors which they contend are "materially false and misleading statements and omissions regarding Massey's regulatory compliance, the safety of its operations, its costs of production, and the ability to maintain or increase the rate of metallurgical coal production at the Company." To summarize Plaintiffs' allegations . . . First, Plaintiffs allege that Defendants consistently made false and misleading statements regarding Massey's nonfatal days lost (NFDL rate) beginning on February 1, 2008, the first day of the class period, through March 24, 2010. Second, Plaintiffs allege that during the class period, Defendants made various false and misleading statements professing Massey's commitment to and focus on safety . . . Third, Plaintiffs allege, notwithstanding Defendants' identification of "risk factors" in its Annual SEC 10-K reporting, its statement that "violations during mining operations occur from time to time" and that Massey's costs and liabilities were impacted by "increasingly strict federal, state, and local environment, health and safety and endangered species laws, regulations and enforcement policies" were misleading given the frequency with which Defendants violated mining regulations. Plaintiffs allege that these categories of statements occurred throughout the entire class period and had an immediate impact on stock pricing.

As a threshold matter, the Court finds that Plaintiffs, in their CAC, adequately identify statements alleged to have been misleading or false. After each such statement, Plaintiffs assert the reason or reasons why the statement is misleading, and then allege a basis to support the materiality of the alleged fact.

(2) SCIENTER

With respect to the second element of a Section 10(b) claim, Defendants assert that Plaintiffs have failed to plead facts sufficient to support a strong inference that any of the Defendants acted with the intent to defraud. A plaintiff seeking to establish liability under Section 10(b) and Rule 10b-5 must allege a defendant "acted with scienter, 'a mental state embracing intent to deceive, manipulate, or defraud.'"

***

The Court finds Defendants' assertions inadequate to persuade the Court that Plaintiffs did not plead particular facts giving rise to the strong inference that Massey and the Director Defendants engaged in conduct with the intent to deceive.

The alleged facts in this case indicate Defendants made frequent statements regarding Massey's commitment to safety and detailed the Company's accomplishments of their safety goals through the use of the NFDL incident rate. The individual directors consistently signed various SEC filings and/or made direct statements to investors during presentations or in press releases applauding the company for its achievement of a lower than national average NFDL rate in 2007–2009 or applauding its use of new safety programs. The NFDL was the sole safety measurement metric used by the company to explain its commitment to safety and its safety success.

The Court's finding is further bolstered by Plaintiffs' allegations that miners made statements indicating Massey engaged in practices that risked the lives of miners (cutting coal into air supply or failing to provide proper mine ventilation), evaded regulatory violation detection (early warning notification system) and regulatory reporting (encouraging injured miners to work in a light duty capacity). Notwithstanding Defendants' assertions that Plaintiffs failed to plead their knowledge of these practices, the Court finds that the frequency in which the NFDL incident rate was used by the Defendants and the manner in which Defendants disseminated this rate to the public supports the "stronger" inference that this metric, which did not measure a company's compliance with safety regulations, was used to defraud the public.

(3) JUSTIFIABLE RELIANCE

Section 10(b) claims require a plaintiff to have relied upon the defendant's deceptive acts. A review of the CAC in this case reveals that Plaintiffs have asserted allegations sufficient to satisfy their invocation of the presumption of reliance. The Court has previously found that Plaintiffs adequately pled that Defendants made various alleged misleading statements or misrepresentations in their communications with the market via SEC filings, press releases, presentations at investor conferences, and conference calls with investors.

***

In light of the foregoing, the Court finds that Plaintiffs' pleading is sufficient to invoke the presumption of reliance on the market, in the context of their "fraud on the market theory."

(4) LOSS CAUSATION

The pleading practice, in this Circuit, requires that a plaintiff, as a precursor to proof, allege loss causation in the complaint, "with sufficient specificity to enable the court to evaluate whether the necessary causal link exists" between the defendant's alleged fraud and the plaintiff's economic harm.

***

The Court finds that Plaintiffs have appropriately pled allegations sufficient to support loss causation . . . In this case, the allegations, accepted by the Court as true, indicate that prior to the tragic UBBM explosion, Defendants did not directly disclose any facts to investors about its safety and compliance record with the exclusion of the lone safety metric of the NFDL. After the April 5, 2010 explosion at the UBBM, MSHA and various media outlets began to release data about the nature of violations cited at UBBM and other Massey mines. This data included the number of violations Massey had amassed in recent years, including at UBBM, and the extent of those violations, which included citations for ventilation and air quality of the mines . . . Therefore, the explosion and the cause of the explosion revealed to the market the fraudulent nature of which Plaintiffs complain, specifically, that Defendants mislead the market about the safety at its mines and its commitment to put production over safety. Therefore, the Court finds that Plaintiffs have sufficiently alleged particular facts supporting an allegation that its losses were caused by Massey's misleading and false statements about the safety of its mines.

B. SECTION 20(A)

Plaintiffs, in their second count, assert a claim under Section 20(a) of the Securities and Exchange Act of 1934 against the Officer Defendants by contending that the Officer Defendants by virtue of their positions, stock ownership, and actions were controlling persons of Massey who "had the power to, and did, directly and indirectly, exercise control over Massey, including the content and dissemination of statements that Plaintiffs' allege are false and misleading." Plaintiffs allege that these Defendants "were provided with and/or had access to reports, filings, press releases and other statements alleged to be misleading prior to and/or shortly after they were issued and had the ability to prevent the issuance or correct the statements" and had an "awareness of the Company's operations and/or intimate knowledge of the false financial statements filed by the Company with the SEC and disseminated to the investing public." Plaintiffs allege these Defendants had the power to influence and control the decision-making of Massey, and did so, including the dissemination of the various statements alleged to be false and misleading. Pursuant to Section 20(a) of the Securities Exchange Act of 1934:

> *Every person who, directly or indirectly, controls any person liable under any provision of this chapter or of any rule or regulation thereunder shall also be liable jointly and severally with and to the same extent as such controlled person to any person to whom such controlled person is liable . . . unless the controlling person acted in good faith and did not directly or indirectly induce the act or acts constituting the violation or cause of action.*

. . . the Court finds that Plaintiffs' Section 20(a) claims survive the instant motions to dismiss.

V.

In conclusion, for the reasons stated herein, the Court does hereby ORDER that Don L. Blankenship, Baxter F. Phillips, Jr., Eric B. Tolbert and Christopher Adkins' Motion to Dismiss Plaintiffs' Consolidated Amended Class Action Complaint (Document 94) and the Joint Motion of Massey Energy Company and the Outside Director Defendants to Dismiss the Consolidated Amended Class Action Complaint (Document 96) be DENIED.

The Court DIRECTS the Clerk to send a copy of this Order to counsel of record and to any unrepresented party.

Questions Presented

1) What is the basis of the plaintiff's theory of recovery for share losses?
2) What were the alleged ethical breaches committed by Massey Energy Company?
3) What elements of the corporate social responsibility metric would Massey Energy Company be viewed as failing under the presented facts of the case?
4) What do the plaintiffs have to prove under section 10(b) of the Securities and Exchange Act in order to establish liability against Massey Energy Company for securities fraud?

❖❖

The Upper Big Branch Mine disaster that killed 29 miners resulted in the governor of West Virginia establishing an independent investigative panel. A report issued by the investigative panel pointed to a corporate culture that was complicit in the disaster's occurrence.[47] In a separate report chapter titled *"The normalization of deviance"* the investigative panel listed and explained each of the company failures that led to the tragic explosion. A patently clear maximization of profit over worker safety was part of the corporate culture precipitating the disaster. The lack of social responsibility exhibited by Massey failed to put people first as part of the "triple bottom-line" equation. An investigative report issued by the federal Mine Safety and Health Administration found similar root causes of the explosion in the deviant corporate culture of Massey Energy.[48]

Failed corporate culture and poor ethical judgment was also responsible for Massey Energy being cited by the Environmental Protection Agency for Clean Water Act violations in 2008. The deposit of coal slurry and wastewater into Kentucky and West Virginia waterways resulted in the company settling with the EPA and paying $20 million in civil fines.[49] Once again, in terms of triple bottom-line assessment of good corporate citizenship, the quest for profits was undermined by an inability to promote an ethical corporate culture wherein environmental impact and community interests were viewed co-equally with economic gain.

SUMMARY

Ethical conduct on the part of a company is integral to its existence as a valued corporate citizen. Corporate scandals of the 20th and 21st centuries have led to major legislative reforms in an attempt to police and regulate corporate malfeasance. As a result corporate consciousness has been raised to the point where major corporations are now embracing their role as good corporate citizens and realizing that economic benefits are tied to more than austere accounting calculations of profit and loss. The corporate social responsibility model, which places importance on the company's role in the community, its treatment of employees, and its impact on the environment,

---

[47] J. Davitt McAteer, *Upper Big Branch: The April 5, 2010 explosion: A failure of basic coal mining safety practices*, Report to the Governor, Governor's Independent Investigative Panel, May 2011.

[48] United States Department of Labor, Mine Safety and Health Administration, https://arlweb.msha.gov/Fatals/2010/UBB/UBBSummary.pdf, December 6, 2011, (last visited June 15, 2017.)

[49] United States Environmental Protection Agency, Massey Energy to Pay Largest Civil Penalty Ever for Water Permit Violations, https://yosemite.epa.gov/opa/admpress.nsf/0/6944ea38b888dd03852573d3005074ba?OpenDocument, January 17, 2008, (last visited June 15, 2017.)

has changed corporate culture for the better. Many companies now look at the triple bottom-line of their economic impact, environmental impact, and the impact on social justice. Studies have found that a large majority of consumers will not support a company that does not meet important ethical goals of sustainability and social justice. Bad ethics have simply become bad for business.

Business ethics as an academic field within professional business programs is still relatively young but it has grown in importance over the last 40 years. The study and understanding of ethical conduct and moral philosophy is fundamental for establishing a proper framework for a corporate ethical model. The field of moral philosophy is divided among three schools of thought: metaethics, normative ethics, and applied ethics. Metaethics studies what it means to be morally good, normative ethics studies whether a particular action is proper and applied ethics seeks how to implement the ethical act and put it into practice.

The ethical company realizes that its profits are not only tied to honest, good services and reputation but that to operate under a corporate culture that does not espouse these values has long term costs. Legal liability and adverse actions against corporate malfeasance has cost many companies millions and billions of dollars in fines and civil damages awards for unethical conduct. Loss of reputation has also resulted in some companies being unable to recover their prior status within an industry due to the negative effects of their corporate malfeasance.

CHAPTER

5

ADMINISTRATIVE LAW

LEARNING OUTCOMES

Upon completion of this chapter the student will be able to:

1 Identify the difference between administrative agency adjudications and civil court adjudications.
2 Explain the powers of administrative agencies and their rulemaking powers.
3 Explain the difference between executive agencies and independent agencies.
4 Discuss the Administrative Procedure Act and its requirements.
5 Explain the exhaustion of administrative remedies rule and the judicial deference rule.

KEY TERMS

Administrative Procedure Act
arbitrary and capricious
delegation of powers
executive agency
exhaustion of remedies
fourth branch of government
independent agency

judicial deference
just cause
mandamus
nondelegation doctrine
rulemaking power
scope of review
substantial evidence review

I. Introduction to Administrative Law

Administrative law is that body of law covering a diverse area of rules, regulations and practice procedures involving different types of federal and state government agencies. Different agencies of the government are created, either by Congress or state legislatures, in order to achieve some government goal. These agencies in turn have the authority to administer the regulations created by the legislature and they have rulemaking power of their own. There are over 100 administrative agencies at the federal level tasked with oversight in diverse areas of our lives. Many aspects of our lives are in some way regulated by federal administrative agencies. Whether it is the regulation of foods and drugs, health care, the environment, workplace safety, or social security benefits, the impact of federal administrative agencies upon us cannot be overlooked. Even at the state level we are impacted by state, county and local administrative agencies that dictate some key aspects of our lives. State departments of motor vehicles administer driving license privileges and motor vehicle registrations and local municipal zoning boards oversee permits and approvals for the use of real property. If you are denied a license to drive or have it suspended your initial recourse is through the Department of Motor Vehicle's administrative adjudicative process. The same process occurs if you are denied a certificate of occupancy for an expansion to your home, a direct appeal is first made to the local zoning board. These are two examples of isolated agency actions in the vast realm of administrative law. The impact of administrative law on our laws and the extensive government regulation in so many areas has led to the description of our government as being an administrative state. Whether or not there is too much government regulation overall or not enough government regulation in some areas has been a subject of political debate in the past, in the present, and will continue on into the future. However, this will not be the focus of the discussion herein, instead we will explore this vast and unique area of law and come to understand its significance to business operations.

There is not a company operating in the United States that is untouched by some form of government regulation. It is vital that business people understand the workings of the different administrative agencies that may regulate their industry and how to challenge agency determinations that may adversely affect their business. For the purpose of simplicity we are going to focus our discussion on federal administrative law and the Administrative Procedure Act (APA), but it should be understood that each state has its own legislation mirroring the federal APA and that there are state agency counterparts to some federal agencies. For instance, even though the federal Occupational Safety and Health Administration (OSHA) administers and enforces workplace safety regulations many states have similar agencies that enforce health and safety standards promulgated under OSHA. An example is New York's Public Employee Safety and Health Bureau (PESH) that enforces public employee health and safety standards under OSHA regulations.

A. Administrative Agencies and their Creation

There are two types of federal administrative agencies, those that are independent agencies and those that are executive agencies. Both Congress and the president have authority to create agencies and provide them with limited powers to carry out their ascribed function. The president has control over executive agencies whose agency leaders serve at the will of the president. The leaders of executive agencies can be removed by the president at any time. Independent agency leaders can only be removed by the president for just cause. Both types of agencies are governed by the federal Administrative Procedure Act, found at 5 U.S.C. 551 et seq.. Section 551(1) of the A.P.A. defines an "agency" as "each authority of the government of the United States whether or not it is within or subject to review by another agency." The A.P.A. explains the process by which administrative agencies are to create and enact their rules and regulations. A failure of an agency to follow this process is one way in which challenges are made to agency rules and regulations.

EXECUTIVE AGENCIES	
Department of Agriculture	Department of the Interior
Department of Commerce	Department of Justice
Department of Defense	Department of Labor
Department of Education	Department of State
Department of Energy	Department of Transportation
Department of Health & Human Services	Department of the Treasury
Department of Housing & Urban Development	Department of Veterans Affairs

An example of a federal executive agency is the Department of Commerce and the leader of the agency appointed by the president is referred to as the Secretary of Commerce. Other examples of federal executive agencies are the Department of Justice, the Department of Labor, and the Department of State. Each of these agency heads, the respective Secretaries of their departments, are cabinet members and assist the president in carrying out the functions of the Executive branch of government. Authority for the president to appoint these executive agency heads does not come from any specific grant of authority but it is an inferred power from Article II, clause 2 of the U.S. Constitution which states that the president may *"require the Opinion, in writing, of the principal Officer in each of the executive Departments, upon any Subject relating to the Duties of their respective Offices."* There are 14 executive department agencies that make up the Cabinet of the Executive branch. The independent federal agencies are those that administer the law within certain designated areas of federal control, such as the environment, small business, Social Security, national security, and consumer protection. The heads of these agencies are not cabinet-level appointments by the president and can only be removed for just cause. The just cause requirement is an employment law standard of reasonableness in the discipline or termination of an employee for misconduct (covered in Chapter 13 Employment Law). This is the same standard required for presidential removal of an independent agency head. Because there were no constitutional provisions for the creation of these agencies they are considered to be extensions of the government by Congress through the "necessary and proper clause" of Article I, section 8 of the Constitution. These different independent agencies are either regulatory in nature, tasked with overseeing different aspects of the national economy, or they are tasked with the administration of special services. Special services may be for the government, as in the General Services Administration which assists with the functioning of other federal agencies by operating and maintaining all government buildings, property and equipment, or they may be for the general population, as with the services provided by the National Foundation of the Arts and Humanities which fosters the development of the arts in the United States. The number of independent agencies far outnumber the executive agencies and their rules and regulations have the force and effect of law. These agencies act as an extension of the federal government and exist in areas where Congress has determined that the regulation is too complex for legislation. Through their delegated powers the administrative agencies act as an arm of the legislative and executive branches. These independent agencies become the acknowledged experts within their respective fields. The creation and subsequent influence of these agencies in government have led to them being referred to as "the Fourth branch" of government.

B. The History of Administrative Law in the United States

The first independent administrative agency created in the United States was the Interstate Commerce Commission in 1887 in an initial effort to regulate railroad fairs.[1] The mission of the ICC was subsequently expanded to include trucking, interstate busing, and telephone companies. The ICC was abolished in 1995 and replaced with the Surface Transportation Board. The original executive agencies were the cabinet departments of the Navy, State, Treasury, and War. As the country grew so too grew the administrative "branch" of the government. Industrialization, technological innovations, and commercial expansion were important catalysts for Congress' need to regulate in significant economic related sectors. A significant increase in industrial growth from 1868 to the early 1900s, accompanied by an increasing immigrant population and concentration of labor in

---

[1] Richard J. McKinney, *Federal Administrative Law: A Brief Overview*, Law Librarians' Society of Washington DC, available at www.llsdc.org/federal-admnistrative-law-a-brief-overview, retrieved June 18, 2017.

major city centers, was the background for the creation of a number of independent regulatory commissions. The Civil Service Commission was re-funded after the passage of the Pendleton Civil Service Reform Act of 1883 established a merit system for government employment. The Food and Drug Administration was created in 1906 to regulate food and drugs sales, and the Federal Trade Commission was created in 1914 to regulate monopolies in response to the Clayton Antitrust Act. But the biggest increase in the size of the regulatory section of government came during the early administration of President Franklin D. Roosevelt. Overall the size of the administrative branch has increased from a mere 1000 federal employees in 1790, to over 2,840,000 employees spread across 15 government departments, 69 agencies and 383 nonmilitary sub-agencies.[2] The federal government employee population grew three-fold in the 12 years from 1789 to 1801 marked as the Federal period. This was the time when the Federalist political party was in control of the government and the federal government was expanded under the newly ratified Constitution. The Federalist period ended in 1801 with the election loss of incumbent John Adams to his vice president, Thomas Jefferson. Government bureaucratic growth continued at an aggressive rate, particularly through the Progressive Period from 1890 to 1920. The Progressive Period was defined as a time of tremendous social and government reform. Even though the period is denoted as ending in 1920 the policies of the progressives were carried forward in the presidential administrations of Calvin Coolidge and Herbert Hoover. As a result the period was also viewed as setting up the subsequent New Deal legislation of the Roosevelt administration and its creation of numerous regulatory agencies in an effort to boost economic growth. Social reform was a major impetus behind the creation of several administrative agencies during the Progressive Period and this same impetus was behind much of the early New Deal legislation in the first 100 days of Roosevelt's first administration following the Great Depression. Derisively referred to as "the alphabet agencies," there were

> **INCREASE IN FEDERAL BUREAUCRACY FROM THE FEDERAL PERIOD TO THE PROGRESSIVE PERIOD**
>
> 1801 – 3,000 EMPLOYEES
>
> 1881 – 95,000 EMPLOYEES
>
> 1925 – 500,000 EMPLOYEES
>
> **Source:** *The Rise of the Bureaucratic State,* James Q. Wilson (1975)

37 agencies created from 1933 to 1935 in Roosevelt's first term in office. Some of these agencies were the creation of Congress, others were by executive order. Of these 37 agencies there are seven that are still in existence today: the Farm Credit Association, the Federal Communications Commission, the Federal Deposit Insurance Corporation, the Federal Housing Association, the Securities and Exchange Commission, the Social Security Board (now merged with the Social Security Administration which was also created in 1935), and the Tennessee Valley Authority. The proliferation of New Deal federal agencies led to even stronger objections and criticisms over the growth of the federal government and the delegation of executive and legislative powers to these agencies.

The Federal Register Act of 1935 required federal government agencies to publish their documents. Section 1501 of the Act defines documents as "Presidential proclamation or Executive order and an order, regulation, rule, certificate, code of fair competition, license, notice, or similar instrument, issued, prescribed, or promulgated by a Federal agency." These documents have been published in print in the Federal Register since July 26, 1935 and online since 1994. In 1946 Congress established the Administrative Procedure Act which mandated the process federal agencies were to

---

[2] Jonathan Turley, *The rise of the fourth branch of government*, Washington Post, May 24, 2013, available at https://www.washingtonpost.com/opinions/the-rise-of-the-fourth-branch-of-government/2013/05/24/c7faaad0-c2ed-11e2-9fe2-6ee52d0eb7c1_story.html?utm_term=.f611ec884b40, retrieved June 18, 2017.

follow for their rulemaking and adjudicative functions. The APA also expanded the information agencies were required to publish in the Federal Register. Twenty years later Congress passed the Freedom of Information Act[3] (FOIA) which also added to the public's ability to access government information. Despite the notice requirements under the Federal Register Act and APA, as well as the more accessible nature of information through the FOIA, the immense spread of government bureaucracy and regulation has led to unabated criticisms (many along political party and ideological lines) over the expanding government infrastructure and the necessity for such extensive government oversight.

C. The Nondelegation Doctrine

The nondelegation doctrine holds that Congress cannot delegate its Article I power to legislate to any entity other than itself. The language of Article 1, section 1 of the U.S. Constitution—"All legislative powers herein granted shall be vested in a Congress of the United States, which shall consist of a Senate and House of Representatives"—has been cited as the authority for this view. The first Supreme Court case to address the nondelegation issue was *Wayman v. Southard*[4] in 1825. In that case Chief Justice Marshall said Congress was permitted to delegate constitutionally authorized powers to the other branches, the executive and judicial, as long as it did not involve the actual legislative power. Marshall distinguished between the important legislative powers and the ability to "fill up the details" while upholding a legislative act that permitted the federal courts to establish rules of practice as long as they did not contradict any laws of the United States.[5] However, it was not until 1928 that the U.S. Supreme Court in *J.W. Hampton Jr. & Co. v. United States* first held that delegation of legislative power to federal agencies was not unconstitutional.[6] Chief Justice William Howard Taft, writing for the 5-3 majority, set out the Court's holding as follows:

> *"If Congress shall lay down by legislative act an intelligible principle to which the person or body authorized to fix such rates is directed to conform, such legislative action is not a forbidden delegation of legislative power."*[7]

Legal Definition

Delegation of authority – administrative agencies are permitted to act only within the grant of authority given to them by legislation. If Congress permissibly delegates authority to an agency to act in a certain area, then that agency cannot extend its authority on its own. Much discretion is given to agency action upon subsequent review by the courts but a clear violation of its delegated authority will be sanctioned by the courts.

The facts of the *J.W. Hampton* case centered on the increase in the tariff rate on the import of barium oxide into New York from four cents per pound to six cents per pound. The increase was made by a proclamation of President Calvin Coolidge under the authority of a section of the Tariff Act of 1922 known as the "flexible tariff provision." The J.W. Hampton Jr. & Co. made a protest claiming

---

[3] 5 USC § 552
[4] 23 U.S. 10
[5] Id. at 43.
[6] 276 U.S. 394.
[7] Id at 409.

that the rise in the tariff rate by the president was an unconstitutional delegation of legislative power to the executive branch. The case came before the U.S. Customs Court which upheld the tariff increase under the provision of the Tariff Act and the U.S. Customs Court of Appeals affirmed the decision of the Customs Court. Chief Justice Taft and the Supreme Court majority reviewed the specific language of the Tariff Act section granting executive authority to increase tariff rates as well as the basis for the proclamation by President Coolidge raising the rate. The Supreme Court also relied on its prior precedent in another nondelegation case, *Interstate Commerce Commission v. Goodrich Transit Company*, when it held that Congress "*having laid down the general rules of action under which a commission shall proceed, it may require of that commission the application of such rules to particular situations and the investigation of facts, with a view to making orders in a particular matter within the rules laid down by the Congress.*"[8] This precedent and comparable state court rulings on the subject of nondelegation, led the Supreme Court to its "intelligible principle" holding in *J.W. Hampton*. However, in two 1935 cases the Supreme Court held that Congress had impermissibly delegated legislative power to the executive branch. In *Panama Refining Co. v. Ryan* the Supreme Court invalidated a provision of the National Industrial Recovery Act of 1933 (NIRA), section 9(c), that allowed the president to "*prohibit the transportation in interstate and foreign commerce of petroleum and the products thereof produced or withdrawn from storage in excess of the amount permitted to be produced or withdrawn from storage by any State law or valid regulation or order prescribed thereunder, by any board, commission, officer, or other duly authorized agency of a State.*"[9] Section 9(c) of the NIRA also contained a criminal penalty for a violation. The Supreme Court held that the section gave the president too much power to regulate commerce and that there were limits on the delegation of Congressional power. Section 9(c) was without any clear guidelines on the importation of oil products, it lacked standards, policies or goals normally associated with a proper delegation of power.[10] Similarly in *A.L.A. Schechter Poultry Corp. v. United States*,[11] decided five months after *Panama Refining*, the Supreme Court found an unconstitutional delegation of Congressional authority. This time the matter involved President Roosevelt's authority under the NIRA to regulate fair competition within the poultry industry by establishing requirements for the sale of whole chickens and regulating minimum work hours of employees. Schechter Poultry Corporation was indicted under 18 different counts relating to the sale of chickens pursuant to the Live Poultry Code which was promulgated by the president according to the authority given to him by section 3 of the NIRA.[12] Chief Justice Charles Evans Hughes, who also wrote the majority opinion in *Panama Refining*, wrote in the *Schechter Poultry* decision that the extent of the government's reach under the NIRA in *Panama Refining* was not as broad as in the present case where the president was trying to regulate against "unfair competition" without any definition from Congress as to what that term means.[13] Chief Justice Hughes wrote that the Act did not establish codes of conduct but rather allowed the president to create codes to prescribe conduct which was a limitless legislative grant of authority to the executive branch. Title I of the NIRA was held to be overbroad and an unconstitutional delegation of Congress' legislative power. The following year the Supreme Court

---

[8] 224 U.S. 194, 212 (1912)
[9] 293 U.S. 388, 406 (1935)
[10] Id. at 430.
[11] 295 U.S. 495 (1935).
[12] Id. at 521.
[13] See Id at 531–32.

extended its delegation oversight of New Deal legislation to the private sector. In *Carter v. Carter Coal Co.* the Supreme Court struck down another New Deal legislative act, the Bituminous Coal Conservation Act of 1935 which sought to create a commission to regulate labor conditions and production standards within the bituminous coal mining industry and promote its interstate commerce.[14] An individual stockholder initiated a lawsuit in order to prevent the company from submitting to federal legislation he saw as injurious to the welfare of the company. He also did not believe the company should become involved in the government's regulatory scheme. Justice Sutherland's narrow 5-4 majority opinion determined the government regulation to be unconstitutional on several grounds but with regard to the delegation of legislative power he said it was "*legislative delegation in its most obnoxious form, for it is not even delegation to an official or an official body, presumptively disinterested, but to private persons whose interests may be and often are adverse to the interests of others in the same business.*"[15] Justice George Sutherland was one of four Justices, including Willis Van Devanter, James McReynolds, and Pierce Butler, who were anti-regulatory and the reason President Roosevelt initiated his court-packing plan in 1937. Known as "The Four Horsemen" because of the their anti-regulatory voting bloc, the Justices often only needed one more vote to join them in blocking Roosevelt's New Deal legislation. In an attempt to nullify the strength of their anti-regulatory voting bloc President Roosevelt came up with a plan to add more New Deal friendly judges to the Supreme Court. The Judicial Procedures Reform Bill sent to Congress on February 5, 1937 sought to alleviate the volume of federal cases and the Supreme Court backlog by allowing the president to add a new judge to any federal court once an incumbent judge reached 10 years of judicial service and were six months past their 70th birthday. This included the U.S. Supreme Court which had a maximum of six additional justices allotted to it under the proposed bill. The fact that each of "The Four Horseman" justices was over 70 years of age gave Roosevelt four new potential appointments to the Supreme Court if the bill was approved. The bill was eventually struck down by the Senate and Roosevelt's plan never came to fruition. In addition, subsequent Supreme Court decisions were friendlier to President Roosevelt's proposed economic regulations under the New Deal. Beginning in early 1937 with *West Coast Hotel Co. v. Parrish*, in which the Supreme Court upheld minimum wage legislation under state law[16], the Supreme Court became more willing to permit legislation that regulated business activity. The *West Coast Hotel* decision was handed down one month after the Judicial Procedures Reform Bill was sent to Congress and is credited with ending the *Lochner* era of Supreme Court jurisprudence. Named for the case of *Lochner v. New York*, 198 U.S. 45 (1905), a liberty of contract case, the subsequent three decade period was marked by a laissez-faire approach to the economy and government regulation.

The nondelegation doctrine's subsequent treatment by the Supreme Court has relied on the "intelligible principle" standard originally announced in *J.W. Hampton*. The New Deal anti-regulation decisions cited above were mostly based on the poor draftsmanship of many of the legislative acts which were quickly written and submitted to Congress in the early days of the first Roosevelt administration. As such they failed to provide the Supreme Court with an intelligible principle upon which to justify their regulation. The need for Congress to delegate as an essential aspect of its legislative

---

[14] 298 U.S. 238 (1936)
[15] Id. at 311.
[16] 300 U.S. 379 (1937)

duties was recognized by the Supreme Court in *Mistretta. v. United States*, 488 U.S. 361 (1989). The Supreme Court found that in an increasingly complex and changing world in which Congress' ability to function would otherwise be crippled delegation was not unconstitutional.[17] *Mistretta v. United States* also set the parameters for valid delegation: (1) Congress must precisely describe the general policy to be carried out by the agency; (2) indicate the agency that is expected to carry out the policy; and (3) set the limits of the delegated authority.[18] While Congress does not have to provide detailed guidance it does have to provide more than agency identification and the general policy.

In the 2015 case of *U.S. Department of Transportation v. Association of American Railroads* the Supreme Court held that the metrics and standards for train scheduling and on-time performance were not unconstitutional due to Congress' granting Amtrak and the Federal Railroad Administration joint authority to establish them.[19] The Supreme Court said that Amtrak was a governmental entity and not a private enterprise since its board was appointed by the President and was created by a legislative act of Congress that required Amtrak (the National Railroad Passenger Corporation) to serve a public objective. Thus, the Supreme Court, in a unanimous decision, said it was not an unconstitutional delegation of legislative power.

D. Creation of Federal Agencies

A federal agency created by Congress results from legislation passed by Congress. The statute creating the federal agency, referred to as an organic statute, not only creates the agency but also establishes a body of rules for the agency to follow. It serves as the foundation of an agency's authority and responsibility. As such it is also a limit on any power that the agency may attempt to exert in a field under its control. The following case examines the limits of agency authority under its organic statute.

Legal Definition

Organic statute – in administrative law this refers to the legislation creating a federal agency from which the agency's power derives. An example would be the National Labor Relations Act of 1935 which created the National Labor Relations Board to enforce the labor laws, and oversee private sector collective bargaining and unfair labor practices and union organizing.

❖❖

Food and Drug Administration v. Brown and Williamson Tobacco Corp.
529 U.S. 120 (2000)

Justice O'Connor delivered the opinion of the Court.

This case involves one of the most troubling public health problems facing our Nation today: the thousands of premature deaths that occur each year because of tobacco use. In 1996, the Food and Drug Administration (FDA), after having expressly disavowed any such authority since its inception, asserted jurisdiction to regulate tobacco products. See 61 Fed. Reg. 44619—45318.

---

[17] 488 U.S. at 372.
[18] Id. at 373.
[19] 135 S. Ct. 1225

The FDA concluded that nicotine is a "drug" within the meaning of the Food, Drug, and Cosmetic Act (FDCA or Act), 52 Stat. 1040, as amended, 21 U.S.C. § 301 *et seq.*, and that cigarettes and smokeless tobacco are "combination products" that deliver nicotine to the body. 61 Fed. Reg. 44397 (1996). Pursuant to this authority, it promulgated regulations intended to reduce tobacco consumption among children and adolescents. The agency believed that, because most tobacco consumers begin their use before reaching the age of 18, curbing tobacco use by minors could substantially reduce the prevalence of addiction in future generations and thus the incidence of tobacco-related death and disease.

Regardless of how serious the problem an administrative agency seeks to address, however, it may not exercise its authority "in a manner that is inconsistent with the administrative structure that Congress enacted into law." *ETSI Pipeline Project v. Missouri,* 484 U.S. 495, 517 (1988). And although agencies are generally entitled to deference in the interpretation of statutes that they administer, a reviewing "court, as well as the agency, must give effect to the unambiguously expressed intent of Congress." *Chevron U.S.A. Inc. v. Natural Resources Defense Council, Inc.,* 467 U.S. 837, 842–843 (1984). In this case, we believe that Congress has clearly precluded the FDA from asserting jurisdiction to regulate tobacco products. Such authority is inconsistent with the intent that Congress has expressed in the FDCA's overall regulatory scheme and in the tobacco-specific legislation that it has enacted subsequent to the FDCA. In light of this clear intent, the FDA's assertion of jurisdiction is impermissible.

I

The FDCA grants the FDA, as the designee of the Secretary of Health and Human Services, the authority to regulate, among other items, "drugs" and "devices." See 21 U.S.C. § 321(g)–(h), 393 (1994 ed. and Supp. III). The Act defines "drug" to include "articles (other than food) intended to affect the structure or any function of the body." 21 U.S.C. § 321(g)(1)(C). It defines "device," in part, as "an instrument, apparatus, implement, machine, contrivance, . . . or other similar or related article, including any component, part, or accessory, which is . . . intended to affect the structure or any function of the body." § 321(h). The Act also grants the FDA the authority to regulate so-called "combination products," which "constitute a combination of a drug, device, or biologic product." § 353(g)(1). The FDA has construed this provision as giving it the discretion to regulate combination products as drugs, as devices, or as both. See 61 Fed. Reg. 44400 (1996).

On August 11, 1995, the FDA published a proposed rule concerning the sale of cigarettes and smokeless tobacco to children and adolescents. 60 Fed. Reg. 41314–41787. The rule, which included several restrictions on the sale, distribution, and advertisement of tobacco products, was designed to reduce the availability and attractiveness of tobacco products to young people. *Id.,* at 41314. A public comment period followed, during which the FDA received over 700,000 submissions, more than "at any other time in its history on any other subject." 61 Fed. Reg. 44418 (1996).

On August 28, 1996, the FDA issued a final rule entitled "Regulations Restricting the Sale and Distribution of Cigarettes and Smokeless Tobacco to Protect Children and Adolescents." *Id.,* at 44396. The FDA determined that nicotine is a "drug" and that cigarettes and smokeless tobacco are "drug delivery devices," and therefore it had jurisdiction under the FDCA to regulate tobacco products as customarily marketed–that is, without manufacturer claims of therapeutic benefit. First, the FDA found that tobacco products "'affect the structure or any function of the body'" because nicotine "has significant pharmacological effects." Specifically, nicotine "exerts psychoactive, or mood-altering, effects on the brain" that cause and sustain addiction, have both tranquilizing and stimulating effects, and control weight. Second, the FDA determined that these effects were "intended" under the FDCA because they "are so widely known and foreseeable that [they] may be deemed to have been intended by the manufacturers," consumers use tobacco products "predominantly or nearly exclusively" to obtain these effects, and the statements, research, and actions of manufacturers revealed that they "have 'designed' cigarettes to provide pharmacologically active doses of nicotine to consumers." Finally, the agency concluded that cigarettes and smokeless tobacco are "combination products" because, in addition to containing nicotine, they include device components that deliver a controlled amount of nicotine to the body.

Having resolved the jurisdictional question, the FDA next explained the policy justifications for its regulations, detailing the deleterious health effects associated with tobacco use. It found that tobacco consumption was "the single leading cause of preventable death in the United States." According to the FDA, "[m]ore than 400,000 people die each year from tobacco-related illnesses, such as cancer, respiratory illnesses, and heart disease." *Ibid.* The agency also determined that the only way to reduce the amount of tobacco-related illness and mortality was to reduce the level of addiction, a goal that could be accomplished only by preventing children and adolescents from starting to use tobacco. The FDA found that 82% of adult smokers had their first cigarette before the age of 18, and more than half had already become regular smokers by that age. It also found that children were beginning to smoke at a younger age, that the prevalence of youth smoking had recently increased, and that similar problems existed with respect to smokeless tobacco. The FDA accordingly concluded that if "the number of children and adolescents who begin tobacco use can be substantially diminished, tobacco-related illness can be correspondingly reduced because data suggest that anyone who does not begin smoking in childhood or adolescence is unlikely ever to begin."

Based on these findings, the FDA promulgated regulations concerning tobacco products' promotion, labeling, and accessibility to children and adolescents. The access regulations prohibit the sale of cigarettes or smokeless tobacco to persons younger than 18; require retailers to verify through photo identification the age of all purchasers younger than 27; prohibit the sale of cigarettes in quantities smaller than 20; prohibit the distribution of free samples; and prohibit sales through self-service displays and vending machines except in adult-only locations. The promotion regulations require that any print advertising appear in a black-and-white, text-only format unless the publication in which it appears is read almost exclusively by adults; prohibit outdoor advertising within 1,000 feet of any public playground or school; prohibit the distribution of any promotional items, such as T-shirts or hats, bearing the manufacturer's brand name; and prohibit a manufacturer from sponsoring any athletic, musical, artistic, or other social or cultural event using its brand name. The labeling regulation requires that the statement, "A Nicotine-Delivery Device for Persons 18 or Older," appear on all tobacco product packages.

The FDA promulgated these regulations pursuant to its authority to regulate "restricted devices." See 21 U.S.C. § 360j(e). The FDA construed § 353(g)(1) as giving it the discretion to regulate "combination products" using the Act's drug authorities, device authorities, or both, depending on "how the public health goals of the act can be best accomplished." 61 Fed. Reg. 44403 (1996). Given the greater flexibility in the FDCA for the regulation of devices, the FDA determined that "the device authorities provide the most appropriate basis for regulating cigarettes and smokeless tobacco." *Id.,* at 44404. Under 21 U.S.C. § 360j(e), the agency may "require that a device be restricted to sale, distribution, or use . . . upon such other conditions as [the FDA] may prescribe in such regulation, if, because of its potentiality for harmful effect or the collateral measures necessary to its use, [the FDA] determines that there cannot otherwise be reasonable assurance of its safety and effectiveness." The FDA reasoned that its regulations fell within the authority granted by § 360j(e) because they related to the sale or distribution of tobacco products and were necessary for providing a reasonable assurance of safety. 61 Fed. Reg. 44405–44407 (1996).

Respondents, a group of tobacco manufacturers, retailers, and advertisers, filed suit in United States District Court for the Middle District of North Carolina challenging the regulations. See *Coyne Beahm, Inc. v. FDA*, 966 F. Supp. 1374 (1997). They moved for summary judgment on the grounds that the FDA lacked jurisdiction to regulate tobacco products as customarily marketed, the regulations exceeded the FDA's authority under 21 U.S.C. § 360j(e), and the advertising restrictions violated the First Amendment. The District Court granted respondents' motion in part and denied it in part. The court held that the FDCA authorizes the FDA to regulate tobacco products as customarily marketed and that the FDA's access and labeling regulations are permissible, but it also found that the agency's advertising and promotion restrictions exceed its authority under § 360j(e). The court stayed implementation of the regulations it found valid (except the prohibition on the sale of tobacco products to minors) and certified its order for immediate interlocutory appeal.

The Court of Appeals for the Fourth Circuit reversed, holding that Congress has not granted the FDA jurisdiction to regulate tobacco products. Examining the FDCA as a whole, the court concluded that the FDA's regulation of tobacco products would create a number of internal inconsistencies. Various provisions of the Act require the agency to determine that any regulated product is "safe" before it can be sold or allowed to remain on the market, yet the FDA found in its rulemaking proceeding that tobacco products are "dangerous" and "unsafe." Thus, the FDA would apparently have to ban tobacco products, a result the court found clearly contrary to congressional intent. This apparent anomaly, the Court of Appeals concluded, demonstrates that Congress did not intend to give the FDA authority to regulate tobacco. The court also found that evidence external to the FDCA confirms this conclusion. Importantly, the FDA consistently stated before 1995 that it lacked jurisdiction over tobacco, and Congress has enacted several tobacco-specific statutes fully cognizant of the FDA's position. In fact, the court reasoned, Congress has considered and rejected many bills that would have given the agency such authority. This, along with the absence of any intent by the enacting Congress in 1938 to subject tobacco products to regulation under the FDCA, demonstrates that Congress intended to withhold such authority from the FDA. Having resolved the jurisdictional question against the agency, the Court of Appeals did not address whether the regulations exceed the FDA's authority under 21 U.S.C. § 360j(e) or violate the First Amendment.

We granted the Government's petition for certiorari to determine whether the FDA has authority under the FDCA to regulate tobacco products as customarily marketed.

II

The FDA's assertion of jurisdiction to regulate tobacco products is founded on its conclusions that nicotine is a "drug" and that cigarettes and smokeless tobacco are "drug delivery devices." Again, the FDA found that tobacco products are "intended" to deliver the pharmacological effects of satisfying addiction, stimulation and tranquilization, and weight control because those effects are foreseeable to any reasonable manufacturer, consumers use tobacco products to obtain those effects, and tobacco manufacturers have designed their products to produce those effects. As an initial matter, respondents take issue with the FDA's reading of "intended," arguing that it is a term of art that refers exclusively to claims made by the manufacturer or vendor about the product. That is, a product is not a drug or device under the FDCA unless the manufacturer or vendor makes some express claim concerning the product's therapeutic benefits. We need not resolve this question, however, because assuming, *arguendo*, that a product can be "intended to affect the structure or any function of the body" absent claims of therapeutic or medical benefit, the FDA's claim to jurisdiction contravenes the clear intent of Congress.

A threshold issue is the appropriate framework for analyzing the FDA's assertion of authority to regulate tobacco products. Because this case involves an administrative agency's construction of a statute that it administers, our analysis is governed by Chevron U.S.A. Inc. v. Natural Resources Defense Council, Inc., 467 U.S. 837 (1984). Under *Chevron*, a reviewing court must first ask "whether Congress has directly spoken to the precise question at issue." If Congress has done so, the inquiry is at an end; the court "must give effect to the unambiguously expressed intent of Congress." *Id*., at 843; see also *United States v. Haggar Apparel Co.*, 526 U.S. 380, 392 (1999); *Holly Farms Corp. v. NLRB*, 517 U.S. 392, 398 (1996). But if Congress has not specifically addressed the question, a reviewing court must respect the agency's construction of the statute so long as it is permissible. See *INS v. Aguirre-Aguirre*, 526 U.S. 415, 424 (1999); *Auer v. Robbins*, 519 U.S. 452, 457 (1997). Such deference is justified because "[t]he responsibilities for assessing the wisdom of such policy choices and resolving the struggle between competing views of the public interest are not judicial ones," *Chevron, supra*, at 866, and because of the agency's greater familiarity with the ever-changing facts and circumstances surrounding the subjects regulated, see *Rust v. Sullivan*, 500 U.S. 173, 187 (1991).

In determining whether Congress has specifically addressed the question at issue, a reviewing court should not confine itself to examining a particular statutory provision in isolation. The meaning–or ambiguity–of certain words or phrases may only become evident when placed in context. See *Brown v. Gardner*, 513 U.S. 115, 118 (1994) ("Ambiguity is a creature not of definitional possibilities but of statutory context"). It is a "fundamental canon of statutory construction that the words of a statute must be read in their context and with a view to their place in the overall statutory scheme." Davis v. Michigan Dept. of Treasury, 489 U.S. 803, 809 (1989). A court must therefore interpret the statute "as a symmetrical and coherent regulatory scheme," *Gustafson v. Alloyd Co.*, 513 U.S. 561, 569 (1995), and "fit, if possible, all parts into an harmonious whole," *FTC v. Mandel Brothers, Inc.*, 359 U.S. 385, 389 (1959). Similarly, the meaning of one statute may be affected by other Acts, particularly where Congress has spoken subsequently and more specifically to the topic at hand. See *United States v. Estate of Romani*, 523 U.S. 517, 530–531 (1998); *United States v. Fausto*, 484 U.S. 439, 453 (1988). In addition, we must be guided to a degree by common sense as to the manner in which Congress is likely to delegate a policy decision of such economic and political magnitude to an administrative agency. Cf. *MCI Telecommunications Corp. v. American Telephone & Telegraph Co.*, 512 U.S. 218, 231 (1994).

With these principles in mind, we find that Congress has directly spoken to the issue here and precluded the FDA's jurisdiction to regulate tobacco products.

*****

Deference under *Chevron* to an agency's construction of a statute that it administers is premised on the theory that a statute's ambiguity constitutes an implicit delegation from Congress to the agency to fill in the statutory gaps. See *Chevron*, 467 U.S., at 844. In extraordinary cases, however, there may be reason to hesitate before concluding that Congress has intended such an implicit delegation. Cf. Breyer, *Judicial Review of Questions of Law and Policy*, 38 Admin. L. Rev. 363, 370 (1986) ("A court may also ask whether the legal question is an important one. Congress is more likely to have focused upon, and answered, major questions, while leaving interstitial matters to answer themselves in the course of the statute's daily administration").

This is hardly an ordinary case. Contrary to its representations to Congress since 1914, the FDA has now asserted jurisdiction to regulate an industry constituting a significant portion of the American economy. In fact, the FDA contends that, were it to determine that tobacco products provide no "reasonable assurance of safety," it would have the authority to ban cigarettes and smokeless tobacco entirely. Owing to its unique place in American history and society, tobacco has its own unique political history. Congress, for better or for worse, has created a distinct regulatory scheme for tobacco products, squarely rejected proposals to give the FDA jurisdiction over tobacco, and repeatedly acted to preclude any agency from exercising significant policymaking authority in the area. Given this history and the breadth of the authority that the FDA has asserted, we are obliged to defer not to the agency's expansive construction of the statute, but to Congress' consistent judgment to deny the FDA this power . . . we are confident that Congress could not have intended to delegate a decision of such economic and political significance to an agency in so cryptic a fashion. To find that the FDA has the authority to regulate tobacco products, one must not only adopt an extremely strained understanding of "safety" as it is used throughout the Act–a concept central to the FDCA's regulatory scheme–but also ignore the plain implication of Congress' subsequent tobacco-specific legislation. It is therefore clear, based on the FDCA's overall regulatory scheme and the subsequent tobacco legislation, that Congress has directly spoken to the question at issue and precluded the FDA from regulating tobacco products.

* * *

By no means do we question the seriousness of the problem that the FDA has sought to address. The agency has amply demonstrated that tobacco use, particularly among children and adolescents, poses perhaps the single most significant threat to public health in the United States. Nonetheless, no matter how "important, conspicuous, and controversial" the issue, and regardless of how likely the public is to hold the Executive Branch politically accountable, *post*, at 31, an administrative agency's power to regulate in the public interest must always be grounded in a valid grant of authority from Congress. And "'[i]n our anxiety to effectuate the congressional purpose of protecting the public, we must take care not to extend the scope of the statute beyond the point where Congress indicated it would stop.'" *United States v. Article of Drug . . . Bacto-Unidisk*, 394 U.S. 784, 800 (1969) (quoting *62 Cases of Jam v. United States*, 340 U.S. 593, 600 (1951)). Reading the FDCA as a whole, as well as in conjunction with Congress' subsequent tobacco-specific legislation, it is plain that Congress has not given the FDA the authority that it seeks to exercise here. For these reasons, the judgment of the Court of Appeals for the Fourth Circuit is affirmed.

It is so ordered.

Questions Presented

1) Why was the FDA regulation of tobacco held by the Supreme Court to be an invalid exercise of agency power?
2) Why did the Supreme Court hold that deference under Chevron was inappropriate to this case?
3) What was the original reasoning of the FDA for its claim that tobacco products were subject to its regulations?

II. The Administrative Procedure Act

As already noted in section 1 above, the Administrative Procedure Act (also referred to as the APA), is a federally enacted statute that serves as a governing guideline for administrative agency functions at the federal level. It was enacted as federal legislation on June 11, 1946 and provided a more stringent guideline upon the activities of federal agencies. In light of the growth of the federal government and its regulatory agencies the passage of the APA was a necessary step in assuring limits upon government power. The New Deal policies of the Roosevelt administration and its reliance on a number of regulatory agencies to carry forth his aggressive economic agenda prompted heated debate on both sides of the issue, those supporting New Deal policies and those against. Passage of the Administrative Procedure Act provided a means to oversee the agencies by policing against improper agency conduct, ensuring fair access and treatment, and protecting public safety. There are four main purposes to the APA that can be discerned from the text of the statute:

1. to mandate federal governmental agencies to provide the public with information regarding their organization, procedure and rules;
2. to allow for public participation in the formal rulemaking process;
3. to set uniform standards for rulemaking and adjudicative process;
4. to define the extent of judicial review.

The APA applies equally to executive and independent federal government agencies.

Many states, but not all, have enacted administrative procedure acts of their own in order to regulate state agencies created under their state constitutions. These state agencies perform under similar restrictions and guidelines as those at the federal level with the difference resting mainly in their designated areas of governance. Typical state administrative agencies are motor vehicle departments, parole boards, state police departments, and education departments. A state agency will be limited in its rulemaking authority by the state administrative procedure act. An example of the purpose behind a state administrative procedure act can be seen in the excerpt below from the Colorado Procedure Act which sets out the legislative intent in creating the act. Note the basic constitutional due process protections alluded to in the "Legislative declaration" and the general assembly's statement about an agency's potential impact on business.

The federal APA, codified at 5 U.S.C. §§ 551–559, includes the Freedom of Information Act (FOIA) contained in § 552, and the Privacy Act contained in § 552a. Both of these were subsequent pieces of legislation added to the APA. The Freedom of Information Act was added in 1967 and the Privacy Act in 1974. The purpose of the Freedom of Information Act is to provide individuals the right of access to information from the federal government, particularly information from and about federal agencies. The law expanded upon the original APA requirement that federal agencies publish their rules in the Federal Register. It is a law designed for government transparency and full disclosure; however, there are exemptions under the FOIA that allow government agencies to withhold certain types of information. These exemptions are listed in § 552 of the Act and include the following:

1. records kept relating to national defense and foreign policy as designated by Executive order;
2. records related to the internal personnel rules and practices of an agency;
3. records specifically exempted from disclosure by statute;
4. records relating to trade secrets and commercial or financial information obtained from a person and privileged or confidential;
5. records that contain or are inter-agency or intra-agency memorandums or letters;

FIGURE 5.1   State Administrative Procedure Act

Colorado State Administrative Procedure Act

24-4-101. Short title.
This article shall be known and may be cited as the "State Administrative Procedure Act".

24-4-101.5. Legislative declaration.
The general assembly finds that an agency should not regulate or restrict the freedom of any person to conduct his or her affairs, use his or her property, or deal with others on mutually agreeable terms unless it finds, after a full consideration of the effects of the agency action, that the action would benefit the public interest and encourage the benefits of a free enterprise system for the citizens of this state. The general assembly also finds that many government programs may be adopted without stating the direct and indirect costs to consumers and businesses and without consideration of such costs in relation to the benefits to be derived from the programs. The general assembly further recognizes that agency action taken without evaluation of its economic impact may have unintended effects, which may include barriers to competition, reduced economic efficiency, reduced consumer choice, increased producer and consumer costs, and restrictions on employment. The general assembly further finds that agency rules can negatively impact the state's business climate by impeding the ability of local businesses to compete with out-of-state businesses, by discouraging new or existing businesses from moving to this state, and by hindering economic competitiveness and job creation. Accordingly, it is the continuing responsibility of agencies to analyze the economic impact of agency actions and reevaluate the economic impact of continuing agency actions to determine whether the actions promote the public interest.

6. records of personnel and medical files and any other files that would be an unwarranted invasion of personal privacy if disclosed;
7. records or information compiled for law enforcement purposes, but only if disclosure would interfere with an ongoing investigation, deprive a person of a fair trial, involve an invasion of privacy, reveal a confidential source, disclose law enforcement techniques or threaten the life or physical safety of an individual;
8. records relating to the regulation of supervision of financial institutions; and
9. records relating to geological and geophysical information and data, including maps, concerning wells.

The FOIA has undergone several amendments to its provisions since its initial passage in 1967. The federal Freedom of Information Act is independent of individual state freedom of information laws designed to provide open access to state governmental agency information.

The Privacy Act of 1974 states that "*[N]o agency shall disclose any record which is contained in a system of records by any means of communication to any person, or to another agency, except pursuant to a written request by, or with the prior written consent of, the individual to whom the record pertains.*"[20] However, certain specific disclosures as enumerated in section (b) of The Privacy Act are permitted, but these are mostly limited to government, agency or court disclosures. The catalyst for the passage of the Act was the Watergate Scandal of 1972 during the second term in office of President Richard Nixon and the Senate investigation's subsequent exposure of illegal Executive branch surveillance and investigation of individuals.[21] The aim of the Act was to establish a "code of fair information practices" governing the collection, maintenance, use and dissemination

---

[20] 5 U.S.C. § 552a(b)
[21] United States Department of Justice, Justice Information Sharing, *Privacy Act of 1974, 5 U.S.C. § 552a*, available at https://it.ojp.gov/PrivacyLiberty/authorities/statutes/1279, retrieved June 22, 2017.

of information about individuals that is maintained by federal agencies.[22] In addition to providing a code of fair practice and restricting government agency disclosure of individual information it contains, the Privacy Act allows individuals access to government records maintained on them and permits them to seek amendment of agency records kept on them by showing they are not accurate, relevant, timely, or complete.[23]

The remainder of the APA covers the three core areas of an administrative agency's functions:

1. rulemaking
2. adjudicative process
3. licensing

Each of these functions is defined in the APA:

§ 551(5) defines "rulemaking" as agency process for formulating, amending, or repealing a rule; § 551(7) defines "adjudication" as agency process for the formulation of an order; and § 551(9) defines "licensing" as agency process respecting the grant, renewal, denial, revocation, suspension, annulment, withdrawal, limitation, amendment, modification, or conditioning of a license.

Within each of these definitions are terms—rule, order, and license—separately defined by the APA that further explain the individual functions. A rule, as defined in subsection 4 of section 551, is an agency statement of general or particular applicability and future effect designed to implement, interpret, or prescribe law or policy or describing the organization, procedure, or practice requirements of an agency; an order, defined in subsection 6, is a final disposition, whether affirmative, negative, injunctive, or declaratory in form, of an agency in a matter other than rule making but including licensing; and, a license, defined in subsection 8, is an agency permit, certificate, approval, registration, charter, membership, statutory exemption or other form of permission.

While the APA is meant to guide all federal government agencies in their core functions there are agencies that are exempt from the Act. The exempt government agencies are Congress, the courts of the United States, governments of the territories and possessions of the United States as well as the District of Columbia, courts martial and military commissions, and naval or military

FIGURE 5.2   The Three Main Administrative Agency Functions

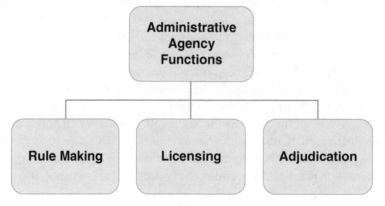

---

[22] Id.
[23] Id.

authority exercised in a time of war. This means that the President, cabinet members and other executive officers, including the military are included under the APA term "agency."[24]

In order for an individual to obtain legal recourse against an administrative agency they must meet the basic prerequisite of standing prior to initiating a civil action. Standing, as may be recalled from Chapter 2, requires an individual to have some stake in the claim to be made, or an injury in fact, and that the interest sought to be protected is within a "zone of interest" meant to be protected or regulated by the relevant statute at issue. Additionally, there must be a causal connection between the agency action and the injury claimed. With regard to agency action there also must be effective relief through the courts. If a claim is not redressable in the courts then standing will fail. The agency adjudicative process and judicial review of agency decisions will be covered below. Before moving onto discussion of the adjudicative process, a reading of the following case, *Perez v. Mortgage Bankers Association*, is necessary in order to understand the complexities involved in agency rule interpretation. The *Perez* case set aside an earlier U.S. Court of Appeals, D.C. Circuit case, *Paralyzed Veterans of America v. D.C. Arena*, requiring agencies to comply with formal administrative procedures when interpreting existing rules. While the APA requires federal agencies to provide for notice and comment prior to adopting "substantive" rules, there is an exemption for "interpretive" rules. However, there has never been a definitive announcement from the courts as to what constitutes an "interpretive" rule.

❖❖

Perez v. Mortgage Bankers Association
135 S. Ct. 1199 (2015)

Justice Sotomayor delivered the opinion of the Court.

When a federal administrative agency first issues a rule interpreting one of its regulations, it is generally not required to follow the notice-and-comment rulemaking procedures of the Administrative Procedure Act (APA or Act). See 5 U.S.C. § 553(b)(A). The United States Court of Appeals for the District of Columbia Circuit has nevertheless held, in a line of cases beginning with *Paralyzed Veterans of Am. v. D. C. Arena L. P.*, 117 F. 3d 579 (1997), that an agency must use the APA's notice-and-comment procedures when it wishes to issue a new interpretation of a regulation that deviates significantly from one the agency has previously adopted. The question in these cases is whether the rule announced in *Paralyzed Veterans* is consistent with the APA. We hold that it is not.

I
A

The APA establishes the procedures federal administrative agencies use for "rule making," defined as the process of "formulating, amending, or repealing a rule." § 551(5). "Rule," in turn, is defined broadly to include "statement[s] of general or particular applicability and future effect" that are designed to "implement, interpret, or prescribe law or policy." § 551(4).

Section 4 of the APA, 5 U.S.C. § 553, prescribes a three-step procedure for so-called "notice-and-comment rulemaking." First, the agency must issue a "[g]eneral notice of proposed rule making," ordinarily by publication in the Federal Register. § 553(b). Second, if "notice [is] required," the agency must "give interested persons an opportunity to participate in the rule making through

---

[24] Frank C. Newman, *What Agencies Are Exempt from the Administrative Procedure Act*, 36 Notre Dame L. Rev. 320 (1961).

submission of written data, views, or arguments." § 553(c). An agency must consider and respond to significant comments received during the period for public comment. See *Citizens to Preserve Overton Park, Inc. v. Volpe*, 401 U.S. 402, 416 (1971); *Thompson v. Clark*, 741 F. 2d 401, 408 (CADC 1984). Third, when the agency promulgates the final rule, it must include in the rule's text "a concise general statement of [its] basis and purpose." § 553(c). Rules issued through the notice-and-comment process are often referred to as "legislative rules" because they have the "force and effect of law." *Chrysler Corp. v. Brown*, 441 U.S. 281–303 (1979) (internal quotation marks omitted).

Not all "rules" must be issued through the notice-and-comment process. Section 4(b)(A) of the APA provides that, unless another statute states otherwise, the notice-and-comment requirement "does not apply" to "interpretative rules, general statements of policy, or rules of agency organization, procedure, or practice." 5 U.S.C. § 553(b)(A). The term "interpretative rule," or "interpretive rule," is not further defined by the APA, and its precise meaning is the source of much scholarly and judicial debate. We need not, and do not, wade into that debate here. For our purposes, it suffices to say that the critical feature of interpretive rules is that they are "issued by an agency to advise the public of the agency's construction of the statutes and rules which it administers." *Shalala v. Guernsey Memorial Hospital*, 514 U.S. 87, 99 (1995) (internal quotation marks omitted). The absence of a notice-and-comment obligation makes the process of issuing interpretive rules comparatively easier for agencies than issuing legislative rules. But that convenience comes at a price: Interpretive rules "do not have the force and effect of law and are not accorded that weight in the adjudicatory process." *Ibid.*

B

These cases began as a dispute over efforts by the Department of Labor to determine whether mortgage-loan officers are covered by the Fair Labor Standards Act of 1938 (FLSA), 52Stat. 1060, as amended, 29 U.S.C. § 201 *et seq*. The FLSA "establishes a minimum wage and overtime compensation for each hour worked in excess of 40 hours in each workweek" for many employees. *Integrity Staffing Solutions, Inc. v. Busk*, 574 U.S. ___, ___ (2014) (slip op., at 3). Certain classes of employees, however, are exempt from these provisions. Among these exempt individuals are those "employed in a bona fide executive, administrative, or professional capacity . . . or in the capacity of outside salesman. . . ." § 213(a)(1). The exemption for such employees is known as the "administrative" exemption.

The FLSA grants the Secretary of Labor authority to "define" and "delimit" the categories of exempt administrative employees. The Secretary's current regulations regarding the administrative exemption were promulgated in 2004 through a notice-and-comment rulemaking. As relevant here, the 2004 regulations differed from the previous regulations in that they contained a new section providing several examples of exempt administrative employees. See 29 CFR § 541.203. One of the examples is "[e]mployees in the financial services industry," who, depending on the nature of their day-to-day work, "generally meet the duties requirements for the administrative exception." § 541.203(b). The financial services example ends with a caveat, noting that "an employee whose primary duty is selling financial products does not qualify for the administrative exemption." *Ibid.*

In 1999 and again in 2001, the Department's Wage and Hour Division issued letters opining that mortgage-loan officers do not qualify for the administrative exemption. In other words, the Department concluded that the FLSA's minimum wage and maximum hour requirements applied to mortgage-loan officers. When the Department promulgated its current FLSA regulations in 2004, respondent Mortgage Bankers Association (MBA), a national trade association representing real estate finance companies, requested a new opinion interpreting the revised regulations. In 2006, the Department issued an opinion letter finding that mortgage-loan officers fell within the administrative exemption under the 2004 regulations. Four years later, however, the Wage and Hour Division again altered its interpretation of the FLSA's administrative exemption as it applied to mortgage-loan officers. Reviewing the provisions of the 2004 regulations and judicial decisions addressing the administrative exemption, the Department's 2010 Administrator's Interpretation concluded that mortgage-loan officers "have a primary duty of making sales for their employers, and, therefore, do not qualify" for the administrative exemption. The Department accordingly withdrew its 2006 opinion letter, which it now viewed as relying on "misleading assumption[s] and selective and narrow analysis" of the exemption example in § 541.203(b). Like the 1999, 2001, and 2006 opinion letters, the 2010 Administrator's Interpretation was issued without notice or an opportunity for comment.

C

MBA filed a complaint in Federal District Court challenging the Administrator's Interpretation. MBA contended that the document was inconsistent with the 2004 regulation it purported to interpret, and thus arbitrary and capricious in violation of § 10 of the APA, 5 U.S.C. § 706. More pertinent to this case, MBA also argued that the Administrator's Interpretation was procedurally in-valid in light of the D.C. Circuit's decision in *Paralyzed Veterans*, 117 F. 3d 579. Under the *Paralyzed Veterans* doctrine, if "an agency has given its regulation a definitive interpretation, and later significantly revises that interpretation, the agency has in effect amended its rule, something it may not accomplish" under the APA "without notice and comment." *Alaska Professional Hunters Assn., Inc. v. FAA,* 177 F. 3d 1030, 1034 (CADC 1999). Three former mortgage-loan officers—Beverly Buck, Ryan Henry, and Jerome Nickols—subsequently intervened in the case to defend the Administrator's Interpretation.

The District Court granted summary judgment to the Department. Though it accepted the parties' characterization of the Administrator's Interpretation as an interpretive rule, the District Court determined that the *Paralyzed Veterans* doctrine was inapplicable because MBA had failed to establish its reliance on the contrary interpretation expressed in the Department's 2006 opinion letter. The Administrator's Interpretation, the District Court further determined, was fully supported by the text of the 2004 FLSA regulations. The court accordingly held that the 2010 interpretation was not arbitrary or capricious.

The D. C. Circuit reversed. Bound to the rule of *Paralyzed Veterans* by precedent, the Court of Appeals rejected the Government's call to abandon the doctrine. In the court's view, "[t]he only question" properly before it was whether the District Court had erred in requiring MBA to prove that it relied on the Department's prior interpretation. Explaining that reliance was not a required element of the *Paralyzed Veterans* doctrine, and noting the Department's concession that a prior, conflicting interpretation of the 2004 regulations existed, the D.C. Circuit concluded that the 2010 Administrator's Interpretation had to be vacated.

We granted certiorari, 573 U.S. ___ (2014), and now reverse.

II

The *Paralyzed Veterans* doctrine is contrary to the clear text of the APA's rulemaking provisions, and it improperly imposes on agencies an obligation beyond the "maximum procedural requirements" specified in the APA, *Vermont Yankee Nuclear Power Corp. v. Natural Resources Defense Council, Inc.,* 435 U.S. 519, 524 (1978) .

A

The text of the APA answers the question presented. Section 4 of the APA provides that "notice of proposed rule making shall be published in the Federal Register." 5 U.S.C. § 553(b). When such notice is required by the APA, "the agency shall give interested persons an opportunity to participate in the rule making." § 553(c). But § 4 further states that unless "notice or hearing is required by statute," the Act's notice-and-comment requirement "does not apply . . . to interpretative rules." § 553(b)(A). This exemption of interpretive rules from the notice-and-comment process is categorical, and it is fatal to the rule announced in *Paralyzed Veterans*.

Rather than examining the exemption for interpretive rules contained in § 4(b)(A) of the APA, the D. C. Circuit in *Paralyzed Veterans* focused its attention on § 1 of the Act. That section defines "rule making" to include not only the initial issuance of new rules, but also "repeal[s]" or "amendments" of existing rules. See § 551(5). Because notice-and-comment requirements may apply even to these later agency actions, the court reasoned, "allowing an agency to make a fundamental change in its interpretation of a substantive regulation without notice and comment" would undermine the APA's procedural framework. 117 F. 3d, at 586.

This reading of the APA conflates the differing purposes of §§ 1 and 4 of the Act. Section 1 defines what a rule-making is. It does not, however, say what procedures an agency must use when it engages in rulemaking. That is the purpose of § 4. And § 4 specifically exempts interpretive rules from the notice-and-comment requirements that apply to legislative rules. So, the D. C. Circuit correctly read § 1 of the APA to mandate that agencies use the same procedures when they amend or repeal a rule as they used to issue the rule in the first instance. See *FCC v. Fox Television Stations, Inc.*, 556 U.S. 502, 515 (2009) (the APA "make[s] no distinction . . . between initial agency action and subsequent agency action undoing or revising that action"). Where the court went wrong was in failing to apply that accurate understanding of § 1 to the exemption for interpretive rules contained in § 4: Because an agency is not required to use notice-and-comment procedures to issue an initial interpretive rule, it is also not required to use those procedures when it amends or repeals that interpretive rule.

B

The straightforward reading of the APA we now adopt harmonizes with longstanding principles of our administrative law jurisprudence. Time and again, we have reiterated that the APA "sets forth the full extent of judicial authority to review executive agency action for procedural correctness." *Fox Television Stations*, Inc., 556 U.S., at 513. Beyond the APA's minimum requirements, courts lack authority "to impose upon an agency its own notion of which procedures are 'best' or most likely to further some vague, undefined public good." *Vermont Yankee*, 435 U.S., at 549. To do otherwise would violate "the very basic tenet of administrative law that agencies should be free to fashion their own rules of procedure." *Id.*, at 544.

These foundational principles apply with equal force to the APA's procedures for rulemaking. We explained in *Vermont Yankee* that § 4 of the Act "established the maximum procedural requirements which Congress was willing to have the courts impose upon agencies in conducting rulemaking procedures." *Id.*, at 524. "Agencies are free to grant additional procedural rights in the exercise of their discretion, but reviewing courts are generally not free to impose them if the agencies have not chosen to grant them." *Ibid*.

The *Paralyzed Veterans* doctrine creates just such a judge-made procedural right: the right to notice and an opportunity to comment when an agency changes its interpretation of one of the regulations it enforces. That requirement may be wise policy. Or it may not. Regardless, imposing such an obligation is the responsibility of Congress or the administrative agencies, not the courts. We trust that Congress weighed the costs and benefits of placing more rigorous procedural restrictions on the issuance of interpretive rules. In the end, Congress decided to adopt standards that permit agencies to promulgate freely such rules—whether or not they are consistent with earlier interpretations. That the D.C. Circuit would have struck the balance differently does not permit that court or this one to overturn Congress' contrary judgment.

***

For the foregoing reasons, the judgment of the United States Court of Appeals for the District of Columbia Circuit is reversed.

It is so ordered.

Questions Presented

1) According to the Supreme Court where did the D.C. Circuit Court err in its ruling?
2) Why was the D.C. Circuit Court's reliance on precedent not a strong position for its holding?
3) What is the separation of powers issue raised by Justice Sotomayor in her opinion?
4) What did the Supreme Court say was the proper application of the APA with regard to notice and comment for interpretive rules?

❖❖❖

III. Agency Rulemaking Power

Rulemaking by a federal agency is a delegated power provided to it by the agency's organic statute. Since there are many areas in which it would be impractical for Congress to regulate the rulemaking function within a specialized area it is delegated to an agency tasked with expertise in that particular area. Executive agencies have their power to exercise executive authority delegated to them by the President. Congressionally created agencies are generally directed by Congress to either regulate within a specific area, such as the Food and Drug Administration's mandate to control and supervise food safety, dietary supplements and drug products, or to problem solve, as in the Environmental Protection Agency's task to curtail pollution and its effects within the United States, or to attain a specific goal, as in the National Aeronautics and Space Administration's mission to explore outer space and engage in scientific experiments in space for the common good.

Section 553 of the Administrative Procedure Act covers agency rulemaking. The agency rulemaking process is referred to as informal rulemaking since it does not go through the more formal and less public procedures of statutorily required public hearing and recording under section 553(c) of the APA. As part of the general rulemaking process agency officials gather information regarding the proposed rule. This information gathering process relates to the need, purpose, and the implementation of the rule. The need for a rule may emanate from the agency itself and its identification of a problem or it may come from a legislative requirement. The public may also petition for the issuance of a rule or to change or rescind an existing rule. The proposed rule is then drafted and notice of the proposed rule has to be published in the *Federal Register*. The *Federal Register* is the daily journal of the United States government containing the rules, proposed rules and notices of the federal government. It can be accessed online at www.federalregister.gov or at the Office of the Federal

Register, www.ofr.gov. Both websites are maintained by the Government Printing Office. The APA requires that notice of the proposed rule contain:

1.   a statement of the time, place, and nature of public rule making proceedings;
2.   reference to the legal authority under which the rule is proposed; and
3.   either the terms or substance of the proposed rule or a description of the subjects and issues involved.

However, these notice requirements do not apply when interpretative rules, general policy statements or rules regarding agency organization, procedure or practice are involved. Further, publication of proposed rulemaking is not required if the agency finds good cause exists that publication and notice of the rules is unnecessary, impractical or contrary to public interest. These exceptions from publication for proposed rules do not negate the need for agencies to publish final rules. This notice of proposed rulemaking (NPRM) is part of the process referred to as "notice and comment rulemaking."

AGENCY PREAMBLE REQUIREMENTS
From 1 C.F.R. § 18.12(b)

AGENCY:
(Name of issuing agency)

ACTION:
(Notice of Intent), (Advance Notice of Proposed Rulemaking), (Proposed Rule), (Final Rule), (Other).

SUMMARY:
(Brief statements, in simple language, of: (i) the action being taken; (ii) the circumstances which created the need for the action; and (iii) the intended effect of the action.)

DATES:
(Comments must be received on or before: _____.) (Proposed effective date: _____.) (Effective date: _____.) (Hearing: _____.) (Other: _____.)

ADDRESSES:
(Any relevant addresses.)

FOR FURTHER INFORMATION CONTACT:
(For Executive departments and agencies, the name and telephone number of a person in the agency to contact for additional information about the document.)

SUPPLEMENTARY INFORMATION:
(any information to be added as per 1 C.F.R. § 18.12(c).)

Once the proposed rule is published in the *Federal Register* there is a public comment period. During this period the public can submit comments to the agency regarding the proposed rule. Submission of written views, data and arguments either with or without oral presentation are accepted.[25] Agencies may hold public hearings, and usually do so for more complex rules, however some agencies are required to hold rulemaking hearings by law. The public comment period lasts from 30 to 60 days,

---

[25] See APA § 553(c)

though the time period can be longer for more complex rules. When the public comment period is concluded the final rule is drafted and published in the *Federal Register*. The final rule has to have an "effective date" and must contain a preamble that contains information regarding the basis and purpose of the rule. Preamble requirements are found in 1 C.F.R. § 18.12(b) and include a specific format for agency preambles. The preamble may also provide the following supplementary information:

1. a discussion of the background and major issues involved;
2. in the case of a final rule, any significant differences between it and the proposed rule;
3. a response to substantive public comments received; and
4. any other information the agency considers appropriate.[26]

The preamble to a final rule contains a summary that includes agency response to comments made during the comment period. Agency rulemaking has to be made based on the rulemaking record which includes public comments, information and data received and expert opinion. When published in the *Federal Register* the final rule's summary will begin by outlining the relevant social issue or problem the rule is aimed at and the regulatory goal of the agency in its rule implementation. Also contained in the summary is the legal authority for the agency's rulemaking. This final publication has to be made 30 days prior to the rule's effective date.

Legal Definition

Arbitrary and capricious – a legal standard used to challenge administrative determinations that have no reasonable legal basis or without adequate consideration of the circumstances of the case.

If formal rulemaking is required then, as per section 553(c) of the APA, sections 556 and 557 control. The requirements of rulemaking then become a trial-like process involving the taking of oaths, subpoenaing of records and individuals, depositions, offers of proof and rules of evidence. The hearing decisions are subject to subsequent review and appeal. Rulemaking can be challenged in court if the final rule is arbitrary, capricious, illegal, unconstitutional, or is an abuse of discretion.

In addition to the informal and formal rulemaking process there are three additional processes: hybrid rulemaking, directed final rulemaking and negotiated rulemaking. Hybrid rulemaking is utilized by some agencies due to requirements of Congress. This process, as hinted at by its name, involves a rulemaking procedure somewhere between the informal and formal process. Hybrid rulemaking is more flexible than the formal rulemaking process covered in sections 556 and 557 but it does require public hearings and comment.[27] An agency must adhere to the hybrid rulemaking requirements only if Congress has by statute placed procedural requirements upon a designated agency, in addition to those found in the APA. Directed final rulemaking foregoes publication of a proposed rule in the *Federal Register* and instead publishes a final rule. An agency will use this form when it does not expect opposition to its rule.[28] If there is opposition the agency will have to withdraw its directed final rule and issue a final rule that addresses the opposition comments.[29] A negotiated rulemaking

---

[26] See 1 C.F.R. § 18.12(c)

[27] Todd Garvey, *A Brief Overview of Rulemaking and Judicial Review*, Congressional Research Service, March 27, 2017

[28] Id.

[29] Id.; See e.g., *Sierra Club v. Environmental Protection Agency*, 99 F.3d 1551, 1554, (10th Cir. 1996).

involves the agency reaching out to constituent interest groups during the informal rulemaking process for input. The involvement of participant groups is aimed at removing opposition to the rule and utilizing the expertise that these groups may possess in the area being regulated. An example would be the Environmental Protection Agency collaborating with an environmental watch group such as the Sierra Club or the Environmental Defense Fund. It allows for consensus rulemaking prior to the final rule. The process resulted from the Negotiated Rulemaking Act of 1996 which sought to encourage federal agencies to employ the assistance in rulemaking from interest groups, potentially expediting the process and removing the potential adversarial nature of the rulemaking process.

The procedures for negotiated rulemaking are found in 5 U.S.C. §§ 561–570. An agency head will first determine the need for a negotiated rulemaking committee. After consideration of a set of criteria outlined in section 563(a) the agency head may utilize the services of a convenor to assist the agency in identifying individuals who will be significantly affected by the rule and to discuss with those

---

CFR TITLES

Title 1 – General Provisions	Title 27 – Alcohol, Tobacco Products and Firearms
Title 2 – Grants and Agreements	Title 28 – Judicial Administration
Title 3 – The President	Title 29 – Labor
Title 4 – Accounts	Title 30 – Mineral Resources
Title 5 – Administrative Personnel	Title 31 – Money and Finance: Treasury
Title 6 – Domestic Security	Title 32 – National Defense
Title 7 – Agriculture	Title 33 – Navigation and Navigable Waters
Title 8 – Aliens and Nationality	Title 34 – Education
Title 9 – Animals and Animal Products	Title 35 – Panama Canal [Reserved]
Title 10 – Energy	Title 36 – Parks, Forests, and Public Property
Title 11 – Federal Elections	Title 37 – Patents, Trademarks, and Copyrights
Title 12 – Banks and Banking	Title 38 – Pensions, Bonuses, and Veterans' Relief
Title 13 – Business Credit and Assistance	Title 39 – Postal Service
Title 14 – Aeronautics and Space	Title 40 – Protection of Environment
Title 15 – Commerce and Foreign Trade	Title 41 – Public Contracts and Property Management
Title 16 – Commercial Practices	Title 42 – Public Health
Title 17 – Commodity and Securities Exchanges	Title 43 – Public Lands: Interior
Title 18 – Conservation of Power and Water Resources	Title 44 – Emergency Management and Assistance
Title 19 – Customs Duties	Title 45 – Public Welfare
Title 20 – Employees' Benefits	Title 46 – Shipping
Title 21 – Food and Drugs	Title 47 – Telecommunication
Title 22 – Foreign Relations	Title 48 – Federal Acquisition Regulations System
Title 23 – Highways	Title 49 – Transportation
Title 24 – Housing and Urban Development	Title 50 – Wildlife and Fisheries
Title 25 – Indians	
Title 26 – Internal Revenue	

FIGURE 5.3 Agency Rulemaking Process

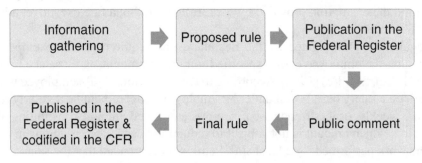

individuals issues of concern and whether a negotiated rulemaking committee is feasible and appropriate.[30] A convenor, defined in section 562(3), is the person who "*impartially assists an agency in determining whether establishment of a negotiated rulemaking committee is feasible and appropriate in a particular rulemaking.*" If a negotiated rulemaking committee is established the committee will select a facilitator to act as an impartial aid in the discussions and negotiations among the members of the negotiated rulemaking committee as they progress toward a final rule.[31] Similar procedures as contained in the APA for publication and comment are provided for in the Negotiated Rulemaking Act.

When a rule is finalized under any of the rulemaking procedures and published in the *Federal Register* it is also codified and made available in the Code of Federal Regulations (CFR). This is a codification of the general and permanent rules of federal departments and agencies. It is published by the Office of the Federal Register, part of the National Archives and Records Administration, and the Government Printing Office. The CFR can be found online at www.ecfr.gov but this is not considered an official legal edition of the CFR, rather it is an editorial compilation of CFR material and *Federal Register* amendments.[32] Bound volumes of the CFR can be found in law libraries. The CFR is divided into 50 titles representing the different areas of federal regulation.

❖❖❖

Auer v. Robbins
519 U.S. 452 (1997)

Justice Scalia delivered the opinion of the Court.

The Fair Labor Standards Act of 1938 (FLSA), 52 Stat. 1060, as amended, 29 U.S.C. §§ 201 *et seq.*, exempts "bona fide executive, administrative, or professional" employees from overtime pay requirements. This case presents the question whether the Secretary of Labor's "salary basis" test for determining an employee's exempt status reflects a permissible reading of the statute as it applies to public sector employees. We also consider whether the Secretary has reasonably interpreted the salary basis test to deny an employee salaried status (and thus grant him overtime pay) when his compensation may "as a practical matter" be adjusted in ways inconsistent with the test.

Petitioners are sergeants and a lieutenant employed by the St. Louis Police Department. They brought suit in 1988 against respondents, members of the St. Louis Board of Police Commissioners, seeking payment of overtime pay that they claimed was owed under § 7(a)(1) of the FLSA,

---

[30] See, 5 U.S.C. § 563(b)(1)

[31] See, 5 U.S.C. § 562(4)

[32] U.S. Government Publishing Office, *Electronic Code of Federal Regulations*, available at https://www.ecfr.gov/cgi-bin/ECFR?page=browse, retrieved June 24, 2017.

29 U.S.C. § 207(a)(1). Respondents argued that petitioners were not entitled to such pay because they came within the exemption provided by § 213(a)(1) for "bona fide executive, administrative, or professional" employees.

Under regulations promulgated by the Secretary, one requirement for exempt status under § 213(a)(1) is that the employee earn a specified minimum amount on a "salary basis." 29 CFR §§ 541.1(f), 541.2(e), 541.3(e) (1996). According to the regulations, "[a]n employee will be considered to be paid 'on a salary basis' . . . if under his employment agreement he regularly receives each pay period on a weekly, or less frequent basis, a predetermined amount constituting all or part of his compensation, which amount is not subject to reduction because of variations in the quality or quantity of the work performed." § 541.118(a). Petitioners contended that the salary basis test was not met in their case because, under the terms of the St. Louis Metropolitan Police Department Manual, their compensation could be reduced for a variety of disciplinary infractions related to the "quality or quantity" of work performed. Petitioners also claimed that they did not meet the other requirement for exempt status under § 213(a)(1): that their duties be of an executive, administrative, or professional nature. See §§ 541.1(a)–(e), 541.2(a)–(d), 541.3(a)–(d).

The District Court found that petitioners were paid on a salary basis and that most, though not all, also satisfied the duties criterion. The Court of Appeals affirmed in part and reversed in part, holding that both the salary basis test and the duties test were satisfied as to all petitioners. We granted certiorari.

The FLSA grants the Secretary broad authority to "define and delimit" the scope of the exemption for executive, administrative, and professional employees. § 213(a)(1). Under the Secretary's chosen approach, exempt status requires that the employee be paid on a salary basis, which in turn requires that his compensation not be subject to reduction because of variations in the "quality or quantity of the work performed," 29 CFR § 541.118(a) (1996). Because the regulation goes on to carve out an exception from this rule for "penalties imposed . . . for infractions of safety rules of major significance," § 541.118(a)(5), it is clear that the rule embraces reductions in pay for disciplinary violations. The Secretary is of the view that employees whose pay is adjusted for disciplinary reasons do not deserve exempt status because as a general matter true "executive, administrative, or professional" employees are not "disciplined" by piecemeal deductions from their pay, but are terminated, demoted, or given restricted assignments.

The FLSA did not apply to state and local employees when the salary basis test was adopted in 1940. In 1974 Congress extended FLSA coverage to virtually all public sector employees and in 1985 we held that this exercise of power was consistent with the Tenth Amendment, *Garcia v. San Antonio Metropolitan Transit Authority*, 469 U.S. 528 (1985) (overruling *National League of Cities v. Usery*, 426 U.S. 833 (1976)). The salary basis test has existed largely in its present form since 1954, and is expressly applicable to public sector employees.

Respondents concede that the FLSA may validly be applied to the public sector, and they also do not raise any general challenge to the Secretary's reliance on the salary basis test. They contend, however, that the "no disciplinary deductions" element of the salary basis test is invalid for public sector employees because as applied to them it reflects an unreasonable interpretation of the statutory exemption. That is so, they say, because the ability to adjust public sector employees' pay— even executive, administrative or professional employees' pay—as a means of enforcing compliance with work rules is a necessary component of effective government. In the public sector context, they contend, fewer disciplinary alternatives to deductions in pay are available.

Because Congress has not "directly spoken to the precise question at issue," we must sustain the Secretary's approach so long as it is "based on a permissible construction of the statute." *Chevron*

U.S.A. Inc. v. Natural Resources Defense Council, Inc., 467 U.S. 837, 842–843 (1984). While respondents' objections would perhaps support a different application of the salary basis test for public employees, we cannot conclude that they compel it. The Secretary's view that public employers are not *so* differently situated with regard to disciplining their employees as to require wholesale revision of his time tested rule simply cannot be said to be unreasonable. We agree with the Seventh Circuit that no "principle of public administration that has been drawn to our attention . . . makes it imperative" that public sector employers have the ability to impose disciplinary pay deductions on individuals employed in genuine executive, administrative, or professional capacities. *Mueller v. Reich,* 54 F. 3d 438, 442 (1995), cert. pending, No. 95-586.

Respondents appeal to the "quasi military" nature of law enforcement agencies such as the St. Louis Police Department. The ability to use the full range of disciplinary tools against even relatively senior law enforcement personnel is essential, they say, to maintaining control and discipline in organizations in which human lives are on the line daily. It is far from clear, however, that only a pay deduction, and not some other form of discipline—for example, placing the offending officer on restricted duties—will have the necessary effect. Because the FLSA entrusts matters of judgment such as this to the Secretary, not the federal courts, we cannot say that the disciplinary deduction rule is invalid as applied to law enforcement personnel.

The more fundamental objection respondents have to the disciplinary deduction rule is a procedural one: The Secretary has failed to give adequate consideration to whether it really makes sense to apply the rule to the public sector. Respondents' *amici* make the claim more specific: The Secretary's failure to revisit the rule in the wake of our *Garcia* decision was "arbitrary" and "capricious" in violation of the Administrative Procedure Act (APA), 5 U.S.C. § 706(2)(A).

It is certainly true that application of the disciplinary deduction rule to public sector employees raises distinct issues that may warrant the Secretary's formal consideration; this much is suggested by the veritable flood of post-*Garcia* litigation against public employers in this area, see, *e.g., Carpenter v. Denver,* 82 F. 3d 353 (CA10 1996), cert. pending, No. 95-2088; *Bankston v. Illinois,* 60 F. 3d 1249 (CA7 1995); *Shockley v. Newport News,* 997 F. 2d 18 (CA4 1993); *Atlanta Professional Firefighters Union, Local 134 v. Atlanta,* 920 F. 2d 800 (CA11 1991). But respondents' complaints about the failure to amend the disciplinary deduction rule cannot be raised in the first instance in the present suit. A court may certainly be asked by parties in respondents' position to disregard an agency regulation that is contrary to the substantive requirements of the law, or one that appears on the public record to have been issued in violation of procedural prerequisites, such as the "notice and comment" requirements of the APA, 5 U.S.C. § 553. But where, as here, the claim is not that the regulation is substantively unlawful, or even that it violates a clear procedural prerequisite, but rather that it was "arbitrary" and "capricious" not to conduct amendatory rulemaking (which might well have resulted in no change), there is no basis for the court to set aside the agency's action prior to any application for relief addressed to the agency itself. The proper procedure for pursuit of respondents' grievance is set forth explicitly in the APA: a petition to the agency for rulemaking, § 553(e), denial of which must be justified by a statement of reasons, § 555(e), and can be appealed to the courts, §§ 702, 706.

A primary issue in the litigation unleashed by application of the salary basis test to public sector employees has been whether, under that test, an employee's pay is "subject to" disciplinary or other deductions whenever there exists a theoretical possibility of such deductions, or rather only when there is something more to suggest that the employee is actually vulnerable to having his pay reduced. Petitioners in effect argue for something close to the former view; they contend that because the

Police Manual nominally subjects all department employees to a range of disciplinary sanctions that includes disciplinary deductions in pay, and because a single sergeant was actually subjected to a disciplinary deduction, they are "subject to" such deductions and hence nonexempt under the FLSA.

The Court of Appeals rejected petitioners' approach, saying that "[t]he mere possibility of an improper deduction in pay does not defeat an employee's salaried status" if no practice of making deductions exists. In the Court of Appeals' view, a "one time incident" in which a disciplinary deduction is taken under "unique circumstances" does not defeat the salaried status of employees. (In this case the sergeant in question, who had violated a residency rule, agreed to a reduction in pay as an alternative to termination of his employment.)

***

The Secretary of Labor, in an *amicus* brief filed at the request of the Court, interprets the salary basis test to deny exempt status when employees are covered by a policy that permits disciplinary or other deductions in pay "as a practical matter." That standard is met, the Secretary says, if there is either an actual practice of making such deductions or an employment policy that creates a "significant likelihood" of such deductions. The Secretary's approach rejects a wooden requirement of actual deductions, but in their absence it requires a clear and particularized policy—one which "effectively communicates" that deductions will be made in specified circumstances. This avoids the imposition of massive and unanticipated overtime liability (including the possibility of substantial liquidated damages, see, *e.g., Kinney v. District of Columbia, supra*, at 12) in situations in which a vague or broadly worded policy is nominally applicable to a whole range of personnel but is not "significantly likely" to be invoked against salaried employees.

Because the salary basis test is a creature of the Secretary's own regulations, his interpretation of it is, under our jurisprudence, controlling unless "'plainly erroneous or inconsistent with the regulation.'" *Robertson v. Methow Valley Citizens Council*, 490 U.S. 332, 359 (1989) (quoting *Bowles v. Seminole Rock & Sand Co.*, 325 U.S. 410, 414 (1945)). That deferential standard is easily met here. The critical phrase "subject to" comfortably bears the meaning the Secretary assigns. See American Heritage Dictionary 1788 (3d ed. 1992) (def. 2: defining "subject to" to mean "prone; disposed"; giving as an example "a child who is subject to colds"); Webster's New International Dictionary 2509 (2d ed. 1950) (def. 3: defining "subject to" to mean "exposed; liable; prone; disposed"; giving as an example "a country subject to extreme heat").

The Secretary's approach is usefully illustrated by reference to this case. The policy on which petitioners rely is contained in a section of the Police Manual that lists a total of 58 possible rule violations and specifies the range of penalties associated with each. All department employees are nominally covered by the manual, and some of the specified penalties involve disciplinary deductions in pay. Under the Secretary's view, that is not enough to render petitioners' pay "subject to" disciplinary deductions within the meaning of the salary basis test. This is so because the manual does not "effectively communicate" that pay deductions are an anticipated form of punishment for employees *in petitioners' category*, since it is perfectly possible to give full effect to every aspect of the manual without drawing any inference of that sort. If the statement of available penalties applied solely to petitioners, matters would be different; but since it applies both to petitioners and to employees who are unquestionably not paid on a salary basis, the expressed availability of disciplinary deductions may have reference only to the latter. No clear inference can be drawn as to the likelihood of a sanction's being applied to employees such as petitioners. Nor, under the Secretary's approach, is such a likelihood established by the one-time deduction in a sergeant's pay, under unusual circumstances.

Petitioners complain that the Secretary's interpretation comes to us in the form of a legal brief; but that does not, in the circumstances of this case, make it unworthy of deference. The Secretary's position is in no sense a "*post hoc* rationalization" advanced by an agency seeking to defend past agency action against attack, *Bowen v. Georgetown Univ. Hospital,* 488 U.S. 204, 212 (1988). There is simply no reason to suspect that the interpretation does not reflect the agency's fair and considered judgment on the matter in question. Petitioners also suggest that the Secretary's approach contravenes the rule that FLSA exemptions are to be "narrowly construed against . . . employers" and are to be withheld except as to persons "plainly and unmistakably within their terms and spirit." *Arnold v. Ben Kanowsky, Inc., 361* U.S. 388, 392 (1960). But that is a rule governing judicial interpretation of statutes and regulations, not a limitation on the Secretary's power to resolve ambiguities in his own regulations. A rule requiring the Secretary to construe his own regulations narrowly would make little sense, since he is free to write the regulations as broadly as he wishes, subject only to the limits imposed by the statute . . .

* * *

Petitioners have argued, finally, that respondents failed to carry their affirmative burden of establishing petitioners' exempt status even under the Secretary's interpretation of the salary basis test. Since, however, that argument was inadequately preserved in the prior proceedings, we will not consider it here. See *Adickes v. S. H. Kress & Co.*, 398 U.S. 144, 147, n. 2 (1970). The judgment of the Court of Appeals is affirmed.

It is so ordered.

Questions Presented

1) What was the first question the Supreme Court had to resolve before making its determination regarding the salary basis test?
2) What was the basis of the petitioners' argument that they were not exempt from overtime under the terms of the FLSA?
3) What did Justice Scalia say with regard to the extent of deference to be accorded the Secretary of Labor's interpretation of agency rules?
4) How did the Supreme Court answer the petitioners' argument regarding the imposition of discipline as a factor in their claim for nonexemption?

❖❖

IV. Agency Adjudication and Judicial Review

Administrative orders are quasi-judicial in character and void if a party is denied a hearing.[33] The agency determination must also be based on the "indisputable character of the evidence" before the agency.[34] A decision entered into by an agency relating to formal rulemaking, licensing, or adjudication is subject to review by a court. Despite the APA not referencing judicial review as applying to informal rulemaking, Congress has by statute also provided for review of informal rulemaking by requiring the use of substantial evidence review for informal agency rulemaking.[35]

---

[33] See, *ICC v. Louisville & N. R.R.*, 227 U.S. 88, 911 (1913).
[34] Id.
[35] Kelly Kunsch, *Standard of Review (State and Federal): A Primer,* Seattle University Law Review, Vol 18:11, 1994.

Title 5 U.S.C. section 706 provides for judicial review of agency decisions pursuant to the Administrative Procedure Act. Under section 706 a reviewing court "*shall decide all relevant questions of law, interpret constitutional and statutory provisions, and determine the meaning or applicability of the terms of an agency action.*" This includes setting aside agency decisions found to be "*arbitrary, capricious, an abuse of discretion, or otherwise not in accordance with law*", unconstitutional, not supported by the facts, a violation of procedure, or outside the statutory jurisdiction of the agency.

Additionally, a reviewing court can compel agency action that is unlawfully withheld or unreasonably delayed. This latter power of review is in the nature of a mandamus action. Mandamus is a judicial writ requiring a lower court or administrative tribunal to perform a statutory duty. The writ can also be directed to an individual, generally a public official, to perform a statutory or legal duty. The word mandamus originates from the Latin meaning "we command" or "we order."

Legal Definitions

Mandamus – a judicial writ requiring a lower court or an individual, such as a public official, to perform a legal or statutory duty.

Substantial evidence – the legal standard of proof required in administrative trials for a party to prove its case. The standard is one of such relevant evidence that a reasonable person would accept as adequate to support a factual result; more than a mere scintilla of evidence.

In order for a reviewing court to overturn an agency decision based on it being arbitrary and capricious there is a four-part test the court must consider. The test requires a reviewing court find the agency action:

1. relied on factors Congress had not intended for it to consider;
2. entirely failed to consider an important aspect of the problem;
3. offered an explanation for its decision that runs counter to the evidence before the agency; or
4. is so implausible that it could not be ascribed to a difference in view or the product of agency expertise.[36]

The Supreme Court in *Citizens to Preserve Overton Park v. Volpe* said that the arbitrary and capricious standard of review was one of whether there was a clear error of judgment in consideration of all the relevant factors before the agency.[37]

Section 554 of the Administrative Procedure Act provides the requirements for agency hearings. These agency adjudications have the potential to deprive an individual or a business of important property interests, therefore constitutional due process protections apply. Subsection (b) of section 554 establishes the procedural due process notice requirements in that all persons entitled to an agency hearing shall be timely informed of:

1. the time, place, and nature of the hearing;
2. the legal authority and jurisdiction under which the hearing is to be held; and
3. the matters of fact and law asserted.

---

[36] See, *Motor Vehicle Manufacturer's Association v. Stae Farm Mutual*, 463 U.S. 29, 43 (1983)
[37] 408 U.S. 402 (1971)

The hearing itself provides the second procedural due process prong of an opportunity to be heard. Even though due process applies to administrative hearings it is not co-equal with the same rights associated with criminal proceedings. The Supreme Court has indicated that *"the extent to which procedural due process must be afforded"* to an individual is influenced to the extent of the loss.[38] Further, the Supreme Court said *"consideration of what procedures due process may require under any given set of circumstances must begin with a determination of the precise nature of the government function involved, as well as of the private interest that has been affected by governmental action."*[39]

The legal standard of proof required in administrative tribunals is one of substantial evidence. This has been defined as more than a mere scintilla of evidence. The U.S. Supreme Court in the 1938 case of *Consolidated Edison v. NLRB* court has defined the substantial evidence standard as *"such relevant evidence as a reasonable mind might accept as adequate to support a conclusion."*[40] The Supreme Court has consistently abided by this definition of substantial evidence when applying it to administrative court determinations.[41] State courts have similarly adhered to the same definition for substantial evidence when applied to state administrative agency determinations.[42] This basis of review is very narrow and if an agency determination is supported by substantial evidence it is considered conclusive. Since this is such a low standard of evidentiary proof it is hard to overcome on the appeal of an agency determination. Substantial evidence review is also narrower than the arbitrary and capricious standard because it is based solely on the record before the reviewing court, while under arbitrary and capricious review the court can consider all factors before an agency, even if not introduced at the hearing.[43]

Legal Definition

Exhaustion of remedies doctrine – a requirement that prior to seeking relief in a state or federal court a litigant must pursue all available nonjudicial or administrative avenues of relief, otherwise a reviewing court will not hear the case.

Prior to seeking court review of an agency determination an aggrieved party must have exhausted all of their administrative remedies. This doctrine, which exists as both a common law and statutory requirement, holds that all nonjudicial or administrative remedies have to be explored prior to a court's involvement. If a litigant attempts to bring a case to a court for review before exhausting all administrative remedies the reviewing court will deny jurisdiction, dismiss the case, and return it to the litigant to seek agency review. Courts will only review administrative actions that are considered to be final. There are several policy reasons for this, not the least of which is the conservation of judicial resources, as well as continuity of agency process and deference to the agency as the subject matter expert in the particular field. The exhaustion of remedies doctrine is codified under the APA is 5 U.S.C. § 704. The section states that unless an agency action has been made directly reviewable by a court it is not final until reviewed by the agency (*"A preliminary, procedural, or intermediate*

---

[38] *Goldberg v. Kelly*, 397 U.S. 254, 262–3 (1970)
[39] Id.
[40] 305 U.S. 197, 229 (1938)
[41] See e.g., *NLRB v. Columbian Enameling & Stamping Co.*, 306 U.S. 292, 300 (1939); *Universal Camera Corp. v. NLRB*, 340 U.S. 474, 477–487 (1951); *Consolo v. Federal Maritime Comm'n*, 383 U.S. 607, 619–620 (1966); *Richardson v. Perales*, 402 U.S. 389, 401 (1971).
[42] See e.g., *Southwestern Pub. Serv. Co. v. Public Util. Comm'n*, 962 S.W.2d 207, 215 (Tex. App., 1998); *Bennett v. Department of Labor & Indus.*, 95 Wash. 2d 531, 534, 627 P.2d 104, 106 (1981).
[43] *Association of Data Processing Serv. Orgs. v. Board of Governors of the Fed. Reserve Sys.*, 745 F.2d 677 (D.C. Cir. 1984).

agency action or ruling not directly reviewable is subject to review on the review of the final agency action.") However, in the case of *Darby v. Cisneros* the Supreme Court said agency review is required "*only when expressly required by statute or when an agency rule requires appeal before review and the administrative action is made inoperative pending that review.*"[44] The facts of this case involved a developer, Darby, who was banned by an administrative law judge from entering into Housing and Urban Development (HUD) projects for 18 months due to allegations of involvement in a fraudulent scheme. HUD regulations said that the decision of an administrative law judge was final unless within 30 days of a decision a request was made to the Secretary of HUD for a review of the administrative law judge's determination. The developer did not file for a review by the Secretary and instead brought an action in federal court for review. The district court found in favor of Darby and HUD appealed. The federal circuit court of appeals reversed on the basis that Darby had not exhausted his administrative remedies. On review the Supreme Court noted that while courts are required to defer to the procedural process established by Congress a litigant cannot be expected to exhaust a remedy when neither the applicable statute nor agency rules require it.[45] In this instance direct review to the courts was appropriate. Exceptions to the exhaustion of remedies doctrine apply in some other limited circumstances. These exceptions include if an agency action is clearly illegal or if the plaintiff is able to adequately plead that seeking agency review would be futile and lead to the same inevitable result being appealed.

Since an administrative agency is established as a de facto subject matter expert in the particular field it is tasked to regulate the courts have largely deferred to agency decision-making and action. The previous case of *Auer v. Robbins* stated that an agency's interpretation of its own regulation is controlling absent it being inconsistent with the regulation or completely erroneous. There have been ideological differences within the Supreme Court regarding the extent of judicial deference and whether it is time to review its general jurisprudence in this area. In addition to *Auer* another Supreme Court case that factors into this discussion over judicial deference is *Chevron U.S.A., Inc. v. National Resource Defense Council, Inc.* In that case the Supreme Court was confronted with a challenge to an ambiguous regulatory statute and the agency's interpretation of the statute. The Supreme Court developed a two-prong analysis in deferring to the agency interpretation. However, in the ongoing judicial debate over deferring to agency interpretation arguments against deference have focused on the surrender of judicial control over coordinate branches by giving them final say in what their laws mean, and the basic textual approach of allowing the courts to decide what the statute means.

❖❖❖

Chevron U.S.A., Inc. v. National Resource Defense Council, Inc.
467 U.S. 837 (1984)

Justice Stevens delivered the opinion of the Court.

In the Clean Air Act Amendments of 1977, Pub. L. 95-95, 91 Stat. 685, Congress enacted certain requirements applicable to States that had not achieved the national air quality standards established by the Environmental Protection Agency (EPA) pursuant to earlier legislation. The amended Clean Air Act required these "nonattainment" States to establish a permit program regulating "new or modified major stationary sources" of air pollution. Generally, a permit may not be issued for a new or modified major stationary source unless several stringent conditions are met. The EPA

---

[44] 509 U.S. 137, 154 (1993)
[45] Id.

regulation promulgated to implement this permit requirement allows a State to adopt a plant wide definition of the term "stationary source." Under this definition, an existing plant that contains several pollution-emitting devices may install or modify one piece of equipment without meeting the permit conditions if the alteration will not increase the total emissions from the plant. The question presented by these cases is whether EPA's decision to allow States to treat all of the pollution-emitting devices within the same industrial grouping as though they were encased within a single "bubble" is based on a reasonable construction of the statutory term "stationary source."

I

The EPA regulations containing the plant wide definition of the term stationary source were promulgated on October 14, 1981. 46 Fed. Reg. 50766. Respondents filed a timely petition for review in the United States Court of Appeals for the District of Columbia Circuit pursuant to 42 U.S.C. 7607(b) (1). The Court of Appeals set aside the regulations. *National Resources Defense Council, Inc. v. Gorsuch*, 222 U.S. App. D.C. 268, 685 F.2d 718 (1982).

The court observed that the relevant part of the amended Clean Air Act "does not explicitly define what Congress envisioned as a `stationary source, to which the permit program . . . should apply," and further stated that the precise issue was not "squarely addressed in the legislative history." Id., at 273, 685 F.2d, at 723. In light of its conclusion that the legislative history bearing on the question was "at best contradictory," it reasoned that "the purposes of the nonattainment program should guide our decision here." Id., at 276, n. 39, 685 F.2d, at 726, n. 39. Based on two of its precedents concerning the applicability of the bubble concept to certain Clean Air Act programs, the court stated that the bubble concept was "mandatory" in programs designed merely to maintain existing air quality, but held that it was "inappropriate" in programs enacted to improve air quality. Id., at 276, 685 F.2d, at 726. Since the purpose of the permit program—its "raison d'etre," in the court's view—was to improve air quality, the court held that the bubble concept was inapplicable in these cases under its prior precedents. Ibid. It therefore set aside the regulations embodying the bubble concept as contrary to law. We granted certiorari to review that judgment and we now reverse.

The basic legal error of the Court of Appeals was to adopt a static judicial definition of the term "stationary source" when it had decided that Congress itself had not commanded that definition. Respondents do not defend the legal reasoning of the Court of Appeals. Nevertheless, since this Court reviews judgments, not opinions, we must determine whether the Court of Appeals' legal error resulted in an erroneous judgment on the validity of the regulations.

II

When a court reviews an agency's construction of the statute which it administers, it is confronted with two questions. First, always, is the question whether Congress has directly spoken to the precise question at issue. If the intent of Congress is clear, that is the end of the matter; for the court, as well as the agency, must give effect to the unambiguously expressed intent of Congress. If, however, the court determines Congress has not directly addressed the precise question at issue, the court does not simply impose its own construction on the statute, as would be necessary in the absence of an administrative interpretation. Rather, if the statute is silent or ambiguous with respect to the specific issue, the question for the court is whether the agency's answer is based on a permissible construction of the statute. "The power of an administrative agency to administer a congressionally created . . . program necessarily requires the formulation of policy and the making of rules to fill any gap left, implicitly or explicitly, by Congress." *Morton v. Ruiz,* 415 U.S. 199, 231 (1974). If Congress has explicitly left a gap for the agency to fill, there is an express delegation of authority to the agency to elucidate a specific provision of the statute by regulation. Such legislative regulations are given controlling weight unless they are arbitrary, capricious, or manifestly contrary to the statute. Sometimes the legislative delegation to an agency on a particular question is implicit rather than explicit. In such a case, a court may not substitute its own construction of a statutory provision for a reasonable interpretation made by the administrator of an agency.

We have long recognized that considerable weight should be accorded to an executive department's construction of a statutory scheme it is entrusted to administer, and the principle of deference to administrative interpretations "has been consistently followed by this Court whenever decision as to the meaning or reach of a statute has involved reconciling conflicting policies, and a full understanding of the force of the statutory policy in the given situation has depended upon more than ordinary knowledge respecting the matters subjected to agency regulations. See, e.g., *National Broadcasting Co. v. United States*, 319 U.S. 190; *Labor Board v. Hearst Publications, Inc.*, 322 U.S. 111; *Republic Aviation Corp. v. Labor Board*, 324 U.S. 793; *Securities & Exchange Comm'n v. Chenery Corp.*, 332 U.S. 194; *Labor Board v. Seven-Up Bottling Co.*, 344 U.S. 344.

". . . If this choice represents a reasonable accommodation of conflicting policies that were committed to the agency's care by the statute, we should not disturb it unless it appears from the statute or its legislative history that the accommodation is not one that Congress would have sanctioned." *United States v. Shimer*, 367 U.S. 374, 382 , 383 (1961). Accord, *Capital Cities Cable, Inc. v. Crisp*, ante, at 699–700.

In light of these well-settled principles it is clear that the Court of Appeals misconceived the nature of its role in reviewing the regulations at issue. Once it determined, after its own examination of the legislation, that Congress did not actually have an intent regarding the applicability of the bubble concept to the permit program, the question before it was not whether in its view the concept is "inappropriate" in the general context of a program designed to improve air quality, but whether the Administrator's view that it is appropriate in the context of this particular program is a reasonable one. Based on the examination of the legislation and its history which follows, we agree with the Court of Appeals that Congress did not have a specific intention on the applicability of the bubble concept in these cases, and conclude that the EPA's use of that concept here is a reasonable policy choice for the agency to make.

*****

Our review of the EPA's varying interpretations of the word "source"—both before and after the 1977 Amendments—convinces us that the agency primarily responsible for administering this important legislation has consistently interpreted it flexibly—not in a sterile textual vacuum, but in the context of implementing policy decisions in a technical and complex arena. The fact that the agency has from time to time changed its interpretation of the term "source" does not, as respondents argue, lead us to conclude that no deference should be accorded the agency's interpretation of the statute. An initial agency interpretation is not instantly carved in stone. On the contrary, the agency, to engage in informed rulemaking, must consider varying interpretations and the wisdom of its policy on a continuing basis. Moreover, the fact that the agency has adopted different definitions in different contexts adds force to the argument that the definition itself is flexible, particularly since Congress has never indicated any disapproval of a flexible reading of the statute.

Significantly, it was not the agency in 1980, but rather the Court of Appeals that read the statute inflexibly to command a plant wide definition for programs designed to maintain clean air and to forbid such a definition for programs designed to improve air quality. The distinction the court drew may well be a sensible one, but our labored review of the problem has surely disclosed that it is not a distinction that Congress ever articulated itself, or one that the EPA found in the statute before the courts began to review the legislative work product. We conclude that it was the Court of Appeals, rather than Congress or any of the decision makers who are authorized by Congress to administer this legislation that was primarily responsible for the 1980 position taken by the agency.

*****

In these cases the Administrator's interpretation represents a reasonable accommodation of manifestly competing interests and is entitled to deference: the regulatory scheme is technical and complex, the agency considered the matter in a detailed and reasoned fashion, and the decision involves reconciling conflicting policies. Congress intended to accommodate both interests, but did not do so itself on the level of specificity presented by these cases. Perhaps that body consciously desired the Administrator to strike the balance at this level, thinking that those with great expertise and charged with responsibility for administering the provision would be in a better position to do so; perhaps it simply did not consider the question at this level; and perhaps Congress was unable to forge a coalition on either side of the question, and those on each side decided to take their chances with the scheme devised by the agency. For judicial purposes, it matters not which of these things occurred.

Judges are not experts in the field, and are not part of either political branch of the Government. Courts must, in some cases, reconcile competing political interests, but not on the basis of the judges' personal policy preferences. In contrast, an agency to which Congress has delegated policymaking responsibilities may, within the limits of that delegation, properly rely upon the incumbent administration's views of wise policy to inform its judgments. While agencies are not directly accountable to the people, the Chief Executive is, and it is entirely appropriate for this political branch of the Government to make such policy choices – resolving the competing interests which Congress itself either inadvertently did not resolve, or intentionally left to be resolved by the agency charged with the administration of the statute in light of everyday realities.

When a challenge to an agency construction of a statutory provision, fairly conceptualized, really centers on the wisdom of the agency's policy, rather than whether it is a reasonable choice within a gap left open by Congress, the challenge must fail. In such a case, federal judges – who have no constituency – have a duty to respect legitimate policy choices made by those who do. The responsibilities for assessing the wisdom of such policy choices and resolving the struggle between competing views of the public interest are not judicial ones: "Our Constitution vests such responsibilities in the political branches." *TVA v. Hill*, 437 U.S. 153, 195 (1978).

We hold that the EPA's definition of the term "source" is a permissible construction of the statute which seeks to accommodate progress in reducing air pollution with economic growth. "The Regulations which the Administrator has adopted provide what the agency could allowably view as . . . [an] effective reconciliation of these twofold ends. . . ." *United States v. Shimer*, 367 U.S., at 383.

The judgment of the Court of Appeals is reversed.

It is so ordered.

Questions Presented

1) What did the Supreme Court state with regard to the EPA's interpretation of "stationary source" under the Clean Air Act?
2) How do Justice Stevens' comments about the role of the judiciary in government process compare with Justice Sotomayor's comments three decades later in *Perez v. Mortgage Bankers' Assn.?*
3) What is the type of deference the Supreme Court espouses in *Chevron*?
4) How does the Supreme Court's deference language in *Auer* differ from this case?

✦✦✦

SUMMARY

Administrative law encompasses an area of government agency regulation that has a broad impact on our everyday lives and the functioning of almost all types of businesses across the country. It is such an integral part of our system of government that it has been critically referred to as "the Fourth Branch" of government. There are a number of federal agencies that are either Executive branch agencies or independent agencies created by Congressional legislation. Due to the increase of federal regulation during the Progressive period and again during the New Deal era of President Roosevelt's administration, Congress, in 1946, passed the Administrative Procedure Act, also known as the APA. The Administrative Procedure Act is a formal guideline for federal agencies to follow in the promulgation and enforcement of their rules. Most states, which have separate administrative agencies and offices of their own, have passed similar statewide administrative procedure acts to guide the functions of their state administrative agencies.

At the federal level administrative agencies exist to implement the powers of either the President or Congress that have been delegated to them by either of the governmental branches. An agency can only act within the boundaries of the power delegated to it. Authority for delegation of Presidential power is found in Article II, clause 2 of the U.S. Constitution and Congress' delegation authority is found in the "necessary and proper" clause contained in Article I, section 8 of the Constitution. The delegation of authority from a constitutional branch of government to an agency was first recognized by the U.S. Supreme Court in the 1825 case of *Wayman v. Southard*. In that case Chief Justice Marshall said delegation was permitted as long as it did not involve the actual legislative power and was not otherwise against the laws of the United States. However, it was not until 1928 in the case of *J.W. Hampton Jr. & Co. v. United States* that the Supreme Court ruled on the constitutionality of the delegation of legislative power to an administrative agency. The Supreme Court in *J.W. Hampton* stated that delegation was permissible as long as there was an "intelligible principle" from Congress directing the actions of the agency.

There are three main functions of an administrative agency—rulemaking, licensing, and adjudication. Each of these activities are defined in the Administrative Procedure Act and any one of them are reviewable by a court if there is an allegation that agency action was arbitrary and capricious, illegal, unconstitutional, or an abuse of discretion. An additional means of agency review is for the courts to compel the agency or an agency official to perform a legal or statutory duty. This type of action is known as a writ of mandamus.

The legal standard of proof required in administrative tribunals is one of substantial evidence which has been defined as the amount of evidence required to convince a reasonable person to reach a factual conclusion. Unless a reviewing court determines there is no substantial evidence to support an agency determination or that the result was arbitrary, capricious, illegal, unconstitutional, or an abuse of discretion, the agency action will be upheld. When reviewing agency determinations relating to its rulemaking or its own administrative adjudications a reviewing court will grant broad judicial deference to the action of the agency unless a petitioner shows one of the above grounds as listed in 5 U.S.C. section 706 is present. Agencies are given broad discretion in their rulemaking and adjudicative powers under the APA.

PROPERTY LAW

LEARNING OUTCOMES

Upon completion of this chapter the student will be able to:

1 Identify the difference between personal property and real property.
2 Distinguish intangible from tangible personal property.
3 Discuss the different means of acquiring personal property.
4 Discuss the different estates in land and possessory interests.
5 Identify nonpossessory estates in land.
6 Discuss lease agreements and the landlord-tenant relationship.
7 Discuss zoning law and the police power of municipal government to regulate zoning.

KEY TERMS

alienation	equitable title	profit-a-prendre
bailment	fee simple	replevin
bona fide purchaser	future interest	trespass
chattel	lease	trover
conversion	legal title	vested right
conveyance	license	
easement	mortgage	

I. Overview of Property Law

The law of property is the study of a diverse set of rights that are specific to the unique nature of the type of property involved. When property rights are asserted by one party claiming a superior right to the property over another the dispute is either over the possession, ownership, or use of the property. However, these legal claims and their enforcement by the courts will depend on the property right asserted. There are two basic types of property: personal property (personalty), like a book or a necklace, and real property, such as land or a structure upon land. Personal property can consist of either tangible property or intangible property. Tangible property is that which we can hold, touch, and feel; we can take physical possession over it. Think of some of the things you possess that are considered tangible property—your car, television, computer, and wallet for example. Intangible property, also referred to as incorporeal property, we cannot physically possess or hold but it carries no less of a legal right or claim to ownership. This type of property includes stocks or bonds, which even though contained on paper we can physically possess, it has no intrinsic value of its own and merely represents a present interest in a company or a future interest in a commodity. The paper represents a value in something but not the thing itself. Other examples of intangible property include intellectual property interests like copyrights, patents, and trademarks. Whatever the type of property involved the law provides an important means to protect ownership, use and possession as well as to enforce rights inherent in the ownership, use and possession of the particular item of property. Of course, the nature of the specific rights to be protected or enforced will depend upon the nature of the property since, for example, there are a distinctly different bundle of rights involved in real estate than in the protection of a trademark.

Before exploring the legal aspects of different types of property and reading case law dealing with these varied property interests let us take a moment to consider the importance of this body of law in our overall legal system, historically and practically. The discussion thus begins with which came first, possession and ownership of property or the system of laws establishing a right of possession to property? This is a slight variation from the classic causality metaphor of the chicken and the egg but one which nonetheless serves the same basic function in seeking to resolve a dilemma. If there is no system of established rights can possession be recognized as anything other than a claim by whoever has the force and will to maintain and hold property? Or was it the establishment of a system for acknowledging possessory and ownership rights that gave property its formal legal classification? We can be certain that interests in property, both personal and real, are not modern concepts that rely on some judicial or statutory recognition before becoming valuable rights worthy of protection. Ancient laws dating back to the Before Common Era Sumerian Code of Urukagina and the Babylonian Code of Hammurabi contained property specific protections against fraud, usury, theft, and claims of right. Later, Common Era codifications, like the influential Justinian Code, also contained similar legal protections and recognition of vested rights. Medieval legal systems, like the Irish Brehon Laws which created a civil system that sought to regulate property and inheritance rights, carried forward the protection of basic property rights as a fundamental aspect of their law. Yet, this historical catalog of legal protections still does not answer the basic question of, from where did property rights first emanate? Perhaps it is best at this point to turn for guidance to the writings of Sir William Blackstone, the great English jurist and legal scholar, whose seminal work, *Commentaries on the Laws of England*, became the foundation of legal education in England and the American colonies in the 18th century. In the Second Book of the *Commentaries*, titled "Of the Rights of Things" Blackstone writes the following in Chapter I Of Property, In General:

There is nothing which so generally strikes the imagination, and engages the affections of mankind, as the right of property; or that sole and despotic dominion which one man claims and exercises over the external things of the world, in total exclusion of the right of any other individual in the universe. And yet there are very few that will give themselves the trouble to consider the original and foundation of this right. Pleased as we are with the possession, we seem afraid to look back to the means by which it was acquired, as if fearful of some defect in our title; or at best we rest satisfied with the decision of the laws in our favour, without examining the reason or authority upon which those laws have been built. We think it enough that our title is derived by the grant of the former proprietor, by descent from our ancestors, or by the last will and testament of the dying owner; not caring to reflect that (accurately and strictly speaking) there is no foundation in nature or in natural law, why a set of words upon parchment should convey the dominion of land: why the son should have a right to exclude his fellow-creatures from a determinate spot of ground, because his father had done so before him: or why the occupier of a particular field or of a jewel, when lying on his death-bed, and no longer able to maintain possession, should be entitled to tell the rest of the world which of them should enjoy it after him. These inquiries, it must be owned, would be useless and even troublesome in common life. It is well if the mass of mankind will obey the laws when made, without scrutinizing too nicely into the reason for making them. But, when law is to be considered not only as a matter of practice, but also as a rational science, it cannot be improper of useless to examine more deeply the rudiments and grounds of these positive constitutions of society.[1]

Blackstone continued his line of reasoning by referencing the Bible and building upon a theory of natural rights to property. In doing so he argued that the simplicity of the natural right theory had to give way to the more permanent and ordered conventions of civilization, that being the creation of a legal system to protect rights in and to property: *"The earth, therefore, and all things therein, are the general property of all mankind, exclusive of other beings, from the immediate gift of the Creator. And, while the earth continued bare of inhabitants, it is reasonable to suppose that all was in common among them, and that everyone took from the public stock to his own use such things as his immediate necessities required. These general notions of property were then sufficient to answer all the purposes of human life; and might perhaps still have answered them had it been possible for mankind to have remained in a state of primeval simplicity . . . But when mankind increased in number, craft, and ambition, it became necessary to entertain conceptions of more permanent dominion; and to appropriate to individuals not the immediate use only, but the very substance of the thing to be used."*[2]

It is no coincidence then that property rights were embedded in the Bill of Rights since the architects of our Constitution would have read Blackstone as part of their legal studies and apprenticeship in the law. The Third Amendment's prohibition against the quartering of soldiers, the Fourth Amendment's "right of the people to be secure in their persons, houses, papers, and effects, against unreasonable searches and seizure," and the Fifth Amendment's due process clause as applied to property and the just compensation clause, are all prominent examples of the Constitution's protection of individual property rights against government infringement and a nod to the Founding Fathers' recognition of the inviolability of those rights. Their reading of John Locke's *Second Treatise of Government* would have also provided a theoretical foundation for these protections since he espoused a natural law theory of rights in property which even in a state of nature had to be respected.[3] This natural law theory of property rights was opposite to that of Thomas Hobbes whose view was that natural rights and natural law do not coexist and respect for individual property rights was not necessary.[4] James Wilson, a Founding Father who represented Pennsylvania at the Constitutional Convention, eventually became one of America's first legal philosophers and as part of a series of lectures on American law he outlined a natural law theory of property rights in his lecture "On the history of property".[5] The natural law theory of property rights and the claim of

---

[1] Sir William Blackstone, *Commentaries on the Laws of England in Four Books, vol. 1* [1753] Online Library of Liberty, http://oll.libertyfund.org/titles/blackstone-commentaries-on-the-laws-of-england-in-four-books-vol-1#lf1387-01_label_2672, retrieved 07/05/17.

[2] Id.

[3] Steven Forde, *John Locke and the Natural Law Tradition,* Natural Law, Natural Rights and American Constitutionalism, http://www.nlnrac.org/earlymodern/locke#_edn2, Witherspoon Publishing, 2011, retrieved July 5, 2017.

[4] Id.

[5] See, James Wilson, *Collected Works of James Wilson, vol. 1* [2007], edited by Mark David Hall and Kermit L. Hall, http://oll.libertyfund.org/titles/wilson-collected-works-of-james-wilson-vol-1, retrieved July 5, 2017.

property pre-existing law was further commented upon in 1850 by French political economist Claude Frederic Bastiat who declared that the law is "the collective organization of the individual right of legitimate defense."[6] Bastiat argued that it was the existence of the natural right to life, liberty and property that prompted men to form laws. The influence of this natural law theory of property was exhibited in early common law cases dealing with possessory rights.

II. The Rights of Possessors

The rule of first possession holds that the first person to take possession of a thing owns it. This has also been referred to as the rule of capture and is an extension of natural law theory. The common law principle of first possession originated from a social structure wherein individuals were dependent upon the land for survival and livelihood. Possession of land was also subject to the rule of first possession—the first person to exercise dominion was vested with legal ownership. Additionally, a possessor or owner of land was also vested with the right to all that is on the land, including wild animals. This was a type of constructive possession legally referred to in Latin as ratio soli ("by reason of the soil.") All animals on the land were the property of the owner until such time as the animals left the land. The rights of land owners voided the right to capture of hunters who would otherwise be trespassing on an owner's land. When it came to the capture of wild animals not on any owned land the rule of first possession applied as long as there was a capture. In the famous New York case of *Pierson v. Post* (1805) the state Supreme Court ruled on a disputed possession case involving the hunting and chasing of a fox by Post, who with his dogs, was in close pursuit of his prey.[7] Pierson, upon seeing this, cut short Post's hunt by killing the fox himself and carrying it off. Post sued for damages and the lower court ruled in his favor. On a writ of review the state Supreme Court reversed and held for Pierson. In doing so the court noted that wild animals on public lands do not belong to anyone and possession cannot be established merely by giving chase. The perfection of the possessory interest is only established by the killing or mortal wounding of the animal. In the court's decision Justice Daniel Tompkins, a future Governor of New York and Vice President of the United States, wrote that ". . . *whatever is not appropriated by positive institutions, can be exclusively possessed by natural law alone. Occupancy is the sole method this code acknowledges.*"[8] Tompkins relied on natural law theory, citing the Justinian Code[9] as one of his legal authorities, but the common law tradition was also significant based on his citation to Blackstone's Commentaries. The judicial opinion in *Pierson v. Post* was authored at a time when a uniquely American legal tradition was still developing; the 18th century codification of laws and the growth of the legal profession would spur further legal developments into the 19th century. The impact on property rights and American jurisprudence in this area would advance as well. The rationale stemming from the *Pierson* decision was that property law should promote certainty and order as well as harmonious relations between individuals. It is necessary that rights to possession and ownership in property be clearly established, otherwise value is diminished. Since ownership

---

[6] Library of Economics and Liberty, http://www.econlib.org/library/Bastiat/basEss3.html, retrieved on July 5, 2017.

[7] See, *Pierson v. Post,* 3 Caines 175, 2 Am. Dec. 264 (1805)

[8] Id.

[9] See, J. Inst. 2.1.12 (5th ed. J. Moyle trans. 1913): "*Wild animals, birds, and fish, that is to say all the creatures which the land, the sea, and the sky produce, as soon as they are caught by any one become at once the property of their captor by the law of nations; for natural reason admits the title of the first occupant to that which previously had no owner.*"

of real property was an early index of wealth the development of the free transferability, or alienation, of land and the publicity of transfer by recording land transfers were significant to creating value by proving ownership.

Legal Definitions

Alienation – the term, as used in property law, refers to the transfer or conveyance of property from ownership of an individual to another. Property is generally termed to be freely alienable, i.e., subject to a transfer of ownership, although there can be a restraint on alienation, such as a provision in a real property deed restricting sale during the life of an individual. The term is primarily used with regard to the transfer of real property but it applies equally to personal property.

Vested right or vested title – refers to an absolute ownership right in real property that is not subject to any contingencies to ownership. A person owning real estate in which another had a life estate would not have completely vested legal title until the death of the life estate owner. The term applies to any form of property ownership wherein a person has an absolute right to some present or future interest in property.

James Wilson listed the three main rights to property as a matter of degrees from the lowest to the highest. The first, the right to possess, was the lowest degree, followed by the right to possess and use, with the right to possess, use and dispose of property as the highest degree of power over property.[10] These different "powers" over property remain as distinct interests in the modern law of property. These are a bundle of rights in which the state offers protection either through the civil or criminal justice systems. Criminal sanctions are not aimed at restoring the property to the owner, though ideally that is a possible outcome. Civil remedies, however, are focused on restoration of the owner to status quo. This may entail replacement, return, or some equitable remedy, such as injunctive relief, impacting property rights. While property is considered to be freely transferable by owners this high degree of power over property is subject to the absolute power of the state to regulate its use and disposition. The state's power to regulate is subject to reasonable restrictions which must be constitutionally valid. Since property ownership and the security of that ownership is a basic right upon which the government cannot infringe the courts must be careful in its review of private agreements that may seek to curtail that right. The following case provides a cogent example of those limits.

❖❖

Shelley v. Kraemer
338 U.S. 1 (1948)

Mr. Chief Justice Vinson delivered the opinion of the Court.

These cases present for our consideration questions relating to the validity of court enforcement of private agreements, generally described as restrictive covenants, which have as their purpose the exclusion of persons of designated race or color from the ownership or occupancy of real property. Basic constitutional issues of obvious importance have been raised.

---

[10] Wilson, supra

The first of these cases comes to this Court on certiorari to the Supreme Court of Missouri. On February 16, 1911, thirty out of a total of thirty-nine owners of property fronting both sides of Labadie Avenue between Taylor Avenue and Cora Avenue in the city of St. Louis, signed an agreement, which was subsequently recorded, providing in part: ". . . the said property is hereby restricted to the use and occupancy for the term of Fifty (50) years from this date, so that it shall be a condition all the time and whether recited and referred to as [*sic*] not in subsequent conveyances and shall attach to the land as a condition precedent to the sale of the same, that hereafter no part of said property or any portion thereof shall be, for said term of Fifty-years, occupied by any person not of the Caucasian race, it being intended hereby to restrict the use of said property for said period of time against the occupancy as owners or tenants of any portion of said property for resident or other purpose by people of the Negro or Mongolian Race."

***

On August 11, 1945, pursuant to a contract of sale, petitioners Shelley, who are Negroes, for valuable consideration received from one Fitzgerald a warranty deed to the parcel in question.

The trial court found that petitioners had no actual knowledge of the restrictive agreement at the time of the purchase.

On October 9, 1945, respondents, as owners of other property subject to the terms of the restrictive covenant, brought suit in the Circuit Court of the city of St. Louis praying that petitioners Shelley be restrained from taking possession of the property and that judgment be entered divesting title out of petitioners Shelley and revesting title in the immediate grantor or in such other person as the court should direct. The trial court denied the requested relief on the ground that the restrictive agreement, upon which respondents based their action, had never become final and complete because it was the intention of the parties to that agreement that it was not to become effective until signed by all property owners in the district, and signatures of all the owners had never been obtained.

The Supreme Court of Missouri, sitting en banc, reversed and directed the trial court to grant the relief for which respondents had prayed. That court held the agreement effective and concluded that enforcement of its provisions violated no rights guaranteed to petitioners by the Federal Constitution. At the time the court rendered its decision, petitioners were occupying the property in question.

The second of the cases under consideration comes to this Court from the Supreme Court of Michigan. The circumstances presented do not differ materially from the Missouri case. In June, 1934, one Ferguson and his wife, who then owned the property located in the city of Detroit which is involved in this case, executed a contract providing in part: "This property shall not be used or occupied by any person or persons except those of the Caucasian race."

"It is further agreed that this restriction shall not be effective unless at least eighty percent of the property fronting on both sides of the street in the block where our land is located is subjected to this or a similar restriction."

The agreement provided that the restrictions were to remain in effect until January 1, 1960. The contract was subsequently recorded, and similar agreements were executed with respect to eighty percent of the lots in the block in which the property in question is situated.

By deed dated November 30, 1944, petitioners, who were found by the trial court to be Negroes, acquired title to the property, and thereupon entered into its occupancy. On January 30, 1945, respondents, as owners of property subject to the terms of the restrictive agreement, brought suit against petitioners in the Circuit Court of Wayne County. After a hearing, the court entered a decree directing petitioners to move from the property within ninety days. Petitioners were further enjoined and restrained from using or occupying the premises in the future. On appeal, the Supreme Court of Michigan affirmed, deciding adversely to petitioners' contentions that they had been denied rights protected by the Fourteenth Amendment.

Petitioners have placed primary reliance on their contentions, first raised in the state courts, that judicial enforcement of the restrictive agreements in these cases has violated rights guaranteed to petitioners by the Fourteenth Amendment of the Federal Constitution and Acts of Congress passed. pursuant to that Amendment. Specifically, petitioners urge that they have been denied the equal protection of the laws, deprived of property without due process of law, and have been denied privileges and immunities of citizens of the United States. We pass to a consideration of those issues.

I

Whether the equal protection clause of the Fourteenth Amendment inhibits judicial enforcement by state courts of restrictive covenants based on race or color is a question which this Court has not heretofore been called upon to consider.

***

It is well, at the outset, to scrutinize the terms of the restrictive agreements involved in these cases. In the Missouri case, the covenant declares that no part of the affected property shall be "occupied by any person not of the Caucasian race, it being intended hereby to restrict the use of said property . . . against the occupancy as owners or tenants of any portion of said property for resident or other purpose by people of the Negro or Mongolian Race."

Not only does the restriction seek to proscribe use and occupancy of the affected properties by members of the excluded class, but, as construed by the Missouri courts, the agreement requires that title of any person who uses his property in violation of the restriction shall be divested. The restriction of the covenant in the Michigan case seeks to bar occupancy by persons of the excluded class. It provides that "This property shall not be used or occupied by any person or persons except those of the Caucasian race."

It should be observed that these covenants do not seek to proscribe any particular use of the affected properties. Use of the properties for residential occupancy, as such, is not forbidden. The restrictions of these agreements, rather, are directed toward a designated class of persons and seek to determine who may and who may not own or make use of the properties for residential purposes. The excluded class is defined wholly in terms of race or color; "simply that, and nothing more."

It cannot be doubted that among the civil rights intended to be protected from discriminatory state action by the Fourteenth Amendment are the rights to acquire, enjoy, own and dispose of property. Equality in the enjoyment of property rights was regarded by the framers of that Amendment as an essential pre-condition to the realization of other basic civil rights and liberties which the Amendment was intended to guarantee . . .

It is likewise clear that restrictions on the right of occupancy of the sort sought to be created by the private agreements in these cases could not be squared with the requirements of the Fourteenth Amendment if imposed by state statute or local ordinance. We do not understand respondents to urge the contrary.

***

Here, the particular patterns of discrimination and the areas in which the restrictions are to operate are determined, in the first instance, by the terms of agreements among private individuals. Participation of the State consists in the enforcement of the restrictions so defined. The crucial issue with which we are here confronted is whether this distinction removes these cases from the operation of the prohibitory provisions of the Fourteenth Amendment.

Since the decision of this Court in the *Civil Rights Cases*, 109 U.S. 3 (1883), the principle has become firmly embedded in our constitutional law that the action inhibited by the first section of the Fourteenth Amendment is only such action as may fairly be said to be that of the States. That Amendment erects no shield against merely private conduct, however discriminatory or wrongful.

We conclude, therefore, that the restrictive agreements, standing alone, cannot be regarded as violative of any rights guaranteed to petitioners by the Fourteenth Amendment. So long as the purposes of those agreements are effectuated by voluntary adherence to their terms, it would appear clear that there has been no action by the State, and the provisions of the Amendment have not been violated.

But here there was more. These are cases in which the purposes of the agreements were secured only by judicial enforcement by state courts of the restrictive terms of the agreements. The respondents urge that judicial enforcement of private agreements does not amount to state action, or, in any event, the participation of the State is so attenuated in character as not to amount to state action within the meaning of the Fourteenth Amendment. Finally, it is suggested, even if the States in these cases may be deemed to have acted in the constitutional sense, their action did not deprive petitioners of rights guaranteed by the Fourteenth Amendment. We move to a consideration of these matters.

II

That the action of state courts and judicial officers in their official capacities is to be regarded as action of the State within the meaning of the Fourteenth Amendment is a proposition which has long been established by decisions of this Court.

***

The action of state courts in imposing penalties or depriving parties of other substantive rights without providing adequate notice and opportunity to defend has, of course, long been regarded as a denial of the due process of law guaranteed by the Fourteenth Amendment.

***

It has been recognized that the action of state courts in enforcing a substantive common law rule formulated by those courts, may result in the denial of rights guaranteed by the Fourteenth Amendment, even though the judicial proceedings in such cases may have been in complete accord with the most rigorous conceptions of procedural due process.

***

The short of the matter is that . . . it has never been suggested that state court action is immunized from the operation of those provisions simply because the act is that of the judicial branch of the state government.

III

Against this background of judicial construction, extending over a period of some three-quarters of a century, we are called upon to consider whether enforcement by state courts of the restrictive agreements in these cases may be deemed to be the acts of those States, and, if so, whether that action has denied these petitioners the equal protection of the laws which the Amendment was intended to insure.

We have no doubt that there has been state action in these cases in the full and complete sense of the phrase. The undisputed facts disclose that petitioners were willing purchasers of properties upon which they desired to establish homes. The owners of the properties were willing sellers, and contracts of sale were accordingly consummated. It is clear that, but for the active intervention of the state courts, supported by the full panoply of state power, petitioners would have been free to occupy the properties in question without restraint.

These are not cases, as has been suggested, in which the States have merely abstained from action, leaving private individuals free to impose such discriminations as they see fit. Rather, these are cases in which the States have made available to such individuals the full coercive power of government to deny to petitioners, on the grounds of race or color, the enjoyment of property rights in premises which petitioners are willing and financially able to acquire and which the grantors are willing to sell. The difference between judicial enforcement and nonenforcement of the restrictive covenants is the difference to petitioners between being denied rights of property available to other members of the community and being accorded full enjoyment of those rights on an equal footing.

The enforcement of the restrictive agreements by the state courts in these cases was directed pursuant to the common law policy of the States as formulated by those courts in earlier decisions. In the Missouri case, enforcement of the covenant was directed in the first instance by the highest court of the State after the trial court had determined the agreement to be invalid for want of the requisite number of signatures. In the Michigan case, the order of enforcement by the trial court was affirmed by the highest state court. The judicial action in each case bears the clear and unmistakable imprimatur of the State. We have noted that previous decisions of this Court have established the proposition that judicial action is not immunized from the operation of the Fourteenth Amendment simply because it is taken pursuant to the state's common law policy. Nor is the Amendment ineffective simply because the particular pattern of discrimination, which the State has enforced, was defined initially by the terms of a private agreement. State action, as that phrase is understood for the purposes of the Fourteenth Amendment, refers to exertions of state power in all forms. And when the effect of that action is to deny rights subject to the protection of the Fourteenth Amendment, it is the obligation of this Court to enforce the constitutional commands.

We hold that, in granting judicial enforcement of the restrictive agreements in these cases, the States have denied petitioners the equal protection of the laws, and that, therefore, the action of the state courts cannot stand. We have noted that freedom from discrimination by the States in the enjoyment of property rights was among the basic objectives sought to be effectuated by the framers of the Fourteenth Amendment. That such discrimination has occurred in these cases is clear. Because of the race or color of these petitioners, they have been denied rights of ownership or occupancy enjoyed as a matter of course by other citizens of different race or color . . . Nor may the discriminations imposed by the state courts in these cases be justified as proper exertions of state police power.

***

The historical context in which the Fourteenth Amendment became a part of the Constitution should not be forgotten. Whatever else the framers sought to achieve, it is clear that the matter of primary concern was the establishment of equality in the enjoyment of basic civil and political rights and the preservation of those rights from discriminatory action on the part of the States based on considerations of race or color. Seventy-five years ago, this Court announced that the provisions of the Amendment are to be construed with this fundamental purpose in mind. Upon full consideration, we have concluded that, in these cases, the States have acted to deny petitioners the equal protection of the laws guaranteed by the Fourteenth Amendment. Having so decided, we find it unnecessary to consider whether petitioners have also been deprived of property without due process of law or denied privileges and immunities of citizens of the United States.

For the reasons stated, the judgment of the Supreme Court of Missouri and the judgment of the Supreme Court of Michigan must be reversed.

Reversed.

Questions Presented

1) What did Chief Justice Vinson say with regard to the Supreme Court's jurisdiction over private agreements concerning the transfer of property?
2) What was the occasion that gave rise to the Supreme Court's ability to intervene in this case and render a decision concerning the private restrictive covenant placed upon the two properties?
3) What did the decision have to say regarding the liberty interest involved in this case?
4) What was the Supreme Court's holding concerning the use of restrictive covenants in the transfer of real property?

❖❖

III. Personal Property

As already mentioned, there are two types of personal property, also known as a chattel: tangible property which is movable, capable of being carried from one place to another; and that which is intangible, something that has worth but is not physical in nature, such as a copyright, trademark, or patent. There are several ways in which someone can come into possession of personal property and we will explore each individually: (1) as a bailee; (2) as a finder of lost or mislaid property; (3) as a gift; and (4) as a bona fide purchaser. One other potential means of acquiring personal property is by way of adverse possession in those jurisdictions that recognize the principle for personal property. New Jersey, for example, recognizes adverse possession over personal property (see the case to follow *O'Keeffe v. Snyder*) while its neighbor New York does not. However, this is generally a means by which title can be acquired to real property and will be covered in the next section on real property.

A. Bailments

Consider the following scenario and the different property interests involved: James is going to see a show downtown and borrows his friend Ed's car. Ed owns the car outright, having just made his last payment on the vehicle. When James gets to his destination he parks the vehicle in a downtown parking garage run by XYZ Corporation. The vehicle will remain with XYZ Corporation in their garage until James returns from the show a few hours later. Who has the superior possessory right to the vehicle in this scenario? Clearly, Ed as the owner of the vehicle has what Wilson would term as the "highest degree" of power over the vehicle since he not only has possession and use of the vehicle as owner, but more importantly has the power to dispose of it as well. The power to dispose of property is referred to as the power of alienation and is superior to the ability to merely possess or use the property. Since Ed has been shown to have the superior right to the vehicle what is the relation between James and Ed with regard to the vehicle and then James and XYZ Corporation? James is what is referred to as a bailee of the property who is receiving it for his sole benefit.

> ### *Legal Definitions*
>
> **Bailment** – an agreement for the temporary placement of control or possession over personal property for a specific purpose as agreed to by the parties to the bailment agreement.
>
> **Bailor** – the person or entity who entrusts the personal property to another, the bailee.
>
> **Bailee** – the person or entity to whom goods are delivered by a bailor for a specified purpose without the transfer of ownership.

James has received from Ed, the bailor, a right to possess and use the vehicle for his trip downtown to see a show. When James parks the car with XYZ Corporation, he is the bailor and XYZ is the bailee who has a right to merely possess the vehicle. However, this is a bailment that is for the sole benefit of the bailor James, who needs someplace to park Ed's vehicle while he is at the show. What is the difference in the duty of care over the property owed by each of the bailee's in this example? As you can see in Table 6.1 the standard of care owed by James as a bailee to Ed is greater than that owed by XYZ as a bailee to James. The possessory and use right have obvious implications in the extent of each party's liability. Suppose that James did not return the vehicle to Ed at the end of his evening and decided to take it on a cross-country tour for several weeks. What would be the legal recourse for Ed? If he were to utilize the criminal justice system the recovery of the vehicle may be secured but the primary criminal justice aim is to apprehend and arrest the offender. A subsequent criminal court proceeding could order restitution for any damage to the vehicle or other losses stemming from James' unauthorized use of the vehicle, but such claims would be limited. However, if Ed were to file a claim in civil court he would be able to recover more extensive potential damages for James' unauthorized use of the vehicle since the available civil remedy is to either return the property, reimburse Ed for lost time, or replace or reimburse him for the value and/or use of the property.

Even though Ed has fully developed rights to use, possess and dispose of his property, his use and disposition of his car is not absolute. Those rights are subject to reasonable regulation by the state. For example, Ed must register his vehicle and have it inspected prior to placing it on public roadways, so his use is not totally without limit. In this case it is reasonable for overall motoring safety and the protection of public health and safety for the state to require licensing. Similarly, Ed is limited in the transfer of his vehicle (his right to dispose of the property) by state laws requiring an exchange of title and satisfaction or transfer of liens prior to the new vesting of title.

The above scenario provides not only an example of Wilson's three different powers over property but it also gives a good example of the nature of a bailment agreement. A bailment is something we enter into everyday of our lives without giving much thought to it. The parking example above is but one of many: dropping clothes off to a dry cleaner, checking a coat at a restaurant, placing

TABLE 6.1 Bailments

Type of bailment	Standard of care	Liability
Sole benefit for bailor	Slight care	For gross negligence
Sole benefit for bailee	Extreme care	For slight negligence
Mutual benefit bailment	Ordinary care	For ordinary negligence

bags with a hotel bellhop or concierge until your room is ready—these are all everyday examples of bailment agreements.

In order to establish a bailment three conditions must be met:

1. delivery by the bailor to the bailee of actual possession or control over the personal property;
2. express or implied acceptance by the bailee to the possession and control over the personal property;
3. the exchange of something of value (consideration) which in this case is the surrendering by the bailor of the possession and control over the property.

Bailments are a type of contractual agreement, therefore acceptance, either express or implied, is an important element in the creation of a bailment. However, an involuntary bailment can be created in certain circumstances. This is known as a constructive bailment and can occur when someone finds lost property and holds it for the owner or when a landlord takes possession of a leased apartment and discovers that the prior tenant left some personal items behind. Liability for involuntary bailments only arises upon negligence in a misdelivery of the property. When the bailment is for the sole benefit of the bailor the standard of care owed by the bailee is one of slight care and liability will result only from gross negligence on the part of the bailee. But, when the bailment is for the bailee's benefit the standard of care shifts and the bailee must exhibit extreme care; this liability will arise upon a showing of a slight degree of negligence. Suppose though that the bailment to the bailee did not result in any benefit to the bailee, what is the standard of care then due the bailor? If a bailee is receiving a fee for the possession of the bailed property then the duty owed is greater than if no fee is received. When there is no fee involved this type of bailment is referred to as a gratuitous or naked bailment agreement. The standard of care in this situation is therefore lower than if the bailee received compensation. Let's explore two fictional scenarios: (1) Jane pays her friend Emily $500.00 to hold and safeguard her expensive designer dress while she is on a weekend get-away with her family. Jane does not trust her new roommate who she is afraid will wear the dress to dance clubs while she is away. Emily agrees to the bailment and takes possession of the dress. The weekend arrives and Emily decides the dress is too nice to keep in a closet and wears it out to a party she is invited to attend. The dress gets stained and torn during a raucous evening of fun and is ruined. Emily will be liable for the value of the dress and the $500.00 paid for the bailment since she owed a duty of extreme care to Jane. Jane will only have to show a slight degree of negligence on the part of Emily in order to succeed in her claim. (2) Now, assume Jane is returning from her weekend away and arrives home to find a large delivery box addressed to her roommate on the front stairs of her apartment building. Jane asks a neighbor who is outside if he can watch her suitcase as she carries the box to her apartment. The neighbor, Joe, says he is waiting on some friends but should be around for the few minutes as Jane carries the box to her apartment. Jane leaves and within a minute a vehicle arrives to pick up Joe, who leaves the suitcase where Jane had place it on the sidewalk in front of the building. After Joe leaves someone comes by and takes Jane's suitcase. Jane returns outside to find that Joe and her suitcase are nowhere to be found. In this instance the standard of care Joe owed to Jane is much less than that owed by Emily who was paid as a bailee. Joe, as a gratuitous bailee, does not owe Jane as much of a duty of care. There are several different factual considerations and defenses on his part that may be a factor in any subsequent lawsuit filed by Jane against him for the loss of her property.

In the above two scenarios it is easy to discern the difference in the standard of care owed in each bailment and the reasoning for it. A clearly stronger legal responsibility rested with Emily rather than Joe based on the nature of the bailment agreement. Here is another scenario for you to contemplate:

a woman leaves a ring with the desk clerk of a hotel where she is a guest. She instructs the clerk that a jeweler she has hired, who also happens to be a guest at the hotel, will stop by to retrieve the ring. The owner needs a missing stone on the ring replaced. The clerk takes possession of the ring but subsequently loses it and does not notify either the owner or the jeweler. A month later the owner finds out from the jeweler that he never received the ring and when an inquiry is made with the hotel the fate of the ring is revealed for the first time. The lost ring is very valuable and its true value, while not in dispute, was never divulged by the owner to the hotel clerk. The immediate questions to be resolved are whether a bailment was created and, if so, what type? Secondly, does the fact that the ring's true value was not disclosed have any bearing on the outcome of the case? The facts recited above are from an actual case, *Peet v. The Roth Hotel*, 191 Minn. 151, 253 N.W. 546 (1934), which has been a favorite in teaching bailments. The Minnesota Supreme Court found that a bailment did exist and that it was a mutual benefit bailment. Mutual assent of the parties, a necessity for creation of a bailment, was found to be present in the owner (Mrs. Peet's) transfer of the ring to the hotel clerk (Ms. Edwards) and the clerk's acceptance of the ring. The mutual benefit of the bailment was exhibited in the hotel's acceptance of the ring as a usual guest service of the hotel rendered in the ordinary course of business. Finally, the true value of the ring was of no consequence since the identity of the bailment item was known and there was no fraud or mistake involved in accepting it as a bailment item.

FIGURE 6.1 Sample Bailment Agreement

BAILMENT AGREEMENT BETWEEN ACME WIDGET COMPANY AND XYZ CORPORATION

THIS BAILMENT AGREEMENT (hereafter referred to as "Agreement") is entered into as of June 26, 2017, by and between ACME WIDGET COMPANY, (hereafter referred to as "Bailee") and XYZ CORPORATION, (hereafter referred to as "Bailor"). In recognition of the mutual promises, and other good and valuable consideration, receipt of which is hereby acknowledged, Bailor agrees to deliver and Bailee agrees to accept the bailment of certain of Bailor's property, at no cost to Bailee, as described herein below.

1. DESCRIPTION OF BAILED PROPERTY
Bailor shall bail to the Bailee property (hereinafter "Property") identified as: [describe here the exact property, and all of it, being bailed.] _____

2. VALUE OF PROPERTY
The value of the Property at the time of bailment to Bailee is: [here itemize the value of each piece of property being bailed and then the total dollar value of the Property]. _____

3. PLACE OF DELIVERY
The Property shall be delivered to Bailee at _____, on or before _____,

4. PLACE OF RETURN
The Property shall be returned by the Bailee to the Bailor at [specify where Property is to be returned] _____ on or before _____, with transportation paid by Bailee. This period of bailment may be extended by the parties.

5. PURPOSE
Bailee shall use the Property only for the purpose of [insert purpose here] _____. Bailee's use shall comply with all applicable laws and regulations, and with applicable requirements and instructions so long as those applicable requirements and/or instructions are provided in writing by Bailor to Bailee.

FIGURE 6.1 *(Continued)*

6. POINT OF CONTACT
The individuals serving as points of contact for the Property are:

Bailor _____   Phone # _____   Fax # _____

Bailor _____   Phone # _____   Fax # _____

7. TITLE AND TRANSFER OF PROPERTY
Title to the Property furnished pursuant to this Agreement shall remain with Bailor and Bailee shall not sell, transfer, lease, mortgage, borrow against, pledge or otherwise create a legal or equitable interest by any third party in the Property.

8. WARRANTY
Bailor warrants that the Property shall be delivered to Bailee in good operating conditions and capable of performing its intended use. **BAILOR MAKES NO OTHER WARRANTIES, EXPRESS OR IMPLIED, AS TO THE PROPERTY'S CONDITION, MERCHANTABILITY, OR FITNESS FOR ANY PARTICULAR PURPOSE.**

9. LIABILITY FOR LOSS OF PROPERTY
Bailee assumes the risk of loss and damage, and shall be responsible for, any loss or damage to the Property while the Property is in Bailee's possession or control. Bailee shall return the Property in as good a condition as possible, except for reasonable wear and tear thereof.

10. LIMITATIONS OF LIABILITY
In no event shall either Bailee or Bailor be liable to the other for special, incidental, or consequential damages arising out of or connected in any way with the bailment, use, or operation of this Property

11. APPLICABLE LAW
This Agreement shall be construed and interpreted in accordance with the laws of the state of California, without resort to said state's Conflicts of Laws rules. If any provision is found to be illegal or otherwise unenforceable by any court or other judicial or administrative body, the other provisions shall not be affected thereby and shall remain in full force and effect.

12. ASSIGNMENT
Neither party shall assign any of its rights or obligations under this Agreement without the prior written consent of the other party.

13. APPLICABLE LAW
This Agreement is not intended by the parties to constitute or create a joint venture, pooling arrangement, partnership, or formal business organization of any kind, and the rights and obligations of the parties shall be only those expressly set forth herein. Neither party shall have the authority to bind the other except to the extent authorized herein

14. COMPLETE AGREEMENT
This Agreement constitutes the complete and final Agreement between the parties and supersedes all prior representations and agreements of the parties with respect to the subject matter hereof.

BAILOR – Acme Widget Company   BAILEE – XYZ Corporation

_____   _____

Signature   Signature

_____   _____

Printed name   Printed name

❖❖

David v. Lose et al.
218 N.E.2d 442 (Ohio 1966)
Supreme Court of Ohio

Prior History: Appeal from the Court of Appeals for Stark County.

On February 22, 1964, the plaintiff delivered his registered Tennessee Walking mare, a show horse, to defendants' stables for breeding purposes. Plaintiff was charged a stud fee. The defendants were notified that the mare was skittish and would kick, especially if she were touched about her rear where a surgical operation had been performed on her tail.

The mare was placed in a box stall adjoining that of defendants' stallion. The walls were of solid board and measured seven feet, four inches high. Wire mesh topped the wall. The stall was the customary and conventional type, well-constructed and in accepted use in the locality. About an hour after the mare had been placed in the stall, she was taken out and led in front of the stallion's stall. When the stallion bit her on the neck, she kicked to indicate her displeasure, and she was thereupon returned to her stall.

After another 45-minute period during which the mare was quiet, the defendants' servant, Woodburn, then left his working area where he could observe the mare and engaged in other duties some distance from the barn. After about 18 minutes, he heard a noise in the barn which he thought was a kick.

Woodburn went to the barn, looked into the mare's stall and found her steaming wet and breathing hard. Her leg was broken. The stallion was standing in his stall and picking at the hay.

The mare was destroyed. The plaintiff filed an action in the Municipal Court of Canton, Ohio, against the defendants for their failure to redeliver the mare. The trial court awarded the plaintiff a judgment for $1,214 and costs. The Court of Appeals for Stark County reversed, stating in its journal 'that the trial court's findings of fact are sufficient to rebut and counterbalance any presumption of negligence on the part of the defendants, and insufficient as a matter of law to establish negligence on the part of said defendants.'

This court allowed plaintiff's motion to certify the record. The cause is now before this court for review.

Opinion: Herbert, J.

When the plaintiff entrusted his mare to the defendants for breeding purposes and paid for this service, a bailment for hire was created. See *7 Ohio Jurisprudence 2d, Bailments, Sections 3 and 6.* The bailee for hire is obligated by law to exercise ordinary care in the safekeeping of the bailor's property, e. g., *Hotels Statler Co., Inc., v. Safier* (1921), 103 Ohio St. 638, 134 N.E. 460, 22 A.L.R. 1190. The bailee also promises to return the property undamaged upon the termination of the bailment, *8 American Jurisprudence 2d, Bailments, Section 164.*

Therefore, the bailor can sue the bailee for breach of either duty, the duty of redelivery or the duty of exercising ordinary care. This was recognized in *Agricultural Ins. Co. v. Constantine* (1944), 144 Ohio St. 275, 58 N.E.2d 658. Paragraph two of the syllabus reads as follows: 'Where a bailor delivers property to a bailee and such bailee fails to redeliver the bailed property upon legal demand therefor, a cause of action, either ex contractu or ex delicto, accrues in favor of the bailor.'

In the case at bar, the bailor's petition states a cause of action in contract for breach of the bailees' duty to return the bailed property undamaged. In order to establish a prima facie case, the bailor need prove only (1) the contract of bailment, (2) delivery of the bailed property to the bailees and (3) failure of the bailees to redeliver the bailed property undamaged at the termination of the bailment.

In order to escape liability, the bailees must then assert and prove some affirmative defense. The bailees in their answer affirmatively plead that 'they exercise that degree of prudent care necessary to safely confine and keep said mare until the acts of performance contemplated by the contract were fulfilled.' The bailees thus assert that the mare was damaged through no fault of their own. In short, they assert nonnegligence as an affirmative defense. The law recognizes this as a legal excuse for failure to redeliver the bailed property undamaged. *8 American Jurisprudence 2d, Bailments, Section 177.* However, the burden of proof on the issue of the bailees' conduct remains with the bailees throughout the trial, *Hanlon v. J. E. Miller Transfer & Storage Co.* (1948), 149 Ohio. St. 387, at 389 and 391, 79 N.E.2d 220; *8 American Jurisprudence 2d, Bailments, Section 311; 7 Ohio Jurisprudence 2d, Bailments, Section 42.* The law on the burden of proof on the issue of negligence in contract cases should be contrasted with that in negligence cases where the bailor, even when proceeding on the basis of res ipsa loquitur, has the burden of proof on the issue of negligence throughout the trial. *8 American Jurisprudence 2d, Bailments, Section 310; 7 Ohio Jurisprudence 2d, Bailments, Section 41.*

The rule in contract cases is stated in the fourth paragraph of the syllabus of *Agricultural Ins. Co. v. Constantine, supra*, as follows: 'In an action by a bailor against a bailee based upon a breach of the contract of bailment, where the bailor proves delivery of the bailed property and the failure of the bailee to redeliver upon legal demand therefor, a prima facie case of want of due care is thereby established and the burden of going forward with the evidence shifts to the bailee to explain his failure to redeliver.'

The Court of Appeals failed to draw the distinction between the tort and contract actions available to a bailor and so confused the two that it erroneously applied the doctrine of res ipsa loquitur to this action in contract. Although such confusion is not without precedent, it should not be encouraged.

The Court of Appeals failed to recognize that the question is not whether the plaintiff has established negligence but whether the defendants have established a legal excuse for breach of the contract. As it was stated in *8 American Jurisprudence 2d, Bailments, Section 166*: 'So far as the particular duty under discussion (i. e., the bailee's duty of redelivery) is concerned, it is erroneous to say that a bailee is liable for negligence. He is liable for not delivering the subject of the bailment, but is excused if it has been lost without fault or want of care on his part.'

In the case at bar, no legal excuse has been shown. The trial court's statement of facts-which is not disputed by either party-indicates that the stall was properly made, and that it was not the customary practice to station an attendant at all times to watch over the horses. No one knows how the injury to the mare occurred. Even if under the circumstances it is consistent with reasonable care for a bailee to put a mare in such a stall and leave her unguarded for a short duration, proof of those facts is not proof of a legal excuse because it is impossible to determine whether such reasonable conduct is at all relevant to how the injury occurred.

Thus, once it is known how the damage to the bailed property occurred, it is incumbent on the bailee to show that he acted reasonably in that regard. Cf. *Agricultural Ins. Co. v. Constantine, supra.* But where, as here, the bailee cannot show how the damage occurred, he must, in order to escape liability, affirmatively prove that he took reasonable precautions under the circumstances to prevent every possibility of damage from actually occurring.

Since the bailees failed to meet that burden and left the question of their conduct in a state of conjecture, the judgment of the trial court is affirmed, and that of the Court of Appeals is reversed.

Judgment reversed.

Reprinted with the permission of LexisNexis.

Questions Presented

1) What are the distinct elements of a bailment agreement that the judge outlined in his decision?
2) What was the standard of care upon the bailee in this case? Why was the bailee held to this standard of care?
3) What did the court state was the error at the Court of Appeals with regard to its review of the issue of liability?

❖❖❖

B. Lost or Mislaid Property

As a general rule the owner of property does not surrender title by losing the property. Ownership rights survive in property that is lost or mislaid. A first finder, however, does retain an interest in the property that is superior to all others except the true owner. If the true owner cannot be found then the finder gains rightful ownership over the property. Under the common law a finder could retain lost property until and unless the original owner came forward. A number of states now have laws in place that modify the common law rule and require a finder of lost property to turn it into the local police to hold for the true owner to claim.[11] If a claim is not made within a set statutory period (usually one year) the property can be claimed by the finder. Every state, Washington D.C., Puerto Rico, and the U.S. Virgin Islands have statutes that protect and provide for the collection of unclaimed financial assets.[12] This relates to assets like forgotten bank accounts containing cash deposits, stock certificates, and bonds.

Lost property, as distinguished from mislaid property, is property that is accidentally and casually lost. Mislaid property is not lost per se but rather placed in a location and then forgotten. There is an assumption in the law that people will attempt to retrace their steps and locate the property, though in reality the same will occur when people lose property if they become aware it is missing. Abandoned property is that in which the owner has relinquished all possession and ownership. A finder has superior rights over all others except for an owner who attempted to reclaim abandoned property, but the latter situation is rare. Whether property is considered lost, mislaid or abandoned is often a question of fact for courts to resolve. Often the claim to the property will be determined by how it is classified. Property that is lost or abandoned will generally go to the finder while mislaid property will go to the possessor of the place where found. Even though real property cannot technically be abandoned since legal ownership is always knowable, it can escheat to the state due to a defect in heirs. In such a case the real

---

[11] See e.g., Conn. Gen. Stat. § 50-1-14; FL Stat. § 705.101-19; Mich. Comp. Law Ann. § 434.21-29; NYS Personal Property Law § 252; 15 Okl. St. Ann. § 511–518; So. Dak. Codified Laws § 43-41-1-11; 27 Vt. Stat. Ann. § 1101-1110; Rev. Code Wash. Ann. § 63.21.010-900; Wisc. Stat. Ann. § 170.01-12

[12] National Association of Unclaimed Property Administrators, The National Association of State Treasurers, https://www.unclaimed.org/what/, retrieved July 8, 2017.

property goes back to the state if an owner dies without a legal heir. The state is able to take title and sell the property.

Treasure trove is a special kind of lost property of value (money, coins, jewels, gold) that is hidden. The finder of treasure trove retains the right of possession and ownership unless the item is found imbedded in the land of another. Any property, regardless of its value, if found on real property is the property of the owner and not the finder. This also generally applies to subsurface mineral rights which belong to the landowner. When thinking of treasure trove imagine those people who walk the beach with metal detectors held out in front of them and headphones wrapped around their ears listening for signals that something of potential value is beneath the sand. Suppose a beachcomber was walking early one morning along the edge of the surf scanning the sandy surface with his machine when suddenly he hears several distinctive blips indicating something solid beneath him. He stops, digs around in the sand, and after scooping down several inches finds three small gold coins one of which is an 1891 Indian Head Double Eagle coin in fair condition valued at $50,000.00. He would be entitled to retain the coin and eventually sell it as the finder/owner.

A finder of property will not prevail if he is a trespasser. The owner of premises upon which an item is found will always prevail over a trespasser. An individual can only maintain an action for recovery of property if the ownership is lawful. A trespasser is thus unable to assert lawful ownership. Similarly, stolen property remains the property of the owner superior to all others except in limited cases where adverse possession is applied to personal property. A thief can otherwise never pass good title. The case of *O'Keeffe v. Snyder* presents an interesting scenario for the New Jersey Superior Court to consider in determining the ownership rights to artwork stolen 30 years prior to a claim by the owner for its return.

❖❖

O'Keeffe v. Snyder
Superior Court of New Jersey, Appellate Division.
170 N.J. Super. 75, 405 A.2d 840 (1979)

The opinion of the court was delivered by J. Morgan.

Three small oil paintings by plaintiff Georgia O'Keeffe, a living American artist of world-wide renown, were stolen from a New York gallery owned by her husband, Alfred Stieglitz, in 1946 by some unknown thief. Their whereabouts remained unknown until March 1976, some 30 years after the theft, when plaintiff discovered them in the possession of defendant Barry Snyder, d/b/a Princeton Gallery of Fine Art, who had purchased them from third party defendant Ulrich A. Frank for $35,000. Plaintiff commenced the present replevin action on May 18, 1976 in an attempt to regain their possession. She appeals from summary judgment entered in defendant's favor adjudging her claim barred by the six-year period of limitations applicable to replevin suits. *N.J.S.A.* 2A:14-1.

The essential facts are relatively free from dispute despite dimmed memories and the death of a prior possessor which has foreclosed knowledge of the date when, and circumstances in which, the paintings passed from the thief to the subsequent possessors. They have been derived from answers to interrogatories and those given by way of oral deposition.

The theft was not reported to the police, plaintiff viewing such official efforts to locate the paintings as being futile. "I was certain [they] could not or would not do anything about what I'm sure they would have thought was a minor theft." Nor did she confront a man by the name of

Estrick, the person she suspected of being the thief. Instead, she hoped that the paintings would be found as were others stolen from the gallery at about the same time. Word of the theft was, however, given to many persons within her artistic circle.

Plaintiff's husband Stieglitz died during the summer of 1946 soon after the theft of the paintings and plaintiff became involved in the settling of his estate over the next three years. As she recited in her affidavit, "I had the burdensome job of settling his estate and could not really pursue the stolen paintings beyond mentioning it to people who were around—the artists—the Stieglitz circle."

In February 1947 one Doris Bry began working as plaintiff's secretary. She and plaintiff discussed the stolen paintings many times over the course of the years although neither reported the loss because plaintiff was convinced such efforts would be unavailing. Eventually, however, in 1972, years before the sale to defendant Snyder, the paintings were listed as stolen with the Art Dealers Association which maintained a registry of stolen paintings.

At some unspecified date and in some unspecified manner after the 1946 theft, the paintings came into possession of third-party defendant's father, Dr. Ulrich Frank, an art collector. According to his son, Ulrich A. Frank, the paintings were displayed "prominently" on the walls of the residences where his father lived during the period of his possession. Information as to Dr. Frank's acquisition of these paintings will probably never be known because he died in 1968 before these facts assumed importance in litigation. Third-party defendant Frank acquired the paintings in February 1965 by gift from his mother and father. For the most part, the paintings remained in his homes on display for the next ten years, during part of which period he lived in Yardley, Pennsylvania. In December 1968 the paintings were displayed at a one-day art exhibit at the Jewish Community Center in Trenton, the owner being there listed as Anonymous. In 1973 all three paintings were consigned to the Danenberg Gallery in New York for sale. Finding no purchaser for them, the Gallery returned them to Frank. In March 1974 they were consigned to defendant Snyder for sale and in March 1975 Snyder purchased the three paintings for $35,000.

O'Keeffe first learned of the whereabouts of the paintings from an associate in New York who informed her that the paintings had been offered for sale to the Andrew Crispo Gallery in New York, presumably when under consignment to the Danenberg Gallery. From this information plaintiff was able to locate the paintings in Snyder's Princeton gallery in March 1976. Her demand for the paintings was rejected and on May 18, 1976 she filed the present suit. Defendant concedes that plaintiff lacked knowledge as to the whereabouts of the paintings between February 1946 and February 1976.

In her complaint plaintiff simply sought possession of the paintings which she alleged to have been stolen from her. Defendant's amended answer denied the essential allegations of the complaint and set out, as separate defenses, that (1) he was the owner of the paintings, (2) plaintiff's claim was barred by laches, (3) plaintiff's claim was barred by limitation, and (4) he held valid title by adverse possession. The record contains no responsive pleadings by third-party defendant Frank and plaintiff has filed no subsequent amendment to the complaint asserting any cause of action against him. Following discovery by way of interrogatories and oral depositions, plaintiff and defendant filed cross-motions for summary judgment.

In an oral opinion granting defendant's motion and denying plaintiff's, the trial judge held that "defendant has simply failed to establish several of the basic requirements of adverse possession." He found that defendant's possession and that of those preceding him and upon which he relies was not a "continual possession which was visible, open and notorious so as to put the plaintiff directly or impliedly on notice of the defendant's possession." Nonetheless, he held plaintiff's suit barred by passage of the statutory six-year period of time (*N.J.S.A.* 2A:14-1), holding that her cause of action accrued at the time of the original theft in 1946. The indulgence of the discovery rule was denied plaintiff because "she failed to confront anyone or take any action at that time [at the time of the theft] against anyone, including a possible thief named Estrick. She simply did nothing." Plaintiff appeals.

We start our consideration of this interesting case with an attempt to focus upon the narrow issue before us. Defendant virtually concedes that plaintiff lost possession of the paintings by theft. Indeed, he has no other choice given plaintiff's uncontradicted testimony, the affidavits of others that record conversations, antedating by years the present controversy, concerning this theft and the whereabouts of the stolen paintings, and the listing of the paintings as stolen in 1972 in a registry of stolen art years before defendant acquired title. Defendant also concedes the indisputable proposition of law that a thief acquires no title to the property stolen by him and can pass none to others regardless of their good faith and ignorance of the theft. *Joseph v. Lesnevich,* 56 N.J.Super. 340, 346 (App.Div. 1959); *Ashton v. Allen,* 70 *N.J.L.* 117, 119 (Sup.Ct. 1903); *Restatement, Torts* 2d, § 229, comment (e) at 448 (1965); *Prosser, Torts* (4 ed. 1971), § 15 at 87. It follows, then, that defendant must concede plaintiff's title to the paintings in question subject to her challenged right to assert that title and claim the paintings. If defendant is to retain the paintings, it is only as a result of the passage of time.

The time within which a suit in replevin must be brought is specified in *N.J.S.A.* 2A:14-1 as being within six years of the date on which the cause of action accrues. The essential question posed for resolution by the trial court and us is when did plaintiff's cause of action accrue. Did the six-year period for suit commence running with the 1946 theft? Did it start running anew with each subsequent transfer of the paintings as against each successive new possessor? Does plaintiff's ignorance concerning the whereabouts of the paintings and in whose possession they were at any given time affect the running of the statutory period? Does the good faith or absence of it on the part of those who acquire possession through the thief affect the manner in which the statutory time period runs? How, if at all, does the doctrine of adverse possession affect the running of the statutory period? These are the areas of inquiry about which we must be concerned.

Although authority concerning limitations of actions to recover possession of chattels is not plentiful, we do not write on a clean slate. The controlling authority of *Redmond v. New Jersey Historical Society,* 132 *N.J. Eq.* 464, 473–476 (E. & A. 1942), held principles of adverse possession, traditionally applicable to real property, to apply as well to personalty.

Dean Ames, in fully considering this question, contrasts the Roman and the English laws on the subject. He persuasively demonstrates, by a wealth of authorities, that other courts, when considering personalty, have consistently applied the same rules of law concerning the necessary requisites of adverse possession that they applied when considering the question of adverse possession of realty. The basis for this like application of principle is, in our opinion, sound and just. We adopt it.

***

One claiming title to property by reason of adverse possession must establish possession for the statutory period which is "actual and exclusive—adverse and hostile—visible or notorious—continued and uninterrupted." *Foulke v. Bond,* 41 *N.J.L.* 527, 545 (E. & A. 1879). With minor changes, not here relevant (see *Mannillo v. Gorski,* 54 N.J. 378 (1969)), those factual requisites of adverse possession have remained unchanged to the present. Moreover, established principles squarely place the burden of proving each of these essential elements of adverse possession on the one claiming title on that basis, and such burden is satisfied only by evidence of a clear and positive nature. *Wilomay Holding Co. v. Peninsula Land Co.,* 36 N.J.Super. 440, 443 (App.Div. 1955); *Redmond v. New Jersey Historical Society, supra* 132 *N.J. Eq.* at 473–474.

Defendant's failure of proof, according to the trial judge, centered on the requirements of visibility and notoriety of the possession. Although not thoroughly discussed, the trial judge apparently viewed the intramural residential display of the paintings and a one-day display at a local art exhibit as insufficient to establish a visible and notorious possession. The conclusion reached is in our view indisputably correct in light of the essential purpose for those requirements.

The requirement of the eight adjectives noted above [actual and exclusive, visible and notorious, continued and interrupted, hostile and adverse] * * * is consequently designed to flag to the true owner the necessity of taking timely legal action * * *. [*Brewer v. Porch*, 98 N.J.Super. 583, 588 (App.Div. 1968), rev'd on other grounds, 53 N.J. 167 (1969)].

Hence, title by adverse possession may never be acquired by mere possession however long continued "which is not such as will give unmistakable notice of the nature of the occupant's claim." *Mannillo v. Gorski,* 54 *N.J.* at 388; 5 *Thompson, Real Property,* § 2546 at 619–624 (1979). Display in one's home provides to the true owner no more notice of the possessor's claim or warning of the need for timely legal action than would its retention in a closet. Neither mode of possession is such as to afford the true owner a realistic opportunity to regain possession by legal action.

***

We fully recognize that by adoption of this view, applying all of the requirements for the adverse possession of land to chattels, we are in many, if not in most, cases foreclosing any real opportunity to acquire adverse title to stolen personalty . . . Many chattels are, of course, small and even when openly held may not give notice of claimant's adverse possession to the true owner. In many cases both the owner and the possessor are equally innocent; one must bear the loss. The question is, and always has been, who of these two innocents must bear the loss? Where adverse possession is concerned, the law favors the owner, at least where he has been deprived of opportunity to defend his title, by the imposition of the several requirements to a title by adverse possession, all of which must be proved by clear and convincing evidence by the adverse claimant. We merely give effect to that policy in applying such law to personalty.

In this case the paintings were very small ones. They were stolen in New York, were thereafter kept out of artistic circulation in the major metropolitan galleries and museums, being displayed only on the walls of the several residences of their successive possessors. We assume that defendant and his predecessors lacked the intention to conceal them. The effect, however, on plaintiff's opportunity to recover them was the same as if they had had that intention. She could not have filed suit in New Jersey or elsewhere. In point of fact, we now know that they were kept for a time in Yardley, Pennsylvania, and thereafter in Princeton, N.J. Plaintiff, living in the far West, could not have known that. And, significantly, once they did appear on the New York art scene, when offered for sale to a New York gallery, plaintiff learned of their whereabouts and the present litigation was commenced. In our view, the trial judge's conclusion that defendant failed to meet his burden of proving that the paintings were possessed in an open, visible and notorious manner was entirely justified.

It yet remains to consider the legal significance of that conclusion. The trial judge apparently viewed as separate the questions of limitation and adverse possession, holding that although title by adverse possession had not been established, plaintiff's claim was nonetheless barred by limitation, the six-year period having commenced running with the theft in 1946. We view these two issues as being the same, and hence reach the contrary result.

With respect to property, real or personal, the bar by limitations extinguishes not only the remedy afforded to recover the property, but the right thereto as well. Indeed, the only vice to the title of the person in possession of such property is the right of the true owner to assert his own title. Once that vice is removed by passage of time, the prescriptive right obtained by the possessor entitles him to pass his own good title to others, including the owner. Indeed, once title to adverse possession vests, the true owner can only regain title by purchase, gift or by himself proving the requisites of an adverse possession . . . actions for the recovery of property, real or personal, of the character required by the law of adverse possession, has persisted throughout the statutory period of limitations. With respect to real property, that period is 20 or 30 years. With respect to personal property, that period is six years. In both cases, however, the property must be possessed for the required period in the required manner. If one of the essential ingredients to adverse possession is missing, the claim for the property is simply not barred.

In this connection it should be observed that neither the statutes of limitation barring rights of entry into real estate nor the statute specifying the period within which suits to recover personal property must be brought recites the requirements for adverse possession. Both types of statutes are essentially couched in terms of limitation similar to the statutes barring personal injury claims. Nonetheless, all judicial authority construing such enactments read into them the essential requirements of adverse possession. See *DeBow v. Hatfield,* 35 N.J.Super. 291 (App.Div. 1955), certif. den. 19 N.J. 327 (1955). Where such elements are not proved, the claim for the property is not barred. *Predham v. Holfester,* 32 N.J.Super. 419 (App.Div. 1954). When the trial judge rejected defendant's claim of title to the paintings by adverse possession, he necessarily disposed of the defense of limitation as well.

***

As applied to the present case, the failure of defendant to establish that his and his predecessors' possession was sufficiently visible and notorious necessarily required not only that his defense of adverse possession be rejected, but the defense of limitation as well. They were, in truth, the same defense.

In direct answer to the questions posed at the outset of this opinion, a cause of action for replevin accrues, in the sense that the statutory time in which suit must be brought starts runnings, when the possession by the defendant, or by those claiming through him, assumes the characteristic elements of adverse possession. See 5 *Thompson, Real Property,* § 2552 at 660 (1979). Although a theoretical cause of action may exist before that time, the statutory period does not run against it. Once it starts running, it continues against subsequent possessors possessing the chattel in the same way; it does not start running anew with each subsequent conversion. *Joseph v. Lesnevich, supra.* Plaintiff's ignorance of the whereabouts of his property does not affect the running of the statute if the possession has the required openness and notoriety; where possession is held clearly and unequivocally, knowledge of the true owner will be presumed. 5 *Thompson, Real Property,* § 2546 at 619 (1979). The good faith of the possessors who nonetheless fail to possess the chattel openly and notoriously has no effect on the running of the statutory period. Finally, the defenses of adverse possession and limitation are the same on the theory that the law refuses to recognize a title it will not protect. 3 *American Law of Property,* § 15.16 at 834 (1952).

In our view, the result reached is the just one given the difficult circumstances of this case. Plaintiff and defendant are assumed to be innocent parties. As to plaintiff the trial judge found, with ample justification, that the manner in which the successive possessors of the paintings held them failed to afford her adequate opportunity to take legal action to protect her interest in them. There is no question but that she is their owner. She should not be deprived of her property without having been afforded such an opportunity. That she did not report the theft to the police in 1946 is beside the point. She may well have been right that such an effort would have proved fruitless. The suspected thief may have been proved entirely innocent. Thirty years later we cannot know one way or the other. In any event, she cannot be deprived of her property on such remote speculation. Moreover, her lack of action did not, as the trial judge suggested it did, deprive defendant or his predecessors of the opportunity of proving their title. Clearly, she has title, and defendants have never seriously asserted otherwise. Had she been successful in earlier recovering her paintings, the result would have been that third-party defendant would never have enjoyed their possession for so many years without paying anything therefor. Although there doubtless will be cases where an innocent converter will be forced to take a substantial loss as a result of our holding, this case does not appear to be one of them.

Moreover, defendant Snyder was not without means of self-protection. He was not a novice in dealing with art works. He purchased the paintings without provenance. He was thus aware of the uncertain history of the paintings' ownership. The artist, however, is alive and it was always open to him to check with her as to their authenticity and the legitimacy of his purchase. He elected to take his chances with this result.

Because we have detected no real dispute concerning the larcenous origin of defendant's possession, and our independent review of his record convinces us of the absence of any genuine controversy concerning that fact, we see no obstacle to entry of a judgment for return of the paintings to plaintiff. All that remains to be tried is the third-party claim wherein defendant seeks to recover from third-party defendant the monies paid for the paintings.

The judgment is reversed, judgment is entered for plaintiff, and the case remanded to the trial court for further proceedings consistent with this opinion.

Reprinted with the permission of LexisNexis.

Questions Presented

1) Why was Georgia O'Keeffe's failure to report the theft of her artwork to the police not held to be a detriment to her claim for a return of her property?
2) What was the court's decision concerning the adverse possession claim made by the defendant?
3) What impact did the court's finding with regard to the adverse possession claim have on the statute of limitations defense asserted by the defendant?

❖❖

C. Remedies for Wrongful Taking of Property

At common law there are several remedies for property that is wrongfully taken from an owner. These common law actions are replevin, trover, conversion and trespass. Modern day statutes of civil procedure have replaced these common law rights of action but the general theory of recovery remains. Replevin is an action for recovery of property that is wrongfully taken when there is a dispute as to ownership and the damages sought is return or restitution of the property that is taken. The true owner (the individual bringing the claim) will be granted possession pending determination by the court and will be entitled to any damages for resulting losses. Trover is also an action for the taking of property but instead of a return of the property sought in a replevin action, trover only looks for the value of the property that was taken. Conversion is the taking of another's property and using it as your own. It is basically a theft of property and an action will lie for the return of the property or the value of its loss to the owner. At common law both trover and conversion involved nonforcible takings of property while replevin was for a forcible or distressed taking. Trespass differs from each of these actions in the fact that there is no loss of property in a trespass. The common understanding of the term is an unlawful entry and remaining onto the real property of another, however, there is a different type of trespass involving the personal property of another. The tort of trespass to chattels is the intentional interference with the personal property of another. In order for a trespass to chattel to be actionable a few elements have to be met:

1. the plaintiff has to have actual possession, or the right to immediate possession, of the property;
2. there must be a volitional act on the part of the defendant that either dispossesses the plaintiff of the property or interferes with the plaintiff's lawful possession of the property;
3. the plaintiff must have suffered actual damages as a result of the trespass.

> ### Legal Definition
>
> **Chattel** – the moveable or immoveable personal property of an individual exclusive of real estate.
>
> **Inter vivos gift** – from the Latin meaning "between the living" this refers to an irrevocable gift made by a donor during the normal course of life.
>
> **Gift causa mortis** – from the Latin meaning "in contemplation of death' this refers to a gift made by a donor in the immediate anticipation of death.

Trespass to chattel is closely related to conversion except conversion is a more severe affront to another's property. Conversion differs in that it is more damaging to a plaintiff's possessory rights than a trespass and the action for conversion forces a sale of the property if damaged to the defendant. A simple example can be shown by returning to the above bailment scenario involving Ed's loan of his vehicle to James. This arrangement we have already established as a bailment agreement for the benefit of James. Instead of just using the vehicle to drive to a show downtown for the night James decides to take it on a cross-country trip for a few weeks. Ed is now without the use of his vehicle which he needs to drive to and from work each day. This loss of the use of his vehicle will factor into his overall damages against James for trespass to chattel. But, what if during the trip James was involved in an accident that totaled the vehicle. Ed obviously would not want a damaged, useless vehicle returned to him so his action would be one of conversion wherein he wants the value of the car plus the loss he sustained in being deprived of the use of his vehicle for several weeks.

D. Gifts

Gifts are voluntary transfers of property or an interest in property from one person to another without any consideration. It is a gratuitous transfer from the donor (the one giving the gift) to the donee (the one receiving the gift.) The gift may be of a future interest in the property instead of an immediate transfer, but this does not impact the validity of the gift. Gift-giving is a common practice which we are familiar with, both as a donor and donee. It is a pleasant way for us to acquire property. However, not all gifts of property are clear and sometimes the issue as to whether a gift was intended ends up in court. These can be troublesome cases for judges and juries alike to decide in favor of a donor seeking a return of or re-payment of property allegedly transferred as a gift. Gifts are considered irrevocable transfers. Courts generally enforce gifts when three conditions are met:

1.   the donor intends to make a present gift of the property;
2.   the donor actually delivers the property to the donee;
3.   the donee accepts the gift.

However, if there is fraud on the part of the donee involved in securing the gift then a gift will not be deemed to have occurred.

The first of these requirements, delivery, is complete when either the donor gives the property directly to the donee or to a third-party acting on behalf of the donee. If the property is given to a third-party on behalf of the donee the gift's delivery will only be complete upon the third-party's delivery of the property to the intended donee. An exception to this rule is if a third-party is holding property for an infant or someone who is not otherwise competent to accept the gift. In either case the third-party can hold the gift for the infant or incompetent and delivery will be considered complete.

Some affirmative act signifying that delivery was made is necessary though actual transfer of the property itself is not necessary. A delivery of property can be actual, symbolic or implied. Actual delivery occurs when a donor gifting property, for instance a family vase, physically presents the vase to the donee. Implied delivery of the same vase occurs if through words or actions the donor manifests an intention to make a gift. Using the above vase example, if an elderly aunt turns to her young niece who is admiring the vase in her home and taking the vase turns to the niece and says, "Here you hold onto it, I have no use for it," an implied gift is made. A symbolic gift is more classically described in the scenario where a person is gifted a car but since it is impractical and impossible to physically hand over a car the transfer of the keys to the car acts as the symbolic delivery of the car. Regardless of the type of delivery, the delivery must be complete for there to be a gift. Completion of the delivery equates to a surrender of control over the property by the donor.

The second element, donative intent on the part of the donor, is a key element of proof in a gift-giving case. Any words, actions, or writings by the donor that not only indicate a transfer of the property to the donee but that the transfer was without any consideration, terms or conditions, will aid in proving donative intent. This is often the element that is challenged in court when there is a dispute over whether a property transfer was a gift or not. In addition to the words or actions of a donor, courts will consider the relationship between the parties, the surrounding circumstances, and the nature of the gifted property, when considering whether or not there was donative intent.

Donative intent requires proof that the donor did not just transfer possession of the property (which would merely create a bailment) but ownership as well to the donee. There has to be a present transfer of the property. Since this requirement of gift-giving involves proof of a mental status to complete delivery of a gift the donor must have the necessary legal capacity to give the property. Thus, infants and incompetents cannot validly gift property. This differs from the ability of the infant or incompetent to be the donee of gift through a third-party.

Since donative intent requires a present intent to make a gift the promise of a future ownership interest is not a gift. This situation is not to be confused with the present transfer of a future interest in property. If parents who owned their home free of debt made a present transfer of their home to their two children but retained a life estate to live in the home until they died this is a completed gift transfer of real property, however, the children cannot sell the property until the parents are deceased. Delivery of the gift of real property though has been completed since a deed transfer will have placed title in the children's names. A different circumstance is present when an individual makes a promise to give an intended donee property in the future but does not effect an immediate transfer of the property. This is at best a contract and clearly lacks the donative intent necessary for a completed gift.

The last element for a gift, acceptance by the donee, requires an unconditional acceptance of the gift on the part of the donee. The acceptance by the donee has to occur at the same time as the delivery of the gift. Until such time as acceptance by the donee the gift may be revoked by the donor. The law presumes that a gift is accepted by the donee if the gift is beneficial to the donee. This last element is easy to prove and usually not in dispute.

There are three types of gift categories: inter vivos gifts, gifts causa mortis and testamentary gifts. An inter vivos gift is one that is made between two living individuals (hence the Latin term inter vivos, which means "between the living") that is irrevocable when made during the normal course of the donor's life. The true nature of an inter vivos gift may not be readily apparent but that does not change the fact that it is a gift. For instance, if someone is indebted to another for $10,000.00 but the creditor decides to forgive the indebtedness due to a long term friendship with the debtor this forgiveness of debt is a gift. Inter vivos gifts may also be given with limiting conditions, as in the life estate example above. The present transfer of title to real property by the parents to their children is an inter vivos gift subject to the limitation of the parents retaining a life estate in the property. Gifts causa mortis and testamentary gifts are similar in the fact that both are given upon the death of the donee, except the nature of the donative intent involved is somewhat different. A gift causa mortis (Latin for "in contemplation of death") is given in anticipation of the imminent death of the donor. It may be accomplished by words, actions or writing. Transfer will be effective immediately upon a donor's death but the gift can otherwise be revoked at any time up to the donor's death. A testamentary gift is one that is made

Legal Definitions

Last will and testament – a legal document that outlines how a person wants their property distributed at death; it only takes legal effect upon the death of the person making the will (testator) and its execution requires by statute certain formalities, such as the presence of at least two witnesses, competency of the testator and a public declaration by the testator that the document is their last will and testament.

Specific bequest – a gift to an individual made in a will of a specific item of property, for example, "I give and bequeath my baseball card collection to my son."

Probate – the legal process by which the validity of a will is proven in court, usually a probate court or similar court of specialized jurisdiction, thereby allowing the distribution of property according to the directions in the will.

Codicil – an addition or addendum to a will that alters, explains, revokes, or supplements the terms of the will without re-execution of the will; a codicil however, must meet the same formal requirements of a will.

in the body of a donor's last will and testament. It too is made on the death of the donor except that there is generally no anticipation of imminent death. A person may complete a will several years in advance of death which makes certain individual gifts (referred to as specific bequests) to persons named in the will. The specific bequests become completed gifts upon the death of the testamentary donor and subsequent probate (proof of validity) of the will. A testamentary gift can be revoked at any time prior to death by the donor. This is accomplished by either drafting a new will or executing an addendum to the will, known as a codicil. The codicil when executed becomes a part of the will. It has to meet the same statutorily required elements for its valid execution as a will. This includes competency of the individual executing (who must be the same person that made the will), the presence of at least two witnesses, and a formal declaration of the document as a codicil to the will (otherwise known, as in the case of a will's execution, as publication.)

E. Bona Fide Purchasers

A bona fide purchaser is an individual who, having paid valuable consideration for property and without any fraud on his part, accepts property believing the seller had a lawful right to sell the property. The bona fide purchaser acts in good faith without any knowledge that a third party has a claim to the property. The bona fide purchaser is also referred to as the bona fide purchaser for value without notice, since this more clearly and completely describes the legal positions of the purchaser. The common law concept of a bona fide purchaser applies equally to an individual who purchases personal property or real property.

The rights of a bona fide purchaser (abbreviated to BFP) to keep the property will be determined by the BFP's good faith in entering into the sale. If a reasonable person would have entered into the transaction with no reasonable belief as to the seller's disputed right to transfer the property then the BFP's right to retain the property will be upheld by a court over the third party claiming a superior right. In such a case the third party claimant, while deprived of their property, is not without recourse against the fraudulent seller. A claim for the value of the property can be made by the third party claimant against the seller. However, a BFP will not be able to maintain possession over a true owner if the property was stolen. In this situation the true owner would be entitled to a return of their property from the BFP but the BFP can seek damages against the fraudulent seller. As in the above case of *O'Keeffe v. Snyder* the true owner of the stolen artwork was restored the possession and ownership of the art despite the innocent purchase of the stolen artwork by Snyder. The remand of the case to the trial court was for a determination of the claim of Snyder, the BFP, against the seller of the artwork.

When dealing with commercial paper—an unsecured, short-term debt instrument, like a promissory note, check, draft, or certificate of deposit—a BFP is referred to as a holder in due course. If a merchant receives a check from a customer for payment of goods and the check is dishonored by the bank for insufficient funds the merchant is still a holder in due course and can obtain payment from the maker of the check. (More on this topic will be covered in chapter 12, Negotiable Instruments.)

We know that a person cannot transfer title to property better than that which he possesses. So in our theft example the thief cannot vest title in a purchaser for property he has stolen since it is not rightfully his. But this also extends to others who, while not having stolen the property, commit some fraud in the transfer, such as a lessee of property who attempts to sell the property. If I lease a new car for three years at $250.00 a month but in the second year of my lease I sell it to a third-party for $18,000.00. I cannot transfer lawful ownership since the leasing company will still be the title owner of the car. However, for the sake of this example assume that the sale goes through and the buyer registers the car in another state. A records check fails to uncover a lien against the car and the buyer is able to register his newly purchased car. I continue to make monthly payments and there is no issue until a year later when the leasing company comes to me for the return of my leased vehicle. What would be the position of the third party who purchased my car once the leasing company tracked them down? The obvious claim would be that they had no idea I did not have title to transfer the vehicle and as an innocent purchaser the legal argument to make is that they are a bona fide purchaser for value. Assuming all other requirements of a BFP can be met the car can be retained by the BFP and my liability would be to the leasing company for the value of the vehicle. However, is there a superior argument to the rights of the BFP that can be made by the leasing company? Certainly it can be argued that a conversion of the property occurred and a theft resulted by my transfer of the car to the third party. In that case the car is returned to the leasing company and I am liable to the third-party purchaser for the $18,000.00.

A common law rule related to a bona fide purchaser is the shelter rule. Under the shelter rule if a bona fide purchaser sells the subject property to another this subsequent grantee is also able to invoke bona fide purchaser status, even if the new grantee would not otherwise qualify as a BFP. The most common scenario used as an example of this rule is when there is a transfer from A to B of property which B purchases unaware of a claim by C as the true owner. B, as a bona fide purchaser, subsequently sells the property to D, still unaware of the disputed nature of the property. However, D is made aware of C's claim prior to the transfer, yet D can still purchase the property despite this knowledge due to B's status as a BFP and the "shelter" it gives to D for his purchase. This rule would not apply if B, as the BFP, sold the property back to A since A, as the original grantor, would have had notice of C's interest in the property. The shelter rule is in place to allow a bona fide purchaser to not only possess and own the property but to be secure in the third leg of property rights, the right to transfer property. The rule applies equally to real property and negotiable instruments.

IV. Real Property

Real property consists of land and the structures upon it. Those structures not only include any buildings, sheds, and garages upon the land but also trees, crops, bodies of water, and sub-surface minerals. It is tangible, immovable property in which is contained a bundle of rights to the property. Real property consists of two types of potential inherited rights, otherwise known as hereditaments: corporeal hereditaments and incorporeal hereditaments. A corporeal hereditament is a tangible, observable, permanent object connected to the land. A house, timber, crops, or minerals are examples of corporeal hereditaments. An incorporeal hereditament is an intangible right derived from the real property. Examples of incorporeal hereditaments include easements, boating rights on a lake, and profits-a-prendre (a right to take something off another's land). Real property differs from personal property in several key aspects:

1. it is permanent and immovable;
2. it has to be transferred by way of a writing (a Statute of Frauds requirement, see chapter 7 on Contracts), with a deed being the typical means of conveyance;
3. the owner has an estate for life (or at least until such time as he decides to transfer the property);
4. it descends upon death to the heir of the owner unlike personal property which comes into the possession of the estate administrator or executor for distribution.

Real property interests are classified according to the type of estate in land the individual possesses. There are three basic categories of estates: freehold, nonfreehold, and concurrent. The difference between the three estates is that freehold estates are inheritable while nonfreehold estates are for a specific duration of time and concurrent estates have simultaneous ownership rights between individuals. Real property, like personal property, is freely transferable but subject to reasonable regulation by the state. One of the chief powers of local municipal governments is over zoning, the control of the use of land and the structures upon it. This is an important police power function of local governments, further explained below, that can limit the use of property which in turn may impact its transferability.

The nonfreehold estate is not an inheritable estate and lacks ownership. The owner interest is known as seisin, a common law term from Medieval England's feudal land system denoting possession and ownership. Nonfreehold estates—an estate for years or an estate from period to period—lack seisin. The only rights conveyed are those of possession and use.

Concurrent estates are found in three different categories, two of which are closely related. A tenancy in common is a concurrent estate wherein each tenant has a unified possession with a separate interest in the property. If there are three tenants in common they may all three own equal shares or one may own a larger share than the other two tenants. They can also each own different shares in the property. A main feature of a tenancy in common is that the separate interest of each tenant in common is inheritable by either the heirs (an individual who receives an ownership interest in real property upon the death of an ancestor) or devisees (an individual who receives a gift of real property by will) of the deceased tenant in common. A joint tenancy differs from a tenancy in common in several key aspects. First and foremost is that a joint tenancy has a right of survivorship which means that upon the death of one joint tenant the remaining joint tenants gain the deceased joint tenant's share by operation of law. The property passes automatically without a probate of the joint tenant's will or administration of the estate if the joint tenant died without a will. If A and B are joint tenants in Blackacre and B dies then A is the full owner. If A, B and C are joint tenants in Blackacre and B dies then A and C are now joint tenants. If A dies five years after B then C is the remaining owner of Blackacre. A joint tenancy also differs from a tenancy in common in that joint tenants cannot possess any divided interests. In a tenancy in common there can be three tenants in common with one tenant possessing a 50% interest and the other two tenants each possessing 25% interest in the property. This cannot happen in a joint tenancy where there is a unity in possession and interest. In fact, there are four unities in a joint tenancy than distinguish it from a tenancy in common:

1. unity in interest – all joint tenants have the same interest in duration, extent and nature;
2. unity in possession – no joint tenant has exclusive control over the property and they each have a simultaneous undivided share;
3. unity of time – requires that each joint tenant came into possession at the same time for the same period of ownership;
4. unity of title – the joint title was vested in the same instrument transferring equal ownership.

If a transferring document does not specify the way in which title is to be taken the law defaults possession to a tenancy in common.

A third type of concurrent estate, closely related to a joint tenancy, is a tenancy by the entirety. This estate is reserved only for married couples and is distinguished from a joint tenancy by the fact that a spouse cannot transfer their interest in the property without the permission of the other spouse. Each spouse possesses an undivided interest with a full right to use and occupy and a right of survivorship. In a tenancy by the entirety the married couple is considered a single entity. Due to this single entity legal fiction the creditors of one spouse cannot force a sale of the property, thereby providing better protection than a joint tenancy. Only about half of the states recognize the tenancy by the entirety. In the other states spouses usually take possession of real property as joint tenants, though there is nothing preventing spouses from taking possession of real property as either joint tenants or tenants in common. The only limit would be state inheritance or estate laws that reserve to a spouse a minimum share of a deceased spouse's property. This statutory right can be waived by a spouse and may be done so in situations involving second marriages.

A. Possessory Estates in Land

There are many different ways in which someone can have title to or possession of real property. These interests are either in the form of a "fee" ownership or a life estate or leasehold estate. A fee ownership is an estate in land that is transferable. The word fee derives from the feudal land relationship of a fief that existed between a medieval landlord and tenant. Fiefs were interests in land

FIGURE 6.2   Concurrent Estates

Tenancy in Common

A tenant in common has unified possession with a separate interest in the property. The property interest of a tenant in common may be unequal but the possessory interest is still unified. Upon the death of a tenant in common that tenant's share passes to the heirs.

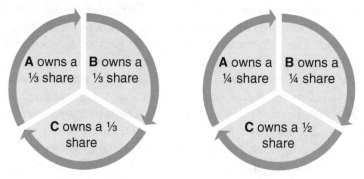

Joint tenancy with right of survivorship

A joint tenant has a unified possession with a joint interest in the property. The interest of the joint tenants are equal and pass to the surviving joint tenants upon the death of any joint tenant.

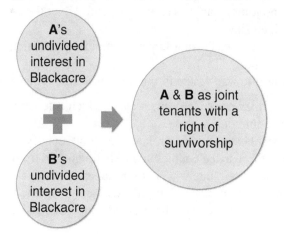

that a tenant would possess on a landlord's property in return for service and loyalty to the landlord as part of the landlord's feudal estate. The fiefs could be large or small and were transferable rights. It was part of a complex land system in the middle ages, the remnants of which we find present in some of the modern terms we use in real property law.

The different possessory fee estates range from the indefeasible fee simple absolute estate, which is the best form of ownership interest, to the defeasible estate of fee simple subject to a condition subsequent. Table 6.2 outlines the different types of possessory fee estates with examples of the words of transfer. All of these possessory fee estates are still viable methods of real property ownership, however the fee tail is only available in four states: Delaware, Maine, Massachusetts and Rhode Island. The fee tail, or entailment, has either been abolished or not recognized in all other states.

The life estate and leasehold estate are also possessory estates in real property, however, these interests are not transferable. In a life estate an owner has a right to possess and own only for the duration of their life. A life estate possessor is referred to as the life tenant and upon the death of the life tenant either a reversionary interest or a remainder interest takes effect. It is used in the United States primarily as an estate planning tool. A typical planning situation involves older parents who own a house that is mortgage-free and want to pass the house and property to their children. By way of the simple execution of a new deed transferring the property from the parents to the children, but reserving in the parents a life estate to the property, the life estate is created. The children have equitable title and the parents have legal title. The property cannot be transferred by the children until such time as the parents die or they surrender the life estate. However, recall from the example above in the section on Gifts that this transfer is a gift of real property from the parents to the children. There are many overlapping concepts that have to be considered when dealing with property transactions.

TABLE 6.2 Possessory Estates

Types of Possessory Estates	Description	Examples of words of transfer
Fee simple absolute	An estate of absolute ownership in land, the highest and best possible type of ownership allowing the owner unlimited right to use, possession and transfer of the property now and into the future.	"A to B"
Fee tail	An estate in land limited to a particular class of heirs.	"To A and the heirs of his body"
Fee simple determinable (or Fee simple defeasible)	An estate in property subject to a transfer with conditions.	"A to B as long B remains sober"
Fee simple subject to condition subsequent	A defeasible estate that may be terminated upon a stated event allowing the grantor to re-enter the land or have it revert back to the grantor.	"A to B on the condition that B marries my niece." or "To B provided that he does not divorce my niece.'
Leasehold estate	Ownership of a temporary right to possess land or property for a fee.	"A to B for 3 years"
Life estate	Ownership of property for the duration of one's life.	"A to B for life"

The leasehold estate is a temporary right to possess property for a term and for a rental price paid to the grantor/lessor. It is a concept that also has its roots in feudal land rights. Under the leasehold agreement the tenant is given a right to use and occupy the landlord's property for an established period of time pursuant to a contractual agreement. The use of the property can be for residential or commercial purposes, farming, or sub-surface mineral extractions from the land. There are several different types of leasehold estates: an estate for years, an estate from period to period (referred to as a periodic tenancy), an estate at will, and an estate at sufferance. The period to period leasehold often results when a lease agreement contains no ending date but specifies a period of tenancy and rental payment for that period. It also commonly occurs when a lease for years expires and the landlord and tenant agree to continue the leasehold month to month without any specific ending date. The estate at will arises when a tenant occupies real property for an indefinite period and the tenancy is terminable by either party at their will without notice. The estate at sufferance occurs when the tenant overstays his lease agreement term but continues to pay rent. The leasehold interest will remain until the landlord tells the tenant to leave. This is commonly referred to as a holdover tenancy.

B. Landlord-Tenant Interests

The landlord-tenant relationship is the form of leasehold estate familiar to most people and one in which many have participated as either a landlord or tenant. Modern day relationships between landlords and tenants are guided by state law. Each state has a specific statutory code defining the landlord-tenant relationship and setting parameters for the eviction process. Twenty-one states have adopted the Uniform Residential Landlord Tenant Act (URLTA).[13] Other states have adopted portions of the URLTA. The URLTA was created in 1972 by the National Conference of Commissioners on Uniform State Laws in order to standardize and modernize state laws relating to landlord-tenant relationships. The URLTA provides a section on relevant definitions and then outlines landlord obligations, tenant obligations, remedies for both the landlord and tenant for failure to abide by the lease agreement, and retaliatory conduct.

Common obligations of the tenant include:

1. maintenance of the premises (not cause any damage, keep property in good condition and clean);
2. reasonable access to the premises will be given to the landlord;
3. adherence to reasonable rules and regulations of the landlord concerning the use and occupancy of the premises;
4. use of the premises by the tenant as a residence or solely for the stated purpose in the lease (in the circumstance of a commercial lease.)

Common obligations of the landlord include:

1. the landlord can only require a reasonable amount as a security deposit, usually no more than one month's rent;
2. the landlord can apply the security deposit at the end of the lease toward unpaid rent by the tenant or toward any damage to the premises caused by the tenant in violation of the tenant's obligation to properly maintain the premises;

---

[13] These states include: Alabama, Alaska, Arizona, Connecticut, Florida, Hawaii, Iowa, Kansas, Kentucky, Michigan, Mississippi, Montana, Nebraska, New Mexico, Oklahoma, Oregon, Rhode Island, South Carolina, Tennessee, Virginia and Washington.

3. prompt return to the tenant of the security deposit at the end of the lease or prompt return of the balance of the security deposit upon satisfaction of past rent due or damage;
4. delivery of the lease premises;
5. maintenance of the leased premises (ensure habitability, make necessary repairs).

Eviction of a tenant and the process a landlord must follow in order to lawfully evict a tenant is explained in the remedies section of the URLTA and in all state statutes covering the landlord-tenant relationship. The failure by a landlord to follow the strict requirements for evicting a tenant can result in the tenant being able to remain on the property beyond the term of the lease.

State laws regulating landlord-tenant relationships impose an implied warranty of habitability upon a landlord to ensure that the property being leased is habitable for humans. This implied warranty under state law is effective even if there is no specific promise of habitability in the lease agreement. The warranty of habitability requires the landlord to provide a structurally sound premises with working electricity and plumbing, water, heat, and other common amenities expected for human habitation. A violation of the implied warranty of habitability can be grounds for a tenant to withhold rent payments and it is often asserted as a defense by tenants in actions initiated by a landlord for past due rent. Within each lease agreement is also an implied covenant of quiet enjoyment. This implied covenant conveys to the tenant a guarantee that his tenancy will not be disturbed by someone with a superior claim or title to the premises.

Federal law becomes involved in the landlord-tenant relationship only if there is discrimination in housing. Title 42 U.S. Code § 3604, as part of the federal Fair Housing Act and Fair Housing Amendments Act, establishes a federal civil violation for anyone to "... *refuse to sell or rent after the making of a bona fide offer, or to refuse to negotiate for the sale or rental of, or otherwise make unavailable or deny, a dwelling to any person because of race, color, religion, sex, familial status, or national origin.*" Discrimination in the rental of real property or the representation that real property is not available because of race, color, religion, sex, familial status, or national origin is also prohibited by federal law. The federal Fair Housing Act also grants rental discrimination protection to the mentally and physically disabled. Disability under federal law includes alcohol or drug addiction, hearing and visual impairments, physical impairment, mental retardation, mental illness, HIV, AIDS, and AIDS-Related Complex.[14] Each state has comparable equal housing and rental laws which, in some cases, extend protections to those discriminated against due to sexual orientation or gender identity.[15] Even though these two latter categories are not specifically covered by the Fair Housing Act discrimination against a lesbian, gay, bisexual, or transgender individual may be covered if it is based on nonconformity with a gender stereotype.[16]

---

[14] FindLaw, Rental Housing Rights for Disabled Tenants, http://civilrights.findlaw.com/discrimination/rental-housing-rights-for-disabled-tenants.html, retrieved July 12, 2017.

[15] Presently only 12 states and the District of Columbia have laws that specifically prohibit discrimination based on sexual orientation. The states are: California, Connecticut, Hawaii, Maryland, Massachusetts, Minnesota, New Hampshire, New Jersey, New Mexico, Rhode Island, Vermont, and Wisconsin. Several major U.S. cities also have housing anti-discrimination laws based on sexual orientation. Only five states have anti-discrimination rental laws based on transgender: California, Connecticut, Minnesota, New Mexico and Rhode Island. Source: http://civilrights.findlaw.com/discrimination/fair-housing-laws-renters-protection-from-sexual-orientation.html

[16] See, U.S. Department of Housing and Urban Development, *Ending Housing Discrimination against Lesbian, Gay, Bisexual and Transgender Individuals and their Families,* https://portal.hud.gov/hudportal/HUD?src=/program_offices/fair_housing_equal_opp/LGBT_Housing_Discrimination, retrieved July 12, 2017.

Commercial real estate leases are a distinctly different form of landlord-tenant agreements. They are generally more complex than residential leasing agreements and include much different rent payment arrangements. Unlike residential leases the commercial lease is not covered by most consumer protection laws and it is for a longer term. Default or breach of a lease term can be more costly than with a residential. The only benefit upon entering a commercial lease is that the terms are more negotiable. There are two ways in which rent is calculated under the terms of a commercial lease. One is by gross rent, the other by a net amount calculation. Gross rent is the most beneficial arrangement for the lessee since it includes all costs associated with the rental wrapped into a set monthly amount. The landlord/lessor pays all utilities and provides for maintenance of the building and this cost is built into the tenant/lessee's rent payment. A net lease may offer a lower base rent but the expenses of the landlord/lessor are also added for a final rent calculation. The net lease will be either a single-net lease, double-net lease or a triple-net lease. In the

FIGURE 6.3 Sample Lease Agreement

LEASE AGREEMENT

By this agreement, made and entered into on December _____, 2017, between **Lawful Properties, LLC**, 1 Main Street, Danbury, CT 06810, Tel. 203-555-1111, referred to below as *Lessor*, and, **Thomas Tenant,** 77 Oak Avenue, Southbury, CT 06810, Tel. # 203-555-2222, referred to below as *Lessee*, the *Lessor* grants, demises, and lets to *Lessee*, and *Lessee* hires and takes as tenant of *Lessor*, the first floor commercial office space located at 80 Main Street, Danbury, CT 06810.

It is further mutually agreed between the parties as follows:

Section I
Term

This lease shall be for a month-to-month tenancy beginning January 1, 2018. *Lessee* agrees to provide thirty (30) days notice to *Lessor* upon termination of the month-to month tenancy.

Section II
Use and Occupancy

The premises leased are to be used and occupied by *Lessee* as a financial planning services office and for no other use or purpose whatsoever. *Lessee* shall not use or permit the use of the premises, or any part of the premises, for any commercial purpose or any purpose other than as above-stipulated without the written consent of *Lessor*.

Section III
Rent

The rental for the premises shall be $1,000.00, payable monthly, on the first day of each month. All payments will be made payable to **Lawful Properties, LLC**, at the following address: 1 Main Street, Danbury, CT 06810, or to any other person or agent and at any other time that *Lessor* may designate. A security deposit of $500.00 is placed on the signing of this lease, said security deposit will be returned at the termination of the lease subject to final inspection of the premises by the *Lessor*. A 10% late payment penalty will be assessed for rent paid after the 15th of each month.

Section IV
Effect of Failure to Deliver Possession of Premises

In the event possession cannot be delivered to *Lessee* on commencement of the lease term, through no fault of *Lessor* or its agents, there shall be no liability on *Lessor* or its agents, but the rental provided shall abate until possession is given. *Lessor* or its agents shall have ten (10) days in which to give possession, and if possession is tendered within such time, *Lessee* agrees to accept the leased premises and pay the rental provided from that date. In the event possession cannot be delivered within such time, through no fault of *Lessor* or its agents, then this lease and all rights under this shall terminate.

FIGURE 6.3 *(Continued)*

Section V
Utilities

Lessor will provide for all utilities which include heat, electricity and water services as part of the rent.

Section VI
Furniture

Lessor has provided office furniture for the use by *Lessee* during the term of the rental. *Lessee* is responsible for the ordinary care of the supplied furniture. Said furniture includes the following: one (1) rectangular solid wood conference table, eight (8) conference table chairs, one (1) round solid wood meeting table, one (1) solid wood desk, one (1) office chair, two (2) solid wood book cases, one (1) copy machine, one (1) copy stand, one (1) wooden coat rack, one (1) metal supply shelf.

Section VII
Snow Removal

Lessor is responsible for snow removal in the front of the premises and for maintaining access to the premises.

Section VIII
Redecoration or Alterations

Lessee shall not make any alterations, additions, or redecorations on the leased premises without the *Lessor's* prior written consent. All additions, fixtures, or improvements made by *Lessee*, except movable household furniture, shall become the property of *Lessor* and remain on the premises as part of the premises, and shall be surrendered with the leased premises at the termination of this lease.

Section IX
Lessor's Right of Entry for Inspection, Repairs, and Alterations

Lessor, or *Lessor's* agents, shall have the right to enter the leased premises during all reasonable hours with reasonable notice to *Lessee* to inspect the premises or to make repairs, additions, or alterations as may be deemed necessary for the safety and comfort of tenants, or for the preservation of the leased premises or the building, or to exhibit the leased premises, and to put and keep upon the doors or windows of the premises a notice indicating that the premises are for rent, at any time within twenty (20) days before the expiration of this lease. The right of entry shall likewise exist for the purpose of removing placards, signs, fixtures, alterations, or additions, which do not conform to this agreement or to the rules and regulations of building.

Section X
Assignment or Sublease

Lessee shall not assign this lease or sublet the premises, or any part of this lease without the prior written consent of the *Lessor*. *Lessor* covenants that such consent shall not be unreasonably or arbitrarily refused.

Section XI
Effect of Failure to Strictly Comply with Provisions of Lease

Lessor's failure to object to any default on the part of *Lessees* shall not be construed as a waiver of such default, nor shall any custom or practice that may grow up between the parties in the course of administering this instrument be construed to waive or to lessen the right of *Lessor* to insist on the performance of the provisions of this lease.

Dated: _____

_____
Lessee – Thomas Tenant

Dated: _____

_____
Lessor – Lawful Properties, LLC by
Larry Landlord as Managing Member

single-net lease the tenant pays rent plus a pro-rata share of the property taxes. The landlord remains responsible for all other property expenses. The double-net lease has the tenant paying rent plus a pro-rata share of the property taxes and insurance. Finally, the triple-net lease requires the tenant to pay rent plus the pro-rata share property taxes and insurance as well as the common maintenance items like landscaping, water, sewer, trash collection, janitorial services, and any property management fees.

❖❖❖

East Haven Assoc. v. Gurian
64 Misc.2d 276 (1970)
Civil Court, City of New York, New York County

LEONARD H. SANDLER, J.

The most important of the several interesting issues presented by the proof in this case is whether or not the doctrine of constructive eviction is available to a residential tenant when a landlord is responsible for conditions that render part of the premises uninhabitable, and the tenant abandons that part but continues to reside in the rest of the premises. Put in another way, the question is whether New York law should recognize the doctrine of partial constructive eviction as a counterpart to partial actual eviction precisely as it has recognized for over a century constructive eviction as a counterpart to actual eviction.

After a careful review of the authorities, I have concluded that the concept of partial constructive eviction is sound in principle, is supported by compelling considerations of social policy and fairness, and is in no way precluded by controlling precedent.

On May 26, 1963, the defendant entered into a lease with the then owner of 301 East 69 Street, with respect to apartment 18E under which the defendant agreed to pay rent for the apartment from December 1, 1963 to November 30, 1966 in the amount of $425 per month. The apartment in question had a terrace.

In April, 1966, the plaintiff acquired the building. At the end of July, 1966, the defendant and his family vacated the apartment and refused to pay rent for the months of August, September, October and November, 1966, the remaining period of the lease. Accordingly, plaintiff sued for the total of the four months rent, for the reasonable value of legal services, and for specific items of damages allegedly caused by the defendants. As to the last, I find the proof wholly deficient and these claims are accordingly dismissed.

The defense to the suit for rent rests upon the claim that the defendant was constructively evicted from the apartment as a result of the misconduct and neglect of the landlord, which allegedly rendered the terrace uninhabitable.

In addition, the defendant sues for damages to his furniture caused by the landlord's neglect, but this claim clearly must fail since the proof established that the damage complained of occurred before the plaintiff acquired the building. Finally, the defendant seeks return of his security in the amount of $425.

The central factual issue turns on the condition of the terrace and the factors causing that condition.

I find that from early 1965 the central air conditioner emitted quite steadily a green fluid and a stream of water overflow that fell in significant quantities on the terrace. I further find that the incinerator spewed forth particles of ash that were deposited in substantial part upon the terrace. The result was to render the terrace effectively unusable for its intended purposes, and the defendant and his family promptly abandoned the terrace, although it had been a prime factor in inducing them to enter the lease.

Nevertheless, I am unable to conclude that the departure of the defendant and his family from the apartment at the end of July, 1966 constituted their constructive eviction from the entire premises. The evidence clearly discloses that the terrace had become unusable no later than the early spring of 1965, and quite possibly earlier. The law is clear that the abandonment must occur with reasonable promptness after the conditions justifying it have developed. (See 1 Rasch, Landlord and Tenant, § 877, and cases cited.)

Unquestionably, this rule should be given a flexible interpretation in light of the practical difficulties these days in finding satisfactory apartments. Moreover, tenants have a right to rely on assurances that the landlord will correct the objectionable conditions.

Although the question is troublesome, I have concluded that a delay of at least 17 months in moving, without any significant proof of an early sustained effort to find other apartments, cannot be reconciled with the current requirements of law.

Turning to the issue of partial eviction, the proof quite plainly established that the terrace had been promptly abandoned once the condition complained of had developed. I am satisfied that conforming the pleadings to the proof to permit consideration of the issue of partial eviction would serve the interests of justice. (CPLR 3025, subd. [c].)

Although the matter is not clear, I am inclined to believe that the proof before me spelled out an actual partial eviction. It seems to me that the tangible and concrete physical character of the substances falling on the terrace provides a substantial basis for such a finding.

However, I do not rest my decision on that ground in view of the decision of the New York Court of Appeals in *Barash v. Pennsylvania Term. Real Estate Corp.* (26 N.Y.2d 77). Although the facts of the *Barash* case do not preclude such a finding, the wording of the opinion plainly suggests a disposition to define actual eviction rather narrowly. I therefore turn to consider the status of partial constructive eviction under New York law.

In his authoritative treatise, Rasch flatly asserted that constructive eviction requires "surrender of the entire possession by the tenant." (See 1 Rasch, Landlord and Tenant, § 876.)

None of the cases he cites, however, supports that sweeping assertion. These cases, with many others, repeat the general formula that constructive eviction requires abandonment of the premises. None of the cases I have examined squarely address the question here presented of the legal effect of abandonment of only that part of the premises rendered uninhabitable.

The doctrine of constructive eviction was developed by analogy to actual eviction on the basis of a very simple and obvious proposition. If a tenant is effectively forced out of leased premises as a result of misconduct by a landlord that substantially impairs enjoyment of the leased premises, the same legal consequences should follow as though the evicted were physically evicted.

In the eloquent landmark decision that firmly established constructive eviction in New York law, *Dyett v. Pendleton* (8 Cow. 727, *supra*) the following was said at page 734: "Suppose the landlord had established a hospital for the small pox, the plague, or the yellow fever, in the remaining part of this house; suppose he had made a deposit of gunpowder, under the tenant, or had introduced some offensive and pestilential materials of the most dangerous nature; can there be any hesitation in saying that if, by such means, he had driven the tenant from his habitation, he should not recover for the use of that house, of which, by his own wrong, he had deprived his tenant? It would need nothing but common sense and common justice to decide it."

Why should a different test be applied where the tenant, through comparable means, is effectively deprived of the use of part of his residence, and abandons that part? Ought not the same consequences to follow as would follow an "actual partial eviction"?

I am unable to see any basis in "common sense and common justice" for treating the two situations differently.

Support for this view appears in the careful phrasing of the first decision to establish the requirement of abandonment in constructive eviction cases (*Edgerton v. Page*, 20 N.Y. 281, 284, 285). The Court of Appeals squarely rested the requirement on the unfairness of suspending rent while the tenant continued to occupy the "entire premises." "I cannot see upon what principle the landlord should be absolutely barred from a recovery of rent, when his wrongful acts stop short of depriving the tenant of the possession of *any portion* of the premises. * * * The true rule, from all the authorities is, that while the tenant remains in possession of the *entire premises* demised, his obligation to pay rent continues."

While some later opinions have been less carefully worded, I know of none that requires a different result.

While the view here expressed seems to me inherent in "common sense and common justice" that gave rise originally to the doctrine of constructive eviction, the result is independently compelled by considerations of fairness and justice in the light of present realities. It cannot be seriously disputed that a major shortage in residential housing has prevailed in our metropolitan area for several decades. The clear effect has been to undermine so drastically the bargaining power of tenants in relation to landlords that grave questions as to the fairness and relevance of some traditional concepts of landlord-tenant law are presented.

The very idea of requiring families to abandon their homes before they can defend against actions for rent is a baffling one in an era in which decent housing is so hard to get, particularly for those who are poor and without resources. It makes no sense at all to say that if part of an apartment has been rendered uninhabitable, a family must move from the entire dwelling before it can seek justice and fair dealing.

Accordingly, I hold that when the defendant and his family ceased to use the terrace, a partial constructive eviction occurred with the same legal consequences as attends a partial "actual" eviction.

These consequences were comprehensively defined in *Peerless Candy Co. v. Halbreich* (125 Misc. 889). It is clear that from the time of the partial eviction, the defendant had the right to stop paying rent. Accordingly, I find against the plaintiff on its action for rent and legal expenses, and for the defendant on his action to recover the security deposit of $425.

Judgment should be entered for the defendant for $425 with interest from August 1, 1966.

Reprinted with the permission of LexisNexis.

Questions Presented

1) What is a constructive eviction?
2) What did the court say were the grounds for the tenant's partial constructive claim?
3) Was the tenant in this case justified in withholding rent? Why?

❖❖

C. Future Interests

Future interests in property, both real and personal, are legal ownership rights that do not permit for present possession or use. They are mainly encountered in trust agreements or deeds of transfer. There are two types of future interests: those retained by the transferor and those retained by the transferee. A future interest retained by a transferor is known as a reversionary interest. An estate is vested in a transferor through a reversionary interest. In Table 6.2 the transferor A has retained a reversionary interest in his property since it is transferred to B as long as B is alive. Upon the death of B the property "reverts" back to A, the original transferor. This is a vested interest A has in the property. A contingent interest is created if A transferred the property to B with the following words: "to B as long as B refrains from the use of alcoholic beverages." If B refrains from drinking alcohol the property is B's but A still has a "possibility of reverter" in the event B gives up on sobriety. This conditional event creates a defeasible estate since the property is transferred subject to conditions. It is known as a fee simple determinable estate, or a fee simple defeasible. A right of entry of termination is created when the grantor transfers property subject to a condition subsequent. If the subsequent condition is not fulfilled the property can be re-entered by the grantor and revert back.

Future interests in a third-party grantee (transferee) are known as remainder interests. A remainder is created through language that passes the property to the third-party grantee upon the completion of the possessory interest of the immediate grantee. Remainder interests are of two types: vested and contingent remainder. The remainder interest exhibited in Table 6.2 illustrates a vested remainder interest. B has a life estate as a result of the transfer and C is said to have a vested remainder that becomes possessory upon the death of B. Since there is no condition precedent to C taking title and the future transfer to C is made in the same transaction, C's interest is vested. A contingent remainder lacks the ability of the remainder interest to vest at the time of transfer. This may be because there is a condition precedent which must be met prior to vesting (as in, "to B for life, then to C as long as C has graduated college and becomes an engineer") or the remainder beneficiary is unknown (for example, when transfer is made to an individual's heirs who are unborn as of the date of transfer). One other type of remainder interest is an executory interest and this interest in property will pass to a grantee only upon the occurrence or nonoccurrence of a stated event. The possibility under an executory interest is also that the property may never pass to the named grantee. Table 6.2 illustrates the executory interest and how it may fail upon the occurrence of a condition subsequent. Since the future interest hinges upon B having heirs it is contingent and only becomes vested upon B producing an heir. C's interest is executory because it is not a true remainder and will only vest if B dies without heirs. There is no reversion with an executory interest. There are two types of executory interests: shifting interest and springing interests. A shifting interest is one in which the grantor of the property gives it to a second party grantee but the second party grantee is divested of the property upon the occurrence of an event that shifts the interest to a third party grantee. An example of this transfer is as follows: "A to B for life, then to C and his heirs, but if C has not married by the time of B's death then to D and his heirs." In this transfer B has a life estate and C has a vested remainder subject to a condition subsequent and D has a shifting executory interest. A springing executory interest is one that jumps or springs from the interest of the grantor to the grantee upon the occurrence of an event. The event which "springs" the grantor's interest in favor of the grantee cuts off the grantor's interest. For example: "A to B if B graduates divinity school." B has a springing executory interest because his graduation from divinity school will divest A from

FIGURE 6.4   Future Interests

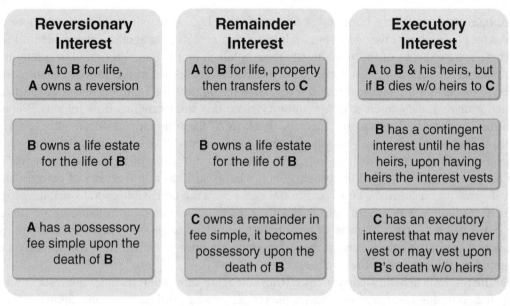

ownership. The condition of grant in the transfer is the subsequent requirement that B complete divinity school and thus spring the interest from A to B.

D. Nonpossessory Estates

Nonpossessory estates in real property give their owners the right to enter property of another or to use another's property without having actual possession of the real property. These estates include easements, profits-a-prendre, licenses, and restrictive covenants.

An easement is a nonpossessory right that allows a holder to use the property of another in a specified manner. There are two main types of easements: an easement appurtenant and easement in gross. An easement appurtenant requires two adjoining land parcels, one the dominant estate which possesses the easement right and the other the servient estate which is the property over which the easement crosses. If one property, Blackacre, is landlocked and access can be gained only by traversing over a second property, Greenacre, and Greenacre's owner gives Blackacre's owner an easement to cross over his property then Greenacre is the servient estate and Blackacre is the dominant estate. The easement once created transfers with the property. An easement in gross only requires one parcel and it is a right given to an individual or entity rather than to an adjoining parcel. A typical easement in gross is one given to a utility company to run underground electrical lines to supply electricity to area homes. This type of easement allows the easement holder to gain access to the property in order to fix or service the underground electrical lines.

A profit-a-prendre is the right of one individual to take from the soil of land someone owns. As described earlier, it is the right to farm and raise crops on another's land, the right to mine for sub-surface minerals, or the right to cut timber from land. A profit-a-prendre can exist with an easement in gross.

A license is simply an authorization from a real property owner to another for access and/or use of real property. It is revocable and may be of a more limited duration than other nonpossessory interests. A person who joins a local gym has a membership that gives the member a license to enter the gym's facilities and use its equipment; otherwise there would be a trespass.

The restrictive covenant limits a landowner in what can be done with the property. It is contained in a clause in a deed that specifies the limits upon the use or possession of the property. This nonpossessory interest is common in the deeds created by real estate developers in the planning of residential subdivisions. A restrictive covenant transfers with the real property and is often used to establish uniformity in a real estate development. For instance, a development of high-end residential homes may contain a restrictive covenant forbidding above-ground swimming pools and clotheslines running from the home to a tree or pole. If a property owner violates the restrictive covenant an adjoining landowner can bring an action to enforce the covenant.

E. Deeds & Mortgages

A deed is a written instrument used to transfer real property. It is a legal document prepared and signed by the transferor/grantor transferring an interest in real property to a transferee/grantee. The deed as an instrument of conveyance needs to be executed by the transferor, delivered to the transferee, accepted by the transferee and then recorded by the transferee in the proper government office for recording, usually a county clerks' office or county recording office. The recording of the deed in a county recording office or county clerk's office provides notice of the ownership interest of the transferee to the exclusion of all others. This act of recording is significant and is guided in each state by a recording statute establishing the method for a property owner in title to perfect their claim to title. There are three different statutory schemes for recognition of the recording act:

1. Race statutes – whoever records their deed first is given priority of title. So if A sells land to B on Monday and the same parcel to C on Tuesday and C files that same day but B doesn't file until Wednesday then C, who took title second, is the owner because he filed first. Even if C knows about the prior transfer to B he is the titled owner by virtue of his recording. This is known as a pure race statute.
2. Notice statutes – a prior recording obviously gives a subsequent purchaser notice of ownership but if a subsequent bona fide purchaser did not have notice and took possession he would be entitled to ownership. In the scenario above if B purchased the property on Monday and did not file and C purchased the same property on Tuesday but knew B had purchased it the day before he would not be entitled to possession as a bona fide purchaser. However, if C purchased the property without knowledge of B's purchase then he is a bona fide purchaser.
3. Race/notice statutes – under this type of statute priority is given to the party who first records but only if they did not have knowledge of a prior transfer. Again, looking to the first scenario under race statutes, C's knowledge that a transfer of the property was made to B the day before will void his recording since even though he was the first to record his deed he did so with knowledge of a prior transfer of the property to another.

Recording is an important part of real property transfer and ownership since it gives a clear indication of who owns the real property and it is relied upon by title companies in determining whether to insure properties, purchasers in determining whether to buy property, and lenders in determining whether to loan money against property.

Deeds are written in one of three forms: either as a bargain and sale deed, a quit claim deed or a general warranty deed. A bargain and sale deed is a form of deed without any covenants. It merely contains the buyer's/grantee's and seller's/grantor's names, the property address and legal description, the date of the conveyance, amount paid for the property and the type of estate transferred. The only representation made is that the seller/grantor has title to the property but there are no representations as to whether the title is free of defects. In another type of bargain and sale deed the seller/grantor can provide a covenant. The covenant states that the seller/grantor has not done anything to encumber the title to the property and it is generally reflected in the following words: "the party of the first part has not done or suffered anything whereby the said premises have been encumbered in any way whatever." Bargain and sale deeds are used sparingly in the United States. The preferred method of transfer is the use of a general warranty deed which gives the buyer/grantee broader protections. In the warranty deed the seller is not only guaranteeing title but also the quality of title, that it is free of defects and if any defects are found that the buyer/grantee can hold the seller/grantor liable. The warranty deed also states that there are no liens, encumbrances, mortgages or encumbrances on the property.

A quit claim deed is a surrender of the property by a grantor to a grantee without any representation other than the release of the grantor's interest to the grantee. There is not even a representation that the grantor has title to the property, just a surrender of the grantor's rights. This type of deed may be used to transfer property to relatives or to add another name to the title as an owner. It may also be used by a property owner who is encountering financial trouble or has lost equity in the property and wishes to unload it quickly. A real estate investor may be willing to take a quit claim deed for a potentially valuable piece of real estate.

Legal Definitions

Mortgagor – the borrower in a mortgage backed financing of real estate.

Mortgagee – the lender in a mortgage backed financing of real estate.

A mortgage is not a document of conveyance like a deed. It is a debt instrument which places the property as collateral for repayment of the loan. The mortgage is used to finance most large real estate purchases and it is based on a set term for a number of years with a calculated amount as a monthly payment based on a yearly interest rate. The lower the interest rate the less the mortgagor will pay in interest over the life of the loan. An alternate type of mortgage loan is an adjustable rate mortgage (ARM) which has a lower entry interest rate but can either rise or lower based on a change in market interest rates. The ARM is attractive due to its lower initial rate but it usually rises over time and can cost as much or more than a conventional mortgage. The financing of real property also involves a note as a companion to the mortgage. The mortgage places the property as collateral on the loan and a foreclosure action by a lender seeks possession of the property. However, the foreclosed property may have depreciated and a subsequent re-sale by the mortgagee may not cover the balance of the loan amount. A promissory note is part of the secured transaction in real estate financing that represents a borrower's promise to re-pay the loan. The note gives the lender (mortgagee) the ability to proceed legally against the borrower (mortgagor) for any money owed on the loan. The lender thereby has two remedies in foreclosure on real property, one against the property on the mortgage the other against the borrower under the promissory note.

A deed of trust is a form of security interest used in some states in lieu of a mortgage. The deed of trust involves three parties in the financing of real property, the borrower, the lender and the trustee who holds legal title to the property for the borrower. If the borrower defaults on the loan the trustee can sell the property under what is termed a foreclosure by power of sale. This type of foreclosure sale, though guided by state statute, differs from a mortgage foreclosure which is guided by a judicial order approving sale of the property. There is no judicial oversight involved in a power of sale foreclosure by a trustee. When a borrower repays a loan subject to a deed of trust the borrower notifies the trustee and requests a reconveyance of title.

FIGURE 6.5   Sample Deed

Bargain and sale deed with covenant against grantor's acts

THIS INDENTURE, made July ____, 2016, among **JACK HILL and JILL HILL**, having an address at 32 Easterbrook Drive, Niagara, New York 14301 ("Grantor"), and **ADAM APPLE and EVE APPLE, as husband and wife**, having an address at 1 Temptation Lane, Pleasantville, New York 10570 ("Grantee").

WITNESSETH, that Grantor, in consideration of Ten Dollars and other valuable consideration, the receipt and sufficiency of which hereby are acknowledged, does hereby grant and release unto Grantees and the heirs, executors, administrators, legal representatives, successors and assigns of Grantees forever,

ALL that certain plot, piece or parcel of land situate, lying and being in the Town of Niagara Falls, County of Erie and State of New York, bounded and described as follows:

BEGINNING at a point on the southwesterly line of Easterbrook Drive, said point being the intersection of the southwesterly line of said Easterbrook Drive with the northwesterly line of lands of Lot No. 9 as shown on a certain map entitled "Easterbrook, Section 2" and recorded in the Erie County Clerk's Office as Map No. 6155 and running thence along the Northwesterly line of lands of said Lot No. 8, South 35-47-45 West 305.49 feet to a point on the easterly line of lands now or formerly Johnson; thence leaving said line and running along the easterly line of lands of now or formerly said Johnson, North 14-35-00 West 231.34 feet to a point; thence leaving said line and running along the southeasterly line of Autumn Road and along the southwesterly line of aforesaid Easterbrook Drive the following: North 32-11-45 East 119.97 feet to a point; thence 38.61 feet on a curve to the right having a radius of 25.00 feet to a point; thence South 58-19-40 East 163.00 feet to the point of BEGINNING.

TOGETHER with all the right, title if intended and interest of, in and to any streets and road abutting the above described premises, to the center line thereof.

SUBJECT TO all laws, ordinances and regulations of governmental authorities affecting said premises, the state of facts a current survey of said premises would show and all matters of record.

TO HAVE AND TO HOLD the premises herein granted unto the Grantees and the heirs, executors, administrators, legal representatives, successors and assigns of Grantee forever.

Grantor covenants that Grantor has not done or suffered anything whereby said premises have been encumbered in any way whatever, except as set forth herein.

Grantor, in compliance with Section 13 of the Lien Law, covenants that Grantor will receive the consideration for this conveyance and will hold the right to receive such consideration as a trust fund to be applied first for the purpose of paying the cost of the improvement before using any part of the total of the same for any other purpose.

IN WITNESS WHERE OF Grantor has duly executed this deed on the date first above written.

_____

JACK HILL

_____

JILL HILL

STATE OF NEW YORK, COUNTY OF _____ } ss.:

On the _____ day of July in the year 2016, before me the undersigned, personally appeared JACK HILL and JILL HILL, personally known to me or proved to me on the basis of satisfactory evidence to be the individuals whose names are subscribed to the within instrument and acknowledged to me that they executed the same in their capacities, and that by their signature on the instrument, the individuals, or the person on whose behalf the individuals acted, executed the instrument.

Place Notary Stamp or Seal Below:

_____

Notary Public

F. Adverse Possession

Adverse possession is a legal doctrine allowing an individual to gain title over the real property of another by meeting certain common law and statutory requirements. State statutes will set the statute of limitations for gaining an adverse possessory right. Depending on the state the period may range from seven to 15 years that an individual has to remain on the property in order to assert an adverse possession claim. The common law requirements necessary to establish an adverse possession claim are that possession be continuous, actual, open and notorious, hostile, and exclusive. These requirements are summarized as follows:

Actual – the adverse possessor must be in actual possession of the property for the required period of time.

Continuous – the adverse possessor must have continuous possession.

Hostile – the adverse possessor infringes on the ownership rights of the true owner and is without permission of the true owner.

Exclusive – the adverse possessor does not share possession with anyone else and excludes all others.

Open and Notorious – the adverse possessor's possession is known to others and puts the true owner on notice he is a trespasser in possession.

Adverse possession claims can be brought by a possessor after the statutory period passes. In an adverse possession action a court will award the adverse possessor legal title to the property over the true owner if all of the statutory and common law requirements are met. This action disseizes the true owner of possession of either the whole property or a portion of the property. At any time during the adverse possessory period the true owner can bring an action for ejectment of the adverse possessor from the real property.

G. Zoning

The first municipal zoning regulation in the United States is largely credited as having been adopted in New York City in 1916. A regulatory scheme was established for the zoning pattern in the City of New York which over time developed, as it did in other municipal codes to follow, into stricter regulations regarding building size, square footage and usage of the property. In order to act as a "safety valve" against rigid governmental regulation of private property an administrative body to oversee governmental zoning regulation was created.[17] Thus was born the zoning board of appeals. The New York State Supreme Court in Oneida County was an early court to uphold the authority and power of the zoning board of appeals in the 1925 case of *People v. Kerner*.[18] This was followed in 1926 by the U.S. Supreme Court's landmark case of *Village of Euclid v. Ambler Realty Co.* which approved a municipal government's power to regulate zoning within its limits as an indispensable police power over the public welfare.[19]

A municipal zoning board of appeals is a governmental administrative agency that has original jurisdiction over matters relating to the municipal zoning codes. It derives its power from state and local laws that establish its existence. The original jurisdiction of the zoning board is limited as are its powers. The zoning board does not have a legislative function, therefore it cannot create new

---

[17] Patricia E. Salkin, New York Zoning Law and Practice, 4 Ed., § 27.08, (2017)
[18] 125 Misc. 526, 533 (Sup. Ct., Oneida Co., 1925)
[19] 272 U.S. 365 (1926)

zoning laws. Further, the board cannot amend the legislative zoning rules or expand or limit the districts to which they apply. The function is limited to one of administrative review to ensure the local zoning regulations are being properly followed and that they are not being applied in a way that onerously restricts the use of real property. Determinations of local zoning officials are reviewable by the zoning board of appeals and the board is permitted to interpret the zoning statutes and their application by the zoning official. Final decisions of a zoning board of appeals are reviewable at the state court level provided that all available administrative remedies have been exhausted. Members of the zoning board of appeals are either appointed by municipal chief executives or elected.

Zoning is an integral part of a municipality's overall plan. In *Village of Euclid v. Ambler Realty* the U.S. Supreme Court found that important municipal concerns and the practicalities of providing efficient government services to residents were met by zoning laws that sought to separate commercial and industrial districts from residential areas:

"The decisions . . . agree that the exclusion of buildings devoted to business, trade, etc., from residential districts bears a rational relation to the health and safety of the community. Some of the grounds for this conclusion are promotion of the health and security from injury of children and others by separating dwelling houses from territory devoted to trade and industry; suppression and prevention of disorder; facilitating the extinguishment of fires and the enforcement of street traffic regulations and other general welfare ordinances; aiding the health and safety of the community by excluding from residential areas the confusion and danger of fire, contagion and disorder which, in greater or less degree, attach to the location of stores, shops and factories. Another ground is that the construction and repair of streets may be rendered easier and less expensive by confining the greater part of the heavy traffic to the streets where business is carried on."[20]

The Supreme Court further found that the need for zoning regulations, an otherwise novel and modern statutory creation, were the result of technological change and the rapidity of societal growth:

"Regulations the wisdom, necessity and validity of which, as applied to existing conditions, are so apparent that they are now uniformly sustained a century ago, or even half a century ago, probably would have been rejected as arbitrary and oppressive. Such regulations are sustained, under the complex conditions of our day, for reasons analogous to those which justify traffic regulations, which, before the advent of automobiles and rapid transit street railways, would have been condemned as fatally arbitrary and unreasonable. And in this there is no inconsistency, for, while the meaning of constitutional guaranties never varies, the scope of their application must expand or contract to meet the new and different conditions which are constantly coming within the field of their operation. In a changing world, it is impossible that it should be otherwise. But although a degree of elasticity is thus imparted not to the meaning, but to the application of constitutional principles, statutes and ordinances which, after giving due weight to the new conditions, are found clearly not to conform to the Constitution of course must fall."[21]

It is upon the foundation of *Village of Euclid v. Ambler Realty* that modern zoning statutes and municipal governance over the development and use within designated zoning districts have been

---

[20] Id at 391.
[21] Id at 387.

Legal Definitions

Zoning – the legislative authority of a municipality, under its police power to regulate public health, safety and welfare, to divide itself geographically into specific areas (or zones) where certain land uses are either permitted or prohibited.

Variance – a municipal zoning board of appeal's exception that provides permission for property to be used in a manner not otherwise allowed by applicable zoning regulations.

Area variance – the authorization of a zoning board of appeals for the use of land in a manner not allowed by the dimensional or physical specifications under the applicable zoning regulations.

Use variance – the authorization of a zoning board of appeals for the use of land for a purpose which is prohibited by applicable zoning regulations.

sustained through the years. Otherwise development could result in a haphazard design negatively impacting both commercial and residential uses of real property to the detriment of their owners.

A key power of the zoning board of appeals, in addition to its power of review, is to provide a variance from existing zoning regulations. Even though the zoning boards do not have a legislative function and are prohibited from changing zoning regulations they can provide permission for property to be used in a manner not allowed by zoning regulations. Only a zoning board of appeals has the power to provide this exception, or variance, from applicable zoning laws. There are two types of variances that can be sought by a property owner: a use variance and an area variance.

A use variance is a permission granted by a zoning board of appeals to allow a use of real property that would otherwise be prohibited under existing zoning regulations. For example, permission to operate a business in a residential area or to convert a one-family residence to a two-family residence in an area of single family homes would be use variances. This is referred to as a nonconforming use of the property. The issuance of a use variance has to be carefully considered by a zoning board due to the overall impact allowing an exception for a prohibited use may have on an area. There are several factors for a zoning board of appeals to consider when deciding whether to issue a use variance:

1. will the property be able to yield a reasonable return if used only for the purpose designated in the zoning regulation;
2. is the property owner's situation due to unique circumstances and not merely due to the general conditions of the zoning district which may reflect the unreasonableness of the zoning regulation; and
3. the use sought by the variance will not alter the essential character of the zoning district.

Each of these factors require the applicant to make a specific offer of proof before the zoning board that meets the requirements for the use variance. The first element is proof of a hardship resulting from an inability to otherwise use the property under any of the designated district zoning uses thereby preempting a reasonable return on the property. This is strictly a monetary element, proof must be in actual dollar figures showing a devaluing of return on the beneficial use of the property. The second element, uniqueness, relates to the hardship which in turn relates to the nature of the land. An undeveloped area may be deemed residential with half-acre zoning for residences but the land owner may have a quarter-acre corner lot on which he wants to construct a small corner market store. This is a unique circumstance that will not permit any permissible use of the property for residential construction under the existing zoning regulations. Additionally, since the neighborhood is still undeveloped the residential character is not adversely impacted by permitting the non-conforming use of a corner market store. The third element pertaining to the essential character of the zoning district ensures that the granting of a use variance will not disturb the comprehensive zoning plan to the point that it is at odds with the purpose of the zoning regulation. Allowing a nightclub and a car wash in the midst of a residential neighborhood would be antagonistic to a rational zoning plan.

An area variance allows variations from established zoning regulations relating to area and physical dimensions outlined in the zoning regulations of a municipality. Zoning may require five acre zoning in an area of a town and a property owner may have a four acre parcel to be improved by construction of a one-family home. An area variance could be granted by the zoning board of appeals for the construction of the home on the four acre lot instead of the required five acre lot. Area variances may be approved for pre-existing structures that were in place prior to the adoption of zoning regulations or that were built years before by a prior homeowner in violation of zoning regulations. A new homeowner in possession may be unaware until served with a notice of violation. As an example, if a homeowner has a shed that is larger than the 10x15 zoning limit for one-family homes an area variance would allow the shed to remain in place, however if the shed were to be replaced any subsequently constructed shed would have to comply with applicable zoning regulations. Area variances may also apply to property line set back requirements. Using the same shed example, if a shed is only 18 inches from the property line of adjoining real property and the municipal zoning code requires a 36 inch set back from the property line an area variance could rectify the issue without having to replace the shed. Once again, if the homeowner does decide to remove the shed then a new shed would have to meet the proper set-back requirements.

In determining whether to issue an area variance a zoning board will consider five factors:

1. whether the variance will create an undesirable change in the character of the neighborhood or be detrimental to adjoining properties;
2. whether the applicant for the variance can achieve the desired result through some means other than the area variance;
3. whether the area variance sought is substantial;
4. whether there will be an adverse environmental or physical impact on the property and the surrounding area within the zoning district;
5. whether the need for the area variance was self-created by the applicant.

This latter consideration, while not fatal to a variance application, does look at the extent to which an applicant is presently seeking the variance due to the applicant's self-created violation of an existing zoning regulation. If an applicant builds an additional home on a lot zoned only for one home there is an element of culpability on the part of the applicant that will not easily resolve his zoning violation with the issuance of an area variance.

Most state statutes regarding municipal implementation of zoning laws empower zoning boards of appeals to impose reasonable conditions or restrictions that are either directly or incidentally related to the proposed use of the property.

SUMMARY

Property law concerns the bundle of rights tied to the use, possession and ownership of property. There are two types of property: personal property (referred to as personalty) and real property. Personal property is divided into two types: tangible property which can be physically possessed and is moveable; and intangible property which cannot be physically possessed. Intangible property, also known as incorporeal property, includes intellectual property interests like patents, copyrights and trademarks.

Historically property interests have been protected by the law dating back to ancient times. Legal codes dating as far back as the Code of Hammurabi have provided protections over individual interests in property. A key aspect of these early property law protections was the inheritability of property interests. Early legal formulations of property rights in the United States were based on natural law theory as it evolved through English common law. Under natural law theory property rights emanate from an individual's own labor in the land which he first claims and possesses over all others. The early common law and natural law theory property protections eventually progressed in the United States into a codification of specific laws guiding use, possessory and ownership interests in property.

Personal property can be acquired by several methods. The most common means is by way of a bailment, a gift, as a finder of lost or mislaid property, or as a bona fide purchaser. There are several common law remedies which can be utilized to recover wrongfully taken personal property. These actions include conversion, replevin, trover, and trespass. Each of these common law actions have been codified in the United States as statutory remedies for the recovery of personal property.

Real property is tangible, immoveable property which includes land and the structures upon it, along with any products of the land. There are two types of inherited rights to real property: corporeal hereditaments and incorporeal hereditaments. Corporeal hereditaments are tangible, observable, permanent objects connected to the land. Incorporeal hereditaments are intangible rights connected to real property. These include easements and profits-a-prendre.

There are different types of possessory and nonpossessory estates in real property. Possessory estates are fee simple absolute, fee tail, fee simple subject to a condition subsequent, fee simple determinable, a life estate and a leasehold interest. Nonpossessory estates include easements, profits-a-prendre, licenses, and restrictive covenants. Future interests in real property exist as either a reversion, a remainder, or an executory interest.

Possession of real property has to be transferred by a written instrument. This is accomplished through a deed which is subsequently recorded in a county clerk's office or recording office. State law designates the type of recording statute followed in each jurisdiction. There are three types of recording statutes: race statutes, notice statutes, and race-notice statutes. The deed as an instrument of conveyance transfers possession and title to real property. Ownership of real property can be held by more than one person either as a tenant in common or a joint tenant. Tenants in common have unified possession with a divided interest in the real property. There is no survivorship element to a tenancy in common. A deceased tenant in common interest passes to the estate of the possessor. A joint tenancy has an undivided, unified interest with a survivorship element. If a joint tenant dies the surviving joint tenant(s) assume undivided, unified ownership. An ownership interest related to joint tenancy is the tenancy by the entirety which is only available to married couples. A tenancy by the entirety has all of the same elements of ownership as a joint tenancy except that the tenant by the entirety cannot sever the tenancy without the permission of the other tenant by the entirety.

Real estate transactions also involve instruments of debt. There are two types of debt instruments common to the financing of real estate: mortgages and deeds of trust. A mortgage is a loan instrument that puts the real property up as collateral for the loan. It is executed in tandem with a promissory note which is an individual pledge of the borrower to repay the loan. A lender will have two remedies upon the default in payment by a borrower: a direct action in foreclosure against the property and a right to proceed individually against the borrower. A foreclosure action involving a mortgage requires judicial approval of the sale of the real property in foreclosure. A deed of trust, used in a number of states in lieu of a mortgage, involves three parties to the financing transaction: the borrower, the lender, and a trustee who holds legal title to the real property until it is paid off. If a borrower defaults on the loan under a deed of trust the trustee can sell the property under a foreclosure power of sale.

Adverse possession is a way by which a nonowner, trespasser can obtain legal title to real property (and to personal property in those states that recognize adverse possession claims to personalty). Adverse possessory rights can be obtained if a trespasser-possessor meets certain common law and statutory requirements. These requirements include possessing the property for a statutorily required period of time and meeting the common law requirements of actual, continuous, hostile, exclusive, open and notorious possession. At any time during the adverse possessory period the true owner can bring an action in ejectment to remove the trespasser-possessor from the property.

Zoning laws represent a local municipal government's exercise of its police power to regulate the public health, safety and welfare. The U.S. Supreme Court has upheld reasonable regulation on the use of real property as part of a comprehensive municipal planning method. Zoning laws set limits and guidelines on the use of real property as well as regulate the dimensions of real property. A zoning board of appeals is established in municipalities as an administrative reviewing body to ensure that zoning regulations are not applied in an unfair manner and that they comply with the overall municipal development plan. Even though a zoning board has no legislative authority it can issue an exception to zoning regulations. This exception is known as a variance. A real property owner can be given a use variance allowing the use of the property in a way not previously zoned for that use or an area variance which allows the property owner an exception to dimensional regulations. Prior to issuing a variance a zoning board will consider several factors not the least of which is the impact that the variance will have on the character of the zoning district.

CHAPTER 7

CONTRACTS

LEARNING OUTCOMES

Upon completion of this chapter the student will be able to:

1 Understand and explain how a contract is formed.
2 Understand and explain defenses to contract enforcement.
3 Understand and explain the kinds of damages that are awarded for breach of contract.
4 Understand when a contract is governed by the common law and when a contract is governed by Article 2 of the Uniform Commercial Code.
5 Understand and explain contract interpretation.

KEY TERMS

acceptance	duress	promissory estoppel
actual damages	expectation damages	reasonably certain terms
bargained-for exchange	incapacity	serious intent to be bound
common law	incidental damages	subjective
communication	legally sufficient value	unconscionability
consequential damages	misrepresentation	unequivocal assent
consideration	mistake	Uniform Commercial Code
contract	objective	void
damages	offer	voidable

I. Purpose and Theory of Contract Law

According to the Restatement (Second) of Contracts, a contract is "a promise or a set of promises for the breach of which the law gives a remedy, or the performance of which the law recognizes as a duty."[1] This is simply a fancy way of saying that a contract is any legally enforceable agreement between two or more people. The key words in this working definition are *legally enforceable*.

Legal Definition

Contract – a legally enforceable agreement between two or more parties.

---

[1] Restatement (Second), Contracts § 1.

The law will not enforce every agreement. For example, it will not enforce an agreement to buy and sell crack cocaine regardless of whether all of the other requirements to enter into a contract are met. The central question of contract law is which agreements should be legally enforceable and the extent to which they can be enforced. This gives rise to the following questions:

1. What are the requirements of a contract?
2. How are the terms of a contract interpreted?
3. What damages should the law award if there is a breach of contract?

A. Sources of Contract Law

Contract law in all 50 states is based on the English Common Law. Unless a state changes a common law rule by statute, the Common Law will apply. In most states, the Common Law typically governs contracts for services/employment, real estate, and insurance.

All 50 states have adopted a form of a statute known as the Uniform Commercial Code ("UCC"). The UCC, first published in 1952, is a "model code" drafted by a group of legal scholars that was led by Karl Llewellyn. In essence, it is a set of suggested laws from legal professionals. Though the UCC started out as a series of suggestions, it has been adopted in substantial form by all 50 states. Article Two of the UCC governs contracts for the sale of goods. A good is defined by the UCC as any tangible item "that is moveable" at the time the contract is entered into.[2] While this may seem narrow, almost every item used in daily life is considered a "good." Virtually everything that can be bought at Walmart, for example, is a good.

B. The Objective Theory of Contracts

To determine whether two (or more) people have entered into a contract, courts look to determine whether the parties intended to enter into a contract. Courts do this objectively, not subjectively. This means that courts do not look to determine what the parties were actually thinking (subjective perspective) when they entered into the contract. Instead, they look to determine whether a *reasonable person* would believe that the parties meant to enter into a contract based on their words and actions in the context of the negotiation (objective perspective).

For instance, imagine if a landscaper were to say to you, "I will mow your lawn for $200" but, by stating "mowing lawns," the landscaper actually believed that he was offering to wash your dishes. In this case, a court would interpret "mowing lawns" as "mowing lawns" rather than washing dishes. A reasonable person would not believe that a landscaper, someone who performs yard

TABLE 7.1   Controlling Law

Type of Contract	Controlling Body of Law
Services/Employment	Common Law
Real Estate	Common Law
Insurance	Common Law
Sale of Goods	Uniform Commercial Code
Lease of Goods	Uniform Commercial Code

---

[2] UCC § 2-105(a).

work for a living, would use the words "mowing lawns" to convey an offer to wash your dishes. While this may seem like a simple concept on the surface, consider the following case.

❖❖

Lucy v. Zehmer
196 Va. 493, 84 S.E.2d 516 (1954)

This suit was instituted by W. O. Lucy and J. C. Lucy, complainants, against A. H. Zehmer and Ida S. Zehmer, his wife, defendants, to have specific performance of a contract by which it was alleged the Zehmers had sold to W. O. Lucy a tract of land owned by A. H. Zehmer in Dinwiddie county containing 471.6 acres, more or less, known as the Ferguson farm, for $50,000. . . .

The instrument sought to be enforced was written by A. H. Zehmer on December 20, 1952, in these words: "We hereby agree to sell to W. O. Lucy the Ferguson Farm complete for $50,000.00, title satisfactory to buyer," and signed by the defendants, A. H. Zehmer and Ida S. Zehmer.

The answer of A. H. Zehmer admitted that at the time mentioned W. O. Lucy offered him $50,000 cash for the farm, but that he, Zehmer, considered that the offer was made in jest; that so thinking, and both he and Lucy having had several drinks, he wrote out "the memorandum" quoted above and induced his wife to sign it; that he did not deliver the memorandum to Lucy, but that Lucy picked it up, read it, put it in his pocket, attempted to offer Zehmer $5 to bind the bargain, which Zehmer refused to accept, and realizing for the first time that Lucy was serious, Zehmer assured him that he had no intention of selling the farm and that the whole matter was a joke. Lucy left the premises insisting that he had purchased the farm.

Depositions were taken and the decree appealed from was entered holding that the complainants had failed to establish their right to specific performance, and dismissing their bill. The assignment of error is to this action of the court.

W. O. Lucy, a lumberman and farmer, thus testified in substance: He had known Zehmer for fifteen or twenty years and had been familiar with the Ferguson farm for ten years. Seven or eight years ago he had offered Zehmer $20,000 for the farm which Zehmer had accepted, but the agreement was verbal and Zehmer backed out. On the night of December 20, 1952, around eight o'clock, he took an employee to McKenney, where Zehmer lived and operated a restaurant, filling station and motor court. While there he decided to see Zehmer and again try to buy the Ferguson farm. He entered the restaurant and talked to Mrs. Zehmer until Zehmer came in. He asked Zehmer if he had sold the Ferguson farm. Zehmer replied that he had not. Lucy said, "I bet you wouldn't take $50,000.00 for that place." Zehmer replied, "Yes, I would too; you wouldn't give fifty." Lucy said he would and told Zehmer to write up an agreement to that effect. Zehmer took a restaurant check and wrote on the back of it, "I do hereby agree to sell to W. O. Lucy the Ferguson Farm for $50,000 complete." Lucy told him he had better change it to "We" because Mrs. Zehmer would have to sign it too. Zehmer then tore up what he had written, wrote the agreement quoted above and asked Mrs. Zehmer, who was at the other end of the counter ten or twelve feet away, to sign it. Mrs. Zehmer said she would for $50,000 and signed it. Zehmer brought it back and gave it to Lucy, who offered him $5 which Zehmer refused, saying, "You don't need to give me any money, you got the agreement there signed by both of us."

The discussion leading to the signing of the agreement, said Lucy, lasted thirty or forty minutes, during which Zehmer seemed to doubt that Lucy could raise $50,000. Lucy suggested the provision for having the title examined and Zehmer made the suggestion that he would sell it "complete, everything there," and stated that all he had on the farm was three heifers.

Lucy took a partly filled bottle of whiskey into the restaurant with him for the purpose of giving Zehmer a drink if he wanted it. Zehmer did, and he and Lucy had one or two drinks together. Lucy said that while he felt the drinks he took he was not intoxicated, and from the way Zehmer handled the transaction he did not think he was either.

*** * ***

Mr. and Mrs. Zehmer were called by the complainants as adverse witnesses. Zehmer testified in substance as follows:

He bought this farm more than ten years ago for $11,000. He had had twenty-five offers, more or less, to buy it, including several from Lucy, who had never offered any specific sum of money. He had given them all the same answer, that he was not interested in selling it. On this Saturday night before Christmas it looked like everybody and his brother came by there to have a drink. He took a good many drinks during the afternoon and had a pint of his own. When he entered the restaurant around eight-thirty Lucy was there and he could see that he was "pretty high." He said to Lucy, "Boy, you got some good liquor, drinking, ain't you?" Lucy then offered him a drink. "I was already high as a Georgia pine, and didn't have any more better sense than to pour another great big slug out and gulp it down, and he took one too."

After they had talked a while Lucy asked whether he still had the Ferguson farm. He replied that he had not sold it and Lucy said, "I bet you wouldn't take $50,000.00 for it." Zehmer asked him if he would give $50,000 and Lucy said yes. Zehmer replied, "You haven't got $50,000 in cash." Lucy said he did and Zehmer replied that he did not believe it. They argued "pro and con for a long time," mainly about "whether he had $50,000 in cash that he could put up right then and buy that farm."

Finally, said Zehmer, Lucy told him if he didn't believe he had $50,000, "you sign that piece of paper here and say you will take $50,000.00 for the farm." He, Zehmer, "just grabbed the back off of a guest check there" and wrote on the back of it. At that point in his testimony Zehmer asked to see what he had written to "see if I recognize my own handwriting." He examined the paper and exclaimed, "Great balls of fire, I got 'Firgerson' for Ferguson. I have got satisfactory spelled wrong. I don't recognize that writing if I would see it, wouldn't know it was mine."

After Zehmer had, as he described it, "scribbled this thing off," Lucy said, "Get your wife to sign it." Zehmer walked over to where she was and she at first refused to sign but did so after he told her that he "was just needling him [Lucy], and didn't mean a thing in the world, that I was not selling the farm." Zehmer then "took it back over there * * * and I was still looking at the dern thing. I had the drink right there by my hand, and I reached over to get a drink, and he said, 'Let me see it.' He reached and picked it up, and when I looked back again he had it in his pocket and he dropped a five dollar bill over there, and he said, 'Here is five dollars payment on it.' * * * I said, 'Hell no, that is beer and liquor talking. I am not going to sell you the farm. I have told you that too many times before.'"

Mrs. Zehmer testified that when Lucy came into the restaurant he looked as if he had had a drink. When Zehmer came in he took a drink out of a bottle that Lucy handed him. She went back to help the waitress who was getting things ready for next day. Lucy and Zehmer were talking but she did not pay too much attention to what they were saying. She heard Lucy ask Zehmer if he had sold the Ferguson farm, and Zehmer replied that he had not and did not want to sell it. Lucy said, "I bet you wouldn't take $50,000 cash for that farm," and Zehmer replied, "You haven't got $50,000 cash." Lucy said, "I can get it." Zehmer said he might form a company and get it, "but you haven't got $50,000.00 cash to pay me tonight." Lucy asked him if he would put it in writing that he would sell him this farm. Zehmer then wrote on the back of a pad, "I agree to sell the Ferguson Place to W. O. Lucy for $50,000.00 cash." Lucy said, "All right, get your wife to sign it." Zehmer came back to where she was standing and said, "You want to put your name to this?" She said "No," but he said in an undertone, "It is nothing but a joke," and she signed it.

She said that only one paper was written and it said: "I hereby agree to sell," but the "I" had been changed to "We". However, she said she read what she signed and was then asked, "When you read 'We hereby agree to sell to W. O. Lucy,' what did you interpret that to mean, that particular phrase?" She said she thought that was a cash sale that night; but she also said that when she read that part about "title satisfactory to buyer" she understood that if the title was good Lucy would pay $50,000 but if the title was bad he would have a right to reject it, and that that was her understanding at the time she signed her name.

On examination by her own counsel she said that her husband laid this piece of paper down after it was signed; that Lucy said to let him see it, took it, folded it and put it in his wallet, then said to Zehmer, "Let me give you $5.00," but Zehmer said, "No, this is liquor talking. I don't want to sell the farm, I have told you that I want my son to have it. This is all a joke." Lucy then said at least twice, "Zehmer, you have sold your farm," wheeled around and started for the door. He paused at the door and said, "I will bring you $50,000.00 tomorrow. * * * No, tomorrow is Sunday. I will bring it to you Monday." She said you could tell definitely that he was drinking and she said to her husband, "You should have taken him home," but he said, "Well, I am just about as bad off as he is."

The waitress referred to by Mrs. Zehmer testified that when Lucy first came in "he was mouthy." When Zehmer came in they were laughing and joking and she thought they took a drink or two. She was sweeping and cleaning up for next day. She said she heard Lucy tell Zehmer, "I will give you so much for the farm," and Zehmer said, "You haven't got that much." Lucy answered, "Oh, yes, I will give you that much." Then "they jotted down something on paper * * * and Mr. Lucy reached over and took it, said let me see it." He looked at it, put it in his pocket and in about a minute he left. She was asked whether she saw Lucy offer Zehmer any money and replied, "He had five dollars laying up there, they didn't take it." She said Zehmer told Lucy he didn't want his money "because he didn't have enough money to pay for his property, and wasn't going to sell his farm." Both of them appeared to be drinking right much, she said.

She repeated on cross-examination that she was busy and paying no attention to what was going on. She was some distance away and did not see either of them sign the paper. She was asked whether she saw Zehmer put the agreement down on the table in front of Lucy, and her answer was this: "Time he got through writing whatever it was on the paper, Mr. Lucy reached over and said, 'Let's see it.' He took it and put it in his pocket," before showing it to Mrs. Zehmer. Her version was that Lucy kept raising his offer until it got to $50,000.

The defendants insist that the evidence was ample to support their contention that the writing sought to be enforced was prepared as a bluff or dare to force Lucy to admit that he did not have $50,000; that the whole matter was a joke; that the writing was not delivered to Lucy and no binding contract was ever made between the parties.

It is an unusual, if not bizarre, defense. When made to the writing admittedly prepared by one of the defendants and signed by both, clear evidence is required to sustain it.

In his testimony Zehmer claimed that he "was high as a Georgia pine," and that the transaction "was just a bunch of two doggoned drunks bluffing to see who could talk the biggest and say the most." That claim is inconsistent with his attempt to testify in great detail as to what was said and what was done. It is contradicted by other evidence as to the condition of both parties, and rendered of no weight by the testimony of his wife that when Lucy left the restaurant she suggested that Zehmer drive him home. The record is convincing that Zehmer was not intoxicated to the extent of being unable to comprehend the nature and consequences of the instrument he executed, and hence that instrument is not to be invalidated on that ground. 17 C.J.S., Contracts, l 133 b., p. 483;

Taliaferro Emery, 124 Va. 674, 98 S.E. 627. It was in fact conceded by defendants' counsel in oral argument that under the evidence Zehmer was not too drunk to make a valid contract.

The evidence is convincing also that Zehmer wrote two agreements, the first one beginning "I hereby agree to sell." Zehmer first said he could not remember about that, then that "I don't think I wrote but one out." Mrs. Zehmer said that what he wrote was "I hereby agree," but that the "I" was changed to "We" after that night. The agreement that was written and signed is in the record and indicates no such change. Neither are the mistakes in spelling that Zehmer sought to point out readily apparent.

The appearance of the contract, the fact that it was under discussion for forty minutes or more before it was signed; Lucy's objection to the first draft because it was written in the singular, and he wanted Mrs. Zehmer to sign it also; the rewriting to meet that objection and the signing by Mrs. Zehmer; the discussion of what was to be included in the sale, the provision for the examination of the title, the completeness of the instrument that was executed, the taking possession of it by Lucy with no request or suggestion by either of the defendants that he give it back, are facts which furnish persuasive evidence that the execution of the contract was a serious business transaction rather than a casual, jesting matter as defendants now contend.

On Sunday, the day after the instrument was signed on Saturday night, there was a social gathering in a home in the town of McKenney at which there were general comments that the sale had been made. Mrs. Zehmer testified that on that occasion as she passed by a group of people, including Lucy, who were talking about the transaction, $50,000 was mentioned, whereupon she stepped up and said, "Well, with the high-price whiskey you were drinking last night you should have paid more. That was cheap." Lucy testified that at that time Zehmer told him that he did not want to "stick" him or hold him to the agreement because he, Lucy, was too tight and didn't know what he was doing, to which Lucy replied that he was not too tight; that he had been stuck before and was going through with it. Zehmer's version was that he said to Lucy: "I am not trying to claim it wasn't a deal on account of the fact the price was too low. If I had wanted to sell $50,000.00 would be a good price, in fact I think you would get stuck at $50,000.00." A disinterested witness testified that what Zehmer said to Lucy was that "he was going to let him up off the deal, because he thought he was too tight, didn't know what he was doing. Lucy said something to the effect that 'I have been stuck before and I will go through with it.'"

If it be assumed, contrary to what we think the evidence shows, that Zehmer was jesting about selling his farm to Lucy and that the transaction was intended by him to be a joke, nevertheless the evidence shows that Lucy did not so understand it but considered it to be a serious business transaction and the contract to be binding on the Zehmers as well as on himself. The very next day he arranged with his brother to put up half the money and take a half interest in the land. The day after that he employed an attorney to examine the title. The next night, Tuesday, he was back at Zehmer's place and there Zehmer told him for the first time, Lucy said, that he wasn't going to sell and he told Zehmer, "You know you sold that place fair and square." After receiving the report from his attorney that the title was good he wrote to Zehmer that he was ready to close the deal.

Not only did Lucy actually believe, but the evidence shows he was warranted in believing, that the contract represented a serious business transaction and a good faith sale and purchase of the farm.

In the field of contracts, as generally elsewhere, "We must look to the outward expression of a person as manifesting his intention rather than to his secret and unexpressed intention. 'The law imputes to a person an intention corresponding to the reasonable meaning of his words and acts.'" First Nat. Bank Roanoke Oil Co., 169 Va. 99, 114, 192 S.E. 764, 770.

At no time prior to the execution of the contract had Zehmer indicated to Lucy by word or act that he was not in earnest about selling the farm. They had argued about it and discussed its terms, as Zehmer admitted, for a long time. Lucy testified that if there was any jesting it was about paying

$50,000 that night. The contract and the evidence show that he was not expected to pay the money that night. Zehmer said that after the writing was signed he laid it down on the counter in front of Lucy. Lucy said Zehmer handed it to him. In any event there had been what appeared to be a good faith offer and a good faith acceptance, followed by the execution and apparent delivery of a written contract. Both said that Lucy put the writing in his pocket and then offered Zehmer $5 to seal the bargain. Not until then, even under the defendants' evidence, was anything said or done to indicate that the matter was a joke. Both of the Zehmers testified that when Zehmer asked his wife to sign he whispered that it was a joke so Lucy wouldn't hear and that it was not intended that he should hear.

The mental assent of the parties is not requisite for the formation of a contract. If the words or other acts of one of the parties have but one reasonable meaning, his undisclosed intention is immaterial except when an unreasonable meaning which he attaches to his manifestations is known to the other party. Restatement of the Law of Contracts, Vol. I, I 71, p. 74.

"* * * The law, therefore, judges of an agreement between two persons exclusively from those expressions of their intentions which are communicated between them. * * *." Clark on Contracts, 4 ed., I 3, p. 4.

An agreement or mutual assent is of course essential to a valid contract but the law imputes to a person an intention corresponding to the reasonable meaning of his words and acts. If his words and acts, judged by a reasonable standard, manifest an intention to agree, it is immaterial what may be the real but unexpressed state of his mind. 17 C.J.S., Contracts, I 32, p. 361; 12 Am. Jur., Contracts, I 19, p. 515.

So a person cannot set up that he was merely jesting when his conduct and words would warrant a reasonable person in believing that he intended a real agreement, 17 C.J.S., Contracts, I 47, p. 390; Clark on Contracts, 4 ed., I 27, at p. 54.

Whether the writing signed by the defendants and now sought to be enforced by the complainants was the result of a serious offer by Lucy and a serious acceptance by the defendants, or was a serious offer by Lucy and an acceptance in secret jest by the defendants, in either event it constituted a binding contract of sale between the parties.

***

The complainants are entitled to have specific performance of the contracts sued on. The decree appealed from is therefore reversed and the cause is remanded for the entry of a proper decree requiring the defendants to perform the contract in accordance with the prayer of the bill.

Reversed and remanded.

Questions Presented

1)   Why did Zehmer contend that he was not bound by his promise to sell the farm?
2)   What test did the Court use to determine whether Zehmer intended to form a contract?
3)   What facts did the Court rely on to hold that Zehmer entered into a contract with Lucy?

❖❖

II. Requirements of a Contract

A contract has three essential elements (requirements): (1) Offer, (2) Acceptance, and (3) Consideration. If even one of these three elements is a missing, an agreement will not likely be legally enforceable.

A. Offers

Every contract has two basics parties to it, the offeror (sometimes called the "promisor") and the offeree (sometimes called the "promisee"). The offeror is the person making the offer. The offeree is the person receiving it. To determine whether an offer is made, courts look only to the objective words and actions of the offeror.

Valid offers have three essential elements: (1) Offeror's Serious Intent to Be Bound, (2) Reasonably Certain Terms, and (3) Communication.

1. Offers: Serious Intent to be Bound

In order for an offer to be valid, a reasonable person must believe that the offeror intends to be bound in contract.[3] While this means that words or actions made in jest or anger cannot lead to an enforceable offer, courts will only look at whether a reasonable person would believe the offeror meant to be bound. For instance, in *Lucy v. Zehmer* (discussed earlier in this chapter), a farmer was bound by his offer to sell his prized farm even though he was intoxicated. The court held that, based on his words and actions, a reasonable person would believe that he was serious. Compare *Lucy v. Zehmer* to the following case.

❖❖❖

Leonard v. Pepsico, Inc.
88 F.Supp.2d 116 (S.D.N.Y. 1999)

KIMBA M. WOOD, District Judge.

Plaintiff brought this action seeking, among other things, specific performance of an alleged offer of a Harrier Jet, featured in a television advertisement for defendant's "Pepsi Stuff" promotion.

I. BACKGROUND

This case arises out of a promotional campaign conducted by defendant, the producer and distributor of the soft drinks Pepsi and Diet Pepsi. (*See* PepsiCo Inc.'s Rule 56.1 Statement ("Def. Stat.") ¶ 2.) The promotion, entitled "Pepsi Stuff," encouraged consumers to collect "Pepsi Points" from specially marked packages of Pepsi or Diet Pepsi and redeem these points for merchandise featuring the Pepsi logo. (*See id.* ¶¶ 4, 8.). . . .

A. The Alleged Offer

Because whether the television commercial constituted an offer is the central question in this case, the Court will describe the commercial in detail. The commercial opens upon an idyllic, suburban morning, where the chirping of birds in sun-dappled trees welcomes a paperboy on his morning route. As the newspaper hits the stoop of a conventional two-story house, the tattoo of a military drum introduces the subtitle, "MONDAY 7:58 AM." The stirring strains of a martial air mark the appearance of a well-coiffed teenager preparing to leave for school, dressed in a shirt emblazoned with the Pepsi logo, a red-white-and-blue ball. While the teenager confidently preens, the military drumroll again sounds as the subtitle "T-SHIRT 75 PEPSI POINTS" scrolls across the screen. Bursting from his room, the teenager strides down the hallway wearing a leather jacket. The drumroll sounds again, as the subtitle "LEATHER JACKET 1450 PEPSI POINTS" appears.

---

[3] *See Leonard v. PepsiCo,* 88 F.Supp.2d 116 (S.D.N.Y. 1999).

The teenager opens the door of his house and, unfazed by the glare of the early morning sunshine, puts on a pair of sunglasses. The drumroll then accompanies the subtitle "SHADES 175 PEPSI POINTS." A voiceover then intones, "Introducing the new Pepsi Stuff catalog," as the camera focuses on the cover of the catalog. (*See* Defendant's Local Rule 56.1 Stat., Exh. A (the "Catalog").)

The scene then shifts to three young boys sitting in front of a high school building. The boy in the middle is intent on his Pepsi Stuff Catalog, while the boys on either side are each drinking Pepsi. The three boys gaze in awe at an object rushing overhead, as the military march builds to a crescendo. The Harrier Jet is not yet visible, but the observer senses the presence of a mighty plane as the extreme winds generated by its flight create a paper maelstrom in a classroom devoted to an otherwise dull physics lesson. Finally, the Harrier Jet swings into view and lands by the side of the school building, next to a bicycle rack. Several students run for cover, and the velocity of the wind strips one hapless faculty member down to his underwear. While the faculty member is being deprived of his dignity, the voiceover announces: "Now the more Pepsi you drink, the more great stuff you're gonna get."

The teenager opens the cockpit of the fighter and can be seen, helmetless, holding a Pepsi. "[L]ooking very pleased with himself," (Pl. Mem. at 3,) the teenager exclaims, "Sure beats the bus," and chortles. The military drumroll sounds a final time, as the following words appear: "HARRIER FIGHTER 7,000,000 PEPSI POINTS." A few seconds later, the following appears in more stylized script: "Drink Pepsi—Get Stuff." With that message, the music and the commercial end with a triumphant flourish.

Inspired by this commercial, plaintiff set out to obtain a Harrier Jet. Plaintiff explains that he is "typical of the 'Pepsi Generation' . . . he is young, has an adventurous spirit, and the notion of obtaining a Harrier Jet appealed to him enormously." (Pl. Mem. at 3.) Plaintiff consulted the Pepsi Stuff Catalog. . . . Conspicuously absent from the Order Form is any entry or description of a Harrier Jet. (*See id.*) The amount of Pepsi Points required to obtain the listed merchandise ranges from 15 (for a "Jacket Tattoo" ("Sew `em on your jacket, not your arm.")) to 3300 (for a "Fila Mountain Bike" ("Rugged. All-terrain. Exclusively for Pepsi.")). It should be noted that plaintiff objects to the implication that because an item was not shown in the Catalog, it was unavailable. (*See* Pl. Stat. ¶¶ 23–26, 29.)

The rear foldout pages of the Catalog contain directions for redeeming Pepsi Points for merchandise. (*See* Catalog, at rear foldout pages.) These directions note that merchandise may be ordered "only" with the original Order Form. (*See id.*) The Catalog notes that in the event that a consumer lacks enough Pepsi Points to obtain a desired item, additional Pepsi Points may be purchased for ten cents each; however, at least fifteen original Pepsi Points must accompany each order. (*See id.*)

Although plaintiff initially set out to collect 7,000,000 Pepsi Points by consuming Pepsi products, it soon became clear to him that he "would not be able to buy (let alone drink) enough Pepsi to collect the necessary Pepsi Points fast enough." (Affidavit of John D.R. Leonard, Mar. 30, 1999 ("Leonard Aff."), ¶ 5.) Reevaluating his strategy, plaintiff "focused for the first time on the packaging materials in the Pepsi Stuff promotion," (*id.,*) and realized that buying Pepsi Points would be a more promising option. (*See id.*) Through acquaintances, plaintiff ultimately raised about $700,000. (*See id.* ¶ 6.)

***

B. Defendant's Advertisement Was Not An Offer

1. *Advertisements as Offers*

The general rule is that an advertisement does not constitute an offer. . . .

The exception to the rule that advertisements do not create any power of acceptance in potential offerees is where the advertisement is "clear, definite, and explicit, and leaves nothing open for negotiation," in that circumstance, "it constitutes an offer, acceptance of which will complete the contract." *Lefkowitz v. Great Minneapolis Surplus Store*, 251 Minn. 188, 86 N.W.2d 689, 691 (1957). . . .

The Court finds, in sum, that the Harrier Jet commercial was merely an advertisement. The Court now turns to the line of cases upon which plaintiff rests much of his argument.

C. An Objective, Reasonable Person Would Not Have Considered the Commercial an Offer

Plaintiff's understanding of the commercial as an offer must also be rejected because the Court finds that no objective person could reasonably have concluded that the commercial actually offered consumers a Harrier Jet.

1. *Objective Reasonable Person Standard*

In evaluating the commercial, the Court must not consider defendant's subjective intent in making the commercial, or plaintiff's subjective view of what the commercial offered, but what an objective, reasonable person would have understood the commercial to convey

***

An obvious joke, of course, would not give rise to a contract. *See, e.g., Graves v. Northern N.Y. Pub. Co.*, 260 A.D. 900, 22 N.Y.S.2d 537 (1940) (dismissing claim to offer of $1000, which appeared in the "joke column" of the newspaper, to any person who could provide a commonly available phone number). On the other hand, if there is no indication that the offer is "evidently in jest," and that an objective, reasonable person would find that the offer was serious, then there may be a valid offer. *See Barnes*, 549 P.2d at 1155 ("[I]f the jest is not apparent and a reasonable hearer would believe that an offer was being made, then the speaker risks the formation of a contract which was not intended."); *see also Lucy v. Zehmer*, 196 Va. 493, 84 S.E.2d 516, 518, 520 (1954) (ordering specific performance of a contract to purchase a farm despite defendant's protestation that the transaction was done in jest as "'just a bunch of two doggoned drunks bluffing'").

***

3. *Whether the Commercial Was "Evidently Done In Jest"*

Plaintiff's insistence that the commercial appears to be a serious offer requires the Court to explain why the commercial is funny. Explaining why a joke is funny is a daunting task; as the essayist E.B. White has remarked, "Humor can be dissected, as a frog can, but the thing dies in the process. . . ." The commercial is the embodiment of what defendant appropriately characterizes as "zany humor." (Def. Mem. at 18.)

First, the commercial suggests, as commercials often do, that use of the advertised product will transform what, for most youth, can be a fairly routine and ordinary experience. The military tattoo and stirring martial music, as well as the use of subtitles in a Courier font that scroll terse messages across the screen, such as "MONDAY 7:58 AM," evoke military and espionage thrillers. The implication of the commercial is that Pepsi Stuff merchandise will inject drama and moment into hitherto unexceptional lives. The commercial in this case thus makes the exaggerated claims similar to those of many television advertisements: that by consuming the featured clothing, car, beer, or potato chips, one will become attractive, stylish, desirable, and admired by all. A reasonable viewer would understand such advertisements as mere puffery, not as statements of fact, *see, e.g., Hubbard v. General Motors Corp.*, 95 Civ. 4362 (AGS), 1996 WL 274018, at *6 (S.D.N.Y. May 22, 1996) (advertisement describing automobile as "Like a Rock," was mere puffery, not a warranty of quality);

Lovett, 207 N.Y.S. at 756; and refrain from interpreting the promises of the commercial as being literally true.

Second, the callow youth featured in the commercial is a highly improbable pilot, one who could barely be trusted with the keys to his parents' car, much less the prize aircraft of the United States Marine Corps. Rather than checking the fuel gauges on his aircraft, the teenager spends his precious preflight minutes preening. The youth's concern for his coiffure appears to extend to his flying without a helmet. Finally, the teenager's comment that flying a Harrier Jet to school "sure beats the bus" evinces an improbably insouciant attitude toward the relative difficulty and danger of piloting a fighter plane in a residential area, as opposed to taking public transportation.

Third, the notion of traveling to school in a Harrier Jet is an exaggerated adolescent fantasy. In this commercial, the fantasy is underscored by how the teenager's schoolmates gape in admiration, ignoring their physics lesson. The force of the wind generated by the Harrier Jet blows off one teacher's clothes, literally defrocking an authority figure. As if to emphasize the fantastic quality of having a Harrier Jet arrive at school, the Jet lands next to a plebeian bike rack. This fantasy is, of course, extremely unrealistic. No school would provide landing space for a student's fighter jet, or condone the disruption the jet's use would cause.

Fourth, the primary mission of a Harrier Jet, according to the United States Marine Corps, is to "attack and destroy surface targets under day and night visual conditions." United States Marine Corps, Factfile: AV-8B Harrier II (last modified Dec. 5, 1995). Manufactured by McDonnell Douglas, the Harrier Jet played a significant role in the air offensive of Operation Desert Storm in 1991. *See id.* The jet is designed to carry a considerable armament load, including Sidewinder and Maverick missiles. *See id.* As one news report has noted, "Fully loaded, the Harrier can float like a butterfly and sting like a bee—albeit a roaring 14-ton butterfly and a bee with 9,200 pounds of bombs and missiles." Jerry Allegood, *Marines Rely on Harrier Jet, Despite Critics*, News & Observer (Raleigh), Nov. 4, 1990, at C1. In light of the Harrier Jet's well-documented function in attacking and destroying surface and air targets, armed reconnaissance and air interdiction, and offensive and defensive anti-aircraft warfare, depiction of such a jet as a way to get to school in the morning is clearly not serious even if, as plaintiff contends, the jet is capable of being acquired "in a form that eliminates [its] potential for military use." (*See* Leonard Aff. ¶ 20.)

Fifth, the number of Pepsi Points the commercial mentions as required to "purchase" the jet is 7,000,000. To amass that number of points, one would have to drink 7,000,000 Pepsis (or roughly 190 Pepsis a day for the next hundred years—an unlikely possibility), or one would have to purchase approximately $700,000 worth of Pepsi Points. The cost of a Harrier Jet is roughly $23 million dollars, a fact of which plaintiff was aware when he set out to gather the amount he believed necessary to accept the alleged offer. (*See* Affidavit of Michael E. McCabe, 96 Civ. 5320, Aug. 14, 1997, Exh. 6 (Leonard Business Plan).) Even if an objective, reasonable person were not aware of this fact, he would conclude that purchasing a fighter plane for $700,000 is a deal too good to be true.

Plaintiff argues that a reasonable, objective person would have understood the commercial to make a serious offer of a Harrier Jet because there was "absolutely no distinction in the manner" (Pl. Mem. at 13,) in which the items in the commercial were presented. Plaintiff also relies upon a press release highlighting the promotional campaign, issued by defendant, in which "[n]o mention is made by [defendant] of humor, or anything of the sort." (*Id.* at 5.) These arguments suggest merely that the humor of the promotional campaign was tongue in cheek. Humor is not limited to what Justice Cardozo called "[t]he rough and boisterous joke . . . [that] evokes its own guffaws." *Murphy v. Steeplechase Amusement Co.,* 250 N.Y. 479, 483, 166 N.E. 173, 174 (1929). In light of the obvious absurdity of the commercial, the Court rejects plaintiff's argument that the commercial was not clearly in jest.

***

III. CONCLUSION

In sum, . . . plaintiff's demand cannot prevail as a matter of law. First, the commercial was merely an advertisement, not a unilateral offer. Second, the tongue-in-cheek attitude of the commercial would not cause a reasonable person to conclude that a soft drink company would be giving away fighter planes as part of a promotion.

Questions Presented

1) Are advertisements considered offers?
2) What element of an offer did the Court say was missing in this case?
3) What facts did the Court use to illustrate that this element of an offer was missing?

❖❖❖

In addition to illustrating that jokes are not binding offers, the *PepsiCo* case illustrates another key point. Advertisements are not usually considered offers unless they are so specific that there is no room for interpretation. They are usually considered invitations to bargain. Similarly, auctions are also usually considered invitations to bargain. The auctioneer is seen as requesting bids from those present.

Much like auctions and advertisements, the language of a communication may also inadvertently result in an invitation to bargain. For instance, if the offeror says something like, "Would you consider mowing my lawn for $150," a court could conclude that the offeror had no serious intent to be bound by stating "would you consider." These words ask only whether the person would entertain an offer and are more likely to be seen as a starting point for a negotiation.

2. Offers: Reasonably Certain Terms

An offer must also contain reasonably certain terms. It is very difficult to write every possible contingency into a contract. Consider the following offer, "I will sell you 50 pens for $50." While this may seem straightforward, this offer is missing several terms. It does not state when the offeror has to deliver the pens. It does not state when the offeree must pay the offeror. It does not state what kind of pens have to be delivered (there are thousands of varieties). Simply because an offer is missing terms does not mean that there is not a contract offer.

The terms required to make an offer reasonably certain differ based on whether the common law or the UCC governs the contract.

a. Offers: Reasonably Certain Terms: Common Law

Under common law, an offer must be definite enough for a court to be able to determine whether a breach occurred and, if a breach occurred, what the remedy for that breach should be.[4] This usually means that the price of the service or property must be included as well as a description of the service or property. The court must also be able to identify the parties to the contract. Courts will also look to

---

[4] Restatement (Second), Contracts § 33(2).

see whether a time has been set for the payment, delivery, or performance in the contract. Though, if the parties have clearly manifested an intent to enter into a contract, a court will provide a "reasonable" term to replace the missing term. Under common law, courts are far less likely to do this than under the UCC.

b. Offers: Reasonably Certain Terms: UCC

The UCC is far more generous with providing missing terms than the common law. The UCC will provide a missing term so long as the parties intended to enter into a contract and the contract is certain enough for the court to be able to apply a remedy if a breach of contract occurs.[5] The terms that the UCC provides to fill in the contract are known as "gapfillers." If a price term is missing, the court will determine what a "reasonable" price is.[6] If the parties do not set a term for when payment for the goods is due, payment is due at the time and place the buyer is to receive the goods from the seller.[7] If the time of delivery is not specified, the goods must be delivered within a "reasonable" time.[8]

Even though the UCC is far more likely to provide missing terms than the common law, it does not usually allow courts to provide a quantity term if one is not stated in the contract.[9]

3. Offers: Communications

The simplest element of an offer to understand is the "communication." An offeree must be actually aware of an offer and its contents to be able to accept it.[10] If a person attempting to accept an offer does not know that an offer was made, the person cannot accept the offer.

4. Offers: Termination

Once made, an offer can usually be terminated before it is accepted. This means that offers can be revoked by the express words or actions of the offeree at any time before acceptance. A revocation of an offer, however, is only effective once it is actually received by the offeree.[11] For instance, imagine the following scenario. Bruce mails an offer to Cory on May 2 reading, "I offer to sell you 100 widgets for $100. To accept, please call 555-1234." On May 3, Bruce sends a revocation of the offer by mail. The offer reaches Cory on May 4, but the revocation of the offer does not reach him until May 5. On May 4, Cory calls the number listed in the offer to accept.

In that scenario, Bruce's revocation would not be effective even though he sent it before Cory accepted because the offeror's revocation does not become effective until the offeree has knowledge of the revocation.

Under the common law, offers become irrevocable only when a person pays the offeror to keep the offer open for a specific period of time (known as an option contract)[12] or the offeree takes a step in reliance on the offer to his or her detriment.[13] For example, imagine that Cory hired Bruce to mow his lawn for $100 a week for a year. During that year, Bruce learns that most lawn

---

[5] UCC § 2-204(3)
[6] UCC § 2-305(1)
[7] UCC § 2-310(a)
[8] UCC § 2-309(1)
[9] UCC § 2-306(1)
[10] *See* 17A Am. Jur. 2d Contracts § 45 (2017).
[11] Restatement (Second), Contracts § 42.
[12] *See* 17A Am. Jur. 2d Contracts § 52 (2017).
[13] *See* Restatement (Second), Contracts § 90.

TABLE 7.2   Ways to Terminate an Offer

Ways to Terminate an Offer
Revocation before acceptance
Rejection by the Offeree
Counteroffer
Lapse of Time
Death of either the Offeror or Offeree
Destruction of the subject matter of the contract
Illegality

mowers in the area are lowering prices and says to Cory, "I will mow your lawn next year for $90 a year." In reliance on Bruce's offer, Cory stops looking for other people to mow his lawn. At the end of the year, Bruce refuses to lower his price as promised.

In that scenario, Bruce's offer would likely be irrevocable because Cory stopped looking for other people to mow his lawn based on Bruce's offer. This is known as "promissory estoppel." We will look at promissory estoppel again in the context of consideration later in this chapter.

Under the UCC, an offer will become irrevocable if it is a "firm" offer made by a merchant. If a merchant puts in a signed writing that an offer will be held open for a certain period of time, that offer will remain open for that period of time. If a signed offer from a merchant states that it will be held open but does not state for how long, the offer will be open for a "reasonable" amount of time not to exceed 90 days.[14]

There are several other ways for an offer to be terminated besides revocation. An offer is terminated when it is rejected by the offeree.[15] Rejection only becomes effective when received by the offeror.[16] Similarly, if the offeree replies with a counter offer, the original offer is terminated.[17] In this scenario, the offeree becomes the offeror, and the offeror becomes the offeree.

If an offer lists a specific amount of time it will remain open (i.e., "This offer is open for 90 days), the offer will be terminated once that period of time lapses. If the period of time to accept the offer remains open, it will be open for a "reasonable" amount of time.

If the subject matter of the offer is destroyed, the offer will be terminated.[18] For instance, if a person offers to buy a house, but the house burns down before the offer is accepted, the offer to buy the house is terminated.

If the offeror or the offeree dies before the offer is accepted, the offer terminates.[19] It also terminates if the subject matter of the offer becomes illegal after the offer is made.[20]

B. Acceptance

The second requirement of a contract is acceptance. An acceptance is a (1) A voluntary act showing (2) unequivocal assent (agreement) to an offer that is (3) communicated to the offeree.

---

[14] UCC § 2-205
[15] Restatement (Second), Contracts § 36.
[16] Restatement (Second), Contracts § 40.
[17] Restatement (Second), Contracts § 36.
[18] Restatement (Second), Contracts § 36, cmt. c.
[19] Restatement (Second), Contracts § 36.
[20] Restatement (Second), Contracts § 36, cmt. c.

1. Acceptance: Voluntary Act

Normally, an acceptance can be accomplished in any manner allowed by the offer. The offeror is the master of the offer.[21] For instance, if an offeror states, "You may accept this offer by jumping up and down ten times," then acceptance can be shown by jumping up and down ten times. Many offers do not state how they are to be accepted. In those cases, acceptance can be accomplished in any manner capable of showing agreement that is reasonable under the circumstances. Words can be used like "yes," "I accept," and "I agree." If you are face-to-face with your offeror, you may be able to accept through gestures like a "thumbs up" or nod of the head. Whether an acceptance is effective will depend on the circumstances.

Even if specifically asked for by the offeror, silence will not be considered a "voluntary act" for the purposes of acceptance.[22] If someone were to walk up to you and say, "By staying silent for three seconds, you agree to wash my car for $1," even if you stayed silent for three seconds, you would not have accepted the offer. Doing nothing is not an action.

Sometimes, courts will allow acceptance by silence if a party accepts the benefit of an offer despite having an opportunity to reject it.[23] For instance, if a stranger begins to wash your car without being asked, and you do nothing to stop it, your silence may be considered acceptance. Under certain circumstances, silence may constitute acceptance if the parties to the contract have had prior dealings.[24] For example, if a buyer receives the same shipment every week from the seller, unless the buyer cancels or rejects the shipment when it is received, the buyer's silence may constitute a voluntary act for the purpose of acceptance.

2. Acceptance: Unequivocal Assent

The voluntary act must show unequivocal assent (agreement) to be an acceptance. The common law is must stricter than the UCC about what constitutes "unequivocal" assent. The common law uses the "mirror image" rule to determine whether an attempted acceptance is unequivocal assent. The mirror image rule requires that the terms of the offer be the same as the terms of the acceptance.[25]

Consider this example. Cory says to Bruce, "I will mow your lawn for $100." Cory replies, "I accept, but it has to be done by March 1." In this case, Cory did not accept Bruce's offer even though his price and quantity term matched because he added a term to it.

Despite being rigid, the mirror image rule does not have a particular formula. In the above example, there were several ways Cory could have accepted the offer. If he had, instead, said, "I accept. I hope that you can do it by March 1," Cory would have accepted Bruce's offer. He would have been merely discussing when it could be done following a mirror image acceptance.

Unlike the common law, the UCC does not require a mirror image for an acceptance. The UCC only requires a clear acceptance of the offer to show unequivocal assent.[26] Therefore, under the UCC, even if an attempted acceptance contains a term that is not in the offer (known as an "additional" term) or a term that conflicts with a term in the offer ("conflicting" term), an acceptance may still be valid.

Consider the following example. Cory sends Bruce a purchase order that reads as follows, "100 widgets, $100, payment by March 6." Bruce receives the purchase order and replies with an order

---

[21] Restatement (Second), Contracts § 50.

[22] Restatement (Second), Contracts § 69.

[23] Restatement (Second), Contracts § 69(1)(a).

[24] Restatement (Second), Contracts § 69(1)(c).

[25] 17A Am. Jur. 2d Contracts § 80 (2017).

[26] UCC § 2-207(1)

acknowledgment stating, "100 widgets, $100, payment by March 1, 5% late fee if not paid on time." In this case, even though Bruce's reply contained an additional term (5% late fee) and a conflicting term (March 1 instead of March 6 as the payment date), a court would likely view this as a clear acceptance. The parties are clearly intending to enter into a contract as both the price and quantity terms match. They just differ on the details.

This example also raises another question. What do we do with additional and conflicting terms in a clear acceptance contract? With conflicting terms, in most states, neither party's version of the conflicting terms becomes part of the contract,[27] and they are "knocked-out" and replaced by the UCC's default terms known as a "gapfillers." In this case, the date of payment would be the date of delivery because that is what the UCC requires if there is no applicable term in the contract.[28]

Additional terms, however, are treated differently than conflicting terms. If one or more of the parties to the contract is not a merchant, additional terms are knocked-out and replaced with gapfillers just like conflicting terms are. So, if either Bruce or Cory is not a merchant in the above example, the additional term in Bruce's acceptance (5% late fee) does not become part of the contract.

If however, both parties to the contract are merchants, the additional term becomes part of the contract unless one of the following three things happens: (1) the offer states that it cannot be altered by an acceptance, (2) the additional term materially alters the contract, or (3) the additional term is objected to by the offeree in a reasonable time.[29] So, unless one of the three listed scenarios occurs, if both Bruce and Cory were merchants, the additional term would have become part of the contract.

In addition to requiring only a clear acceptance instead of a mirror image, the UCC also allows unequivocal assent to be shown through conduct if the writings of the parties do not create a clear acceptance. Imagine that Cory sends Bruce a purchase order that reads as follows, "100 widgets, $100, payment by March 6. Acceptance is limited to and conditioned on acceptance of the terms of this order." Bruce receives the purchase order and replies with an order acknowledgment stating, "100 widgets, $100, payment by March 1, 5% late fee if not paid on time." Bruce then ships the widgets to Cory who begins to sell them.

In this scenario, Bruce did not accept Cory's offer because he put a conflicting term and an additional term in his attempted acceptance, which Bruce's offer did not allow for by stating, "Acceptance is limited to and conditioned on acceptance of the terms of this order." However, the parties would still have a contract because their conduct (Bruce shipping and Cory selling the goods) would lead a reasonable person to believe that they had a contract.

Determining what terms to use when a contract is formed by conduct is much simpler than determining the terms to use when a contract is formed by clear acceptance. All terms that the parties do not agree on are knocked out and replaced by gapfillers. It does not matter whether the disagreed-upon terms are conflicting terms or additional terms or whether the parties to the contract are merchants.

Legal Definition

Unequivocal Assent – the unambiguous and unqualified agreement of the offeree to the terms of the offer.

---

[27] *See Richardson v. Union Carbide Ind. Gases, Inc.*, 790 A. 2d 962, 967–68 (NJ App. Div. 2002).

[28] UCC § 2-310(a)

[29] UCC § 2-207(2)

3. Acceptance: Communication

An acceptance must also be communicated to the offeror by the offeree. This can be done in any manner allowed by the offer.[30] Unlike the termination of a contract offer, which is considered effective when received by the offeree, an acceptance is considered to be sufficiently communicated when it is dispatched.[31] This is known as the "mailbox" rule.

Consider the following example. Bruce mails an offer to Cory on May 2 reading, "I offer to sell you 100 widgets for $100. To accept, please mail the accompanying form to the return address on the envelope." The offer reaches Cory on May 4, and, on the same day, Cory mails the form back to the return address. On May 5, Bruce calls Cory to revoke the offer. On May 6, Bruce receives the form.

In the above example, Cory validly accepted Bruce's offer even though Bruce had not received the acceptance when he attempted to revoke the offer because acceptances are valid when dispatched.

C. Consideration

The third element of a contract is consideration. Consideration is the (1) bargained-for exchange of (2) items or services of legally sufficient value.[32] What this means is that both sides must suffer a detriment from entering into the contract. Consider the following example. Bruce enters into an agreement with Cory to sell 100 widgets for $100. Cory gives up $100. Bruce gives up 100 widgets. Because both gave something up as part of the bargain, there is sufficient consideration to support a contract.

Legal Definition

Consideration – anything of legally sufficient value exchanged for something else of legally sufficient value as part of the same bargain.

---

1. Consideration: Legally Sufficient Value

Consideration need not be money to be legally sufficient. It can be almost any promise, performance, or forbearance (not doing something). Consider this example. Bruce promises to mow Cory's lawn if Bruce washes Cory's car. In that case, no money is exchanged. However, there is still legally sufficient value. Cory gets his car washed. Bruce receives a promise from Cory that he will mow his lawn.

Forbearance (not doing something) is also legally sufficient value. In the famous nineteenth century case of *Hamer v. Sidway*, a court held that an uncle's promise to pay his nephew $5,000 if the nephew refrained from drinking alcohol, using tobacco, swearing, playing cards, and playing pool until he was 21 was of legally sufficient value. Even though there was no obvious benefit to the uncle and avoiding nineteenth century vice benefitted the nephew, because the nephew gave up things he had the legal right to do, the uncle received legally sufficient value.[33]

It is also important to note that a court will not consider whether the exchange of consideration is fair. It will only look to see if both parts of the exchange have legally sufficient value. Consider this example. Bruce owns a watch worth $1,000. Cory promises to buy the watch from Bruce for $500. In that case, Cory is giving up $500. Bruce is giving up a watch. Even though the consideration

---

[30] Restatement (Second), Contracts § 50.
[31] Restatement (Second), Contracts § 63(a).
[32] Restatement (Second), Contracts § 71.
[33] *Hamer v. Sidway*, 124 N.Y. 538, 27 N.E. 256 (NY App. Div. 2d 1891)

is not equal, it is still of legally sufficient value because courts will not find a lack of consideration even if one side gets the much better end of the bargain.

2. Consideration: Bargained-for Exchange

In order for there to be a bargained-for exchange, each party must give up something of legally sufficient value in exchange for something of legally sufficient value. In the above-mentioned *Hamer v. Sidway*, the uncle gave up $5,000 in exchange for the nephew giving up his right to drink alcohol, use tobacco, swear, play cards, and play billiards. The uncle's promise induced the nephew to give up those things. By giving up those things, the nephew induced his uncle to give him $5,000.

In contrast, consider this scenario. Bruce and Cory are good friends. Bruce says to Cory, "Because you are my friend, I promise to give you $500." In this scenario, there is no bargained-for exchange. Though Bruce gave Cory $500 because of their friendship, Cory's friendship with Bruce was not induced by the promise of $500. One was not exchanged for the other. Contract law will not enforce gifts.

3. Consideration: Things that are not Usually Consideration

There are several common scenarios that will not create consideration. These include "past" consideration, pre-existing duties, and illusory promises.

a. Past Consideration

Past consideration is a promise made in return for something that has already occurred. Because consideration requires bargained-for exchange, past events will not count as consideration.

Consider this example. When Cory was in elementary school, Bruce saved him from a bully. Fifteen years later, Cory becomes a rich entrepreneur after designing the next great social media platform, "InstaFaceChatMachine." After hitting it big, he tells Bruce, "Because you saved me from that bully, I am going to pay you $50,000."

In that case, because Bruce had saved Cory from the bully before Cory's promise to pay him was made, there was no bargained-for exchange, which means that there was no consideration.

b. Pre-Existing Duty

If a party promises to do something it is already obligated to do, it will not be considered of legally sufficient value. As discussed earlier in this chapter, in *Hamer v. Sidway*, an uncle gave up $5,000 in exchange for his nephew giving up his right to drink alcohol, use tobacco, swear, play cards, and play billiards.[34] The nephew not doing those things was of legally sufficient value because he had the right to do them. Imagine that, instead of giving up drinking and smoking, the nephew had to promise to not use crack cocaine. In that situation, because the law already places everyone under a duty not to use crack cocaine, the nephew would be under a pre-existing duty not to use crack cocaine. This means that he would not be giving up something of legally sufficient value.

---

[34] *Hamer v. Sidway*, 124 N.Y. 538, 27 N.E. 256 (NY App. Div. 2d 1891)

The common law and the UCC differ on whether a previous contract will create a pre-existing duty. Under common law, if a person promises to do something as part of a contract, a promise to do that thing cannot serve as consideration for a second contract between those parties.[35]

Imagine this scenario. Bruce promises to mow Cory's lawn for $150 on Saturday. Bruce then gets an offer to mow Dillon's lawn for $200 on Saturday. Bruce then goes to Cory and says, "I will only mow your lawn on Saturday if you pay me $225."

In that case, even if Cory agreed to the price increase, it would not create a legally binding agreement. Bruce was already under a pre-existing duty to mow Cory's lawn on Saturday by contract. A contract to mow lawns is governed by the common law because lawn mowing is a service. Therefore, a promise to "mow Cory's lawn on Saturday" cannot be consideration in a second contract that merely increases the price.

The UCC, however, allows parties to modify their contract without consideration if the parties make the modification in good faith.[36] Imagine that Bruce promises to deliver 100 widgets to Cory in exchange for $100. Bruce enters into this contract believing that each widget will cost him $0.95. Bruce later finds out that he would have to pay $1.05 for each widget, which would result in a loss on his contract with Cory. He explains this to Cory, and Cory agrees to pay $110 for the widgets to make up the extra costs for Bruce.

In that case, even though Bruce was under a pre-existing contractual duty to Cory to deliver the widgets, Cory's promise to pay $110 instead of $100 would be considered legally sufficient value. Cory and Bruce made a modification in good faith based on a change in the market conditions. However, if Bruce had simply decided to raise the price to get more money from Cory without any other reason, the pre-existing duty rule would likely apply because he would have no good faith basis for modiciation.

c. Illusory Promises

An illusory promise is a promise that is not sufficiently definite enough to constitute consideration. Consider the following example. Bruce says to Cory, "If you pay me $500, I will give you my watch if I feel like it."

In that case, there is no certainty as to whether Bruce will ever suffer a legal detriment because his "promise" does not require him to do so. His promise only requires that he give Cory the watch if he "feels like it," a feeling that Bruce will likely never experience. This is not legally sufficient value.

4. Promissory Estoppel

There are still some promises that will be enforced even if they are not supported by consideration. The most common exception to the rule that consideration is required is promissory estoppel, which is also known as "detrimental reliance." If one person relies on another person's promise to his or her detriment, a court will likely enforce the promise.[37] Promissory estoppel has three elements: (1) A clear and definite promise, (2) justified reliance on the promise, (3) and the advancement of justice by enforcement of the promise.

Consider the following example. Bruce, a landscaper, promises to mow Cory's lawn every week on Saturday for free because Cory once saved him from a bully in elementary school. Relying

---

[35] Restatement (Second), Contracts § 73.
[36] UCC § 1-203.
[37] Restatement (Second), Contracts § 90.

on Bruce's promise, Cory sold his lawn mower to Dillon, rendering him unable to mow his lawn. Bruce then decides that mowing Cory's lawn every week for free is too much and refuses to do it.

In that case, even though there is no consideration (Cory saving Bruce from a bully is not consideration because it is past consideration), a court could still enforce Bruce's promise under the doctrine of promissory estoppel. Bruce made a clear promise to mow Cory's lawn every week. Cory also justifiably relied on that promise by selling his lawn mower, something that he would not have done without Bruce's promise. A court would also likely find that justice would be served by enforcing Bruce's promise because Cory would otherwise be worse off because of it.

Legal Definition

Promissory Estoppel – the doctrine allowing enforcement of a promise made without consideration on which the promisee relied to his or her detriment.

III. Contract Interpretation

Once a contract is made, a court may be asked to determine the meaning of its terms. Even the most well written contracts can have vague and missing terms. When it is difficult to determine what a contract means, a court will consider the plain meaning of the words first and not look to any external factors if a meaning can be derived from the words of the contract itself.[38] Consider the following case.

❖❖

White City Shopping Ctr., LP v. PR Restaurants LLC
21 Mass. L. Rptr. 565 (2006)

BACKGROUND

Defendant, PR, is a Massachusetts limited liability company that operates 22 Panera Bread ("Panera") restaurants in the New England area. Panera is a cafe-style restaurant chain that sells sandwiches, coffee, and soup. Mitchell J. Roberts is the manager of PR. PR is a tenant under a commercial lease for approximately 4,469 square feet of retail space in the Shopping Center located on Route 9, in Shrewsbury. White City, a limited partnership, is the landlord of the Shopping Center. Chair 5, the intervening party, is a Delaware limited liability company and franchisee of Qdoba, a Mexican-style restaurant chain that sells burritos, quesadillas, and tacos. Both Panera and Qdoba compete in the same "fast-casual" restaurant market.

On March 14, 2001, White City entered into a ten-year lease ("the Lease") with PR for retail space to operate a Panera restaurant in the Shopping Center. Lease negotiations lasted several months partly because of PR's request to include an exclusivity clause in the Lease. PR authored the clause which underwent three revisions prior to the Lease's execution. The exclusivity clause that both parties initially agreed to restricted White City from entering into new leases with businesses that primarily sell sandwiches. In its first iteration, Section 4.07 of the Lease states, in relevant part:

> Landlord *agrees not* to enter into a lease, occupancy agreement or license affecting space in the Shopping Center or consent to an amendment to an existing lease permitting use . . . for a bakery

---

[38] *See White City Shopping Ctr., LP v. PR Rests., LLC,* 2006 Mass. Super. LEXIS 544 (Mass. Super. Ct. 2006)

or restaurant reasonably expected to have annual sales of *sandwiches* greater than ten percent (10%) of its total sales or primarily for the sale of high quality coffees or teas, such as, but not limited to, Starbucks, Tea-Luxe, Pete's Coffee and Tea, and Finagle a Bagle . . . The foregoing *shall not* apply to (i) the use of the existing, vacant free-standing building in the Shopping Center for a Dunkin Donuts-type business, or for a business serving near-Eastern food and related products, (ii) restaurants primarily for sit-down table service, (iii) a Jewish delicatessen or (iv) a KFC restaurant operating in a new building following the demolition of the existing, freestanding building. No new building shall violate the no-build provision of this Lease.

Lease § 4.07 (emphasis supplied).

The Lease contained no definition of "sandwiches" or "near-Eastern" food. During lease negotiations, PR and White City did not discuss the definition of "sandwiches" or the type of food products they intended the term to cover. Furthermore, the parties never indicated, specified, or agreed that the term "sandwiches" included tacos, burritos, and quesadillas.

Following the Lease's execution in March, the parties amended the exclusivity clause to include additional restrictions. On December 30, 2005, Section 4.07 of the Lease was amended, as follows:

The foregoing restriction shall also apply (without limitation) to a Dunkin Donuts location and to a Jewish-style delicatessen within the Shopping Center, but shall not apply to (i) use of the existing, freestanding building in the Shopping Center partially occupied by Strawberries and recently expanded for a business serving near-eastern food and related products, (ii) restaurants for primarily for sit down table service or (iii) a Papa Gino's restaurant (provided the same continues to operate with substantially the same categories of menu items as now apply to its stores and franchisees generally).

Lease § 4.07.

Sometime after the amendment, PR learned that White City had entered into discussions with Chair 5 to lease commercial space. Chair 5 planned to develop and construct a Qdoba restaurant in the same Shopping Center as Panera. After learning of the parties' plans, PR had its attorney contact White City to express concern and seek an assurance that White City would not enter into a lease with Chair 5. PR believed that White City's leasing of space to Chair 5 violated Section 4.07 of the Lease. Specifically, PR believed, and later asserted that tacos, burritos, and quesadillas fell within meaning of "sandwiches" and therefore, White City was prohibited from leasing to Chair 5 under the Lease. White City refused to provide the requested assurance when PR's attorney contacted it about the pending Chair 5 lease. On or around August 22, 2006, White City executed a lease with Chair 5 for 2,100 square feet of retail space in the Shopping Center. On September 28, 2006, White City filed an action against PR, seeking a declaratory judgment that it did not breach its lease with PR.

***

A contract is construed to be given reasonable effect to each of its provisions. *Id.* "The object of the court is to construe the contract as a whole in a reasonable and practical way, consistent with its language, background and purpose." *USM Corp. v. Arthur D. Little Systems, Inc., 28 Mass. App. Ct. 108, 116, 546 N.E.2d 888 (1989).* The starting point must be the actual words chosen by the parties to express their agreement. *Id.* If the words of the contract are plain and free from ambiguity, they must be construed in accordance with their ordinary and usual sense. See *Ober v. National Casualty Co., 318 Mass. 27, 30, 60 N.E.2d 90 (1945).*

Given that the term "sandwiches" is not ambiguous and the Lease does not provide a definition of it, this court applies the ordinary meaning of the word. New Webster Third International

Dictionary describes a "sandwich" as "two thin pieces of bread, usually buttered, with a thin layer (as of meat, cheese, or savory mixture) spread between them." Merriam-Webster, 2002. Under this definition and as dictated by common sense, this court finds that the term "sandwich" is not commonly understood to include burritos, tacos, and quesadillas, which are typically made with a single tortilla and stuffed with a choice filling of meat, rice, and beans. As such, there is no viable legal basis for barring White City from leasing to Chair 5. Further, PR has not proffered any evidence that the parties intended the term "sandwiches" to include burritos, tacos, and quesadillas. As the drafter of the exclusivity clause, PR did not include a definition of "sandwiches" in the lease nor communicate clearly to White City during lease negotiations that it intended to treat burritos, tacos, quesadillas, and sandwiches the same. Another factor weighing against PR's favor is that it was aware that Mexican-style restaurants near the Shopping Center existed which sold burritos, tacos, and quesadillas prior to the execution of the Lease yet, PR made no attempt to define, discuss, and clarify the parties' understanding of the term "sandwiches." Accordingly, based on the record before the court, PR has not shown a likelihood of success on the merits.

Question Presented

1) What rule(s) of law did the court rely on to reach its decision?
2) What evidence did the court rely on to find that a burrito was not a sandwich within the meaning of the contract?
3) How could this contract have been drafted to avoid this problem?

❖❖

IV. Breach of Contract

A breach of contract occurs when one or both parties does not perform a contractual duty. There are two kinds of breach of contract. A material breach, also called a "total" breach, is a breach of the contract so serious that the non-breaching party can terminate the contract. A partial breach is any breach that is not a material breach.[39]

Under common law, a breach will not be considered material if the breaching party substantially performs the contract.

Jacobs & Young v. Kent is a classic illustration of a partial breach under common law. In that case, a contractor agreed to use a particular brand of pipe to construct a house. Due to an oversight, he used a different brand. The court held that, because the two brands were virtually identical and no other breaches were brought to the attention of the court, the contract was substantially performed. Because the contract was substantially performed, the non-breaching party (the homeowner) was only entitled to the difference in value between the pipe used and the pipe for which the contract called, which was little to nothing.[40]

To determine whether a breach is material or partial, the court will look at a number of factors, including the purpose of the contract, the reasons the breach of contract occurred, and the effect that a finding of material breach would have on the parties.[41]

---

[39] Restatement (Second), Contracts § 236.
[40] *Jacobs & Young v. Kent*, 230 N.Y. 239, 129 N.E. 889 (NY 1921).
[41] Restatement (Second), Contracts § 241.

The UCC does not apply the substantial performance doctrine. It uses the "perfect tender rule." Under UCC § 2-601, a seller must provide "conforming" goods to the buyer. If the goods do not meet every aspect of the contract, the buyer may choose to accept the shipment, reject some of the goods, or reject all of the goods. However, if there is still time to perform under the contract, the seller has the right to "cure" the defective performance and provide conforming goods if it so notifies the buyer.

For example, Bruce orders "100 green widgets to be delivered on March 15" from Cory. On March 1, Bruce delivers 100 blue widgets to Cory. The blue widgets are identical in every way to the green widgets except color. Even though this might meet the common law standard of substantial performance, Bruce can choose to reject any or all of the widgets. However, if Bruce rejects the blue widgets, Cory still can perform under the contract and provide him with 100 green widgets because he still has another two weeks to perform under the contract.

A. Breach of Contract: Anticipatory Repudiation

In some cases, a party will breach a contract before he or she has to perform under the contract. This is called an "anticipatory repudiation." For example, Bruce agrees to mow Cory's lawn on Saturday for $100. On Thursday, Bruce calls Cory and says, "I won't be mowing your lawn on Saturday, Bro. I'm going to Yankee Stadium."

When an anticipatory repudiation occurs, the non-breaching party can choose to consider it a material breach even before performance is due.[42] Until the non-breaching party makes the breaching party aware that he or she considers the anticipatory repudiation to be a material breach or materially changes his or her position because of the anticipatory repudiation, the breaching party may retract his or her anticipatory repudiation.[43]

In the above example, Bruce repudiates his promise to mow Cory's lawn two days before performance is due. If Cory does not inform him that he considers the breach material or take some other step based on Bruce's breach, such as hiring another landscaper, Bruce could retract his repudiation and perform the contract.

B. Breach of Contract: Time to Perform

Unless the agreement specifically states that "time is of the essence," a delay in performance (by the date specified in the contract) will be considered a partial breach.

V. Defenses to Contract Enforcement

Even though a party breaches a contract that was formed by offer, acceptance, and consideration, the breaching party may still be able to avoid liability if he or she has a defense to enforcement.

Legal Definitions

Void Contract – a contract that can never be enforced.

Voidable Contract – a contract that may be made void by one or more of the parties.

---

[42] Restatement (Second), Contracts § 253(1); UCC § 2-610.
[43] Restatement (Second), Contracts § 256(1); UCC § 2-611.

TABLE 7.3   Effect of Void and Voidable Contracts

Void	No one can enforce the contract
Voidable	The injured party can choose to ratify or disaffirm the contract

Contract defenses generally have one of two effects. They render the contract void or voidable. If a defense renders a contract void, the contract cannot be enforced by either party under any circumstances. If a defense renders a contract voidable, the injured party may choose to enforce the contract, but the uninjured party cannot choose to enforce the contract unless the injured party ratifies the contract (chooses to enforce it).

A. Defenses to Contract Enforcement: Capacity

Every party to a contract must be of sufficient mental capacity to enter into a contract. There are three categories of people who may lack capacity to enter into contracts: (1) minors, (2) the mentally incapable and, (3) only in rare circumstances, intoxicated persons.

1. Defenses to Contract Enforcement: Capacity: Minors

With few exceptions, any contract entered into by a minor (a person under 18 or who is legally emancipated from his or her parents) will be voidable at the option of the minor.[44] A minor has the choice to disaffirm the contract as long as he or she is still a minor and for a reasonable period after becoming an adult.[45]

The most common exception to this rule is a contract for the "necessities" of the minor.[46] If the contract is for a necessity, the adult is entitled to the reasonable value of the contract.

The definition of "necessity" varies based on the needs of the minor. If a minor is under the care of a guardian, even if the contract is for something like food or clothing, it may not be considered a necessity for the purposes of this rule. Necessities also only include those things that provide for a minor's subsistence and may include food, medical care, shelter, and clothing.

In some states, a minor may not be able to disaffirm a contract if he or she lies about his or her age. In others, minors may not be able to disaffirm a contract if they are unable to return the goods or are doing business as an adult. Minors also cannot disaffirm contracts for military service.

2. Defenses to Contract Enforcement: Capacity: Mental Capacity

If a contract is made with a person who has been declared mentally incompetent to enter into a contract by a court of law, any contract entered into by that person is void.[47] This means that not even the person's guardian can enforce the contract no matter how beneficial it is to the mentally incompetent person. Only a guardian can enter into a contract to bind someone declared mentally incompetent by a court of law.

If someone is mentally incompetent but has not been so declared by a court of law, under some circumstances, the contract may become voidable at the option of the mentally incompetent person. The contract will only become voidable if the mentally incompetent person lacks the ability to

---

[44] Restatement (Second), Contracts § 14.
[45] *See Rivera v. Reading Housing Authority,* 819 F.Supp. 1323 (E.D. Pa. 1993).
[46] Restatement (Second), Contracts § 12, cmt. f.
[47] Restatement (Second), Contracts § 13.

understand that he or she is entering into or contract or to understand the nature, consequences, and purposes of the contract.[48]

All other contracts entered into by someone alleging mental incompetence will be enforceable. Like contracts entered into by minors, contracts entered into by those who are mentally incompetent for "necessaries" will be enforceable for the reasonable value of the contract.[49]

3. Defenses to Contract Enforcement: Capacity: Intoxicated Persons

In most cases, a contract entered into by an intoxicated person will be enforceable. Unlike criminal law, there is no distinction made based on whether the intoxication was voluntary or involuntary. A contract entered into by an intoxicated person will only become voidable if the intoxicated person lacks the ability to understand that he or she is entering into or contract or to understand the nature, consequences, and purposes of the contract.[50] This is the same standard the court uses for those who are mentally incompetent. If the contract becomes voidable, it is only voidable at the option of the intoxicated person.

Like contracts entered into by minors and those who are mentally incompetent, contracts entered into by intoxicated persons for "necessaries" will be enforceable for the reasonable value of the contract.[51]

B. Defenses to Contract Enforcement: Public Policy

Contracts that violate public policy are void.[52] Contracts are essentially agreements that society chooses to enforce. Any agreement that violates the public policy of the state in which enforcement is sought will not be enforced.

The most common form of public policy is statute. Any contract for something that violates a statute will not be enforced. For instance, if Bruce agrees to sell Cory 100 kilograms of crack cocaine for $100,000, the law will not enforce that agreement if one of them refuses to perform.

States may also find contracts that do not violate a statute violate the state's public policy nonetheless. For instance, in *In Re Baby M*, the New Jersey Supreme Court refused to enforce a surrogacy contract that required a woman to surrender her parental rights after agreeing to carry a child for another couple. The court held that the state's public policy was to make custody determinations only based on the best interests of the child. The court ultimately held that it was in the best interests of the child to terminate the parental rights of the surrogate mother, but it did so based on basic family law principles, not the unenforceable void contract.[53]

C. Defenses to Contract Enforcement: Duress

For a party to be able to raise duress as a defense, the person must enter into the contract as the result of a "wrongful act."

---

[48] Restatement (Second), Contracts § 15.
[49] Restatement (Second), Contracts § 12, cmt. f.
[50] Restatement (Second), Contracts § 16.
[51] Restatement (Second), Contracts § 12, cmt. f.
[52] Restatement (Second), Contracts § 178.
[53] *In Re Baby M*, 2 17 N.J. Super. 313, 525 A.2d 1128 (NJ 1987).

Illegal acts are wrongful acts for the purposes of duress. For instance, if Bruce threatened to "beat Cory senseless" if he did not enter into a contract with him, Cory could raise duress as a defense because the assault committed by Bruce qualifies as a wrongful act.

A wrongful act need not be illegal. Though tough negotiating, like threatening to exercise your legal right to sue another, will not be considered duress. However, some economic acts will be considered wrongful acts. If someone creates a situation that provides the injured party no reasonable alternatives, a wrongful act may have occurred.

Consider the following example. Bruce enters into a contract with Cory to provide 100 customized golf shirts for $500 for a charity golf tournament on Saturday. On Friday, Bruce contacts Cory and informs him that he will not perform the contract unless he gets an additional $500. Bruce knows that Cory cannot obtain these custom t-shirts anywhere else on one day's notice.

In that case, Bruce's act will be considered wrongful by a court. He created the situation giving rise to Cory's problem by refusing to perform a valid contract. Cory also lacks reasonable alternatives as there is no way for him to get the custom t-shirts in time for the charity tournament.

Duress renders a contract void if the wrongful act giving rise to the duress was violent. Duress renders a contract voidable at the option of the injured party if the wrongful act was not violent.[54]

D. Defenses to Contract Enforcement: Undue Influence

Closely related to duress, undue influence occurs when a person in a position of trust with another uses that trust or power in a way that deprives that person of free will and substitutes his or her own desires and goals.[55] This essentially means that one person takes advantage of a close relationship with another so deeply that the person being taken advantage of no longer has the ability to act for himself or herself. A contract entered into as a result of undue influence is voidable at the option of the innocent party.[56]

Undue influence must result from a legally recognized position of trust. This may include the parent—child relationship, doctor—patient relationship, guardian—ward relationship, husband—wife relationship, priest—penitent relationship, or trustee—beneficiary relationship.

Courts will especially consider the mental state of the dependent person. Mental incapacity is not required for a finding of undue influence, but, the more feeble the mind of the dependent person, the more likely that undue influence will be found.

E. Defenses to Contract Enforcement: Mistake

In limited circumstances, if one or both of the parties made a material mistake of fact about the contract, the contract becomes voidable. Whether the mistake renders the contract voidable depends on whether the mistake made is one of fact or one of value and whether the mistake is bilateral or unilateral.

A mistake of value is a mistake made by one (unilateral) or both (bilateral) of the parties about the worth of the subject matter of the contract. A mistake of fact is a mistake about the nature, matter, or kind of the subject matter of the contract. Imagine the following two scenarios.

---

[54] Restatement (Second), Contracts §§ 174, 175.
[55] *See* Undue Influence, Black's Law Dictionary (9th Ed. 2009).
[56] Restatement (Second), Contracts § 177.

SCENARIO A: Bruce finds a Vincent Van Gogh painting in his attic. He agrees to sell it to Cory for $50,000. Both Bruce and Cory mistakenly believe that the painting is worth $50,000 when they sign the contract. They later find out that the painting is worth $100,000.

SCENARIO B: Bruce finds what he believes to be a Vincent Van Gogh painting in his attic. He agrees to sell it to Cory for $50,000. Both Bruce and Cory mistakenly believe it was painted by Vincent Van Gogh. They later find out that the painting was made by an artist named Vincent Van Bro.

Scenario A is a mistake of value. Mistakes of value will not render a contract voidable. Both Bruce and Cory knew exactly what the subject matter of the contract is, a Vincent Van Gogh painting. They were simply wrong about how much it was worth. Therefore, the contract was not voidable.

Scenario B is a mistake of fact. Both mistakenly believe the painting was made by Vincent Van Gogh.

Whether a mistake of fact renders a contract voidable depends on whether the mistake was bilateral or unilateral and whether the mistake was material. A mistake is bilateral if it is made by both parties to the contract. A mistake is unilateral if it is made by only one of the parties to the contract.

In Scenario B above, the mistake was a bilateral mistake of fact. That is, both Bruce and Cory were mistaken about what the painting was. A bilateral mistake of fact renders the contract voidable at the option of either party.[57] So, in Scenario B, either Bruce or Cory could choose to disaffirm the contract.

Unilateral mistakes of fact are usually not considered a defense to contract enforcement. However, a unilateral mistake of fact will render a contract voidable at the option of the mistaken party if the non-mistaken party had reason to know that a mistake was made.[58] Imagine if, instead of Bruce and Cory being mistaken about the "Van Bro" painting in Scenario B, only Cory was mistaken and that Bruce knew that Cory thought the "Van Bro" painting was a Van Gogh. In that scenario, Cory could probably rescind the contract.

Most importantly, a mistake of fact must be material to render the contract voidable, regardless of whether the mistake is bilateral or unilateral. A mistake of fact is material when it is significant or essential to the case.[59] This means the fact must be one of the reasons that the parties entered into the contract.

In *Sherwood v. Walker*, two men entered into a contract to buy and sell a cow. Both believed the cow was unable to have offspring when they entered into the contract. As a result of their bilateral mistake of fact, the cow's price was greatly reduced because a fertile cow is worth significantly more than a barren cow. The parties later discovered that the cow was indeed fertile. The Michigan Supreme Court held that the mistake of fact was material because the farmer would not have sold the cow for such a low price, if at all, if it was capable of having offspring.[60]

F. Defenses to Contract Enforcement: Misrepresentation

A misrepresentation is a false or leading assertion that does not accord with the facts.[61] If the misrepresentation is material, meaning that it is a statement "likely to induce a reasonable person to assent or that the maker knows is likely to induce the recipient to assent,"[62] the contract becomes voidable at the option of the innocent party.[63] Even if a misrepresentation is not material, if the

---

[57] Restatement (Second), Contracts § 152.

[58] Restatement (Second), Contracts § 152.

[59] *See* Material Fact, Black's Law Dictionary (9th Ed. 2009)

[60] *Sherwood v. Walker*, 66 Mich. 568, 33 N.W. 919 (Mich. 1887).

[61] *See* Misrepresentation, Black's Law Dictionary (9th Ed. 2009)

[62] Material Misrepresentation, Black's Law Dictionary (9th Ed. 2009)

[63] Restatement (Second), Contracts § 164.

misrepresentation is fraudulent (intentional), the contract becomes voidable at the option of the injured party.[64]

If the misrepresentation was made intentionally, recklessly, or negligently, and the innocent party was damaged as a result of entering into the contract, the innocent party may also get money damages from the misrepresenting party on top of being able to rescind the contract.[65]

A misrepresentation can occur by words, actions, active concealment of material facts, and non-disclosure of material facts.[66] Further, a misrepresentation will render a contract voidable only when the party is justified in relying on the other party's representation. Mere statements of opinion are not considered representations except if an inexperienced purchaser is relying on the opinion of an expert.[67] Consider the following two examples.

SCENARIO A: Bruce, an experienced art dealer, finds a painting in his attic and invites Cory to look at it. He tells Cory, "This is a Vincent Van Gogh painting." Bruce knows that the painting was made by Vincent Van Bro. Based on his misrepresentation that the painting was made by Vincent Van Gogh, Cory pays $100,000 for the painting.

SCENARIO B: Bruce, an insurance salesman, finds a painting in his attic that was made by Vincent Van Gogh. He invites Cory to look at the painting and says, "This is Vincent Van Gogh's finest piece. You have to buy it from me." Cory buys the painting from Bruce for $100,000 only because Bruce represented to him that it was Van Gogh's best painting. He later learns that art critics universally consider the painting to be Van Gogh's worst.

In Scenario A, Bruce's misrepresentation would render the contract voidable at Cory's option and expose him to any damages Cory may have incurred as a result. He knew the painting was not done by Van Gogh and that Cory would not have bought it without that representation.

In Scenario B, Bruce made a statement of opinion when he said that it was Van Gogh's "finest piece." An opinion is not considered a misrepresentation unless made by an expert to a novice. Bruce is an insurance salesman in Scenario B, not an art dealer like in Scenario A. Thus, his statement of opinion is not considered a misrepresentation. Cory cannot rescind the contract or sue for damages.

G. Defenses to Contract Enforcement: Unconscionability

Though courts do not normally look at whether a contract is "fair," in extreme situations, some contracts or terms of a contract are considered so "unconscionable" (unfair) that they will not be enforced. If a contract term is found to be unconscionable, a court may declare the entire contract void, remove the unconscionable term and enforce the rest of the contract without it, or re-write the unconscionable term so that it is fair.[68]

A contract or contract term may be unconscionable for one or both of two reasons. A term may be substantively unconscionable or procedurally unconscionable. A term is substantively unconscionable if it is unduly harsh or oppressive in the eyes of the court.

More frequently, courts look to see if there was procedural unconscionability. Procedural unconscionability occurs when one party is in such a superior bargaining position to the other that enforcement of the contract would not be fair.

---

[64] Restatement (Second), Contracts § 164.

[65] This is because fraudulent misrepresentation is also a tort. *See* Section IV.H of Chapter 9 for a more detailed explanation.

[66] Restatement (Second), Contracts §§ 160-162.

[67] *See, e.g., Shore Builders, Inc. v. Dogwood, Inc.*, 616 F.Supp. 1004, 1017 (D. Del. 1985).

[68] Restatement (Second), Contracts § 208; UCC § 2-302.

TABLE 7.4 Contract Defenses

Defense	Requirements	Effect
Mistake	Bilateral material mistake of fact **or** unilateral material mistake of fact if the non-mistaken party knows of the mistaken party's mistake	Bilateral = Voidable by both parties Unilateral = Voidable by the mistaken party
Misrepresentation	A false or misleading assertion regarding a material fact	Voidable by the innocent party
Duress	Wrongful Act causes someone to enter into a contract. The wrongful act can be illegal or economic. If a wrongful act is economic it must be (1) a result of a situation caused by the party applying duress that (2) leaves no reasonable alternative for the innocent party	Void if the wrongful act giving rise to the duress is violent Voidable by the innocent party if the wrongful act giving rise to the duress is non-violent
Undue Influence	(1) Special relationship (2) used to take over the will of the dependent person in that relationship	Voidable by the innocent party
Incapacity by age	Party to the contract is under 18	Voidable by the minor child until a reasonable time after reaching adulthood
Incapacity declared by Court	Party to the contract is declared incapable to enter into a contract by a court	Void
Incapacity by intoxication or mental disability not declared by a court	Party to the contract lacks the ability to understand that he or she is entering into a contract **or** lacks the ability to understand the nature, consequences, and purposes of the contract.	Voidable at the incapacitated person's option
Public Policy	The contract violates a statute or other public policy	Void
Unconscionability	(1) Procedural (unfair bargaining position because of the relationship of the parties) **or** (2) Substantive (term or terms are grossly unfair)	A court may (1) Void the entire contract (2) Void just the offensive term(s) (3) Rewrite the offensive terms to be fair

For instance, in *Jones v. Star Credit Corp.*, a New York trial court found that a contract to purchase a freezer for $1234.80 (after credit charges) from a rent-to-own furniture store was unconscionable because the freezer was only worth $300, and the purchaser was a welfare recipient without bargaining power.[69] The court found that the amount paid by the welfare recipient was unfair relative to the value but also noted,

---

[69] *Jones v. Star Credit Corp.*, 59 Misc. 2d 189, 298 N.Y.S.2d 264 (N.Y. Sup. 1969)

No doubt, the mathematical disparity between $300, which presumably includes a reasonable profit margin, and $900, which is exorbitant on its face, carries the greatest weight. Credit charges alone exceed by more than $100 the retail value of the freezer. These alone, may be sufficient to sustain the decision. Yet, a caveat is warranted lest we reduce the import of [unconscionability] solely to a mathematical ratio formula. It may, at times, be that; yet it may also be much more. The very limited financial resources of the purchaser, known to the sellers at the time of the sale, is entitled to weight in the balance. Indeed, the value disparity itself leads inevitably to the felt conclusion that knowing advantage was taken of the plaintiffs. In addition, the meaningfulness of choice essential to the making of a contract can be negated by a gross inequality of bargaining power.[70]

Legal Definition

Unconscionability – a defense to the enforcement of a contract that is extremely unfair.

H. Defenses to Contract Enforcement: Statute of Frauds

Most contracts do not have to be in writing. However, there are several categories of contracts that must be in writing to be enforceable. First passed by the English parliament in 1677, the Statute of Frauds is the list of contracts that must be in writing.[71] It has been modified since 1677, especially by the UCC.[72] The following types of contracts must be made in writing:

1. Contracts relating to marriage
2. Contracts that cannot be performed within a year by their terms
3. Contracts for the transfer of an interest in land
4. Contracts by the executor of an estate to pay the estate's debt with his or her own money
5. Contracts for the sale of goods in excess of $500
6. Contracts for surety

1. Defenses to Contract Enforcement: Statute of Frauds: What is a "Signed Writing"?

Before getting into the types of contracts covered by the statute of frauds, it is important to know what kinds of writings will satisfy it. There is no magic formula required to make a writing. In most states, the writing must name the parties, the subject matter of the contract, the consideration being

FIGURE 7.1 Statute of Frauds

Remember the acronym "MY LEGS" for the Statute of Frauds. It covers:

M : Contracts relating to **marriage**
Y : Contracts that cannot be performed within a **year** by their terms
L : Contracts for the transfer of an interest in **land**
E : Contracts entered into by an **executor** to pay the debts of an estate with his or her own money
G : Contracts for the sale of **goods** in excess of $500
S : Contracts for **surety**

---

[70] *Jones v. Star Credit Corp.*, 59 Misc. 2d 189, 298 N.Y.S.2d 264 (N.Y. Sup. 1969)
[71] Statute of Frauds, Black's Law Dictionary (9th Edition 2009)
[72] *See* UCC § 2-201

exchanged between the parties, and any other term essential to the contract under the circumstances.[73] Under the UCC, the writing need only contain the quantity of the goods being purchased.[74] Under both the common law and the UCC, the writing does not even have to be the contract itself. It can even be a memorandum reciting the terms required under the statute of frauds. The writing, however, must be signed by the party against whom enforcement is sought.[75]

In some states, the statute of frauds will not be enforced if the party admits that a contract exists or if a party takes a detrimental step in reliance on the agreement (promissory estoppel).[76] There are other exceptions that apply to particular types of contracts under the statute of frauds that will be discussed below.

2. Defenses to Contract Enforcement: Statute of Frauds: Contracts Relating to Marriage

Any contract relating to marriage must be in writing. In earlier times, these types of contracts were far more frequent than they are now. Dowries were often paid to prospective husbands by fathers in consideration for marrying their daughters. In the modern context, the most common application of this rule is to prenuptial agreements.

3. Defenses to Contract Enforcement: Statute of Frauds: Contracts that Cannot be Performed Within a Year by Their Terms

If a contract cannot be performed within a year after it is formed, it must be in writing. The clock starts the day after the contract is made. Consider the following examples.

SCENARIO A: Bruce hires Cory to mow his lawn for 2 years.
SCENARIO B: Bruce hires Cory to mow his lawn for as long as he wants to mow his lawn. He intends to have Cory mow his lawn for years.

The contract in Scenario A must be in writing. The contract, by its terms, cannot be performed in a year. It has to take two years. The contract in Scenario B does not need to be in writing. Though both intend the contract to take years to perform, it could be performed in less than a year by its terms as Cory can quit at any time. Therefore, it does not have to be in writing.

4. Defenses to Contract Enforcement: Statute of Frauds: Contracts Involving the Transfer of an Interest in Land

Contracts regarding the sale or lease of an interest in real property (land and houses) must be in writing. There is an exception to this rule however. If a party pays part or all of the purchase price, that party can enforce the contract even if it is not in writing.

5. Defenses to Contract Enforcement: Statute of Frauds: Contracts by the Executor of an Estate to Pay the Debts of the Estate With His or Her Own Money

When a person dies, everything he or she owns becomes the property of a mythical entity known as his or her "estate." The estate is administered by an executor, which is usually a friend or family

---

[73] Restatement (Second), Contracts § 131.
[74] UCC § 2-201, cmt. 1.
[75] Restatement (Second), Contracts § 131.
[76] For a fuller discussion of promissory estoppel, (see section II.C.4 of this chapter.)

member of the deceased appointed by the Probate Court. The Executor is not personally liable for the debts of the estate. In other words, the executor does not have to use his or her own money to pay the debts of the deceased.

If the executor chooses to pay this debt despite not being legally obligated to do so, that contract must be in writing under the statute of frauds.

6. Defenses to Contract Enforcement: Statute of Frauds: Contracts for the Sale of Goods in Excess of $500

Any contract for the sale of goods in excess of $500 must be in writing. The UCC, however, has created several exceptions to this rule.

Under the UCC, the statute of frauds will not apply if a merchant sends an unsigned order confirmation stating the essential terms of the contract to another merchant that is not objected to within 10 days.[77] Further, if a person pays for goods or accepts delivery of the goods, the statute of frauds will not apply.[78]

There is also an exception for "specially manufactured goods." If a seller makes custom goods that can only be sold to the buyer, and the seller begins manufacturing the goods before the buyer breaches the agreement, the statute of frauds will not apply.[79]

Finally, if the party against whom enforcement is sought admits under oath that a contract exists, the statute of frauds will not apply.[80]

7. Defenses to Contract Enforcement: Statute of Frauds: Surety Contracts

Contracts for surety must be in writing. A surety contract is a contract that makes one person liable for the debt of another if that person cannot pay the debt. The person who becomes liable as a surety is often called a co-signer.

Imagine the following scenario. Bruce wants to sign a lease promising to pay Dillon $500 a month to rent an apartment. Bruce has bad credit and was evicted from his last apartment. Dillon refuses to let Bruce live in his apartment unless someone else promises to pay him if Bruce defaults on his rent. Because they are friends, Cory agrees to co-sign Bruce's lease.

In that scenario, Cory's promise to pay Dillon if Bruce does not must be in writing. Cory gets no benefit from the contract other than seeing his friend not be homeless.

VI. Contract Damages

Perhaps the most important question in contract law is what a party is entitled to after a breach of contract occurs. Contract law usually awards "expectation damages." Expectation damages are "compensation awarded for the loss of what a person reasonably anticipated from a transaction that was not completed."[81] Essentially, after a breach of contract occurs, a court aims to put the parties in the position they would have been in had the contract been performed. Consider the following case.[82]

---

[77] UCC § 2-201(2)
[78] UCC § 2-201(3)(c)
[79] UCC § 2-201(3)(a)
[80] UCC § 2-201(3)(b)
[81] Expectation Damages, Black's Law Dictionary (9th Edition 2009)
[82] *Hawkins v. McGee* was discussed prominently in *The Paper Chase*, a film that was available on Netflix at the time of this writing.

❖❖

Hawkins v. McGee
84 N.H. 114, 146 A. 641 (1929)

Branch, J.

1. The operation in question consisted in the removal of a considerable quantity of scar tissue from the palm of the plaintiff's right hand and the grafting of skin taken from the plaintiff's chest in place thereof. The scar tissue was the result of a severe burn caused by contact with an electric wire, which the plaintiff received about nine years before the time of the transactions here involved. There was evidence to the effect that before the operation was performed the plaintiff and his father went to the defendant's office and that the defendant in answer to the question, "How long will the boy be in the hospital?", replied, "Three or four days, . . . not over four; then the boy can go home, and it will be just a few days when he will be able to go back to work with a perfect hand." Clearly this and other testimony to the same effect would not justify a finding that the doctor contracted to complete the hospital treatment in three or four days or that the plaintiff would be able to go back to work within a few days thereafter. The above statements could only be construed as expressions of opinion or predictions as to the probable duration of the treatment and plaintiff's resulting disability, and the fact that these estimates were exceeded would impose no contractual liability upon the defendant. The only substantial basis for the plaintiff's claim is the testimony that the defendant also said before the operation was decided upon, "I will guarantee to make the hand a hundred per cent perfect hand" or "a hundred per cent good hand."

***

2. The substance of the charge to the jury on the question of damages appears in the following quotation: "If you find the plaintiff entitled to anything, he is entitled to recover for what pain and suffering he has been made to endure and what injury he has sustained over and above the injury that he had before." To this instruction the defendant seasonably excepted. By it, the jury was permitted to consider two elements of damage, (1) pain and suffering due to the operation, and (2) positive ill effects of the operation upon the plaintiff's hand. Authority for any specific rule of damages in cases of this kind seems to be lacking, but when tested by general principle and by analogy, it appears that the foregoing instruction was erroneous.

***

"By 'damages' as that term is used in the law of contracts, is intended compensation for a breach, measured in the terms of the contract." Davis v. Company, 77 N.H. 403, 404. The purpose of the law is to "put the plaintiff in as good a position as he would have been in had the defendant kept his contract." 3 Williston, Cont., s. 1338; *Hardie etc. Co. v. Company*, 150 N.C. 150. The measure of recovery "is based upon what the defendant should have given the plaintiff, not what the plaintiff has given the defendant or otherwise expended." 3 Williston, Cont., s. 1341. "The only losses that can be said fairly to come within the terms of a contract are such as the parties must have had in mind when the contract was made, or such as they either knew or ought to have known would probably result from a failure to comply with its terms." *Davis v. Company*, 77 N.H. 403, 404; *Hurd v. Dunsmore*, 63 N.H. 171.

***

The extent of the plaintiff's suffering does not measure this difference in value. The pain necessarily incident to a serious surgical operation was a part of the contribution which the plaintiff was willing to make to his joint undertaking with the defendant to produce a good hand. It was a legal detriment suffered by him which constituted a part of the consideration given by him for the contract. It represented a part of the price which he was willing to pay for a good hand, but it furnished no test of the value of a good hand or the difference between the value of the hand which the defendant promised and the one which resulted from the operation.

It was also erroneous and misleading to submit to the jury as a separate element of damage any change for the worse in the condition of the plaintiff's hand resulting from the operation, although this error was probably more prejudicial to the plaintiff than to the defendant. Any such ill effect of the operation would be included under the true rule of damages set forth above, but damages might properly be assessed for the defendant's failure to improve the condition of the hand even if there were no evidence that its condition was made worse as a result of the operation.

***

Questions Presented

1) What facts did the Court say gave the only grounds for the Plaintiff to obtain damages?
2) How did the Court say that plaintiff's damages should be measured in this case?
3) Why were the instructions given to the jury wrong?

❖❖

What constitutes expectation damages depends on the type of contract that is involved. There are several types of damages that tend to be a part of the expectation damages calculation.

A. Contract Damages: Actual Damages

Actual damages, which are also known as "compensatory damages," are the damages a party incurs that are the direct result of the breach of contract. They usually take one of two forms when a seller breaches a contracts, "cover cost" and "market damages."

The cover cost is the cost to find a replacement service or replacement goods. For instance, if Bruce breaches a contract with Cory to mow his lawn for $50, and Cory hires Dillon instead to mow his lawn for $60, Cory's cover damages are $10. It is the difference between the contract price and the replacement cost.

Market damages are the difference between the contract price and the market price of the goods or services that are the subject matter of the contract. The market price is measured on the day that the innocent party learns about the breach. For instance, if Bruce informs Cory on May 15 that he is breaching a contract to mow his lawn on May 17 for $50, Cory's market damages would be whatever the market price for lawn mowing services was on May 15 minus the contract price.

When a buyer breaches the contract, the seller's actual damages are often the contract price itself or, in the case of the sale of goods, the difference between the contract price and the resale price of the goods.

B. Contract Damages: Incidental Damages

Incidental damages are losses that are "reasonably associated with or related to actual damages."[83] These are essentially damages incurred by a party to complete the objective of the contract.

---

[83] Incidental Damages, Black's Law Dictionary (9th Ed. 2009)

For instance, imagine that Bruce breaches a contract with Cory to mow his lawn for $50. To find another landscaper, Cory places an ad online at the cost of $10. The cost of the advertisement is incidental damages. Cory placed the ad in the newspaper to get his lawn mowed, the original objective of his contract with Bruce.

C. Contract Damages: Consequential Damages

Consequential damages are losses indirectly incurred as a result of the breach of contract. Unlike incidental or actual damages, consequential damages must also be reasonably foreseeable.

Imagine that Bruce is a gardener for "Bushy Hedges," a company that specializes in trimming hedges to look like members of the Presidential Bush family. Cory is an affluent businessman who has long admired the Bush clan. He agrees to pay Bruce $500 to trim the hedges in his front lawn to look like Jeb Bush. He says to Kyle, "You need to do this right because I'm holding a lawn expo next week to show off my Jeb hedge. I've pre-sold 50 tickets for $50 each. That's $2,500 I will have to refund if this is not done properly." On the day he set aside to create the Jeb hedge, Bruce gets so caught up in his crossfit routine that he forgets to do the hedge. As a result, Cory has to cancel his show and refund all the money he collected in advance."

In the above scenario, Cory could likely collect $2,500 from Bruce as a result of his breach. The loss is indirectly related to the contract. The purpose of the contract between Cory and Bruce was to produce a hedge, not put on a show in his garden. However, if Bruce did not breach, the show would have gone on, and Cory would have collected $2,500.

Just as importantly, Cory's loss of revenue was reasonably foreseeable. Cory told Bruce about the potential loss before he breached. If he had not done this, Bruce would have no way of reasonably foreseeing Cory's loss, rendering Cory unable to collect consequential damages.

D. Contract Damages: Specific Performance

Specific performance is a remedy that requires the breaching party to actually perform the contract for the contract price. No money damages are awarded as a part of specific performance. Courts will only award specific performance if money damages will not put the parties in the position they would have been in had the contract been performed.

Imagine that Bruce agrees to sell his home to Cory for $250,000. Bruce then breaches the contract and refuses to sell to Cory. If a court ordered specific performance, Bruce would have to sell his home to Cory in exchange for $250,000.

Courts will almost never award specific performance when a service contract is breached. Courts are hesitant to do this because forcing someone to perform a service is essentially involuntary servitude, which, since the Constitution prohibited it via the Thirteenth Amendment in 1865, is considered a violation of public policy. Further, as a practical matter, people often do not do a good job when forced to perform.

Courts also rarely grant specific performance when a contract for the sale of goods is breached. There are few goods unique enough to qualify for specific performance.

E. Contract Damages: Expenses Saved

Any expenses the non-breaching party saves as a result of the breach of contract will be subtracted from his or her total damage award. Consider the following example.

TABLE 7.5 Contract Remedies

Type of Expectation Damage	Requirements
Actual	The losses directly flowing from the breach of contract
Incidental	The losses closely associated with actual losses
Consequential	The (1) reasonably foreseeable (2) indirect losses resulting from the breach of contract
Specific performance	A court requiring the parties to actually perform the contract

Bruce agrees to paint Cory's house for $100. Cory then breaches the contract by hiring another painter. Bruce would have had to spend $20 on paint had he painted Cory's house.

Bruce would receive $80. His actual loss is the contract price, which is $100. However, he saved $20 by not having to buy paint, which is subtracted from his total award. This puts Bruce and Cory in the position they would have been in had the contract been performed.

F. Contract Damages: Mitigation

The non-breaching party is under a duty to reasonably mitigate (reduce) damages. Consider the following example.

Cory is Bruce's landlord. Bruce signs a one-year lease to pay $500 a month in rent. After three months, Bruce breaches the contract. A month after Bruce breaches, Dillon offers to rent Bruce's former room for $490 a month.

If Cory was not able to find someone to replace Bruce, Bruce would owe him $500 a month for nine months. However, now that Dillon has offered to rent the apartment after one missed payment by Bruce for $10 less a month than what Bruce was paying, Bruce will only owe $580 over 9 months ($10 a month for the 8 months Dillon offered to pay plus $500 for the missed month). Cory is under a duty to mitigate his damages. Either he accepts Dillon's offer, which reduces Cory's actual loss, or he rejects Dillon's offer, which violates his duty to mitigate (reduce) damages.

G. Contract Damages: Liquidated Damages

Expectation damages can be difficult to measure. In situations where that is the case, parties often include a clause in the contract stating what the damages will be in the event of a breach. For a liquidated damages clause to be enforceable, it must be a reasonable estimate of what the innocent party's damages would have been. Frequently, the parties must know that damages would be difficult to measure at the time the contract was formed.[84]

H. Contract Damages: Formulas for Damages

General Formula for Damages

Actual Damages + Incidental Damages + Consequential Damages − Expenses Saved

---

[84] *See*, e.g., *Winthrop Resources Corp. v. Eaton Hydraulics, Inc.*, 361 F.3d 465 (8th Cir. 2004).

Most contracts will allow the non-breaching party to collect whatever the actual damages, incidental damages, and consequential damages are but will subtract whatever expenses are saved as a result of the breach.

1. Contract Damages: Formulas for Damages: Service Contracts

The actual damages for a service contract depend on which party breaches and whether that party breaches before, during, or after the performance. If a seller of a service breaches a service contract before performance begins, the buyer will receive his or her cover cost (replacement cost minus the contract price). If a seller of a service contract does not complete the work, the buyer's actual loss will be the actual cost of completion minus what the buyer would have paid seller to complete it.

If a seller of a service renders a defective performance, the buyer's remedy will depend on whether the breach was material. As discussed earlier in this chapter, in *Jacobs & Young v. Kent*, a contractor agreed to use a particular brand of pipe to construct a house. Due to an oversight, he used a different kind of brand. The court held that, because the two brands were virtually identical and no other breaches were brought to the attention of the court, the contract was substantially performed. Because the contract was substantially performed, the buyer (the homeowner) was only entitled to the difference in value between the pipe used and the pipe for which the contract called, which was little to nothing.[85]

If, unlike in the case above, the breach is substantial, the buyer's damages will be the cost to repair the seller's defective performance.

If a buyer breaches a service contract, a seller's actual damages will be the contract price minus whatever damages the seller was able to mitigate by finding alternate work.

2. Contract Damages: Formulas for Damages: Real Estate Contracts

Every piece of real estate is considered unique. So, if a seller breaches a real estate contract, the buyer's remedy is specific performance (getting a court order to force the seller to sell the house). However, if specific performance is not available (most commonly, the seller sells the house to someone else), the buyer's actual loss is the difference between the market value of the house on the day the buyer learned about the breach minus the contract price.

Cover (replacement) cost can never serve as the basis for a buyer's actual loss when the seller damages a real estate contract because every piece of real estate is considered unique.

If a buyer breaches a real estate contract, a court will award the difference between the contract price and the market price to the seller. However, the seller must likely still continue to maintain the property and pay the mortgage. Though these are arguably incidental damages, they are usually not compensable.[86] It is very common for a liquidated damages clause to be included in the contract for the sale of real estate that allows the seller to keep the buyer's deposit in the event of buyer's breach of contract.

FIGURE 7.2 Sample Liquidated Damages Clause

Sample Liquidated Damages Clause Allowing Seller to Keep Buyer's Deposit

If BUYER is in default hereunder, or, on or before the date of closing as set forth herein, BUYER indicates that he or she is unable or unwilling to perform and SELLER stands ready to perform SELLER's obligations, SELLER's sole remedy shall be the right to terminate this Agreement by written notice to BUYER or BUYER's attorney and retain the down payment as reasonable liquidated damages for BUYER's inability or unwillingness to perform.

---

[85] *Jacobs & Young v. Kent*, 230 N.Y. 239, 129 N.E. 889 (NY 1921).
[86] *See*, e.g., *Roesch v. Bray*, 46 Ohio App. 3d 49 (Ohio App. Ct. 1988).

3. Contract Damages: Formulas For Damages: Sale of Goods

The Uniform Commercial Code offers a number of remedies when a contract for the sale of goods is breached.

If a seller refuses to provide goods to buyer, the buyer has two choices of remedy. If the buyer covers his costs and buys replacement goods, the buyer may choose either to obtain the difference between the contract price and the cover cost from the seller[87] or to obtain the difference between the contract price and the market price of the goods from the seller.[88]

Similarly, under the perfect tender rule, the buyer has two options if the seller provides nonconforming goods. The buyer can reject the goods and proceed to obtain the remedies listed in the paragraph above, or it can accept the goods and recover the difference between the value of the goods it expected to receive and the value of the goods that it actually received.[89]

A seller has many choices if the buyer improperly rejects the goods or repudiates the contract while the seller still has the goods. The seller can resell the goods.[90] If the seller resells the goods, the seller can obtain the difference between the resale price and the contract price.[91] The seller can also stop delivery of the goods,[92] cancel the contract,[93] or sue for the difference between the market value of the goods and the contract price.[94] If the difference between the contract price and the market price is not enough to put the seller in the place he or she would have been in had the contract been performed, the seller can obtain lost profits instead of market value.

If a buyer accepts the goods but refuses to pay for them, the seller may sue the buyer for the contract price.[95] It may also hold on to any other goods not yet delivered to the buyer and, if he cannot resell them, collect the contract the price.[96]

I. Contract Damages: Quasi-Contract

Even if a contract is not formed, a party can sometimes still recover damages under the theory of "quasi-contract." A quasi-contract is not a contract. Rather, it is simply a remedy to provide compensation to a party to avoid unjustly enriching another party. If a quasi-contract is found, the plaintiff may recover *quantum meruit* damages, meaning that the benefitted party must pay a reasonable amount of money for those services.

Imagine that Bruce is a pizza delivery boy. He delivers a pizza to Cory at 1201 Fictional Place that was paid for in advance by Alex, who lives at 1203 Fictional Place. Bruce mistakenly delivers the pizza to Cory at 1201 Fictional Place. Despite not paying for the pizza, Cory accepts it.

Even though Cory did not enter into a contract to buy the pizza, because he accepted it knowing that it was not his, a court could require Cory to pay for it under the doctrine of quasi-contract.

---

[87] UCC § 2-712
[88] UCC § 2-713
[89] UCC § 2-714
[90] UCC §§ 2-703(d), 2-709
[91] UCC § 2-709
[92] UCC § 2-703(a)-(b)
[93] UCC § 2-703(f)
[94] UCC § 2-708(1)
[95] UCC § 2-709
[96] UCC § 2-709

J. Reliance Damages

In some cases, a court may opt not to place the injured party in the position that it would have been in had the contract been performed and, instead, award the injured party damages sufficient to put it in the position it would have been in had the contract never been made. This is especially common in promissory estoppel cases.[97]

For example, imagine that Bruce offers to mow Cory's lawn for free. Relying on that promise, Cory turns down Alex's offer to mow his lawn for $50. Bruce refuses to mow Cory's lawn, and Cory cannot find someone to mow his lawn for less than $60.

In that case, Bruce's promise is enforceable even though it lacks consideration (Bruce received nothing in return from Cory). It is enforceable under promissory estoppel because Cory relied on the promise to his detriment (He turned down a below market offer to have his lawn mowed by Alex).

If the contract had never been made, Cory would have paid $50 to Alex to have his lawn mowed. However, because of Bruce's promise to Cory, Cory has to pay $60 to someone else to have his lawn mowed. A court could choose to award Cory the $10 difference as reliance damages, placing him in the position he would have been in had the contract never been made.

Under a theory of expectation damages, Cory would be awarded $60 because his lawn would have been mowed for free if Bruce had performed as promised. However, because this is a promissory estoppel case, a court has the option to choose between expectation damages and reliance damages.

In some circumstances, reliance damages can be awarded even when consideration is present.[98] For example, a court may award an injured party reliance damages in the case of a contract on which it would have otherwise taken a loss.[99]

For example, imagine that Cory agrees to build Bruce a new building in exchange for $200,000. The building would have cost Cory $250,000 in materials and labor—a $50,000 loss. Cory nonetheless performs under the contract and, without receiving payment from Bruce, spends $10,000 on materials for the job. Bruce then breaches the contract and refuses to let Cory build the new building.

In this case, Cory has no expectation damages because he would have lost money had the contract been performed. However, a court may award him $10,000 for the materials that he expended in reliance on the contract—placing him in the position that he would have been in had the contract not been performed.

K. Restitution Damages

In some cases, a court may also award restitution damages. Restitution damages seek to prevent a party from improperly gaining a benefit.[100] For example, imagine that Cory signs a written contract to buy Bruce's house for $150,000 even though the house's market value is only $100,000. Cory pays Bruce a $20,000 deposit. Bruce then breaches the contract.

In this case, Cory could sue for specific performance of the contract. However, that would not be to his advantage given that the market value of the house is lower than the purchase price. Instead, he may choose to sue Bruce for restitution damages of $20,000 (his deposit) as Bruce would have essentially received it for nothing if Cory did not sue for specific performance.[101]

---

[97] Restatement (Second), Contracts § 90.
[98] Restatement (Second), Contracts § 347.
[99] Restatement (Second), Contracts § 347, cmt. a.
[100] Restatement (Second), Contracts § 370.
[101] Restatement (Second), Contracts § 373, Illus. 1.

A party who breached the contract may also seek restitution damages to the extent that it provided a benefit to the non-breaching party.[102] For example, imagine that Bruce promises to mow Cory's lawn for $50 a month for a year. Under the contract, payment is not due until the end of the year. Cory mows the lawn for 11 months but breaches the contract by not mowing Bruce's lawn in the twelfth month. Bruce refuses to pay Cory at the end of the year for the 11 months that he mowed Bruce's lawn.

In this case, even though Cory breached the contract, he could sue Bruce for restitution damages of $550—payment for the 11 months that he mowed Bruce's lawn. Without restitution damages, Bruce would have improperly received 11 months of free lawn mowing.

SUMMARY

A contract is a legally enforceable agreement between two or more parties and is the backbone of business law. If the law did not enforce contracts, far fewer people would be trusting enough to enter into commercial agreements.

The law will not enforce every agreement however. A contract is formed by one party accepting another's offer that is supported by consideration. This means that both sides have to give something up for it be a legally enforceable contract. There are also several defenses to enforcement. For example, illegal contracts and contracts with those declared mentally incompetent by a court are never enforceable. Some agreements are enforceable at the option of an aggrieved party. For instance, someone who enters into a contract as the result of a misrepresentation may choose whether to enforce the agreement.

It is also essential to remember what damages parties are entitled to upon breach of the contract. As a general rule, courts like to put parties in the position they would have been in had the contract been performed, a concept called *expectation damages*.

It is also important to remember that contracts are interpreted objectively. This means that they are interpreted from the perspective of a reasonable person. The whole point of enforcing contracts, after all, is to enforce the reasonable expectations of the parties as best as possible.

---

[102] Restatement (Second), Contracts § 374.

CHAPTER 8

AGENCY

LEARNING OBJECTIVES

Upon completion of this chapter the student will be able to:

1 Explain and identify the ways that agency relationships are created.
2 Explain and identify the different types of agency authority.
3 Explain and identify when principals, agents, and third parties are liable to each other.
4 Understand the duties owed by principals and agents.
5 Explain and identify the ways an agency relationship is terminated.

KEY TERMS

actual authority
agency relationship
agent
apparent authority
authority by estoppel
detour
disclosed principal
employee
frolic

independent contractor
inherent authority
partially disclosed principal
principal
ratification
respondeat superior
scope of employment
third party
undisclosed principal

I. Introduction

Have you ever asked someone to do something for you? Imagine that you are hungry at work but cannot get away from your desk. So, you hand a co-worker who is going on a break $2.00 and say, "Be a friend, and buy me a candy bar." Your co-worker agrees and says, "I will go the cafeteria and bring it back to you after my break." Unknowingly, you just created an agency relationship with your co-worker.

Agency is the name for the relationship that arises when one person agrees to act on behalf of another. In the example above, your co-worker agrees to work on your behalf, which makes him your agent. The law of agency is vital because it governs most transactions entered into in a commercial setting. Consider the example above. The person your co-worker buys the candy bar from probably does not own the cafeteria. She is likely working as an employee on behalf of the cafeteria's owner, making her the owner's agent. In fact, the cafeteria is likely not even owned by a natural person. It is probably owned by a company like a corporation or LLC. Without agents, companies could accomplish nothing.

While this seems like a straightforward concept, agency law is often quite complex. Think about the above example. You authorized your coworker to buy you a candy bar. However, you did not specify the kind of candy bar that you wanted or how much you wanted your friend to spend on the candy bar. Could your coworker have used any change leftover on his own behalf? With agency, the devil is in the details.

We will answer the following questions in this chapter:

1. How is an agency relationship formed?
2. What is the scope of an agent's authority?
3. Who can be held liable for the acts of an agent?
4. How is an agency relationship ended?

II. Terminology and Governing Law

A. The Parties

In every agency relationship, there are two major players, the principal and the agent. Neither can exist without the other. The agent is the person who acts on behalf of the principal.[1] That is, the principal is the one who gives the orders (in theory), and the agent is the one who follows those orders and acts on behalf of the principal. In the example in the introduction of our chapter in which you ask a co-worker to buy you a candy bar, you are the principal and the co-worker is the agent because the co-worker is acting on your behalf.

Legal Definitions

Principal – someone who authorizes and allows another to act on his or her behalf.

Agent – a person acting on behalf of someone else.

There is also usually another important person within agency law. Every time an agent acts on behalf of a principal, the agent is dealing with a third person. In the example in the introduction of our chapter in which you ask a co-worker to buy a candy bar on your behalf, the co-worker is buying the candy bar from the cafeteria. Without the cafeteria, there would be no reason for the agent to act on the principal's behalf at all. For the purposes of this chapter, the person with whom the agent interacts will be called "the third party."

Legal Definition

Third Party – in agency law, the third party is the person or entity with whom the agent interacts with on behalf of the principal.

---

[1] *See* Restatement (Third), Agency § 1.01; Restatement (Second), Agency § 1.

B. Governing Law

Every state has a slightly different take on agency law. However, because agency existed at common law, agency law is relatively uniform throughout the United States. Though not binding, courts in all 50 states frequently cite a treatise called the "Restatement of Agency" when discussing agency law. First developed in the first half of the 20th century, the Restatement of Agency seeks to summarize the general principles of agency law as laid out in state court decisions and statutes. The Restatement (Second) of Agency was published in 1958 and has been heavily relied on by judges. The Restatement (Third) of Agency was published in 2006 and incorporates most of the principles from the Restatement (Second) of Agency. Both remain influential on modern courts. Both will be cited in this chapter.

C. Who Can be a Principal and an Agent

Agency relationships are not limited to natural persons. Business entities like corporations and LLCs can serve as principals and agents.[2] For instance, Jamie Justice can be an agent for Smooth Creations, LLC. Conversely, Smooth Creations, LLC can be an agent for Jamie Justice. An agency relationship can even exist without a natural person's involvement. For example, Smooth Creations, LLC can be an agent of Rotten Apples Partnership.

III. Creation of an Agency Relationship

Agency relationships are created by the words and actions of the principal and the agent. The principal's words and actions must show that it wants the agent to act on its behalf, and the agent's words and actions must show that it will act on behalf of the principal. There is no magical formula to make this happen. This can happen by the express agreement of the parties or by accident. The parties do not need to intend to have an agency relationship to have one.[3] Similarly, one of the parties may intend an agency relationship without one resulting. Consider the following case.

❖❖

Harts v. Farmers Ins. Exchange
461 Mich. 1, 597 N.W.2d 47 (1999)

TAYLOR, J.

We granted leave in this case to determine whether a licensed insurance agent owes an affirmative duty to advise or counsel an insured about the adequacy or availability of coverage. We hold that, except under very limited circumstances not present in this case, an insurance agent owes no such duty to an insured. We therefore affirm the decision of the Court of Appeals, which affirmed the trial court's grant of summary disposition in favor of defendants.

I. FACTS AND PROCEEDINGS

In early 1993, plaintiffs, Tyrone and Gloria Harts owned a Chevrolet Cavalier that was covered by a policy of no-fault automobile insurance they had purchased from defendant Farmers Insurance

---

[2] *See* Restatement (Third), Agency §§ 1.01; 1.04(5); Restatement (Second), Agency § 1, cmt. a.
[3] *See* Restatement (Third), Agency § 1.01, cmt. b; Restatement (Second), Agency § 1, cmt. b.

Exchange, through defendant Gregory Pietrzak, a licensed insurance agent selling insurance exclusively for Farmers. The policy covering the Cavalier did not include optional uninsured motorist coverage.

While driving the Cavalier on February 15, 1993, Mrs. Harts was involved in an automobile accident with an uninsured vehicle. Mrs. Harts was injured, and plaintiffs' six-year-old son was killed. The Harts received from Farmers the personal injury protection benefits due them under the Cavalier policy. They also subsequently obtained a $2 million default judgment against the driver and owner of the uninsured vehicle. However, they have never collected any money on this judgment.

The Harts then filed suit against Mr. Pietrzak and Farmers. They contended that Mr. Pietrzak was negligent in selling them an insurance policy that was inadequate because it did not contain uninsured motorist coverage. They also contended that Farmers was vicariously liable for Mr. Pietrzak's negligence and actively negligent for its own failure to properly supervise Mr. Pietrzak.

The discovery phase of the case revealed the extent of the parties' prior dealings. Beginning in 1989, the Harts had insured a series of six vehicles, including the Cavalier, with Farmers, first with agent John Straub and then beginning in 1992 with Mr. Pietrzak. During the time that they had insured with Mr. Straub, they had purchased for one of their vehicles, a Buick Century, uninsured motorist coverage. This coverage, however, was canceled by Mrs. Harts when the policy on the Century was reinstated after it had lapsed for nonpayment.

On the applications for coverage with respect to vehicles other than the Century, including the application for the Cavalier that was signed by plaintiffs less than one month before the accident, plaintiffs did not select uninsured motorist coverage on the space provided on the application form. Moreover, the record reflects that, some three months before the accident, Farmers notified plaintiffs about the availability of uninsured motorist coverage. The availability of this coverage was made in a November 7, 1992, renewal notice for one of plaintiffs' vehicles. That notice specifically advised plaintiffs that uninsured motorist coverage was available and that they should contact their agent if interested.

While Mr. Harts had no recollection of any conversations with Mr. Pietrzak concerning the nature or extent of the coverage obtained on the Cavalier, Mr. Harts did recall an earlier conversation in which he discussed "full coverage" for the Century with Mr. Pietrzak. However, Mr. Harts did not at that time request uninsured motorist coverage on the Century even though the Harts had earlier had such coverage on this vehicle. Further, it is noteworthy that yet another conversation concerning "full coverage" occurred when the policy on the Century was transferred to an Aerostar, and again Mr. Harts made no request for uninsured motorist coverage.

Defendants moved for summary disposition pursuant to MCR 2.116(C)(10), contending that there was no special relationship between plaintiffs and Mr. Pietrzak as required by Bruner v. League General Ins. Co., 164 Mich.App. 28, 416 N.W.2d 318 (1987), and that therefore Mr. Pietrzak did not owe plaintiffs a duty to advise them about uninsured motorist coverage or the adequacy of their coverage. Finding Bruner dispositive, the trial court granted the motion in favor of defendants. The Court of Appeals affirmed. This Court granted plaintiffs' application for leave to appeal. 459 Mich. 895, 589 N.W.2d 279 (1998).

II. STANDARD OF REVIEW

A motion pursuant to MCR 2.116(C)(10) tests the factual support of a plaintiff's claim and is subject to de novo review. Smith v. Globe Life Ins. Co., 460 Mich. 446, 597 N.W.2d 28 (1999).

In reviewing a motion for summary disposition pursuant to MCR 2.116(C)(10), the court considers the pleadings, affidavits and other documentary evidence filed in the action or submitted by the parties, MCR 2.116(G)(5), in the light most favorable to the nonmoving party. Id. The motion is properly granted if the documentary evidence presented shows that there is no genuine issue with respect to any material fact and the moving party is therefore entitled to judgment as a matter of law. Id.

III. ANALYSIS

On appeal, plaintiffs acknowledge that no special relationship as required by Bruner exists in this case. However, they contend that this Court should reject Bruner's requirement of a special relationship and allow them to sue Mr. Pietrzak for his negligence in failing to offer them any advice or counsel concerning uninsured motorist coverage. In short, they ask this Court to determine that a licensed insurance agent has a duty to offer advice or counsel concerning uninsured motorist coverage.

Whether a duty exists is a question of law that is solely for the court to decide. Murdock v. Higgins, 454 Mich. 46, 53, 559 N.W.2d 639 (1997). In considering this question of duty and its potential expansion, it is appropriate to first look at the common-law duties inherent in an insurer-agent-insured relationship and then to consider the extent to which this relationship has been affected by certain Michigan statutes that are relevant to the establishment of an agent's duty.

It is uncontested, indeed it is essential to the cause of action pleaded by plaintiffs, that Mr. Pietrzak was Farmers' agent. As such, under the common law, he had a duty to comply with the various fiduciary obligations he owed to Farmers and to act for its benefit. Hawkeye Casualty Co. v. Frisbee, 316 Mich. 540, 548, 25 N.W.2d 521 (1947); 1 Restatement Agency, 2d, § 13, p. 52; 2 Restatement Agency, 2d, § 387, p. 201. Moreover, because he was Farmers' agent, he had no common-law duty to advise plaintiffs. . . . This general common-law rule is no doubt premised, at least in part, on the nature of the relationship of the parties. . . . . Specifically, the relationship between the insurer and insured is a contractual one. . . . . The relationship between the insurer and its agent is controlled by the principles of agency. . . . .

***

Thus, under the common law, an insurance agent whose principal is the insurance company owes no duty to advise a potential insured about any coverage. Such an agent's job is to merely present the product of his principal and take such orders as can be secured from those who want to purchase the coverage offered. Our Legislature also recognizes the limited nature of the agent's role. Those who offer insurance products have been regulated by statute in Michigan for at least 120 years, with insurance agents and insurance counselors being in fact subject to licensure before they can offer their services to the public. The most recent revisions to these regulatory statutes became effective in 1973. What is clear from these provisions is that the Legislature has long distinguished between insurance agents and insurance counselors, with agents being essentially order takers while it is insurance counselors who function primarily as advisors.

However, as with most general rules, the general no-duty-to-advise rule, where the agent functions as simply an order taker for the insurance company, is subject to change when an event occurs that alters the nature of the relationship between the agent and the insured. This alteration of the ordinary relationship between an agent and an insured has been described by our Court of Appeals as a "special relationship" that gives rise to a duty to advise on the part of the agent.

Bruner, supra; see also Marlo Beauty Supply, Inc. v. Farmers Ins. Group of Cos., 227 Mich.App. 309, 314–315, 575 N.W.2d 324 (1998); Stein v. Continental Casualty Co., 110 Mich.App. 410, 416–417, 313 N.W.2d 299 (1981); Palmer v. Pacific Indemnity Co., 74 Mich.App. 259, 267, 254 N.W.2d 52 (1977).

While we agree with Bruner that there must be "some type of interaction on a question of coverage," id. at 34, 416 N.W.2d 318, we do not subscribe to the possible reading of Bruner that holds reliance on the length of the relationship between the agent and the insured is the dispositive factor in transforming the relationship into one in which the traditional common-law "no duty" principle is abrogated. We thus modify the "special relationship" test discussed in Bruner and the other cases cited above so that the general rule of no duty changes when (1) the agent misrepresents the nature or extent of the coverage offered or provided, (2) an ambiguous request is made that requires a clarification, (3) an inquiry is made that may require advice and the agent, though he need not, gives advice that is inaccurate, or (4) the agent assumes an additional duty by either express agreement with or promise to the insured.

In this case, there is no documentary evidence suggesting that Mr. Pietrzak misrepresented the coverage offered or provided. As stated, plaintiffs had in fact received notice that uninsured motorist coverage was available for the Cavalier only three months before the accident. Further, there is no evidence that Mr. Harts made a request about insurance coverage on the Cavalier that might be construed as ambiguous or that would have required clarification. Mr. Harts never requested or inquired about "full coverage" on the Cavalier. Finally, Mr. Pietrzak did not expressly agree or promise to advise Mr. Harts about insurance coverage generally or uninsured motorist coverage specifically. Thus, with respect to the coverage obtained on the Cavalier, no event occurred that could or would take this case outside the general rule that Mr. Pietrzak owed plaintiffs no duty to advise them about coverage.

***

Accordingly, because plaintiffs have failed to establish the duty element of their negligence claim against Mr. Pietrzak, summary disposition in favor of Mr. Pietrzak was proper. Smith, supra; Schultz, supra at 449, 506 N.W.2d 175. Because plaintiffs cannot establish liability against Mr. Pietrzak, the agent, they likewise cannot establish vicarious liability against Farmers, the principal. Kerry v. Turnage, 154 Mich.App. 275, 281, 397 N.W.2d 543 (1986); Lincoln v. Gupta, 142 Mich. App. 615, 622, 370 N.W.2d 312 (1985). And, because Mr. Pietrzak was under no obligation to give advice about uninsured motorist coverage, Farmers cannot be liable for any alleged negligent supervision. Accordingly, summary disposition in favor of Farmers was proper. Therefore, for the reasons stated in this opinion, we affirm the decision of the Court of Appeals.

***

Questions Presented
1) Was there an agency relationship between the insurance agent and the customer? Why or why not?
2) Was there an agency relationship between the insurance agent and the insurance company? Why or why not?
3) What could plaintiffs have done to change the outcome of this case?

An agency relationship can be created in a number of ways. It can be created by the express agreement of the principal and agent.[4] It can be implied by the conduct of the principal and the agent.[5] These types of agency are known as "Actual Agency." Agency can even be created by the principal's actions towards the third party or by the nature of the situation giving rise to the agent's actions.[6] This doctrine is known as "Agency by Estoppel," "Apparent Agency," or "Ostensible Agency."[7]

A. Actual Agency

Actual agency is the most common form of agency. It is created when the principal and agent agree to enter into an agency relationship. This can be done either with words or by conduct.[8]

An agency agreement made by words can either be written or unwritten. For instance, imagine that Jamie Justice agrees to mow Alec Irons' lawn. An actual agency relationship is created between the two because Alec and Jamie have agreed that Jamie will perform a particular task on Alec's behalf. Their agreement can either be written or oral.

An agency agreement can also be implied by the conduct of the parties without an express agreement. For instance, imagine that Alec Irons begins to wash Jamie Justice's windows without being asked. Jamie sees him doing this as she leaves her house, gives him a "thumbs up," and continues on her way. Though neither Alec nor Jamie expressly made an agreement for her windows to be washed, the conduct of both Alec and Jamie shows that they desire that Alec perform an action on her behalf, creating an actual agency in which Jamie is the principal and Alec is the agent.

B. Agency by Estoppel

Agency by estoppel arises when the actions of the principal lead a third party to believe the agent has authority when the agent actually has no authority.[9]

If a principal does something to make a third person reasonably believe that the agent has authority to act on its behalf, courts will hold that a principal created an agency relationship with the agent for the purposes of the transaction in question.[10] Imagine that Alec Irons, the President of Smooth Creations, Inc., gives Jamie Justice company letterhead to write her own recommendation for graduate school. Instead of writing a recommendation, Jamie Justice uses the letterhead to write a purchase order for 1,000 cupcakes, which is sent to and accepted by Death by Cupcake, LLC. Because Alec, as President of Smooth Creations, Inc., gave Jamie Smooth Creations, Inc.'s letterhead, Smooth Creations, Inc. created a situation in which a third person could reasonably believe Jamie had authority to act on its behalf, creating an agency by estoppel.

IV. Types and Scope of Agency Authority

An agent can be acting pursuant to actual authority, apparent authority, authority by estoppel, inherent authority, or authority by ratification.

---

[4] Restatement (Third), Agency § 1.03; Restatement (Second), Agency §§ 15, 26.

[5] Restatement (Third), Agency § 1.03; Restatement (Second), Agency §§ 15, 26.

[6] Restatement (Third), Agency § 2.05; Restatement (Second), Agency § 267

[7] *See Baptist Hospital Memorial System v. Sampson*, 969 SW 2d 945, 948, n. 2 (TX 1998) ("Many courts use the terms ostensible agency, apparent agency . . . and agency by estoppel interchangeably.")

[8] Restatement (Third), Agency § 1.03; Restatement (Second), Agency §§ 15, 26.

[9] Restatement (Third), Agency § 2.05; Restatement (Second), Agency § 267

[10] Restatement (Third), Agency § 2.05; Restatement (Second), Agency § 267

A. Actual Authority

There are two kinds of actual authority, express and implied.[11] Express authority is the authority the agent gains from the principal's direct authorization. It can be either written or oral. For example, Alec Irons, the CEO of Smooth Creation, Inc., makes Jamie Justice the manager of its New York store and tells her to hire three cashiers. Jamie hires Midhat, Arusha, and Ana as cashiers. In doing so, she acted according to express authority because the principal (Smooth Creations, Inc.) authorized her to do so.

An agent may also have actual implied authority. Implied authority is the unspoken and unwritten authority the agent receives from the principal. Most agents' actions are taken pursuant to this kind of authority. Consider the following example.

Alec Irons, the CEO of Smooth Creation, Inc., makes Jamie Justice the manager of its New York store. He tells Jamie to hire three cashiers. She hires Midhat, Arusha, and Ana. She then sets a schedule in which Midhat works 20 hours a week for $11.00 an hour, Arusha works 30 hours a week for $12.00 an hour, and Ana works 40 hours a week for $13.00 an hour.

Although Alec does not specifically tell Jamie to set their schedules or their pay rates, Jamie nonetheless has the implied authority to do so. It is impossible for the principal to list out every single thing it wants the agent to do. So, instead, agents have the authority to take actions that a reasonable agent would believe the principal would desire to be taken in that instance.[12] In the above example, a reasonable manager, especially if given the authority to hire, would clearly believe that she had the authority to set the employees schedules and pay rates unless otherwise ordered by the principal.

In determining whether implied authority exists, it is very important to consider the customs of the field the agent is acting in, prior dealings between the agent and principal, and what the principal has told the agent to do or not to do.[13] The determination is made on a case-by-case basis. For instance, in the above example in which Jamie had authority to hire three employees, if it was not customary for managers in that industry to set cashier pay rates and Jamie had no indication from Alec to the contrary, then Jamie likely would not have had implied authority.

Actual implied authority should not be confused with "authority implied in law." In some rare situations, a person who had never contemplated entering into an agency relationship with another may be in one. This is known as authority implied in law. For instance, each spouse can be held liable for the necessary expenses, like food or medical services, of the other even if they did not intend to act as agents for one another.[14] This is different from implied authority despite the similarity in name because implied authority requires an actual agency relationship. Authority implied in law requires the lack of an agency relationship.

B. Apparent Authority

Apparent authority is the authority an agent derives from the principal's actions towards and words to the third party.[15] An agent has almost nothing to do with its creation. It is designed for the

---

[11] Restatement (Third), Agency § 2.01, cmt. b; Restatement (Second), Agency § 7, cmt. c.

[12] Restatement (Third), Agency § 2.02; Restatement (Second), Agency § 7, cmt. c.

[13] Restatement (Third), Agency, § 2.02, cmt. e; Restatement (Second), Agency § 7, cmt. c.

[14] *See, e.g.*, *Jersey Shore Medical Center-Fitkin Hospital v. Estate of Sidney Baum*, 84 N.J. 137, 141 (NJ 1980); *see also* Restatement (Second), Agency § 7, cmt. c.

[15] Restatement (Third), Agency § 2.03; Restatement (Second); Agency § 27.

protection of the third party. In other words, if the principal creates a situation in which the third party reasonably believes the agent has authority, the agent has apparent authority.

Consider the following example. Alec Irons, CEO of Smooth Creations, Inc., hires Jamie to be the manager of the New York store. He tells Jamie, "You cannot sell a widget for less than $100 even if someone wants to buy a lot of widgets in bulk." While talking to Midhat, a potential client, Alec tells him, "Contact Jamie in the New York branch. She will take care of you and get you what you need." Midhat then calls Jamie, and they enter into a contract in which Smooth Creations, Inc. agrees to sell Midhat 100 widgets for $75 each.

In the above example, Jamie did not have actual authority to enter into a contract with Midhat. Alec, her boss, specifically told her that she could not sell widgets at that price. However, Jamie nonetheless had apparent authority to enter into the contract with Midhat. Alec, by making Jamie a manager and telling Midhat that Jamie will take care of him and get him what he needs, Alec created a situation in which Midhat could reasonably believe that Jamie could sell him widgets at the reduced price. Midhat had no reason to believe Jamie did not have the authority because of Alec's actions.

REQUIREMENTS OF APPARENT AUTHORITY
Restatement (Third), Agency § 3.03; Restatment (Second), Agency § 27.

1. Agent does not have actual authority
2. Principal makes manifestations that cause the third party to *reasonably* believe that the agent has actual authority

---

Apparent authority can be vested in an agent who exceeds his or her authority, like in the above example when Jamie made a contract beyond her authority as manager. It can also vest in a person who is not actually an agent of the principal. For instance, imagine that Alec, the owner of Smooth Creations, Inc. is allowing his friend Jamie Justice to shadow him for the day. He takes her on a sales call and introduces her to the potential customer as a junior salesperson to make it seem more professional. Later in the day, Jamie goes back to the potential customer without Alec and makes a sale. In that case, Jamie would have apparent authority. She was not Alec's agent, so she did not have actual authority. Alec told the potential customer that Jamie was a salesman, which the customer reasonably relied on to place an order.

C. Authority by Estoppel

Authority by estoppel is very similar to apparent authority, and the terms are sometimes used interchangeably by courts. However, the concepts are distinct. Authority by estoppel has different requirements than apparent authority. The major difference is what a principal must do to create the authority. Apparent authority requires that the principal represent to the third party that the agent is an agent. Authority by estoppel requires only that the principal know of the third party's mistaken belief or otherwise intentionally or carelessly cause the third party's mistaken belief.[16] This can be done in a number of ways and is a much lower bar for a third party wishing to hold a principal accountable. Consider the following case.

---

[16] Restatement (Third), Agency § 2.05; Restatement (Second), Agency § 8B(1).

❖❖

Hoddeson v. Koos Bros.
47 N.J.Super. 224, 135 A.2d 702 (1957)

The opinion of the court was delivered by JAYNE, J.A.D.

The occurrence which engages our present attention is a little more than conventionally unconventional in the common course of trade. Old questions appear in new styles. A digest of the story told by Mrs. Hoddeson will be informative and perhaps admonitory to the unwary shopper.

The plaintiff Mrs. Hoddeson was acquainted with the spacious furniture store conducted by the defendant, Koos Bros., a corporation, at No. 1859 St. George Avenue in the City of Rahway. On a previous observational visit, her eyes had fallen upon certain articles of bedroom furniture which she ardently desired to acquire for her home. It has been said that "the sea hath bounds but deep desire hath none." Her sympathetic mother liberated her from the grasp of despair and bestowed upon her a gift of $165 with which to consummate the purchase.

It was in the forenoon of August 22, 1956 that Mrs. Hoddeson, accompanied by her aunt and four children, happily journeyed from her home in South River to the defendant's store to attain her objective. Upon entering, she was greeted by a tall man with dark hair frosted at the temples and clad in a light gray suit. He inquired if he could be of assistance, and she informed him specifically of her mission. Whereupon he immediately guided her, her aunt, and the flock to the mirror then on display and priced at $29 which Mrs. Hoddeson identified, and next to the location of the designated bedroom furniture which she had described.

Upon confirming her selections the man withdrew from his pocket a small pad or paper upon which he presumably recorded her order and calculated the total purchase price to be $168.50. Mrs. Hoddeson handed to him the $168.50 in cash. He informed her the articles other than those on display were not in stock, and that reproductions would upon notice be delivered to her in September. Alas, she omitted to request from him a receipt for her cash disbursement. The transaction consumed in time a period from 30 to 40 minutes.

Mrs. Hoddeson impatiently awaited the delivery of the articles of furniture, but a span of time beyond the assured date of delivery elapsed, which motivated her to inquire of the defendant the cause of the unexpected delay. Sorrowful, indeed, was she to learn from the defendant that its records failed to disclose any such sale to her and any such monetary credit in payment.

Such were the essentialities of the narrative imparted to the judge and jury in the Union County District Court, where Mrs. Hoddeson and her husband obtained a final judgment against the defendant in reimbursement of her cash expenditure. The testimony of her aunt was corroborative of that of Mrs. Hoddeson.

Although the amount of money involved is relatively inconsiderable, the defendant has resolved to incur the expense of this appeal. This Division has heretofore had occasion to state that justice is not qualified by the monetary importance of the controversy. *Series Publishers, Inc. v. Greene,* 9 *N.J. Super.* 166 *(App. Div.* 1950). Obviously, the endeavor of the defendant is to elicit from us a precedential opinion concerning a merchant's liability in the exceptional circumstances disclosed by the evidence to which we have already alluded, and by the supplementary evidence to which we shall presently refer.

It eventuated that Mrs. Hoddeson and her aunt were subsequently unable *positively* to recognize among the defendant's regularly employed salesmen the individual with whom Mrs. Hoddeson had arranged for the purchase, although when she and her aunt were afforded the opportunities to gaze intently at one of the five salesmen assigned to that department of the store, both indicated a resemblance of one of them to the purported salesman, but frankly acknowledged the incertitude of their identification. The defendant's records revealed that the salesman bearing the alleged resemblance was on vacation and hence presumably absent from the store during the week of August 22, 1956.

As you will at this point surmise, the insistence of the defendant at the trial was that the person who served Mrs. Hoddeson was an impostor deceitfully impersonating a salesman of the defendant without the latter's knowledge.

It was additionally disclosed by the testimony that a relatively large number of salesmen were employed at the defendant's store, and that since they were remunerated in part on a sales commission basis, there existed considerable rivalry among them to serve incoming customers; hence the improbability of the unnoticed intrusion of an impersonator.

Fortifying the defense, each of the five salesmen, but not every salesman, denied that he had attended Mrs. Hoddeson on the stated occasion, and the defendant's comptroller and credit manager verified the absence in the store records of any notation of the alleged sale and of the receipt of the stated cash payment.

The credibility of the testimony of both Mrs. Hoddeson and her aunt was thus shadowed. The trial judge transmitted to the jury for determination the simple factual issue whether Mrs. Hoddeson and her co-plaintiff had established by a preponderance of the credible evidence that the $168.50 was paid in fact to an employee of the defendant; otherwise, the defendant should be acquitted of liability.

The jury resolved that controversial issue in favor of the plaintiffs. The defendant's application for a new trial was denied by the trial judge, who announced:

"It is my conclusion that the evidence of the circumstances proved by the plaintiff warranted a finding by the jury that the person who received the money was an employee of the defendant."

Does it clearly and unequivocally appear that the action of the trial judge constituted a manifest denial of justice under the law? *Hartpence v. Grouleff,* 15 N.J. 545. 549 (1954).

The ground now asserted on behalf of the defendant for a reversal of the judgment is that there was a deficit of evidence to support the conclusion that a relationship of master and servant existed between the man who served and received the money from Mrs. Hoddeson and the defendant company.

There can be no doubt that the existence of the alleged relationship, or in the alternative an estoppel by the defendant to deny its existence, was an essential element of the legal right of the plaintiff, Mrs. Hoddeson, to recover her monetary disbursement from the company. Neither is it to be doubted that such a relationship of agency, actual or apparent, can be proved by means of circumstantial evidence.

We do not hastily yield to the temptation immediately to adopt the postulate that the person who waited upon Mrs. Hoddeson was without question a humbugger unassociated with the defendant. We recognize that the jurors, pursuant to the directions of the court, weighed on the scales of reasonable probabilities the inferences anent that issue which were to them derivable from the circumstantial evidence relating on the one hand to the described behavior and deportment of the individual and on the other to the revelatory state of the defendant's records.

Perhaps in reality the jurors did not read the scales mistakenly, and so initially we pause to examine the probative range of the circumstantial evidence. True, in the present case there was evidence that the person whose identity is undisclosed approached Mrs. Hoddeson and her aunt in the store, publicly exhibiting the mannerisms of a salesman; inquired if he could be of service; upon being informed of the type of the articles in which Mrs. Hoddeson was interested, he was not only sufficiently acquainted with their description, but also where in the department they were respectively on display, guiding them without hesitation to the location of the mirror and then to that of the indicated bedroom furniture; he represented that those articles were not then available in stock, which significantly the store records disclosed to be true; his prophetic representation concerning their prospective arrival in stock proved to be prescient, unless he gleaned that information from the price tag; he accurately calculated their true sales prices and openly received the cash. Those activities precisely characteristic of the common experiences and practices in the trade were conspicuously pursued in market overt during a period of 30 to 40 minutes.

In the consideration of the propriety of the defendant's motion for an involuntary dismissal of the action, we are not at liberty to suspect that the verified narrative of Mrs. Hoddeson, corroborated by her aunt, was purely imaginative or artfully inventive, but rather to regard it as a trustworthy revelation of the factual events to the extent of her knowledge. *Gentile v. Public Service Coordinated Transport*, 12 *N.J. Super.* 45, 49 (*App. Div.* 1951).

In the study of the circumstantial evidence, its perceptible legal deficiency and inadequacy inhere in the limitations of its disclosures. Obviously it confines its information solely to the activities of the supposed salesman. It does not embrace or, indeed, touch any manifestations whatever emanating *from the defendant* tending to indicate *its conference of authority,* actual or apparent, upon the alleged salesman.

Where a party seeks to impose liability upon an alleged principal on a contract made by an alleged agent, as here, the party must assume the obligation of proving the agency relationship. It is not the burden of the alleged principal to disprove it.

Concisely stated, the liability of a principal to third parties for the acts of an agent may be shown by proof disclosing (1) express or real authority which has been definitely granted; (2) implied authority, that is, to do all that is proper, customarily incidental and reasonably appropriate to the exercise of the authority granted; and (3) apparent authority, such as where the principal by words, conduct, or other indicative manifestations has "held out" the person to be his agent.

Obviously the plaintiffs' evidence in the present action does not substantiate the existence of any basic express authority or project any question implicating implied authority. The point here debated is whether or not the evidence circumstantiates the presence of apparent authority, and it is at this very point we come face to face with the general rule of law that the apparency and appearance of authority must be shown to have been created by the manifestations of the alleged principal, and not alone and solely by proof of those of the supposed agent. Assuredly the law cannot permit apparent authority to be established by the mere proof that a mountebank in fact exercised it.

The plaintiffs here prosecuted an action in *assumpsit*, alleging a privity of contract with the defendant through the relationship of agency between the latter and the salesman. The inadequacy of the evidence to prove the alleged essential element of agency obliges us to reverse the judgment.

But prelude, as we may do here, a case in which a reconciliation of the factual circumstances disclosed by the evidence of both the plaintiffs and the defendant exhibits an unalleged and an undetermined justiciable cause of action, should the plaintiffs, by our reversal of the judgment, be conclusively denied the opportunity, auspicious or not, appropriately and not mistakenly, to seek judicial relief?

Let us hypothesize for the purposes of our present comments that the acting salesman was not in fact an employee of the defendant, yet he behaved and deported himself during the stated period in the business establishment of the defendant in the manner described by the evidence adduced on behalf of the plaintiffs, would the defendant be immune as a matter of law from liability for the plaintiffs' loss? **The tincture of estoppel that gives color to instances of apparent authority might in the law operate likewise to preclude a defendant's denial of liability.**

***

Our concept of the modern law is that where a proprietor of a place of business by his dereliction of duty enables one who is not his agent conspicuously to act as such and ostensibly to transact the proprietor's business with a patron in the establishment, the appearances being of such a character as to lead a person of ordinary prudence and circumspection to believe that the impostor was in truth the proprietor's agent, in such circumstances the law will not permit the proprietor defensively to avail himself of the impostor's lack of authority and thus escape liability for the consequential loss thereby sustained by the customer.

***

Let it not be inferred from our remarks that we have derived from the record before us a conviction that the defendant in the present case was heedless of its duty, that Mrs. Hoddeson acted with ordinary prudence, or that the factual circumstances were as represented at the trial. In reversing the judgment under review, the interests of justice seem to us to recommend the allowance of a new trial with the privilege accorded the plaintiffs to reconstruct the architecture of their complaint appropriately to project for determination the justiciable issue to which, in view of the inquisitive object of the present appeal, we have alluded. . . .

Questions Presented

1) Why did the purported phony salesman not have any actual or apparent authority?
2) Why did the court state that the store could be held liable for the actions of the phony salesman even though there was no actual or apparent authority?
3) How did the court distinguish between estoppel and apparent authority?

❖❖

Authority by Estoppel also differs from apparent authority in another key way. It requires that the third party change its position in reliance on the purported agent's authority.[17] Essentially, the third party must make itself worse off by interacting with the purported agent. This includes "payment of money, expenditure of labor, suffering a loss or subjection to legal liability."[18]

Reliance can take many forms, such as paying the purported agent or giving up an opportunity in reliance on the purported agent's actions. For instance, in *Hoddeson v. Koos Bros.*, a third party walked into a department store to buy furniture. She ended up purchasing furniture from someone falsely claiming to be a salesman. By paying the phony salesman, she changed her position for the worse. If she had not paid the phony salesman, she would not have changed her position in reliance on the contract and would not have been able to claim agency by estoppel.

---

[17] Restatement (Third), Agency § 2.05; Restatement (Second), Agency § 8B.
[18] Restatement (Third), Agency § 2.05, cmt. b; Restatement (Second), Agency § 8B(3).

The reliance must also be reasonable.[19] In *Hoddesson v. Koos Bros.*, the phony salesman dressed and talked like a sales person. None of the other salesmen at the store stopped and intervened. The customer had no reason to know the phony salesman was phony. However, if the person who claimed to be the salesman had an unkempt appearance and dressed differently than all the other salesman, the customer's reliance probably would not have been reasonable as a reasonable person would know the salesman was an impostor.

REQUIREMENTS OF AGENCY BY ESTOPPEL
Restatement (Third), Agency § 2.05; Restatement (Second), Agency § 8B.

1. Agent does not have actual authority
2. Principal knows about or causes (either intentionally or carelessly) the third party to *reasonably* believe that the agent had authority
3. The third party takes a step in reliance on the agent's actions

---

TABLE 8.1 Apparent Authority v. Authority by Estoppel

Requirement	Type of Authority	
	Apparent Authority	**Authority by Estoppel**
Actual Authority	Agent has none	Agent has none
Principal's Action	Manifestation to third party that agent has authority	(a) Knowledge of third party's belief that agent has authority **or** (b) Causes third party to believe agent has authority (either intentional or careless)
Third Party's Belief	Third party's belief in the agent's authority must be reasonable	Third party's belief in the agent's authority must be reasonable
Step in Reliance	None required	Third party must change its position by taking a step in reliance on the agent's actions

D. Inherent Authority

Inherent authority is also very similar to apparent authority and authority by estoppel. It is so similar that it was intentionally excluded from the Restatement (Third) of Agency.[20] However, many cases that rely on the Restatement (Second) of Agency remain good law. According to the Restatement (Second) of Agency, inherent authority is the authority an agent derives "not from [actual] authority, apparent authority or estoppel, but solely from the agency relation."[21]

Essentially, inherent authority is the authority an agent derives solely from its position of being an agent. Consider the following example. Alec Irons, CEO of Smooth Creations, Inc., hires Jamie to be the manager of the New York store. He tells Jamie, "You cannot sell a widget for less than $100." Jamie notices that sales at her store are slow, so she starts selling widgets at $75 each. Midhat purchases 100 widgets for $75 each from Jamie. Assume that managers in the widget industry typically control their stores' pricing.

---

[19] Restatement (Third), Agency § 2.05; Restatement (Second), Agency § 8B.
[20] Restatement (Third), Agency § 2.01, cmt. b.
[21] Restatement (Second), Agency § 8A

Here, Jamie probably has inherent authority because it is customary for managers to have control over the pricing. Jamie's position as a manager, which is her role as an agent, gives her the ability to bind the principal even though the principal told her not to sell widgets at that price.

The argument can also be made that authority by estoppel exists in this case. Jamie did not have actual authority to sell the widgets for $75 each because the principal told her not to. The principal also arguably caused the situation by making Jamie the manager and putting her in a position to reduce prices. Midhat also could likely reasonably rely on her because she was the manager of the store. Assuming that he paid for the widgets, he also probably took a step in reliance on her authority.

In many cases, inherent authority overlaps with agency by estoppel and apparent authority. However, there are some situations in which it does not. For instance, imagine that Jamie is selling widgets on behalf of Alec but Alec directs Jamie to tell customers that she owns the business. Alec instructs her not to sell widgets for less than $100. Jamie then sells a widget to a customer for $75.

In this situation, Alec is something known as an "undisclosed principal." That is, the third party has no idea the agent is acting on behalf of someone else. In these situations, there can be no apparent authority or authority by estoppel because the third party does not know a principal is involved. However, Jamie will likely have inherent authority given that most salesman have the authority to make sales. Though inherent agency is excluded from the Restatement (Third) of Agency, it specifically states that an undisclosed principal is liable if its agent disregards instructions and the other elements of authority by estoppel exist.[22] So, Alec would still likely be liable in this situation.

E. Authority by Ratification

Ratification occurs when the principal subsequently approves an agent's unauthorized action.[23] This binds the principal as if the act had been authorized. Ratification requires the following:

1. Affirmation[24]
2. Capacity[25]
3. Timeliness[26]
4. Completeness[27]
5. Knowledge of All Material Facts[28]
6. Disclosed Principal (Second Restatement only)[29]

1. Affirmation

The principal must affirm the agent's unauthorized action.[30] Affirmation can be either express or implied.[31] Express affirmation, which can be either written or oral,[32] occurs when the principal explicitly states that it is affirming the unauthorized agent's act. For instance, imagine that, without

---

[22] *See* Restatement (Third), Agency § 2.06
[23] Restatement (Third), Agency § 4.01; Restatement (Second) § 82.
[24] Restatement (Third) Agency § 4.01(2); Restatement (Second), Agency § 83
[25] Restatement (Third) Agency § 4.04; Restatement (Second), Agency § 86
[26] Restatement (Third) Agency § 4.05; Restatement (Second), Agency § 88
[27] Restatement (Third) Agency § 4.07; Restatement (Second), Agency § 96
[28] Restatement (Third) Agency § 4.06; Restatement (Second), Agency § 91
[29] *Cf.* Restatement (Second) Agency, § 85(1) *with* Restatement (Third), Agency § 4.03
[30] Restatement (Third) Agency § 4.01(2); Restatement (Second), Agency § 83
[31] Restatement (Third) Agency § 4.01(2); Restatement (Second), Agency § 93
[32] Restatement (Third) Agency § 4.01(2); Restatement (Second), Agency § 93

authorization, Jamie agrees to sell 100 widgets for $75 each to Midhat on behalf of Smooth Creations, Inc. At a meeting of the board of directors, the directors discuss Jamie's deal and issue a corporate resolution stating that they will honor the contract with Midhat. Smooth Creations, Inc. has expressly affirmed the contract with Midhat by this act.

Implied affirmation is conduct by the principal that would lead a reasonable person to believe that an agent's actions have been ratified. For instance, imagine that, without authorization, Jamie agrees to sell 100 widgets for $75 each to Midhat on behalf of Smooth Creations, Inc. Jamie collects payment from Midhat and passes the payment along to the accounting department, which notifies the shipping department to fulfill Midhat's order and does not return the payment to Midhat. In that case, by keeping the benefit of the contract, Smooth Creations, Inc. impliedly affirmed Jamie's contract with Midhat. It is reasonable to believe that a principal has affirmed a contract when it keeps the benefit of the contract.

2. Capacity

The principal must have the legal capacity to enter into the contract made by the agent both when the contract was entered into and when it was affirmed.[33] For instance, if the principal was declared mentally incapable by a court of law[34] when he or she entered into a contract, the principal cannot later ratify the transaction. Similarly, if a principal is declared mentally incapable by a court of law after an agent enters into a contract without authority, the principal cannot ratify the contract until a court rules he or she once again is mentally capable.

There is an exception to this rule. When the principal is only partially incapacitated when he or she enters into a contract, the principal can ratify the contract when that partial incapacity is cured.[35] For instance, if a minor enters into a contract, the minor can ratify the contract upon reaching adulthood.

3. Timeliness

A ratification must be made in a timely manner. For example, a principal cannot ratify a transaction once the third party has withdrawn from the transaction.[36]

4. Completeness

A ratification must ratify the entire transaction, not just part of it.[37] For instance, if Jamie enters into a contract with Midhat on Smooth Creations, Inc.'s behalf without authorization to sell 100 widgets for $75 each and 100 trinkets for $50 each, Smooth Creations, Inc. must ratify the sale of both the widgets and trinkets, not just one or the other.

5. Knowledge of All Material Facts

A principal must have knowledge of all the material facts relating to a contract in order to be able to affirm it.[38] If a principal does not have knowledge of all the material facts, it may rescind the

---

[33] Restatement (Third), Agency § 4.04; Restatement (Second), Agency §§ 84,86.

[34] A person who is declared mentally incapable by a court of law cannot enter into a contract. *See* Restatement (Second), Agency § 84, cmt. c.

[35] Restatement (Third), Agency § 4.04, Official Comment b; Restatement (Second), Agency § 84, cmt. c.

[36] Restatement (Third), Agency § 4.05(1); Restatement (Second), Agency § 88

[37] Restatement (Third), Agency § 4.07; Restatement (Second), Agency § 96

[38] Restatement (Third), Agency § 4.06; Restatement (Second), Agency § 91

contract the agent entered into without authorization. For instance, imagine that Alec hires Jamie to purchase used cars on his behalf. He orders Jamie not to pay more than $10,000 per car. Jamie then enters into a contract to buy a used Ford Pinto for $12,000 and a used Smart Car for $13,000 from Midhat. Before Jamie tells Alec, Midhat contacts him to make arrangements for delivery of the Ford Pinto. Alec agrees to accept the Pinto. Midhat does not mention the Smart Car.

In this case, Alec does not know about the second car, which is a material fact. However, once he finds out about the second car, he can rescind the contract for the cars if he desires.[39]

6. Disclosed Principal

The Second and Third Restatement differ as to what kind of principal can ratify an unauthorized act. Under the Second Restatement, a contract can only be ratified if the principal is disclosed to the third party.[40] That is, the third party must know that the agent is acting on behalf of the principal and cannot believe the agent is acting of his or her own accord. Under the Third Restatement, the principal does not need to be disclosed to ratify the contract. Consider the following scenario.

Alec hires Jamie to purchase used cars on his behalf. He orders Jamie not to pay more than $10,000 per car. Jamie then enters into a contract to buy a used Ford Pinto for $12,000 from Midhat. She does not tell Midhat that she is acting on Alec's behalf, and Midhat believes that Jamie is purchasing the car for herself. Under the Restatement (Second) approach, Alec would not be able to ratify the contract. Under the Restatement (Third) approach, he would be able to ratify the contract.

V. Liability in Contract

Because multiple parties are involved in any contract made by an agent, questions arise as to when a principal can be bound in contract by an agent, when an agent can be held liable for a contract made on behalf of a principal, and when a principal can hold a third party liable for breach of a contract made with an agent.

Liability in contract depends on two things. It depends on what type of principal the agent is acting on behalf of and what type of authority the agent exercises. There are three basic types of principals.

A. Types of Principal

When a third party is aware that the agent is acting on behalf of a principal and knows the identity of that principal, the principal is a disclosed principal.[41] For example, suppose that Jamie enters into a contract on behalf of Smooth Creations, Inc. with Midhat to sell 100 widgets for $75 each. When Midhat enters into the contract, he knows that Jamie is the manager of the store. In this case, Smooth Creations, Inc. is a disclosed principal because Midhat knows that Jamie is acting in her capacity as an agent of Smooth Creations, Inc.

The second type of principal is an undisclosed principal. When the third party is unaware that the agent is acting on behalf of a principal and believes the agent is acting on its own behalf, the

---

[39] Remember that a ratification cannot be partial. So, if he wishes to rescind, he will have to give back the Pinto.

[40] Restatement (Second), Agency § 85(1)

[41] Restatement (Third), Agency § 1.04(2)(a); Restatement (Second), Agency § 4(1)

principal is an undisclosed principal.[42] For example, imagine that Alec wants to buy Midhat's Ford Pinto but that Midhat and Alec are arch enemies. To induce Midhat to sell him the car, Alec hires Jamie to be his agent to buy the car from Midhat. She tells Midhat that she is buying the car for herself. In this case, Alec is an undisclosed principal because Midhat has no idea that Jamie is acting as an agent.

The third kind of principal is a partially disclosed principal. When the third party is aware that the agent is acting on behalf of a principal but does not know the identity of the principal, the principal is a partially-disclosed principal.[43] For example, imagine that Alec wants to buy Midhat's Ford Pinto but that Midhat and Alec are arch enemies. To induce Midhat to sell him the car, Alec hires Jamie to be his agent to buy the car from Midhat. She tells Midhat that she is buying the car on behalf of someone else but does not tell him who the principal is. In this case, Alec is a partially-disclosed principal because Midhat knows that Jamie is acting on the behalf of a principal but does not know who that principal is.

TABLE 8.2 Types of Principals.

Type of Principal	Characteristics of Principal	
	Third Party Knows the Agent is Acting on Behalf of a Principal	Third Party Knows Who the Principal is
Disclosed Principal	Yes	Yes
Undisclosed Principal	No	No
Partially-Disclosed Principal	Yes	No

B. Liability of the Principal to the Third Party

The principal will be liable for contracts entered into with a third party if the principal acts with any of the authorities discussed earlier in the chapter, even if the principal did not want or authorize the agent to act. So, a principal can be held liable when the agent acts according to actual express authority, actual implied authority, apparent authority, authority by estoppel, inherent authority, or authority by ratification.[44] It does not matter whether the principal is disclosed, undisclosed, or partially-disclosed.

There is an important exception to this rule known as the equal dignity rule. The equal dignity rule is not mentioned expressly by any section of the Restatement of Agency (except in the official comments of the Third Restatement), but a version of it is applicable in many states. If a contract must be in writing to be valid under the statute of frauds,[45] an agent's authority to enter into that contract must also be in writing.[46] The consequence of a violation of the equal dignity rule is that the contract becomes voidable at the option of the principal.

For instance, imagine that Alec orally tells Jamie to sell his house. Under the statute of frauds, a contract for the sale of land must be in writing.[47] Jamie approaches Midhat and offers to sell him

---

[42] Restatement (Third), Agency § 1.04(2)(b); Restatement (Second), Agency § 4(3).

[43] Restatement (Third), Agency § 1.04(2)(c); Restatement (Second), Agency § 4(2). The Restatement (Third) refers to a partially-disclosed principal as an "unidentified principal."

[44] *See* Restatement (Third), Agency §§ 2.01, 2.02, 2.03, 2.06, 3.01, 3.03, 4.01, 4.02, 4.03, 6.01, 6.02; Restatement (Second), Agency §§ 7, 8, 8A, 25, 26, 27, 32-34, 49, 82, 83, 85, 100, 143 159.

[45] *See* Section V.H of Chapter 7 for a discussion of the Statute of Frauds.

[46] *See* Restatement (Third), § 3.02, cmt. b.

[47] Restatement (Second), Contract, § 110(d).

the house for $250,000 and executes a contract on Alec's behalf to sell the house. Even though Jamie had actual authority to sell Alec's house, because the authority was not in writing, Alec may choose to avoid the contract.

This rule is easily misconstrued. It does not apply to all written contracts. It applies only to contracts that *must* be in writing to be enforceable. For instance, imagine that Alec tells Jamie to sell 100 widgets for $400. Jamie enters into a written contract with Midhat to sell him the 100 widgets for $400. A contract for the sale of goods only has to be in writing if it is for $500 or more.[48] Because Jamie's authority did not have to be in writing, the equal dignity rule is not violated even though she entered into a written contract pursuant to oral authority.

There are some exceptions to the equal dignity rule as well in most states. If the agent acting pursuant to oral authority is an officer of the principal corporation, the equal dignity rule does not apply.[49] Further, a principal may be estopped from asserting the equal dignity rule if it creates the appearance that the agent has authority.[50] For instance, in the example above in which Jamie entered into a contract with Midhat to sell Alec's house pursuant to Alec's oral authorization, if Alec had told Midhat that Jamie had the authority to sell the house, a court may prevent the principal from asserting the equal dignity rule as a defense.

If an agent operates outside the scope of any authority, the principal will not be held liable. It does not matter whether the principal is disclosed, undisclosed, or partially-disclosed. For instance, imagine if the facts of *Hoddeson v. Koos Brothers* were a little different. In that case, a customer went to a department store to buy furniture. She bought the furniture from someone pretending to be a salesman and tried to sue the mattress store. The court held that the mattress store could be liable to the customer for the phony salesman's act on an authority by estoppel theory. Imagine that, instead of paying the fake salesman, she agreed with the fake salesman to pay the store later. Authority by estoppel requires a step in reliance on the contract by the third party, such as paying for a product. If she did not pay the mattress salesman or take any other step in reliance, the phony salesman would not have had any authority to sell her the mattress. Because the phony salesman would have had no authority at all to rely on, the principal could not be held liable.

C. Liability of the Agent to Third Party

While a principal's liability to a third party turns on whether the agent possessed authority, an agent's liability to a third party turns on whether the principal was disclosed, undisclosed, or partially-disclosed. If an agent is acting on behalf of a disclosed or partially-disclosed principal pursuant to actual authority, either express or implied, the third party can sue only the principal.[51]

Imagine that Alec Irons, the CEO of Smooth Creations, Inc., makes Jamie Justice the manager of its New York store. He tells Jamie to hire a cashier. She hires Midhat and enters into a contract with him on behalf of Smooth Creations, Inc. to be a cashier for $13.00 an hour. In this case, if Smooth Creations, Inc. were to breach its employment contract with Midhat, Midhat would not be able to hold Jamie liable for that breach of contract because Jamie was acting with actual authority

---

[48] *See* Uniform Commercial Code § 2-201(1).
[49] Restatement (Third), Agency § 3.02, cmt. c.
[50] Restatement (Third), Agency § 3.02, cmt. d.
[51] Restatement (Third), Agency § 6.01(2), Restatement (Second), Agency § 320.

and Smooth Creations, Inc. was obviously a disclosed principal as Midhat knew that he would be working for Smooth Creations, Inc.

If the principal is undisclosed, the third party may sue the agent or the principal if the agent had actual authority or inherent authority.[52] For instance, imagine that Alec wants to buy Midhat's Ford Pinto but that Midhat and Alec are arch enemies. To induce Midhat to sell him the car, Alec hires Jamie to be his agent to buy the car from Midhat. She tells Midhat that she is buying the car for herself. In this case, Alec is an undisclosed principal because Midhat has no idea Jamie is acting as an agent. If Alec breaches the contract, Midhat can elect to sue either Jamie or Alec.

An undisclosed principal cannot exist outside of actual authority, inherent authority, or ratification. By definition, the agent cannot act according to apparent authority because apparent authority requires the principal to tell the third party that the agent is acting on behalf of the principal. Similarly, authority by estoppel cannot be created when there is an undisclosed principal because it requires the principal to know about or unintentionally contribute to the appearance that the agent has authority.[53] Once a principal has ratified a contract, it is treated as if the agent had actual authority. This means that the third party cannot sue the agent regardless of the type of authority the agent originally had.

If the principal is disclosed or partially disclosed but the agent lacks authority, the third party cannot hold the agent liable on the contract but can hold the agent liable under another theory. Every time that an agent makes a contract with a third party on behalf of a principal, the agent makes a warranty to the third party that he or she has the authority to bind the principal.[54] If the agent exceeds its authority or has no authority, the third party may hold the agent liable for breach of that warranty unless the contract is later ratified by the principal, the third party knew the agent lacked authority, or the agent disclaims warranty liability to the third party.[55] The liability for breach of warranty includes the benefit of the bargain the third party expected to receive from the contract,[56] which is also the most common measure of damages for breach of contract.[57] Furthermore, if an agent intentionally misrepresents his or her authority, the agent may be liable to the third party for the tort of misrepresentation.[58]

D. Liability of Third Party to Principal

When an agent makes a contract with a third party, regardless of the type of principal, the third party will be liable to the principal to perform the contract if the agent acted with actual authority, apparent authority, inherent authority, or authority by ratification.[59] A third party will not be held liable for contracts entered into with agents acting pursuant to authority by estoppel because authority by estoppel only prevents the principal from denying the agent's authority.[60]

There are exceptions to the general rule, however, when the principal is undisclosed. If the contract specifically excludes the possibility that the undisclosed principal can be a party to the contract, the undisclosed principal cannot be a party to the contract and, therefore, cannot hold the third

---

[52] Restatement (Third), Agency §§ 6.02(2), 6.03(2), 6.09; Restatement (Second), Agency §§ 321, 322.
[53] Restatement (Third), Agency § 4.02(1), Restatement (Second), Agency § 319.
[54] Restatement (Third), Agency § 6.10; Restatement (Second), Agency § 329.
[55] Restatement (Third), Agency § 6.10; Restatement (Second), Agency § 329, 338.
[56] Restatement (Third), Agency § 6.10; Restatement (Second), Agency § 329, cmt. j.
[57] Restatement (Second), Contracts § 347.
[58] *See* Restatement (Third), Agency § 6.10, Official Comment a; Restatement (Second) Agency § 330.
[59] Restatement (Third), Agency § 6.01, 6.02; Restatement (Second), Agency § 292.
[60] Restatement (Third), Agency § 2.05; Restatement (Second) Agency § 8B.

TABLE 8.3 Liability in Contract for Principals and Agents to Third Party

Type of Principal	Type of Authority				
	Actual	**Apparent**	**Estoppel**	**Inherent**	**Ratification**
Disclosed	Principal only for breach of contract	Principal for breach of contract; Agent for breach of warranty	Principal for reliance damages; Agent for breach of contract and warranty	Principal for breach of contract; Agent for breach of warranty	Principal only for breach of contract
Undisclosed	Principal and Agent for breach of contract	N/A	N/A	Principal for breach of contract; Agent for breach of warranty	Principal only for breach of contract
Partially-disclosed	Principal and Agent for breach of contract	Principal for breach of contract; Agent for breach of warranty	Principal for reliance damages; Agent for breach of contract and warranty	Principal for breach of contract; Agent for breach of warranty	Principal only for breach of contract

party liable.[61] For instance, imagine that Jamie tries to enter into a contract with Midhat on behalf of Alec without telling him that she is Alec's agent. The contract has a clause stating, "Jamie represents that she is acting solely on her own behalf and not for another party." In this case, the contract forbids an undisclosed principal, so Alec cannot be a party to the contract and hold Midhat liable.

Further, if an agent falsely represents to the third party that it is not acting on behalf of the undisclosed principal, the third party, unless it chooses not to avoid the contract, is not liable to the principal.[62]

VI. Liability in Tort

An agent is always liable for his or her own torts. However, there are several occasions in which a principal will also be held liable for the tortious actions of its agents. Generally, a principal can be held liable for the torts of its agents that it authorized, that it negligently allowed the agent to commit, or that the agent committed within the scope of its employment.

A. Torts Authorized by the Principal

A principal is liable for the torts that it authorizes its agents to commit.[63] For instance, imagine that Alec, CEO of Smooth Creations, Inc., orders Jamie to beat up Midhat in order to get him to pay his overdue bill to Smooth Creatons, Inc. Because Smooth Creations, Inc. authorized Jamie to beat up

---

[61] Restatement (Third), Agency § 6.03(1); Restatement (Second) Agency, § 189.
[62] Restatement (Third), Agency § 6.11(4); Restatement (Second) Agency, § 304.
[63] Restatement (Third), Agency § 7.04; Restatement (Second) Agency, §§ 212, 215, 218.

Midhat through its subagent Alec, Smooth Creations, Inc. can be held liable if Midhat wishes to sue for the intentional tort of battery.

B. Torts a Principal Negligently Allows an Agent to Commit

If a principal is negligent in how it chooses its agent, supervises its agent, or controls its agent, the principal can be held liable for torts committed by its agent.[64] For example, imagine that Alec, CEO of Smooth Creations, Inc., despite knowing that Jamie did not have a license to drive a forklift, orders Jamie to drive a forklift. Jamie accidentally hits Midhat, a visiting delivery truck driver, with the forklift and injures him. Smooth Creations, Inc. could be held liable for Jamie's actions because Alec improperly chose, controlled, and supervised Jamie.

C. Torts Committed Within the Scope of Employment

The most common way a principal is held liable for the actions of its agents is through the doctrine of *respondeat superior*. *Respondeat superior* holds a principal liable for the actions that its agents take within the scope of their agency. To create vicarious liability under the doctrine of *respondeat superior*, the agent must be the principal's employee,[65] not its independent contractor,[66] and the tort must be committed within the scope of employment.[67]

1. Difference between Employees and Independent Contractors

Not all agents are employees. An employer has the right to control the manner and means by which an employee works.[68] By contrast, an independent contractor is someone hired by the principal to work on its behalf but whose manner and means of work are not controlled by the principal.[69] While this may seem simple, this issue can become quite complex in the real world. Consider the following two examples.

EXAMPLE 1: Alec, CEO of Smooth Creations, Inc., hires Jamie Justice to be the manager of Smooth Creations, Inc.'s New York office. Alec tells her where to work, at what prices she must sell products, and when she can hire and fire other employees. He also obligates her to follow a host of policies listed in the company handbook.

EXAMPLE 2: Alec, CEO of Smooth Creations, Inc., hires Midhat, a plumber who owns his own business, to come in and install several new toilets in Smooth Creations, Inc.'s New York office. He tells Midhat the color and make of the toilets that he wants and tells him when and where to install the toilets. He does not, however, provide Midhat's tools and has no intention of Midhat performing other tasks for Smooth Creations, Inc. immediately after the toilets are installed, though he is considering hiring him for work in the future if he does a good job.

In Example 1, Jamie is almost certainly an employee of Smooth Creations, Inc. In Example 2, Midhat is almost certainly an independent contractor of Smooth Creations, Inc. In both scenarios, Alec has a great deal of control over some of the manner and means by which both Jamie and

---

[64] Restatement (Third), Agency § 7.05; Restatement (Second) Agency, § 213.

[65] This is the term used by the Restatement (Third) of Agency. The Restatement (Second) of Agency uses the term "servant" instead of employee.

[66] This is the term used by the Restatement (Second) of Agency. The Restatement (Third) of Agency frames agents as either employees or non-employees.

[67] Restatement (Third), Agency § 7.07(1); Restatement (Second) Agency, §§ 243-249

[68] Restatement (Third), Agency § 7.07(3)(a); Restatement (Second) Agency, § 2(2).

[69] Restatement (Second), Agency § 2(3). The Restatement (Third) does not specifically refer to independent contractors but excludes a principal's liability for their torts by only holding a principal liable for the torts of employees. *See* Restatement (Third), Agency § 7.07.

Midhat work. He tells them when and where to work, how much money they make, and what work they must perform. However, what differentiates Midhat from Jamie is the degree of control that Alec has. Alec is not telling Midhat by what methods to install the toilets or providing him tools. Midhat is also only working for a short time.

These scenarios can get infinitely more complex. Imagine that Smooth Creations, Inc. needed plumbing services 5 days a week or its CEO told Midhat the method by which to install the toilets or asked him to use special tools provided by the company. What if Jamie was a part-time manager and that Alec spent more hours a week at the New York office than she did?

That's why whether an agent is an employee or independent contractor depends on the facts and circumstances present in each case.

Factors used to determine whether an agent is an employee or an independent contractor include:[70]

1. The method by which the agent is selected
2. Whether the work performed is part of the employer's business
3. Whether payment is made by wages
4. How much control the principal has over the work
5. Whether the parties intended to create an employment relationship

2. Scope of Employment

Whether an employee is acting within the scope of employment is also decided on a case-by-case basis. An employee is acting within the scope of employment when he or she is working to further the employer's interests.[71]

In some instances, it is very clear whether an employee is acting within the scope of employment. For instance, imagine that Jamie is the manager of Smooth Creations, Inc.'s New York office. She is personally helping her favorite customer Midhat load the widgets he just bought into his car, which is parked in the company parking lot. While loading the widgets, she accidentally drops the widgets onto his left foot, breaking it in three places. Midhat sues Smooth Creations, Inc. for his injuries.

In the above scenario, Jamie is clearly within the scope of her employment. She is helping a customer on company property during work hours with a product that she just sold him. However, imagine now that Jamie, who has developed a personal relationship with Midhat, decides to visit him on her way home from work. Using her own car, she drives into his driveway and runs over his foot by accident. This is a much closer call. On the one hand, Jamie is on her own time, using her own car, and on Midhat's property. On the other hand, Midhat is her customer. Whether she is acting within the scope of employment depends on a number of factors. The Restatement (Second) of Agency lays out a series of factors that has proved influential with courts. Under its approach, the following factors are considered when determining whether an agent is acting within the scope of employment:

1. Whether the act is normally performed by the kind of employee performing it
2. Where and when the act occurred
3. Whether the principal has asked the employee to perform the action taken before
4. The extent to which other employees perform the same type of action

---

[70] *See, e.g., Rubin v. Weissman*, 475 A. 2d 1235 (MD Ct. App. 1984).
[71] Restatement (Third), Agency § 7.07(2); Restatement (Second), Agency § 229.

5. Whether the act is outside of the employer's regular course of business
6. Whether the employer expects the employee to perform the act
7. Whether the employer provided the tools by which the act was done
8. Whether the agent performed the work in a normal and customary manner[72]

One of the most common situations in which a principal may claim an agent is not working within the scope of employment is when the agent is driving during working hours. Usually, employees are not considered to be acting within the scope of their employment when driving to and from work. However, an employee may also be driving during working hours. Consider the following scenario.

Alec tells his employee Jamie to use a company car to drive a widget to his customer Midhat. On the way to Midhat's house, Jamie takes a turn in the opposite direction toward the post office to mail a personal letter to her pen pal. While turning into the post office, she negligently causes a car accident. In this situation, even though Jamie is acting on her own behalf and not according to Alec's instructions, she is probably still within the scope of her employment for the purposes of *respondeat superior*. When an agent takes a mere detour while still working for a principal, the agent will still be considered to be within the scope of employment. If an agent goes on a "frolic," the agent is acting outside the scope of her authority. For instance, if Jamie delayed her delivery to go to a baseball game in the next town, she would likely have been on a frolic.

Legal Definitions

Detour – an employee's insubstantial deviation from the principal's instructions while working within the scope of his or her employment.

Frolic – an employee's substantial deviation from the principal's instructions that takes the principal outside the scope of his or her employment.

The more substantial the deviation, the more likely it is to be considered a frolic. Courts make this determination on a case by case basis. Consider the following case

❖❖

O'Connor v. McDonald's Restaurants
269 Cal.Rptr. 101 (1990)

OPINION, KREMER, P.J.

Plaintiff Martin K. O'Connor appeals summary judgment favoring defendants McDonald's Restaurants of California, Inc., and McDonald's Corporation (together McDonald's) on his complaint for damages for personal injuries on a theory of McDonald's vicarious liability for the negligence of its employee Evans. O'Connor, injured when his motorcycle collided with an automobile driven by Evans, contends the superior court erred in determining Evans had completely departed from a special errand on behalf of McDonald's and was not acting within the scope of his employment at the time of the accident. Determination whether Evans merely "diverted" rather than "completely departed" from his special errand when the accident occurred requires resolution of disputed triable factual issues. Therefore, we reverse the summary judgment.

---

[72] Restatement (Second), Agency § 299. The Restatement (Third) of Agency does not give a suggested list of factors for courts to consider.

I. FACTS

In reviewing the propriety of the summary judgment, we state the facts in the light most favorable to O'Connor.

From about 8 p.m. on August 12, 1982, until between 1 and 2 a.m. the next day, Evans and several McDonald's coworkers scoured the children's playground area of McDonald's San Ysidro restaurant. The special cleaning prepared the restaurant for inspection as part of McDonald's "spring-blitz" competition. Evans—who aspired to a managerial position—worked without pay in the cleanup party at McDonald's request. Evans's voluntary contribution of work and time is the type of extra effort leading to advancement in McDonald's organization.

After completing the cleanup, Evans and four fellow workers went to the house of McDonald's employee Duffer. Duffer had also participated in the evening's work. At Duffer's house, Evans and the others talked shop and socialized into the early hours of the morning. About 6:30 a.m., as Evans drove from Duffer's house toward his own home, his automobile collided with O'Connor's motorcycle.

II. SUPERIOR COURT PROCEEDINGS

O'Connor filed a lawsuit for negligence against Evans, McDonald's and others. O'Connor complained of serious injuries resulting in permanent disability and the loss of his left leg below the knee. The suit claimed McDonald's was liable for negligence on a theory of respondeat superior.

Essentially, O'Connor claimed Evans was on a "special errand" for his employer McDonald's when he worked on the spring-blitz cleanup on his own time. (2) According to O'Connor, if Evans were on a special errand, then his driving would be exempt from the "going and coming" rule by which an employer ordinarily is not liable for an employee's negligence while commuting. Under O'Connor's theory, the special errand began when Evans left his own home and continued until he returned home.

McDonald's sought summary judgment, contending as a matter of law Evans was acting outside the scope of his employment at the time of the accident.

The superior court found Evans was on a special errand for McDonald's when he voluntarily reported for cleanup duties at the San Ysidro restaurant. However, the superior court further found Evans's stop at Duffer's house was a "complete departure" from his special errand. Thus, the court concluded any responsibility of McDonald's for Evans's driving terminated before the accident. The court granted summary judgment for McDonald's. O'Connor appeals.

III. ANALYSIS

The central issue before us is of some antiquity. In 1834 Baron Parke addressed the issue: "The master is only liable where the servant is acting in the course of his employment. If he was going out of his way, against his master's implied commands, when driving on his master's business, he will make his master liable; but if he was going on a frolic of his own, without being at all on his master's business, the master will not be liable." (*Joel v. Morison* (1834) 6 Car. & P. 501, 503, 172 Eng.Rep. 1338, 1339.)

Unfortunately, as an academic commentator observed in 1923, "It is relatively simple to state that the master is responsible for his servant's torts only when the latter is engaged in the master's business, or doing the master's work, or acting within the scope of his employment; but to determine in a particular case whether the servant's act falls within or without the operation of the rule presents a more difficult task." (Smith, *Frolic and Detour* (1923) 23 Colum.L.Rev. 444, 463.)

Here we must determine whether the superior court properly concluded as a matter of law that Evans's activity in attending the gathering at Duffer's house constituted a complete departure from a special errand for McDonald's (a frolic of his own) rather than a mere deviation (a detour).

(3a) Whether there has been a deviation so material as to constitute a complete departure by an employee from the course of his employment so as to release employer from liability for employee's negligence, is usually a question of fact. (*Loper v. Morrison* (1944) 23 Cal.2d 600, 605 [145 P.2d 1].)

(4a) "In determining whether an employee has completely abandoned pursuit of a business errand for pursuit of a personal objective, a variety of relevant circumstances should be considered and weighed. Such factors may include the intent of the employee, the nature, time and place of the employee's conduct, the work the employee was hired to do, the incidental acts the employer should reasonably have expected the employee to do, the amount of freedom allowed the employee in performing his duties, and the amount of time consumed in the personal activity. [Citations.] (3b) While the question of whether an employee has departed from his special errand is normally one of fact for the jury, where the evidence clearly shows a complete abandonment, the court may make the determination that the employee is outside the scope of his employment as a matter of law. [Citations.]" (*Felix v. Asai, supra*, 192 Cal. App.3d at p. 932–933.)

(4b) Here the evidence does not clearly show complete abandonment. Instead, the evidence raises triable issues on the factors bearing on whether Evans completely abandoned the special errand in favor of pursuing a personal objective.

A. Evans's Intent

In its motion for summary judgment, McDonald's did not identify any evidence Evans intended to abandon his special errand when he decided to join his coworkers in the gathering at Duffer's house. However, in opposing McDonald's motion, O'Connor presented evidence bearing on Evans's intent from which a jury might reasonably infer Evans did not completely abandon his special errand when he went to Duffer's house.

The record contains evidence McDonald's encourages its employees and aspiring managers to show greater dedication than simply working a shift and going home. O'Connor presented McDonald's operations and training manual and employee handbook to demonstrate McDonald's fosters employee initiative and involvement in problem solving. Such evidence could reasonably support a finding of "a direct and specific connection" between McDonald's business and the gathering at Duffer's because the gathering was consistent with the "family" spirit and teamwork emphasized by McDonald's in its communications with employees. Such evidence could also reasonably support a finding McDonald's emphasis on teamwork made a group discussion of McDonald's business at Duffer's house a foreseeable continuation of Evans's special errand. The record also contains evidence supporting a reasonable inference Evans went to Duffer's house intending to continue his work on the spring blitz for McDonald's. Much of the conversation during the gathering centered on McDonald's business or concerned employee-manager relations. A "main inspection" was scheduled for the day after the spring blitz cleanup of the playground area. The persons at Duffer's house continued their mental inventory of last minute things they could do to improve their chances in the spring blitz competition. According to Evans, the group was concerned about whether "we were going to win [the spring blitz], and we did." The group discussed the cleaning activities of the spring blitz to determine whether they might return to the restaurant to correct any deficiencies. According to Duffer, the activity during the gathering at his house consisted of "sitting around talking about the blitz and relaxing." The group also "talked about other stores, how they had been doing [and] about passing the quality checks that we had or spot checks that we had."

Thus, evidence and reasonable inferences bearing on Evans's intent raise triable factual issues about whether he completely abandoned the special errand.

B. Nature, Time, and Place of Evans's Conduct

McDonald's contends the gathering at Duffer's house after normal business hours was an informal social function unconnected to Evans's special errand for his employer. However, O'Connor submitted evidence suggesting the gathering benefited McDonald's, occurred at Evans's fellow employee's house immediately after McDonald's place of business closed, consisted of continuation of employees' discussion about the spring blitz, and was inspired by the spirit of competition engendered by McDonald's. That evidence and reasonable inferences bearing on the nature, time and place of Evans's conduct raise triable factual issues about whether he completely abandoned the special errand.

C. Work Evans Was Hired to Do

McDonald's contends the asserted managerial discussions at Duffer's house went beyond the scope of work Evans was hired to do. However, O'Connor introduced evidence suggesting Evans was in training to become a manager and was expected to show initiative in his work to be worthy of future promotion. Such evidence raises an inference Evans's participation in discussions at Duffer's house did not exceed the scope of his assigned work.

D. McDonald's Reasonable Expectations

In a declaration supporting McDonald's motion for summary judgment, Evans's direct supervisor Cardenas asserted Evans "was under no instruction from me, or any other authorized employee of McDONALD'S, with respect to his activities after he left the restaurant. [¶] . . . I had no knowledge that other co-employees would go to Joe Duffer's house after the final clean-up." McDonald's also presented evidence it required official employee conferences be attended by a salaried manager and no such salaried manager attended the Duffer gathering. However, these facts do not compel a finding as a matter of law contrary to O'Connor's claim McDonald's implicitly encouraged Evans to continue his special errand by conferring with co-employees on what they might do to win the spring blitz competition.

E. Evans's Freedom in Performing Duties

O'Connor presented evidence Evans had considerable latitude in performing his duties. Evans was not paid for his performance of the special errand. His work was voluntary and consistent with other occasions where he and fellow workers were expected to pitch in to help the team effort without punching in on the time clock.

F. Amount of Time Consumed in Personal Activity

McDonald's contends Evans stopped at Duffer's home for four hours on his own volition, for his own enjoyment and without McDonald's explicit direction or suggestion. However, O'Connor presented evidence showing much of the discussion at Duffer's home was related to Evans's employment at McDonald's. Such evidence raises a triable factual issue about the combination of personal entertainment and company business at Duffer's house. (5) "Where the employee may be deemed to be pursuing a business errand and a personal objective simultaneously, he will still be acting within the scope of his employment." (*Felix v. Asai, supra*, 192 Cal. App.3d at p. 932.)

G. Conclusion

The superior court found—and the parties here do not challenge—Evans's voluntary participation in the spring blitz until after midnight constituted a special errand on McDonald's behalf. The question here is whether the gathering at Duffer's to discuss the spring blitz and socialize constituted a complete departure from the special errand.

Because disputed factual questions and reasonable inferences preclude determination as a matter of law of the issue whether Evans completely abandoned his special errand, the court should have denied McDonald's motion for summary judgment.

DISPOSITION

The summary judgment is reversed. O'Connor to have costs on appeal.

Questions Presented

1) What factors did the court consider to determine whether the employee was acting within the scope of his employment?
2) What facts led the court to believe that the employee could be acting within the scope of his employment?
3) What facts led the court to believe that the employee might not be acting within the scope of his employment?

❖❖

VII. Duties Owed Between Agents and Principals

An agent is considered a fiduciary of the principal.[73] This means that agent owes certain duties to the principal. The most important of these duties are the duty of care, the duty of loyalty, and the duty of obedience.

A. Agent's Duty of Care

An agent owes a duty of care to the principal to act like a reasonable agent of that kind would act.[74] For instance, imagine that Alec, the President of Smooth Creations, Inc., hires Jamie to be the manager of Smooth Creations, Inc.'s New York branch. Jamie enters into a contract with a customer on the company's behalf to sell him 100 widgets for $1,000 by June 8. Jamie then forgets to tell the delivery company to deliver the widgets, and Midhat cancels the contract on June 9. Because a reasonable manager ensures delivery of her sales, Jamie violated her duty of care.

---

[73] Restatement (Third), Agency §§ 1.01, 8.01; Restatement (Second), Agency § 13.
[74] Restatement (Third), Agency § 8.08; Restatement (Second), § 379.

B. Agent's Duty of Loyalty

An agent must also act with loyalty towards the principal. This means the agent must act only in the principal's interest, not its own best interests or the best interests of a third party.[75] For example, imagine that Alec hires Jamie to find an investment property suitable for him to purchase. Jamie discovers a house that she believes will turn a huge profit after slight repairs are made. If Jamie either buys the house herself or acts to buy it for another one of her clients without Alec's consent, Jamie will have violated her duty of loyalty and be subject to liability to Alec. Release of the principal's confidential information also violates the duty of loyalty.[76]

C. Agent's Duty to Obey

An agent must obey all reasonable, clear instructions from the principal.[77] An agent also owes the principal the duty to act only as authorized.[78] Even if the principal's orders are not in the principal's best interests, the agent is under a duty to follow them. An agent may even be held liable for a loss caused by failure to obey or act as authorized if, in doing so, the agent saves the principal from an even bigger loss.[79]

For example, imagine that Jamie is Alec's stock broker. He owns shares in Smooth Creations, Inc. Jamie notices that the share price of Smooth Creations, Inc. is plummeting. Alec orders his agent Jamie not to sell. She disobeys and sells the shares. Alec lost $1,000 as a result of the sale of his shares. However, if Alec had not sold when he did, he would have lost $5,000. Even though Jamie saved Alec $4,000, he could still hold her liable for the loss resulting from the sale of the stock because she disobeyed his orders.

D. Duties Owed by the Principal to the Agent

The duties a principal owes to an agent are not as extensive as the duties owed by an agent to a principal. However, a principal owes a duty of indemnity and, therefore, must still reimburse an agent for any expenses or losses it incurred as a result of acting on behalf of a principal.[80] A principal is also under a duty to perform any obligation it has to the agent it agreed to in the agency contract, such as paying the agent.[81] A principal can also not interfere with the agent's work unreasonably and must act in good faith towards the agent and give the agent all the information that it reasonably needs.[82]

VIII. Termination of Agency Relationship

An agent's authority can be terminated in a number of ways. It can be terminated by an act of the principal or agent, and it can be terminated by operation of law.

---

[75] Restatement (Third), Agency §§ 8.02—8.04; Restatement (Second), Agency § 390—393.
[76] Restatement (Third), Agency § 8.05(2); Restatement (Second), Agency §§ 395—396.
[77] Restatement (Third), Agency § 8.09; Restatement (Second), Agency § 385.
[78] Restatement (Third), Agency § 8.09; Restatement (Second), Agency § 383.
[79] *See* Restatement (Third), Agency § 8.09, cmt. b.
[80] Restatement (Third), Agency § 8.14; Restatement (Second), Agency §§ 438-440.
[81] Restatement (Third), Agency § 8.13; Restatement (Second), Agency §§ 432, 441.
[82] Restatement (Third), Agency § 8.15; Restatement (Second), Agency §§ 434, 435, 437.

A. Termination by Voluntary Action

An agent's authority to act on behalf of a principal is most commonly terminated because one or both of the parties chooses to end the agency relationship. If both agree to end the relationship, the agency relationship ends.[83] The agent ceases to have authority and neither owes any duties to the other. Neither party is liable to the other for breaching the agency agreement when both chose to end it.

However, if only the agent or only the principal decides to terminate the agency agreement, one may be liable for breach of contract. Though the agent's authority ceases on its renunciation of it or the principal's revocation of it, further analysis under contract law is required to determine if either is liable to the other.[84] For instance, if the principal fired its employee for refusing to commit perjury, the employer principal would likely be liable to the former employee agent for wrongful termination.[85]

There is one notable exception to this general rule. An agent's apparent authority is not terminated as to third parties who do not have notice of the termination of the agent's authority.[86]

An agent's authority will also be terminated if the agency contract specifies when the agency terminates.[87] For instance, if an employment contract specifies that the employment is to last for one year, the employee agent's authority to act for the principal ends after one year.

An agent's authority can also be terminated when a specified event occurs.[88] For instance if the agency agreement states that the agent is only employed to achieve a particular objective, such as the purchase of a house, the agent's authority terminates when the objective is achieved. Similarly, an agency agreement can also specify an event which terminates an agent's authority. For example, an agency agreement may specify that the agent's authority ends when the principal returns from vacation. Once the principal returns from vacation, the agent's authority is terminated.

B. Termination by Operation of Law

An agent's authority may also terminate by operation of law. An agent's authority automatically terminates if the agent or principal dies[89] or the agent or principal becomes legally insane.[90]

Circumstances can also terminate an agent's authority. For instance, if the principal and agent's countries go to war, the agent's authority is terminated if exercise of the agent's authority is illegal, too dangerous, or too impracticable.[91] If circumstances so change that an agent could reasonably conclude that the principal would not want the agent to act, the agent's authority may terminate.[92] For example, imagine that Alec hires Jamie to sell his home for $250,000. While preparing to sell the home, Jamie discovers a giant, previously undiscovered gold deposit on Alec's property. Jamie's authority to sell the house terminates.[93]

---

[83] Restatement (Third) Agency § 3.09; Restatement (Second), Agency § 117

[84] Restatement (Third), Agency § 3.10; Restatement (Second), Agency § 118

[85] *See, e.g., Petermann v. International Brotherhood of Teamsters,* 174 Cal. App. 2d 184, 189, 344 P.2d 25 (1959)

[86] Restatement (Third), Agency § 3.11; Restatement (Second), Agency § 125

[87] Restatement (Third), Agency § 3.09; Restatement (Second), Agency § 105

[88] Restatement (Third), Agency § 3.09; Restatement (Second), Agency §§ 106, 107.

[89] Restatement (Third), Agency § 3.07; Restatement (Second), Agency §§ 120-121

[90] Restatement (Third), Agency § 3.08; Restatement (Second), Agency § 122.

[91] Restatement (Third), Agency § 3.06, cmt. b; Restatement (Second), Agency § 115, cmt. b.

[92] Restatement (Third), Agency § 3.09; Restatement (Second), Agency § 108(1).

[93] *See* Restatement (Second), Agency § 108, Illus. 1.

An agent's authority also terminates when the subject matter of the agent's authority is lost or destroyed.[94] For example, imagine that Alec hires Jamie to sell his car. Before she sells his car, Alec gets into an accident in it and totals the car. In this situation, Jamie's authority to sell the car is terminated.

An agent's authority can also terminate if the agent or principal declares bankruptcy or is otherwise insolvent (unable to pay debts when due). If an agent declares bankruptcy or becomes insolvent, its authority terminates if its financial condition affects its ability to act on behalf of the principal.[95] If a principal goes bankrupt or otherwise has its assets substantially impaired, an agent's authority is terminated if the agent has notice of the bankruptcy or impairment and if a reasonable agent would believe a principal would not desire the agent to act on its behalf.[96]

TABLE 8.4   Agency Termination

Ways to Terminate Agency	
Act of the Parties	**Operation of Law**
Mutual Consent	Principal or Agent's Death
Principal's revocation	Principal or Agent's Insanity
Agent's Renunciation	Change of Circumstances
Lapse of Time	War
Specified Event	Bankruptcy

SUMMARY

Agency law is crucial to commercial transactions. Almost all commercial transactions are conducted by agents because business entities only act through agents. It is especially important to know when an agency relationship exists. It can be created by agreement of the parties or by estoppel to protect the interests of third parties.

It is also very important to know when agent is acting within or outside the scope of its authority. Agents can act according to actual authority (either express or implied), apparent authority, authority by estoppel, inherent authority, and authority by ratification. Knowing what type of authority, if any, the agent is acting pursuant to will help principals, agents, and third parties know who is liable to the others.

Agents must be especially careful to act within the scope of their authority and to disclose the principal to the third party whenever possible as an agent cannot be held liable for its authorized actions with third parties when the third party knows who the principal is. Principals must also be careful that their agents act within the scope of their authority as the principal can be held liable by the third party for acts it did not authorize if apparent authority, inherent authority, or authority by

---

[94] Restatement (Third), Agency § 3.06; Restatement (Second), Agency § 110
[95] Restatement (Third), Agency § 3.06; Restatement (Second), Agency § 113
[96] Restatement (Third), Agency § 3.06; Restatement (Second), Agency § 113

estoppel exists. Third parties must be careful to ensure that agents have the authority to bind principals as well. If a third party's belief in the agent's authority is not reasonable, it will not be able to hold the principal liable for the agent's actions.

Employers must also carefully monitor their employees' actions. An employer is liable for the torts of its employees committed within the scope of their employment.

Agents and principals should be especially careful when acting in relation to one another. The agent owes the principal the duties of care, loyalty, and obedience. The principal owes the agent the duty of indemnification and the duty to act reasonably in their dealings with one another.

In short, the agency relationship is very powerful. The modern commercial structure would not exist without it. However, the agency relationship is fraught with many details and pitfalls to which everyone involved must pay attention.

CHAPTER 9

TORTS

LEARNING OUTCOMES

Upon completion of this chapter the student will be able to:

1   Understand the difference between intentional torts, negligence, and strict liability torts.
2   Understand the elements of each intentional tort.
3   Understand the elements of negligence.
4   Understand strict liability torts.
5   Understand the difference between tort law, criminal law, and contract law.

KEY TERMS

appropriation	conversion	negligence
assault	damages	proximate causation
assumption of the risk	defamation	strict liability
battery	duty	tortfeasor
breach of duty	false imprisonment	trespass to chattel
causation	fraudulent misrepresentation	trespass to land
cause in fact	intentional infliction of	
comparative negligence	emotional distress	
contributory negligence	invasion of privacy	

I. Introduction

It is difficult to precisely define what a "tort" is.[1] Tort law has been described as "not a unified subject but a complex of diverse wrongs whose policy implications point in different directions."[2] For the purposes of this chapter, a tort is essentially any violation of another's legal right, except for breach of contract, for which the law provides a remedy. This incredibly broad definition is necessary because the word *tort* is used to classify almost every kind of civil wrong committed. Torts include wrongful acts committed intentionally (such as battery and assault) and unintentionally (like causing a car accident). The only civil wrong that is not tortious (the adjective form of *tort*) is breach of contract. It is important to distinguish between torts and

---

[1] Speiser, S, Krause, C, & Gans, A, American Law of Torts § 1:1 (2017) (citing Prosser, Law of Torts (4th ed.) p 1 § 1 note 1 (1971)).
[2] Speiser, S, Krause, C, & Gans, A, American Law of Torts § 1:15 (2017)

breaches of contract because they provide a very different set of remedies that serve different purposes.

Breach of contract is the violation of a voluntary agreement between private parties. The damages usually awarded are known as "expectation damages." This measure of damages looks to place parties in the position they would have been in had the contract been performed.[3] A breach of contract requires that a person voluntarily enter into a private agreement. Without that agreement, no liability can be imposed for its breach.

By contrast, torts universally apply to society. That is, they apply to everyone, not just people who voluntarily agree to be bound by a particular set of rules like those who enter into a contract. For example, battery (which will be discussed more completely later in this chapter) is the intentional, offensive touching of another.[4] Any person who intends to offensively touch another (such as by a punch to the face) can be sued for battery regardless of whether he or she agrees to be bound by tort law. By contrast, no one is under a duty to perform the terms of a contract before entering into one. A person only becomes subject to liability by consent.

Tort damages serve different purposes than contract damages serve. Tort law is primarily designed to compensate the innocent victims of torts for their injuries, but it has also been stated that tort law is designed to shift the damages resulting from a tort to the most culpable party possible as well as to deter wrongful conduct.[5]

Tort law is also different from criminal law even though a lot of conduct that is criminal is also tortious. For example, battery is both a crime and a tort. The difference is that criminal law seeks to punish individuals who have committed wrongs against society. The offenses are prosecuted by the government and cannot be prosecuted by individuals. Torts, on the other hand, provide a remedy for the harm to the individual even if the act also harms society as a whole. Unlike criminal prosecutions, tort lawsuits are prosecuted by the individuals involved.

II. Types of Torts

There are many ways to classify torts. Torts can be classified by the type of harm that result from their commission. For example, torts that result in harm to a person are called personal injury torts, and torts that result in harm to property are called property torts. This chapter will classify torts by the state of mind required for their commission. Intentional torts are those torts that require the person to intend a particular consequence from his or her action.[6] The most common unintentional tort is negligence. Negligence is committed when a person violates a societally imposed duty and unintentionally causes an injury.[7] For strict liability torts, the state of mind of the person committing the tort is not relevant, and liability is automatically imposed if the act is committed.[8] In other words, the person is liable for the act no matter what state of mind he or she was in when committing the act.

---

[3] *See*, e.g., *Hawkins v. McGee*, 84 N.H. 114, 146 A. 641 (N.H. 1929). *See* Section VI of Chapter 7 for a full discussion of the purpose of contract remedies.

[4] Restatement (Second), Torts § 13 (1965)

[5] *See* 74 Am. Jur. 2d Torts § 2 (2017)

[6] Restatement (Second), Torts § 8A (1965).

[7] *See* Restatement (Second), Torts §§ 281-282 (1965).

[8] *Strict Liability*, Black's Law Dictionary (10th Ed. 2014)

III. Sources of Law

Most of American tort law originally derives from English common law. Today, tort law is primarily governed by individual states. Though every state's tort law is different, because most state torts arise from a common source, tort law is very similar in most states. Many states have added torts by statute that did not exist at common law, but common law torts predominate the field.[9]

The best formulation of common law torts is found in the Restatement (Second) of Torts. The Restatement (Second) of Torts, published in 1965 by the American Law Institute, is a summary of common law torts as they have been applied by American courts. Courts in all states often cite it in their decisions, especially when a court faces an issue for the first time (known as an issue of first impression).[10] Some parts of the Restatement (Third) of Torts, an update of the Restatement (Second), have been published by the American Law Institute, but the Restatement (Second) has been cited so frequently since it was published that it is the better statement of law at this time. That may change in the future.

IV. Intentional Torts

For an intentional tort to be committed, the tortfeasor (person committing the tort) must intend the consequences of his or her actions.[11] An intentional tort cannot result by accident. There are several kinds of intentional torts. Each will be discussed in turn in this section.

Legal Definitions

Intentional Torts – the class of torts that requires the tortfeasor to intend the consequences of his or her actions.

Tortfeasor – a person who commits a tort.

A. Assault and Battery

Assault and battery are often confused because they are inter-related. Each, however, is a unique and separate intentional tort. Battery is the offensive, non-consensual, and intentional touching of another.[12] An assault is intentional conduct that creates the imminent apprehension of a battery.[13] In other words, it is a threatened battery. Both can be committed in the same course of conduct. Consider the following example.

James walks up to Dante, points a gun in his face, and says, "I'm going to murder you." As Dante begins to run away, James shoots Dante in the knee and injures him. In this example, James committed battery by intentionally shooting Dante. He also committed an assault before he shot the gun by placing Dante in apprehension of imminent physical harm.

---

[9] *See* Speiser, S, Krause, C, & Gans, A, American Law of Torts § 1:16 (2017)

[10] *See* Speiser, S, Krause, C, & Gans, A, American Law of Torts § 1:18 (2017)

[11] Restatement (Second), Torts § 8A (1965)

[12] Restatement (Second), Torts § 13 (1965)

[13] Restatement (Second), Torts § 21 (1965)

Like all torts, assault and battery are best studied by breaking them down to their base parts, which are known as elements.

The elements of battery are (1) harmful or offensive touching and (2) intent to cause a harmful or offensive touching. The elements of assault are (1) apprehension of battery and (2) intent to cause an apprehension of battery.

1. Offensiveness and Harmfulness of Touching

A touching will give rise to battery when it is either harmful or offensive. A touching is harmful when it causes pain, illness, or physical impairment.[14]

The offensiveness of a touching for the purposes of battery (and, therefore, the inter-related tort of assault) is determined from the perspective of a reasonable person.[15] For example, imagine that James goes to pat Dante on the back for a job well done. Dante finds this extremely offensive because he thinks that James is gross. The touching in this case is not likely offensive as reasonable people do not find most pats on the back to be offensive.

2. Apprehension and Intent Elements of Assault

For an assault to occur, the victim must be placed in "apprehension" of a battery. This is not the same thing as fear. A person need not be scared of the consequences of the assault. A person need only be placed in apprehension that a battery will occur. This means that the person must believe a battery will occur.

Unlike the offensiveness of a touching, the apprehension element of assault does not look to whether a reasonable person would be placed in fear of an assault. So long as the assaulter intended to place the victim in apprehension of a battery and the victim actually believed a battery would occur, the intent element of assault is satisfied.

For example, imagine that James knows that Dante incorrectly and irrationally believes that he is allergic to dog hair and will break out in hives if exposed to it. James takes a batch of dog hair and chases Dante around the room telling him, "You're going to itch for weeks, sucker, when I get a hold of you!" Even though Dante would not actually be harmed by the dog hair and a reasonable person would not believe that he would be, James has nonetheless placed Dante in apprehension because he intended Dante's fear of a battery, and Dante actually was afraid a battery would occur.

3. Intent Element of Battery

The intent required to commit a battery is usually the intent to touch the other person. It does not matter whether the person intended the contact to be offensive or to cause bodily harm. For instance, James could punch Dante on the arm meaning to playfully say hello, but, he could nonetheless be held liable for battery if a reasonable person would find his arm punch offensive.[16]

Further, there are some circumstances in which a person could not even intend to touch another person but still be held liable for battery. If a person intends to merely assault another and

---

[14] Restatement (Second), Torts § 15 (1965).
[15] *See* Restatement (Second), Torts § 19 (1965)
[16] *See* Restatement (Second), Torts § 16 (1965)

accidentally touches that person in the process, the intent requirement of battery is met. For instance, imagine that James walks up to Dante and pretends that he is about to punch him just to scare him but accidentally hits Dante when Dante moves to avoid contact. In that case, even though James did not intend to touch Dante, the intent requirement of battery is met because he intended to assault him. Consider the following case.

❖❖

Nelson v. Carroll
355 Md. 593, 735 A.2d 1096 (1999)

CHASANOW, Judge.

This case requires that we determine the extent to which a claim of accident may provide a defense to a civil action for battery arising out of a gunshot wound. Charles A. Nelson, the plaintiff in this case and the petitioner here, asserts that the trial court should have held Albert Carroll, the defendant and respondent, liable for the tort of battery as a matter of law, sending to the jury only the issue of damages. We agree with Nelson that a claim of "accident" provides no defense to a battery claim where the evidence is undisputed that Nelson was shot by Carroll as Carroll threatened and struck him on the side of his head with the handgun.

I.

This is the second time this case has been before us. In our earlier decision, we addressed the Court of Special Appeals' conclusion that Nelson had failed to preserve his motion for judgment under Maryland Rule 8-131(a) because he had not stated with particularity all the reasons why the motion should be granted. *See* Md. Rule 2-519(a). We reversed, holding that Nelson had properly raised his reasons for seeking a motion for judgment. *See Nelson v. Carroll*, 350 Md. 247, 711 A.2d 228 (1998).

We summarized the essential facts of this case in our earlier decision:

"Carroll shot Nelson in the stomach in the course of an altercation over a debt owed to Carroll by Nelson. The shooting occurred on the evening of July 25, 1992, in a private nightclub in Baltimore City that Nelson was patronizing. Carroll, who was described as being a 'little tipsy,' entered the club and demanded repayment by Nelson of the $3,800 balance of an $8,000 loan that Carroll had made to Nelson. Nelson immediately offered to make a payment on account but that was unsatisfactory to Carroll. At some point Carroll produced a handgun from his jacket.

Carroll did not testify. There were only two witnesses who described how the shooting came about, Nelson and Prestley Dukes (Dukes), a witness called by Carroll. Dukes testified that when Nelson did not give Carroll his money Carroll hit Nelson on the side of the head with the handgun and that, when Nelson did not 'respond,' Carroll 'went to hit him again, and when [Carroll] drawed back, the gun went off.' Nelson, in substance, testified that he tendered $2,300 to Carroll, that Carroll pulled out his pistol and said that he wanted all of his money, and that the next thing that Nelson knew, he heard a shot and saw that he was bleeding." *Nelson*, 350 Md. at 249, 711 A.2d at 229.

* * *

Nelson testified to undergoing extensive medical treatment resulting from his gunshot wound. Immediately after being shot, Nelson lost consciousness as a result of blood loss and did not fully regain consciousness for three or four months, until November 1992. He continued to spend months in various hospitals and rehabilitation facilities, undergoing multiple operations. He testified to the nearly complete loss of his eyesight.

Carroll was subsequently arrested and charged with shooting Nelson. Carroll pled guilty to assault and illegal possession of a handgun, was convicted, and was serving a seven-year sentence at the time of the civil trial.

II.

A.

Nelson's sole contention before this Court is that he was entitled to a motion for judgment on the issue of liability for battery. He contends that the evidence that Carroll committed a battery is uncontested. Specifically, Nelson asserts that Carroll's primary defense on the issue of liability—that the discharge of the handgun was accidental—is unavailable under the circumstances of this case.

* * *

Since the only disputed fact relates to whether Carroll shot Nelson accidentally as he was striking him, we need only address the narrow question of whether, under the facts of this case, the defense that the shot was fired accidentally is capable of exonerating Carroll of liability.

B.

A battery occurs when one intends a harmful or offensive contact with another without that person's consent. *See* RESTATEMENT (SECOND) OF TORTS § 13 & cmt. d (1965). "The act in question must be some positive or affirmative action on the part of the defendant." *Saba v. Darling*, 320 Md. 45, 49, 575 A.2d 1240, 1242 (1990). *See also* PROSSER & KEETON, THE LAW OF TORTS § 9, at 39 (5th ed.1984).

A battery may occur through a defendant's direct or indirect contact with the plaintiff. In this case, Carroll unquestionably committed a battery when he struck Nelson on the side of his head with his handgun. *See Saba*, 320 Md. at 49, 575 A.2d at 1242 (observing that defendant's striking of plaintiff in the face, causing injury to his jaw, was "the *sine qua non* of an intentional tort"). Likewise, an indirect contact, such as occurs when a bullet strikes a victim, may constitute a battery. "[I]t is enough that the defendant sets a force in motion which ultimately produces the result. . . ." PROSSER & KEETON, THE LAW OF TORTS § 9, at 40 (5th ed.1984). Thus, if we assume the element of intent was present, Carroll also committed a battery when he discharged his handgun, striking Nelson with a bullet.

Nelson's action in the instant case focuses on the indirect contact of the bullet and not the battery that occurred when Carroll struck him on the head. It is the bullet that allegedly caused the harm for which Nelson seeks damages. As the analysis that follows suggests, however, the circumstances surrounding the gunshot are relevant in determining whether a battery occurred.

C.

Carroll's defense that he accidentally discharged the handgun requires us to examine the "intent" requirement for the tort of battery. It is universally understood that some form of intent is required for battery. *See* RESTATEMENT (SECOND) OF TORTS § 13 (1965)("An actor is subject to liability to another for battery if . . . he acts *intending* to cause a harmful or offensive contact. . . ." (Emphasis added)); PROSSER & KEETON, THE LAW OF TORTS § 9, at 39 (5th ed. 1984) (Battery requires "an act *intended* to cause the plaintiff . . . to suffer such a contact. . . ." (Emphasis added)); HARPER, JAMES & GRAY, THE LAW OF TORTS § 3.3, at 3:9 (3d ed. 1996) ("[T]o constitute a battery, the actor must have *intended* to bring about a harmful or offensive contact or to put the other party in apprehension thereof." (Emphasis added) (footnote omitted)).

* * *

The intent element of battery requires not a specific desire to bring about a certain result, but rather a general intent to unlawfully invade another's physical well-being through a harmful or offensive contact or an apprehension of such a contact.

* * *

Thus, innocent conduct that accidentally or inadvertently results in a harmful or offensive contact with another will not give rise to liability, but one will be liable for such contact if it comes about as a result of the actor's volitional conduct where there is an intent to invade the other person's legally protected interests.

* * *

The only reasonable inference that can be drawn from the circumstances of this shooting, which in essence are uncontested, is that Carroll's actions evidenced an intent to commit a battery. Carroll presented no evidence disputing the fact that he carried a loaded handgun and that he struck Nelson on the head with the gun. The merely speculative evidence upon which Carroll claims the shot was an accident was Dukes' testimony that when Carroll "went to hit him again . . . the gun went off." In contrast, the evidence is undisputed that Carroll possessed a handgun which he openly carried into the nightclub, that Carroll struck Nelson with the handgun, and that the handgun discharged simultaneously as Carroll went to strike Nelson again. Indeed, taking every possible inference in favor of Carroll, the gunshot occurred as he attempted to strike Nelson with the gun. Under such circumstances, no reasonable inference can be drawn that Carroll lacked the required intent to commit the battery.

Finally, we observe that the uncontested facts also evidence an assault from which the intent element of battery will be implied as a matter of law. The rule is widely recognized that when one commits an assault, and in the course of committing the assault that person comes into contact with the person assaulted, the intent element of battery may be supplied by the intent element of the assault. Professors Prosser and Keeton explain:

"Although a contact . . . is . . . essential, the intent element of the cause of action [of battery] is satisfied not only if the defendant intends a harmful contact . . . upon the plaintiff . . . *but also if the defendant intends only to cause apprehension that such a contact is imminent (an assault-type consequence).*" (Emphasis added) (footnotes omitted). PROSSER & KEETON, THE LAW OF TORTS § 9, at 39 (5th ed.1984). *See also* RESTATEMENT (SECOND) OF TORTS § 13 (1965) ("An actor is subject to liability to another for battery if (a) he acts intending to cause a harmful or offensive contact with the person of the other or a third person, *or an imminent apprehension of such a contact. . . .*" (Emphasis added)).

Because the defendant has committed an assault, the intent element of assault is subsumed into the battery claim even though the defendant contends that the actual harm was accidental or otherwise unintentional. "The intent required [for battery] is only the intent . . . to cause apprehension that such a contact is imminent. . . ." PROSSER & KEETON, THE LAW OF TORTS § 9, at 42 (5th ed.1984). Therefore, one who intends to frighten another by assaulting him or her, and touches this person in a harmful or offensive manner and claims the touching was inadvertent or accidental, is liable for battery, notwithstanding the contention that the actual touching was never intended. *See, e.g., Alteiri v. Colasso,* 168 Conn. 329, 362 A.2d 798, 801 (1975) (affirming liability for battery when minor plaintiff was injured by defendant's throwing of an object into the yard where minor was playing, even though defendant had only attempted to scare the minor). *Cf. Steinman,* 109 Md. at 65, 71 A. at 518 (observing, in denying liability in battery claim, that "[i]t would not be possible . . . that an action for assault alone could be maintained"). Thus, the risk is mitigated that a wrongdoer will be found free from liability while the innocent victim suffers the consequences of the wrongful conduct.

* * *

The evidence is uncontested that Carroll angrily wielded a handgun at Nelson and that he struck Nelson on the side of his head at least once with the loaded hand gun. These undisputed facts evidence an assault and battery from which the intent to commit the battery caused by the gunshot may be implied as a matter of law. This conclusion becomes obvious if we assume, for the moment, a modest variation of the facts of this case: Carroll never struck Nelson on the head, but only had pointed the gun at Nelson, not intending to shoot him, only to scare him into paying his debt. If under these revised facts the gun accidentally went off, injuring Nelson, the intent to commit the assault would allow Nelson to recover for the battery; Carroll's assault would fulfill the intent element for battery. Even though under this variation of the facts Carroll never struck Nelson on the head, the evidence would still conclusively demonstrate that a battery occurred because of Carroll's admission and the undisputed evidence that Carroll entered the nightclub wielding the handgun threateningly at Nelson for his failure to pay a debt. Indeed, Carroll's attorney conceded at trial that "[Carroll] shouldn't have gone in there with a gun. He was wrong. *But what he intended to do was to scare him.*" (Emphasis added). Thus, by his own admission, Carroll intended to frighten Nelson into paying his debt by carrying a handgun into the nightclub. Had Carroll shot Nelson without ever striking him, the assault he committed by carrying a weapon into the nightclub with the present ability to use it and with the admitted desire to "scare him" would have been sufficient to establish the intent element for battery.

It is clear then that, where the only factual difference between our hypothetical and the actual facts of the instant case is the additional fact that a separate battery occurred (Carroll's striking of Nelson on the side of the head), the necessary intent is present so as to result in Carroll's liability for battery for shooting Nelson. The facts are not disputed that Carroll struck Nelson on the head with the handgun, thus committing a battery. *See Saba,* 320 Md. at 49, 575 A.2d at 1242; Part II.B., *supra.*

Viewing the facts most favorably to Carroll, the gun discharged accidentally as Carroll went to strike Nelson again. But whether the discharge itself was actually an accident is not germane under these facts, since it is clear that in striking Nelson initially, Carroll committed a volitional act with the "inten[t] to violate the legally protected interest of another in his person." HARPER, JAMES & GRAY, THE LAW OF TORTS § 3.3, at 3:14 (3d ed.1996).

* * *

Therefore, the motion for judgment as to liability should have been granted, with the only question remaining for the jury being the damages resulting from the discharge of the gun.

Questions Presented
1) Which of the Defendant's actions constituted the intent to commit battery?
2) In what situations did the court say the intent for battery could be satisfied?
3) Would the case have been different if the shooter never showed the gun to his victim before accidentally shooting him?

❖❖

4. Defenses to Assault and Battery

There are several defenses available both to assault and battery. First, a person acting in self-defense, in defense of others, or in defense of property may also be exempt from liability for assault and battery.[17] It is crucial, however, that the force used be proportionate to the threat.[18] Force that threatens great bodily harm cannot be used to defend property.[19]

Consent may also be a defense to assault and battery.[20] For example, when a patient gives consent to a surgeon to remove a kidney, the patient cannot successfully sue the surgeon for battery even though the removal of kidney would certainly be considered an intentional, harmful touching in most contexts.

For the consent to be valid, the person consenting must understand the nature, extent, or probable consequences of the conduct.[21] For example, a minor who is too young to realize the dangers of boxing cannot consent to taking part in a boxing match. Consent also cannot be given to a criminal act by someone the criminal law seeks to protect.[22] For example, imagine that a state requires boxing matches to be licensed. Consent will not be a defense against a battery claim brought by anyone that was injured in that boxing match.

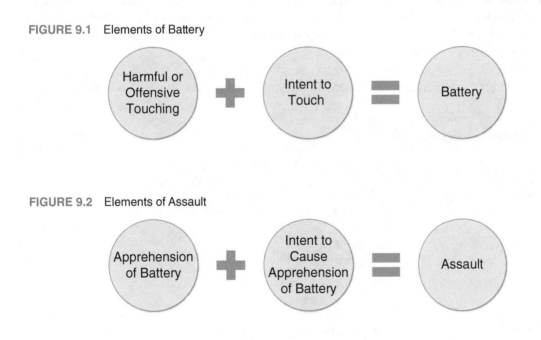

FIGURE 9.1 Elements of Battery

FIGURE 9.2 Elements of Assault

---

[17] *See* Restatement (Second), Torts §§ 63-76, 890 (1965).

[18] Restatement (Second), Torts § 70 (1965)

[19] Restatement (Second), Torts § 66 (1965). This section specifies that deadly force or force that will inflict great bodily harm can only be used in defense of a person who is in danger of death or great bodily harm. It omits defense of property from the definition.

[20] *See* Restatement (Second), Torts § 49 (1965), Restatement (Second), Torts § 892A(1) (1965)

[21] *See* Restatement (Second), Torts § 59 (1965), Restatement (Second), Torts § 892A(2), cmt. b (1965)

[22] Restatement (Second), Torts § 61 (1965), Restatement (Second), Torts § 892 (2), cmt. b (1965)

B. False Imprisonment

False imprisonment is the tort equivalent of kidnapping. It occurs when a person intentionally confines another in a particular space without his or her consent. It has three essential elements, (1) confinement, (2) intent to confine, and (3) awareness of the confinement by the victim.[23]

Confinement defies easy definition. The place of confinement can be very large or it can be very small. The confinement can be caused indirectly or directly.[24] The confinement can be done by erecting physical barriers, using physical force upon another, or even threatening the use of physical force on another.[25] The confinement may even be for a short time.[26]

For example, imagine that Dante is dating James's daughter and that James does not like it. Dante comes to pick James' daughter up from James' house. James grabs a gun from his mantle and says to Dante while he points the gun at him, "You won't move from this chair until I say you do, son. Do you understand me?" Dante then sits in the chair not knowing when he will be able to get up. This is most likely false imprisonment. It does not matter that Dante is in a comfortable chair or is confined for just a short period of time.

The confined person must also be aware of the confinement to be able to recover for false imprisonment.[27] For example, imagine that Dante is dating James' daughter and that James does not like it. Dante comes to pick James' daughter up from James' house. James tells Dante, "Sit in this chair while my daughter gets ready." Dante does not know it, but James does not intend to let him out of the chair and has a gun in his boot to ensure it. After talking to his daughter, James changes his mind, and Dante is let out of the chair none the wiser. Because Dante was not aware of his confinement, he was not falsely imprisoned.

Shopkeepers have a defense to false imprisonment if they detain a suspected shoplifter in a reasonable manner for a short period of time who they reasonably believe stole from the store.[28]

FIGURE 9.3   Elements of False Imprisonment

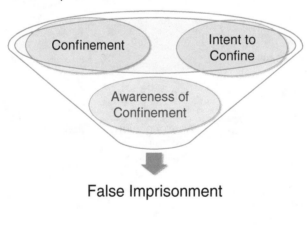

False Imprisonment

---

[23] Restatement (Second), Torts § 35 (1965)

[24] Restatement (Second), Torts § 37 (1965)

[25] Restatement (Second), Torts §§ 38-40 (1965)

[26] *See* Restatement (Second, Torts § 35, cmt. h (1965)

[27] Restaement (Second), Torts § 42 (1965).

[28] Restatement (Second), Torts § 120A (1965); *see also Gortarez v. Smitty's Super Valu, Inc.*, 140 Ariz. 91, 101-03, 680 P.2d 807 (AZ 1984) (explaining the history of shopkeeper's privilege).

C. Intentional Infliction of Emotional Distress

Intentional infliction of emotional distress (IIED) occurs when a tortfeasor intentionally causes *severe* emotional distress through outrageous and extreme conduct.[29] The elements of IIED are (1) severe emotional distress, (2) extreme and outrageous conduct, and (3) intent to cause severe emotional distress.

This tort does not cover garden-variety insults. For instance, if James were to call Dante a "stupid loser" for getting a "mullet" haircut, even if Dante cried, he would be unlikely to be able to recover damages from James for the burning jab. The conduct must be so extreme and outrageous that it goes beyond the bounds of decency.[30]

The early case of *Brooker v. Silverthorne* is a classic illustration of the extreme and outrageous conduct. In that case, a man was held liable for IIED who called a telephone operator but was unable to get the telephone connection and then screamed at the operator, "You God damned woman! None of you attend to your business. . . . You are a God damned liar. If I were there, I would break your God damned neck."[31] The operator lost sleep, became ill, and missed work as a result of the incident.[32]

Because bodily harm is a hallmark of severe emotional distress, it can be very difficult to recover for IIED without it. However, under the Restatement (Second) of Torts, bodily harm is not an element of IIED and recovery is possible without it.[33]

For example, imagine that James brings an angry mob to Dante's door and threatens to lynch him if he does not leave town in 10 days. Dante suffers emotional distress as a result. Even if Dante did not suffer bodily harm as a result of the threat, James would nonetheless be liable for intentional infliction of emotional distress.[34]

FIGURE 9.4 Elements of Intentional Infliction of Emotional Distress

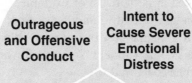

Outrageous and Offensive Conduct

Intent to Cause Severe Emotional Distress

Severe Emotional Distress

[29] Restatement (Second), Torts § 46(1) (1965).
[30] Restatement (Second), Torts § 46, cmt. d (1965).
[31] *Brooker v. Silverthorne*, 99 S.E. 350, 351 (SC 1919).
[32] *Brooker v. Silverthorne*, 99 S.E. 350, 351 (SC 1919).
[33] *See* Restatement (Second), Torts § 46, cmt. k (1965).
[34] *See* Restatement (Second), Torts § 46, Illus. 20 (1965).

D. Trespass to Chattel and Conversion

Trespass to chattel and conversion are torts committed against personal property, which is essentially any moveable property. Trespass to chattel occurs when a person intentionally interferes with another's right to possession of his or her personal property.[35] A conversion is essentially a trespass to chattel that is so severe that the tortfeasor must pay the owner of the property its full value.[36]

Legal Definition

Chattel – moveable personal property.

A trespass to chattel is a minor interference with another's personal property. It can be accomplished by causing another to lose possession of personal property temporarily, by improperly touching another's personal property, or by using personal property without authorization.[37]

For example, imagine that James and Dante are in a book club. The night before a meeting, because he forgot to get a copy of his own, James takes Dante's copy of the book that will be discussed at the meeting and does not return it until after the book club meets. In this case, James has committed trespass to chattel by both using the book without authorization and by taking it without James' permission.

The concept of trespass to chattel has even made it to the digital age. In *Sotello v. DirectRevenue, LLC*, a court held that a software developer can be liable for trespass to chattel if it allows spyware to be downloaded onto to a user's computer.[38]

Conversion is closely related to trespass to chattel. It is essentially a severe trespass to chattel. An act becomes a conversion rather than a trespass to chattel when the interference is so severe that the tortfeasor must pay the owner the fair market value of the personal property. This can take many forms.

The classic example of conversion is theft.[39] For example, imagine that James steals one of Dante's books without permission and sells it to another person. This is obviously a conversion. Similarly, conversion occurs when someone destroys or irreparably damages another's property.[40] For example, if James takes Dante's book without his permission and throws the book on the fire at a book-burning rally, a conversion has occurred.

Conversion even occurs when someone receives stolen property that he or she did not realize was stolen.[41] For example, imagine that someone steals one of James' books and sells it to Dante. Even if Dante did not know the book was stolen, Dante is liable for conversion. The only intent required for conversion is the intent to commit the act that results in conversion. In this case, that is taking possession of someone else's book without authorization.

---

[35] Restatement (Second), Torts § 217 (1965)
[36] Restatement (Second), Torts § 220A (1965)
[37] Restatement (Second), Torts § 217 (1965)
[38] *Sotelo v. DirectRevenue, LLC*, 384 F.Supp.2d 1219, 1229, 1232 (N.D. Ill. 2005).
[39] Restatement (Second), Torts §§ 221, 223 (1965)
[40] Restatement (Second), Torts § 226 (1965)
[41] Restatement (Second), Torts § 229 (1965)

FIGURE 9.5 Comparison of Trespass to Chattel and Conversion

Trespass to Chattel	Conversion

A minor interference with another's personal property.
 	
Can be accomplished by:
  1. Unauthorized use of personal property
  2. Improperly Touching another's personal property
  3. Causing another to temporarily lose personal property
	An interference with another's personal property so severe that the tortfeasor must pay the entire fair market value of the property to the owner.
	
	Can be accomplished by:
	  1. Destroying personal property
	  2. Stealing another's property

Essentially, any time an owner is permanently dispossessed of or can no longer effectively use his or her personal property, a conversion has occurred.[42]

E. Trespass to Land

Trespass to land occurs when a person intentionally enters the land owned by another or causes someone or something else to enter the land without the legal right to do so.[43] There is no requirement that the property itself be damaged.[44]

For example, imagine that James walks across Dante's yard on his way to go to school without Dante's permission. Even if he causes no damage, James has committed trespass because he intended to walk on Dante's yard. Even if he mistakenly believed he had the right to walk on Dante's yard, James is still liable in trespass.[45]

A person who accidentally enters the land of another, however, will only be liable for trespass if damage to the property occurs.[46] For example, if James got into a car accident with Dante, which caused him to land on the property of another unintentionally, James would be liable for trespass only if damages occurred to the property.[47]

Trespass also includes staying on a property after one's invitation has expired. For example, if a person buys a ticket to a baseball game but remains in the stadium overnight after the game has ended, a trespass has been committed.

Causing objects to enter another's land is also a trespass. For example, if James crop dusts Dante's farm without his permission, James has committed trespass by dropping a substance onto the property without authorization.

At common law, a person's land included everything above it and beneath it, a doctrine known as *ad coelum*.[48] Some exceptions to this rule have been made over time, such as for airplanes flying over residential areas at a high altitude.[49]

---

[42] *See* Restatement (Second), Torts §§ 222A, 223 (1965)

[43] Restatement (Second), Torts § 158 (1965)

[44] Restatement (Second), Torts § 163 (1965)

[45] Restatement (Second), Torts § 164 (1965)

[46] Restatement (Second), Torts § 165 (1965)

[47] *See* Restatement (Second), Torts § 165, Illus. 5 (1965)

[48] *See* Restatement (Second), Torts § 159, cmt. g (1965)

[49] Restatement (Second), Torts § 159(2) (1965)

F. Defamation

Legal Definition

Defamation – a cause of action allowing recovery for false statements made (either written or oral) that harm another's reputation.

The tort of defamation is designed to protect a person's reputation from false statements. Defamation occurs when a person makes a harmful false statement. The elements of defamation are as follows:

1. A Statement that is
    a. False,
    b. Defamatory, *and*
    c. Published
2. Fault of the person publishing the statement
3. In *some* cases, harm to the aggrieved party.[50]

1. Types of Defamation and When Special Harm is Required to Establish Defamation

There are two basic kinds of defamation, slander and libel. Libel is defamation made in a permanent form, such as a writing or recording. Slander is defamation made in a non-permanent form, such as an unrecorded statement.[51]

The distinction between slander and libel is important. In libel cases, no harm is required to establish a claim for defamation.[52] Slander requires proof of harm unless the slander is (1) a statement made about a person committing a crime, (2) a statement about a person having a "loathsome disease" (such as a sexually transmitted infection), (3) a statement that affects another person's profession or job, or (4) a statement alleging sexual misconduct.[53]

2. The Statement Requirement

Defamation requires that a statement be made that is false, defamatory, and published.

Truth is an absolute bar to defamation. A statement must be false to be defamatory.[54]

If a statement is not published, defamation has not been committed. "Published" is a term of art meaning that the statement has been communicated to someone else.[55] This is an incredibly low bar. The communication can even be accidental.

A person does not even need to be the person who originally made the statement to be liable for defamation. A claim for defamation may arise against someone who has re-published the statement of another that he or she has reason to know is defamatory.[56]

---

[50] *See* Restatement (Second), Torts § 558 (1965)
[51] Restatement (Second), Torts § 568 (1965)
[52] Restatement (Second), Torts § 569 (1965)
[53] Restatement (Second), Torts § 570 (1965)
[54] Restatement (Second), Torts § 581A (1965)
[55] Restatement (Second), Torts § 577 (1965)
[56] Restatement (Second), Torts § 581 (1965)

The statement must also be defamatory. A statement is defamatory if it harms another's reputation or causes others to think less of or not associate with the subject of the statement.[57] This includes any statement likely to lead to ridicule, hatred, or contempt.[58] For example, if James were to call his bookkeeper Dante "a scandalous liar who embezzled money from my company," his statement would almost certainly be defamatory.

3. Fault Requirement

For defamation to occur, the person making the statement must be at fault for making the statement. This requirement's origin comes from the famous 1964 Supreme Court case *New York Times v. Sullivan*.[59] In *Sullivan*, the Supreme Court held that the First Amendment prohibits a person from being held liable for the defamation of a public figure while speaking about a matter of public concern unless the person made the statement knowing it was false or with reckless disregard for its truth.[60]

The U.S. Supreme Court went on to hold in cases after *Sullivan* that there must be a fault requirement for all forms of defamation regardless of whom the statement is about.[61] Under the Restatement (Second) of Torts, a defamatory statement made about a private citizen or about a public figure not regarding a matter of public concern must be made at least negligently to give rise to defamation.[62]

4. Defense of Privilege

Privilege is a defense to defamation. There are several forms of privileged statements. A statement that is made with a person's consent, even if it is otherwise defamatory, is privileged.[63] Statements made during a judicial proceeding[64] or in some government proceedings are privileged.[65] A statement made by one spouse to another is also privileged even if it is defamatory.[66]

There are also statements that can receive *qualified* privilege, which means that they are only privileged under some circumstances. So long as the privilege is not abused and the statement meets the requirements of the privilege, the statement will remain privileged. For example, a person who reprints a defamatory statement by someone at a public proceeding in the official report of that public proceeding will not be liable for defamation.[67]

G. Privacy Torts

Privacy torts are a relatively recent invention in Anglo-American law. Invasion of privacy was not recognized as a tort at common law. However, in 1890, future Supreme Court Justice Louis Brandeis and his then law partner Samuel Warren published a law review article arguing for the recognition of

---

[57] Restatement (Second), Torts § 559 (1965)

[58] Restatement (Second), Torts § 559, cmt. b (1965)

[59] 376 U.S. 254 (1964)

[60] *New York Times v. Sullivan*, 376 U.S. 254 (1964). This constitutional requirement is shown in the Restatement (Second), Torts § 580A (1965)

[61] *See Gertz v. Robert Welch, Inc.*, 418 U.S. 323 (1974)

[62] Restatement (Second), Torts § 580B (1965)

[63] Restatement (Second), Torts § 583 (1965)

[64] Restatement (Second), Torts §§ 585-589 (1965)

[65] Restatement (Second), Torts §§ 590-591 (1965)

[66] Restatement (Second), Torts § 592 (1965)

[67] Restatement (Second), Torts § 611 (1965)

the right to privacy as a tort.[68] In 1905, the Georgia Supreme Court became the first court to be persuaded by the famous article and recognize a cause of action for invasion of privacy.[69]

Following a law review article written by influential legal scholar William Prosser,[70] modern privacy law has largely been grouped into four categories.

1. Intrusion Upon Seclusion

The first is called "intrusion upon seclusion." A person commits this tort when he or she:

1. Intentionally intrudes (physically or otherwise)
2. upon the solitude or seclusion of another
3. in a manner that would be highly offensive to a reasonable person[71]

For example, imagine that James breaks into Dante's house and searches his medicine cabinet to find out what medicines Dante is taking. Other examples include eavesdropping, wiretapping, and unwanted, embarrassing photographing.[72]

2. Appropriation of Name or Likeness

The second category is the appropriation of a person's name or likeness without authorization. This tort is committed when a person uses (1) another's name or likeness (2) for his own benefit (3) without authorization.[73]

A person need not even use the exact likeness of another to commit this tort. The most famous example of this is the "Robot Vanna White" case. In *White v. Samsung Electronics America, Inc.*, the Ninth Circuit Federal Court of Appeals held that Samsung tortiously appropriated Vanna White's likeness by placing a wig, gown, and jewelry on a robot and placing it in a setting that closely resembled "Wheel of Fortune," the famous show on which White regularly appears in a fancy gown and jewelry.[74]

3. Publicity Given to Private Life

The third type of invasion of privacy occurs when someone improperly publishes a private fact about another person. The publication of the fact must be highly offensive to a reasonable person and not be made about a matter of public concern.[75] The communication must be made to a relatively large of number of people to be tortious.

For example, this tort is committed when a newspaper publishes the details of an individual's sex life that is not a matter of public concern. This tort is also committed when a creditor mails a letter to everyone in a debtor's town stating that the debtor did not pay his debts.[76]

---

[68] Brandeis, L & Warren, S, *The Right to Privacy*, 4 Harv. L. Rev. 193 (1890).

[69] *Pavesich v. New England Life Insurance Co.*, 122 Ga. 190, 50 S.E. 68 (GA 1905). *See also* Restatement (Second), Torts § 652, cmt. a (1965).

[70] Prosser, W., *Privacy*, 48 Calif. L. Rev., 383 (1960)

[71] Restatement (Second), Torts § 652B (1965)

[72] *See* Restatement (Second), Torts § 652B, cmt. b (1965)

[73] Restatement (Second), Torts § 652C (1965)

[74] *White v. Samsung Electronics, Inc,*, 971 F.2d 1395 (9th Cir. 1992).

[75] Restatement (Second), Torts § 652D (1965)

[76] *See* Restatement (Second), Torts § 652D, cmts. a and b (1965).

4. False Light

The fourth privacy tort is the publication of material that places another in a false light. The false light a person is placed in must be highly offensive to a reasonable person, and the tortfeasor must either know that the statement would place the victim in a false light or recklessly believe that it would not place the victim in a false light.[77]

For example, imagine that Dante is a famous poet and that James publishes a horrific poem entitled "Rhyme Time for Mimes" under Dante's name. This would clearly place Dante in a false light.

H. Fraudulent Misrepresentation

Fraudulent Misrepresentation, also known as fraud, occurs when someone intentionally misrepresents a material (important) fact upon which another justifiably relies that causes damage.[78]

For example, James is a used car dealer who offers to sell Dante a car. Without Dante's knowledge, James rolls the odometer back from 200,000 miles to 20,000 miles. This is clearly a fraudulent misrepresentation. James misrepresented the condition of the automobile, which is a material fact any time a car is purchased. Dante was justified in relying on the odometer as he had no reason to doubt its accuracy. He was also damaged by purchasing a car in a different condition than he reasonably believed it was in.[79]

Usually, inflated statements of a seller, known as "puffery," are not considered misrepresentation. For example, a misrepresentation does not occur when a car salesman states, "This car is going to be hugely popular." However, if the seller falsely said, "We have sold 100 cars of this make and model," fraudulent misrepresentation occurred (assuming the other elements are met).

Most opinions are not misrepresentations. However, if the person making the statement has significantly superior knowledge of the subject matter compared to the person that the statement is made to, such as a banker making a statement about a loan to an unsophisticated customer, the opinion may give rise to a claim for misrepresentation.[80]

I. Tortious Interference with Advantageous Economic Relationships

Competition is an essential part of the American economic structure. It is as natural as it is unsurprising that businesses compete with each other for the same customers. However, there are certain circumstances in which the law will consider intensely aggressive business tactics impermissible.

If a person intentionally *and* improperly interferes with a known contractual relationship between two other parties, he or she commits tortious interference with a contractual relationship. The torts occurs when (1) a person intentionally (2) and knowingly (3) causes another to breach a contract (4) in an improper manner. The rule may apply to prospective contractual relationships as well in some circumstances.[81]

For example, James knows that Dante has a contract to buy a car from Kaylee. He calls Kaylee and offers her the same car for $5,000 less than her contract price with Dante on the condition that she breach her contract with Dante. This is clearly a tortious interference with a contractual relationship.

---

[77] Restatement (Second), Torts § 652E (1965)

[78] Restatement (Second), Torts § 525 (1965)

[79] *See* Restatement (Second), Torts § 525 Illus. 1 (1965)

[80] *See*, e.g., *Jolley v. Chase Home Finance, LLC*, 213 Cal.App.4th 872, 893, 153 Cal.Rptr.3d 546, 563 (Cal. App. 2013).

[81] Restatement (Second), Torts § 766B (1965)

Courts weigh several factors when determining whether an interference is improper. They will weigh factors like the relationship between the parties, the interferer's motivation, the nature of the interferer's conduct, the interests of the parties, and the interests of society.[82]

V. Negligence

Negligence is likely the most commonly committed tort. Unlike intentional torts, by definition, negligence is committed unintentionally. Negligence is the violation of a duty of care owed to another that causes damage to the person to whom the duty is owed.[83] It is most often committed when damage results from a person's unreasonable actions. Consider the following example.

James is driving behind Dante. Dante stops at a stop sign. Because James is sending a text message on his cell phone, he does not see the stop sign or Dante's stopped car, causing the front of his car to hit Dante's car. As a result, Dante's car suffers damage, and Dante's neck is injured.

In the above example, James did not want to hurt Dante or his car. He did not intend for the collision to happen. However, James has nonetheless committed a tort—negligence. One need not intend damage to be liable for it. Here, James' actions were clearly not those of a reasonable person. Driving is a dangerous enough activity without distraction. Because James distracted himself while driving, Dante was injured. The law allows recovery for the negligent acts of others to place the burden of injury on the party it deems more at fault.

Negligence traditionally has four elements:

1. A duty owed to another
2. Breach of that duty
3. Causation
4. Damages[84]

A. Duty to Another

A negligence action cannot succeed unless the Defendant owed the Plaintiff a duty of care. Fortunately for plaintiffs, at every moment of every day, almost every adult person owes to every other person the duty to act like a reasonable person would under the same or similar circumstances.[85] In some situations, however, a heightened or lesser duty applies.

1. Duty to Act Like a Reasonable Person

Almost every adult person owes to every other adult person the duty to act like a reasonable person under the same or similar circumstances. What constitutes what a "reasonable person" would do under the circumstances is intensely fact intensive and varies from case to case.

For example, imagine that James and Dante are facing one another in an intersection while driving. James is intending to turn left. Dante is intending to continue going straight. Local traffic customs dictate that the person going straight has the right of way. James does not see Dante's car coming, and he is struck by Dante's car. Damage is caused to both cars and both men.

---

[82] *See* Restatement (Second), Torts § 767 (1965)
[83] *See* 57A Am. Jur. 2d Negligence § 5 (2017)
[84] *See*, e.g., *Burgess v. Superior Court of Los Angeles Cnty.*, 831 P.2d 1197, 1200 (Cal. 1992)
[85] Restatement (Second), Torts § 283 (1965)

James is clearly liable for negligence in this case as reasonable people follow the prescribed rules for rights-of-way. However, imagine now that James sees Dante before turning but that Dante motioned at him to go first. Thinking that James would clear the intersection more quickly, Dante hits the gas and hits James' car.

This scenario is much like the first in that Dante hit James' car while James was turning left. However, Dante is the one more likely to be found negligent as he waived his right of way. James likely acted reasonably by turning pursuant to Dante's gesture. Dante likely acted unreasonably by going before James cleared the intersection.

The reasonable man standard is objective. That is, it is viewed from the perspective of what society believes is reasonable under the circumstances.[86] It does not matter whether the individual actually believed his actions were reasonable at the time.

In the above example in which James hit Dante's car because he did not see it, James likely thought that his turn was reasonable when made it. He probably would not have turned had he seen Dante. However, that is completely irrelevant to the determination of negligence. The reasonable man standard looks at what society believes a reasonable person should do under the same or similar circumstances. Reasonable people do not turn left when they do not have the right of way, rendering James liable for negligence.

2. Duty Owed by Children

There is an important exception to the "reasonable-person standard." It does not usually apply to children who accidentally cause damage. A child only owes the duty to act like a reasonable child of that age would under the same or similar circumstances.[87] For example, a 12-year-old child is held to the standard of what a reasonable 12-year-old child would do under the same or similar circumstances. An eight-year-old child is held to the standard of what a reasonable eight-year-old child would do under the same or similar circumstances.

There is, however, a very important exception to this rule. A child who is engaged in an activity that is normally only performed by adults or that requires adult qualifications will be held to the normal reasonable adult person standard.[88]

For example, imagine that James, who is 15 years old and does not have a driver's license, and Dante are facing one another in an intersection while driving. James is intending to turn left. Dante is intending to continue going straight. Local traffic custom dictates that the person going straight has the right of way. James does not see Dante's car coming, and he is struck by Dante's car, causing damage to both cars and personal injury to both.

In this case, James will be held to the standard of a reasonable adult person because he is engaged in an activity requiring adult qualifications.[89]

3. Duty Owed by a Person with a Disability

Negligence law makes a distinction between those with a physical disability and those with a mental disability. A person with a physical disability, such as a person missing a limb, only owes the

---

[86] Restatement (Second), Torts § 283, cmt. c (1965)

[87] Restatement (Second), Torts § 283A (1965)

[88] Restatement (Second), Torts § 283A, cmt. c (1965)

[89] *See* Restatement (Second), Torts § 283A, cmt. c (1965)

duty to act like a reasonable person with that disability would act under the same or similar circumstances, a lower standard than the reasonable adult standard.[90]

However, a person with a mental disability, including any mental illness or intellectual disability, is usually held to the standard of a reasonable person that does not have that disability.[91] The only time a mental disability lowers the duty that a person owes is when the person with a mental disability is a child, in which case the child is held to the standard of a reasonable child with that disability.[92]

4. Duty Owed by Professionals and Skilled Tradesmen

A person acting within the scope of his or her employment, trade, or profession is held to the standard of what a reasonable member of that trade would do under the same or similar circumstances.[93] For example, an attorney owes a duty to act like a reasonable attorney would under the same or similar circumstances when providing legal advice.

This duty does not extend outside the professional context however. For example, when driving a car, an attorney is held to the standard of a reasonable person driving a car, not the standard of how a reasonable attorney would drive.

5. Negligence *Per Se*

An action can be both tortious and illegal.[94] Sometimes, a statute or administrative regulation can create a duty.[95] This is called "negligence *per se*."

For example, imagine that James is driving his car down the road. He sees a stop sign but decides not to stop and hits Dante's car. A local ordinance states, "All drivers must completely stop their automobiles at a stop sign. All violators will pay a fine of $50.00."

In this case, the law has created a duty for James to stop at the stop sign. By not doing so, he has breached that duty. It does not matter that there is also a $50 fine owed to the city.

Not all violations of a law will lead to negligence *per se*. A statute only becomes a duty when the person injured is someone the statute seeks to protect and the injury is the type of injury that the statute seeks to prevent.[96]

For example, imagine that the local building code requires that every factory's elevator have a special safety device in it and that legislative history proves that the safety device was meant only to protect factory workers from physical injuries. James and Dante are in a factory elevator without this safety device. The elevator then breaks, injuring both James and Dante. James is an employee of the factory. Dante is merely a visiting customer. Dante misses work as a result of the medical injuries from his accident.

In this case, the factory is under a duty to James to put the safety device in the elevator because the statute is meant to protect against physical injuries to employees. James is an employee, the class the statute seeks to protect, and he was physically injured, the type of injury the statute seeks to prevent.

---

[90] Restatement (Second), Torts § 283C (1965)

[91] Restatement (Second), Torts § 283B (1965)

[92] Restatement (Second), Torts § 283B, cmt. a (1965)

[93] Restatement (Second), Torts § 299A, cmt. c (1965)

[94] Restatement (Second), Torts § 287 (1965)

[95] Restatement (Second), Torts § 286 (1965)

[96] Restatement (Second), Torts § 286 (1965)

On the other hand, the factory is likely not under a duty to Dante to put the safety device in the elevator. Dante is a customer, which is not a class the statute seeks to protect. He also misses work, which is not an injury that the statute seeks to prevent. That does not mean the factory will not ultimately be liable to Dante. Regular negligence duties, such as the duty to act like a reasonable person and premises liability duties (which will be discussed in the next section) still apply. It just means that no duty to follow the statute is established under the "negligence *per se*" doctrine.[97]

6. Premises Liability

Premises liability law addresses what duties the owner or possessor of real property (land and buildings) owes to those on the property. This area of the law is currently undergoing a transformation. Under common law, and under the Restatement (Second) of Torts, premises liability turns on whether the injured person was a trespasser, licensee, or invitee (these will be discussed shortly). However, there has been a trend among states to abolish the common law rule and replace it with a "unitary standard." This standard, which was adopted by the Restatement (Third) of Torts, does not distinguish between trespassers, licensees, and invitees. It merely requires that a landowner's actions be reasonable under the circumstances, except in the case of "flagrant trespassers."[98]

a. Duties Owed to Trespassers

A trespasser is essentially anyone on the land of another without the right to be there.[99] Under the common law and Restatement (Second) approach, a landowner does not owe a trespasser any duty to keep the land safe from conditions that may cause injury.[100]

However, there are some exceptions to this rule. Most involve situations in which the landowner knows that his or her land is trespassed upon. For example, when a landowner knows that his or her land is frequently trespassed upon, a landowner must warn trespassers about non-obvious conditions that may cause death or serious injury.[101]

Also, if a landowner is conducting a dangerous activity, he or she must take reasonable steps to keep known trespassers safe from the activity.[102]

There is also an exception known as the "attractive nuisance doctrine." If a dangerous condition exists on a landowner's property that he or she knows is likely to attract trespassing children, the landowner is liable for the injuries of trespassing children if the following conditions are met:

1. The children could not realize the risk created by the condition because of their age
2. The benefits of eliminating the conditions outweigh the burdens of removing it
3. The landowners does not take reasonable precautions to keep the children safe from injury.[103]

The Restatement (Third) of Torts usually holds that a landowner must act reasonably under the circumstances to trespassers. The only exception to this rule is that of the "flagrant trespasser."

---

[97] *See* Restatement (Second), Torts § 286, Illus. 1 and Illus. 3 (1965)
[98] Restatement (Third), Torts: Phys. & Emot. Harm §§ 51-52 (2012)
[99] Restatement (Second), Torts § 329 (1965)
[100] Restatement (Second), Torts § 333 (1965)
[101] Restatement (Second), Torts § 335 (1965)
[102] Restatement (Second), Torts § 336 (1965)
[103] Restatement (Second), Torts § 339 (1965)

A landowner only owes the duty not to intentionally or recklessly cause injury to a "flagrant trespasser" under this approach. This term has not been extensively litigated. The drafters of the Restatement (Third) stated in its comments, however,

> *"Flagrant" is used here in the sense of egregious or atrocious rather than in its alternative meaning of conspicuous. Nevertheless, no single word can capture the concept, which is further explained in this Comment. This Section leaves to each jurisdiction employing the concept to determine the point along the spectrum of trespassory conduct at which a trespasser is a "flagrant" rather than an ordinary trespasser. The critical aspect of this Section is that a distinction is made, and different duties of care are owed depending on whether a trespasser is a flagrant trespasser or an ordinary trespasser.*[104]

Thus, a flagrant trespasser will likely be defined as one that continues trespassing after frequent warnings to the contrary or that trespasses for a bad purpose.

b. Duties Owed to Invitees and Licensees

An invitee falls into one of two categories. An invitee may be a member of the general public in a place for a public purpose for which the land is open. An invitee may also be anyone on the premises for business purposes. A licensee is someone who is on the land only because of the owner's consent.[105] For example, most social guests are licensees. However, most business customers are invitees.

Under the Restatement (Second) approach, a landowner owes invitees the duty to keep them safe from certain conditions that a reasonable person would not discover, understand the danger of, or protect themselves against. This duty applies only to conditions that the landowner either knew about or, following a reasonable inspection, should have known about.[106]

Under the Restatement (Second) approach, a landowner owes licensees the duty to warn them about conditions that the landowner knows or should know about and that the licensees do not know or have no reason to know about.[107]

The Restatement (Third) approach does not distinguish between licensees and invitees. The landowner owes a duty to keep the premises reasonably safe under the circumstances to all people on his or her property.[108]

7. The Duty to Rescue

A person is not normally under a duty to rescue another person in peril or in need of aid.[109] For example, if James sees Dante dying on the side of the road, he is under no duty to call him an ambulance.

However, there are some exceptions to this general rule. If someone creates the dangerous situation the person is in, he or she is under a duty to aid.[110] For example, if James runs over Dante with his car, he is under a duty to help him get medical care.

---

[104] Restatement (Third), Torts: Phys. & Emot. Harm § 52, cmt. a (2012)
[105] Restatement (Second), Torts § 330 (1965)
[106] Restatement (Second), Torts § 343 (1965)
[107] Restatement (Second), Torts § 342 (1965)
[108] Restatement (Third), Torts: Phys. & Emot. Harm § 51 (1965)
[109] Restatement (Second), Torts § 314 (1965)
[110] Restatement (Second), Torts § 322 (1965)

Another exception is the "special relationship" rule. Some types of people are required to help others because of the status of their relationships. This duty applies generally to business persons who have customers or employees on their premises.[111]

A third exception to this rule applies to those who voluntarily attempt to rescue others.[112] When someone begins a rescue attempt, he or she is under a duty to act reasonably in that attempt. For example, imagine that Dante is dying on the side of the road. A crowd gathers around Dante. To look good in front of the crowd, James screams, "I'll go get help!" Once he is out of the crowd's sight, he makes no attempt to get help. In that case, James may be liable for acting unreasonably because he volunteered to help rescue Dante but did not actually help.

B. Breach of Duty

Once a duty has been established, it is up to the Plaintiff to also prove that the Defendant violated that duty. This is known as "breach of duty." The jury (or judge in the case of a bench trial) determines whether the duty has been breached.[113] The judge always determines what duty applies.[114]

For example, imagine that Dante is dying on the side of the road. A crowd gathers around Dante. To look good in front of the crowd, James screams, "I'll go get help!" Once he is out of the crowd's sight, he makes no attempt to get help. A judge will determine whether James owes a duty to Dante, which is especially important because a duty to rescue does not normally exist but may exist based on the facts of this case given James' voluntary assumption of responsibility. A jury will decide whether James breached that duty to Dante.

Breach of duty can be proven with direct evidence. It can also be proven with indirect evidence under the doctrine of *res ipsa loquitur* (Latin for "the thing speaks for itself"). Normally, the Plaintiff must prove his or her case by a preponderance of the evidence, however, under the doctrine of *res ipsa loquitur*, a plaintiff can shift the burden of proof to the Defendant by showing that (1) the incident that occurred does not ordinarily happen without negligence and (2) no one else but the Defendant could have been responsible. When the Plaintiff makes this showing, it is up to the Defendant to prove that he or she was not negligent.[115]

For example, imagine that Dr. James is operating on Dante. Dante later claims that he is experiencing pain. After an x-ray, it is discovered that there is a sponge in Dante's lower intestine. Dr. James and his nurses claim that Dr. James did not leave the sponge in Dante after surgery, leaving no direct evidence. However, under the doctrine of *res ipsa loquitur*, Dante need only show that there was no other reason a sponge would be inside of him other than the surgery performed by Dr. James and that sponges are only left inside of people when surgeons are negligent. If Dante makes this showing (which is very likely), Dr. James will have to prove that he was not negligent.

C. Causation

Causation is an essential element of negligence.[116] If the Defendant's breach of duty is not the cause of Plaintiff's injuries, the Defendant will not be held liable for negligence. For example, imagine

---

[111] *See* Restatement (Second) §§ 314A(3), 314B (1965)

[112] Restatement (Second), Torts § 323 (1965)

[113] Restatement (Second), Torts § 328C (1965)

[114] Restatement (Second), Torts § 328B (1965)

[115] *See* Restatement (Second), Torts § 328D (1965)

[116] *See* Restatement (Second), Torts § 430 (1965)

that James is the owner of a store and does not place a "caution: wet floor" sign on the area he mopped, leaving it wet. Dante walks over the area without incident but later falls trying to jump over a tall display of cans in the store for fun, injuring his left shoulder. Although James was arguably negligent for not placing a warning sign about the wet floor, Dante's injuries were caused by his own actions, not the wet floor. This means that James cannot be held liable for negligence.

There are two essential elements of causation, cause in fact and proximate causation. Both must be present to hold someone liable for negligence.[117]

Cause in fact, also known as "but for" causation, exists when the Defendant's actions were a substantial factor in Plaintiff's injuries and, but for the Defendant's actions, the Plaintiff would not have been injured.[118] For example, imagine that James is the owner of a store and does not place a "caution: wet floor" sign on the area he mopped, leaving it wet. Dante walks over the area without incident but later falls trying to jump over a tall display of cans in the store for fun, injuring his left shoulder. James' actions are not what directly caused Dante's injuries. That is, regardless of whether the floor was wet, Dante would have been injured.

Cause in fact can arguably be very broad. For example, in the above scenario, imagine that Dante argues that he would have gone to a different area of the store than the one where the can display was stacked if he had seen a "caution: wet floor" sign. He could argue that, but for the lack of a sign, he would not have been in the place he was injured. This is why proximate cause, also known as "legal cause," is required to prove causation.

Proximate cause requires that the Plaintiff's injury be a reasonably foreseeable result of the defendant's actions.[119] In above example, no reasonable person would foresee that not placing a "caution: wet floor" sign would result in a customer injuring himself jumping over a can display. Thus, there is no proximate causation, which means that there is no liability for negligence. Consider the following case.

❖❖❖

Palsgraf v. The Long Island Railroad Company
248 N.Y. 339, 162 N.E. 99 (1928)

CARDOZO, C. J.

Plaintiff was standing on a platform of defendant's railroad after buying a ticket to go to Rock-away Beach. A train stopped at the station, bound for another place. Two men ran forward to catch it. One of the men reached the platform of the car without mishap, though the train was already moving. The other man, carrying a package, jumped aboard the car, but seemed unsteady as if about to fall. A guard on the car, who had held the door open, reached forward to help him in, and another guard on the platform pushed him from behind. In this act, the package was dislodged, and fell upon the rails. It was a package of small size, about fifteen inches long, and was covered by a newspaper. In fact it contained fireworks, but there was nothing in its appearance to give notice of its contents. The fireworks when they fell exploded. The shock of the explosion threw down some scales at the other end of the platform many feet away. The scales struck the plaintiff, causing injuries for which she sues.

---

[117] *See* 57A Am. Jur. 2d Negligence § 414 (2017); *see also Fedorczyk v. Caribbean Cruise Lines, Ltd.*, 82 F. 3d 69, 73 (3rd Cir. 1996) ("Causation includes cause in fact and legal causation, which is often referred to as proximate cause. Courts have often conflated cause in fact and legal causation into 'proximate cause,' but the two are conceptually distinct.")

[118] *See* 57A Am. Jur. 2d Negligence § 415 (2017)

[119] *See* 57A Am. Jur. 2d Negligence § 413 (2017)

The conduct of the defendant's guard, if a wrong in its relation to the holder of the package, was not a wrong in its relation to the plaintiff, standing far away. Relatively to her it was not negligence at all. Nothing in the situation gave notice that the falling package had in it the potency of peril to persons thus removed. Negligence is not actionable unless it involves the invasion of a legally protected interest, the violation of a right. 'Proof of negligence in the air, so to speak, will not do.' Pollock, Torts (11th Ed.) p. 455; Martin v. Herzog, 228 N. Y. 164, 170, 126 N. E. 814. Cf. Salmond, Torts (6th Ed.) p. 24. 'Negligence is the absence of care, according to the circumstances.' Willes, J., in Vaughan v. Taff Vale Ry. Co., 5 H. & N. 679, 688; 1 Beven, Negligence (4th Ed.) 7; Paul v. Consol. Fireworks Co., 212 N. Y. 117, 105 N. E. 795; Adams v. Bullock, 227 N. Y. 208, 211, 125 N. E. 93; Parrott v. Wells-Fargo Co., 15 Wall. [U. S.] 524, 21 L. Ed. 206. The plaintiff, as she stood upon the platform of the station, might claim to be protected against intentional invasion of her bodily security. Such invasion is not charged. She might claim to be protected against unintentional invasion by conduct involving in the thought of reasonable men an unreasonable hazard that such invasion would ensue. These, from the point of view of the law, were the bounds of her immunity, with perhaps some rare exceptions, survivals for the most part of ancient forms of liability, where conduct is held to be at the peril of the actor. Sullivan v. Dunham, 161 N. Y. 290, 55 N. E. 923, 47 L. R. A. 715, 76 Am. St. Rep. 274. If no hazard was apparent to the eye of ordinary vigilance, an act innocent and harmless, at least to outward seeming, with reference to her, did not take to itself the quality of a tort because it happened to be a wrong, though apparently not one involving the risk of bodily insecurity, with reference to some one else. 'In every instance, before negligence can be predicated of a given act, back of the act must be sought and found a duty to the individual complaining, the observance of which would have averted or avoided the injury.' McSherry, C. J., in West Virginia Central & P. R. Co. v. State, 96 Md. 652, 666, 54 A. 669, 671 (61 L. R. A. 574). Cf. Norfolk & W. Ry. Co. v. Wood, 99 Va. 156, 158, 159, 37 S. E. 846; Hughes v. Boston R. R. Co., 71 N. H. 279, 284, 51 A. 1070, 93 Am. St. Rep. 518; U. S. Express Co. v. Everest, 72 Kan. 517; Emry v. Roanoke Navigation & Water Power Co., 111 N. C. 94, 95, 16 S. E. 18, 17 L. R. A. 699; Vaughan v. Transit Development Co., 222 N. Y. 79, 118 N. E. 219; Losee v. Clute, 51 N. Y. 494; Di Caprio v. New York Cent. R. Co., 231 N. Y. 94, 131 N. E. 746, 16 A. L. R. 940; 1 Shearman & Redifield on Negligence, § 8, and cases cited; Cooley on Torts (3d Ed.) p. 1411; Jaggard on Torts, vol. 2, p. 826; Wharton, Negligence, § 24; Bohlen, Studies in the Law of Torts, p. 601. 'The ideas of negligence and duty are strictly correlative.' Bowen, L. J., in Thomas v. Quartermaine, 18 Q. B. D. 685, 694. The plaintiff sues in her own right for a wrong personal to her, and not as the vicarious beneficiary of a breach of duty to another.

A different conclusion will involve us, and swiftly too, in a maze of contradictions. A guard stumbles over a package which has been left upon a platform. It seems to be a bundle of newspapers. It turns out to be a can of dynamite. To the eye of ordinary vigilance, the bundle is abandoned waste, which may be kicked or trod on with impunity. Is a passenger at the other end of the platform protected by the law against the unsuspected hazard concealed beneath the waste? If not, is the result to be any different, so far as the distant passenger is concerned, when the guard stumbles over a valise which a truckman or a porter has left upon the walk? The passenger far away, if the victim of a wrong at all, has a cause of action, not derivative, but original and primary. His claim to be protected against invasion of his bodily security is neither greater nor less because the act resulting in the invasion is a wrong to another far removed. In this case, the rights that are said to have been violated, are not even of the same order. The man was not injured in his person nor even put in danger. The purpose of the act, as well as its effect, was to make his person safe. It there was a wrong to him at all, which may very well be doubted it was a wrong to a property interest only, the safety of his package. Out of this wrong to property, which threatened injury to nothing else, there has passed, we are told, to the plaintiff by derivation or succession a right of action for the invasion of an interest of another order, the right to bodily security. The diversity of interests emphasizes the futility of the effort to build the plaintiff's right upon the basis of a wrong to some one else. The gain is one of emphasis, for a like result would follow if the interests were the same. Even then, the orbit of the danger as disclosed to the eye of reasonable vigilance would be the orbit of the duty. One who jostles one's neighbor in a crowd does not invade the rights of others standing at the outer fringe when the unintended contact casts a bomb upon the ground. The wrongdoer as to them is the man who carries the bomb, not the one who explodes it without suspicion of the danger. Life will have to be made over, and human nature transformed, before prevision so extravagant can be accepted as the norm of conduct, the customary standard to which behavior must conform.

The argument for the plaintiff is built upon the shifting meanings of such words as 'wrong' and 'wrongful,' and shares their instability. What the plaintiff must show is 'a wrong' to herself; i. e., a violation of her own right, and not merely a wrong to some one else, nor conduct 'wrongful' because unsocial, but not 'a wrong' to any one. We are told that one who drives at reckless speed through a crowded city street is guilty of a negligent act and therefore of a wrongful one, irrespective of the consequences. Negligent the act is, and wrongful in the sense that it is unsocial, but wrongful and unsocial in relation to other travelers, only because the eye of vigilance perceives the risk of damage. If the same act were to be committed on a speedway or a race course, it would lose its wrongful quality. The risk reasonably to be perceived defines the duty to be obeyed, and risk imports relation; it is risk to another or to others within the range of apprehension. Seavey, Negligence, Subjective or Objective, 41 H. L. Rv. 6; Boronkay v. Robinson & Carpenter, 247 N. Y. 365, 160 N. E. 400. This does not mean, of course, that one who launches a destructive force is always relieved of liability, if the force, though known to be destructive, pursues an unexpected path. 'It was not necessary that the defendant should have had notice of the particular method in which an accident would occur, if the possibility of an accident was clear to the ordinarily prudent eye.' Munsey v. Webb, 231 U. S. 150, 156, 34 S. Ct. 44, 45 (58 L. Ed. 162); Condran v. Park & Tilford, 213 N. Y. 341, 345, 107 N. E. 565; Robert v. United States Shipping Board Emergency Fleet Corp., 240 N. Y. 474, 477, 148 N. E. 650. Some acts, such as shooting are so imminently dangerous to any one who may come within reach of the missile however unexpectedly, as to impose a duty of prevision not far from that of an insurer. Even to-day, and much oftener in earlier stages of the law, one acts sometimes at one's peril. Jeremiah Smith, Tort and Absolute Liability, 30 H. L. Rv. 328; Street, Foundations of Legal Liability, vol. 1, pp. 77, 78. Under this head, it may be, fall certain cases of what is known as transferred intent, an act willfully dangerous to A resulting by misadventure in injury to B. Talmage v. Smith, 101 Mich. 370, 374, 59 N. W. 656, 45 Am. St. Rep. 414. These cases aside, wrong is defined in terms of the natural or probable, at least when unintentional. Parrot v. Wells-Fargo Co. (The Nitro-Glycerine Case) 15 Wall. 524, 21 L. Ed. 206. The range of reasonable apprehension is at times a question for the court, and at times, if varying inferences are possible, a question for the jury. Here, by concession, there was nothing in the situation to suggest to the most cautious mind that the parcel wrapped in newspaper would spread wreckage through the station. If the guard had thrown it down knowingly and willfully, he would not have threatened the plaintiff's safety, so far as appearances could warn him. His conduct would not have involved, even then, an unreasonable probability of invasion of her bodily security. Liability can be no greater where the act is inadvertent.

Negligence, like risk, is thus a term of relation. Negligence in the abstract, apart from things related, is surely not a tort, if indeed it is understandable at all. Bowen, L. J., in Thomas v. Quartermaine, 18 Q. B. D. 685, 694. Negligence is not a tort unless it results in the commission of a wrong, and the commission of a wrong imports the violation of a right, in this case, we are told, the right to be protected against interference with one's bodily security. But bodily security is protected, not against all forms of interference or aggression, but only against some. One who seeks redress at law does not make out a cause of action by showing without more that there has been damage to his person. If the harm was not willful, he must show that the act as to him had possibilities of danger so many and apparent as to entitle him to be protected against the doing of it though the harm was unintended. Affront to personality is still the keynote of the wrong. Confirmation of this view will be found in the history and development of the action on the case. Negligence as a basis of civil liability was unknown to mediaeval law. 8 Holdsworth, History of English Law, p. 449; Street, Foundations of Legal Liability, vol. 1, pp. 189, 190. For damage to the person, the sole remedy was trespass, and trespass did not lie in the absence of aggression, and that direct and personal. Holdsworth, op. cit. p. 453; Street, op. cit. vol. 3, pp. 258, 260, vol. 1, pp. 71, 74. Liability for other damage, as where a servant without orders from the master does or omits something to the damage of another, is a plant of later growth. Holdsworth, op. cit. 450, 457; Wigmore, Responsibility for Tortious Acts, vol. 3, Essays in Anglo-American Legal History, 520, 523, 526, 533. When it emerged out of the legal soil, it was thought of as a variant of trespass, an offshoot of the parent stock. This appears in the form of action, which was known as trespass on the case. Holdsworth, op. cit. p. 449; cf. Scott v. Shepard, 2 Wm. Black. 892; Green, Rationale of Proximate Cause, p. 19. The victim does not sue derivatively, or by right of subrogation, to vindicate an interest invaded in the person of another. Thus to view his cause of action is to ignore the fundamental difference between tort and crime. Holland, Jurisprudence (12th Ed.) p. 328. He sues for breach of a duty owing to himself.

The law of causation, remote or proximate, is thus foreign to the case before us. The question of liability is always anterior to the question of the measure of the consequences that go with liability. If there is no tort to be redressed, there is no occasion to consider what damage might be recovered if there were a finding of a tort. We may assume, without deciding, that negligence, not at large or in the abstract, but in relation to the plaintiff, would entail liability for any and all consequences, however novel or extraordinary. <u>Bird v. St. Paul Fire & Marine Ins. Co., 224 N. Y. 47, 54, 120 N. E. 86, 13 A. L. R. 875;</u> <u>Ehrgott v. Mayor, etc., of City of New York, 96 N. Y. 264, 48 Am. Rep. 622;</u> <u>Smith v. London & S. W. R. Co., [1870–1871] L. R. 6 C. P. 14; 1</u> Beven, Negligence, 106; Street, op. cit. vol. 1, p. 90; Green, Rationale of Proximate Cause, pp. 88, 118; cf. Matter of Polemis, L. R. 1921, 3 K. B. 560; 44 Law Quarterly Review, 142. There is room for argument that a distinction is to be drawn according to the diversity of interests invaded by the act, as where conduct negligent in that it threatens an insignificant invasion of an interest in property results in an unforeseeable invasion of an interest of another order, as, e. g., one of bodily security. Perhaps other distinctions may be necessary. We do not go into the question now. The consequences to be followed must first be rooted in a wrong.

The judgment of the Appellate Division and that of the Trial Term should be reversed, and the complaint dismissed, with costs in all courts.

Questions Presented

1) Why was the railroad not held responsible for the Plaintiff's injury?
2) What hypothetical scenario did the court compare the facts of this case to? Why did it make that analogy?
3) Would the outcome have been different if the railroad workers knew the packages contained fireworks?

❖❖

Legal Definitions

Cause in fact – in a negligence action, cause in fact is the requirement that Plaintiff's injuries would not have occurred but for Defendant's conduct.

Proximate Causation – in a negligence action, proximate cause is the requirement that the Plaintiff's injuries be a foreseeable result of Defendant's breach of duty.

D. Damages

The final element of negligence is damages. Damages are essentially a legal term of art meaning both injury and compensation for injury.[120] There are several kinds of damages a Plaintiff can be awarded for a Defendant's negligence.

A Plaintiff may be awarded "general damages." General damages are those that occur so frequently from an injury that they are presumed to have occurred.[121] General damages are often not easily calculated. For example, as a result of negligence, there is often pain and suffering, mental anguish, and the loss of the ability to perform activities. For example, imagine that a Plaintiff loses a foot. How does one determine what the loss of that foot is worth? The answer is probably different to and for almost everyone. Despite the uncertain value of the types of injuries for which general damages are awarded, they are a major part of many Plaintiffs' damges.

A Plaintiff may also be awarded special damages. Special damages are damages that result from the Defendant's actions but do not necessarily always occur because of the particular harm committed. For example, if a Plaintiff misses work, has medical bills, or suffers a diminished earning capacity because of Defendant's conduct, those damages are special damages. They must be able to be measured precisely in money to be awarded.[122] For instance, a Plaintiff can collect damages for medical bills as special damages because the exact cost of the medical care can be determined.

A Plaintiff may also be awarded punitive damages in exceptional cases. Punitive damages are damages awarded to punish the Defendant's conduct. They are not tied to the Plaintiff's actual injuries. These damages are optional and are only awarded when there is outrageous conduct with reckless or evil motives. For example, in *Olson v. Hyundai Motor Co.*,[123] Hyundai was required to pay $73,000,000 in punitive damages for a mechanical malfunction caused by severe manufacturing defects that resulted in the death of two teenagers. Punitive damages are not awarded in the vast majority of cases.

E. Defenses

There are several defenses to a negligence action. Most revolve around the Plaintiff's actions during the incident that gave rise to his or her claims.

---

[120] *See* Damages, Black's Law Dictionary (10th ed. 2014)
[121] Restatement (Second), Torts § 904(1) (1965)
[122] Restatement (Second), Torts § 904(2), cmt. b (1965)
[123] *Olson v. Hyundai Motor Co.*, Order on Plaintiffs' Joint Motion for Review of Punitive Damages, DV-11-304 (Mont. Dist. September 9, 2014).

1. Contributory v. Comparative Negligence

The most common defense to a negligence action is that Plaintiff's own actions caused or contributed to the cause of his or her injuries. There are two different versions of this defense, contributory negligence and comparative negligence.

Contributory negligence was the rule at common law, but it is now only the rule in a small number of states.[124] Under the doctrine of contributory negligence, if the Plaintiff's injuries were caused in any way by his or her own actions, the Plaintiff could not recover anything from the Defendant.[125] For example, imagine that James is driving while intoxicated and gets into a car accident with Dante. Just before the accident, Dante's driver's side front tire crosses the yellow line. Under the doctrine of contributory negligence, because Dante was arguably negligent himself, he might not be able to recover for his injuries even though James was driving while intoxicated.

Because of the harshness of the contributory negligence doctrine, the vast majority of courts now use the comparative negligence doctrine.[126] Under the comparative negligence doctrine, a jury awards damages based on the relative fault of each party and awards damages accordingly.[127] For example, if a jury finds the Defendant 70% at fault for the Plaintiff's injury, the Plaintiff recovers 70% of his or her damages from the Defendant.

There are two approaches to comparative negligence, pure and modified. In states that use the pure comparative negligence doctrine, a Plaintiff may recover damages regardless of how at fault he or she was.[128] For example, if the jury finds that the Plaintiff was 70% responsible for his or her own injuries and the Defendant was 30% at fault, the Plaintiff recovers 30% of the cost of his or her injuries from the Defendant.

In states that use the modified comparative negligence doctrine, a Plaintiff may only recover if the Plaintiff is less liable for his or her injuries than the Defendant.[129] In the above example, even though the Defendant was 30% at fault according to the jury, the Plaintiff would recover nothing because the Plaintiff was more responsible than the Defendant. When multiple Defendants are involved, some states require that the Plaintiff be less liable than all the Defendants combined. Others allow the Plaintiff to recover from any Defendant who was more negligent than the Plaintiff was.[130]

Legal Definitions

Comparative Negligence – a defense to negligence in which the Plaintiff's damages are reduced (or eliminated) proportionately to the degree to which Plaintiff contributed to his or her own injuries.

Contributory Negligence – a defense to negligence that prohibits a Plaintiff from recovering damages if he or she contributed to his or her own injuries.

---

[124] 57B Am. Jur. 2d Negligence § 956 (2017)
[125] 57B Am. Jur. 2d Negligence § 799 (2017)
[126] *See* 57B Am. Jur. 2d Negligence § 956 (2017)
[127] *See* 57B Am. Jur. 2d Negligence § 954 (2017)
[128] 57B Am. Jur. 2d Negligence § 962 (2017)
[129] 57B Am. Jur. 2d Negligence § 965 (2017)
[130] 57B Am. Jur. 2d Negligence § 965 (2017)

2. Assumption of the Risk

When a Plaintiff consents to participate in an activity knowing that a particular risk of injury is involved, the Defendant may raise a defense known as "assumption of the risk." Though many jurisdictions merely consider whether the Plaintiff assumed the risk of injury as a factor in comparative negligence, at common law and in some modern jurisdictions, assumption of the risk may still bar recovery.[131] To establish that the Plaintiff assumed the risk, the Plaintiff must prove the Defendant knew about the risk, understood the risk, and voluntarily agreed be exposed to the risk.[132]

There are two kinds of assumption of the risk, express and implied. Express assumption of the risk occurs when the Plaintiff consents either orally or in writing to undertake a risk.[133] This is most frequently done through a written liability waiver. Liability waivers can be difficult to enforce however. Many states limit what liability can be waived by statute or in court decisions. Liability waivers are also strictly construed, meaning that anything not expressly stated in them will not be waived.[134]

Implied assumption of the risk occurs when Plaintiff voluntarily exposes himself or herself to a known, understood danger. For example, in *Murphy v. Steeplechase Amusement Co.*, the court held that the Plaintiff voluntarily assumed the risk of injuries resulting from falling when he went on an amusement ride called "The Flopper" that was designed to make its riders fall down.[135] The following case is another great example of implied assumption of the risk.

❖❖

Sutton v. Eastern New York Youth Soccer Ass'n, Inc.
8 A.D.3d 855 (3d Dept. 2004)

SPAIN, J.

While attending a soccer tournament in which his son was a participant, plaintiff D. James Sutton (hereinafter plaintiff) was struck by a soccer ball kicked by a 16-year-old boy practicing on one of the soccer fields between games. Thereafter, plaintiff and his wife, derivatively, commenced this personal injury action against organizations and teams sponsoring and/or participating in the tournament, as well as the boy who kicked the ball, seeking to recover damages for injuries he sustained to his knee as a result of the accident. Supreme Court granted summary judgment to all defendants, finding that plaintiff had assumed the risk of being struck by a soccer ball, and dismissed the complaint. On plaintiffs' appeal, we affirm.

According to plaintiff, May 30, 1999 was a sunny, exceedingly hot day and his son, a member of defendant Latham Circle Soccer Club, was participating in a Highland Soccer Club Tournament at Maalyck Park in the Town of Glenville, Schenectady County. Plaintiff attended as a spectator and had just finished watching his son's second game of the day from one of the sidelines when he walked to the end of the field to a tent which had been erected by his son's team some 30 to 40 yards behind the goal line in order to provide shade for the players while they were not engaged on the field. While walking past the field, plaintiff noticed six or seven players from defendant Guilderland Soccer Club

---

[131] *See* 57B Am. Jur. 2d Negligence § 761 (2017)

[132] *See* 57B Am. Jur. 2d Negligence § 761 (2017)

[133] *See Knight v. Jewett*, 834 P. 2d 696, 715 (Cal. 1992)

[134] *See Scott v. Pacific West Mt. Resort*, 834 P. 2d 6, 9 (Wash. 1992)

[135] *Murphy v. Steeplechase Amusement Co.*, 250 N.Y. 479, 166 N.E. 173 (N.Y. 1929)

on the field "hacking around" and warming up for the next game. Once under the tent, plaintiff was in the process of removing a sandwich from his son's cooler when he was struck in the chest and knocked off his feet by a soccer ball kicked from the field by a Guilderland player, defendant Ian Goss.

The first argument raised on appeal is that plaintiff was not a voluntary spectator of the soccer match at the point in time when he was injured; accordingly, plaintiffs argue, he cannot be found to have assumed the risk of injury (*see Hawkes v. Catatonk Golf Club*, 288 AD2d 528, 529–530 [2001]). In support of this contention, plaintiffs point to the fact that a game was not in progress on the field and that, when injured, he was standing some 30 to 40 yards away from the field of play. We are unpersuaded. The doctrine of assumption of risk can apply not only to participants of sporting events, but to spectators and bystanders who are not actively engaged in watching the event at the time of their injury (*see Sutfin v. Scheuer*, 145 AD2d 946, 947–948 [1988], *affd* 74 NY2d 697 [1989]). Indeed, "the spectator at a sporting event, no less than the participant, 'accepts the dangers that inhere in it so far as they are obvious and necessary, just as a fencer accepts the risk of a thrust by his antagonist or a spectator at a ball game the chance of contact with the ball. . . . The timorous may stay at home' " (*Akins v. Glens Falls City School Dist.*, 53 NY2d 325, 329 [1981], quoting *Murphy v. Steeplechase Amusement Co.*, 250 NY 479, 482–483 [1929] [Cardozo, Ch. J.]). Here, plaintiff admitted that he was at the tournament as a spectator and was aware that players were practicing on the field when he walked past them. Furthermore, although plaintiff's son's team had just finished a game, the tournament involved hundreds of players with teams playing at various times on at least five fields and plaintiff had been at the tournament all morning, surrounded by this activity. Under these circumstances, we find that plaintiff's presence at the tournament rendered him a voluntary spectator to the soccer play in progress throughout the day (*cf. Hawkes v. Catatonk Golf Club, supra* at 530).

Next, plaintiffs contend that the placement of the tent behind the goal line of one of the soccer fields enhanced the risk to spectators at the game, thereby undermining the argument that plaintiff assumed the risk of getting struck by a ball. Plaintiffs rely on evidence in the record that spectators at soccer games should, for their safety, observe the game from the sidelines and that standing behind the goal line increases the chance of being struck by a kicked ball. This Court has not previously had occasion to address directly the duty of care owed to spectators at a soccer match (*but see Honohan v. Turrone*, 297 AD2d 705 [2d Dept 2002]). Existing jurisprudence surrounding the duty owed to spectators at a baseball game, though not controlling given the differences in the games of baseball and soccer, is nonetheless helpful to our analysis.

In *Akins v. Glens Falls City School Dist.* (*supra*), for the first time, the Court of Appeals defined a circumscribed duty of care owed by the proprietor of a baseball field to its spectators. Taking into consideration the independence of spectators who might want to watch a game from an unprotected vantage point, and recognizing that "even after the exercise of reasonable care, some risk of being struck by a ball will continue to exist" (at 331), the Court held that "the proprietor of a ball park need only provide screening for the area of the field behind home plate where the danger of being struck by a ball is the greatest" (at 331). Recently, we followed and held that the municipal owner of a baseball park which has provided adequate space for spectators to view the game from behind the backstop did not owe a duty to install screens or netting above a fence running along the first baseline to protect spectators walking in the area between the fence and bathrooms against the risk of being struck by foul balls (*Wade-Keszey v. Town of Niskayuna*, 4 AD3d 732, 733–735 [2004]). We stated that "[w]e discern nothing in, its progeny or its antecedents to require ballpark owners to install protective screening to shield spectators on their way to bathrooms, concession stands and parking lots" (at 734).

Unlike baseball parks, outdoor soccer fields typically have no protective screening or fencing for spectators, presumably because the ball is larger and moves slower, enabling the spectator who observes a ball coming his or her way to avoid being struck. Indeed, plaintiffs do not suggest that, in the exercise of reasonable care, defendants had a duty to provide any protective measures along the sidelines (*see Honohan v. Turrone, supra* at 705). Instead, plaintiffs assert that defendants unreasonably enhanced the risk of injury to plaintiff by essentially inviting him to stand at the end of the field through their placement of the team tent. Although we agree that a factual question has been presented as to whether the risk of being struck by a soccer ball is enhanced when a spectator is standing behind the goal line, we find that question immaterial to the disposition of this action. There is no suggestion that there was not adequate room for the spectators to remain along the sidelines; in fact, plaintiff was seated along the sidelines prior to moving to the tent to get a sandwich (*see Wade-Keszey v. Town of Niskayuna, supra* at 403–404; *see also Davidoff v Metropolitan Baseball Club*, 61 NY2d 996, 998 [1984]). Accordingly, just as the owner of a baseball park is not responsible for the spectator who leaves his or her seat and walks through a potentially more hazardous zone to reach a bathroom or concession stand, thereby assuming the open and obvious risk of being hit by a ball, defendants here cannot be held responsible for the risk assumed by plaintiff when he, aware that players were active on the field, left the sidelines and stood in the tent positioned in the arguably more dangerous zone behind the goal line (*see Wade-Keszey v. Town of Niskayuna, supra* at 402).

We also reject plaintiffs' contention that the risk of being struck while some 40 yards away from a field upon which no formal game was in progress was not open and obvious. In the context of a sporting event, where the risks "are fully comprehended or perfectly obvious" a participant will be deemed to have consented to such risk (*Turcotte v. Fell*, 68 NY2d 432, 439 [1986]; *see Sutfin v. Scheuer*, 145 AD2d 946, 947 [1988], *supra*). As discussed, plaintiff had been in attendance for hours at a tournament where soccer games were almost continuously in progress and had actual knowledge that players were kicking the ball around on the field when he opted to move to the tent behind the goal line. Further, he was familiar with the game of soccer having admittedly been a frequent spectator of the game for over 14 years (*see Sutfin v Scheuer, supra* at 947). Under these circumstances, we hold that plaintiff should have appreciated the risk of being hit by an errant soccer ball when he opted to enter the tent in the area behind the goal (*see id; see also Honohan v. Turrone, supra* at 705).

Finally, while it is true that participants and spectators of sporting events are not deemed to have consented to reckless or intentional acts (*see Turcotte v. Fell, supra* at 439), contrary to plaintiffs' contentions, we find no record evidence that Goss acted recklessly when he misfired the ball in plaintiff's direction, inasmuch as it is questionable whether it is "even arguably negligent" for youngsters participating in sporting events to make an errant throw or kick (*Sutfin v. Scheuer, supra* at 948; *see Bierach v. Nichols*, 248 AD2d 916, 918 [1998]).

We have considered plaintiffs' remaining contentions and find them to be without merit.

Questions Presented

1) What analogies did the court draw to other sports and why?
2) What risks did the Plaintiff assume?
3) Why did the court hold that the Plaintiff assumed those risks?

❖❖

FIGURE 9.6   Elements of Negligence

Duty	Breach of Duty	Causation	Damages
Duty that applies depends on the situation and can include: • Reasonable Person • Reasonable Child • Reasonable Person with Physical Disabilities • Reasonable Professional • Negligence Per Se • Premises Liability Duties	• Provable by direct evidence • Provable by indirect evidence under the doctrine of *res ipsa loquitur*	Requires: • Cause in Fact ("But For" Causation): Defendant's actions actually cause the injury **and** • Proximate Causation: Defendant's injuries are the foreseeable result of Plaintiff's breach of duty	Types: • General: Damages that are normally associated with the injury. • Special: Damages that are not always associated with the injury. Must be monetary • Punitive: Damages designed to punish Defendant, not tied to Plaintiff's actual loss

VI. Strict Liability

Though intentional torts and negligence make up the great majority of torts, there is a third category of torts known as "strict liability" torts. Strict liability means that the tortfeasor is held to be at fault regardless of what the tortfeasor's state of mind was or how much care the tortfeasor exercised.[136] Intentional torts require that that the tortfeasor intend the specific consequences of his or her action. Negligence requires that the tortfeasor not take reasonable care. Strict liability torts impose liability on the tortfeasor for merely causing damage.

There are several kinds of torts that fall under the strict liability umbrella. Some pertain to animals. A person who owns a wild animal (like a bear) is strictly liable for the injuries caused by the dangerous propensities of the animal.[137] For example, if James owns a tiger that mauls Dante, James must pay for Dante's injuries even if he took the most stringent and extreme precautions possible. Similarly, the owner of livestock is strictly liable for most damage caused by the livestock on another's property.[138]

Anyone who carries on an abnormally dangerous activity is strictly liable for the injuries resulting from the things that make that activity dangerous.[139] For example, if James is using dynamite on his property and his dynamite causes damage to Dante's property, he will be strictly liable for that damage. However, if the explosion were to scare the neighbor's dog into a violent frenzy, causing the dog to maul Dante, James would not be strictly liable for Dante's injuries because they were caused by something that is not what makes dynamite abnormally dangerous.

There is also a category of torts known as products liability. Products liability deals with who is liable for a defectively manufactured or defectively designed product. Products liability torts are usually strict liability torts.[140] For example, imagine that a manufacturer creates a toy called

---

[136] *Strict Liability*, Black's Law Dictionary (10th Ed. 2014)

[137] Restatement (Second), Torts § 507 (1965)

[138] Restatement (Second), Torts § 504 (1965)

[139] Restatement (Second), Torts § 519 (1965)

[140] Restatement (Third) of Torts: Prod. Liab. § 1 (1998). Most courts now rely on the Restatement (Third) for products liability law.

"Raccoon Man," which becomes the Christmas season's hottest toy. Unfortunately, without management's knowledge, the wrong kind of paint is used on raccoon man. The paint turns out to be toxic and causes injury to several children. In that case, the manufacturer would likely be held strictly liable for the children's injuries even if it exercised reasonable care in the manufacture of "Raccoon Man." It would also be strictly liable if "Raccoon Man" had a faulty design that caused injury.

It is important to note that products liability cases can be brought against manufacturers, distributors, or retailers of the defective product.[141] This means that a retailer or wholesaler who had nothing to do with the error can be held strictly liable for the manufacturer's mistake, although it may be able to sue the manufacturer for damages after being sued by the purchaser if the defect truly rested with the manufacturer.[142]

SUMMARY

A tort is essentially a cause of action that provides a civil remedy for any wrongful conduct other than breach of contract. This means that there are many different kinds of torts. They generally fall into three categories.

There are intentional torts. These torts, like battery, assault, intentional infliction of emotional distress, and tortious interference with business relationships (to name a few of many) require that the tortfeasor intend the consequences of his or her actions. For example, false imprisonment requires that the tortfeasor intend to improperly confine someone to a limited area without his or her consent.

Negligence is the most commonly committed tort. It is incredibly broad and encompasses many different kinds of wrongful behavior. At its heart, negligence law essentially seeks to compensate those harmed by the unreasonable actions of others. Negligence is committed every day by well meaning people who do not desire the negative consequences of their actions.

Strict liability imposes liability regardless of the intent or reasonableness of the tortfeasor's actions. Though these torts are few in number compared to intentional torts and negligence-based torts, they are nonetheless important and can create liability even for people who act with the greatest degree of care.

Torts are litigated every day in the United States. Combined with breach of contract, they account for essentially all of the actions brought by private persons in court. Knowledge of their elements is especially essential to anyone engaging in business.

---

[141] Restatement (Third) of Torts: Prod. Liab. § 1, cmt. e (1998).
[142] *See* Restatement (Third) of Torts: Prod. Liab. § 1, cmt. e (1998).

CHAPTER

10

BUSINESS ENTITIES

LEARNING OUTCOMES

Upon completion of this chapter the student will be able to:

1   Understand the advantages and disadvantages of different types of common business entities.
2   Understand how common business entities are formed.
3   Understand how common business entities are taxed.
4   Understand when the owners of common business entities are liable for business losses.
5   Understand the rights of owners of common business entities.

KEY TERMS

board of directors
"C" corporation
closely-held corporation
corporation
double taxation
general partnership
limited liability company
limited liability partnership
limited liability limited partnership
limited partnership
member

nonprofit corporation
officer
operating agreement
pass through entity
partner
partnership
partnership agreement
"S" corporation
shareholder
sole proprietorship
ultra vires

I. Introduction

One of the most important choices a business owner makes is the legal form that his or her business takes. This chapter will discuss forms of the four most common business entities: (1) Partnerships, (2) Corporations, (3) Limited Liability Companies, and (4) Sole Proprietorships. Different types of business entities are best in different situations. For instance, obviously, a partnership cannot be formed if only one person owns the business.[1]

---

[1] UPA § 101(6) (1997).

When determining what form a business should take, owners should ask themselves the following questions:

1. How should the entity be formed?
2. Who should be in control of the entity?
3. Who should be liable for the entity's losses?
4. How should the entity's profits be distributed?
5. How should the entity be taxed?

II. Partnerships

The partnership is the most basic and oldest form of business association. Partnerships, then known as *societas*, first appeared in Europe in the Middle Ages. The concept eventually made its way into English mercantile courts, then English equity courts, and then English courts of law. The concept was not put into statute in England until the 1890s. This eventually spurred the creation of American partnership statutes.[2]

There are two main kinds of partnerships, general partnerships and limited partnerships. A general partnership is a partnership in which all the partners take part in the management of the business. A limited partnership is one in which only some of the partners are actively involved in the management of the business.

A. General Partnership

A general partnership (hereinafter "partnership") is any association of two or more people who agree to run a for-profit business together.[3] They are governed by state law. However, every state but Louisiana has adopted a version of the Uniform Partnership Act (UPA), a set of statutes recommended by academics and lawyers to all states. Since it was first proposed in 1914, the UPA has been amended several times. The 1997 version has been substantially adopted by 39 different states and the District of Columbia as of the time of this writing.[4] Because this version is used by the overwhelming majority of states, all references to the UPA in this chapter will be to the 1997 version unless otherwise stated.

The most important thing to remember about the UPA is that it is essentially a set of default rules to be used when the partnership agreement, which is the agreement between the partners to run the for-profit business, is incomplete.[5] For instance, imagine that Shreya and Angelica agree to start a business selling cattle. Their partnership agreement states that Shreya and Angelica agree to split the profits equally, but it does not state how losses will be shared. While the parties are allowed to agree to a set division of losses, they did not do so, which means the UPA rule regarding losses will apply (which will be discussed later in this chapter).

---

[2] *See* Callison & Sullivan, Partnership Law & Practice: General and Limited Partnerships § 1:2 (2016)

[3] *See* UPA § 101(6) (1997)

[4] National Conference of Commissioners on Uniform State Laws, Legislative Fact Sheet – Partnership Act (1997), available at http://uniformlaws.org/LegislativeFactSheet.aspx?title=Partnership%20Act%20(1997)%20(Last%20Amended%202013)

[5] UPA § 103(a) (1997) ("[R]elations among the partners and between the partners and the partnership are governed by the partnership agreement. To the extent the partnership agreement does not otherwise provide, this [Act] governs relations among the partners and between the partners and the partnership")

1. Formation

There is no set of magic words that creates a partnership. In most cases, a partnership does not even need to be in writing. A partnership can even be created unintentionally.[6] Because a partnership is merely two or more persons running a for-profit business together, there are only two requirements to start a partnership. First, two or more people must be partners. Second, those people must be running a for-profit business.

It is usually easy to determine whether two or more persons are involved. It is worth noting that a partner need not be a natural person. It can be a business entity like a corporation, LLC, or another partnership.[7]

The second element is usually the harder element to satisfy. This element immediately removes all nonprofit entities from consideration. A nonprofit entity that is run by two or more people, unless it intentionally takes another business form like a corporation, is known as an Nonprofit unincorporated association ("NUA").[8] NUAs are not partnerships.

Even if an entity is being run for-profit, a partnership still might not exist. To determine whether a partnership exists, courts will look to the circumstances of each particular case. Courts will typically look to a series of factors to determine if the parties intended to carry on a partnership. Courts will first look to see whether the parties are sharing profits and/or losses from the business. They will also look to see if parties share management power and ownership of the business as well as whether all the parties invested capital in the business.[9] All of these factors need not be present to create a partnership. Courts look to the unique circumstances of each case and weigh the factors to determine whether a partnership was formed.[10] Consider the following two scenarios:

SCENARIO A: Kristina and Adnan decide to buy a farm together. Each pays 50% of the purchase price. They agree that Kristina will get 60% of the profit and Adnan will get 40% of the profit and both agree that all business decisions must be unanimous.

SCENARIO B: Kristina buys a farm. She leases the farm to Adnan in exchange for 50% of his profit each year. Kristina has no say in the operation of the farm.

Scenario A clearly creates a partnership. Scenario B clearly does not. In both scenarios, they are splitting profits from the farm. In fact, in Scenario B, they are splitting the profits more equitably than in Scenario A (50/50 instead of 60/40). The difference is in the management of the farm and in who invested in the farm. In Scenario A, both parties invested in the farm and get to make decisions about it. However, in Scenario B, neither of those factors are present.

Usually, a court will presume profit sharing creates a partnership, but the UPA lists several types of profit sharing that are not included in this presumption. This list includes payments made to employees and independent contractors, payment of rent, payment of a debt (including debt paid in installments), annuities paid to surviving spouses of deceased partners, and the sale of a business' goodwill.[11]

Parties can even create a written agreement that states the parties are forming a partnership and still not create a partnership. Consider the following case.

---

[6] UPA § 202(a) (1997)

[7] UPA § 101(10)(1997)

[8] *See* Revised Uniform Unincorporated Nonprofit Association Act § 2(8) (2008)

[9] *See, e.g., Ingram v. Deere,* 288 S.W.3d 886 (2009)

[10] *See, e.g., Holmes v. Lerner,* 88 Cal.Rptr.2d 130, 138 (Cal. App. 1999)

[11] UPA § 202(c)(3) (1997).

❖❖

Fenwick v. Unemployment Compensation Commission
133 N.J.L. 295, 44 A.2d 172 (1945)

OPINION

DONGES, Justice.

This is an appeal from a judgment of the Supreme Court reversing a determination of the Unemployment Compensation Commission. The question involved is whether one Arline Chesire was, from January 1, 1939, to January 1, 1942, a partner or an employee of the prosecutor-respondent, John R. Fenwick, trading as United Beauty Shoppe. If she was an employee, then she was the eighth and deciding employee for the purpose of determining the status of the respondent for the year 1939 as an employer subject to the terms of the statute. N.J.S.A. 43:21–1 et seq. It is not the contention of the appellant commission that there was a fraudulent intent to avoid the act but the case is submitted as one of legal construction of the relation between Mrs. Chesire and the respondent.

Respondent Fenwick commenced operation of the beauty shop in Newark in November, 1936. In either 1937 or early 1938 he employed Mrs. Chesire as a cashier and reception clerk. Apparently her duties were to receive customers, take their orders for services to be performed by the operators, and collect the charges therefor. The shop did not work on an appointment basis but on a 'first come-first served' plan. Mrs. Chesire was employed at a salary of $15 per week and continued at that salary until December, 1938, when she requested an increase. Respondent expressed a willingness to pay higher wages if the income of the shop warranted it. Thereupon an agreement was entered into by the parties. This agreement was drawn by a lawyer who had offices nearby and provided:

1) That the parties associate themselves into a partnership to commence January 1, 1939.
2) That the business shall be the operation of the beauty shop.
3) That the name shall be United Beauty Shoppe.
4) That no capital investment shall be made by Mrs. Chesire.
5) That the control and management of the business shall be vested in Fenwick.
6) That Mrs. Chesire is to act as cashier and reception clerk at a salary of $15 per week and a bonus at the end of the year of 20% of the net profits, if the business warrants it.
7) That as between the partners Fenwick alone is to be liable for debts of the partnership.
8) That both parties shall devote all their time to the shop.
9) That the books are to be open for inspection of each party.
10) That the salary of Fenwick is to be $50 per week and at the end of the year he is to receive 80% of the profits.
11) That the partnership shall continue until either party gives ten days' notice of termination.

The relationship was terminated on January 1, 1942, at the request of Mrs. Chesire who desired to cease work and remain at home with her child.

The Commission held that the agreement was nothing more than an agreement fixing the compensation of an employee. The Supreme Court held that the parties were partners. The court apparently gave great weight to the fact that the parties had entered into the agreement, had called themselves partners, had designated the relationship one of partnership, and held that the surrounding circumstances, the conduct of the parties, etc., were not such as to overcome the force and effect to be given the declaration of the agreement.

Most of the cases wherein the courts have undertaken to determine whether or not a partnership existed, or whether certain persons were members of existing partnerships, have been those in which creditors have sought to impose liability upon alleged partners. In most cases, too, there have been no written partnership agreements to assist in fixing the status. However, the principles of law to be applied are the same. We think there can be no doubt of the right of the Commission, in the circumstances of this case, to raise the question and have a determination of the question of whether a partnership exists in law even though there is this agreement which is called a partnership agreement. We need not consider here what the effect of the agreement on the parties inter sese would be, but only its effect on the application of the unemployment compensation law.

There are several elements that the courts have taken into consideration in determining the exercise or non-existence of the partnership relation. The first element is that of the intention of the parties and here, of course, the agreement itself is evidential although not conclusive. Light on the intent of the parties is shed by the testimony of the respondent as follows:

'Q. When was she first hired by you?

A. That is what I said, either 1937 or 1938, I can't say definitely what it was without looking it up: I couldn't give you the exact date. And she felt as though she was not getting enough money. Well, we were doing a lot of business, but the prices were very low at the time; it was in the depression and you had to bring your prices down to get business. And I told her I did not want to lose her because she was a very very good girl to me in that office, she was what I needed. I told her I couldn't see where I could afford to give her any more. And I did not want to lose her. So it went back and forth, back and forth. Finally I said, 'I will tell you what I will do: If we make any more money I will pay you more, if you want to go along on that agreement.' And that is where the partnership thing came in; that is how we started to be on the partnership concern at that time; that is when that was all discussed and arranged.'

That statement is persuasive that the intention of the parties was to enter into an agreement that would provide a possibility of increase of compensation to Mrs. Chesire and at the same time protect Fenwick from being obliged to pay such increase unless business warranted it. The whole thing was prompted and instigated by the demand of the employee for an increase. The employer valued her services and did not wish to lose her. He wished to retain her in the exact same capacity as before but was afraid to promise a straight increase for fear it might mean loss to him. There is no suggestion that anything but the financial relation between the parties, with respect to compensation for services, was the thing they had in mind. After January 1st, 1939, the date the alleged partnership became effective, the operation of the business continued as before. Mrs. Chesire continued to serve in precisely the same capacity as before and Fenwick continued to have complete control of the management of the business. It would seem that, as far as the intention of the parties is concerned, the effect of the statements in the agreement has been met and overcome by the sworn testimony of Fenwick and by the conduct of the parties.

Another element of partnership is the right to share in profits and clearly that right existed in this case. However, not every agreement that gives the right to share in profits is, for all purposes, a partnership agreement. Wild v. Davenport, 48 N.J.L. 129, 132, 7 A. 295, 57 Am.Rep. 552; Cornell v. Redrow, 60 N.J.Eq. 251, 47 A. 56. Therefore, this point is not conclusive.

Another factor is the obligation to share in losses, and this is entirely absent in this case because the agreement provides that Mrs. Chesire is not to share in the losses.

Another is the ownership and control of the partnership property and business. Fenwick contributed all the capital and Mrs. Chesire had no right to share in capital upon dissolution. He likewise reserved to himself control.

The next is community of power in administration, and the reservation in the agreement of the exclusive control of the management of the business in Fenwick excludes this element so far as Mrs. Chesire is concerned. In Wild v. Davenport, supra, Mr. Justice Depue, speaking for this court, said [48 N.J.L. 129, 7 A. 297]:

'In Voorhees v. Jones [29 N.J.L. 270], the decision that a servant or agent who had a share of profits simply as compensation for services was neither a partner, nor liable for partnership debts, was placed by Chief Justice Whelpley on the ground that such a person had no control over the operation of the firm, and could not direct its investments, nor prevent the contracting of debts; in other words, had none of the prerogatives of a principal in the management and control of the business.'

The law as stated in these opinions has been followed by our courts.

Another element is the language in the agreement, and although the parties call themselves partners and the business a partnership, the language used excludes Mrs. Chesire from most of the ordinary rights of a partner.

The conduct of the parties toward third persons is also an element to be considered and the conduct of the parties here does not support a finding that they were partners. They did file partnership income tax returns and held themselves out as partners to the Unemployment Compensation Commission, and Fenwick in his New York state income tax return reported that his income came from the partnership. But to no one else did they hold themselves out as partners. They did not inform the persons they purchased materials from, although Fenwick says this was not necessary since all purchases were for cash and they neither sought nor gave credit. The right to use the trade name had apparently come to Fenwick from one Florence Meola, by lease, and the partnership was given that name by Fenwick. There is no evidence that the trade name was ever registered as that of the partnership.

Another element is the rights of the parties on dissolution and apparently in this case the result of the dissolution, as far as Mrs. Chesire is concerned, was exactly the same as if she had quit an employment. She ceased to work and ceased to receive compensation and everything reverted to the condition it was in prior to 1939, except that Fenwick carried on with a new receptionist.

Under all these circumstances, giving due effect to the written agreement and bearing in mind that the burden of establishing a partnership is upon the one who alleges it to exist, Cornell v. Redrow, 60 N.J.Eq. 251, 47 A. 56, we think that the partnership has not been established, and that the agreement between these parties, in legal effect, was nothing more than one to provide a method of compensating the girl for the work she had been performing as an employee. She had no authority or control in operating the business, she was not subject to losses, she was not held out as a partner. She got nothing by the agreement but a new scale of wages.

The question as presented to this court is one of law and not one of fact. The facts are really not in dispute. The contest concerns the inferences of law to be drawn from the facts as found by the Supreme Court.

The Uniform Partnership Act defines a partnership as an association of 'two or more persons to carry on as co-owners a business for profit.' N.J.S.A. 42:1–6. Essentially the element of co-ownership is lacking in this case. The agreement was one to share the profits resulting from a business owned by Fenwick. He contributed all the capital, managed the business and took over all the assets on dissolution. Ownership was conclusively shown to be in him.

The Act further provides that sharing of profits is prima facie evidence of partnership but 'no such inference shall be drawn if such profits were received in payment * * * as wages of an employee.' R.S. 42:1–7, N.J.S.A., and it seems that is the legal inference to be drawn from the factual situation here.

The judgment is reversed.

Questions Presented

1) What factors did the court believe weighed in favor of partnership?
2) What factors did the court believe weighed against partnership?
3) What could the parties have done to create a partnership in this case?

❖❖

2. Partnership Control

A partnership is controlled by its partners. As discussed above, the partnership is normally controlled in the manner specified by the partnership agreement. However, wherever the partnership agreement is silent, the rules of the UPA apply.[12]

Where the partnership agreement is silent, the UPA provides that every partner has an equal say in the management of the partnership.[13] This means that, for ordinary decisions, each partner has one vote.[14] A partner's voting share is not affected by what percentage of the profit share the partner is entitled to or by how much capital a partner invests in the partnership.

For example, imagine that Shreya, Angelica, Damon, and Tucker form a partnership to sell widgets. The partnership agreement provides that Shreya, Angelica, and Damon are each entitled to 30% of the profits and that each is to contribute $300 to start the partnership. The partnership agreement also provides that Tucker is entitled to 10% of the profit and that he is to contribute $100 to start the partnership. The agreement is silent on decision-making power. At a meeting of the partners, they originally unanimously agree to set the price of widgets at $9. At a later meeting, Shreya and Angelica vote to set the price of widgets at $10. Damon and Tucker vote against setting the price of widgets at $10.

In the above example, the price of widgets will not change. Even though Shreya and Angelica receive a combined 60% of the profit and contributed 60% of the startup capital, because the agreement is silent as to voting, the UPA's default rule takes effect, which gives each partner one vote regardless of the size of his or her partnership interest and requires a majority of partners to make a decision. Because a majority requires *more* than 50% of the partners, 2 partners (50%) is not enough to make a decision in this case.

There are, however, some circumstances in which the UPA will require unanimous consent of the partners. When a decision is outside the ordinary course of business, a decision must be

---

[12] UPA § 103(a) (1997)
[13] UPA § 401(f) (1997)
[14] UPA § 401(j) (1997)

made unanimously.[15] The following decisions almost always require unanimous consent under the UPA:

1. Admitting a new partner to the business[16]
2. Changing the nature of the partnership's business
3. Engaging in new lines of business
4. Changing the capital structure of the partnership
5. Amending the partnership agreement
6. Confessing a judgment (allowing a judgment to be entered against the partnership without legal proceedings)
7. Disposing of the goodwill of the partnership
8. Performing an act making it impossible to do partnership business
9. Assigning partnership interests to a trust for the benefit of creditors[17]

Each partner is also an agent of the partnership. This means that, to the outside world, the partner may have the apparent authority to bind the partnership in contract even if the partner exceeds his or her authority.[18] If a partner enters into a contract on behalf of the partnership, even if the partner does not have the authority to do so, the partnership will be bound to it unless the other party to the contract knew or should have known the partner lacked authority or the matter is outside the ordinary course of business (the type of matter requiring unanimous consent), or, in the case of the sale of partnership real estate, a statement of partnership authority is filed with the appropriate state or municipal office.[19]

3. Partnership Losses

The major drawback to forming a partnership is how losses are allocated. Unlike corporations and LLCs, which will be discussed later in this chapter, each partner can be held personally liable for the losses and debts of a partnership incurred in the ordinary course of business or with the partnership's authority.[20] This means that a partner's personal assets, like his or her house and personal bank accounts, can be taken involuntarily by creditors using the judicial process to satisfy debts of the partnership.[21] Consider the following example.

Imagine that Shreya, Angelica, Damon, and Tucker form a partnership to sell widgets. The partnership agreement provides that Shreya, Angelica, and Damon are each entitled to 30% of the profits and that each is to contribute $300 to start the partnership. The partnership agreement also provides that Tucker is entitled to 10% of the profit and that he is to contribute $100 to start the partnership. Shreya is given authority by the other partners to enter into contracts to buy widgets. Shreya buys widgets from American Pride, Inc. for $10,000 to be paid in a year. The widgets turn out not to be as popular as Shreya thought and are only sold for $1,000.

---

[15] UPA § 401(j) (1997)

[16] UPA § 401(i) (1997)

[17] The original UPA proposed in 1914 contained a list in Section 9 of actions that required unanimous consent. The 1997 UPA has no such list to allow more flexibility but states in its official comments that most of these likely still require unanimous consent to bind the partnership. *See* UPA § 301, cmt. 4 (1997).

[18] For a more detailed discussion of apparent authority, see Section IV of Chapter 8.

[19] UPA §§ 301, 303 (1997)

[20] UPA §§ 305(a), 306(a) (1997)

[21] UPA § 306(a) (1997)

If American Pride, Inc. is not paid, it has several options. In most states, partners are jointly and severally liable for the debts of the partnerships.[22] This means that American Pride, Inc. can sue any combination of the partners as well as the partnership. It could choose to sue only Tucker, even though he is a minority partner, if it so chooses. Usually, however, creditors must first seek the assets from the partnership before suing the partners.[23] Further, partners who joined the partnership after the conduct giving rise to the lawsuit occurred cannot be held liable for the debts the partnership incurred before they joined the partnership.[24]

A partner who pays more than his or her share of the debt has the right to be reimbursed by the partnership or other partners.[25] Each partner is liable for the percentage of losses it agreed to in the partnership agreement. If the agreement makes no provision for loss sharing, losses are shared in the same proportion as profits are shared.[26] Consider the following example.

Shreya, Angelica, Damon, and Tucker form a partnership to sell widgets. The partnership agreement provides that Shreya, Angelica, and Damon are each entitled to 30% of the profits and that each is to contribute $300 to start the partnership. The partnership agreement also provides that Tucker is entitled to 10% of the profit and that he is to contribute $100 to start the partnership.

In this example, because the partnership agreement does not state how losses are to be shared, they are shared in the same percentage as profits, which is 30% each to Shreya, Angelica, and Damon and 10% to Tucker.

4. Partnership Profits and Property

If the partnership agreement is silent as to profits, each partner will receive an equal share of the profits.[27]

A partner, however, is not usually entitled to compensation for services performed for the partnership, such as a salary, unless the partners otherwise agree.[28] The only exception to this rule is that a partner is entitled to compensation for services performed in the winding down of the partnership when it is dissolved.[29]

Every partner also has a right to inspect the partnership books and records as well as all the information pertaining to the business.[30] Each partner is also entitled to an accounting of partnership assets during the term of the partnership and upon dissolution.[31]

A partner also has the right to use partnership property for partnership purposes.[32] However, a partner does not have the right to dispose of or sell partnership property without authorization from the partnership.[33] A partner may also not sell his or her management rights in the

---

[22] UPA § 306(a) (1997)
[23] UPA § 307(d) (1997)
[24] UPA § 306(b) (1997)
[25] UPA § 401(c), cmt. 4 (1997)
[26] UPA § 401(b) (1997)
[27] UPA § 401(b) (1997)
[28] UPA § 401(h) (1997).
[29] UPA § 401(h) (1997).
[30] UPA §§ 401(h)(2)-(3) (1997)
[31] UPA § 405(b) (1997)
[32] UPA § 401(g) (1997)
[33] UPA § 501 (1997)

partnership.[34] A partner may only transfer his or her right to profits and distributions from the partnership.[35]

5. Partnership Taxation

Partnerships have a relatively advantageous tax structure. Though a partnership is usually treated as a separate business entity from its individual owners,[36] it is considered a *pass through* entity for tax purposes.[37] A pass through entity is a business organization that is not taxed. The entity's profits are passed through to its owners who are then taxed at the income tax rate on their earnings from the partnership.

Legal Definition

Pass through entity – a business entity that is not directly taxed as an entity but whose owners pay taxes on their individual earnings from the entity.

---

6. Partnership Duties

Every partner owes a duty of care and a duty of loyalty to the partnership.[38] These duties cannot be eliminated by the partnership agreement.[39]

The duty of care prohibits each partner from acting grossly negligently or recklessly. It also prohibits a partner from intentionally engaging in misconduct and knowingly violating the law during the course of partnership business.[40]

The duty of loyalty prohibits three things. It prohibits partners from competing against the partnership (a partner of a bakery cannot own a similar bakery in the same mini-mall).[41] A partner also cannot represent someone having an interest adverse to the partnership (a partner cannot represent the interests of a partnership creditor for example).[42] Finally, a partner must hold all partnership property in trust and cannot usurp the opportunities of the partnership. For example, if a partner learns of an opportunity to buy a property through partnership business, if the partnership would buy the house, the partner cannot buy it for himself or herself.[43]

7. Partnership Dissociation and Dissolution

Dissociation is the process by which a partner leaves the partnership. Dissolution is the process by which a partnership ends. Once a partnership is dissolved, its affairs must be "wound up," which means that the partnership continues until all of its outstanding business at the time of dissolution is completed.

---

[34] UPA § 502, cmt. (1997)
[35] UPA § 502 (1997)
[36] UPA § 201 (1997)
[37] *See* 26 U.S.C. § 701
[38] UPA § 404(a) (1997)
[39] UPA § 103(b) (1997)
[40] UPA § 404(c) (1997)
[41] UPA § 404(b)(3) (1997)
[42] UPA § 404(b)(2) (1997)
[43] UPA § 404(b)(1) (1997)

a. Dissociation of a Partner

Under the original UPA proposed in 1914, whenever a partner was dissociated from a partnership, the partnership had to be dissolved.[44] The revised Uniform Partnership Act that is in effect in the vast majority of states has a different rule. A partnership is usually allowed to continue once a partner leaves.[45] However, there are some circumstances in which a partnership must be dissolved if a partner is dissociated.

It is also important to know whether a partner wrongfully dissociates. Wrongful dissociation is a partner's removal from the partnership because of a violation of the partnership agreement, because of a court order, because the partner entered bankruptcy, or because the partner, if it is a business entity like an LLC or corporation, dissolved.[46] A partner who wrongfully dissociates is liable to the partnership for any damages resulting from the dissociation, including the cost to replace the partner's expertise and experience.[47]

Any partner may choose to dissociate from the partnership voluntarily.[48] If a partner voluntarily dissociates from an at-will partnership (one without a definite term or specific undertaking), the partnership must dissolve. However, the partnership need not wind up its affairs and can continue doing business by unanimous vote of the partners (including the dissociating partner) after the partner's withdrawal.[49] The consent of the dissociating partner to continue business is not required if that partner wrongfully dissociated.[50]

The partnership agreement may also provide for the dissociation of partners. If any event specified in the partnership agreement requiring a partner's dissociation occurs, that partner will be dissociated.[51]

In some circumstances, a partner may be dissociated by a unanimous vote of the other partners. A unanimous vote of other partners will dissociate a partner if it is no longer lawful to do business with that partner, a partner transfers all or nearly all of his or her interest in the partnership, or the dissociated partner is a business entity that has been dissolved.[52]

Other partners may also get a court order to remove a partner if that partner has acted wrongfully. This includes material (significant) breaches of the duties of loyalty and care and any conduct that negatively materially affected the business or makes it impracticable to do business with that partner.[53]

A partner will also be automatically dissociated in the event of that partner's death, financial insolvency (through bankruptcy, assigning his or her interest for the benefit of creditors, or entering receivership), physical incapacity, or mental incapacity.[54] In the event the partnership was for a specific, limited period of time or just for a specific, particular reason when a partner is dissociated because of one of these events, the partnership may be dissolved by a majority vote of the remaining partners.

---

[44] *See* UPA § 31 (1914); *See also* UPA § 601, cmt. 1 (1997).

[45] *See* UPA § 601, cmt. 1 (1997).

[46] *See* UPA § 602 (1997)

[47] *See* UPA § 602(c), cmt. 3 (1997).

[48] UPA § 601(1) (1997).

[49] UPA § 802(b) (1997)

[50] UPA § 802(b) (1997)

[51] UPA § 601(2)-(3) (1997)

[52] UPA § 601(4) (1997)

[53] UPA § 601(5) (1997)

[54] UPA § 601(6)-(7) (1997).

Once dissociation occurs, the dissociated partner loses his or her right to manage the business.[55] The dissociated partner's duty of loyalty is also terminated, though his or her duty of care remains in effect with respect to pre-dissociation events.[56]

Following dissociation, a partner's share must also be bought out. The buyout price is based on what the partner would have received had the business been wound up on the day of dissociation unless otherwise agreed to beforehand (which is a fairly common practice).[57]

A dissociated partner also remains liable for any actions taken by the partnership before dissociation.[58] The dissociated partner may also be held liable for two years after dissociation for actions taken by the partnership if the debt arose from a creditor who reasonably believed that the partner had not been dissociated.[59] A partner can limit his or her exposure to liability to 90 days by filing a statement of dissociation with the appropriate state or municipal office.[60]

Partnerships should also file a statement of dissociation with the appropriate state or municipal offices and make creditors and customers aware that a partner was dissociated. A dissociated partner can have apparent authority to enter into transactions on behalf of the partnership for two years following dissociation if the creditor or customer reasonably does not know that the partner was dissociated.[61] While the partnership has the right to sue the dissociated partner for damages if this occurs, it is far better to stop the problem before it occurs.

b. Partnership Dissolution

Dissolution is the termination of the partnership's existence. It is essentially its death. Following dissolution, the partnership is no longer allowed to enter into new business and must be wound up.[62] A partnership is wound up by using the partnership assets to pay the partnership's debts. If the partnership's assets are not sufficient to pay back the partnership's debts, the partners must pay the debts in the method specified by the operating agreement. If there is no operating agreement, the losses will be shared in the same proportion as profits are shared. If there are assets left after dissolution, the assets are paid to the partners.[63]

A partnership need not wind up its affairs and can continue doing business by unanimous vote of the partners if the partnership is dissolved.[64] The consent of a dissociating partner to continue business is not required if that partner wrongfully dissociated.[65]

The UPA lays out the events that require dissolution of a partnership. If the partnership is at will, it must be dissolved if a partner voluntarily dissociates from the partnership.[66]

If the partnership is for a specific, limited period of time or just for a specific, particular reason, the partnership will be dissolved following a unanimous vote of the partners in the event of a

---

[55] UPA § 603(b)(1) (1997)
[56] UPA § 603(b)(2)-(3) (1997)
[57] UPA § 701(a) (1997)
[58] UPA § 703(a) (1997)
[59] UPA § 703(b) (1997)
[60] UPA § 704(c) (1997)
[61] UPA § 702(a) (1997)
[62] UPA § 602(a) (1997)
[63] *See* UPA § 807 (1997)
[64] UPA § 801(1) (1997)
[65] UPA § 802(b) (1997)
[66] UPA § 801(1) (1997)

TABLE 10.1   Partnership Dissolution

Event	Dissolution Required?
Voluntary Withdrawal of a partner	Yes if a partnership at will (but partners may unanimously vote not to wind up the business and continue the entity after dissolution. This includes the dissociated partner unless that partner wrongfully dissociated)
Manner specified by the partnership agreement	No
Unanimous vote +	No
(a) no longer lawful to do business with that partner, (b) a partner transfers all or nearly all of his or her interest in the partnership, **or** (c) the dissociated partner is a business entity that has been dissolved	
Court order for	No
(a) material breach of duty of care or loyalty, (b) conduct negatively affecting the partnership, **or** (c) conduct making it impracticable to do business with that partner	
Partner's Death	Only if
	(a) The partnership is for a specific period of time or specific undertaking **and** (b) a majority of partners vote to dissolve
Partner's Mental or Physical Incapacity	Only if
	(a) The partnership is for a specific period of time or specific undertaking **and** (b) a majority of partners vote to dissolve
Financial Insolvency of a partner	Only if
	(a) The partnership is for a specific period of time or specific undertaking **and** (b) a majority of partners vote to dissolve

partner's death, financial insolvency (through bankruptcy, assigning his or her interest for the benefit of creditors, or entering receivership), physical incapacity, or mental incapacity.[67]

A partnership's dissolution can also be controlled by the partnership agreement. A partnership will be dissolved if an event specified by the partnership agreement that requires dissolution occurs.[68]

---

[67] UPA § 801(2) (1997).
[68] UPA § 801(3) (1997)

A partnership will dissolve if its business becomes illegal unless the partnership can find a legal purpose for its partnership within 90 days of the partnership's activities becoming illegal.[69]

A partnership can be dissolved by court order in certain circumstances as well. The court may order a partnership to dissolve upon application by a partner if it finds that the partnership's economic purpose has been frustrated (such as when the partnership cannot make profit anymore), another partner has engaged in wrongful conduct towards the partnership or other partners, or business can no longer be carried on in accordance with the partnership agreement.[70]

TABLE 10.2   Reasons for Partnership Dissolution

Reasons for Dissolution
Voluntary dissociation of a partner (if an at-will partnership)
Death, incapacity, or insolvency of a partner + majority vote of the partners (if a partnership for a specific time or purpose)
Event specified in a partnership Agreement
Illegality of partnership business (unless cured in 90 days)
Court order if economic purpose is frustrated, a partner acts wrongfully, or the partnership agreement cannot be practicably performed anymore

B. Limited Liability Partnership

The limited liability partnership (LLP) is a relatively new business entity. First established in the 1990's, the limited liability partnership is an attempt by states to create a kind of partnership that provides the tax advantages of a general partnership while reducing the partners' personal liability. LLPs are also governed by the UPA, and most of the same rules apply to general partnerships and LLPs.

Unlike a general partnership, an LLP cannot be created by accident. It must be formed by filing the appropriate paperwork with the secretary of state for the state it wishes to be created in.[71] A general partnership also can be converted to an LLP by amending the partnership agreement and filing the appropriate paperwork with the state.[72]

An LLP allows its partners to avoid personal liability for the debts of the LLP.[73] That is, partners' personal assets cannot be reached by the LLPs creditors. However, there is an important exception in most state laws that is not in the UPA. A person who is a professional, such as a doctor, attorney, or accountant, can still be sued for his or her own negligence even if the professional was working on behalf of the LLP. However, many states allow innocent partners to avoid personal liability for the negligent act of other partners.[74] This is especially important because many LLPs are run by professionals.

---

[69] UPA § 801(4) (1997)
[70] UPA § 801(5) (1997)
[71] UPA § 1001(c) (1997)
[72] UPA § 1001(c) (1997)
[73] UPA § 306(c) (1997)
[74] *See, e.g.,* Del. Code tit. 6 § 15-306(b)

C. Limited Partnership

A limited partnership is a partnership in which only some partners manage the partnership and in which only some of the partners are liable for the debts of the partnership. These kinds of partnerships did not exist at common law but are now created by statute in some form in every state.[75]

State laws vary regarding limited partnerships. Most states have some version of the Uniform Limited Partnership Act (ULPA), but there have been several significant revisions to the act. Only some states have adopted these revisions.[76] The most current version of the ULPA was proposed in 2001, but it has only been adopted in 21 states and Washington, D.C. as of the time of this writing.[77]

The major differences between a limited partnership and a general partnership are in formation, management structure, and liability. A limited partnership cannot be formed accidentally. It can only be formed by filing a certificate of limited partnership with the appropriate state office (usually the secretary of state).[78] It is vital that all statutory requirements for forming a limited partnership be met. If they are not, a limited partnership could potentially not be formed.[79]

Every limited partnership must have at last one general partner and one limited partner. The general partner has the right and responsibility to manage the limited partnership. The limited partner has no management rights but is otherwise entitled to partnership rights.[80] However, a limited partner has limited liability. That is, except for the limited partner's capital contribution, a limited partner cannot be held personally liable for the limited partnership's debts.[81]

D. Limited Liability Limited Partnership

Many states provide for limited liability limited partnerships (LLLPs). An LLLP is a hybrid between a limited partnership and a limited liability partnership. An LLLP is essentially just a limited partnership in which both the general and limited partners are not personally liable for the debts of the partnership.[82]

III. Corporations

The modern corporation is a fairly recent development in the Anglo-American legal system. In England, for example, corporations were originally chartered only by special acts of a legislature or the crown for special purposes. For instance, many of England's overseas colonies were founded by corporations chartered for that purpose. For instance, King James I chartered the "Virginia Company of London" to found colonial settlements in North America, including the first permanent British settlement in North America at Jamestown, Virginia.[83]

---

[75] *See* 59A Am. Jur. 2d Partnership § 762 (2017)
[76] *See* 59A Am. Jur. 2d Partnership § 762 (2017)
[77] National Conference of Commissioners on Uniform State Laws, Legislative Fact Sheet – Limited Partnership Act (2001), available at http://www.uniformlaws.org/LegislativeFactSheet.aspx?title=Limited%20Partnership%20Act%20(2001)%20(Last%20Amended%202013)
[78] *See* 59A Am. Jur. 2d Partnership § 774 (2017)
[79] *See, e.g., Miller v. Department of Revenue, State of Oregon,* 958 P.2d 833 (1998)
[80] *See* 59A Am. Jur. 2d Partnership § 820 (2017)
[81] *See Pear v. Grand Forks Motel Associates,* 553 N.W.2d 774 (N.D. 1996).
[82] *See, e.g.,* N.D. Cent. Code § 45-23-01 et seq. (2017).
[83] Colossus: How the Corporation Changed America, p. 1 (Jack Beatty ed., 2001).

The corporation as we know it, the one that is a common business entity that almost anyone can form, did not begin to appear in America until the early nineteenth century.[84] Much like those early corporations, however, modern corporations technically still require special permission from the state to come into existence. Influential nineteenth-century Chief Justice John Marshall described the nature of the corporation as follows:

> *A corporation is an artificial being, invisible, intangible, and existing only in contemplation of law. Being the mere creature of law, it possesses only those properties which the charter of creation confers upon it, either expressly, or as incidental to its very existence. These are such as are supposed best calculated to effect the object for which it was created.*[85]

Essentially, he described the corporation as a state-created business entity that can only be formed with the state's permission and only has the power to perform acts allowed by the state. Keep this in mind while reading the rest of this section. Because corporations are state creatures subject to state restriction, every state has its own version of corporate laws. The basic tenets of corporate law remain the same throughout the states, but each state has its own unique provisions.

A. Corporate Formation

As discussed above, a corporation is formed by an act of the state. In the modern world, legislatures do not often create corporations by special act. Instead, they have passed general acts allowing parties to apply to form a corporation,[86] which are then approved by a government agency other than the legislature (such as the state's secretary of state).[87] A majority of states base their general incorporation laws on the Revised Model Business Corporation Act, but every state has its own unique corporate laws.

1. Incorporators

Anyone who is a part of forming the corporation is known as an incorporator.[88] The incorporator's primary duty is to file the necessary paperwork with the secretary of state to create the corporation. It does not need to be a shareholder (owner), corporate officer, or member of the board of directors. Requirements vary from state to state. For example, in some states, a person must be 21 years old to be an incorporator, but, in most states, a person need only be 18 years old to be an incorporator.[89] In many states, a business entity like a corporation or partnership may serve as an incorporator.[90] However, in some states, only a natural person may be an incorporator.[91]

2. What the Incorporator Must File

An incorporator's main duty is to file and sign the articles of incorporation. The articles of incorporation is essentially the incorporator's application to the state to create a corporation. It must

---

[84] Colossus: How the Corporation Changed America, p. 1 (Jack Beatty ed. 2001).
[85] *Dartmouth College v. Woodward,* 4 Wheat. 518, 636 (1819).
[86] *See* 18A Am. Jur. 2d Corporations § 152 (2017)
[87] *See, e.g.,* Ark. Code § 4-26-201
[88] Black's Law Dictionary, *Incorporator* (9th Ed.)
[89] *See* Ark. Code § 4-26-201; Col. Rev. Stat. § 7-102-101
[90] *See, e.g.,* Cal. Corp. Code § 200
[91] *See, e.g.,* Minn. Stat. § 336.1-101

include the corporation's proposed name (it cannot be the same or deceptively similar to a pre-existing corporation's name), a statement of the nature and purpose of the corporation, the duration of the corporation, the capital structure of the corporation, and the corporation's management structure.

a. Statement of the Nature and Purpose of the Corporation

Every corporation must have a purpose. Most corporations are now "general purpose corporations." That is, the corporation's statement of purpose allows the organization to do anything that is lawful.[92] The statement of purpose reads something like this, "This corporation is formed to engage in any lawful act or activity for which corporations may be formed under the laws of this state."

However, organizations may also be formed for special and particular purposes. For instance, a corporation may be organized to "buy and sell commodities." Many corporations also choose to exist only for nonprofit purposes. Most nonprofit corporations, which are often called "501(c)(3)s" (the section of the tax code that governs them), are usually organized for charitable or similar purposes.[93]

Some states create certain kinds of corporations that can only be organized for special purposes. For instance, many states only allow banks to organize as corporations to perform banking activities and only allow insurance companies to organize to perform insurance-related activities.[94]

Many states also allow for a specialty purpose corporation called a professional corporation. A professional corporation is one organized specifically to perform a particular professional service like accounting, medical, or legal services.[95]

b. Duration of the Corporation

A corporation usually lasts for an indefinite amount of time from when it is incorporated.[96] However, a corporation may choose to exist for a shorter period of time in its articles of incorporation if it so desires or a statute so requires.

c. Capital Structure of a Corporation

A corporation's owners are known as shareholders. A share, also known as a stock, is an ownership interest in the corporation. Most states require that the articles of incorporation state how many shares and what types of shares of a corporation will exist.[97] A corporation is free to create as many classes and kinds of shares as it likes. For instance, some shares may include the right to vote on certain company matters and the right to dividends. Some shares may be nonvoting shares but carry the right to receive a dividend.

---

[92] *See* 18A Am. Jur. 2d Corporations § 159 (2017)
[93] *See* 26 U.S.C. § 501(c)(3)
[94] *See, e.g.* Conn. Gen. Stat. § 33-645.
[95] *See, e.g.* Cal. Corp. Code § 13400 *et seq.*
[96] *See* 18A Am. Jur. 2d Corporations § 71 (2017)
[97] *See, e.g.,* Mo. Rev. Stat. § 351-055

d. Management Structure of the Corporation

Often times, the articles of incorporation will provide the corporation's management structure. A corporation is managed differently than a partnership. Unlike a partnership, a corporation is not managed directly by its owners (the shareholders). Rather, management is vested in a board of directors. The board of directors then delegates its power to run the day to day operations of the corporation to a team of corporate officers like a Chief Executive Officer and Chief Operating Officer. Officers are not appointed by the articles of incorporation, but the articles of incorporation can provide guidance regarding their election.

e. First Organizational Meeting

Once the corporation's articles of incorporation is approved by the state, the state will issue a certificate of incorporation. Following this, the organization holds its first meeting, known as the first organizational meeting.

The first order of business at these meetings is usually to adopt the corporation's bylaws, which are essentially the corporation's internal rules. They usually specify who can be a shareholder of the corporation, the voting procedures for shareholders, rules for the board of directors, and how often the shareholders and board of directors must meet. A board of directors is then elected, and stock is issued.[98]

f. Defective Incorporation

State laws lay out very specific ways to create a corporation. When a corporation successfully completes all the statutory requirements of incorporation, it is known as a *de jure* corporation, and its existence cannot be attacked by someone the corporation did business with or the state.[99] However, because corporations are state-created creatures, mistakes made in the incorporation process can have very serious consequences. As will be discussed later in the chapter, a corporation's shareholders, board of directors, and officers are not normally liable for the losses of the corporation personally, which means that their personal assets cannot be taken to satisfy corporate debts. Under the *de facto* corporation doctrine, there are only limited protections for corporations that failed to properly comply with corporate formation statutes.

A *de facto* corporation is a defectively formed organization that meets certain requirements. To invoke the doctrine, the defectively formed corporation must show that (1) there was a valid statute

---

[98] Revised Model Business Corporations Act § 2.05
[99] *Robertson v. Levy,* 197 A.2d 443, 445 (D.C. Cir. 1964) ("A de jure corporation is not subject to direct or collateral attack either by the state in a quo warranto proceeding or by any other person.")

the corporation could have been organized under, (2) an attempt to incorporate was made under that statute, and (3) there was an attempt to do business under that corporate name. If this doctrine is applied, only the state may attempt to attack the corporation's existence, not third parties who attempted to do business with the defective corporation.[100] This doctrine does not exist in every jurisdiction however.[101]

Similar to the doctrine of *de facto* corporation, the doctrine of corporation by estoppel can prevent a party who seeks to deny the existence of a defectively formed corporation from doing so if justice so requires. The situations in which this doctrine arises are heavily varied and usually involve a person trying to escape liability because the corporation it made a contract with was defectively formed. These doctrines also do not exist in every state.[102]

The following case illustrates the importance of forming a corporation properly. It is from a jurisdiction that does not recognize the doctrines of *de facto* or estoppel corporations.

❖❖

Robertson v. Levy
197 A.2d 443 (D.C. 1964)

On December 22, 1961, Martin G. Robertson and Eugene M. Levy entered into an agreement whereby Levy was to form a corporation, Penn Ave. Record Shack, Inc., which was to purchase Robertson's business. Levy submitted articles of incorporation to the Superintendent of Corporations on December 27, 1961, but no certificate of incorporation was issued at this time. Pursuant to the contract an assignment of lease was entered into on December 31, 1961, between Robertson and Levy, the latter acting as president of Penn Ave. Record Shack, Inc. On January 2, 1962, the articles of incorporation were rejected by the Superintendent of Corporations but on the same day Levy began to operate the business under the name Penn Ave. Record Shack, Inc. Robertson executed a bill of sale to Penn Ave. Record Shack, Inc. on January 8, 1962, disposing of the assets of his business to that "corporation" and receiving in return a note providing for installment payments signed "Penn Ave. Record Shack, Inc. by Eugene M. Levy, President." The certificate of incorporation was issued on January 17, 1962. One payment was made on the note. The exact date when the payment was made cannot be clearly determined from the record, but presumably it was made after the certificate of incorporation was issued. Penn Ave. Record Shack, Inc. ceased doing business in June 1962 and is presently without assets. Robertson sued Levy for the balance due on the note as well as for additional expenses incurred in settling the lease arrangement with the original lessor. In holding for the defendant the trial court found that Code 1961, 29-950, relied upon by Robertson, did not apply and further that Robertson was estopped to deny the existence of the corporation.

The case presents the following issues on appeal: Whether the president of an "association" which filed its articles of incorporation, which were first rejected but later accepted, can be held personally liable on an obligation entered into by the "association" before the certificate of incorporation has been issued, or whether the creditor is "estopped" from denying the existence of the

---

[100] *Robertson v. Levy,* 197 A.2d 443, 445 (D.C. Cir. 1964)

[101] *See American Vending Services, Inc. v. Morse,* 881 P.2d 917, 922 (UT Ct. App. 1994) (compiling cases from different jurisdictions' approach to the de facto corporation doctrine)

[102] *See American Vending Services, Inc. v. Morse,* 881 P.2d 917, 923-24 (UT Ct. App. 1994) (compiling cases from different jurisdictions' approach to corporation by estoppel doctrine)

"corporation" because, after the certificate of incorporation was issued, he accepted the first installment payment on the note.

The Business Corporation Act of the District of Columbia, Code 1961, Title 29, is patterned after the Model Business Corporation Act which is largely based on the Illinois Business Corporation Act of 1933. On this appeal, we are concerned with an interpretation of sections 29-921c and 29-950 of our act. Several states have substantially enacted the Model Act, but only a few have enacted both sections similar to those under consideration. A search of the case law in each of these jurisdictions, as well as in our own jurisdiction, convinces us that these particular sections of the corporation acts have never been the subject of a reported decision.

For a full understanding of the problems raised, some historical grounding is not only illuminative but necessary. In early common law times private corporations were looked upon with distrust and disfavor. This distrust of the corporate form for private enterprise was eventually overcome by the enactment of statutes which set forth certain prerequisites before the status was achieved, and by court decisions which eliminated other stumbling blocks. Problems soon arose, however, where there was substantial compliance with the prerequisites of the statute, but not complete formal compliance. Thus the concepts of de jure corporations, de facto corporations, and of "corporations by estoppel" came into being.

Taking each of these in turn, a de jure corporation results when there has been conformity with the mandatory conditions precedent (as opposed to merely directive conditions) established by the statute. A de jure corporation is not subject to direct or collateral attack either by the state . . . or by any other person.

A de facto corporation is one which has been defectively incorporated and thus is not de jure. The Supreme Court has stated that the requisites for a corporation de facto are: (1) A valid law under which such a corporation can be lawfully organized; (2) An attempt to organize thereunder; (3) Actual user of the corporate franchise. Good faith in claiming to be and in doing business as a corporation is often added as a further condition. A de facto corporation is recognized for all purposes except where there is a direct attack by the state . . . . The concept of de facto corporation has been roundly criticized.

Cases continued to arise, however, where the corporation was not de jure, where it was not de facto because of failure to comply with one of the four requirements above, but where the courts, lacking some clear standard or guideline, were willing to decide on the equities of the case. Thus another concept arose, the so-called "corporation by estoppel." This term was a complete misnomer. There was no corporation, the acts of the associates having failed even to colorably fulfill the statutory requirements; there was no estoppel in the pure sense of the word because generally there was no holding out followed by reliance on the part of the other party. Apparently estoppel can arise whether or not a de facto corporation has come into existence. Estoppel problems arose where the certificate of incorporation had been issued as well as where it had not been issued, and under the following general conditions: where the "association" sues a third party and the third party is estopped from denying that the plaintiff is a corporation; where a third party sues the "association" as a corporation and the "association" is precluded from denying that it was a corporation; where a third party sues the "association" and the members of that association cannot deny its existence as a corporation where they participated in holding it out as a corporation; where a third party sues the individuals behind the "association" but is estopped from denying the existence of the "corporation"; where either a third party, or the "association" is estopped from denying the corporate existence because of prior pleadings.

One of the reasons for enacting modern corporation statutes was to eliminate problems inherent in the de jure, de facto and estoppel concepts. Thus sections 29-921c and 950 were enacted as follows:

"§ 29-921c. Effect of issuance of incorporation.

"Upon the issuance of the certificate of incorporation, the corporate existence shall begin, and such certificate of incorporation shall be conclusive evidence that all conditions precedent required to be performed by the incorporators have been complied with and that the corporation has been incorporated under this chapter, except as against the District of Columbia in a proceeding to cancel or revoke the certificate of incorporation."

"§ 29-950. Unauthorized assumption of corporate powers.

"All persons who assume to act as a corporation without authority so to do shall be jointly and severally liable for all debts and liabilities incurred or arising as a result thereof."

The first portion of section 29-921c sets forth a *sine qua non* regarding compliance. No longer must the courts inquire into the equities of a case to determine whether there has been "colorable compliance" with the statute. The corporation comes into existence only when the certificate has been issued. Before the certificate issues, there is no corporation de jure, de facto or by estoppel. After the certificate is issued under section 921c, the de jure corporate existence commences. Only after such existence has begun can the corporation commence business through compliance with section 29-921d, by paying into the corporation the minimum capital, and with section 921a(f), which requires that the capitalization be no less than $1,000. These latter two sections are given further force and effect by section 29-918 (a) (2) which declares that directors of a corporation are jointly and severally liable for any assets distributed or any dividends paid to shareholders which renders the corporation insolvent or reduces its net assets below its stated capital. (See also, Code 1961, § 29-917).

***

We hold, therefore, that the impact of these sections, when considered together, is to eliminate the concepts of estoppel and de facto corporateness under the Business Corporation Act of the District of Columbia. It is immaterial whether the third person believed he was dealing with a corporation or whether he intended to deal with a corporation. The certificate of incorporation provides the cut off point; before it is issued, the individuals, and not the corporation, are liable.

Turning to the facts of this case, Penn Ave. Record Shack, Inc. was not a corporation when the original agreement was entered into, when the lease was assigned, when Levy took over Robertson's business, when operations began under the Penn Ave. Record Shack, Inc. name, or when the bill of sale was executed. Only on January 17 did Penn Ave. Record Shack, Inc. become a corporation. Levy is subject to personal liability because, before this date, he assumed to act as a corporation without any authority so to do. Nor is Robertson estopped from denying the existence of the corporation because after the certificate was issued he accepted one payment on the note. An individual who incurs statutory liability on an obligation under section 29-950 because he has acted without authority, is not relieved of that liability where, at a later time, the corporation does come into existence by complying with section 29-921c. Subsequent partial payment by the corporation does not remove this liability.

The judgment appealed from is reversed with instructions to enter judgment against the appellee on the note and for damages proved to have been incurred by appellant for breach of the lease.

Questions Presented

1)   What would the result have been if the jurisdiction recognized the *de facto* corporation doctrine?
2)   What should the parties have done to protect themselves?

❖❖❖

B. Control of a Corporation

A corporation's day to day business is conducted by officers elected by the board of directors. The board of directors is elected by the shareholders. Officers, shareholders, and boards of directors are limited by several things however. They are subject to the articles of incorporation, the corporate bylaws, and certain duties owed to the corporation.

FIGURE 10.1   Corporate Hierarchy

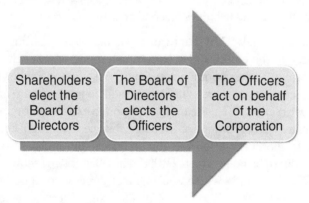

1. *Ultra Vires* Doctrone

Every officer and member of the board of directors can only act with the authority granted by the articles of incorporation and bylaws. Officers are also only allowed to act as authorized by the Board of Directors. When an officer or director acts in a manner beyond his or her power, the action is *ultra vires*, which is Latin for "beyond the power."

For instance, imagine that the articles of incorporation for American Pride, Inc. state that the purpose of the corporation is only to buy and sell alcohol. If its CEO, Dillon Mellencamp, or the Board of Directors enters into a contract to buy a house in a residential neighborhood, the act would be considered *ultra vires*.

Similarly, if the Board of Directors prohibits officers from acting in a certain way, the acts the officers perform contrary to the Board of Directors' orders are *ultra vires*. For instance, imagine that the Board of Directors of American Pride, Inc. prohibits its CEO, Dillon Mellencamp, from selling the company's real estate without board approval. Any contract Dillon enters into for American Pride, Inc. to sell real estate without board approval is *ultra vires*.

Ultra Vires acts are treated differently in every state. The Revised Model Business Corporations Act (RMBCA) provides that the acts are presumptively valid exercises of corporate power but allows shareholders, the corporation itself, or the state's attorney general to sue to prohibit or obtain damages for *ultra vires* acts.[103]

---

[103] Revised Model Business Corporations Act § 3.04

2. Roles of the Officers and Directors

Officers generally make most of the day to day decisions for corporations while the board of directors authorizes the "big picture" decisions. The board of directors sets the strategic vision, and the officers implement it. The types of decisions often made by boards of directors include major financial decisions like declaring dividends and issuing new shares (if authorized to do so by the articles of incorporation). They also elect the officers of the corporation and authorize major policy initiatives. For instance, the board of directors usually must approve the corporation's major contracts, new lines of business, and the sale of substantial corporate assets.

3. Duties Owed by Officers and Directors

Officers and members of the board of directors owe several duties to the corporation. They are considered to be in a fiduciary relationship with the corporation. They owe duties of care and loyalty to the corporation and cannot have conflicts of interest.

a. Duty of Care

Every state has its own version of the duty of care owed by officers and directors of the corporation, but the duty of care is somewhat similar in most states. Directors and officers must act in the best interests of the corporation and exercise the amount of care a reasonable person would in the same or similar circumstances.[104] Directors and officers must also make informed decisions.[105] Directors and officers are usually allowed to rely on the information provided by officers and outside experts to make their decisions.[106]

A director or officer who fails to exercise due care may be held liable for the breach of that duty. However, the officers' and directors' judgment need not be perfect. Most states employ a version of the business judgment rule when examining whether a director or officer's bad decision violated the duty of care. Under the business judgment rule, a court will presume that the directors and officers acted in good faith and in the best interests of the corporation so long as there is no evidence of fraud, illegality, self-dealing, or unreasonable failure to obtain necessary information.[107] If evidence of those things are shown, the presumption does not apply and courts will examine the directors' and officers' decision much more closely.

b. Duty of Loyalty

Officers and directors must also act with loyalty to the corporation. This means that the officer or director must place the corporation's interest before any personal interest.[108] This means that the director or officer cannot be a part of any business in competition with the corporation, engage in self-dealing, or usurp a corporate opportunity for personal use.

---

[104] *See* 18A Am. Jur. 2d Corporations §§ 1444, 1445 (2017)

[105] *See, e.g., Shoen v. SAC Holding Corp.,* 122 Nev. 621, 137 P.3d 1171 (Nev. 2006)

[106] *See, e.g., Brehm v. Eisner,* 746 A.2d 244 (Del. 2000).

[107] *See* 18A Am. Jur. 2d Corporations § 1454 (2017)

[108] *See, e.g., In re Amerco Derivative Litigation,* 252 P.3d 681, 127 Nev. Adv. Op. No. 17 (Nev. 2011), *Carsanaro v. Bloodhound Technologies, Inc.,* 65 A.3d 618 (Del. Ch. 2013).

If an officer or director has a personal interest and stands to gain from a corporate transaction, he or she must fully disclose that benefit to the board of directors. Many states will allow contracts from which an officer or director personally benefits to stand so long as the contract is fair, reasonable, and made following full disclosure.[109]

4. Duties and Rights of Shareholders

Shareholders are those who own the stock of the corporation. They are often split into classes. Some shareholders may hold stock that does not carry the right to vote for instance. Unlike officers and directors, no matter what class of stock the shareholder owns, the shareholders do not have the right to manage the corporation (although a shareholder can serve as an officer or member of the board of directors). However, their main responsibility is to elect a board of directors to manage the corporation. They may also vote to remove a director for cause (such as a breach of the duty of loyalty or care) in most states.

They also can challenge actions of the officers and board of directors as well. If the shareholders believe that the officers and directors are taking actions to hurt the corporation, such as violating the duties of care and loyalty, shareholders may bring a lawsuit known as a shareholder derivative suit to assert the rights of the corporation against the directors and/or officers. The shareholders bringing the suit do not personally derive benefits from a shareholder derivative suit. Any amount won goes directly to the corporation.[110]

5. Closely-Held Corporations

There is one notable exception to the rules outlined above. Closely-held corporations are not held to the same rules as other corporations. A closely-held corporation is a corporation in which all of the shares are held by a small number of people, usually a family. The board of directors and officers of the corporation are usually also shareholders.

> ### Legal Definition
>
> **Closely-held corporation** – a corporation that is managed by its shareholders and in which all of the shares are held by a small number of people.

Closely-held corporations are not held to the same standards as other private corporations. They are far less formal. In most states, if the shareholders agree, the corporation can be run without a board of directors, without bylaws, and without shareholder meetings.[111] Often times, closely-held corporations will contain restrictions in the articles of incorporation or through a separate agreement between the shareholders that any shareholder who wishes to sell his or her stock must first offer it to the other shareholders of the corporation.

---

[109] *See* RMBCA § 8.62
[110] *See* 18A Am. Jur. 2d Corporations § 1932 (2017)
[111] *See, e.g.,* RMBCA § 732

C. Liability for the Corporation's Losses

Officers, members of the board of directors, and shareholders are not normally held liable for the losses of the corporation. This is the great advantage of creating a corporation. However, there are some circumstances in which officers, members of the board of directors, or shareholders will be held liable for losses of the corporation.

Officers and directors are liable for losses resulting from their breaches of the duties of care and loyalty. Because the corporation is an entity separate from its shareholders, shareholders are rarely held liable for the debts and liabilities of the corporation. This is the great advantage of the corporate form. However, there are some situations in which courts have nonetheless held shareholders liable. Known as "piercing the corporate veil," a shareholder will be held liable if a court deems it necessary to prevent fraud or achieve equity.[112] There are many reasons courts have pierced the corporate veil, but common factors considered by courts include:

1. Whether the corporation was used to commit fraud or a crime
2. Whether corporate formalities like meetings of the board of directors were disregarded
3. Whether corporate funds were frequently commingled (mixed together) with the personal funds of the shareholders
4. Whether a sufficient amount of capital was kept by the corporation to run the business[113]

D. Distribution of Corporate Profits

The board of directors makes the ultimate determination concerning what to do with the corporation's earnings. The board of directors may save some of the profit to create operating reserves, reinvest the profits within the corporation itself for upgrade or expansion, or declare a dividend.[114] A dividend is a share of profits paid to shareholders. While shareholders do not choose whether to declare a dividend, they do hold some power in seeing that one is declared. Shareholders elect the board of directors, which is responsible for declaring dividends. If directors do not declare dividends frequently enough, the shareholders may well not reelect the directors at the next shareholder meeting.

E. Corporate Taxation

Most corporations are known as "C" corporations for the section of the tax code under which they are taxed. Shareholders of "C" corporations are at a major tax disadvantage compared to owners of sole proprietorships, partnerships, and most LLCs. Profits from a "C" Corporation are subject to "double taxation." Because the corporation is considered a separate entity from its owners, a corporation's earnings are taxed every year at the corporate taxation rate. Further, shareholders must also pay personal taxes on the dividends that they receive from the corporation at the capital gains taxation rate.

In some circumstances, a corporation is eligible to become an "S" corporation rather than a "C" corporation. An "S" corporation is only taxed once. While shareholders must still pay personal

---

[112] *See Morris v. Dept. of Taxation,* 82 N.Y.2d 135, 140-41, 623 NE 2d 1157 (NY 1993)
[113] *See, e.g., Castleberry v. Branscum,* 721 SW 2d 270-72 (TX 1986)
[114] *See* 18A Am. Jur. 2d Corporations § 1008 (2017)

taxes on dividends, there is no taxation of the corporation's profits before dividends are paid out. To be an "S" corporation, the corporation must be domestic (in the United States). All its shareholders must be individuals (in most cases) who are not nonresident aliens, and there must be no more than 100 shareholders. There must also only be one class of stock.[115]

F. Termination of a Corporation

A corporation can be terminated in a number of ways. The official legal term for this is "dissolution." Following a corporation's dissolution, its assets must be distributed, a process known as "liquidation."

Legal Definitions

Dissolution – the process by which a business entity ceases to exist.

Liquidation – the process by which a dissolved business entity's assets are distributed.

---

1. Dissolution

A corporation can be dissolved voluntarily or involuntarily. It can be done voluntarily by a unanimous vote of the shareholders. In some states, a corporation may be dissolved by a vote of the board of directors *and* a certain proportion of shareholders.[116] In most cases, a majority of the stockholders may also dissolve a corporation so long as they act in good faith towards the minority stockholders.[117]

A corporation may also be dissolved involuntarily by court decree. For example, in many states, failure to pay taxes may result in dissolution of the corporation. Engaging in *ultra vires* actions or failing to begin performing or abandoning the corporation's purpose may also lead to the dissolution of the corporation.[118] In very limited circumstances in some states, minority stockholders may ask the court to dissolve a corporation for extreme mismanagement of the corporation, fraud, insolvency of the corporation, or deadlock of the directors.[119]

2. Liquidation

Once a corporation is dissolved, its remaining assets must be liquidated. The board of directors, acting as trustees, must pay the corporation's creditors first. If any assets remain, they are split amongst the shareholders on a *pro rata* basis (equal amount per share in each class of share).[120] Profitable corporations, however, do not often dissolve. Thus, shareholders do not often walk away with a share of the corporate assets.

---

[115] *See* 26 U.S.C. § 1361
[116] *See* 18A Am. Jur. 2d § 2344 (2017)
[117] *See Grato v. Grato,* 272 N.J. Super. 140, 158, 639 A.2d 390 (N.J. App. Div. 1994)
[118] *See* RMBCA § 14.20
[119] *See* 18A Am. Jur. 2d § 2350 (2017)
[120] *See* 18A Am. Jur. 2d § 2440 (2017)

IV. Limited Liability Company (LLC)

The limited liability company (LLC) is a relatively recent invention. Wyoming became the first state where LLCs could be formed in 1977.[121] However, LLCs did not become popular until an IRS revenue ruling in 1988 held that they would be taxed like partnerships in most cases.[122] Every state now has a set of LLC statutes. However, they vary significantly given that the concept is so new.

Seventeen states and Washington, D.C. have passed a version of the Uniform Limited Liability Company Act (ULLCA) as of the time of this writing.[123] Given the wide variation of LLC laws, it is very important to know the laws for the state in which you live. Despite the variation on specific details of the LLC statutes, all of the LLC statutes have several of the most important elements in common.

At their hearts, all LLCs are hybrid creatures. They are hybrids of partnerships and corporations. They are also hybrids of statute and contract.[124] This provides for an incredible amount of flexibility when organizing the business. Given this flexibility, it is likely to become more and more important in the future.[125]

A. Formation

Like a corporation, an LLC is entirely a creature of statute. Without a state statute allowing its formation, an LLC cannot exist.[126] One of the LLC's most attractive features is the flexibility with which it can be organized. To create an LLC, the organizers must file articles of organization with the appropriate state office, which is usually the secretary of state for the state under whose laws the LLC is organized. The articles of organization must specify information like the name of the LLC (which usually must contain the words "limited liability company" or one of its variations such as "LLC" or "Ltd. Liab. Co."), the business address of the LLC, and the members (owners) of the LLC.[127]

If an LLC has one member, it is known as a "single-member" LLC. If it has more than one member, it is called a "multi-member" LLC. Regardless of whether the LLC is a single-member or multi-member LLC, the members should create an operating agreement. An operating agreement is very similar to a partnership agreement. A good one specifies how profits and losses will be distributed, what the members' capital contributions are, how the LLC will be managed, how new members may be admitted to the LLC, and how the operating agreement itself can be amended.

State statutes usually give great latitude to members to organize their LLCs as they wish through operating agreements, which is why an LLC also is very much a creature of contract as well as statute.

---

[121] Wayne M. Gazur & Neil M. Goff, Assessing the Limited Liability Company, 41 Case W. Res. L. Rev. 387, 391 (1991)

[122] *See* IRS Rev. Rul. 88-76, 1988-2 C.B. 360 (1988).

[123] National Conference of Commissioners on Uniform State Laws, Legislative Fact Sheet – Limited Liability Company (2006), available at http://www.uniformlaws.org/LegislativeFactSheet.aspx?title=Limited%20Liability%20Company%20(2006)%20(Last%20Amended%202013)

[124] 59A Am. Jur. 2d Limited Liability Companies § 1 (2017)

[125] *See* Maizes, R, Limited Liability Companies: A Critique, 70 St. John's L. Rev. 575, 576 (2012).

[126] *Spurlock v. Begley,* 308 S.W.3d 657, 659 (KY 2010)

[127] *See, e.g.,* Conn. Gen. Stat. § 34-37 (2017). Connecticut enacted the Revised Uniform Limited Liability Company Act in 2017.

B. Management of an LLC

In the operating agreement (or articles of organization in some states), the members must specify whether the LLC is to be a member-managed LLC or a manager-managed LLC. If an operating agreement does not state whether the LLC will be member-managed or manager-managed, an LLC will be member-managed. A member-managed LLC is an LLC that is managed directly by its members (like a partnership). A manager-managed LLC is managed by a team of managers (similar to the board of directors of a corporation). The team of managers can consist of any combination of members and nonmembers.[128] Members who are not managers do not possess management rights in a manager-managed LLC.[129]

Unless otherwise specified in the operating agreement, LLC management rules usually follow partnership rules in most states. For instance, for ordinary decisions in a LLC, most states require a simple majority of members (or managers in case of a manger-managed LLC) regardless of their capital contributions or profit shares to pass a resolution.[130] However, some states have a different rule, such as requiring a majority of the ownership interest to pass an ordinary resolution in a member-managed LLC.[131] For decisions not in the ordinary course of business, unanimity is usually required.[132]

C. Losses in an LLC

One of the great advantages of an LLC is that, just like a corporation, its members and managers are not held personally liable for the LLC's debts in most cases.[133] Like a corporation, however, in some circumstances, the "veil may be pierced," and members and managers may be held personally liable for the debts of the LLC. Much like a corporation's shareholders or members of the board of directors, an LLC's members or managers may be liable for the losses of the LLC if they use the LLC to perpetrate a fraud, do not provide enough capital to sufficiently operate the business, do not observe business formalities (such as having meetings when required), or intermingle personal and LLC funds repeatedly.[134] LLC members must also be careful to disclose that they are doing business as an LLC or risk having the veil pierced. Consider the following case.

❖❖❖

Irrigation Mart, Inc. v. Gray
965 So.2d 988 (La. Ct. App. 2007)

BROWN, C.J.

This action to collect on an open account was filed by Irrigation Mart, Inc., against defendant, Michael Gray d/b/a Plantasia f/k/a Clearwater Irrigation. Between March 2004 and February 2005, Plantasia purchased on account drainage materials from plaintiff. Following Plantasia's failure to

---

[128] *See* 51 Am. Jur. 2d Limited Liability Companies § 7 (2017)

[129] *See* 1 Close Corp and LLCs: Law and Practice § 5:11 (Rev. 3d ed.) (2017)

[130] RULLCA § 407 (2006)

[131] *See, e.g.,* Del. Code Ann. tit. 6, § 18-402; Cal. Corp. Code § 17103(a)(3); N.Y. Limited Liab. Cos. § 402(f).

[132] RULLCA § 407

[133] 51 Am. Jur. 2d Limited Liability Companies § 16 (2017)

[134] 51 Am. Jur. 2d Limited Liability Companies § 20 (2017)

pay on the account, plaintiff sued Gray for the principal sum, judicial interest from date of demand, and attorney fees. The trial court found that Gray did not disclose his agency capacity to Irrigation Mart and was thus liable for the $16,741.82 due on the open account, plus judicial interest from the date of demand, all costs, and attorney fees. Gray now appeals. For the reasons contained herein, we affirm.

FACTS

Michael Gray was a landscaper. Gray filed articles of organization for MDG Enterprises, LLC, d/b/a Clearwater Irrigation, with the Louisiana Secretary of State on June 21, 2000. Gray, operating as Clearwater Irrigation, opened an account with Irrigation Mart, Inc., for the purchase of landscaping supplies in 2001. Later, Gray filed articles of organization for Arborscapes, LLC, d/b/a Plantasia, and changed the name on his account with Irrigation Mart from Clearwater Irrigation to Plantasia. Gray never disclosed the existence or identities of the two LLCs, MDG Enterprises or Arborscapes.

On August 12, 2005, plaintiff filed a petition seeking to collect the amount due on the open account, which included Plantasia's purchase of drainage materials between March 25, 2004, and February 10, 2005.

Plaintiff obtained a default judgment on February 22, 2006. Gray filed a motion for new trial. Irrigation Mart agreed to a new trial in exchange for Gray's agreement to pay attorney fees of $1,000 incurred in connection with the default judgment.

The matter was tried on September 11, 2006. The trial court rendered judgment on October 2, 2006, ruling in favor of Irrigation Mart and against Gray for the amount on the open account of $16,741.82, plus judicial interest from the date of demand, all costs, and attorney fees as the parties stipulated at 15%.

DISCUSSION

The trial court's written opinion states:

> The issue before the court is whether the defendant should bear personal liability for the debts he incurred on behalf of several businesses he operated using trade names for two undisclosed limited liability companies. The court finds the following facts as proven by a preponderance of the evidence. The defendant took no affirmative steps at the beginning or during the course of the business relationship to disclose to the plaintiff the legal nature of his businesses or his relationship with them. There was insufficient evidence to indicate that the plaintiff should have known that the defendant was operating his businesses other than as a sole proprietorship using various trade names. The very existence of the defendant's two limited liability companies as well as their names was first learned by plaintiff at the trial. The business documents used by the defendant during this period did not indicate a limited liability status of any kind. The business card of the defendant introduced into evidence named the defendant simply as owner for the named businesses (Clearwater and Plantasia) with no indication of a limited liability status. Similarly, the business checks used by the defendant for payment on account gave no indication of a limited liability status. Finally, the defendant testified that he at no time communicated formally or informally to the plaintiff the true nature of his legal relationship with his businesses. In the court's opinion, these actions served to foster the plaintiff's reasonable belief that the defendant was conducting his businesses as a sole proprietor using different trade names.

The defense places much emphasis on the testimony of a former salesman of the plaintiff, Mr. Mobley. During the cross-examination of Mr. Mobley, it became apparent to the court, that Mr. Mobley knew only that the defendant operated as a business. He was unfamiliar with the legalities of defendant's businesses or the defendant's legal relationship with them. The defense also strongly urges the court to consider the fact that the plaintiff sought a continuing guaranty from the defendant and that this therefore imputes knowledge of defendant's adverse legal status to the plaintiff. Considering the testimony of the parties, the time frame and unresponsiveness of defendant toward plaintiff's attempts at collection, the court views the actions of plaintiff as an attempt in their mind to improve their position by having the defendant "sign something else" acknowledging the debt, and as nothing more.

Gray argues that he acted in an agency capacity when contracting with plaintiff. Further, Gray contends that Irrigation Mart received sufficient constructive knowledge of this agency relationship to the extent that he, Gray, never became personally liable for any debts incurred.

A mandatary who contracts in the name of the principal within the limits of his authority does not bind himself personally for the performance of the contract. La. C.C. art. 3016. On the other hand, a mandatary who contracts in his own name without disclosing his status as a mandatary does bind himself personally for the performance of the contract. La. C.C. art. 3017. Generally, an agent will be held to have bound himself personally when he enters into an agreement without disclosing the identity of his principal. _American Bank and Trust Co. of Coushatta v. Boggs and Thompson, 36,157 (La. App.2d Cir.06/12/02), 821 So.2d 585_. The agent has the burden of proving that he disclosed his agency status and the identity of his principal if he wishes to avoid personal liability. _Id._ However, express notice of the agent's status and the principal's identity is not required to escape personal liability if the agent proves that sufficient evidence of the agency relationship was known by the third party so as to put him on notice of the principal-agent relationship. _Id._

Both plaintiff and defendant have framed the issue, as did the trial court, as a factual question. Both sides have strongly supported their positions with recitation of testimony and documentary evidence. A reviewing court may not set aside a district court's finding of fact in the absence of manifest error or unless it is clearly wrong, and where there is conflict in the testimony, inferences of fact should not be disturbed upon review, even though the reviewing court may feel that its own evaluations and inferences are as reasonable. _Hanks v. Entergy Corp., 06-477 (La.12/18/06), 944 So.2d 564_. In order to reverse a district court's determination of a fact, a reviewing court must review the record in its entirety and conclude that reasonable factual basis does not exist for the finding, and further determine that the record establishes that the fact finder is clearly wrong or manifestly erroneous. _Bonin v. Ferrellgas, Inc., 03-3024 (La.07/02/04), 877 So.2d 89_. Where there are two permissible views of the evidence, the fact finder's choice between them cannot be manifestly erroneous or clearly wrong. _Id._

The trial court found, the record supports, and, indeed, it is not contested that plaintiff was not aware of the existence of Gray's two limited liability companies, MDG Enterprises, LLC, and Arborscapes, LLC, until trial. Further, the business documents, business cards, and checks used by Gray during his dealings with Irrigation Mart did not indicate a limited liability status. Gray even testified that he at no time communicated formally or informally to the plaintiff that he operated a LLC. Plaintiff's knowledge of the trade names Clearwater Irrigation and Plantasia cannot equate to disclosure of MDG Enterprises, LLC, or Arborscapes, LLC. Generally, an agent will be held to have bound himself personally when he enters into an agreement without disclosing the identity of his principal. Gray had the burden of proving that he disclosed his agency status to plaintiff and the identity of his principal (MDG Enterprises, LLC, and later Arborscapes, LLC) if he wished to avoid personal liability, and, given the facts listed above, the trial court did not commit manifest error in holding that he failed to so do. *See* <u>American Bank and Trust Co. of Coushatta, supra</u>.

CONCLUSION

For the reasons set forth above, the judgment of the trial court ordering Michael Gray to pay Irrigation Mart, Inc., $16,741.82 on Gray's open account, with judicial interest from the date of judicial demand until paid, together with all costs of this suit, and attorney fees as stipulated by the parties, is affirmed. Costs of this appeal are to be borne by appellant, Michael Gray.

AFFIRMED.

Questions Presented

1) Why did the court pierce the corporate veil in this case?
2) What would have happened if the veil had not been pierced?
3) How could the defendant have avoided having the veil pierced?

❖❖❖

D. Profits in an LLC

An LLC's profits are split in accordance with a manner specified in the operating agreement. If the operating agreement is silent about profits, most states require that the profits be split in proportion to each member's capital contribution.[135] For example, if Shreya made a capital contribution of $2,000 to start an LLC and Angelica made a capital contribution of $1,000 to start an LLC, Angelica would receive 2/3 of the profits and Shreya would receive 1/3 of the profits if the operating agreement did not state how profits would be shared.

Unless the operating agreement otherwise specifies, the decision to distribute LLC profits will be made by vote of the members in a member-managed LLC or by a vote of the managers in a manger-managed LLC.[136]

E. LLC Taxation

The members of an LLC have a choice with regard to taxation. The LLC may choose to be taxed either like a partnership or a corporation. An LLC that is taxed like a partnership is a *pass through* entity, meaning that the LLC itself is not taxed but that each member is taxed individually on his or her share of the profits at the income tax rate. If its members elect to be taxed like a corporation, the LLC income is taxed twice. The LLC itself is taxed at the corporate tax rate, and, after those taxes are paid, each member is taxed on his or her share of the profits at the capital gains tax rate.[137]

---

[135] *See* Callison, J. & Sullivan, M, Limited Liability Companies: A State-by-State Guide To Law And Practice § 7.5 (2017).
[136] *See* Callison, J. & Sullivan, M, Limited Liability Companies: A State-by-State Guide To Law And Practice § 7.2 (2017).
[137] *See* Callison, J. & Sullivan, M, Limited Liability Companies: A State-by-State Guide To Law And Practice § 12.1 (2017).

LLCs rarely choose to be taxed as a corporation. However, there are occasional instances when paying the corporate tax rate and the capital gains tax on the LLC's profits is less expensive than the income tax members would pay if they chose to be taxed once.

F. LLC Members' Duties

Like officers and members of the board of directors of a corporation and the partners of a partnership, LLC members owe certain duties to the LLC. Members who also manage the LLC (either in a member-managed LLC or manager-managed LLC) and managers of a manager-managed LLC owe duties to the LLC in particular. What duties these members and managers owe varies from state to state. Most states impose duties similar to, if more nuanced than, the duties owed by a partner to a partnership.

Virtually all states require that managers and member-managers act in good faith towards the LLC, in its best interests, and with some degree of skill in business judgment. Virtually every state also has a version of the duty of loyalty for LLC managers and member-managers, meaning that they cannot engage in self-dealing, usurp business opportunities from the LLC, or compete with the LLC. This area of law is still developing and is in a state of flux.[138]

G. LLC Termination

Like a partnership and a corporation, an LLC can be dissolved. Like the partners of a partnership, its members can also be dissociated (removed).

1. Dissociation of Members

Every state has its own unique twist on how a member of an LLC can be dissociated. The operating agreement may specify ways in which an LLC member may be dissociated such as the occurrence of a specific event or by a vote of a particular percentage of the other members.[139] Members may also voluntarily withdraw without wrongfully dissociating (often with notice provisions) in most states unless the operating agreement otherwise states that dissociation is prohibited.[140]

Though most LLC statutes do not state ways in which a member can be dissociated against his or her will, in many states, a court order can be obtained to dissociate a member in some circumstances.[141] An LLC member may also be dissociated upon death, bankruptcy, or mental incapacity.[142]

2. Dissolution of the LLC

State statutes also vary regarding what events will cause an LLC to dissolve. The following events have led to dissolution in several states:

1. Use of a method specified in the operating agreement
2. An event specified in the operating agreement

---

[138] *See* Callison, J. & Sullivan, M, Limited Liability Companies: A State-by-State Guide To Law And Practice § 8.7 (2017).

[139] 51 Am. Jur. 2d Limited Liability Companies § 24 (2017)

[140] *See* Callison, J. & Sullivan, M, Limited Liability Companies: A State-by-State Guide To Law And Practice § 9.1 (2017).

[141] *See, e.g., Tully v. McLean,* 948 N.E.2d 714 (Ill. App. Div. 2011)

[142] *See* Callison, J. & Sullivan, M, Limited Liability Companies: A State-by-State Guide To Law And Practice § 9.2 (2017).

3. Unanimous consent of the members
4. Business becomes impracticable
5. Dissociation of a member[143]

Once an LLC is dissolved, its affairs must be wound up. Creditors of the LLC must be paid first. If money remains after this, members' capital contributions are paid back. If money remains after this, the remaining profits are split among the members.[144]

V. Sole Proprietorships

A sole proprietorship is the most basic form of business entity imaginable. It is essentially one person operating and owning a business who has not otherwise created an entity like a corporation or an LLC.[145] The vast majority of businesses in the United States are organized as sole proprietorships. In 2014, there were approximately 23 million sole proprietorships.[146]

Sole proprietorships have several advantages. They are easily formed and managed and are taxed favorably. Their major disadvantages relate to the owner's liability for losses and the owner's difficulty in raising capital.

A. Advantages of a Sole Proprietorship

Sole proprietorships are easy to form. No paperwork is needed. All a person has to do to form a sole proprietorship is to engage in business without any partners and without otherwise creating a business entity. If the sole proprietor wishes, he or she may do business under a particular name and register it with an appropriate local office. This is known as a "D/B/A" (doing business as) name.[147]

A sole proprietorship is also easy to manage. All decisions are made by the sole proprietor. The sole proprietor's profits are also all his or her own.

A sole proprietor's income is also taxed only once. The business is treated as if it does not exist, and all of its profits are taxed as personal income by the IRS.[148]

B. Disadvantages of a Sole Proprietorship

The major disadvantage of the sole proprietorship is that the sole proprietor has unlimited liability. That is, the sole proprietor is personally liable for all of the business' debts.

Sole proprietors also frequently have trouble raising capital. Because the business has no other owners, the sole proprietor's only sources of funds are his or her own personal funds and proceeds from any loans the business might be able to obtain.

---

[143] *See* Callison, J. & Sullivan, M, Limited Liability Companies: A State-by-State Guide To Law And Practice § 10.1 (2017).

[144] *See, e.g.,* Conn. Gen. Stat. 34-247 (2017).

[145] *See Ladd v. Scudder Kemper Investments, Inc.,* 741 N.E.2d 47, 49-50 (Mass. 2001)

[146] Dungan, A., Sole Proprietorship Returns, Tax Year 2014, IRS Statistics of Income Bulletin (2014), available at https://www.irs.gov/pub/irs-soi/soi-a-inpr-id1614.pdf (This figure was reached subtracting the number of LLC's filing sole proprietorship tax returns from the total number of sole proprietorship tax returns).

[147] *See* Clemons, R. & Lassila, D, *Choice of Entity Issues: Single-Member LLC's v. 'Regular' Sole Proprietorships,* 117 J. Tax'n 259, 260 (2012)

[148] Alberty, S., Advising Small Businesses § 4:3 (2017)

VI. Tables Comparing Business Entities

TABLE 10.3   Business Formation

	General Partnership	Corporation	LLC	Sole Proprietorship
Formation	The act of 2 or more people running a for profit business no paperwork required but a partnership agreement is strongly advisable	Filing of the articles of incorporation with the appropriate state authority (usually the secretary of state) Bylaws adopted at the first organizational meeting should be specific	Filing of the articles of organization with the appropriate state authority Operating agreement between the members is optional but strongly advisable	The act of doing business without others and without forming an entity Can file for a D/B/A name

TABLE 10.4   Business Management

	General Partnership	Corporation	LLC	Sole Proprietorship
Management	Unless the partnership agreement provides otherwise, a majority of the partners for ordinary business and unanimous consent of the partners for matters outside the ordinary course of business	By the board of directors, which usually delegates much of its authority to the officers of the corporation	If a member-managed LLC, by the members. Unless the operating agreement provides otherwise, a majority of members wins in the ordinary course of business. Unanimous consent is required for matters outside the ordinary course of business If a manager-managed LLC, unless otherwise provided by the operating agreement, a majority of managers wins in the ordinary course of business. Unanimous consent is required for matters outside the ordinary course of business	Managed by the sole proprietor

TABLE 10.5   Business Profits

	General Partnership	Corporation	LLC	Sole Proprietorship
Profits	Unless otherwise specified by the agreement, shared equally by the partners	Distributed to shareholders through dividends declared by the board of directors	Unless specified otherwise by the operating agreement, split by the members in accordance with their capital contributions in most states	Solely belong to the sole proprietor

TABLE 10.6   Business Losses

	General Partnership	Corporation	LLC	Sole Proprietorship
Losses	Losses are to be shared in the same manner as profits are shared unless the agreement specifies otherwise. Partners have unlimited liability to third parties for the acts of the partnership and other partners. However, partners paying more than their share under the agreement to third parties have the right to be reimbursed by the partners who paid less than their share of the losses	Only the corporation is liable for its debts. Shareholders, members of the board of directors, and officers cannot be sued unless the corporate veil is pierced.	Only the LLC is liable for its debts. Managers and members cannot be sued unless the corporate veil is pierced.	The sole proprietor is personally liable for all losses of the sole propietorship

TABLE 10.7   Business Taxation

	General Partnership	Corporation	LLC	Sole Proprietorship
Taxation	Each partner is taxed on his or her share of the profits The partnership itself is not taxed	The corporation's income is taxed at the corporate rate The shareholders also pay taxes on the dividends they receive at the capital gains rate	The LLC may choose to be taxed as a partnership (if 2 or more members), sole proprietorship (if only one member), or a corporation	The sole proprietor is taxed on the business' profits personally The business itself is not taxed

SUMMARY

It is essential for a business owner to weigh all of his or her options when deciding what legal form his or her business should take. There are several forms that a business can take. The four main categories are partnerships, corporations, LLCs, and sole proprietorships. Each has its own advantages and disadvantages.

General partnerships allow for direct control of the business by the partners. They are also only taxed once. However, each partner is liable for the acts of the partnership and other partners in the course of partnership business. It is vital that the partners spell out their rights and duties in a written partnership agreement whenever possible.

Corporations allow their shareholders, boards of directors, and officers to avoid personal liability for the corporation's debts in most instances. However, their income is taxed twice, and shareholders do not have as much control over the business because it is managed by a board of directors.

LLCs tend to present the best of both worlds. They provide limited liability for its members like corporations do and also allow the LLC to be taxed in the manner most favorable to it. Businesses are increasingly choosing this form because of the great advantages and flexibility that it provides.

Most businesses are still organized as sole proprietorships. Sole proprietorships take no work to form. The sole owner has the right to manage the business as he or sees fit, takes all the profits from the business, and is taxed only once. However, the sole proprietor has unlimited liability for the debts of the business and is solely responsible for them.

When choosing an entity, it is vital to find the one that is right for your business after weighing all of the advantages and disadvantages of each entity. The choice can be the difference between success and financial ruin.

CHAPTER 11

SECURED TRANSACTIONS

LEARNING OUTCOMES

Upon completion of this chapter the student will be able to:

1 Explain how a security interest is created and attached.
2 Explain how to perfect a security interest.
3 Understand which security interests have priority.
4 Understand how a security interest is enforced.
5 Understand the remedies available to a secured party.

KEY TERMS

account	general intangible
attachment	instrument
authentication	inventory
chattel paper	perfection
collateral	priority
consumer goods	purchase money security interest
debtor	secured party
deposit account	security agreement
equipment	security interest
farm goods	secured transaction

I. Introduction

Imagine that your friend Julie wants to borrow $100. However, just last month, she borrowed $100 from you and did not pay it back. You say to Julie, "I'd love to loan you another $100, but I am just not sure that you will pay me back." Julie replies, "I need this money. Tell you what. Here is my birth stone ring. It's worth $100. Hold onto it until I pay you back, and, if I don't pay you back by next month, keep it." As Julie hands you the ring, you reply, "You've got a deal!" You both sign an agreement stating that Julie will give you her ring if she does not pay you back. Then, you hand her $100.

This simple transaction is known as a secured transaction. A secured transaction is any transaction "by which a buyer or borrower gives collateral to the seller or lender to guarantee payment of an obligation."[1] Essentially, a secured transaction guarantees that the creditor will get paid at least something if the debtor does not make payment. In the above case, you are guaranteed to get paid something because you have a security interest in the collateral—Julie's ring—which you will be able to sell if she does not pay you. Collateral is basically the property used to secure payment. A security interest is an "interest in personal property or fixtures which secures payment or performance of an obligation."[2] In other words, it is a right to the collateral in the event of non-payment. A security interest also gives a creditor priority in bankruptcy proceedings over creditors who do not have a security interest in that piece of personal property.

In this chapter, we will discuss secured transactions involving personal property and answer the following questions:

1. How is a security interest created and attached?
2. How is a security interest perfected?
3. Which security interests take priority in the event of a conflict?
4. How can a security interest be enforced?
5. What remedies are available to the secured party?

A. Applicable Law

The law of secured transactions for personal property is governed by Article 9 of the Uniform Commercial Code,[3] which every state has substantially adopted in some form. For real property, the law of secured transactions is governed by the common law and varies from state to state.

B. Parties to a Secured Transaction

Every secured transaction involves at least two parties, the secured party and the debtor.

The secured party is the person who gains an interest in the collateral.[4] The secured party is often also called the seller when the secured party is selling the thing in which it takes a security interest (like a car dealer taking a security interest in a car after its sold on credit). The secured party is also often called the "lender" when the secured party is making a loan after receiving collateral (like when a bank takes a security interest in a car after it gives the buyer a loan to purchase it).

The debtor is any person who has an interest in the collateral that is involved in the secured transaction.[5] The debtor usually owes payment to the secured party, which is the reason all secured transactions occur anyway.

Legal Definitions

Debtor – person pledging collateral to pay a debt.

Secured Party – a person who has a security interest in the debtor's collateral.

---

[1] Secured Transactions, Black's Law Dictionary (9th Ed. 2009).
[2] Uniform Commercial Code § 1-201(35)
[3] Uniform Commercial Code § 9-101(a)(1)
[4] Uniform Commercial Code § 9-102(a)(72)
[5] *See* Uniform Commercial Code § 9-102(a)(28)

II. Creation and Attachment of a Security Interest

A security interest becomes enforceable when it attaches to the collateral.[6] The three requirements to create a valid security interest are as follows:

a. The debtor must have rights in the collateral
b. The secured party must give value to the debtor
c. Either (1) the debtor gives up possession of the collateral to the secured party or (2) a valid security agreement is executed.[7]

The first requirement is relatively self-explanatory. The debtor must actually have the right to put up the collateral as security. For instance, a person cannot put up a stolen ring as collateral.

The second requirement is also relatively straightforward. The secured party must do something for the debtor in order to gain a security interest in collateral. Usually, this involves a loan from the secured party to the debtor.

The third requirement, the secured party's possession of the collateral or a written security agreement, is easy to satisfy in theory but can become somewhat complex in practice.

In many cases, a security agreement need not be in writing if the secured party obtains possession of the collateral.[8] However, most agreements are reduced to writing as a practical matter.

Written security agreements have a few requirements. First, the agreement must be authenticated by the debtor.[9] This means that the debtor must sign the agreement. The harder requirement to satisfy is the requirement that the security agreement adequately describe the collateral provided. The agreement must "reasonably identify" the collateral involved.[10] While it is relatively easy to describe something like a piece of jewelry, as will be discussed later in the chapter, security agreements often create a security interest in several items at once. This can lead to overly broad and vague descriptions of collateral. Inadequate descriptions of collateral include "all the debtor's personal property" and "all the debtor's assets."[11]

III. Perfection of a Security Interest

Perhaps the most important concept in the law of secured transactions is perfection. Perfection is the "validation of a security interest as against other creditors."[12] Merely creating an attached security interest is not enough to ensure that the security interest will be honored. Often times, a debtor

FIGURE 11.1 Formula to Create an Attached a Security Interest

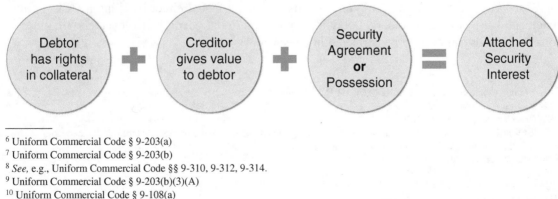

---

[6] Uniform Commercial Code § 9-203(a)
[7] Uniform Commercial Code § 9-203(b)
[8] *See,* e.g., Uniform Commercial Code §§ 9-310, 9-312, 9-314.
[9] Uniform Commercial Code § 9-203(b)(3)(A)
[10] Uniform Commercial Code § 9-108(a)
[11] Uniform Commercial Code § 9-108(c)
[12] Perfection, Black's Law Dictionary (9th Ed.).

will owe more than one person money and declare bankruptcy. Even if the security interest is attached, if a security interest is not perfected, the secured party will usually be treated as an unsecured party (someone without a security interest) in bankruptcy.[13] A perfected security interest also almost always takes priority over an unperfected security in the same property, even if the perfected security interest attached after the unperfected security interest did.[14]

A security interest can be perfected in several ways. It is most often perfected by filing a UCC-1 financing statement with the proper authorities (usually the secretary of state) in the state in which the personal property is located. Some security interests can also be perfected by possession or control of the collateral. Some security interests even perfect automatically the moment that they attach. The correct method to perfect a security interest depends on the type of collateral that the secured party is attempting to perfect its security interest in.

There are two broad categories of collateral, tangible collateral and intangible collateral. Tangible collateral is usually goods, anything moveable at the time the security interest is granted.[15] Intangible collateral is any collateral that exists only because it is connected to non-tangible property. This includes things like obligations under a promissory note and rights to the money in a bank account.

Legal Definition

Perfection – the process by which a secured party validates its security interest.

A. Perfection of Tangible Collateral

There are four main categories of tangible collateral, (1) consumer goods, (2) inventory, (3) farm products, and (4) equipment.[16]

1. Perfection of Consumer Goods

Consumer goods are defined by the UCC as "goods that are used or bought for use primarily for personal, family, or household purposes."[17] A good is defined very broadly as anything "movable when a security interest attaches."[18] This includes common household items like furniture, televisions, microwaves, and the like. It also includes items used by families, like automobiles and boats. Essentially, it is anything not attached to real property that a family uses.

A security interest in most consumer goods can be perfected either by filing a UCC-1 filing statement[19] or by the secured party obtaining possession of the goods.[20] However, certain kinds of consumer goods can or must be perfected in other ways.

---

[13] *See* Uniform Commercial Code § 9-317(a)(2)(A), 11 U.S.C. § 544.

[14] *See* Uniform Commercial Code § 9-317.

[15] Uniform Commercial Code § 9-102(a)(44)

[16] The UCC discusses other categories of tangible goods including agricultural liens and accessions, but the rules for perfecting security interests in them do not significantly differ from the major categories.

[17] Uniform Commercial Code § 9-102(a)(23)

[18] Uniform Commercial Code § 9-102(a)(44)

[19] Uniform Commercial Code § 9-310(a)

[20] Uniform Commercial Code § 9-313(a)-(b).

A purchase money security interest (PMSI) in consumer goods is automatically perfected the moment it attaches. A PMSI is a security interest given to the secured party by the debtor in something that the secured party extended credit to the debtor to buy. For instance, if a bank loaned Julie $5,000 to buy a boat on the condition that she give the bank a security interest in the boat, the bank's security interest is a PMSI. Commonly, the seller of a good receives a PMSI from the buyer of the good. For instance, imagine that an electronics retailer sells a television to Julie for $1,000. The electronics retailer allows Julie to pay for the TV over five years in exchange for a security interest in the TV. In that case, the electronics retailer's security interest is a PMSI.

As stated above, a PMSI in consumer goods is perfected the moment the security interest attaches. No filing statement or possession is required to perfect it.

There is a notable exception to the rules of perfection for consumer goods however. Consumer goods subject to a certificate of title laws have unique perfection rules. This exception covers anything for which a certificate of legal title is required to own under state law. It usually includes cars, boats, and mobile homes. If a good requires a certificate of title, a security interest cannot be perfected by filing a UCC-1 statement, by possession, or by attachment.[21] A security interest in a consumer good requiring a certificate of title can only be perfected by another method allowed by state law. State laws on how to perfect certificate of title goods vary. However, state laws often require a notation of a security interest on the title itself.

State laws also differ as to what happens if a certificate of title is improperly issued without noting a security interest on it. Consider the example provided by the following case.

❖❖

Bank v. Parish
46 Kan.App.2d 422, 264 P.3d 491 (2011)

STANDRIDGE, J.

Robert A. Bazin (Robert) and Bazin Excavating, Inc. (Bazin Excavating) appeal the district court's decision to grant summary judgment in favor of Stanley Bank (Bank) in this dispute over proceeds from the sale of a 2006 GMC Yukon, which was seized by Bazin Excavating in order to satisfy a judgment despite the Bank's purchase money security interest in the truck. For the reasons stated below, we affirm in part, reverse in part, and remand with directions.

Facts

In early 2006, the Bank loaned Johnny and Kellie Parish $40,000 to purchase a 2006 GMC Yukon. As security for the loan, Johnny and Kellie granted the Bank a security interest in the Yukon. The Bank properly filed its notice of this security interest with the Kansas Department of Revenue (KDR) and, thereafter, the lien was on record in KDR's electronic lien filing system known as E-lien and recorded on the truck's paper title and registration receipt.

In a lawsuit unrelated to either the Yukon or the Bank, the district court in Johnson County, Kansas, granted default judgment against Johnny Parish in favor of Bazin Excavating. Following judgment, Bazin Excavating levied on the Yukon and proceeded to have it sold at public auction.

In March 2008, the Bank filed suit against Robert and Bazin Excavating in conjunction with the levy and sale of the Yukon. Both parties filed motions for summary judgment. After considering the

---

[21] Uniform Commercial Code § 9-311(a)(2)

motions and arguments of counsel, the district court granted summary judgment in favor of the Bank. The court found the statement of facts in the Bank's motion to be uncontroverted and adopted the facts and reasoning set forth therein. The court ultimately awarded damages to the Bank in an amount equal to the monetary value of the Yukon at the time of the sale.

***

A Brief Overview of Kansas Law on Secured Transactions in the Context of Personal Property Subject to Certificates of Title in Kansas

Commercial transactions in Kansas are governed by the Kansas Uniform Commercial Code (UCC). K.S.A. 84-1-101 *et seq*. More specifically, the laws relating to secured transactions and the creation, attachment, perfection, priority, and enforcement of a security interest are set forth in Article 9 of the UCC. K.S.A. 84-9-101 *et seq*.

A security interest is a legal interest in personal property that secures the performance of an obligation, usually the payment of a debt. K.S.A. 2010 Supp. 84-1-201(35). The personal property subject to the security interest is commonly referred to as collateral. K.S.A. 2010 Supp. 84-9-102(12). A security interest attaches to collateral when it becomes enforceable against the debtor. To be enforceable, the secured party must give value to the debtor, the debtor must acquire legal rights in the collateral or the power to transfer rights in the collateral to a secured party, and the debtor must authenticate a security agreement that provides a description of the collateral. K.S.A. 2010 Supp. 84-9-203(a)-(b). Upon default of the underlying debt, a secured creditor is entitled to take possession and dispose of the collateral. K.S.A. 2010 Supp. 84-9-609.

In order to protect a secured interest in collateral against third parties who may claim a secured or unsecured interest in the same collateral, a secured creditor typically must file a financing statement with the appropriate government agency setting forth the name of the debtor, the name of the secured party, and the description of the collateral. K.S.A. 2010 Supp. 84-9-310(a). The process of filing this financing statement, usually referred to as "perfecting" the security interest, provides public notice to interested parties that a prior security interest exists.

The UCC creates an exception to the required filing of a financing statement when the secured transaction involves a purchase money security interest, which is created when the secured collateral is purchased by the debtor with money provided by the creditor just for that purpose. K.S.A. 2010 Supp. 84-9-103(b)(1); K.S.A. 2010 Supp. 84-9-309(1); K.S.A. 2010 Supp. 84-9-310(b)(2). A purchase money security interest ordinarily is deemed perfected at the time it attaches to the collateral. K.S.A. 2010 Supp. 84-9-309.

Notably, and relevant to the facts presented here, the UCC provides a secondary exception to the underlying exception, which as noted above deems perfection of a purchase money security interest to automatically occur upon attachment. More specifically, a purchase money security interest in property that is subject to any certificate-of-title law in Kansas, including automobiles, will not be perfected upon attachment but instead can be perfected only by compliance with K.S.A. 2010 Supp. 8-135(c)(5), the Kansas statute applicable to certificates of title and security interests in motor vehicles. K.S.A. 2010 Supp. 84-9-311(a)(2).

***

Although more procedural than substantive, we believe it important to mention the relatively new statute pertaining to the electronic certificate of title. To that end, the division of motor vehicles (Division) is now required to issue a secured certificate of title only in electronic form when

(1) a secured creditor files a valid notice of security interest; (2) when a purchaser applies for certificate of title for a vehicle that is subject to an existing lien. K.S.A. 2010 Supp. 8-135d(a). The Division retains sole possession of the electronic certificate of title until the lien is lawfully released.

We conclude our legal overview by providing a two-point summary of the perfection procedure based on the statutes discussed above when they are construed in conjunction with each other. First and foremost, Kansas law provides that a purchase money security interest in an automobile held by a secured creditor is perfected when the certificate of title issues with the lien noted thereon. Secondly, and because purchasers do not always register and title their vehicles in a timely manner, Kansas law affords a secured creditor the opportunity to perfect its purchase money security interest during the interim time period between purchase and issuance of a certificate of title by timely mailing or delivering a formal notice of security interest, along with the applicable fee, to the Division.

APPLICATION OF FACTS TO LEGAL CONCLUSION

The issue presented in this first count is whether the Bank's security interest in the Yukon takes priority over legal interests previously or currently held by Robert and/or Bazin Excavating. In order to determine priority, we first must determine the type of interest held by each of the parties in the Yukon. To do so, we review the undisputed material facts, which are set forth below.

In early 2006, the Bank loaned Johnny and Kellie Parish $40,000 to purchase the Yukon. The transaction was made pursuant to a note and security agreement executed by the parties, within which the Yukon was designated as collateral to secure the loan. Because Johnny and Kellie Parish purchased the Yukon with the money loaned to them by the Bank for that very purpose, the Bank held a purchase money security interest in the Yukon. K.S.A. 2010 Supp. 84-9-103(b)(1).

On January 31, 2006, the Bank properly completed and timely mailed to the Division a notice of security interest in the Yukon. In doing so, the Bank properly perfected its purchase money security interest in the Yukon on that date. On April 3, 2006, the Division registered Johnny and Kellie Parish as owners of the Yukon subject to the Bank's lien and issued an electronic certificate of title with the Bank's lien noted thereon. By operation of law, the electronic certificate of title noting the Bank's lien necessarily preserved the Bank's previously perfected purchase money security interest in the Yukon.

On June 26, 2007, over a year after the Bank's purchase money security interest in the Yukon was perfected, Bazin Excavating recovered a money judgment against Johnny Parish as the result of a lawsuit unrelated to either the Yukon or the Bank. On July 2, 2007, the district court entered an order in conjunction with this separate lawsuit that authorized the sheriff to attach designated real and personal property owned by Johnny Parish to satisfy the judgment against Parish held by Bazin Excavating. The order of attachment was executed on July 3, 2007, and the sheriff seized the Yukon as part of that order.

On August 29, 2007, Bazin Excavating filed a notice of sale for the Yukon, which designated the sale to be held at auction on September 21, 2007. Two days before the sale was to take place, Robert, the president and sole owner of Bazin Excavating, drove to Topeka in order to obtain a certificate of title for the Yukon. According to Robert, he was told to have the title available at the time of the sale, but he did not recall who told him this. After telling the clerk about the impending sheriff's sale of the Yukon and the need for a certificate of title prior to such a sale, Robert presented the clerk with paperwork, which presumably consisted of a certified copy of the judgment, the order of attachment, the order of execution, the attachment inventory, and the order of sale. Notably, Robert did not inform the clerk that he knew the Bank had a lien on the Yukon. When the clerk handed Robert a paper certificate of title to the Yukon void of any lien, Robert reportedly said:

"'I was under the presumption there possibly could have been a lien on one of these [Robert also seized a motor home].'" The clerk allegedly responded with the comment: "'not any more [*sic*].'" At the September 21, 2007, auction, Robert—on his own behalf and not on behalf of Bazin Excavating — was the high bidder and purchased the Yukon for $23,000.

At some point after Johnny and Kellie Parish defaulted on their loan, the Bank discovered the Yukon had been sold and thereafter made a demand against Robert and Bazin Excavating for the proceeds from the sale. In support of this demand, the Bank highlighted the fact that the electronic certificate of title for the Yukon held by the Division, which the Bank had accessed via the Division's website, properly reflected that the Yukon continued to be subject to a lien by the Bank. Both Robert and Bazin Excavating refused to yield to the Bank's demand, referring to the paper certificate of title for the Yukon that Robert received on behalf of Bazin Excavating from the clerk in Topeka prior to the sale upon which there was no notice of existing lien.

***

From the above, we conclude as a matter of law that the Bank had a security interest in the Yukon that was superior to all other prior and existing interests; thus, the district court did not err in granting summary judgment in favor of the Bank on this issue.

***

Count I: Declaratory Judgment Prioritizing the Bank's Security Interest

The issue presented in this first count is whether the Bank's security interest in the Yukon takes priority over legal interests previously or currently held by Robert and/or Bazin Excavating. . . .

At some point after Johnny and Kellie Parish defaulted on their loan, the Bank discovered the Yukon had been sold and thereafter made a demand against Robert and Bazin Excavating for the proceeds from the sale. In support of this demand, the Bank highlighted the fact that the electronic certificate of title for the Yukon held by the Division, which the Bank had accessed via the Division's website, properly reflected that the Yukon continued to be subject to a lien by the Bank. Both Robert and Bazin Excavating refused to yield to the Bank's demand, referring to the paper certificate of title for the Yukon that Robert received on behalf of Bazin Excavating from the clerk in Topeka prior to the sale upon which there was no notice of existing lien. . . .

From the above, we conclude as a matter of law that the Bank had a security interest in the Yukon that was superior to all other prior and existing interests . . . .

Although not critical to our decision, we note in closing that the conclusion we have reached today is supported by an important legal principle articulated by the legislature in K.S.A. 2010 Supp. 84-9-337, which by its title governs the priority of security interests in goods covered by certificate of title. Relevant to the issue presented here, this statute governs those situations when a security interest in goods is perfected pursuant to applicable certificate of title laws but a certificate of title subsequently is issued by the state that does not reflect the security interest. In this situation, a buyer (other than a dealer) of the goods is entitled to rely on the unencumbered certificate of title and to take free of the perfected security interest only if the buyer (a) gives value for the goods; (b) receives delivery of the goods after the unencumbered certificate of title is issued; and (c) receives delivery of the goods without knowledge of the security interest. K.S.A. 2010 Supp. 84-9-337(1). Although this statute by its language applies only when "a security interest in goods is perfected by any method under the law of another jurisdiction," the qualified nature of the protection reflects an intention by the legislature to assure that only an innocent purchaser will qualify for the exceptional safeguards afforded by this section. (Emphasis added.) K.S.A. 2010 Supp. 84-9-337.

Applying this legal principle to the facts here, we find Robert is not entitled to rely on the unencumbered certificate of title and to take free of the Bank's perfected security interest. As to the first prerequisite for protection, Robert has failed to come forward with any evidence to controvert the Bank's claim that Robert gave value for the Yukon at the auction. As to the second prerequisite for protection, the undisputed facts establish that the Yukon was delivered to Robert on July 3, 2007, immediately after the order of attachment was executed, which was before the unencumbered certificate of title was issued on September 20, 2007. As to the third prerequisite for protection, the undisputed facts show that Robert knew about the Bank's security interest in the Yukon, both when the Yukon was delivered to him on July 3, 2007, and when he retained possession and/or received delivery of the Yukon after he purchased at the auction on September 21, 2007.

Questions Presented

1) Why was it important that the bank perfected its security interest?
2) How did the bank perfect its security interest in this case?
3) What could Bazin Excavating have done differently to avoid this situation?

❖❖

2. Perfection of Inventory

Inventory is any good that is being held for sale or lease by the debtor or any raw materials held for production or works in progress.[22] This essentially includes most things a debtor intends to sell to someone else. For instance, any television an electronics retailer has in stock for sale is considered inventory.

A security interest in inventory is almost always perfected by filing a UCC-1 statement.[23] However, a security interest in inventory can be perfected by the secured party taking possession of the inventory.[24] This, however, is not common considering that businesses sell their inventory to make the money that they use to pay back the secured party.

Security interests in inventory can often become complex. They are often granted by very broad security agreements describing inventory as "all the debtor's inventory now or hereafter acquired." This can lead to multiple creditors having a security interest in the same inventory. Consider the following example.

Julie's Widgets, LLC borrows $100,000 from Great National Bank and Trust. The loan is secured by a security interest in "all Julie's Widgets, LLC's inventory now or hereinafter acquired." Business is going well for Julie's Widgets, LLC. She now wants to expand her business and sell trinkets as well as widgets. To do so, Julie's Widgets, LLC contacts Spencer's Trinkets, LLC. Spencer's Trinkets, LLC agrees to sell Julie's Widgets, LLC 10,000 trinkets for $10,000. Julie's Widgets, LLC does not have $10,000, so Spencer's Trinkets, LLC agrees to loan Julie's Widgets, LLC the money to buy trinkets. To secure the loan, Spencer's Trinkets, LLC receives a security interest from Julie's Widgets, LLC in "all trinkets in her inventory now or hereinafter acquired." For reasons that will be discussed later in this chapter, if both Spencer's Trinkets, LLC and Great National Bank and Trust both perfect their security interests in the inventory (the trinkets), Spencer's Trinkets, LLC's security interest will have priority because it is a PMSI (Spencer's Trinkets, LLC loaned Julie's Widgets, LLC the money to buy the trinkets).

---

[22] Uniform Commercial Code § 9-102(a)(48)
[23] Uniform Commercial Code § 9-310(a)
[24] Uniform Commercial Code § 9-313(a)

The rules to perfect a PMSI for inventory are very strict. A PMSI in inventory is only perfected after the following conditions are met:

1. A UCC-1 statement is filed *before* the debtor receives the inventory
2. The debtor receives possession of the inventory
3. An authenticated notification, describing the inventory and stating that the secured party is taking or will take a PMSI in the inventory, is sent to anyone else who has a security interest in the inventory
4. The notification sent by the secured party to the conflicted secured party is received within five years before the debtor receives possession of the inventory[25]

3. Perfection of Farm Products

Farm Products are goods other than timber involved in a farming operation.[27] Farm products include mostly crops and livestock.[26]

A security interest in farm goods is almost always perfected by filing a UCC-1 statement.[28] However, a security interest in farm goods can be perfected by the secured party taking possession of the farm products.[29] This, however, is not common considering that farms use their farm products to make the money that they use to pay back the secured party.

To perfect a PMSI in farm products, usually a UCC-1 financing statement must be filed within 20 days of when the debtor receives the farm products.[30] However, to perfect a PMSI in livestock, the following requirements must be met:

1. The UCC-1 filing statement must be filed *before* the debtor receives the livestock
2. The debtor receives possession of the livestock
3. The secured party sends an authenticated notification to anyone else who has a security interest in the livestock describing the livestock and stating that the secured party is taking or will take a PMSI in the livestock
4. The notification sent by the secured party to the conflicted secured party is received within the six months before the debtor takes possession of the livestock.[31]

4. Perfection of Equipment

Equipment is essentially any good that is not farm products, inventory, or consumer goods.[32] Equipment is usually goods purchased for use in a business. This category is very broad and can include almost anything a business uses. Examples include a cash register used by a grocery store, a delivery truck used by a parcel service, and computers used by an insurance agency.

A security interest in equipment is almost always perfected by filing a UCC-1 statement.[33] However, a security interest in equipment can be perfected by the secured party taking possession

[25] Uniform Commercial Code § 9-324(b)
[26] Uniform Commercial Code § 9-102(a)(34)
[27] Uniform Commercial Code § 9-102(a)(34)
[28] Uniform Commercial Code § 9-310(a)
[29] Uniform Commercial Code § 9-313(a)
[30] Uniform Commercial Code § 9-324(a)
[31] Uniform Commercial Code § 9-324(d)
[32] Uniform Commercial Code § 9-102(a)(33)
[33] Uniform Commercial Code § 9-310(a)

of the equipment.[34] This, however, is not common considering that businesses use equipment to make the money that they use to pay back the secured party.

To perfect a PMSI in equipment, a UCC-1 financing statement must be filed within 20 days of when the debtor receives the equipment.[35]

5. How to Determine Which Type of Collateral a Good is

To determine what type of collateral a good is, the UCC looks at how the good is used by the debtor. This is particularly important because the same good can be many different types of collateral. Take, for example, an automobile. An automobile, for most people, is a consumer good because, in the hands of the average person, an automobile is used for personal purposes. However, the same automobile used by the consumer for personal use was likely inventory when it was held by the car dealership for sale. The same automobile could also be equipment if it is used, for example, by a parcel service to make deliveries.

TABLE 11.1   How to Perfect a Security Interest in Tangible Goods

Type of Good	Basic Definition	Example	How to Perfect Non-PMSI Security Interest	How to Perfect PMSI
Consumer Goods	Goods that are used for personal, family, or household purposes.	Family car; Household microwave; Personal computer	Filing or Possession	Automatically perfected on attachment
Inventory	Goods being held for sale or lease by the debtor	Cars a car dealership intends to sell; Microwaves to be sold by an appliance store; Computers to be sold by an electronics store	Filing or Possession	(1) Filing before debtor receives goods (2) Send notice to junior lienholders received within the 5 years before debtor receives goods
Farm Products	Goods other than timber involved in a farming operation	Crops; Livestock	Filing or Possession	(1) Filing before debtor receives goods (2) Send notice to junior lienholders within the 6 months before debtor receives goods
Equipment	Goods used in a business	Delivery Truck used by parcel service; break room microwave; Computer used by a company	Filing or Possession	Filing within 20 days of when debtor receives the goods

---

[34] Uniform Commercial Code § 9-313(a)
[35] Uniform Commercial Code § 9-324(a)

B. Perfection of Intangible Collateral

Intangible Collateral is any collateral that exists only because it is connected to non-tangible property. It is split into 5 broad categories: (1) Chattel Paper, (2) Instruments, (3) Accounts, (4) Deposit Accounts, and (5) General Intangibles.[36]

Legal Definitions

Tangible Collateral – types of collateral that can be touched.

Intangible Collateral – types of collateral that only exist because of their connection to intangible property.

---

1. Perfection of Chattel Paper

Chattel paper is defined by the UCC as a "record or records that evidence both a monetary obligation and a security interest in specific goods, a security interest in specific goods and software used in the goods, a security interest in specific goods and license of software used in the goods, a lease of specific goods, or a lease of specific goods and license of software used in the goods."[37] Essentially, chattel paper is a record of a transaction showing that the debtor owes money for a good that the secured party has a security interest in.

For instance, imagine that you buy a car from a dealership. The dealership agrees to let you pay for the car in $500.00 per month installments on the condition that you grant it a security interest in the car. The secured party (the car dealer) then obtains a loan from a bank and uses your contract to pay for the car in installments as collateral. In this case, the installment contract between you and the dealer is chattel paper.

There are two kinds of chattel paper, tangible and electronic. Tangible chattel paper is physical paper. Electronic chattel paper is exactly what it sounds like. It is chattel paper stored in an electronic medium like a computer rather than on physical paper.

Tangible chattel paper can usually be perfected either by filing a UCC-1 statement[38] or by taking possession of the tangible chattel paper.[39]

Like a security interest in tangible chattel paper, a security interest in electronic chattel paper can be perfected by filing a UCC-1 statement.[40] However, unlike tangible chattel paper, no one can be in physical possession of the chattel paper. Instead, a security interest in electronic chattel paper can be perfected by the secured party taking control of the electronic chattel paper.[41] There must only be one *authoritative* copy of the electronic chattel paper if perfection is to be done by taking control.[42]

---

[36] The UCC recognizes security instruments in other intangibles like commercial tort claims.

[37] Uniform Commercial Code § 9-102(11)

[38] Uniform Commercial Code § 9-312(a)

[39] Uniform Commercial Code § 9-313(a)

[40] Uniform Commercial Code § 9-312(a)

[41] Uniform Commercial Code § 9-314(a)

[42] Uniform Commercial Code § 9-105

2. Perfection of Instruments

An instrument is defined by the UCC as "a negotiable instrument or any other writing that evidences a right to the payment of a monetary obligation, is not itself a security agreement or lease, and is of a type that in ordinary course of business is transferred by delivery with any necessary indorsement or assignment."[43] Essentially, it is any document showing money is owed from one person to another for something that is not secured by a security interest. The most common examples are checks and promissory notes.[44]

A security interest in an instrument can usually be perfected by filing a UCC-1 statement.[45] It can also usually be perfected by taking possession of the instrument.[46] If the instrument is obtained for "new value" (money, money's worth in property, services, credit, or release of an obligation),[47] it is automatically perfected for a temporary period of 20 days. On the 21st day after attachment, the security interest in the instrument is no longer perfected unless a UCC-1 financing statement is filed or the secured party gets possession of the instrument.

3. Perfection of Accounts

An account is defined very technically by the UCC as "right to payment of a monetary obligation, whether or not earned by performance, (i) for property that has been or is to be sold, leased, licensed, assigned, or otherwise disposed of, (ii) for services rendered or to be rendered, (iii) for a policy of insurance issued or to be issued, (iv) for a secondary obligation incurred or to be incurred, (v) for energy provided or to be provided, (vi) for the use or hire of a vessel under a charter or other contract, (vii) arising out of the use of a credit or charge card or information contained on or for use with the card, or (viii) as winnings in a lottery or other game of chance operated or sponsored by a State, governmental unit of a State, or person licensed or authorized to operate the game by a State or governmental unit of a State. The term includes health-care-insurance receivables."[48] The definition goes on to specifically exclude other kinds of collateral like chattel paper, instruments, and deposit accounts.[49]

Essentially an account is the right to receive a payment for a service, good, or other item. The most common type of account is known as an account receivable, which is the amount of money a customer owes for purchasing something on credit that is not secured by collateral. For instance, imagine that Julie's Widgets, LLC buys 1,000 trinkets from Spencer's Trinkets, LLC for $1,000 payable in 30 days. Spencer's Trinkets, LLC does not take a security interest in the trinkets. The $1,000 Julie's Widgets, LLC owes to Spencer's Trinkets, LLC is an account receivable, which is simply known as an "account" under UCC terminology.

A security interest in an account is perfected by filing a UCC-1 financing statement in most cases.[50] However, in some very limited cases, a security interest in an account may be perfected automatically. A security interest in a health-care-insurance account receivable, for instance, is perfected automatically upon attachment.[51]

---

[43] Uniform Commercial Code § 9-102(a)(47)

[44] For a more extensive discussion of what constitutes a negotiable instrument, see Section III of Chapter 12.

[45] Uniform Commercial Code § 9-312(a)

[46] Uniform Commercial Code § 9-313(a)

[47] Uniform Commercial Code § 9-102(a)(57)

[48] Uniform Commercial Code § 9-102(a)(2)

[49] Uniform Commercial Code § 9-102(a)(2)

[50] Uniform Commercial Code § 9-310(a).

[51] Uniform Commercial Code § 9-309(5). *See also* Uniform Commercial Code § 9-309(2) (automatic perfection of some minor accounts)

4. Perfection of Deposit Accounts

Deposit accounts are any "demand, time, savings, passbook, or similar account maintained with a bank."[52] Essentially, a deposit account is a bank account.

A security interest in a deposit account is not perfected in the usual ways that security interests in other collateral are perfected. A security interest in a deposit account cannot be perfected by filing a UCC-1 filing statement. It cannot be perfected by possession because bank accounts are intangible and exist only on paper.

The only way a security interest in a deposit account can be perfected is by the secured party taking control of the deposit account.[53] A secured party, unless it is the bank with whom the account is held, may take control by entering into an authenticated agreement with the bank and the debtor that gives the secured party the right to dispose of the funds in the deposit account without the debtor's consent.[54] If the secured party is the bank with whom the account is held, the bank's security interest in the account is perfected as long as the account remains there.[55]

5. Perfection of General Intangibles

A general intangible is defined more by what it is not than what it is. It is a residual ("catch-all") category that is designed to cover everything that is not one of the other recognized forms of collateral.[56] The most common kinds of general intangibles are intellectual property rights (like copyrights, patents, and trademarks) and computer software.[57]

With one exception, security interests in general intangibles are perfected by filing.[58] Usually, a UCC-1 statement is the appropriate statement. However, for filing to perfect a security interest in a copyright, the agreement itself should be filed with the U.S. Copyright Office.[59]

The exception to the filing-by-perfection requirement is the sale of a payment intangible. A security interest obtained in the sale of a payment intangible is automatically perfected upon attachment.[60] A payment intangible is any "general intangible under which the account debtor's principal obligation is a monetary obligation."[61] This narrow category includes any general intangible that is a right to receive money from the debtor.[62] For example, imagine that Julie hits Spencer with her car. Spencer sues Julie for negligence. Before trial, Spencer agrees to a settlement and drops his claim against Julie in exchange for $250,000. Julie's obligation to pay Spencer is now a contractual obligation under which Spencer has the right to receive payment and is considered a payment intangible.[63]

---

[52] Uniform Commercial Code § 9-102(a)(29)

[53] Uniform Commercial Code § 9-312(b)(1)

[54] Uniform Commercial Code § 9-104(2)

[55] Uniform Commercial Code § 9-104(1)

[56] Uniform Commercial Code § 9-102 cmt. 5.d.

[57] Uniform Commercial Code § 9-102 cmt. 5.d.

[58] Uniform Commercial Code § 9-310(a)

[59] *See,* e.g., *In re Peregrine Entm't, Ltd.,* 116 B.R. 194 (C.D. Cal. 1990)

[60] Uniform Commercial Code § 9-309(3)

[61] Uniform Commercial Code § 9-102(a)(61)

[62] Payment intangibles are easily confused with accounts and chattel paper. *See, e.g., In Re Commercial Money Center, Inc.,* 350 BR 465 (B.A.P. 9th Cir. 2006) (reversing a lower court's finding that a payment stream resulting from a debtor's rights as lessor were chattel paper and not payment intangibles)

[63] *See* Uniform Commercial Code § 9-109 cmt. 15.

TABLE 11.2   How to Perfect a Security Interest in Intangible Collateral

Type of Good	Basic Definition	Example	How to Perfect Regular Security Interest
Chattel Paper	Records evidencing a monetary obligation and security interest in a good	Secured Installment contract	If tangible, filing or possession. If intangible, filing or control.
Instrument	Negotiable documents or other uncategorized writing showing a right to payment	Check; Unsecured Promissory note	Filing or Possession If obtained for new value, it is automatically perfected for a temporary 20 day period
Accounts	Right to payment from another for goods or services	Company's accounts receivable	By filing; automatically in very limited circumstances
Deposit Accounts	Bank Accounts	Savings Account	Only Control
General Intangibles	All uncategorized intangibles	Intellectual Property; Software	Filing; automatic if it is a payment intangible

C. Perfection of Proceeds from the Sale of Collateral

Imagine the following scenario. Julie's Widgets, LLC grants a security interest in "all its inventory now or hereafter acquired" to Giant National Bank in exchange for a loan of $100,000. Giant National Bank files a UCC-1 filing statement with the proper authorities to perfect its security interest. Julie's Widgets, LLC has 10,000 widgets in her inventory and sells them to Spencer for $10,000. Julie then refuses to pay her loan to Giant National Bank when the loan balance is $10,000.

In that scenario, even though the inventory was sold, Giant National Bank would be able to collect the $10,000 that Julie's Widgets, LLC received for the widgets. That is because a security interest attaches to the proceeds from the sale of collateral.[64] The security interest in the cash proceeds of the sale collateral is also considered perfected the day that the security interest in the original collateral was considered perfected[65] and remains perfected.[66] So, in the above example, even though a security interest in the cash proceeds of the sale of the widgets did not attach until the widgets were sold, the security interest was considered perfected retroactively to the day the security interest in the widgets themselves was perfected (the filing day).

Proceeds of the sale are also not limited to the cash received from the sale of the original collateral. Consider the following example. Julie's Widgets, LLC grants a security interest in "all its inventory now or hereafter acquired" to Giant National Bank in exchange for a loan of $100,000. Giant National Bank files a UCC-1 filing statement with the proper authorities to perfect its security interest. Julie's Widgets, LLC has 10,000 widgets in its inventory and sells them to Spencer for $10,000. Julie's Widgets, LLC then uses that $10,000 to buy a new truck to deliver widgets. After buying the truck, Julie's Widgets, LLC refuses to pay her loan to Giant National Bank when the loan balance is $10,000.

---

[64] Uniform Commercial Code § 9-315(a)
[65] Uniform Commercial Code § 9-315(c)
[66] Uniform Commercial Code § 9-315(d)(2)

In this case, even though the truck is a step removed from the cash that was received for the widgets, a security interest in Giant National Bank still attaches to the truck because it is considered proceeds subject to a security interest. The security interest in this case, however, will only remain perfected for 20 days. A security interest in proceeds from collateral will only remain perfected after 20 days if the proceeds are cash proceeds or the original filing that perfected the security interest covered the type of collateral that the proceeds is.[67]

In this case, Giant National Bank only filed a UCC-1 financing statement showing a security interest in the inventory of Julie's Widgets, LLC. However, the truck that Julie's Widgets, LLC bought for delivery with the cash received for selling the widgets in inventory is considered equipment, which is not covered by the financing statement. Therefore, rendering the security interest in the truck only perfected for 20 days. If Giant National Bank's UCC-1 financing statement stated the bank's security interest had been for "all inventory and equipment," the truck would remain perfected past 20 days because the truck is being used as equipment, which the UCC-1 financing statement covers.

D. Perfection of Acquired Collateral and Future Advances

After-acquired collateral is "a debtor's property that is acquired after a security transaction and becomes additional security for payment of a debt."[68] A future advance is "money secured by an original security agreement even though it is lent after the security agreement is attached."[69] Consider the following example.

Imagine that Julie's Widgets, LLC takes out a line of credit with Giant National Bank that allows Julie's Widgets, LLC to borrow up to $50,000 at any time. To secure the line of credit, Giant National Bank takes a security interest in "all inventory, now and hereafter acquired." The security agreement also specifically provides that all of Julie's Widgets, LLC's inventory will serve as security for future advances from the line of credit. A month later, Julie takes $5,000 out of the line of credit to buy 1,000 widgets to sell.

The 1,000 widgets acquired after the security agreement are inventory because the debtor intends to sell the them. Julie's Widgets, LLC also acquired them after it entered into a security agreement with Giant National Bank for its inventory. It is, therefore, considered after-acquired collateral.

The $5,000 Julie's Widgets, LLC took out of its line of credit is a future advance because it was money lent subject to the security agreement after the parties entered into the security agreement.

With the exception of most consumer goods and commercial tort claims, a security agreement may include future advances and after-acquired collateral.[70] In the above example, the security agreement specifically included after-acquired inventory, so Giant National Bank has a security interest in the 1,000 widgets acquired by Julie's Widgets, LLC as inventory after the security agreement was entered into.

The $5,000 Julie borrowed from the line of credit is secured by all of Julie's Widgets, LLC's inventory, not just the 1,000 widgets the $5,000 was used to buy, because the security agreement covered future advances.

A security interest in after-acquired collateral is considered perfected on the day the security interest attaches to the after-acquired collateral if it is the type of collateral that was covered by the original financing statement.[71]

---

[67] Uniform Commercial Code § 9-315(d)

[68] After-acquired property, Black's Law Dictionary, § 1 (9th Ed. 2009).

[69] Future Advance, Black's Law Dictionary (9th Ed.)

[70] Uniform Commercial Code § 9-204.

[71] Uniform Commercial Code § 9-502, Official Comment 2; § 9-308(a).

In the above example, assume Giant National Bank perfected its original security interest by filing a UCC-1 financing statement describing the collateral subject to the statement as "all debtor's inventory." The bank's interest in the widgets acquired after the statement was filed would be considered perfected on the day the widgets were acquired because Giant National Bank's financing statement's description of collateral included inventory, which is the type of collateral the widgets are in this case. However, with a few very technical exceptions, future advances are considered perfected on the date that the original security interest was perfected.[72]

E. Perfection by Filing

Most types of collateral are and can be perfected by filing a financing statement.[73] The most common type of financing statement is the UCC-1 financing statement, and it is usually filed with the secretary of state for the state the collateral is in. Filing is the preferred method of perfection because it puts other parties on notice that the secured party has a security interest in the collateral. A filing fee is usually required as well before the filing becomes effective.

A filing statement can even be filed before the security interest in the collateral attaches. In that case, the security interest is usually considered perfected on the day that the security interest attaches.[74] Consider the following example.

Julie agrees to grant Giant National Bank a security interest in her favorite diamond ring in exchange for a loan of $10,000. They sign the security agreement on March 8. On March 9, the bank files a UCC-1 financing statement to perfect its interest in the ring. On March 10, the bank gives Julie the $5,000 promised under the loan.

In the above case, the bank's security agreement did not attach to the ring until March 10, the date it gave value for the security interest. Even though the UCC-1 financing statement was filed the day before attachment, the bank's security interest in the ring is still perfected because perfection became effective upon attachment on March 10.

While filing a financing statement seems simple, filling out a UCC-1 form correctly can be a tricky endeavor. There are some common pitfalls that prevent financing statements from perfecting a security interest.

Much like the collateral subject to the security agreement must be described in the security agreement, the collateral must also be described in the financing statement. The description in the financing statement need not be the same as the description in the security agreement. The description only needs to allow others to reasonably identify what collateral is described.[75] For instance, a description like, "all of the debtor's inventory now and hereinafter acquired" is sufficient.[76]

The standard for the description of collateral in the financing statement is also lower than the standard for the description of collateral in the security agreement. A security agreement's description of collateral does not allow the "supergeneric" descriptions "all the debtor's assets" and "all the debtor's personal property."[77] However, a financing statement can describe collateral as "all assets" or "all personal property."[78]

---

[72] UCC § 9-322(a)(1)
[73] *See* Uniform Commercial Code § 9-310(a)
[74] *See* Uniform Commercial Code § 9-308(a)
[75] Uniform Commercial Code §§ 9-108(a), 9-504(1)
[76] Uniform Commercial Code §§ 9-108(b), 9-504(1)
[77] Uniform Commercial Code § 9-108(c)
[78] Uniform Commercial Code § 9-504(2)

Though there is a provision in the UCC stating that minor errors on a financing statement do not render it ineffective,[79] it is absolutely essential that the debtor's name is complete and spelled correctly.[80] This can become especially problematic when the debtor is a business entity. Consider the following case.

❖❖

Receivables Purchasing Co., Inc. v. R & R Directional Drilling, LLC
263 Ga.App. 649, 588 S.E.2d 831 (2003)

RUFFIN, Presiding Judge.

Receivables Purchasing Company, Inc. (Receivables) and R & R Directional Drilling, LLC (R & R) each claim entitlement to $32,136.84 deposited into the registry of the trial court by Dillard Smith Construction Company (Dillard Smith). The trial court found in favor of R & R. Receivables appeals . . . . For reasons that follow, we affirm.

"Under the clearly erroneous test, we will not disturb the trial court's factual findings if there is any evidence to sustain them." The record shows that Dillard Smith hired Network Solutions, Inc. as a subcontractor on several projects. Network later assigned all rights that it had to payment for this work to Receivables. On April 2, 2001, Receivables filed a UCC-1 financing statement in Bartow County to perfect Receivables' security interest in these payments and thus its entitlement to the payments. In an error that has now become the crux of this dispute, the financing statement listed the debtor as "Net work Solutions, Inc." rather than the correct name "Network Solutions, Inc."

R & R subsequently performed drilling services for Network, for which R & R was not paid. On May 23, 2002, R & R obtained a judgment against Network in the amount of $40,993.74. According to R & R's counsel, R & R performed a UCC search under the name "Network Solutions, Inc." to determine if any individual or entity held a superior claim to the funds. When the search failed to reveal any debtor named Network Solutions, Inc., R & R filed a summons and affidavit of garnishment on July 12, 2002, against Network and Dillard Smith for the amount owed to R & R. Dillard Smith answered the summons, stating that it was holding a sum of $32,136.84 which was owed to Network, but that these funds were also being claimed by Receivables. Accordingly, it requested the court to allow these funds to be deposited with the court. Dillard Smith also filed a counterclaim requesting that the court order that R & R and Receivables interplead their respective claims.

Subsequent to Dillard Smith's motion to interplead, which was the first notice to R & R that there might be a superior claim to the funds, R & R requested that the Georgia Superior Court Clerks Cooperative Authority (GSCCCA) perform a UCC search pursuant to [UCC § 9-523(c)]. The GSCCCA did a certified search under the correct name Network Solutions, Inc. The search did not reveal Receivables' financing statement, which, as noted above, was filed incorrectly under "Net work Solutions, Inc."

On October 8, 2002, based on consent of the parties, the trial court entered an order directing Dillard Smith to pay $32,136.84 into the court's registry and making Receivables a party to the interpleader counterclaim. Receivables then filed a motion for withdrawal of the $32,136.84, contending that Receivables had a superior right to these funds by virtue of the UCC-1 financing statement it filed on April 2, 2001. R & R responded, arguing that Receivables' UCC-1 statement was not a perfected security interest that could defeat R & R's lien on the proceeds because Receivables failed to properly name Network Solutions, Inc. as the debtor on the financing statement.

---

[79] Uniform Commercial Code § 9-506(a)
[80] Uniform Commercial Code § 9-502(a)(1)

This case turns on whether Receivables has a perfected security interest by virtue of its financing statement. If the security interest is not perfected, R & R is entitled to the funds pursuant to its lien on the proceeds, which dates from the service of the summons and garnishment. Following a hearing on October 10, 2002, the trial court entered a lengthy findings of fact and conclusions of law. The trial court concluded that the incorrect name made the financing statement "seriously misleading" pursuant to [UCC § 9-506(b)] and thus the statement was not sufficient to perfect Receivables' security interest. Accordingly, the court found in favor of R & R and ordered that R & R could withdraw the $32,136.84 deposited with the court.

Receivables appeals, contending that the trial court erred in making a factual determination that R & R conducted a diligent search. Receivables also contends that the trial court erred in finding that "Net work Solutions, Inc." is seriously misleading pursuant to [UCC § 9-506(b)].

Under Georgia law, a financing statement is sufficient to perfect a security interest only if it provides the name of the debtor. With respect to a registered organization, as in the present case, the debtor's name is deemed sufficient if the financing statement provides the name of the debtor indicated on the public record of the debtor's jurisdiction of organization which shows the debtor to have been organized.

Accordingly, to be sufficient under the statute, Receivables needed to correctly identify Network Solutions, Inc. on the financing statement. As we have noted, however, Network is incorrectly listed as "Net work Solutions, Inc." [UCC § 9-506] defines the effects of such an error:

(a) **Minor errors and omissions.** A financing statement substantially satisfying the requirements of this part is effective, even if it has minor errors or omissions, unless the errors or omissions make the financing statement seriously misleading.

(b) **Financing statement seriously misleading.** Except as otherwise provided in subsection (c) of this Code section, a financing statement that fails sufficiently to provide the name of the debtor in accordance with subsection (a) of [UCC § 9-503] is seriously misleading.

(c) **Financing statement not seriously misleading.** If a search of the records of the filing office under the debtor's correct name, using the filing office's standard search logic, if any, would disclose a financing statement that fails sufficiently to provide the name of the debtor in accordance with subsection (a) of [UCC § 9-503], the name provided does not make the financing statement seriously misleading.

***

As set forth above, however, these sections specifically define what makes an error or omission in a financing statement seriously misleading. Accordingly, a party filing a financing statement now acts at his peril if he files the statement under an incorrect name.

In the present case, it is undisputed that a search through the Bartow County Superior Court Clerk's Office using the correct name did not reveal the financing statement. Thus, the plain language of [UCC § 9-503(b) and (c)] mandates the result reached by the trial court. Because the name of the debtor on the financing statement is seriously misleading, Receivables does not have a perfected security interest. Accordingly, we find that the trial court ruled correctly in favor of R & R.

Questions Presented

1) Why did the Court find the UCC-1 financing statement "seriously misleading"?
2) What did R&R try to do to determine whether anyone else had a security interest in Network Solutions, Inc.'s right to payment from Dillon Smith?
3) What could Receivables Co.'s attorney have done differently to avoid this issue?

FIGURE 11.2   UCC-1 Financing Statement Form

UCC FINANCING STATEMENT
FOLLOW INSTRUCTIONS

A. NAME & PHONE OF CONTACT AT FILER (optional)

B. E-MAIL CONTACT AT FILER (optional)

C. SEND ACKNOWLEDGMENT TO: (Name and Address)

THE ABOVE SPACE IS FOR FILING OFFICE USE ONLY

1. DEBTOR'S NAME: Provide only one Debtor name (1a or 1b) (use exact, full name; do not omit, modify, or abbreviate any part of the Debtor's name); if any part of the Individual Debtor's name will not fit in line 1b, leave all of item 1 blank, check here ☐ and provide the Individual Debtor information in item 10 of the Financing Statement Addendum (Form UCC1Ad)

1a. ORGANIZATION'S NAME			
1b. INDIVIDUAL'S SURNAME	FIRST PERSONAL NAME	ADDITIONAL NAME(S)/INITIAL(S)	SUFFIX
1c. MAILING ADDRESS	CITY	STATE / POSTAL CODE	COUNTRY

2. DEBTOR'S NAME: Provide only one Debtor name (2a or 2b) (use exact, full name; do not omit, modify, or abbreviate any part of the Debtor's name); if any part of the Individual Debtor's name will not fit in line 2b, leave all of item 2 blank, check here ☐ and provide the Individual Debtor information in item 10 of the Financing Statement Addendum (Form UCC1Ad)

2a. ORGANIZATION'S NAME			
2b. INDIVIDUAL'S SURNAME	FIRST PERSONAL NAME	ADDITIONAL NAME(S)/INITIAL(S)	SUFFIX
2c. MAILING ADDRESS	CITY	STATE / POSTAL CODE	COUNTRY

3. SECURED PARTY'S NAME (or NAME of ASSIGNEE of ASSIGNOR SECURED PARTY): Provide only one Secured Party name (3a or 3b)

3a. ORGANIZATION'S NAME			
3b. INDIVIDUAL'S SURNAME	FIRST PERSONAL NAME	ADDITIONAL NAME(S)/INITIAL(S)	SUFFIX
3c. MAILING ADDRESS	CITY	STATE / POSTAL CODE	COUNTRY

4. COLLATERAL: This financing statement covers the following collateral:

5. Check only if applicable and check only one box: Collateral is ☐ held in a Trust (see UCC1Ad, item 17 and Instructions) ☐ being administered by a Decedent's Personal Representative

6a. Check only if applicable and check only one box: ☐ Public-Finance Transaction ☐ Manufactured-Home Transaction ☐ A Debtor is a Transmitting Utility   6b. Check only if applicable and check only one box: ☐ Agricultural Lien ☐ Non-UCC Filing

7. ALTERNATIVE DESIGNATION (if applicable): ☐ Lessee/Lessor ☐ Consignee/Consignor ☐ Seller/Buyer ☐ Bailee/Bailor ☐ Licensee/Licensor

8. OPTIONAL FILER REFERENCE DATA:

FILING OFFICE COPY — UCC FINANCING STATEMENT (Form UCC1) (Rev. 04/20/11)

A UCC-1 financing statement is usually only effective to perfect a security interest for five years from the date that it is filed.[81] However, a continuation statement can be filed within the six months prior to the expiration of the five-year period that will make the financing statement effective for another five years (from the date the last financing statement would have expired).[82]

If a financing statement is not continued, upon the expiration of the five-year period, the security interest becomes unperfected.[83]

IV. Priority of Security Interests

The most important question about a security interest is whether it has priority over other claims against the debtor. For instance, imagine that two people claim a security interest in the same collateral from the same debtor. Imagine that someone has a lien and someone has a security interest in the same property. There are innumerable situations in which two or more parties could have a claim against the same property.

A. Perfected Secured Creditors vs. Unperfected Secured Creditors

A perfected secured creditor has priority over an unperfected secured creditor. Consider the following example.

Julie grants a security interest in her diamond ring to Giant National Bank to secure a loan of $50,000 on June 25. Giant National Bank does not perfect its security interest in the diamond ring. On June 26, Julie grants a security interest in the same diamond ring to Spencer to secure a $1,000 loan. Spencer perfects his security interest by filing a UCC-1 financing statement on June 30. Julie fails to make payments to both.

In this case, Spencer would have priority over Giant National Bank even though Giant National Bank's security interest attached first because Spencer perfected his security interest, and Giant National Bank did not.

B. Perfected Secured Creditors vs. Perfected Secured Creditors

Between two creditors who have perfected security interests, the first one of them to have perfected or filed a UCC-1 financing statement has priority over the other[84] unless one of the creditors has a perfected PMSI.

Consider the following example. Julie grants a security interest in her diamond ring to Giant National Bank to secure a loan of $50,000. The bank files a UCC-1 filing statement to perfect its security interest on July 1. It disburses proceeds of the loan to Julie on June 25. On June 26, Spencer grants a security interest in the same diamond ring to Spencer to secure a $1,000 loan. Spencer perfects his security interest by filing a UCC-1 financing statement on June 30. Julie fails to make payments to both.

In this case, Spencer would have priority over Giant National Bank even though Giant National Bank's security interest attached first because Spencer perfected his security interest first.

---

[81] Uniform Commercial Code § 9-515(a)
[82] Uniform Commercial Code § 9-515(d), (e)
[83] Uniform Commercial Code § 9-515(c)
[84] Uniform Commercial Code § 9-322(1)

Perfected PMSI Exception

The most notable exception to the "first-to-perfect/file" rule is the perfected PMSI priority rule. A perfected PMSI always has priority over a perfected non-PMSI security interest.[85] For instance, imagine that Julie's Widgets, LLC gives a security interest in all its equipment to secure a loan from Giant National Bank of $50,000 not used to buy equipment. Giant National Bank perfects its security interest by filing on June 25. Julie's Widgets, LLC then buys equipment from Spencer's Trinkets, LLC and only pays for part of it. To secure payment for the rest of the equipment, Spencer's Trinkets, LLC takes a security interest in the equipment that it sold to Julie's Widgets, LLC. This security interest is a PMSI. Spencer's Trinkets, LLC then perfects its PMSI in the equipment by filing a financing statement on August 25, which was within 20 days of the date Julie's Widgets, LLC received the equipment. Julie's Widgets, LLC then defaults on payments to both Giant National Bank and Spencer's Trinkets, LLC.

In the above case, Giant National Bank perfected its non-PMSI security interest on June 24. Spencer's Trinkets, LLC perfected its PMSI security interest on August 25. Although Spencer's Trinkets, LLC security interest was perfected after Giant National Bank's security interest, Spencer's Trinkets, LLC will have priority in the equipment because its security interest was a perfected PMSI.

If a seller's perfected PMSI conflicts with a lender's perfected PMSI, the seller's perfected PMSI will have priority.[86]

C. Perfected Secured Creditors vs. Lien Creditors

In most cases, a perfected secured creditor only has priority over a lien creditor if the secured creditor perfected its security interest before the lien holder executed and levied (enforced) its lien.[87]

Consider the following example. Julie grants a security interest in her diamond ring to Giant National Bank to secure a loan of $50,000. The bank files a UCC-1 filing statement to perfect its security interest on July 30. It disbursed proceeds of the loan to Julie on June 25. On June 26, Spencer wins a lawsuit against Julie who had hit him with a car. Spencer obtains a writ of execution from the Court to levy Julie's diamond ring on July 10 and has it served by a Sheriff on Julie on July 15.

In this case, Spencer would have priority over Giant National Bank even though Giant National Bank's security interest attached first because Spencer obtained a levy on his judgment lien before Giant National Bank perfected its interest in the diamond ring. If Giant National Bank had perfected its security interest (probably by filing) before Spencer had his writ of execution served on Julie by the sheriff, Giant National Bank would have had priority.

It is very important to note that the UCC's definition of lien creditor includes bankruptcy trustees.[88] A bankruptcy trustee is the person the bankruptcy court appoints to dispose of a person's assets in bankruptcy.[89] What this means practically is that, because a bankruptcy trustee is a lien creditor for the purposes of secured transactions, if a security interest is not perfected by the time the debtor goes into bankruptcy, the bankruptcy trustee can void the unperfected security interest, making the secured party just another unsecured creditor unlikely to get paid.[90]

---

[85] Uniform Commercial Code § 9-324
[86] UCC § 9-324(g)
[87] Uniform Commercial Code § 9-317(a)
[88] Uniform Commercial Code § 9-102(a)(52)(C)
[89] *See* 11 U.S. Code § 704
[90] *See* 11 U.S. Code § 544

FIGURE 11.3   Basic Priority of Creditors

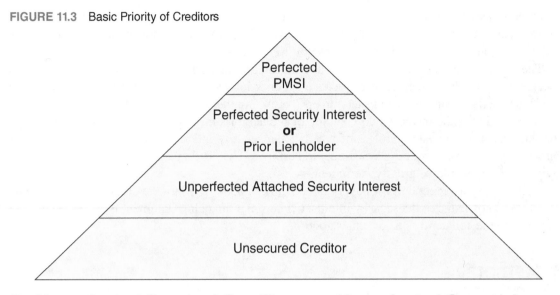

D. Unperfected Secured Creditors vs. Unperfected Secured Creditors

Between two unperfected security interests, the first to attach will have priority.[91] Consider the following example.

Julie enters into a security agreement with Giant National Bank in which she agrees to grant a security interest in her diamond ring to Giant National Bank to secure a loan of $50,000 on June 20. It disbursed proceeds of the loan to Julie on June 25. On June 23, Julie enters into a security agreement with Spencer in which she agrees to grant a security interest in her diamond ring to Spencer to secure a loan of $1,000. Spencer disburses the proceeds of the loan to Julie on June 24. Neither perfects its security interest. Julie fails to make payments to both.

In this case, Spencer would have priority over Giant National Bank even though Giant National Bank entered into a security agreement first. Spencer's security interest attached first because Spencer gave value before Giant National Bank did by disbursing its loan before Giant National Bank did.

E. Secured Creditors vs. Subsequent Buyers of Collateral

Usually, if the debtor sells the collateral without consent of the secured party to a third party, the secured party will continue to have a security interest in the collateral, which means the debtor can take action against the third party.[92]

For instance, imagine that Julie enters into a security agreement with Giant National Bank in which she agrees to grant a security interest in her diamond ring to Giant National Bank to secure a loan of $50,000 on June 20. Giant National Bank files a UCC-1 financing statement to perfect its interest on the same day. On June 25, Spencer, who did not perform a UCC-1 financing statement search, buys the ring from Julie for $10,000.

In that case, the bank would be able to take action against Spencer (discussed later in this chapter) to enforce its security interest in the ring because the item was sold without its consent. There are, however, exceptions to this general rule.

---

[91] Uniform Commercial Code § 9-322(a)(3)
[92] *See,* e.g., *Bank v. Parish*, 46 Kan.App.2d 422, 264 P. 3d 491 (Kansas Court of Appeals, 2011)

Often times, the secured party will want a debtor to dispose of collateral so that the debtor can pay the secured party back. A third party will take collateral free from a security interest if the secured party agrees to allow the debtor to sell it free from the security interest.[93]

The other common exception is the "buyer in the ordinary course of business exception." For instance, imagine that a secured party takes a security interest in "all of debtor's inventory." The debtor then sells the inventory to its customers. Assuming the sale was part of the debtor's regular course of business, the buyer would take any of the debtor's inventory that he or she bought free from any security interest regardless of whether the security interest was perfected.[94] This is, of course, very practical. Requiring a customer to perform a UCC-1 financing statement search before buying anything would be grossly inefficient.

There is also an exception for buyers of consumer goods who buy the collateral (1) for value (2) without knowledge of the security interest (3) before a financing statement is filed (4) with the intent to use the collateral as a consumer good.[95]

V. Remedies

When a debtor defaults on the obligation underlying the secured party's security interest (most often by not making payments on the loan), the secured party has several options. Most commonly, the secured party will engage in "self-help" and attempt to repossess the collateral.[96]

To repossess collateral, all the secured party must do is not "breach the peace."[97] A secured party must be incredibly careful with how it repossesses collateral. First, a secured party will be liable for any damages resulting from a breach of peace during a repossession, such as injuries resulting from the debtor trying to stop the repossession.[98] Secondly, the UCC does not define what it means to breach the peace. This means that what a breach of peace is will vary somewhat from state to state. Consider the following case.

❖❖

Duke v. Garcia
No. 11–CV–784–BRB/RHS, 2014 U.S. Dist. LEXIS 48062 (D.N.M. Feb. 28, 2014)

BOBBY R. BALDOCK, Circuit Judge.

Gustavo Soto owns and operates Access Auto Recovery, LLC, a New Mexico business specializing in the repossession of motor vehicles. Plaintiff Tiar Duke sued Soto and Access Auto, among other Defendants, on a number of claims involving the April 2011 repossession of her car. This opinion deals solely with Plaintiff's motion for summary judgment on her claims that, while repossessing her car: (1) Soto and Access Auto trespassed on her land; (2) Access Auto violated New Mexico's Uniform Commercial Code (UCC); and (3) Access Auto violated New Mexico's Unfair Practices Act (UPA). See Doc. #157.

---

[93] Uniform Commercial Code § 9-315(a)(1)

[94] Uniform Commercial Code § 9-320(a)

[95] Uniform Commercial Code § 9-320(b)

[96] Uniform Commercial Code § 9-609(b)(2)

[97] Uniform Commercial Code § 9-609(b)(2)

[98] Uniform Commercial Code § 9-609 cmt. 3.

I.

The relevant, undisputed facts are as follows. On April 15, 2011, Defendant Soto drove his Access Auto tow truck to Plaintiff's home in Rio Rancho, New Mexico, intending to repossess her Dodge Charger due to her failure to make payments. With Soto was Jerome Baca, an Access Auto employee. At Plaintiff's home, the duo spotted the Charger, and Plaintiff spotted the duo. Baca then exited the truck and approached Plaintiff's garage. A confrontation ensued, the details of which are fiercely disputed. Most significantly for purposes here, Soto testified he saw Plaintiff push Baca several times, whereas Plaintiff testified it was in fact Baca who pushed her several times. At some point during this fracas, Soto left his truck and approached Plaintiff and Baca. Minutes later, Plaintiff and Soto each called 9-1-1. While waiting for the police, Soto and Baca did not leave Plaintiff's property. Several Rio Rancho police officers eventually arrived, separated the parties, interviewed them, and then coordinated Soto and Baca's repossession of the vehicle.

***

III. TRESPASS TO LAND & UNIFORM COMMERCIAL CODE

A. Repossession

Plaintiff first claims Defendants Soto and Access Auto trespassed on her land. This is a state-law claim brought under 28 U.S.C. § 1367, so the Court applies New Mexico statutory law and common law. See BancOklahoma Mortg. Corp. v. Capital Title Co., 194 F.3d 1089, 1103 (10th Cir. 1999). "Trespassing, both at common law and by statute, is the entry onto another's property without permission of the owner." State v. Tower, 59 P.3d 1264, 1265 (N.M. App. 2002). Both sides agree Soto and Baca's initial entry onto Plaintiff's property was *not* a trespass to land because it was privileged under N.M. Stat. Ann. § 55-9-609. This statute, which copies UCC § 9-609 verbatim, authorizes a secured party to take possession of a collateral "without judicial process, if it proceeds without a breach of the peace." No one disputes Access Auto and Soto were pursuing a collateral on behalf of Defendant Automobile Acceptance Corp., a secured party. So Plaintiff's trespass claim is actually that Defendants failed to leave her land *after* they lost their UCC-based privilege to be there because of a breach of the peace. Plaintiff's second claim—closely related to the first—is brought under the UCC directly, which "supports the recovery of actual damages for committing a breach of the peace in violation of Section 9-609." Id. § 55-9-625 cmt. 3. In short, Plaintiff asserts Soto and Baca violated § 55-9-609 by repossessing her car after a breach of the peace.

The parties agree a breach of the peace occurs when a debtor orally protests repossession. See, e.g., State v. Trackwell, 458 N.W.2d 181, 185 (Neb. 1990)(citing Dixon v. Ford Motor Credit Corp., 391 N.E.2d 493 (Ill. App. 1979)); see also Brophy v. Ament, 2009 WL 5206041, at *21 (D.N.M. Nov. 20, 2009) (unpublished). Plaintiff asserts she breached the peace by orally protesting Soto and Baca's repossession efforts. Defendants, on the other hand, assert Plaintiff never told Soto and Baca to leave her property. The Court disagrees, at least in regard to Baca, and by extension, Access Auto. See Tercero v. Roman Catholic Diocese, 48 P.3d 50, 58 (N.M. 2002) ("[I]t is the law in New Mexico that an employer is liable for intentional torts of his employee if the torts are committed in the course and scope of the employment[.]"). On the record presented, a reasonable jury would have no choice but to conclude Plaintiff demanded Baca leave her property. Indeed, evidence indicates Plaintiff made *numerous* such demands. In deposition, Plaintiff testified her first words to Baca were "Get out of my garage." Doc. #157-5, at 2. Plaintiff also testified she told Baca "if he didn't leave, I was going to call the police." *Id.* at 3. Furthermore, Officer Benjamin Sanchez, himself a Defendant, testified when he arrived at the scene Plaintiff was "irate" and repeatedly screaming "I want them off my property!" Doc. #157-2, at 3. Officer Adrian Garcia, also a Defendant, similarly stated he heard Plaintiff "in an escalated voice speaking to Mr. Sanchez that she wanted them off her property." Doc. #189-1, at 2. Finally, the transcript of Plaintiff's three 9-1-1 calls leaves zero doubt—an oral demand was made:

***

These calls document *nine* different times where Plaintiff directly tells a man attempting to repossess her car to either leave her property or get out of her garage. An additional *six* times Plaintiff tells the operator she wants this man to leave. Access Auto and Soto do not contest the transcript's authenticity. Nor do they argue the operator's (highly questionable) assurance that the repossession was lawful affects the analysis. Rather, they first assert Plaintiff's statements, in the recording and otherwise, are self-serving. That may be so, but the question at this point is whether her statements are contradicted, not whether they are self-serving. Regardless, Defendants Sanchez and Garcia support Plaintiff's account, and their statements are assuredly not self-serving. Access Auto and Soto also assert "the meaning of the dialogue recorded on these tapes is not clear." Doc. #169, at 3. The Court disagrees. The tapes are crystal clear—Plaintiff unequivocally demanded, at minimum, that a male repossessor vacate her garage and property.

More significantly, Access Auto and Soto assert the above evidence is contradicted—and thus, an issue of fact exists—because Soto testified he never heard Plaintiff say anything about leaving her property. See Doc. 169-1, at 6. Soto, however, also admitted he did not hear the initial conversation between Baca and Plaintiff because he was in his truck, id. at 3, and that he could only "sort of" hear her 9-1-1 calls because he was back inside his truck calling 9-1-1 when she made them, id. at 6. Thus, his own failure to hear a demand, even if true, does not contradict the abundant evidence indicating demands were made and Baca heard them. Again, this directly implicates Access Auto. See Tercero, 48 P.3d at 58.

Even assuming a genuine dispute exists on whether Soto (somehow) failed to hear Plaintiff's demands, and assuming his own employee's knowledge is not imputed to him (a point which Plaintiff does not raise), Soto still testified he saw Plaintiff shove Baca almost immediately after Baca entered her property. See Doc. 157-1, at 5-6. Similarly, in his 9-1-1 call, Soto stated Plaintiff was "pushing [Baca] because she is trying to shut the garage." Doc. #157-4. Pushing is physical violence, and actual violence means a breach of the peace has occurred, regardless of who initiated it. See, e.g., Williams v. Ford Motor Credit Co., 674 F.2d 717, 718-20 (8th Cir. 1982) (finding repossession lawful because it "was accomplished without any incident which might tend to provoke violence"); Marine Midland Bank-Cent. v. Cote, 351 So. 2d 750, 752 (Fla. Dist. Ct. App. 1977) ("[T]he debtor's physical objection bars repossession even from a public street."); Thompson v. Ford Motor Credit Co., 324 F. Supp. 108, 115 (D.S.C. 1971) ("[A] breach of the peace is a violation of public order, a disturbance of public tranquility, by any act or conduct inciting to violence." (citation omitted))

***

In response, Access Auto and Soto contend Plaintiff's "crazy" and "bizarre behavior when she pushed Baca" did not revoke the privilege to be on her land because she gave no indication she was opposed to the repossession. Again, this is undeniably false in regard to Baca. As to Soto,

Defendants cite his testimony that Plaintiff did not "act like she was opposed" to the taking of the vehicle because she "told us that she had it worked out with the bank." Doc. #169-1, at 5. Soto's testimony is self-contradictory, as pushing someone who enters your property to repossess your car is almost the definition of opposing repossession. We could reject Soto's testimony because of this contradiction and the fact that the rest of the evidence here—most importantly, the 9-1-1 tapes and Sanchez and Garcia's testimony—renders it utterly implausible. See <u>Seshadri v. Kasraian, 130 F.3d 798, 802 (7th Cir. 1997)</u> ("[T]estimony can and should be rejected without a trial if, in the circumstances, no reasonable person would believe it."). Regardless, Soto himself *admits* he viewed the push as a breach of the peace, and he has cited no case law where physical violence occurred and a court nevertheless declined to find breach of the peace as a matter of law. At the end of the day, Soto witnessed a breach of the peace and yet did not leave Plaintiff's property until he repossessed her car.

Two additional arguments raised by Access Auto and Soto should be addressed. First, they argue, seemingly in the alternative, that they cannot be liable for trespass to land or violation of § 55-9-609 because they abandoned repossession once Plaintiff called the police, and the subsequent repossession was a separate attempt to which Plaintiff voluntarily agreed. Access Auto and Soto again rely on Soto's deposition, where he disclaimed any intent or hope to repossess the vehicle after the police were called. Said Soto, "We stopped for the cops. . . . [I]f it wasn't going to happen to get [the] vehicle, we were—you know, that was it." Doc. #169-1.

As above, this narrative is utterly implausible. Even if accepted as true, however, Access Auto and Soto would still be liable on the claims here as a matter of law. Soto's testimony would not affect the trespass to land claim because it is undisputed Soto and Baca never left Plaintiff's property while waiting for the police, even though the breach of peace unquestionably terminated their privilege to be there. This was a trespass to land. And in regard to § 55-9-609, not only did Soto testify the police were present during the eventual repossession, but he essentially concedes they controlled the process.

> "[Attorney]:   Who told you that [Plaintiff] was giving up the vehicle for repossession?
> [Soto]:   The cops. . . .
> [Attorney]:   Did you overhear any conversations that [led] you to understand what it was that [led] Ms. Duke to decide to give up the vehicle voluntarily?
> [Soto]:   No." Doc. #169-1, at 9-10.

According to the New Mexico Supreme Court, a non-judicial repossession is automatically wrongful when "a repossessor is . . . assisted by law enforcement officials in order to prevent a breach of the peace. . . . [T]he imprimatur of the state evinced by the presence of a law enforcement official, without judicial process, removes a repossession from the ambit of [the previous version of § 55-9-609]." <u>Waisner v. Jones, 755 P.2d 598, 602 (N.M. 1988)</u> (citations omitted). As such, even if Access Auto and Soto totally abandoned their first repossession attempt, their later, successful effort did not comply with § 55-9-609. Thus, they are directly liable under the UCC, in addition to being liable for trespass to land.

Second, Access Auto and Soto argue Plaintiff's motion should be denied even if they lose on these issues. To reach this fanciful conclusion, Access Auto and Soto assert a judicial resolution at this juncture would not streamline litigation because a trial on damages would cover the same territory as a trial on the merits. Defendants cite no binding or even remotely persuasive law for this wishful thinking, so the Court declines to exercise its discretion in such a manner.

In summary, the Court finds as a matter of law that Defendants Access Auto and Soto intentionally trespassed on Plaintiff's land when they repossessed her vehicle, and that Access Auto violated N.M. Stat. Ann. § 55-9-609 when Soto and Baca continued with the repossession after a breach of the peace. We therefore grant Plaintiff summary judgment on these claims.

***

V.

No genuine dispute of fact exists as to Plaintiff's claims that Defendants Soto and Access Auto trespassed on her land and that Access Auto violated the UCC, N.M. Stat. Ann. § 55-9-609, and UPA, N.M. Stat. Ann. § 57-12-3. Accordingly, Plaintiff's motion for summary judgment on these claims, Doc. #156, is GRANTED.

Questions Presented

1) What actions constituted a "breach of peace?"
2) What body of law did the court use to determine what a "breach a peace" was?
3) What could the repossessers have done differently in this case to achieve a different outcome?

❖❖

A. Disposing of Repossessed Collateral

Repossessing collateral is only the first step to a secured party getting repaid. After it repossesses the collateral, the secured party has many options. The secured party may "sell, lease, license, or otherwise dispose of any or all collateral in its present condition or following any reasonably preparation or processing."[99]

If the secured party chooses to sell the collateral, it must do so in a "commercially reasonable manner."[100] The sale can be either private or public.[101] However, if the secured party wishes to purchase the collateral, it must do so at a public sale unless the collateral is something normally sold on a particular market or is "the subject of widely distributed price quotations."[102]

The secured party may also choose to keep the collateral to satisfy the debt in most circumstances.[103] If it does so, it must send notice of the proposal to all junior lienholders and, usually, the debtor.[104]

B. Distribution of Proceeds

Once collateral is sold by the secured party, the proceeds are applied with the following priority:

1. Expenses incurred by the secured party to repossess and sell the collateral
2. The rest of the debt the repossessing party is owed
3. Amounts owed to junior lienholders (in the order of priority specified earlier in this chapter)

---

[99] Uniform Commercial Code § 9-610(a)
[100] Uniform Commercial Code § 9-610(b)
[101] Uniform Commercial Code § 9-610(b)
[102] Uniform Commercial Code § 9-610(c)
[103] Uniform Commercial Code § 9-620
[104] Uniform Commercial Code §§ 9-620—621

All remaining amounts are given to the debtor in most circumstances. However, frequently, the sale of the collateral will not cover the above-listed expenses, which means that the debtor still owes the secured party money. A secured party can sue the debtor for this leftover money, which, once granted by the court, is called a *deficiency judgment.*

C. Other Judicial Remedies

A secured party can also choose not to enforce its security agreement and simply sue the debtor on the underlying debt as if it had no security interest.[105] This practice, while rare, can be more beneficial to the secured party than enforcing the security interest in some cases.

Imagine that Julie gets a loan from Giant National Bank to buy a 1985 Ford Pinto. To secure the loan, the bank takes a security interest in the car. Julie does not insure the car and gets into a car accident that completely totals the car. Julie also owns a diamond ring that the bank did not take a security interest in. Julie defaults on her payments to the bank and still owes the bank $5,000.

In the above case, the bank would be foolish to enforce its security interest. The car is totaled, rendering it worthless. Instead, the bank can sue Julie as if it had no security interest and, after receiving a judgment, obtain a writ of execution and levy for the diamond ring to satisfy its debt.

SUMMARY

The law of secured transactions is incredibly technical and complex. Article 9 of the UCC lays out a very formulaic and (usually) precise way to create and enforce security interests.

First and foremost, a security interest must be created and attached. This is done once the secured party gives value to the debtor, and the secured party either takes possession of the collateral or executes a valid authenticated (usually signed) security agreement.

To be sure a security interest is enforceable, it must also be perfected. This is most often done by filing a UCC-1 financing statement, although each type of collateral has its own rules for perfection. The first perfected security interest usually has payment priority over other types of claims made by other creditors, and it will preserve the secured party's claim if the debtor enters bankruptcy.

Beware, however, of the power of the Purchase-Money Security Interest (PMSI). A perfected PMSI takes payment priority over almost all other security interests.

The law of secured transactions is also unique because it allows the secured party to use "self-help" and repossess the collateral if the debtor defaults on the underlying obligation. The secured party must be careful and ensure that it does not "breach the peace" when repossessing the collateral. There are also non-Article 9 remedies at the secured party's disposal as well. If the collateral has no value, other avenues for relief are better to pursue.

In short, the secured party in particular must be careful to pay attention to detail. Article 9 is very precise. The smallest slip-up could result in the secured party not getting paid at all.

---

[105] Uniform Commercial Code § 9-601(a)(1)

CHAPTER
12

NEGOTIABLE INSTRUMENTS

LEARNING OUTCOMES

Upon completion of this chapter the student will be able to:

1 Explain and understand what a negotiable instrument is.
2 Identify the elements of negotiability.
3 Know the different types of negotiable instruments.
4 Understand what a holder in due course is and why becoming one is important.
5 Understand who is liable on a negotiable instrument.

KEY TERMS

acceptance
bearer instrument
check
demand instrument
discharge
draft
drawee
drawer
holder
holder in due course
indorsee
indorsement

indorser
negotiable instrument
order instrument
payee
personal defense
presentment
presentment warranty
promissory note
signature liability
time instrument
transfer warranty
universal defense

I. Introduction

A negotiable instrument is a signed writing that evidences an unconditional promise or order to pay a fixed amount of money on demand or at a specific time in the future.[1] Negotiable instruments serve two main purposes. First, a negotiable instrument, most commonly a check, serves as a safe replacement for cash. Second, it serves as a way to extend credit, most commonly in the form of a promissory note.

    The most important thing about a negotiable instrument is that a holder (person lawfully in possession of the instrument with the right to receive payment) may negotiate (transfer) his or her right to receive payment to a third person. A way to transfer money safely became necessary as the world

---

[1] UCC § 3-104(a)

became more connected. Modern negotiable instruments trace their roots to medieval Europe where, instead of transporting gold coins, merchants traded written bills of sale. The rules surrounding these early negotiable instruments became part of the *Lex Mercatoria* (also known as "Law Merchant"), which was a set of customs and rules developed over time by medieval merchants to settle disputes quickly.

Today, negotiable instruments are governed by state law. Every state has adopted a version of the Uniform Commercial Code (UCC), which itself was heavily influenced by the *Lex Mercatoria.* Negotiable instruments are governed by Article 3 of the UCC and, to a lesser extent, Article 4 of the UCC. There are three versions of Article 3 of the UCC currently enacted by the states. Article 3 of the UCC was first revised in 1990. Only New York has not enacted the revisions made in 1990. Article 3 of the UCC was revised again in 2002, but only 12 states have enacted those revisions as of the time of this writing. The vast majority of states (37) use only the 1990 revisions. Because the overwhelming majority of states use the 1990 version of Article 3, unless specifically mentioned in this chapter, references to Article 3 of the UCC are references to the 1990 edition.

This chapter will answer the following questions:

1. What qualifies as a negotiable instrument?
2. How is a negotiable instrument transferred?
3. Who can a negotiable instrument be enforced by and against?

II. Important Terms and Concepts

There are two broad categories of negotiable instruments, orders to pay and promises to pay. An order to pay is an instrument in which one person (the drawer) commands another person (the drawee) to pay a third person (a payee) a fixed amount of money. For example, an instrument stating "Shelby orders Michael to pay $1,000 to the order of Derick" is an order to pay. The two main kinds of orders to pay are drafts and checks.

A promise to pay typically only involves two parties. An instrument is a promise to pay if one person (the maker) promises to pay another person (a payee). The two most common promises to pay are promissory notes and certificates of deposit (CDs).

FIGURE 12.1 Sample Draft

August 8, 2017 $1,000

30 days after the above-date _____

PAY TO THE ORDER OF: Derick Fiction _____

One thousand and 00/100 _____ DOLLARS

VALUE RECEIVED AND CHARGE THE SAME TO ACCOUNT OF

Michael Thunder

To: Shelby Danger, Inc.   By: *Michael Thunder*

*In this draft, Derick Fiction is the payee, Shelby Danger, Inc. is the drawee, and Michael Thunder is the drawer.

FIGURE 12.2 Sample Promissory Note

August 8, 2017

MICHAEL THUNDER, the undersigned, promises to pay *one thousand dollars ($1,000)* to the order of SHELBY DANGER, INC. on or before 90 days from the above for value received with interest of six percent (6%) per year (computed on the basis of actual days and a year of 360 days) with the interest to be paid on maturity of the note.

By: Michael Thunder
Michael Thunder

*In this promissory note, Shelby Danger, Inc. is the payee and Michael Thunder is the Maker

TABLE 12.1 Table of Parties to a Negotiable Instrument

Orders to Pay	
Payee	Person to Whom Payment is Made
Drawee	Person Whom Drawer Orders to Pay
Drawer	Person Who Orders the Drawee to Pay
Promises to Pay	
Maker	Person Who Promises to Pay
Payee	Person Whom the Maker Pays

Orders to pay and promises to pay both have a payee. If an instrument is payable to anyone, it is known as a "bearer instrument." This is evidenced by using language like "pay to the order of bearer" or "pay to the order of Cash." An instrument payable to a specific person is an "order instrument." It contains language like, "Pay to the order of Shelby Danger." Bearer instruments are normally paid to whoever is in possession of the instrument. Order instruments are only payable to the party named by the instrument.[2]

Negotiable instruments are also classified in terms of when they are payable. A *time* instrument is payable at a specific date in the future. For instance, an instrument payable "on or after January 8, 2017" is a time instrument. A *demand* instrument is one that is payable immediately after it is first issued. An instrument is issued when it is delivered "for the purpose of giving rights" to the payee.[3]

The most important feature of a negotiable instrument is that it can be transferred to another person by the payee. That is, the payee can give up its rights under the instrument to another person. This is done by a process known as indorsement. Indorsement occurs when the payee signs the negotiable instrument over to another person.[4] The person whom the instrument is indorsed to (indorsee) then receives the payee's rights under the negotiable instrument and becomes the holder of the instrument.

---

[2] *See* UCC § 3-109
[3] UCC § 3-105. Under the pre-1990 version of the UCC, issue occurred when it was first delivered to the holder of the instrument.
[4] UCC § 3-201(b)

> ### *Legal Definition*
>
> **Holder** – a person or entity in possession of a negotiable instrument who has the right to receive payment under it.

A. Types of Orders to Pay

The two most common types of orders to pay are drafts and checks. A draft is an order for one person (the drawee) to pay another (the payee).[5] Checks are technically a kind of draft, but they are so ubiquitous that special rules apply to them that do not apply to other drafts. Checks are demand drafts (meaning they are payable immediately when issued) in which the drawee is a bank.[6]

1. Types of Noncheck Drafts

A draft that is payable on demand is known as both a demand draft and a sight draft. One that is payable at a particular time is known as a time draft. The most common kind of draft other than a check is known as a trade acceptance. A trade acceptance, which is used most frequently in the sale of goods, is a draft in which the payee and the drawer are both the seller of the goods. Consider the following example.

Shelby Danger, Inc. is selling 5,000 widgets to Michael Thunder, LLC for $5,000. They enter into a contract on March 1 that specifies that the widgets will be delivered on April 1 and paid for on May 1. Shelby Danger, Inc. creates a draft to secure payment that reads as follows, "Shelby Danger, Inc. orders Michael Thunder, LLC to pay $5,000 to the order of Shelby Danger, Inc. on May 1."

The above draft is a trade acceptance. Shelby Danger, Inc. is both the drawer (person ordering payment) and the payee (person to whom payment is to be made). If Shelby Danger, Inc. wishes to get paid sooner than May 1, it can sell the draft in the commercial money market to obtain payment faster.

A banker's acceptance is similar to a trade acceptance. In a banker's acceptance, the drawee is a bank, the payee is the seller, and the drawer is the buyer. To distinguish it from a check, a banker's acceptance must be a time draft. In a banker's acceptance, the buyer of goods orders the bank to pay the seller from its account at the bank.

2. Types of Checks

Checks are ubiquitous. A check is a demand instrument in which the drawee is a bank. When the drawer is a consumer at the bank, the check is often referred to as a personal check. Because it is difficult to verify whether the account a personal check is drawn on has enough money to pay the amount owed to the payee, business is often done using something called a cashier's check (also known as a bank check). A cashier's check is a check in which both the drawer and the drawee are a bank. To obtain a cashier's check, the bank's customer typically gives the bank money for the

---

[5] UCC § 3-104(e)
[6] UCC § 3-104(f)

check (as well as an additional fee) from its personal account. The bank then transfers that money to its cashier's check account and makes a check payable on that account to whoever the customer requests. Because banks are considered more reliable than their customers, cashier's checks are treated as nearly the equivalent of cash in commercial transactions.

B. Types of Promises to Pay

The most common promise to pay instrument is the promissory note. Promissory notes (often just called "notes") are written promises made by one person (the maker) to pay another (the payee). Promissory notes are usually payable to a specific person, but they can be made payable to the bearer. They are frequently secured using personal or real property as collateral (collateral notes).

While promissory notes can be payable on demand, they are usually payable over a period of time. If a promissory note is payable in installments over time, it is known as an installment note.

Certificates of Deposit (CD's) are "note[s] on the bank."[7] To create a CD, a customer deposits a fixed amount of money with the bank, and the bank promises to pay back that amount plus interest after a certain amount of time has passed. They are very similar to regular bank accounts. The key difference is that a CD is technically a loan from the customer to the bank. A regular bank account is not.

III. Requirements for Negotiability

An instrument is negotiated when it is transferred by someone other than the issuer. For orders to pay, the issuer is the drawer. For promises to pay, the issuer is the maker.

Legal Definition

Negotiation – "a transfer of possession, whether voluntary or involuntary, of an instrument by a person other than the issuer to a person who thereby becomes its holder." UCC § 3-201(a).

In order for an instrument to be negotiable, it must meet certain criteria. It must be in writing[8] and signed by the issuer.[9] It must contain an unconditional promise[10] to pay a fixed amount of money,[11] and it must be payable on demand or at a definite time.[12] Except for checks,[13] an instrument must also be payable to a specific person's order or to the bearer (possessor) of the instrument.[14]

---

[7] UCC § 3014(j)
[8] UCC § 3-103(a)(6),(9)
[9] UCC § 3-103(a)(3),(5)
[10] UCC § 3-104(a)
[11] UCC § 3-104(a)
[12] UCC § 3-104(a)(2)
[13] UCC § 3-104(c)
[14] UCC § 3-104(a)(1)

A. Writing Requirement

A negotiable instrument must be in written form.[15] Because the whole point of creating a negotiable instrument is to transfer it, the writing must be both capable of being permanent and portable. A writing need not be on paper. It can be on anything that "can be reduced to tangible form."[16] While the writing need not be absolutely permanent (nothing truly is), some forms of writing are better than others. For instance, writing a negotiable instrument in pencil is not advisable because it is more easily altered.

NEGOTIABILITY REQUIREMENTS
1. Must be Written
2. Must be signed by the issuer
3. Unconditional promise/order to pay
4. Be for a fixed amount of money
5. Be payable on demand or at a specific time
6. Be payable to order or bearer if not a check

It should be also noted that words that are written out will outweigh figures written on the instrument if they conflict. For instance, most checks require the drawer to write out the sum of money in words as well as write the amount payable as a number. If the amount written in words conflicts with the amount written in numbers, the instrument will be for the amount written in words.[17]

However, with the exception of checks, the writing cannot state that the instrument is "non-negotiable" or "not governed by Article 3."[18]

B. Signature Requirement

The writing must be signed by the issuer.[19] For orders to pay, the issuer is the drawer. For promises to pay, the issuer is the maker. There is no precise formula to determine what a signature is. It only needs to be a symbol showing the signer's intent to authenticate the agreement.[20] It does not need to be hand-signed under Article 3 either and can be done using a machine.[21] It does not have to be a person's name. It can be as simple as an "X." The signature can appear anywhere on the document, but it is usually in the bottom right-hand corner of the document.

While the signature requirement is easy to satisfy, deviating from the normal practices of common negotiable instruments may make your instrument harder or more expensive to sell because irregular instruments are often fraudulent.

C. Unconditional Promise to Pay

The writing cannot contain any conditions making payment of the obligation uncertain.[22] It cannot state, "Pay to the order of Michael Thunder if he eats 100 hot dogs." It also cannot be a mere acknowledgment of the debt. It must specifically order a person to pay or specifically promise to pay a particular sum. For instance, a note stating, "I owe Shelby Danger $500" is not negotiable. Owing someone money and promising someone money are two very different things.

---

[15] UCC § 3-103(a)(6),(9)
[16] UCC § 1-201(43)
[17] UCC § 3-114
[18] UCC § 3-104(d). Under the pre-1990 version of Article 3, this was not true.
[19] UCC § 3-103(a)(3),(5)
[20] UCC § 1-209(39)
[21] UCC § 3-401(b)
[22] UCC § 3-104(a)

While the instrument can reference another writing, such as a promissory note for money borrowed to buy a house referencing the mortgage securing payment of the note, the instrument cannot state that it is governed by another writing or state that it is subject to the terms and conditions of another writing.[23]

D. Fixed Amount of Money

To be negotiable, an instrument must promise or order to pay a fixed amount of money. This requirement has two parts. The amount must be fixed, and the note must be payable in money.

To be considered a fixed amount of money, the sum owed must be ascertainable on the instrument's face. All the amount has to be is determinable with certainty. Thus, a instrument can be for a fixed amount of money even if it requires the maker or drawer to pay with interest. The interest can be for a fixed amount or for a variable amount tied to a specific formula, such as the LIBOR rate, or to market conditions.[24] If the instrument states that it is to be paid with interest but an amount cannot be ascertained from the instrument, the interest rate is the judgment rate in effect at the place the instrument was first set to be paid.[25]

The instrument must also be payable in money. Money is "a medium of exchange authorized or adopted by a domestic or foreign government as part of its currency."[26] Instruments are not negotiable if they are payable in precious metals like gold or silver, or things of value other than money, like crops or livestock.

E. Payable on Demand or at a Specific Time

An instrument must be payable on demand (when issued) or at a specific time in order to be negotiable.[27] If no time is specified on the instrument, the instrument is payable on demand. However, an instrument is a time instrument if the date upon which payment is due can be ascertained when it is issued.[28] An instrument can state it is payable on specific date or within a specific time period (30 days from issue for example). However, an instrument stating that it is "payable on or after the day my sister gets married" is not negotiable because, when the instrument was issued, there was no way to know for certain when the sister would be married.

The instrument does not need to be dated unless a date is needed to determine the time it is to be paid, such as an instrument stating "payable 30 days after issue." An instrument can also be antedated (dated before issue) or post-dated (dated after issue) and still be negotiable.

F. Payable to the Order or Bearer

Other than a check, an instrument must state either that it is payable to a particular person or entity (order instrument) or be payable to bearer (bearer instrument) to be negotiable.

---

[23] UCC § 3-106(a)
[24] UCC § 3-112
[25] UCC § 3-112(b)
[26] UCC § 1-201(24)
[27] UCC § 3-104(a)(2)
[28] UCC § 3-108(b)

To be negotiable, an order instrument must specifically identify a person to be paid. For instance, an instrument stating, "Payable to the Order of My Best Friend" is not negotiable because it does not name a specific person or entity.

Bearer instruments do not need to identify a specific person to be negotiable. However, the instrument must clearly be payable to someone like "Bearer," "Cash," or "Shelby Danger or Bearer."

IV. How to Negotiate an Instrument

A. Bearer Instruments

A bearer instrument (one not payable to a particular person or entity) is negotiated (transferred) when it is intentionally delivered from one person to another. This gives bearer instruments a certain amount of risk. Imagine that Shelby Danger pays Michael Thunder for services performed on his lawn with a check that states "Payable to Cash." If Michael loses this check, and it is found by Derick Fiction, Michael runs the risk of not being able to cash his check. Technically, no negotiation occurred because Derick stole the check. However, if Derick delivered the check to a third person, a negotiation would have occurred, and Michael, for reasons discussed later in this chapter, would be at an even greater risk of not getting paid. For now, consider the following case.

❖❖❖

Chung v. New York Racing Association
186 Misc. 2d 9, 714 N.Y.S.2d 429 (2000)

KENNETH L. GARTNER, J.

A published news article recently reported that an investigation into possible money laundering being conducted through the racetracks operated by the defendant New York Racing Association was prompted by a small-time money laundering case in which a Queens bank robber used stolen money to purchase betting vouchers and then exchanged the vouchers for clean cash. (Newsday, Sept. 28, 2000, at A33, col 1.) The instant case does not involve any such question of wrongdoing, but does raise a novel legal issue regarding the negotiability of those same vouchers when their possession is obtained by a thief or finder. The defendant concedes that "there are no cases on point."

The defendant is a private stock corporation incorporated and organized in New York as a non-profit racing association pursuant to section 202 of the Racing, Pari-Mutuel Wagering and Breeding Law. The defendant owns and operates New York's largest thoroughbred racetracks—Belmont Park Racetrack, Aqueduct Racetrack, and Saratoga Racetrack—where it stages thoroughbred horse races and conducts pari-mutuel wagering on them pursuant to a franchise granted to the defendant by the State of New York.

The plaintiff was a Belmont Park Racetrack horse player. He attended the track and purchased from the defendant a voucher for use in SAMS machines. As explained in *Seminole Tribe v State* (1993 WL 475999, *9 [SD Fla, Sept. 22, 1993, Marcus, J.]): "In addition to accepting bets placed at parimutuel facility windows staffed by facility employees, [some] facilities use SAMS. SAMS are automated machines which permit a bettor to enter his bet by inserting money, vouchers or credit cards into the machine, thereby enabling him to select the number or combination he wishes to purchase. A ticket is issued showing those numbers." When a voucher is utilized for the purpose of placing a bet at a SAMS machine, the SAMS machine, after deducting the amount bet by the horse player during the particular transaction, provides the horse player with, in addition to his betting ticket(s), a new voucher showing the remaining balance left on the voucher.

In the instant case, the unfortunate horse player departed the SAMS machine with his betting tickets, but without his new voucher—showing thousands of dollars in remaining value—which he inadvertently left sitting in the SAMS machine. Within several minutes he realized his mistake and hurried back to the SAMS machine, only to find the voucher gone. He immediately notified a security guard. The defendant's personnel thereafter quickly confirmed the plaintiff as the original purchaser of the lost voucher. The defendant placed a computerized "stop" on the voucher. However, whoever had happened upon the voucher in the SAMS machine and taken it had acted even more quickly: the voucher had been brought to a nearby track window and "cashed out" within a minute or so of the plaintiff having mistakenly left it in the SAMS machine.

The plaintiff now sues the defendant, contending that the defendant should be liable for having failed to "provide any minimal protection to its customers" in checking the identity and ownership of vouchers prior to permitting their "cash out." The defendant, in response, contends that the voucher consists of "bearer paper," negotiable by anyone having possession, and that it is under no obligation to purchasers of vouchers to provide any such identity or ownership checks.

As opposed to instruments such as ordinary checks, which are typically made payable to the order of a specific person and are therefore known as "order paper," bearer paper is payable to the "bearer," i.e., whoever walks in carrying (or "bearing") the instrument. Pursuant to section 3-111 of the Uniform Commercial Code, "[a]n instrument is payable to bearer when by its terms it is payable to . . . (c) 'cash' or the order of 'cash', or any other indication which does not purport to designate a specific payee."

Each New York Racing Association voucher is labeled "Cash Voucher." Each voucher contains the legend "Bet Against the Value or Exchange for Cash." Each voucher is also encoded with certain computer symbols which are readable by SAMS machines. The vouchers do by their terms constitute "bearer paper."

There is no doubt that under the Model Uniform Commercial Code the defendant would be a "holder in due course" of the voucher, deemed to have taken it free from all defenses that could be raised by the plaintiff. As observed in 2 White and Summers, Uniform Commercial Code (at 225-226, 152-153 [4th ed 1995]):

"Consider theft of bearer instruments . . . [T]he thief can make his or her transferee a holder simply by transfer to one who gives value in good faith. If the thief's transferee cashes the check and so gives value in good faith and without notice of any defense, that transferee will be a holder in due course under 3-302, free of all claims to the instrument on the part . . . of any person and free of all personal defenses of any prior party. Therefore, the holder in due course will not be liable in conversion to the true owner . . . Of course, the owner of the check will have a good cause of action against the thief, but no other cause of action . . .

"If an instrument is payable to bearer . . . the possessor of the instrument will be a holder and, if he meets the other tests, a holder in due course. This is so even though the instrument may have passed through the hands of a thief; the holder in due course is one of the few purchasers in Anglo-Saxon jurisprudence who may derive a good title from a chain of title that includes a thief in its links."

However, the Model Uniform Commercial Code in its present form is not in effect in New York. In 1990, the National Conference of Commissioners on Uniform State Laws and the American Law Institute approved a revised article 3. (Model Uniform Commercial Code art 3.) This revised article 3 has never been enacted in New York. . . .

[For the purposes of this case,] the old Code (as still in effect in New York) has the same meaning as the new Model Uniform Commercial Code, which represents a clarification rather than a change in the law.

This result makes sense. A contrary result would require extensive verification procedures to be undertaken by all transferees of bearer paper. The problem with imposing an identity or ownership check requirement on the negotiation of bearer paper is that such a requirement would impede the free negotiability which is the essence of bearer paper. As held in *Tonelli v Chase Manhattan Bank* (41 NY2d 667, 671-672 [1977]): "[Where] the instrument entrusted to a dishonest messenger or agent was freely negotiable bearer paper . . . the drawee bank [cannot] be held liable for making payment to one presenting a negotiable instrument in bearer form who may properly be presumed to be a holder [citations omitted]." (See also, Bunge Corp. v Manufacturers Hanover Trust Co., 31 NY2d 223 [1972].) In *Bunge Corp.*, the dishonest employee of the remitter of an official bank check delivered the check to the named payee but then (with the assistance of a confederate in the payee's employ) stole it back and returned it to the bank, which cancelled it and gave the remitter a credit. The Court of Appeals determined that while an action could presumably be maintained by the payee against the remitter, equitable estoppel would bar the payee from pursuing a claim against the bank. The Court held that upon the check's return by the remitter the bank had no obligation to the named payee to make any inquiry of the named payee before cancelling the check. In a dissent, Judge Breitel objected that freeing the bank of the obligation to make some inquiry of the specific person to whose order the check was made would obliterate the "distinction between order paper and bearer paper." (31 NY2d, at 236.) Implicit in Judge Breitel's objection (as well as the majority's holding) is that in the case of bearer paper there certainly would be no obligation on the issuing bank to make any investigation before accepting its return, and giving value for it. (See also, *Heinike Assocs. v Liberty Natl. Bank*, 166 AD2d 922 [4th Dept 1990] [drawee bank was a holder in due course and thus not liable to drawer for permitting drawer's faithless employee to cash bearer instruments].)

Moreover, the plaintiff in the instant case knew that the voucher could be "Exchange[d] for cash." The plaintiff conceded at trial that (1) when he himself utilized the voucher prior to its loss, no identity or ownership check was ever made, and (2) he nevertheless continued to use it. The plaintiff could therefore not contend that he had any expectation that the defendant had in place any safeguards against the voucher's unencumbered use, or that he had taken any actions in reliance on the same.

This court is compelled to render judgment denying the plaintiff's claim, and in favor of the defendant.

Questions Presented

1) Why was the betting slip considered bearer paper?
2) Were the betting slips considered negotiable instruments?
3) Why did the court not require the racetrack to provide greater protections for customers?

❖❖

B. Order Instruments

Order instruments (those payable to specific people or entities) are negotiated in a two-step process. First, the instrument must be indorsed by the payee. Then, the instrument must be delivered to the new holder. An indorsement is essentially the signature of the payee somewhere on the instrument (usually the back). An indorsement can also be signed on a separate piece of paper attached to the instrument called an allonge.[29]

Legal Definitions

Indorser – the person signing and delivering an instrument by indorsement.

Indorsee – the person to whom an instrument is indorsed and delivered.

C. Types of Indorsement

There are four different ways a check can be indorsed, some of which can be combined into a single indorsement.

1. Blank Indorsement

A blank indorsement is an indorsement accompanied without any further instructions or requirements.[30] It does not list a new payee and usually consists of a stand-alone signature. If an instrument is indorsed in blank, even if it was an order instrument before indorsement, it becomes a bearer instrument following the indorsement, making it negotiable only by delivery.[31]

> **BLANK INDORSEMENT**
>
> *SHELBY DANGER*

2. Special Indorsement

A special indorsement is an indorsement made to a particular payee.[32] It states something like, "Pay to the Order of Shelby Danger" above the signature. Even if the instrument was a bearer instrument before the special indorsement, the instrument becomes an order instrument upon the special indorsement.

> **SPECIAL INDORSEMENT**
>
> PAY TO THE ORDER OF MICHAEL THUNDER
>
> *SHELBY DANGER*

3. Restrictive Indorsement

A restrictive indorsement is an indorsement that requires the indorsee to comply with the written instructions of the indorser. These types of indorsements are often not enforceable against the indorsee or any subsequent indorsees.

---

[29] UCC § 3-204(a). The allonge must be firmly attached. Paper clips will not due, but staples are generally permissible.

[30] UCC § 3-205(b)

[31] UCC § 3-205(b)

[32] UCC § 3-205(a)

For instance, an indorsement containing the restriction "No further indorsement" is not enforceable and cannot prevent further indorsement and negotiation. Article 3 specifically prohibits this kind of restrictive indorsement.[33]

Conditional indorsements are also often not enforceable. A conditional indorsement is one that makes further indorsement conditional on some future event.[34] Conditional indorsements will not be enforced against any future indorsee who takes the instrument for value.[35] For instance, if an indorsement states, "Payable to Shelby Danger on the condition that his Mother bakes me a cake" will not be enforced against any person who takes the instrument for value.

The most common type of restrictive indorsement is known as a collection (or deposit) indorsement. These indorsements require a bank to serve as a collecting agent for the indorser. This kind of indorsement is accomplished by writing "For Deposit Only" or "For Collection Only" above the indorsement signature. These indorsements are effective and lock the instrument into the bank collection process.[36]

COLLECTION INDORSEMENT
FOR COLLECTION ONLY
SHELBY DANGER

Another common restrictive indorsement is the trust indorsement. A trust indorsement requires the indorsee to use the funds to benefit a third person named in the indorsement.[37] This indorsement will state something like, "Pay to the Order of Shelby Danger in Trust for Michael Thunder."

TRUST INDORSEMENT
PAY TO THE ORDER OF MICHAEL THUNDER IN TRUST FOR DERICK FICTION
SHELBY DANGER

4. Qualified Indorsements

As we will discuss later in the chapter, an indorser may become liable to pay the indorsee and any subsequent indorsees the amount of the instrument if it is not paid to the payee. A qualified indorsement is an indorsement in which the indorser disclaims liability on the instrument. There are two ways in which an indorser can become liable, signature liability and warranty liability. Signature liability renders the indorser liable because he or she signed the instrument. Warranty liability renders the indorser liable for transferring and/or presenting the instrument for payment.

A qualified indorsement will relieve the indorser of signature liability but not warranty liability.[38] A qualified indorsement is accomplished by writing the words "Without Recourse" above the indorser's signature. A qualified indorsement can be done either in blank or by special indorsement.

QUALIFIED INDORSEMENT
WITHOUT RECOURSE
SHELBY DANGER

D. Misspelled Indorsements

An indorser should sign his or her name exactly as it appears on the instrument. However, a payee or indorsee's name that is misspelled has three options. He or she can sign his or her name as it appears on the instrument, how his or her name is actually spelled, or both.[39]

---

[33] UCC § 3-206(a). The pre-1990 version of Article 3 would have allowed this kind of indorsement.
[34] UCC § 3-206(b)
[35] UCC § 3-206(b)
[36] UCC § 3-206(c)
[37] UCC § 3-206(d)
[38] UCC § 3-415(b)
[39] UCC § 3-204(d)

E. Instruments Made Out to Multiple Parties

Instruments and their indorsements are often made out to two or more people. If the instrument or indorsement clearly intends that both signatures are required to pay the instrument, such as an instrument or indorsement made out to "Shelby Danger and Michael Thunder," both must indorse the instrument to make it transferrable. If it states the instrument can be paid to either party ("Shelby Danger or Michael Thunder") or it is unclear whether both signatures are required ("Shelby Danger; Michael Thunder"), then the instrument can be transferred by either one or both of their signatures.[40]

F. Instruments Payable to Legal Entities

An instrument payable to a legal entity like "Shelby Danger, Inc." or "Michael Thunder, LLC" can be indorsed by someone authorized by the entity (usually an officer of the entity).

V. Holders vs. Holders in Due Course

Because negotiable instruments are transferrable, it is especially important to know what rights in the instrument the person in possession of it has. Consider the following example.

Shelby Danger, Inc. enters into a contract with Michael Thunder, LLC to purchase 1,000 widgets for $1,000. Shelby Danger, Inc. executes a promissory note to Michael Thunder, LLC for $1,000. Michael Thunder, LLC then sells the promissory note to Derick Fiction and negotiates it to him by properly indorsing the note. Michael Thunder, LLC refuses to deliver the widgets to Shelby Danger, Inc. as promised. When it comes time for Shelby Danger, Inc. to pay, Derick Fiction seeks to collect payment.

Whether Derick Fiction can collect from Shelby Danger, Inc. will depend on what kind of possessor Shelby Danger, Inc. is. A holder is a person in possession of a negotiable instrument with the right to receive payment on the instrument. There are two basic kinds of holders, "ordinary holders" and "holders in due course." Ordinary holders take an instrument subject to any defense to enforcement of the instrument the issuer (maker or drawer) has. For instance, in the above case, Shelby Danger, Inc. has a valid defense to enforcement of the note because Michael Thunder, LLC did not provide the widgets promised.

By contrast, a holder in due course (HDC) takes a note subject only to a small subset of the defenses the issuer has known as universal defenses. In the above example, Derick Fiction would be able to enforce the note against Derick Fiction if he was a HDC because breach of contract is not a universal defense (universal defenses will be discussed later in this chapter). An ordinary holder is essentially any holder who is not a holder in due course. A holder in due course must meet very stringent requirements.

A. How to Become a Holder in Due Course

Holders in due course must meet several requirements. The possessor of the instrument must be a holder (person entitled to enforce he instrument) who has acquired the instrument for value in good faith. The possessor must also take the instrument without notice that it has been dishonored,

---

[40] UCC § 3-110(d)

TABLE 12.2   How to Become a Holder in Due Course

HDC REQUIREMENTS The possessor of the instrument must:
1. Be a holder
2. Give value for the instrument
3. Take it in good faith

4. Take without notice of the following:
   a. The instrument being overdue
   b. The instrument being dishonored
   c. Claims to and defenses against the instrument
   d. Alteration of the instrument
   e. Unauthorized signatures on the instrument

5. Instrument is not so irregular or incomplete that its authenticity should be called into question

without notice that the instrument is overdue, without notice that any person has a claim against or defense to enforcement of the instrument, without notice that the instrument has been altered, and without notice that any of the signatures (including indorsements) were unauthorized.[41] A person cannot become a holder in due course of an instrument that is so irregular or incomplete that its authenticity is questionable.

B. Being a Holder

A person cannot be a holder in due course without first becoming a holder. The holder is any person authorized to enforce the instrument who is in possession of it. A holder of an order instrument is almost always the instrument's original payee or a subsequent indorsee. If the instrument is a bearer instrument, the holder is anyone who took possession of the note by delivery.

C. Acquiring for Value

Value for the purposes of becoming a holder in due course is similar to but different from the concept of consideration in contract law. Not everything that is considered value for the purposes of becoming a HDC would satisfy the consideration element of contract formation.[42] Similarly, not everything that would be considered value under the consideration element of contract formation would meet the UCC HDC requirements for value.

Article 3 of the UCC lists five categories of things that will be considered value and allow an ordinary holder to become a holder in due course.

The most common way of satisfying the HDC value requirement is performing the promise that the instrument was given to pay for.[43] For instance, if Shelby Danger, Inc. signs a promissory note

---

[41] UCC § 3-302(a)
[42] *See* Section II.C of Chapter 7 for a full discussion of consideration
[43] UCC § 3-203(a)(1)

promising to pay Michael Thunder, LLC $1,000 for 1,000 widgets, and Michael Thunder, LLC sells the note to Derick Fiction for $900, Derick Fiction would not become a holder in due course until he paid Michael Thunder, LLC the $900 that he promised to pay for the note. Unlike contract consideration, a promise is not enough to constitute value. There must be performance of the promise to become a holder in due course.

The only exception to this rule is if the promise made is for an irrevocable obligation, such as a bank issuing a letter of credit (a bank's guarantee to a seller that the buyer will pay for goods or services).[44]

With the exception of liens arising from judicial process (like judgment liens), value can also be given by the holder taking a security interest in the instrument.[45] For instance, imagine that Shelby Danger, Inc. needs to purchase new inventory. It obtains a promissory note from Michael Thunder, LLC to pay for $1,000 of the new inventory Shelby Danger, Inc. wishes to purchase. To secure a $1,000 loan from Giant National Bank, Shelby Danger, Inc. transfers the Michael Thunder, LLC promissory note to Giant National Bank as collateral to repay the loan. Because Giant National Bank took a security interest in the promissory note, it has given value.

Banks also frequently become holders in due course by obtaining security interests in the checks presented to them by customers.[46] For instance, imagine that Shelby Danger deposited a check into his account at Local Bank for $1,000. Before depositing the check, Shelby Danger had $100 in his account. The drawer of the check was Michael Thunder, and the drawee was Giant National Bank. In order to deposit the check with Local Bank, Shelby Danger indorsed the check to Local Bank. When Local Bank attempted to collect the check from Giant National Bank, Giant National Bank refused to pay because Michael Thunder did not have enough funds in his account to pay the check. Before letting Local Bank know the check could not be paid, Local Bank cashed a check drawn on Shelby Danger's account for $1,050, resulting in a balance of -$950 for Shelby Danger. Shelby Danger was unable to pay his negative balance to the bank.

In the above example, Local Bank would be a holder in due course for $950 on the check because it gave value by automatically receiving a security interest in the check Shelby deposited up to the amount that it paid out. This is known as the "first-in, first-out" rule.[47]

Value can also be given by taking the instrument as payment for an antecedent claim (claim existing before the instrument was issued).[48] For instance, imagine that Michael Thunder, LLC owes Shelby Danger, Inc. $1,000 for goods it received but never paid for. Instead of suing Michael Thunder, LLC, Shelby Danger, Inc. accepts a promissory note from Michael Thunder, LLC for $1,000 plus interest. In this case, Shelby Danger, Inc. gives value because it took the instrument for a service already provided. While this constitutes value for the purposes of becoming a holder in due course, taking something for a prior claim is often not considered consideration under contract law.

---

[44] UCC § 3-203(a)(5), cmt. 5.
[45] Security interests are discussed in Chapter 11
[46] *See* UCC § 4-210
[47] UCC § 4-210, cmt. 2
[48] UCC § 3-303(a)(3)

A person can become a holder in due course by trading one negotiable instrument for another.[49] For instance, if Shelby Danger owed Michael Thunder $1,000 on a promissory note, and Michael Thunder sold his right to collect the promissory note to Derick Fiction for a check in the amount of $400, the value requirement would be satisfied.

D. Taking in Good Faith

Article 3 of the UCC defines good faith as "honesty in fact and the observance of reasonable commercial standards of fair dealing."[50] This is determined on a case-by-case basis by the courts as the standard is very subjective. However, it does require the holder to honestly believe the instrument is valid and not subject to claims and defenses.

This requirement only applies to the holder of the instrument, not to the transferor. For instance, if a check made out to Michael Thunder was stolen by Shelby Thunder and sold to Derick Fiction, Derick Fiction could still become a holder in due course if he acted in good faith when he purchased the check. It does not matter that Shelby, the transferor, did not act in good faith.

E. Taking without Notice

The instrument must be taken without notice that it is overdue, that it has been dishonored, that it contains an unauthorized signature, that it has been altered, or that defenses and claims to the instrument exist.

1. Taking without Notice that the Instrument is Overdue

Whether an instrument is overdue depends on whether the instrument is a demand instrument or a time instrument. A demand instrument is overdue if someone previously made a demand for payment.[51] A check is overdue 90 days after it is dated.[52] All other demand instruments are overdue if they have been outstanding for an unreasonable amount of time.[53] Reasonableness is determined on a case-by-case basis "in light of the nature of the instrument and the usage of the [instrument in the] trade."[54]

Time instruments become overdue when payment on them is not received by the due date.[55] If the time instrument requires installment payments, the instrument is considered overdue when an installment payment is missed.[56] There is also a special rule for a note that is part of a series of notes for the same debt. Failure to pay even one of those notes on time results in the entire set of notes being considered overdue for the purposes of determining whether the possessor is a holder in due course.

2. Taking without Notice of Dishonor

In order to collect payment for an instrument, the holder must "present" the note to the issuer (drawee or maker). Presentment occurs when demand for payment is made or a demand for

---

[49] UCC § 303(a)(4)
[50] UCC § 3-103(a)(4)
[51] UCC § 3-304(a)(1)
[52] UCC § 3-304(a)(2)
[53] UCC § 3-304(a)(3)
[54] UCC § 3-304(a)(3)
[55] UCC § 3-304(b)(2)
[56] UCC § 3-304(b)(1)

acceptance of a draft is made.[57] Acceptance is the drawee's promise to pay a draft when the draft becomes payable. Dishonor essentially occurs when the party to whom presentment is made refuses to pay the instrument.[58]

Legal Definitions

Presentment – when a holder of an instrument makes a timely demand to the drawee that the instrument be paid or accepted.

Acceptance – promise of a drawee to pay an instrument when it becomes due.

Dishonor – refusal of the drawee to pay a properly presented instrument.

For instance, imagine that Michael Thunder writes Shelby Danger a check drawn on his account at Giant National Bank for $500. Shelby Danger deposits the check at Local Bank. Local Bank seeks to collect on the check from Giant National Bank. Giant National Bank refuses to pay because Michael Thunder does not have enough money in his account to pay the check.

In the above case, Local Bank presented the check when it asked Giant National Bank to pay it. Giant National Bank dishonored the check by refusing to pay it. Dishonor does not mean that the drawee was wrong not to pay the instrument. It just means it refused to do so when the instrument was properly presented to it.

If a holder has notice that an instrument has been dishonored, it cannot become a holder in due course.[59]

3. Taking without Notice of Claims or Defenses

A holder cannot become a holder in due course if he or she has knowledge that another person has a claim against an instrument or that anyone has a valid defense to the enforcement of the instrument.[60] For instance, imagine that Shelby Danger executes a promissory note in favor of Michael Thunder as a promise to pay for goods. Michael Thunder never delivers the goods, but he sells the note to Derick Fiction. Derick Fiction can only become a holder in due course if he did not know that Michael breached his contract with Shelby.

If multiple defenses are available, such as a case where both breach of contract and fraud are available, notice of a single defense serves as notice of all defenses.

F. Irregular and Incomplete Instruments

A holder cannot become a holder in due course if the instrument is so irregular or incomplete that its authenticity is in doubt.[61] An instrument is only too incomplete to prevent a holder from being a holder in due course if it is missing essential information, such as the amount of the instrument or the signature of the maker or drawer. Even if the holder did not know the instrument was incomplete

---

[57] UCC § 3-501(a)

[58] *See* UCC § 3-502

[59] UCC § 3-304(a)(2)

[60] UCC §§ 3-302(a)(iv)-(v), 3-305(a), 3-306

[61] UCC § 3-302(a)(1)

when issued, it can become a holder in due course if the instrument was completed by the time it took possession,[62] even if that completion was fraudulent.[63]

An instrument is too irregular to make a holder a holder in due course if it contains obvious signs of forgery or alteration. However, if reasonable examination would result in knowledge of the forgery, a holder cannot become a holder in due course. Consider the following case.

❖❖

Triffin v. Somerset Valley Bank
343 N.J.Super. 73, 777 A.2d 993 (2001)

The opinion of the court was delivered by CUFF, J.A.D.

This case concerns the enforceability of dishonored checks against the issuer of the checks under Article 3 of the Uniform Commercial Code (UCC), as implemented in New Jersey in N.J.S.A. 12A:3-101 to 3-605.

Plaintiff purchased, through assignment agreements with check cashing companies, eighteen dishonored checks, issued by defendant Hauser Contracting Company (Hauser Co.). Plaintiff then filed suit in the Special Civil Part to enforce Hauser Co.'s liability on the checks. The trial court granted plaintiff's motion for summary judgment. . . .

In October 1998, Alfred M. Hauser, president of Hauser Co., was notified by Edwards Food Store in Raritan and the Somerset Valley Bank (the Bank), that several individuals were cashing what appeared to be Hauser Co. payroll checks. Mr. Hauser reviewed the checks, ascertained that the checks were counterfeits and contacted the Raritan Borough and Hillsborough Police Departments. Mr. Hauser concluded that the checks were counterfeits because none of the payees were employees of Hauser Co., and because he did not write the checks or authorize anyone to sign those checks on his behalf. At that time, Hauser Co. employed Automatic Data Processing, Inc. (ADP) to provide payroll services and a facsimile signature was utilized on all Hauser Co. payroll checks.

Mr. Hauser executed affidavits of stolen and forged checks at the Bank, stopping payment on the checks at issue. Subsequently, the Bank received more than eighty similar checks valued at $25,000 all drawn on Hauser Co.'s account.

Plaintiff is in the business of purchasing dishonored negotiable instruments. In February and March 1999, plaintiff purchased eighteen dishonored checks from four different check cashing agencies, specifying Hauser Co. as the drawer. The checks totaled $8,826.42. Pursuant to assignment agreements executed by plaintiff, each agency stated that it cashed the checks for value, in good faith, without notice of any claims or defenses to the checks, without knowledge that any of the signatures were unauthorized or forged, and with the expectation that the checks would be paid upon presentment to the bank upon which the checks were drawn. All eighteen checks bore a red and green facsimile drawer's signature stamp in the name of Alfred M. Hauser. All eighteen checks were marked by the Bank as "stolen check" and stamped with the warning, "do not present again." Each of the nine payees on the eighteen checks are named defendants in this case.

Plaintiff then filed this action against the Bank, Hauser Co., and each of the nine individual payees. Plaintiff contended that Hauser Co. was negligent in failing to safeguard both its payroll checks and its authorized drawer's facsimile stamp, and was liable for payment of the checks.

---

[62] UCC § 3-115(b)
[63] *See* UCC § 3-407(c)

The trial court granted plaintiff's summary judgment motion, concluding that no genuine issue of fact existed as to the authenticity of the eighteen checks at issue. Judge Hoens concluded that because the check cashing companies took the checks in good faith, plaintiff was a holder in due course as assignee. Judge Hoens also found that because the checks appeared to be genuine, Hauser Co. was required, but had failed, to show that plaintiff's assignor had any notice that the checks were not validly drawn.

***

Hauser Co. argues that summary judgment was improperly granted because the court failed to properly address Hauser Co.'s defense that the checks at issue were invalid negotiable instruments and therefore erred in finding plaintiff was a holder in due course.

***

As a threshold matter, it is evident that the eighteen checks meet the definition of a negotiable instrument. N.J.S.A. 12A:3-104. Each check is payable to a bearer for a fixed amount, on demand, and does not state any other undertaking by the person promising payment, aside from the payment of money. In addition, each check appears to have been signed by Mr. Hauser, through the use of a facsimile stamp, permitted by the UCC to take the place of a manual signature. N.J.S.A. 12A:3-401(b) provides that a "signature may be made manually or by means of a device or machine . . . with present intention to authenticate a writing." It is uncontroverted by Hauser Co. that the facsimile signature stamp on the checks is identical to Hauser Co.'s authorized stamp.

Hauser Co., however, contends that the checks are not negotiable instruments because Mr. Hauser did not sign the checks, did not authorize their signing, and its payroll service, ADP, did not produce the checks. Lack of authorization, however, is a separate issue from whether the checks are negotiable instruments. Consequently, given that the checks are negotiable instruments, the next issue is whether the checks are unenforceable by a holder in due course, because the signature on the checks was forged or unauthorized.

[UCC §] 3-203 and [UCC §] 3-302 discuss the rights of a holder in due course and the rights of a transferee of a holder in due course. Section 3-302 establishes that a person is a holder in due course if:

(1) the instrument when issued or negotiated to the holder does not bear such apparent evidence of forgery or alteration or is not otherwise so irregular or incomplete as to call into question its authenticity; and

(2) the holder took the instrument for value, in good faith, without notice that the instrument is overdue or has been dishonored or that there is an uncured default with respect to payment of another instrument issued as part of the same series, without notice that the instrument contains an unauthorized signature or has been altered, without notice of any claim to the instrument described in 12A:3-306, and without notice that any party has a defense or claim in recoupment described in subsection a. of 12A:3-305.

Section 3-203 deals with transfer of instruments and provides:

> a. An instrument is transferred when it is delivered by a person other than its issuer for the purpose of giving to the person receiving delivery the right to enforce the instrument.
> b. Transfer of an instrument, whether or not the transfer is a negotiation, vests in the transferee any right of the transferor to enforce the instrument, including any right as a holder in due course, but the transferee cannot acquire rights of a holder in due course by a transfer, directly or

indirectly, from a holder in due course if the transferee engaged in fraud or illegality affecting the instrument.

***

The record indicates that plaintiff has complied with the requirements of both sections 3-302 and 3-203. Each of the check cashing companies from whom plaintiff purchased the dishonored checks were holders in due course. In support of his summary judgment motion, plaintiff submitted an affidavit from each company; each company swore that it cashed the checks for value, in good faith, without notice of any claims or defenses by any party, without knowledge that any of the signatures on the checks were unauthorized or fraudulent, and with the expectation that the checks would be paid upon their presentment to the bank upon which the checks were drawn. Hauser Co. does not dispute any of the facts sworn to by the check cashing companies.

The checks were then transferred to plaintiff in accordance with section 3-203, vesting plaintiff with holder in due course status. Each company swore that it assigned the checks to plaintiff in exchange for consideration received from plaintiff. Plaintiff thus acquired the check cashing companies' holder in due course status when the checks were assigned to plaintiff. See N.J.S.A. 12A:3-203, Comment 2. Moreover, pursuant to section 3-203(a)'s requirement that the transfer must have been made for the purpose of giving the transferee the right to enforce the instrument, the assignment agreements expressly provided plaintiff with that right, stating that "all payments [assignor] may receive from any of the referenced Debtors . . . shall be the exclusive property of [assignee]." Again, Hauser Co. does not dispute any facts relating to the assignment of the checks to plaintiff.

Hauser Co. contends, instead, that the checks are per se invalid because they were fraudulent and unauthorized. Presumably, this argument is predicated on section 3-302. This section states a person is not a holder in due course if the instrument bears "apparent evidence of forgery or alteration" or is otherwise "so irregular or incomplete as to call into question its authenticity." N.J.S.A. 12A:3-302(a)(1).

In order to preclude liability from a holder in due course under section 3-302, it must be apparent on the face of the instrument that it is fraudulent. The trial court specifically found that Hauser Co. had provided no such evidence, stating that Hauser Co. had failed to show that there was anything about the appearance of the checks to place the check cashing company on notice that any check was not valid. Specifically, with respect to Hauser Co.'s facsimile signature on the checks, the court stated that the signature was identical to Hauser Co.'s authorized facsimile signature. Moreover, each of the check cashing companies certified that they had no knowledge that the signatures on the checks were fraudulent or that there were any claims or defenses to enforcement of the checks. Hence, the trial court's conclusion that there was no apparent evidence of invalidity was not an abuse of discretion and was based on a reasonable reading of the record.

To be sure, [UCC] section 3-308(a) does shift the burden of establishing the validity of the signature to the plaintiff, but only if the defendant specifically denies the signature's validity in the pleadings. The section states:

In an action with respect to an instrument, the authenticity of, and authority to make, each signature on the instrument is admitted unless specifically denied in the pleadings. If the validity of a signature is denied in the pleadings, the burden of establishing validity is on the person claiming validity, but the signature is presumed to be authentic and authorized unless the action is to enforce the liability of the purported signer and the signer is dead or incompetent at the time of trial of the issue of validity of the signature.

[UCC §] 3-308(a) (emphasis added).]

Comment 1 explains that a specific denial is required to give the plaintiff notice of the defendant's claim of forgery or lack of authority as to the particular signature, and to afford the plaintiff an opportunity to investigate and obtain evidence. . . . In the absence of such specific denial the signature stands admitted, and is not in issue. Nothing in this section is intended, however, to prevent amendment of the pleading in a proper case.

[[UCC §] 3-308, Comment 1.]

Examination of the pleadings reveals that Hauser Co. did not specifically deny the factual assertions in plaintiff's complaint.

Even if Hauser Co.'s general denial was sufficient, the presumption that the signature is valid still remains, unless Hauser Co. satisfies the evidentiary requirements of [UCC §] 3-308. Comment 1 to that section explains that even when the defendant has specifically denied the authenticity of a signature, the signature is still presumed to be authentic, absent evidence of forgery or lack of authorization. Comment 1 states:

The burden is on the party claiming under the signature, but the signature is presumed to be authentic and authorized except as stated in the second sentence of subsection(a). "Presumed" is defined in Section 1-201 and means that until some evidence is introduced which would support a finding that the signature is forged or unauthorized, the plaintiff is not required to prove that it is valid. The presumption rests upon the fact that in ordinary experience forged or unauthorized signatures are very uncommon, and normally any evidence is within the control of, or more accessible to, the defendant. The defendant is therefore required to make some sufficient showing of the grounds for the denial before the plaintiff is required to introduce evidence. The defendant's evidence need not be sufficient to require a directed verdict, but it must be enough to support the denial by permitting a finding in the defendant's favor. Until introduction of such evidence the presumption requires a finding for the plaintiff. [UCC §] 3-308, Comment 1 (emphasis added).]

Here, Hauser Co. has not provided any evidence of the invalidity of the signature. Hauser Co.'s reliance on conclusory statements does not constitute such a "sufficient showing." *See Coupounas v. Madden*, 401 Mass. 125, 514 N.E.2d 1316, 1320 (1987) (defendant disputing validity of notes "had to do more than 'call into question' the 'integrity' of the notes").

***

Hauser Co. provided no factual evidence tending to disprove the authenticity of the signature, relying instead on self-interested and conclusory statements. Consequently, the trial court did not err in finding that Hauser Co. had failed to provide any evidence of the invalidity of the checks.

In conclusion, we hold that Judge Hoens properly granted summary judgment. There was no issue of material fact as to: (1) the status of the checks as negotiable instruments; (2) the status of the check cashing companies as holders in due course; (3) the status of plaintiff as a holder in due course; and (4) the lack of apparent evidence on the face of the checks that they were forged, altered or otherwise irregular. Moreover, Hauser Co.'s failure to submit some factual evidence indicating that the facsimile signature was forged or otherwise unauthorized left unchallenged the UCC's rebuttable presumption that a signature on an instrument is valid. Consequently, the trial court properly held, as a matter of law, that plaintiff was a holder in due course and entitled to enforce the checks.

Affirmed.

Questions Presented

1) Why was the Plaintiff a holder in due course?
2) Why did it matter that Plaintiff was a holder in due course?
3) What could the forgery victim have done to change the outcome of this case?

❖❖❖

G. Situations in Which There Can be no Holder in Due Course

Even if all the requirements of a holder in due course are met, there are some situations in which a holder cannot become a holder in due course. A person cannot become a holder in due course by purchasing an instrument through legal process (such as a judicial or bankruptcy sale).[64] A person cannot become a holder in due course if it purchases the instrument in a bulk acquisition if it is not within the person's ordinary course of business.[65] A person also cannot become a holder in due course by taking over an estate as an administrator.[66]

There are also some situations in which other statutes outside of the UCC have made it essentially impossible to become a holder in due course. For instance, FTC Rule 433, which governs consumer credit transactions, requires consumer creditors to place a statement in every credit contract that states that any subsequent holders will be subject to the claims and defenses the consumer has or had against the creditor. This puts every holder on notice of possible defenses, which effectively prohibits subsequent creditors from becoming holders in due course in consumer credit transactions because one must have no notice of defenses to become a holder in due course.

FIGURE 12.3   FTC Rule 33 Notice

> **FTC RULE 33 NOTICE**
>
> ANY HOLDER OF THIS CONSUMER CREDIT CONTRACT IS SUBJECT TO ALL CLAIMS AND DEFENSES WHICH THE DEBTOR COULD ASSERT AGAINST THE SELLER OF GOODS OR SERVICES OBTAINED PURSUANT HERETO OR WITH THE PROCEEDS HEREOF. RECOVERY HEREUNDER BY THE DEBTOR SHALL NOT EXCEED AMOUNTS PAID BY THE DEBTOR HEREUNDER.

H. The Shelter Principle

The shelter principle is powerful. It allows someone who would not ordinarily become a holder in due course to become one. Under the shelter principle, any holder who obtains the note from a holder in due course becomes a holder in due course, even if that person could not become a holder in due course under normal rules.[67]

For instance, imagine that Michael Thunder and Shelby Danger enter into a contract. Michael Thunder promises to pay $5,000. Shelby Danger promises to deliver 5,000 widgets. Michael Thunder executes a promissory note to Shelby Danger for $5,000 before delivery. Delivery is never made. Before Michael Thunder breaches the contract, he sells the note to Derick Fiction for $4,000. Derick Fiction sells the note to Tito Hurricane in exchange for $3,000. Tito Hurricane, however, knows that Michael breached the contract when he buys the note.

------

[64] UCC § 3-302(c)(i)
[65] UCC § 3-302(c)(ii)
[66] UCC § 3-302(c)(iii)
[67] UCC § 3-203(b)

In the above example, Tito Hurricane becomes a holder in due course under the shelter principle. Normally, he would have not been a holder in due course because he had notice of Shelby's defense to payment. However, because Derick was a holder in due course, he became a holder in due course.

The shelter principle would even make anyone Tito Hurricane sold the note to a holder in due course. As long as title can be traced back to a holder in due course, the holder becomes a holder in due course.

There is one notable exception to the shelter principle. If a holder obtains an instrument by fraud, the holder cannot become a holder in due course.[68] For instance, if someone obtained a note by fraud and later sold it to a holder in due course, the person who committed fraud could not later buy the note back and become a holder in due course.

VI. Defenses to Enforcement

There are several defenses that can be asserted against holders of a negotiable instrument. They fall into two broad categories, universal defenses and personal defenses. Universal defenses are those defenses that are effective against everyone, including holders in due course. They are also known as real defenses. Personal defenses are those defenses that are only effective against ordinary holders and are not effective against holders in due course.

A. Universal Defenses

The following are universal defenses that can be asserted even against holders in due course: (1) Forgery, (2) Fraud in the Execution, (3) Material Alteration, (4) Discharge in bankruptcy, (4) Minority, (5) Illegality, (6) Mental Capacity, and (7) Extreme Duress.

1. Forgery

If the maker or drawer's signature is forged, even if the person seeking to enforce the negotiable instrument is a holder in due course, the maker or drawer has a defense to enforcement.[69] A holder in due course may be able to hold prior indorsers liable, but neither a holder in due course nor an ordinary holder will be able to collect the instrument from the maker or drawee.

There is one exception to this rule. If a maker or drawer's negligence led to the forgery, the maker or drawer can be held liable for some or all of the forgery.[70] For instance, if a company president leaves the company check book in the company's public lobby along with her signature stamp, the company may be liable to pay the resulting forged checks because the company president acted negligently.

2. Fraud in the Execution

Fraud in the execution occurs when the drawer or maker is induced to sign the negotiable instrument without the knowledge that or the reasonable opportunity to learn that the document signed is a negotiable instrument.[71] For instance, imagine that Shelby Danger is blind and his best friend,

---

[68] UCC § 303(b)
[69] UCC § 3-401(a)
[70] UCC § 3-406(a)
[71] UCC § 3-305(a)(1)(iii)

Michael Thunder, has him sign a document that he claims is a delivery receipt but is, in fact, a check. In that case, even if Michael Thunder sold the check to a holder in due course, Shelby Danger would be able to successfully assert the defense of fraud in the execution.

3. Material Alteration

Material alteration occurs when a person changes an instrument so that it changes the terms between the parties to the instrument.[72] This includes changing the amount owed under the instrument, changing the due date on the instrument, or changing the amount of interest paid. Material alteration can only be asserted partially asserted against a holder in due course. Holders in due course can enforce the instrument according to the terms of the instrument before it was altered. Ordinary holders cannot enforce the instrument at all, even on the original terms.[73] If the alteration was simply another party completing the instrument, the HDC can enforce the instrument as completed. However, if the alteration-by-completion was obvious on its face, the holder would not qualify as a holder in due course and would remain an ordinary holder.

4. Other Universal Defenses

Other universal defenses include discharge in bankruptcy,[74] minority of the drawer or maker (usually the drawer or maker is under 18),[75] illegality of the instrument (assuming state contract law renders the instrument void),[76] duress (assuming state contract law renders the instrument void),[77] and lack of mental capacity (assuming state contract law renders the instrument void).[78]

B. Personal Defenses

Personal defenses are defenses that are always effective against ordinary holders but are usually not effective against holders in due course. They include breach of contract,[79] breach of warranty,[80] lack of consideration,[81] fraud in the inducement,[82] discharge by prior payment,[83] nondelivery of the instrument,[84] and ordinary duress.[85]

   Breach of contract is the most common defense raised that will not be effective against the holder in due course. If the contract for which the negotiable instrument was given was breached, the payee will only be able to assert a defense against ordinary holders. For instance, if Michael promises to mow Shelby's lawn and Shelby pays him by check, if Michael breaches the contract by

---

[72] *See* UCC § 3-407(a)
[73] UCC § 3-407(b)
[74] UCC § 3-305(a)(1)(iv)
[75] UCC § 3-305(a)(1)(i)
[76] UCC § 3-305(a)(1)(ii)
[77] UCC § 3-305(a)(1)(ii)
[78] UCC § 3-305(a)(1)(ii)
[79] UCC § 3-305(a)(2)
[80] UCC § 3-305(a)(2)
[81] UCC §§ 303(b), 3-305(2)
[82] UCC § 3-305(2)
[83] UCC § 3-601(b)
[84] UCC §§ 1-105(b), 3-305(a)(2)
[85] UCC § 3-305(a)(1)(iii)

TABLE 12.3   Table of Defenses

Universal Defenses
Forgery
Fraud in the Execution
Material Alteration
Bankruptcy Discharge
Minority (assuming state law recognizes it as a defense)
Illegality (if state law makes it void)
Mental Incapacity (if state law makes it void)
Extreme Duress (if state law makes it void)

Personal Defenses
Breach of contract
Breach of warranty
Lack of consideration
Fraud in the Inducement
Discharge by Prior Payment
Nondelivery

not mowing the lawn, Shelby will only be able to assert his defense of breach of contract against ordinary holders. If Michael sells the instrument to a holder in due course, Shelby will have to pay the holder in due course.

Fraud in the inducement occurs when fraud is committed that causes the drawer or maker to issue the instrument. Unlike fraud in the execution, which is when the maker or drawer is led to believe the negotiable instrument is not a negotiable instrument, fraud in the inducement can be raised as a defense when the maker or drawer of the instrument intentionally issued the instrument but was fraudulently induced into entering into the underlying transaction.

For instance, imagine that Shelby sells Michael 1,000 widgets knowing that they are defective. Despite this, he assures Michael that they are not defective, and the widgets are not obviously defective upon inspection. Michael enters into a contract for the widgets secured by a promissory note. Because Michael entered into the contract because of Shelby's fraudulent inducement, he has a defense against ordinary holders, but he does not have a valid defense against holders in due course.

VII. Liability

There are two kinds of liability on a negotiable instrument, signature liability and warranty liability. Signature liability takes effect when a person signs the negotiable instrument. Warranty liability takes effect when someone transfers the instrument to another party or the instrument is presented to the drawee or the maker for payment.

A. Signature Liability

When a person signs an instrument, including an indorser, he or she is essentially agreeing to pay the instrument to subsequent holders in certain situations. There are two categories of signature liability, primary liability and secondary liability.

1. Primary Liability

A party who is primarily liable on the instrument must pay the instrument when it is properly presented unless that party has a valid defense to enforcement discussed in the previous section of this chapter. His or her liability is immediate upon issue of the instrument and becomes effective when the instrument becomes due.

On a note, the only party that is primarily liable is the maker.[86] On a draft, only an acceptor will be held primarily liable in most cases.[87] As discussed earlier in the chapter, an acceptance is a promise by the drawee to pay the draft when it becomes due. For instance, imagine that Shelby Danger, Inc. issued a draft ordering Derick Fiction, Inc. to pay Michael Thunder, LLC $5,000 on May 3. In order to make Michael Thunder, LLC more comfortable, Derick Fiction, Inc., on April 15, promised to pay the draft. Derick Fiction, Inc.'s promise to pay the draft is called an acceptance.

Once a draft is accepted by the drawee, the drawee becomes primarily liable on the draft. If the draft is one for which the drawer and drawee are the same person, like a cashier's check, the drawer/drawee becomes primarily liable when he or she issues the check.[88]

2. Secondary Liability

Parties that have secondary liability are only liable on the negotiable instrument if the instrument is dishonored by the party with primary liability. A secondary party also only becomes liable only after proper presentment and notice of the dishonor is given in a timely manner to the secondary party. Drawers of a draft[89] and indorsers[90] of either a draft or a note can become secondarily liable.

a. Presentment

As discussed earlier in the chapter, proper presentment occurs when a holder brings an instrument to the drawee or maker in a proper and timely manner for payment or acceptance.[91] An acceptance is the promise of the drawee to pay an instrument before it is due. Presentment can be made in any manner that is commercially reasonable.[92]

Time instruments must be presented for acceptance on or before the due date or for payment on the due date to be properly presented.

---

[86] UCC § 3-412
[87] UCC § 3-413
[88] UCC § 3-412
[89] *See* UCC § 3-414
[90] *See* UCC § 3-415
[91] *See* UCC § 3-501
[92] *See* UCC § 3-501(b)(1)

Demand instruments must be presented within a reasonable time for either acceptance or payment to be considered presented in a timely manner. However, checks must be presented within 30 days of the indorser's signature to hold the indorser secondarily liable.[93]

b. Dishonor

For a secondary party to be liable, the instrument must also be dishonored. Dishonor of a note occurs when it is not paid after it becomes due by the maker.[94] If a draft is accepted, dishonor occurs when the acceptor refuses to pay the instrument after it becomes due.[95] An unaccepted draft (other than a check) is dishonored when the drawee refuses to pay the draft on or after the date it becomes due.[96]

There are special rules to determine whether a check was dishonored. In most cases, checks are deposited in a bank that is not the drawee. For instance, imagine that Michael Thunder has a checking account at Giant National Bank and Shelby has a checking account at Local Bank. If Michael Thunder writes Shelby a check for $500, Giant National Bank would be the drawee. Shelby would not likely take that check (although he could) to Giant National Bank to get what he is owed from Michael. Instead, he would likely take the check to Local Bank and deposit the check there after he indorsed it. Local Bank would then present the check to Giant National Bank for payment. Before presenting the check, Local Bank has no way of knowing whether the check is good or whether it will be dishonored. In this situation, Local Bank is known as the depository bank (because that's where the check is deposited) and also the presenting bank (because it is presenting the check to Giant National Bank). Giant National Bank is the Drawee Bank and is also known as the payor bank (because it is paying the check). Giant National Bank as the drawee/payor bank will then take the money out of Michael Thunder's (the drawer's) account and send it to Local Bank as the depository/payee bank. It can also dishonor the check if Michael Thunder does not have enough money in his account to pay the check.

Under Article 4 of the UCC, there are special rules to determine when a check is considered dishonored after it is paid. A bank has until midnight following the day the check was presented to it to decide whether to pay the item. If it wishes to dishonor the check, it must either return the check, return an image of the check, or give notice to the presenting bank of its desire to dishonor the check.[97] If it fails to do so, the payor bank will be liable to pay the item unless there is a breach of presentment warranties (which will be discussed later in the chapter) or the payor bank can prove fraud.[98]

There is one notable instance when a maker or drawer's refusal to pay an item will not be considered dishonor. If a signature of an indorser is missing from the instrument and the maker or drawee refuses to pay the instrument for that reason, dishonor has not occurred.[99]

---

[93] UCC § 3-415(e)
[94] UCC § 3-502(a)
[95] UCC § 3-502(d)
[96] *See* UCC § 3-502(b)
[97] UCC § 4-301(a)
[98] UCC § 4-302
[99] UCC § 3-501(b)(3)(i)

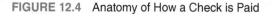

FIGURE 12.4   Anatomy of How a Check is Paid

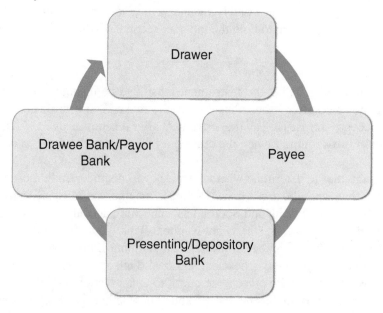

c. *Notice of Dishonor*

To hold a party secondarily liable, notice must also be given to that party in a timely manner. Any party other than a bank must give notice of dishonor to the drawer or other party it wishes to hold liable under the instrument within 30 days after it receives notice of dishonor.[100] A depository/payor bank (also known as a collecting bank) must give notice of dishonor by midnight of the business day following the day it received notice of dishonor.[101]

3. Unauthorized Signatures

If a person signs another's name to an instrument without authorization, the person's whose name was forged will not be liable to anyone on the instrument unless one of two exceptions applies. The forger will be liable and treated as if he or she signed the instrument in his or her own name if the holder gives value for the instrument and takes it in good faith.[102] A person will be liable if he or she agrees to pay the instrument by ratifying the forged signature.[103] A person may also be liable for some or all of the instrument if his or her negligence made the forgery possible, such as by leaving a signature stamp and checkbook out in public.[104] However, if a party is negligent in paying the check, the drawer may once again be off the hook. Consider the following case.

---

[100] UCC § 3-503(c). Under § 3-508(2) of the pre-1990 version of the UCC, notice of dishonor had to be given by non-banks by midnight of the third business day following notice of dishonor.

[101] UCC § 3-503(c).

[102] UCC § 3-403(a)

[103] UCC § 3-403(a)

[104] UCC § 3-406

❖❖

Triffin v. Pomerantz Staffing Services, LLC
370 N.J.Super. 301, 851 A.2d 100 (2004)

The opinion of the court was delivered by FISHER, J.A.D.

In this case, we are called upon to determine whether an innocent party, whose check stock was imitated and whose signature was forged, can be held liable when another innocent party pays that check in good faith. We answer that question in the negative and affirm.

On April 20 and 21, 2002, Friendly Check Cashing Corp. was presented with eighteen counterfeit checks, in amounts ranging between $380 and $398, purporting to have been issued by defendant Pomerantz Staffing Services, LLC on its account with defendant Bank of New York. Each check bore Pomerantz's full name and address and a facsimile signature of "Gary Pomerantz." Also printed on the face of each check was a warning: "THE BACK OF THIS CHECK HAS HEAT SENSITIVE INK TO CONFIRM AUTHENTICITY." Without examining the checks as suggested by this warning, Friendly cashed the checks, which the bank returned unpaid and stamped: "COUNTERFEIT" and "DO NOT PRESENT AGAIN."

Friendly assigned any causes of action arising from the dishonoring of these checks to plaintiff Robert J. Triffin, who filed suit against Pomerantz, the Bank of New York and the individual payees on the eighteen checks. Plaintiff made no attempt to effect service on the payees and voluntarily dismissed his claim against the bank. Plaintiff and Pomerantz, the remaining parties, filed cross-motions for summary judgment. The trial judge granted Pomerantz's motion and dismissed the action.

We start with the signatures on the face of the checks, which purport to have been made by Pomerantz. Pomerantz claimed, and plaintiff did not dispute, that it did not sign the checks which also did not come from its check stock. Since "[a] person is not liable on an instrument unless the person signed the instrument," or the instrument was signed by another in a representative or authorized capacity, N.J.S.A. 12A:3-401(a), the Uniform Commercial Code must be examined to determine what constitutes a signature which will obligate a drawer in these circumstances to pay an instrument.

The Uniform Commercial Code, with its interest in the expeditious movement of funds through the use of checks and other negotiable instruments, declares that a document is "signed" when it includes "any symbol executed or adopted by a party with present intention to authenticate a writing."[UCC §] 1-201(39). The importance of the authentication requirement was explained by the drafters of the Code in the following way:

The inclusion of authentication in the definition of "signed" is to make clear that as the term is used in this Act a complete signature is not necessary. Authentication may be printed, stamped or written; it may be by initials or by thumbprint. It may be on any part of the document and in appropriate cases may be found in a billhead or letterhead. No catalog of possible authentications can be complete and the court must use common sense and commercial experience in passing upon these matters. The question always is whether the symbol was executed or adopted by the party with present intention to authenticate the writing.

[UCC §] 1-201(39) Uniform Commercial Code comment (emphasis added).]

See also [UCC §] 3-401(b) ("A signature may be made manually or by means of a device or machine, and by the use of any name, including a trade or assumed name, or by a word, mark, or symbol executed or adopted by a person with present intention to authenticate a writing.").

Since the emphasis is not on the manner in which a symbol, representing a signature, is made, but is on the signer's "present intention to authenticate the writing," it is clear that a forged signature cannot convey the intention of the drawer to authenticate the writing.

Even forged signatures, however, have some significance in determining liability and the risk of loss imposed by the Uniform Commercial Code. That is, the Code does not place forgeries in a class by themselves but includes them within the definition of "unauthorized" signatures. [UCC §] 1-201(43) ("'Unauthorized' signature or indorsement means one made without actual, implied, or apparent authority and includes a forgery."). In setting the bounds of liability regarding an instrument containing an "unauthorized" signature, [UCC §] 3-403(a) declares that an "unauthorized signature is ineffective except as the signature of the unauthorized signer in favor of a person who in good faith pays the instrument or takes it for value," N.J.S.A. 12A:3-403(a).

The drafters' comments to the Code have not entirely clarified the extent to which this provision applies. There is also scant case law on the subject. Nevertheless, we conclude, as the plain language of [UCC §] 3-403(a) demonstrates, that only the malefactor can be held liable on a forged or counterfeit instrument; that is, as the statute expressly states, the unauthorized signature is ineffective "except as the signature of the unauthorized signer." See Perini Corp. v. First Nat'l Bank, 553 F.2d 398, 404 (5th Cir.1977) ("The forgery does not operate as the ostensible drawer's signature.") Since some malefactor signed Pomerantz's name on these checks, then that malefactor can be held liable, but not Pomerantz. See Henry J. Bailey and Richard B. Hagedorn, Brady on Bank Checks: The Law of Bank Checks,¶ 28.01 (Pratt ed., 2004); Payne v. White, 101 A.D.2d 975, 477 N.Y.S.2d 456, 458-59 (App.Div.1984).

Plaintiff presented no sworn statements or other evidential material in opposition to Pomerantz's sworn statements that the checks did not come from its check stock and the signatures embossed on the instruments were not Pomerantz's. Accordingly, it was undisputed that the forged signatures were "unauthorized" and could not impose liability on Pomerantz for these counterfeit checks. We, thus, affirm the summary judgment entered in favor of Pomerantz.

Even if the Code were to permit liability on a drawer whose signature has been forged, plaintiff would still be obligated to show that Friendly was a holder in due course. For the following reasons, we conclude that the undisputed facts do not permit Friendly to claim the status of holder in due course.

A holder in due course is "one who takes an instrument for value, in good faith, and without notice of dishonor or any defense against or claim to it on the part of any person." Triffin v. Quality Urban Hous. Partners, 352 N.J.Super. 538, 541, 800 A.2d 905, 907 (App.Div.2002). Of particular importance [UCC §] 3-302(a)(1), which further defines "holder in due course" as "the holder of an instrument if . . . the instrument when issued or negotiated to the holder does not bear such apparent evidence of forgery or alteration or is not otherwise so irregular or incomplete as to call into question its authenticity."

Our resolution of the application of [UCC §] 3-302(a)(1), and the claim that Friendly was a holder in due course, is illuminated by our earlier decision in *Triffin v. Somerset Valley Bank*, 343 N.J.Super. 73, 777 A.2d 993 (App.Div. 2001). There, we affirmed a summary judgment entered in favor of plaintiff where, like here, he was assigned the rights of a check cashing entity to sue on dishonored checks. The checks in Somerset Valley were allegedly issued by Hauser Co., which in the ordinary course of its business, signed its checks through the use of a facsimile signature, like Pomerantz. While Hauser argued that the checks were unauthorized and forged, we also recognized that Hauser failed to oppose plaintiff's summary judgment motion with "anything about the appearance of the checks to place the check cashing company on notice that any check was not valid" and that an examination of the checks revealed that the forged signature "was identical to Hauser Co.'s authorized facsimile signature." Id. at 85, 777 A.2d at 1000. In the absence of any question or irregularity about the checks themselves or the circumstances surrounding the transactions, we concluded in Somerset Valley that plaintiff's assignor was a holder in due course as defined by [UCC §] 3-302(a)(1). The case at hand, however, presents the obverse counterpart to Somerset Valley, differing significantly because the record here contains undisputed evidence that the checks were counterfeit, and appeared to be so, when presented to Friendly, plaintiff's assignor.

Once the validity of a signature is denied in the pleadings, the burden of "establishing validity is on the person claiming validity." N.J.S.A. 12A:3-308(a); Somerset Valley, supra, 343 N.J.Super. at 85, 777 A.2d 993. Because Pomerantz disputed the validity of the signatures on the checks, it became incumbent upon plaintiff to show that the signatures were valid by showing an absence of "evidence of forgery or alteration" on the face of the instruments. In addition, a holder in due course must satisfy both a subjective and an objective test of good faith, Maine Fam. Fed. Credit Union v. Sun Life Assur. Co. of Canada, 727 A.2d 335, 340 (Me.1999), requiring a consideration of the holder's honesty in fact and observance of reasonable commercial standards, [UCC §] 3-103(a)(4); Travelers Indem. Co. v. Good, 325 N.J.Super. 16, 24, 737 A.2d 690, 695 (App.Div.1999). When the Uniform Commercial Code placed the burden of proving the validity of a signature upon the person asserting validity, N.J.S.A. 12A:3-308(a), it created a standard by which the legitimacy of a check is judged by its appearance, N.J.S.A. 12A:3-302(a)(1), and in requiring that the holder take the instrument in good faith, N.J.S.A. 12A:3-302(a)(2), the Code deemed relevant an examination of the honesty, the state of mind, the experience, and the reasonableness of the conduct of the alleged holder in due course.

In this case, plaintiff did not claim that Friendly examined the checks to determine whether they had heat sensitive ink and plaintiff made no attempt to explain this failure. Each check directed the holder to touch the check to confirm its authenticity, advising that, because of the heat sensitive ink, the logo "should fade when touched." Plaintiff did not dispute Pomerantz's assertion that the counterfeit checks did not contain heat sensitive ink and that their bogus nature would have been revealed by simply touching the checks. Unlike Somerset Valley, the evidence in this case was undisputed that the checks bore, when presented to Friendly, evidence that they were not authentic. We are satisfied that the failure to utilize the heat sensitive test described on the face of the instruments—which, if utilized, would have unquestionably revealed that the checks were counterfeit—precluded Friendly, as a matter of law, from claiming holder in due course status. A party who fails to make an inquiry, reasonably required by the circumstances of the transaction, so as to remain ignorant of facts that might disclose a defect cannot claim to be a holder in due course. General Inv. Corp. v. Angelini, 58 N.J. 396, 403-04, 278 A.2d 193, 196-97 (1971).

This result is further compelled by the fact that the party claiming to be a holder in due course was in the business of cashing checks. It is reasonable, in considering whether the instruments were received in good faith and whether the holder comported with reasonable commercial standards, that the holder be expected to fully examine the front and back of the instrument and, where the instrument purports to contain a method by which its authenticity may be tested, that the holder actually utilize that method. While this failure would likely preclude any holder of these instruments from claiming holder in due course status, it particularly precludes entities in the business of cashing checks. Accordingly, we reject plaintiff's contention that this information was irrelevant. Instead, we hold that it is commercially unreasonable for a check cashing entity to fail to utilize the heat sensitive test when so cautioned on the face of the check.

Plaintiff also misguidedly argues that Pomerantz's contract with the bank impacts upon these issues. This contract authorized the bank to honor and pay, without limit and without inquiry, checks drawn on the account "regardless of by whom or by what means the actual or purported facsimile signature thereon may have been affixed thereto, if such a signature resembles the facsimile specimen filed with the Bank." Contrary to plaintiff's contentions, the contract governs only the relationship between the account holder and the bank, and purports to place the risk of loss on the account holder if the bank were to pay a check containing a signature resembling the filed facsimile specimen. The rights and liabilities of Pomerantz and the bank governed by this contract were never triggered since the bank dishonored all the checks in question.

Affirmed.

Questions Presented

1)   How is this case different from *Triffin v. Somerset Valley Savings,* a case presented earlier in this chapter?

2)   What could the check cashing company have done differently to change the outcome of the case?

3)   What prevented the Plaintiff from becoming a holder in due course?

❖❖

When an indorsement is forged, the indorser is not usually held liable for the forged indorsement. In most situations, the first party to take the instrument following the forged indorsement will end up paying the loss. A holder can only inherit the rights given to it by the transferee. A forger has no rights in the instrument, so the person who takes it from the forger will end up taking the loss because the instrument cannot be properly paid by the drawee or maker unless all of the indorsements are valid.

There are two notable exceptions to this rule. If the drawer of a check or maker of a note issues an instrument to an impostor and the impostor forges an indorsement, the drawer of the check will be liable to the payor bank unless the bank was negligent, such as by not asking for identification.[105] For example, imagine that, pretending to be Derick Fiction, Shelby Danger convinces Michael Thunder to give him a check made out to Derick Fiction. Shelby then indorses the check as Derick and presents it to the bank for payment. If the bank pays the check, unless it was negligent, Michael Thunder will be liable despite the forged indorsement because he gave the check to an impostor.

If a check is paid to a fictitious payee, someone without right to receive payment, even if there is a forged indorsement, the drawer will still be liable to pay the instrument.[106] Consider the following example. Shelby Thunder is an employee of Michael Thunder, LLC. He hands his boss a fake invoice from Derick Fiction, Inc. for services Derick Fiction, Inc. did not perform. Michael Thunder, LLC then pays the invoice with a check made out to Derick Fiction, Inc. Shelby then takes the check and forges an indorsement for Derick Fiction, Inc. and deposits the check in an account in his name. If the check is paid by the drawee, Michael Thunder, LLC will still be liable for the amount of the check because Derick Fiction, Inc. is a fictitious payee.

---

[105] UCC § 3-404(a)
[106] UCC § 3-404(b)

While any indorser who pays a forged instrument can still technically sue the forger, the indorser is not likely to yield a recovery. Forgers are often difficult to locate and are out of money by the time they are sued by their victims.

4. Qualified Indorsements

If an indorser writes the words "without recourse" above his or her name, the indorser has no signature liability.[107] The indorser will still, however, have warranty liability, which will be discussed in the next section.

B. Warranty Liability

When a person transfers an instrument to someone else, he or she makes certain warranties that apply once the note is transferred. It does not matter if the instrument is presented, dishonored, or timely notice of its dishonor is given. One does not even need to indorse the check to be subject to warranty liability. These warranties are not written. They are implied.

There are two sets of warranties, transfer warranties and presentment warranties.

1. Transfer Warranties

When an instrument is transferred for consideration, the transferor makes 5 warranties:

1. The transferor is entitled to enforce the instrument
2. All signatures are authentic and authorized
3. The instrument has not been altered
4. There are no claims or defenses to enforcement of the instrument against the transferor
5. The transferor does not have knowledge of a bankruptcy proceeding against the maker, acceptor or, in the event of an unaccepted draft, the drawer[108]

If consideration is given to the transferor and the transferor indorses the instrument, these warranties are made to all subsequent transferees. If consideration is given to the transferor and the transferor transfers the instrument without indorsing it (always a bearer instrument), the warranty is only made to the immediate transferee.[109] These warranties, however, are never made to the drawee.

Transfer warranties cannot be disclaimed by a qualified indorsement (one made "without recourse").[110] They cannot be disclaimed at all if the instrument is a check but can be disclaimed if the instrument is not a check by writing something like "without warranties."[111]

If any of these warranties are violated, the transferor can sue any prior indorser that made transfer warranties to it. The warrantee (person to whom the warranty was made) is eligible to recover damages in the amount that it lost. So, if the amount lost by the warrantee is less than the value of instrument, the warrantee will not receive the full value of the instrument and will only receive the amount it was damaged.[112]

---

[107] UCC § 3-415(b)

[108] UCC § 3-416(a). Under the 2002 revisions to Article 3, a sixth warranty is made that remotely created items (like a telecheck) are authorized for the amount shown on the instruments

[109] UCC § 3-416(a)

[110] UCC § 3-415(b)

[111] UCC § 3-416(c)

[112] UCC § 3-416(b)

2. Presentment Warranties

Presentment warranties are warranties made by a transferor to the party receiving presentment (usually the maker or drawee). Any person who transfers the instrument, even if he or she does not present the instrument to the maker or drawee, makes the following warranties to the party that eventually receives presentment:

1. The transferor is authorized to receive payment or acceptance (if an indorsement is missing or not authorized, this warranty will be breached)
2. The instrument has not been altered
3. The transferor has no knowledge that the drawer's signature is not authorized[113]

Presentment warranties do not require consideration. They also cannot be disclaimed by a qualified indorsement (one made "without recourse").[114] They cannot be disclaimed at all if the instrument is a check but can be disclaimed by writing something like "without warranties"[115] if the instrument is not a check.

If any of these warranties are violated, the drawee or maker can sue any prior indorser that made presentment warranties. The warrantee (person to whom the warranty was made) is eligible to recover damages in the amount that it lost. So, if the amount lost by the warrantee is less than the instrument, the warrantee will not receive the full value of the instrument and will only receive the amount in which it was damaged.[116]

VIII. Discharge

Discharge is the release of liability. A party can be discharged from liability on a negotiable instrument in a variety of ways.

The most common reason a party's liability is discharged is because the instrument has been paid by the party that is primarily liable.[117] Consider the following scenario.

Shelby Danger is the maker of a promissory note payable to Michael Thunder. Michael Thunder indorses the note and transfers it to Derick Fiction. Shelby Danger pays Derick Fiction. Because payment was made by the party that was primarily liable (Shelby Danger) both Shelby and Michael are discharged and no longer liable on the note.

There are a few exceptions to this general rule. Most notably, if a party pays someone he or she knows acquired the instrument by theft and is not a holder in due course, no discharge will result from payment.[118]

Payment by an indorser will only release the indorser and any subsequent indorsers from liability.

Tender (offer) of payment will also discharge the person attempting to make payment if the offer of payment is rejected (assuming the tender is made to the party entitled to enforce the instrument).[119]

---

[113] UCC § 3-417(a). Under the 2002 revisions to Article 3, a fourth warranty is made that remotely created items (like a telecheck) are authorized for the amount shown on the instruments
[114] UCC § 3-415(b)
[115] UCC § 3-417(e)
[116] UCC § 3-417(b)
[117] UCC § 3-602
[118] UCC § 3-602(b)(2)
[119] UCC § 3-603(b)

Discharge can also occur if the instrument is cancelled by a person entitled to enforce the instrument. The following actions can be considered intentional cancellations:

1. Surrendering the instrument (the party who receives the instrument is discharged)
2. Intentional destruction or mutilation of the instrument (all parties discharged)
3. Agreeing not to sue on the instrument in writing (the parties specified in the agreement are discharged)
4. Striking out the name of a prior indorser (only that indorser is discharged)[120]

Similar to when a person voluntarily surrenders an instrument, any person who reacquires an instrument (such as a prior payee or indorser) is discharged along with all prior indorsers. However, if that person sells the instrument again, the party is once again liable along with all subsequent indorsers.[121]

Striking out an indorser's name can also have effects on other indorsers. If an indorser's right to collect reimbursement from a prior indorser is impaired, the impaired indorser is discharged.[122]

SUMMARY

Negotiable instruments are essentially written promises to pay someone that can be transferred. They are used in everyday consumer transactions like when a tenant pays rent to the landlord with a check. They are also used extensively in commercial transactions, such as when a promissory note is signed to pay back a loan.

Negotiable instruments are incredibly flexible. They can be due on demand or in the future. They can be transferred by parties seeking to obtain payment faster. They also are a convenient way to move large sums of money without having to physically move the money.

To create a negotiable instrument, strict requirements must be met. Because negotiable instruments can be transferred, a number of different parties can become involved in a transaction. It is important to know the type of negotiable instrument created, who the parties to the instrument are, and how each is liable to the other.

It is especially important for those purchasing instruments to become holders in due course. Holders in due course can enforce an instrument even if the original payee would not be able to enforce the instrument in many cases. They are only subject to universal defenses, not personal defenses.

It is also important to remember who can be held liable to pay a negotiable instrument. While parties like drawees and makers are primarily liable, indorsers and drawers are secondarily liable and can be forced to pay the instrument if the primarily liable party does not pay the instrument.

Even parties that do not sign the instrument and merely transfer it can be held liable as well for breaching transfer and presentment warranties. Until discharge occurs, usually by payment of the instrument, no one who has signed the instrument or transferred the instrument is safe from liability.

---

[120] UCC § 3-604(a)
[121] UCC § 3-207
[122] UCC § 3-605(c)

13

EMPLOYMENT LAW

LEARNING OUTCOMES

Upon completion of this chapter the student will be able to:

1 Provide a brief history of employment law in the United States.
2 Distinguish between an employee and an independent contractor.
3 Discuss at-will employment and the difference with just cause employment.
4 Discuss the impact of unions in the workplace and collective bargaining rights.
5 Identify the variety of protections available to employees in the workplace.
6 Identify and discuss the main forms of workplace discrimination and remedies for abuse.

KEY TERMS

at-will employment
Beck rights
covenant
disparate impact
disparate treatment

implied contract
just cause employment
respondeat superior
right-to-work

I. History and Overview of Employment Law

There is much that is taken for granted these days with regard to the employment relationship in the United States. Employees at any level and in any industry can begin their workday knowing that they are relatively secure in their employment and that the law protects them from a host of potential workplace evils. In the event an employee feels aggrieved by a workplace condition or the conduct of another employee or a supervisor, that employee has a process available to seek an appropriate remedy. If there is an unsafe work condition a complaint can be made to the federal Occupational, Safety and Health Administration or a comparable state agency that will come in and investigate to ensure safe working conditions and employee safety. If a male supervisor is harassing a female employee because she spurned his romantic advances and he is now giving her poor job evaluations she can file an internal complaint with her Human Resources Department or Equal Employment Office. If she does not obtain a satisfactory resolution of her complaint she can seek assistance from a state equal employment or human rights agency established to assist employees who are discriminated against in the workplace. The federal Equal Employment Opportunity Commission is an alternate means for filing a complaint and as a last resort a remedy can be sought through the courts. These are but a few examples of the extent to which employee workplace rights are presently accorded not only a form of recognition but a viable means to enforce those rights. The history of employment law in the United States discloses a much different viewpoint of the employee in relation to the employer and the security of the employee's job.

When discussing employment law the term labor law is sometimes used interchangeably but this is a misnomer. At the outset we want to distinguish between the two distinct but interrelated fields of law. Labor law deals primarily with unions, collective bargaining rights, and any other issue relating to organized labor. The activities of unions, which will be discussed a bit more in-depth in the section below, are regulated by federal and state law. Employment law is focused more on the employer–employee relationship (though in workplaces where the employees are unionized the employer–employee relationship is greatly impacted), hiring and retention practices, human resource issues, wages and benefits, workplace safety, and workplace discrimination and harassment. This chapter's discussion will focus mainly on the area of employment law but a quick overview of labor law will be covered below.

Prior to the advent of the 19th century the idea of employee rights was a foreign concept in the American workplace. There were no regulations covering topics such as child labor, working hours, and overtime. Employees toiled at the will and mercy of their employers. The concept of workplace rights eventually began to slowly evolve in 18th century Europe during the industrial revolution. Demographic shifts to major cities for manufacturing jobs and less reliance upon an agrarian economy changed the nature of employment. Workplace rules and regulations began to take shape in 19th century Europe and the emerging industrialization in the United States brought a similar response. The post-Revolution period in the United States from 1787 to 1830 was a time of awakened interest in personal rights. The economic shift from a self-contained agrarian economy to a manufacturing economy required legislatures to respond to increasing workplace issues with specific laws targeting the employment relationship.[1] However, the resulting legislation was not often supportive of employee rights, nor were the judicial interpretations of resulting disputes. The focus was not on protecting the employee but on binding the employee to the employer.[2] The common law concept of master–servant was initially used by the courts to define the employment relationship, but it finally gave way to the terms "employer" and "employee" in latter 19th century legal language.[3] According to the master–servant rule there was an implied contract whereby one person agreed to be under the control of another for work purposes. The master could dictate the terms and conditions of employment and the servant was bound to obey the work orders and rules of the master. From this arrangement the principles of agency relationship arose and the legal doctrine that a master was vicariously liable for the acts of his servant while the servant was employed by the master. This is the common law doctrine of respondeat superior. Over time the master–servant relationship developed within American law to represent a more formalized status between the two parties, one in which the employee was able to obtain severability from the master. The paternalistic nature of the master–servant relationship gave way to the recognized legal status of the employee, but this would not spring into place immediately. Important workplace rights that were to be eventually granted to employees would slowly develop over the course of several decades.

---

[1] See e.g., James Gray Pope, *A Brief History of United States Labor and Employment Law*, The Oxford International Encyclopedia of Legal History 477–86 (Stanley N. Katz ed.) (2009)

[2] Id.

[3] Id.

One of the first legislative efforts to improve workplace conditions and regulate employment was in the area of child labor. A combination of efforts between the burgeoning labor movement and legislative efforts during the mid-19th century led to the passage of laws in several states that set minimum age requirements for child workers, limited the hours children could work, and set mandatory school attendance requirements for child workers. These initial state legislative acts eventually led to passage of federal law restricting child labor, culminating in the passage of the Fair Labor Standards Act in 1938 which, in addition to regulating other forms of labor, placed restrictions on child labor. However, attempts at reforms in the workplace for older employees paralleled those of child labor but did not garner as sympathetic a response. At the forefront of the worker reform movement were various labor organizations that began to gain a following among workers in the United States. These labor organizations were not welcome by employers and were treated as criminal conspiracies. A case from the Philadelphia Mayor's Court in 1806, *Commonwealth v. Pullis*,[4] also known as the Philadelphia Cordwainer's Case, was the first U.S. court case to arise from a labor strike. In that case the court found that the eight members of a guild of shoemakers who went on strike against their employer engaged in a criminal conspiracy in restraint of trade. According to the court's decision the attempt by the workers to benefit themselves was injurious to those who did not belong to their guild and this was held to be culpable criminal conduct for which the defendants were fined.[5] This concept of a trade union as a criminal conspiracy was later rejected by the Supreme Judicial Court of Massachusetts in the 1842 case of *Commonwealth v. Hunt*.[6] In that case the court held that "*associations may be entered into, the object of which is to adopt measures that may have a tendency to impoverish another, that is, to diminish his gains and profits, and yet so far from being criminal or unlawful, the object may be highly meritorious and public-spirited. The legality of such an association will therefore depend upon the means to be used for its accomplishment.*"[7] While not totally rejecting the idea that a trade union or labor association could be a criminal conspiracy, the Massachusetts court was the first court to establish that unions organized to improve employee rights and working conditions were not in themselves criminal. In order for a criminal conspiracy to be applied there had to be "falsehood or force" involved.[8] Thus, in *Hunt* Chief Justice Lemuel Shaw created the "illegal purposes doctrine" to determine whether the activities of a labor union were a conspiracy. If the purpose of the union activity and its tactics were not illegal then no criminal conspiracy could be maintained by state prosecutors. The criminal conspiracy doctrine used by employers to limit employee rights in the workplace was an early example of the impact of natural rights theory and the prevailing laissez-faire approach toward government involvement in business.[9] The equal liberty of employer and employee, under the doctrine, to negotiate freely and individually was infringed upon by collective, coercive efforts.[10] However, with the weakening of the criminal conspiracy argument by *Hunt* and subsequent court cases that followed its lead, employers resorted to other means to limit the organizational rights of employees.

---

[4] 3 Doc. Hist. of Amer. Ind. Soc. 59 (2d Edition, Commons 1910)

[5] Id.

[6] 45 Mass. 111 (1842)

[7] Id.

[8] Id.

[9] Walter Nelles, "*Commonwealth v. Hunt*" (1932). Faculty Scholarship Series. Paper 4495. http://digitalcommons.law.yale.edu/fss_papers/4495

[10] Id.

During the latter part of the 19th century and into the early 20th century workers began utilizing economically impactful methods to express their grievances and push for reforms and work-place benefits. These methods included boycotts, picketing, production slow-downs, and strikes.[11] Employer responses to these methods were to enlist the services of professional strike-breakers or to "blacklist" an employee or group of employees thereby denying them work. Employers also resorted to the use of criminal conspiracy prosecutions against employees involved in labor unions or associations. However, these prosecutions were not as effective or as efficient as the employers desired.[12] Employer attacks upon collective employee actions were shifted to enjoining employee activities through court ordered injunctions. These injunctions were a civil hybrid of the criminal conspiracy doctrine that sought to use equitable relief as means of controlling employee behavior. The U.S. Supreme Court sanctioned the use of injunctions in labor disputes in the 1895 case of *In re Debs*.[13] An important feature of many of these injunctions was the enforcement of "yellow dog" contracts wherein the employer had the employee sign an agreement that they either would not join a union while employed by the employer or that they would resign from the union if already a member. These "yellow dog" contracts were made a condition of employment. Under a theory of contractual interference courts issued injunctions against collective employee action.

An 1896 Massachusetts case *Vegelahn v. Guntner* found the coordinated strike methods used by employees of a furniture factory were "*an unlawful interference with the rights of both employer and of the employed.*"[14] The court further noted that the "*employer has a right to engage all persons who are willing to work for him, at such prices as may be mutually agreed upon, and persons employed or seeking employment have a corresponding right to enter into or remain in the employment of any person or corporation willing to employ them. These rights are secured by the Constitution itself.*"[15] The *Vegelahn* case though is better known for the dissent of Oliver Wendell Holmes who was still six years away from his appointment as an Associate Justice of the U.S. Supreme Court. Holmes acknowledged the natural conflict bound to exist between employer and employee in an often cited section of his dissent: "*If the policy on which our law is founded is too narrowly expressed in the term of free competition, we may substitute free struggle for life. Certainly the policy is not limited to struggles between persons of the same class competing for the same end. It applies to all conflicts of temporal interests.*"[16] He followed this with a strenuous argument on behalf of an equality of freedom of employees to pursue their liberty interests as well as those of the employers to pursue theirs: "*One of the eternal conflicts out of which life is made up is that between the effort of every man to get the most he can for his services, disguised under the name of capital to get his services for the least possible return. Combination on the one side is patent and powerful. Combination on the other is necessary and desirable counterpart, if the battle is to be carried on in a fair and equal way.*"[17] Holmes' view was not shared in subsequent cases, particularly those of the U.S. Supreme Court.

In *Adair v. United States* the 1908 U.S. Supreme Court, of which Holmes was a member, struck down a federal law protecting collective employee action from the use of "yellow dog"

---

[11] Pope at 480.
[12] Id.
[13] 158 U.S. 564 (1895)
[14] 167 Mass. 92, 97 (1896)
[15] Id.
[16] Id at 107.
[17] Id at 108.

contracts by employers.[18] The *Adair* decision was based on the holding that banning "yellow dog" contracts was unconstitutional as a violation of the liberty of contract. *Adair* re-affirmed the Supreme Court's recognition of a liberty of contract under the due process clause of the 14th Amendment first announced in *Allgeyer v. Louisiana*.[19] This occurred during the 40-year period known as the Lochner Era (see Chapter 3, section III) in which the U.S. Supreme Court limited its involvement in economic regulation by the states. This often worked to the detriment of workers as in the case of *Lochner v. New York* which relied on the liberty of contract theory to strike state laws seeking to limit the working hours of bakers. Later in 1915 and then again in 1917 the U.S. Supreme Court in *Coppage v. Kansas*[20] and *Hitchman Coal & Coke Co., v. Mitchell*[21] held in favor of employer use of "yellow dog" contracts. Holmes was a dissenter in both cases.

The use of injunctions in labor disputes was restricted by the Anti-Injunction Act of 1931 (also referred to as the Norris-LaGuardia Act).[22] One of the act's goals was to prohibit judicial enforcement of "yellow dog" contracts. This was followed in 1933 by the National Industrial Recovery Act (NIRA)[23] which recognized employee rights to bargain collectively. Although the NIRA was later ruled unconstitutional by the Supreme Court in *Schecter Poultry Corp. v. United States*[24] the restrictions upon collective employee bargaining were slowly disappearing. The passage of the National Labor Relations Act of 1935 (also known as the Wagner Act)[25] initiated a period of growth for the U.S. labor movement and the corresponding recognition of employee rights.[26] The Wagner Act's constitutionality was upheld by the U.S. Supreme Court in *NLRB v. Jones & Laughlin Steel Corporation*.[27] Workplace protections for employees continued to progress, first with the passage of the Taft-Hartley Act of 1947 granting employees a set of rights against unfair union labor practices as well as providing for judicial enforcement of collective bargaining agreements. Employees in the United States were eventually provided remedies against discrimination (Title VII to the Civil Rights Act of 1964), ensured workplace safety (Occupational Safety and Health Act of 1970), guaranteed the security of pensions (Employee Retirement Income Security Act of 1974), and other rights in the workplace previously unimagined a century earlier. The modern workplace is now a balance of the competing interests of employer and employee originally articulated by Holmes in *Vegelahn v. Guntner*, rather than the one-sided expression of the will of the employer over the workforce. Disputes that arise in the workplace are initially handled by trained human resource professionals and, ideally, resolved to the satisfaction of employer and employee without any court intervention. However, if the matter cannot be settled "in-house," alternative dispute resolution forums and the courts remain available for workplace grievances and operate in an environment that is theoretically less antagonistic to employee rights than the courts during the Lochner Era.

---

[18] 208 U.S. 161 (1908).

[19] 165 U.S. 578, 589 (1897): *"The "liberty" mentioned in that amendment means not only the right of the citizen to be free from the mere physical restraint of his person, as by incarceration, but the term is deemed to embrace the right of the citizen to be free in the enjoyment of all his faculties, to be free to use them in all lawful ways, to live and work where he will, to earn his livelihood by any lawful calling, to pursue any livelihood or avocation, and for that purpose to enter into all contracts which may be proper, necessary, and essential to his carrying out to a successful conclusion the purposes above mentioned."*

[20] 236 U.S. 1 (1915).

[21] 245 U.S. 229 (1917).

[22] 29 USCA § 101 et seq.

[23] 48 Stat. 195 (1933).

[24] 295 U.S. 495 (1935). See also, Chapter, 5, section I above for a discussion of *Schecter Poultry Corp.*

[25] 29 USCA § 151 et seq.

[26] Pope at 482.

[27] 301 U.S. 1 (1937).

Table 13.1, though not inclusive of all federal laws, highlights some of the major federal legislation of the 20th century benefitting employees in the workplace.

TABLE 13.1 Major Federal Legislation Benefitting Employees

Law	Year	Employee Benefit
National Labor Relations Act	1935	Protects employees from unfair labor practices by unions and employers
Social Security Act	1935	Provides retirement, disability, Medicare health insurance, Supplemental Security Income, family, and survivors' benefits
Fair Labor Standards Act	1938	Regulates employee minimum wages, overtime pay, equal pay, and child labor
Labor Management Relations Act	1947	Makes it unlawful for employers to interfere with, discipline or discriminate against employees and job candidates for legitimate, union-related activities
Labor Management Reporting and Disclosure Act	1959	Grants employee union members certain rights and protects their interests by guaranteeing democratic union process
Equal Pay Act	1963	Prohibits wage disparity on the basis of gender; amended the FLSA
Civil Rights Act – Title VII	1964	Prohibits employer discrimination on the basis of race or sex in hiring, promoting, or firing of employees
Age Discrimination in Employment Act	1967	Prohibits age discrimination in employment against anyone 40 or over and provides equal opportunity, thus covering protections not provided in Title VII
Occupational Safety and Health Act	1970	Protects employees from safety and health hazards in the workplace
Employee Retirement, Income and Security Act	1974	Requires private employers who establish pension plans to maintain fiscal responsibility and accountability over the plans
Consolidated Omnibus Reconciliation Act	1985	Requires employers to offer continued health-care insurance benefits at group rates to employees and their qualified beneficiaries when there has been a layoff or reduction in work force
Worker Adjustment Retraining and Notification Act	1988	Requires certain employers to issue advance notification of plant closings and mass layoffs to qualified, affected employees
Employee Polygraph Protection Act	1988	Prohibits most private sector employers from conducting polygraph tests on employees or applicants
Americans with Disabilities Act	1990	Prohibits certain employers from discriminating against individuals on the basis of their disabilities
Family Medical Leave Act	1993	Gives eligible employees up to 12 weeks of unpaid, job-protected leave in a 12-month period to care for their own serious health conditions or those of qualified family members
Lilly Ledbetter Fair Pay Act	2009	Amended the Civil Rights Act of 1964 and overruled the U.S. Supreme Court decision in *Ledbetter v. Goodyear Tire & Rubber Co.*, 550 U.S. 618 (2007) by stating that the 180 day statute of limitations for filing an equal pay lawsuit begins with each new paycheck following the discriminatory period

II. The Employer–Employee Relationship

A. Employee vs. Independent Contractor

In order to determine the extent of an individual's protection in the workplace and what rights they may have it is necessary to ascertain whether or not they are in fact an employee. If they are not an employee then the individual is most likely an independent contractor. An independent contractor is someone who contracts with an employer to undertake a particular job for the employer. The independent contractor can be an individual, a separate independent business, a corporation or other established business entity. There is no uniform definition of independent contractor—it is based mostly on common law, state statutory guidelines, court interpretations, and Internal Revenue Service guidelines.

The distinction between an employee and an independent contractor is important for several reasons. If the individual is an employee then the employer is responsible for paying the employee's federal and state unemployment tax, social security tax, and worker's compensation and disability premiums. These payments are not made by an employer if the individual is an independent contractor. Additionally, the employer is bound by certain statutory duties and labor related restrictions when an individual is an employee. Federal laws like the NLRA, FLSA, and ERISA will apply to employees but not to independent contractors. Furthermore, employers are responsible for the negligent acts of its employees under the common law doctrine of respondeat superior. An independent contractor will generally be solely liable for its own acts and will have a separate insurance policy in place to protect against its own negligent acts.

Legal Definition

Respondeat superior – a common law legal doctrine holding that master is responsible for the acts of his servant; this doctrine has subsequently been applied to the legal relationship between a principal and an agent, and in employment an employer is legally responsible for the acts of the employee.

Whether or not someone is defined as an employee may rely on common law principles separate from a statutory definition. In the following case the U.S. Supreme Court had to determine the meaning of the term "employee" according to a contractual agreement for retirement benefits under ERISA. As you read the case note the procedural history and the District Court and Court of Appeals decisions prior to the Supreme Court's involvement.

❖❖❖

Nationwide Mutual Ins. Co. v. Darden
503 U.S. 318 (1992)

Justice Souter delivered the opinion of the Court.

In this case we construe the term "employee" as it appears in § 3(6) of the Employee Retirement Income Security Act of 1974 (ERISA), 88 Stat. 834, 29 U.S.C. § 1002(6), and read it to incorporate traditional agency law criteria for identifying master–servant relationships.

I

From 1962 through 1980, respondent Robert Darden operated an insurance agency according to the terms of several contracts he signed with petitioners Nationwide Mutual Insurance Co. and others Darden promised to sell only Nationwide insurance policies, and, in exchange, Nationwide agreed to pay him commissions on his sales and enroll him in a company retirement scheme called the "Agent's Security Compensation Plan" (Plan). The Plan consisted of two different programs: the "Deferred Compensation Incentive Credit Plan," under which Nationwide annually credited an agent's retirement account with a sum based on his business performance, and the "Extended Earnings Plan," under which Nationwide paid an agent, upon retirement or termination, a sum equal to the total of his policy renewal fees for the previous 12 months.

Such were the contractual terms, however, that Darden would forfeit his entitlement to the Plan's benefits if, within a year of his termination and 25 miles of his prior business location, he sold insurance for Nationwide's competitors. The contracts also disqualified him from receiving those benefits if, after he stopped representing Nationwide, he ever induced a Nationwide policyholder to cancel one of its policies.

In November 1980, Nationwide exercised its contractual right to end its relationship with Darden. A month later, Darden became an independent insurance agent and, doing business from his old office, sold insurance policies for several of Nationwide's competitors. The company reacted with the charge that his new business activities disqualified him from receiving the Plan benefits to which he would have been entitled otherwise. Darden then sued for the benefits, which he claimed were nonforfeitable because already vested under the terms of ERISA. 29 U.S.C. § 1053(a).

Darden brought his action under 29 U.S.C. § 1132(a), which enables a benefit plan "participant" to enforce the substantive provisions of ERISA. The Act elsewhere defines "participant" as "any employee or former employee of an employer . . . who is or may become eligible to receive a benefit of any type from an employee benefit plan. . . ." § 1002(7). Thus, Darden's ERISA claim can succeed only if he was Nationwide's "employee," a term the Act defines as "any individual employed by an employer." § 1002(6).

It was on this point that the District Court granted summary judgment to Nationwide. After applying common-law agency principles and, to an extent unspecified, our decision in *United States v. Silk*, 331 U.S. 704 (1947), the court found that "'the total factual context' of Mr. Darden's relationship with Nationwide shows that he was an independent contractor and not an employee." App. to Pet. for Cert. 47a, 50a, quoting *NLRB v. United Ins. Co. of America*, 390 U.S. 254 (1968).

The United States Court of Appeals for the Fourth Circuit vacated. *Darden v. Nationwide Mutual Ins. Co.*, 796 F.2d 701(1986). After observing that "Darden most probably would not qualify as an employee" under traditional principles of agency law, *id.*, at 705, it found the traditional definition inconsistent with the "'declared policy and purposes'" of ERISA, *id.*, at 706, quoting *Silk, supra*, at 713, and *NLRB v. Hearst Publications, Inc.*, 322 U.S. 111, 131–132 (1944), and specifically with the congressional statement of purpose found in § 2 of the Act, 29 U.S.C. § 1001. It therefore held that an ERISA plaintiff can qualify as an "employee" simply by showing "(1) that he had a reasonable expectation that he would receive [pension] benefits, (2) that he relied on this expectation, and (3) that he lacked the economic bargaining power to contract out of [benefit plan] forfeiture provisions." 922 F.2d 203, 205 (CA4 1991) (summarizing 796 F.2d 701 (CA4 1986)). The court remanded the case to the District Court, which then found that Darden had been Nationwide's "employee" under the standard set by the Court of Appeals. 717 F. Supp. 388 (EDNC 1989). The Court of Appeals affirmed. 922 F.2d 203 (1991).

In due course, Nationwide filed a petition for certiorari, which we granted on October 15, 1991. 502 U.S. 905. We now reverse.

II

We have often been asked to construe the meaning of "employee" where the statute containing the term does not helpfully define it . . .

ERISA's nominal definition of "employee" as "any individual employed by an employer," 29 U.S.C. § 1002(6), is completely circular and explains nothing. As for the rest of the Act, Darden does not cite, and we do not find, any provision either giving specific guidance on the term's meaning or suggesting that construing it to incorporate traditional agency law principles would thwart the congressional design or lead to absurd results. Thus, we adopt a common-law test for determining who qualifies as an "employee" under ERISA, a test we most recently summarized in *Community for Creative Non-Violence v. Reid, 490* U.S. 730 (1989): "In determining whether a hired party is an employee under the general common law of agency, we consider the hiring party's right to control the manner and means by which the product is accomplished. Among the other factors relevant to this inquiry are the skill required; the source of the instrumentalities and tools; the location of the work; the duration of the relationship between the parties; whether the hiring party has the right to assign additional projects to the hired party; the extent of the hired party's discretion over when and how long to work; the method of payment; the hired party's role in hiring and paying assistants; whether the work is part of the regular business of the hiring party; whether the hiring party is in business; the provision of employee benefits; and the tax treatment of the hired party." 490 U.S., at 751–752.

In taking its different tack, the Court of Appeals cited *NLRB v. Hearst Publications, Inc.*, 322 U.S., at 120–129, and *United States v. Silk*, 331 U.S., at 713, for the proposition that "the content of the term 'employee' in the context of a particular federal statute is 'to be construed "in the light of the mischief to be corrected and the end to be attained."'" *Darden*, 796 F. 2d, at 706, quoting *Silk, supra*, at 713, in turn quoting *Hearst, supra*, at 124. But *Hearst* and *Silk*, which interpreted "employee" for purposes of the National Labor Relations Act and Social Security Act, respectively, are feeble precedents for unmooring the term from the common law. In each case, the Court read "employee," which neither statute helpfully defined, to imply something broader than the common-law definition; after each opinion, Congress amended the statute so construed to demonstrate that the usual common-law principles were the keys to meaning.

To be sure, Congress did not, strictly speaking, "overrule" our interpretation of those statutes, since the Constitution invests the Judiciary, not the Legislature, with the final power to construe the law. But a principle of statutory construction can endure just so many legislative revisitations, and *Reid's* presumption that Congress means an agency law definition for "employee" unless it clearly indicates otherwise signaled our abandonment of *Silk's* emphasis on construing that term "'in the light of the mischief to be corrected and the end to be attained.'" *Silk, supra*, at 713, quoting *Hearst, supra*, at 124. . . .

Quite apart from its inconsistency with our precedents, the Fourth Circuit's analysis reveals an approach infected with circularity and unable to furnish predictable results. Applying the first element of its test, which ostensibly enquires into an employee's "expectations," the Court of Appeals concluded that Nationwide had "created a reasonable expectation on the 'employees' part that benefits would be paid to them in the future," *Darden*, 796 F. 2d, at 706, by establishing "a comprehensive retirement benefits program for its insurance agents," *id.*, at 707. The court thought it was simply irrelevant that the forfeiture clause in Darden's contract "limited" his expectation of receiving pension benefits, since "it is precisely that sort of employer-imposed condition on the *employee's* anticipations that Congress intended to outlaw with the enactment of ERISA." *Id.*, at 707, n. 7 (emphasis added). Thus, the Fourth Circuit's test would turn not on a claimant's actual "expectations," which the court effectively deemed inconsequential, *ibid.*, but on his statutory entitlement to relief, which itself depends on his very status as an "employee." This begs the question.

This circularity infects the test's second prong as well, which considers the extent to which a claimant has relied on his "expectation" of benefits by "remaining for 'long years,' or a substantial period of time, in the 'employer's' service, and by foregoing other significant means of providing for [his] retirement." *Id.*, at 706. While this enquiry is ostensibly factual, we have seen already that one of its objects may not be: to the extent that actual "expectations" are (as in Darden's case) unnecessary to relief, the nature of a claimant's required "reliance" is left unclear. Moreover, any enquiry into "reliance," whatever it might entail, could apparently lead to different results for claimants holding identical jobs and enrolled in identical plans. Because, for example, Darden failed to make much independent provision for his retirement, he satisfied the "reliance" prong of the Fourth Circuit's test, see 922 F. 2d, at 206, whereas a more provident colleague who signed exactly the same contracts, but saved for a rainy day, might not.

Any such approach would severely compromise the capacity of companies like Nationwide to figure out who their "employees" are and what, by extension, their pension-fund obligations will be. To be sure, the traditional agency law criteria offer no paradigm of determinacy. But their application generally turns on factual variables within an employer's knowledge, thus permitting categorical judgments about the "employee" status of claimants with similar job descriptions. Agency law principles comport, moreover, with our recent precedents and with the common understanding, reflected in those precedents, of the difference between an employee and an independent contractor.

III

While the Court of Appeals noted that "Darden most probably would not qualify as an employee" under traditional agency law principles, *Darden, supra*, at 705, it did not actually decide that issue. We therefore reverse the judgment and remand the case to that court for proceedings consistent with this opinion.

So ordered.

Questions Presented

1) What standard did Justice Souter use in determining whether or not an employer–employee relationship existed between Darden and Nationwide Mutual Insurance Company?
2) What fault did Justice Souter find with the Fourth Circuit Court of Appeals' definition of employee and its ruling in favor of Darden?
3) Whether or not Darden is determined to be an "employee" impacts his right to bring an ERISA claim and therefore goes to a jurisdictional issue of standing. What is the underlying substantive claim in the case that was not an issue on Supreme Court review?

❖❖

There are a number of common law factors used by the courts to determine whether someone is an employee or an independent contractor. Method of payment is one. If the person is on a company's payroll and receives steady wages then that person is an employee. The nature of the work to be performed is another test. If the individual's work is considered integral to the business then that person is considered an employee. For example, if XYZ Corporation, a financial services company, pays three individuals to complete work for the company, the nature of that work can be indicative of the person's status as an employee. Mike is employed by XYZ Corporation as a certified financial planner and he possesses a Series 7 trading license. He maintains a list of clients whose accounts he services for XYZ Corporation. In return he receives bi-weekly salary and commissions on the sales of financial products. Mike is clearly an employee of XYZ Corporation. He performs work that is integral to the company's business and significantly tied to the overall company purpose. Dan is another person who works at XYZ Corporation. He is a computer technician who services the company computers and overall network which is in use twenty-four hours a day, seven days a week. Depending on the circumstances Dan may either be an employee or an independent contractor. If Dan is working for another company, Financial Tech Services, Inc., that is hired by XYZ Corporation to service its computers then he is an independent contractor. However, if XYZ Corporation has its own computer and technology division specifically tasked with the service and maintenance of its computer network, an activity integral to its business, then Dan would be considered an employee who is compensated by XYZ Corporation. A third individual, Jake is hired by XYZ Corporation to paint the company lobby, boardroom and lunchroom. The job will take a month to complete and his compensation is based on a quote for each room including the cost of paint and materials. Halfway through the job while painting the boardroom Jake falls off a ladder and injures his back, thus putting him out of work for several months. Since Jake is not an employee there is no liability on the part of XYZ Corporation for Jake's worker's compensation claim. Any liability of XYZ Corporation would be limited to its own negligence in causing Jake's injury, but the typical workplace protections an employer owes to an employee with regard to worker's compensation and disability claims would not apply in this situation. Suppose Jake attempted to make an arguable claim that he was an employee of XYZ Corporation when he was injured? Several factors would work against his claim—he was not performing work integral to the company's business and he was not supplied the materials for his work by the company. While there is much more that has to be considered when determining an individual's employment status the foregoing is just a simple example of the differences in the working relationship that can exist between individuals and employers.

A more comprehensive test of employment status is the common law standards used by the Internal Revenue Service (IRS). Employers are keenly attentive to the criteria since the mislabeling of an individual as an independent contractor rather than as an employee can render an employer liable for back taxes on unemployment, social security and worker's compensation. The IRS test is merely a guideline referred to as "the Twenty-factor test." The test guidelines are as follows:

1. If the person is trained by the employer then that person is usually an employee;
2. If the person is required by the employer to comply with instructions about when, where and how they are to work then that person is an employee;
3. If the person's activities are integrated into business operations indicating that the person is subject to company direction and control then that person is an employee;
4. If the person's services must be rendered personally, indicating employer interest and oversight, then the person is an employee;
5. If a person has assistants hired, supervised and paid by the employer then the person is an employee;
6. If there is a continuing relationship between the person and the employer tending to show an employer–employee relationship;
7. If the employee sets specific working hours for the person this tends to show control over the person and the existence of an employer–employee relationship;

8. If the person works mostly full-time for the employer and is not free to pursue work from other employers then the person is an employee;

9. If the work is done primarily on the employer's premises and cannot be done elsewhere then the person may be considered an employee;

10. If a person is required to submit regular written or oral reports to an employer then the person is considered an employee;

11. Wages paid by the employer on an hourly, weekly or monthly basis, instead of by job or on strict commission, indicate an employer–employee relationship;

12. If the employer pays for business or travel expenses then the person is likely an employee;

13. If the employee supplies the person with tools, materials, or equipment for the job then the person is likely an employee;

14. If there is an order or sequence that a person is required to complete their work established by an employer then that person is considered an employee;

15. A person who, for the purpose of performing services, has invested in work space and maintains it on his own is generally an independent contractor;

16. A person who is able to determine a profit or loss based on his services is generally an independent contractor;

17. A person who performs services for more than one company at any one time is generally an independent contractor;

18. If a person on a regular and consistent basis makes his services available to the general public then he is considered an independent contractor;

19. If an employer has a right to discharge a person then that person is generally considered an employee;

20. If a person has the right to terminate their relationship with an employer at any time without incurring a breach of contract claim then that person is considered an employee.

Under common law and IRS rules an employer can consider someone an employee if the employer can control what will be done and how it will be done.[28] An individual who is not an employee and is defined as an independent contractor must pay self-employment tax, consisting of Social Security and Medicare taxes, on income of $400.00 or more. The self-employment tax rate is 13.3% to 10.4% for Social Security and 2.9% for Medicare.

The IRS "Twenty-factor test" essentially divides the common law factors into three categories for determining whether an employer–employee relationship exists. These factors are: behavioral, financial, and relationship based.[29] Behavioral factors look to the degree of control an employer has over an employee. Is there training, an evaluation system for employees, are work instructions provided and what is the degree of oversight? Financial factors consider how the individual is paid, whether the worker is reimbursed for expenses, does the worker share in profit and loss? The relationship test is based on whether there is a contractual agreement between the employer and the worker, how permanent is the relationship, does the employer provide the worker benefits, and whether the worker provides services that are a key activity of the business? These test categories are also based on two basic tests used by courts for determining if an individual is an

---

[28] See, IRS, Employee (Common Law Employee), https://www.irs.gov/businesses/small-businesses-self-employed/employee-common-law-employee, retrieved July 22, 2017.

[29] See generally, IRS, Type of Relationship, https://www.irs.gov/businesses/small-businesses-self-employed/type-of-relationship, retrieved July 22, 2017.

employee—the "economic realities test" and the "right to control test." The first test, "economic realities", like the IRS financial test, considers the dependence of the worker on the company for salary, benefits and expenses. If the majority of payment comes from the company the person is generally considered an employee. The "right to control" test is the behavioral test determining the extent to which the worker's job function is controlled by the employer.

B. At-will Employment vs. Just Cause Employment

An at-will employee has very little legal protection from termination, other than if the termination was for an illegal reason, and serves "at the will" of the employer. This type of employment agreement exists in every state except Montana where there is a statutory protection for probationary employees from being fired for any reason other than good cause. The at-will employee can be terminated from employment at any time for any lawful reason by the employer. Correspondingly the at-will employee can leave his employment without notice to the employer but this reciprocal right is of little consequence to the overall job security of the employee.

Unless the terms of employment are otherwise clearly stated in an agreement between an employer and an employee the courts will presume the existence of an at-will employment. The employer though will likely define the nature of the employment relationship in any one of a number of documents—applications, handbooks, employment agreements, policy manuals—provided to the employee. The clearest indication of at-will employment and notice to the employee will be provided in an agreement or contract signed by the employee acknowledging the nature of the employment. However, in 2014 the National Labor Relations Board case of *American Red Cross Arizona Blood Services Division*[30] an administrative law judge found that section 7 of the National Labor Relations Act protecting employees' right to engage in concerted activity was violated by having the employee sign an acknowledgement regarding certain terms of the at-will employment. At issue and found to be a violation of section 7 was the following statement: "I further agree that the at-will employment relationship cannot be amended, modified or altered in any way."[31] This provision was held by the ALJ as being able to be interpreted to limit employees' rights to engage in collective action to change their at-will employment status. Since section 7 of the NLRA protects employee rights to engage in "concerted activity" to change the terms and conditions of employment the employer was ordered by the NLRB to remove the provision from its handbook. The employer was also directed to post a notice to all employees that the company would not violate their rights under the NLRA. This move by the NLRB to limit employers' at-will disclaimers required many U.S. employers to revise their handbooks and other personnel documents concerning at-will employment. As long as there is no express or implied limitation in an employer's disclaimer regarding an employee's right to engage in protected workplace activities an acknowledgement that an employee's status is that of an at-will employee will not be held to violate section 7 of the NLRA.

The at-will employee, however, still works under the most tenuous of conditions since there is no job security and the terms of employment can be altered by the employer without notice. This means that wages, scheduling, reduction of paid time off, and termination of benefits can be effectuated by the employer without consequence. Termination can be arbitrary and sudden. The only limit upon an at-will employee being terminated is if the termination were for an unlawful reason.

---

[30] Case No. 28-CA-23443 (February 1, 2012)(ALJ Meyerson)
[31] Id.

This would entail terminations based upon a discriminatory basis or in violation of specific statutory protections such as whistleblower statutes.

Despite the limited legal protections for at-will employees the law recognizes three main exceptions to the at-will employment doctrine: an implied covenant of good faith and fair dealing exception, an implied contract exception, and a public policy exception. The implied covenant of good faith and fair dealing exception is recognized in a minority of states and prohibits terminations based on bad faith or malice. It is sometimes interpreted by courts as requiring an element of just cause for dismissal. An example of a bad faith dismissal would be the firing of a long term employee without any reason. This was the reasoning of a California appellate court in the 1980 case of *Cleary v. American Airlines, Inc.* in which American Airlines terminated an 18-year employee for no stated reason.[32] The appellate court said that the length of the employee's service to the company, his satisfactory work record, and the company's policy of internally resolving workplace disputes prevented the employee's termination on any basis other than just cause. The *Cleary* case points to several factors a reviewing court will consider in finding an implied covenant of good faith:

1. length of employee service;
2. record of employee work performance;
3. any employment representations made to the employee by the employer;
4. did the company follow its internal policies?

The implied contract exception is recognized in three-quarters of the U.S. states and will apply when the employer makes either oral or written representations to the employee regarding the security of the employment relationship or provides procedures to be followed when adverse job actions are taken against an employee. In the case of *Pine River State Bank v. Mettille* the Minnesota Supreme Court found an implied contract in an employee handbook under the traditional contract terms of offer, acceptance and consideration.[33] Mettille, the employee, was hired as an indefinite, at-will employee for the position of loan officer. There was no contract of employment, just an oral agreement. An employee handbook was given to Mettille after he began working for Pine River State Bank. The handbook contained a section entitled "Disciplinary Policy" that provided a progressive disciplinary procedure for employee misconduct. The Minnesota Supreme Court found the policy to create an offer of a unilateral contract in which the bank promised employment in exchange for the employee's labor. The employee's labor was the acceptance and necessary consideration for the formation of a contract. The court held that the bank's termination of the employee without the benefit of a progressive disciplinary procedure violated the terms of the implied contract.

Legal Definitions

Implied contract – a legally enforceable agreement arising from the conduct between two parties, the relationship between the parties, or principles of equity.

Covenant – an agreement or undertaking for the performance of some action.

The public policy exception is the most widely recognized exception to the employment at-will doctrine and is followed in a majority of states. The exception holds that an employee is wrongfully

---

[32] 111 Cal.App.3d 443 (1980)
[33] 333 N.W.2d 622 (1983)

discharged when the employer terminates the employee against a specific, well-established policy of the state. This can involve terminations that violate a provision of the state constitution, administrative rule or state statute. Examples would be the termination of an employee for refusing to engage in forced political speech[34], for an employee filing a worker's compensation claim,[35] for an employee's jury service,[36] or for an employee refusing to violate a state statute.[37]

Legal Definitions

Just Cause – in the employment context is a standard for employee dismissal for violating terms of an employment contract; it is generally based on some form of employee conduct that is incompatible with the employer's workplace expectations or for employee misconduct that is culpable, blameworthy, subject to censure, and can include intentional as well as negligent acts.

Progressive Discipline – an employee disciplinary structure that provides an increasing range of responses to employee misconduct based on the frequency, repetition, or severity of the employee acts or behavior; also may be referred to as corrective action procedures or performance improvement plans.

Just cause employment is the polar opposite of employment at-will. Under a just cause employment relationship an employee can only be terminated upon a finding of "just cause" by the employer. The "just cause" standard refers to employee conduct that is inconsistent or irreconcilable with the contract of employment. Upon a finding of "just cause" the employer may terminate the employee. This type of employment is generally established through an employment agreement or contract between the employer and employee. Oftentimes the employer will have an established internal disciplinary policy that it will follow prior to terminating an employee for misconduct. The disciplinary procedure is based on the concept of progressive discipline wherein an employee's initial, minor infractions will be used as a warning and corrective steps will be taken to make the employee a productive member of the workplace. As employee infractions mount, the severity of the punishment increases eventually leading to termination for the employee who cannot or does not correct his or her behavior or workplace performance. However, if the infraction is serious enough it can lead to prompt termination despite no prior disciplinary record.

"Just cause" has been interpreted by the courts as amounting to a fair and honest reason for termination made in good faith.[38] Examples of "just cause" grounds for discipline and potential termination are insubordination, incompetence, excessive lateness or absences, neglect of workplace duties, and certain criminal offenses. When it comes to criminal offenses there are crimes that should not impact the employment contract but others that will definitely go to the core of the employment relationship. Certainly crimes committed in the workplace or against the employer or a co-worker are terminable offenses. Theft offenses or other crimes that reflect upon an employee's honesty and trustworthiness may be cause for discipline or termination.

---

[34] See e.g., *Novosel v. Nationwide Insurance Co.*, 721 F.2d 894 (3d Cir. 1983)

[35] See e.g., *Firestone Textile Co. Division, Firestone Tire & Rubber Co. v. Meadows*, 666 S.W.2d 730 (1983)

[36] See e.g., *Reuther v. Fowler and Williams, Inc.*, 255 Pa.Super. 28, 386 A.2d 119 (1978)

[37] See e.g., *Woodson v. AMF Leisureland Centers, Inc.*, 842 F.2d 699 (3d Cir., 1988)

[38] See e.g., *Uintah Basin Medical Center v. Hardy*, 179 P. 3d 786 (2008)

C. Unions & Collective Bargaining Activities in the Workplace

The first section of this chapter provided an overview of the history of U.S. employee rights in the workplace. Significant to that history from the mid-19th century up to the latter part of the 20th century was the growth and advocacy of unions. However, the present day reality is that union membership is on the decline in the United States. Union membership in 2016 was at 10.7% of wage earners.[39] Of those members the percentage of unionized workers were higher in the public sector, exceeding the private sector by five times as many workers who were union members.[40] Unionization rates were higher in education, training and library occupations (34.6%) and in protective services occupations (34.5%).[41] Furthermore, union membership was highest in New York State (23.6%) and half of all union members in the United States live in just seven states: California, New York, Pennsylvania, Michigan, New Jersey, Illinois and Ohio.[42]

Despite decreasing numbers and the perceived hostility to organized labor that has existed in this country over the last few years, union members can be found in every state and the District of Columbia. Even though union membership is overwhelmingly weighted toward the public sector there are an estimated 7.4 million private sector workers nationwide who are unionized.[43] This number is actually slightly higher than the 7.1 million unionized public sector workers in the United States.

Union membership offers several advantages to employees. One of these advantages is collective bargaining which permits a group of employees to bargain with the employer over mutual salary, benefits and other conditions of employment. Studies have shown that unionized employees earn more on average than nonunion employees.[44] This increase in wages was across the board in blue-collar and white-collar positions. The collective bargaining agreement is a voluntary agreement between the employer and the union, represented by selected employees, that is guided by federal and state laws. An additional advantage to union membership that is addressed in the collective bargaining agreement is job security and the provisions for "just cause" dismissal. The disciplinary procedure established in the collective bargaining agreement is an important employee protection that insures against arbitrary and capricious punishments.

Collective bargaining in the private sector for businesses involved in interstate commerce only is regulated by the National Labor Relations Act (NLRA). All employees of a qualified employer under the NLRA are entitled to organize and bargain collectively for wages and other conditions of employment. Excluded from the definition of employer for NLRA purposes is the federal government or any state or political subdivision of the state. Thus, employees of these government entities are also excluded from NLRA coverage.[45] Also excluded under the definition of employees under the NLRA are independent contractors, supervisory and managerial employees.

---

[39] U.S. Bureau of Labor Statistics, Union Members 2016, https://www.bls.gov/news.release/pdf/union2.pdf, retrieved July 23, 2017.

[40] Id.

[41] Id.

[42] Id.

[43] Id.

[44] See e.g., George I. Long, Monthly Labor Review, April 2013, *Differences between union and nonunion compensation, 2001–2011*, https://www.bls.gov/opub/mlr/2013/04/art2full.pdf, retrieved July 23, 2017.

[45] State labor laws and federal law pertaining to government employees cover the collective bargaining rights of these employees.

Under the terms of the NLRA there are four basic rules to the collective bargaining process:

1. the employer has to bargain with an NLRB certified employee collective bargaining representative[46];
2. the bargaining has to be over what are termed mandatory subjects of negotiation: wages, hours, leave, and other conditions of employment[47];
3. the bargaining by both sides has to be done in good faith over these mandatory subjects of bargaining until they either reach an agreement or impasse[48];
4. the employer has to abide by a collective bargaining agreement that is in place and cannot unilaterally change a mandatory bargaining term contained within the agreement[49].

If an employer fails to negotiate with a certified employee collective bargaining representative this is an unfair labor practice and subject to the aggrieved employee representative filing an unfair labor practice charge with the National Labor Relations Board (NLRB). The NLRB will review unfair labor practice charges, determine if there is in fact an unfair labor practice taking place, and then intervene if it is determined that an employer has acted in bad faith or refused to negotiate. The NLRB has no independent enforcement powers but it can seek enforcement of its orders through its Office of General Counsel in the U.S. Courts of Appeals.

One of the more contentious aspects of union membership is union security clauses contained in collective bargaining agreements. These clauses, also referred to as a union-shop agreement, require employees working under a collective bargaining agreement to join the incumbent union as a condition to continual employment. Under section 8(a)(3) of the National Labor Relations Act union membership must be completed within 30 days of employment under a union-shop agreement. The membership requirement, however, does not mandate full membership, only dues-paying membership. Thus, the union initiation fee and monthly union dues are required but all other indicia of membership need not be joined by the employee. The rationale for mandatory dues collection is that an employee should not be able to enjoy the benefits of collective bargaining without funding those efforts of the union. This includes the costs and expenses involved in the handling of grievances, employee disciplinary cases, contract negotiation and administration. An alternate arrangement to the union-shop agreement is the agency shop agreement under which all employees, union and nonunion, pay an agency fee, a sort of representation fee, as a condition of employment. This arrangement also comes under the theory no employee workplace benefit should be derived from the union without paying for it. The U.S. Supreme Court in *National Labor Relations Board v. General Motors Corp.* upheld the use of agency shop agreements.[50] The Supreme Court opinion found that such agreements did not violate the NLRA and in doing so Justice White provided a comparison of the union-shop and agency-shop relationship: "*If an employee in a union shop unit refuses to respect any union-imposed obligations other than the duty to pay dues and fees, and membership in the union is therefore denied or terminated, the condition of "membership" for § 8(a)(3) purposes is nevertheless satisfied, and the employee may not be discharged for nonmembership even though he is not a formal member. Of course, if the union chooses to extend membership even though the employee will meet only the minimum financial burden, and refuses to support*

---

[46] 29 U.S.C.A. § 159(a)
[47] 29 U.S.C.A. § 158(d)
[48] Id.
[49] Id.
[50] 373 U.S. 734 (1963)

or "join" the union in any other affirmative way, the employee may have to become a "member"
under a union shop contract, in the sense that the union may be able to place him on its rolls. The
agency shop arrangement proposed here removes that choice from the union and places the option
of membership in the employee, while still requiring the same monetary support as does the union
shop. Such a difference between the union and agency shop may be of great importance in some
contexts, but, for present purposes, it is more formal than real. To the extent that it has any signifi-
cance at all, it serves, rather than violates, the desire of Congress to reduce the evils of compulsory
unionism while allowing financial support for the bargaining agent."[51]

Paying for a union's service under a collective bargaining agreement in which an employee
derives a benefit does not seem to be unfair, but what about other union expenditures of employee
dues that are not related to employee benefits, such as political campaigns? In 1988 the U.S.
Supreme Court held that forcing nonunion employees to contribute union dues to activities beyond
the negotiation and administration of a union contract was illegal and unconstitutional. In *Commu-*
nications Workers of America v. Beck the Supreme Court affirmed a Fourth Circuit Court of Appeals
decision finding the expenditure of agency collected fees on the campaigns of two political candi-
dates was illegal.[52] The Supreme Court held that the NLRA restricted a union from collecting
agency dues for political activities if a member decided to opt out. The right to opt out became
known as "Beck rights" and their enforcement depended on the state where an employee lived and
the union they belonged to. If an employee resided in a "right-to-work-state" they could totally opt
out of union membership or agree to pay only a representational portion of the dues. In these states
unions would be left with the option of continuing to represent the members who opted out or to
completely sever their ties with the union. In non-right-to-work states employee choice is limited
to paying only the portion of dues related to contract negotiation and administration.

Legal Definition

Beck rights – the right of a union member to opt out of paying the portion of union dues that
go toward political activity.

Right-to-work states are jurisdictions that forbid employers and unions from entering into agreements requiring employees to join a union and pay dues as a condition to continued employment.
These states are found mostly in the south and western part of the United States with forced unionism
prevailing in the Northeast and Pacific coast. Presently there are 28 right-to-work states with Kentucky
and Missouri as the most recent states to pass right-to-work legislation.[53] If a state has passed right-to-
work legislation section 14(b) of the NLRA allows the state to prohibit union-shop and agency-shop
agreements. While unions have attempted to challenge the validity of right-to-work legislation their
efforts have mostly been unsuccessful. The main crux of union challenges has been based on the
argument that the legislation denies the unions a property right without due process of law since the
denial of union dues requires the union to otherwise enter into costly contract negotiations which are
unsustainable without proper funding. The legal battle between unions and state legislators continues
with little sign of support coming from the U.S. Supreme Court. A 2015 report by the Economic

---

[51] Id at 743–44

[52] 487 U.S. 735 (1988)

[53] National Right to Work Legal Defense Foundation, *Right to Work States*, http://www.nrtw.org/right-to-work-states, retrieved July 27, 2017

Policy Institute showed that employees in right-to-work states had lower wages than their non-right-to-work state colleagues.[54] Despite the lower salary trend for employees the majority of U.S. states and their legislators at the local and national level remain ideologically committed to right-to-work laws.

III. Employee Workplace Rights

Table 13.1 contains a list of significant federal legislation of the 20th century that has had a positive impact on employee rights and in many instances created specific statutory grounds for the filing of legal actions claiming a violation of workplace rights. As evidenced by the brief historical outline in section I above, many of the basic workplace rights that modern day employees often take for granted were not available in the past. Like so many rights and freedoms that we enjoy in a democratic society the path to their achievement was long and arduous. The securing of these workplace rights and protections was no different.

There are some fundamental protections which can be expected in the workplace, many of which were realized as a result of the Civil Rights Act of 1964 and the overall movement toward civil rights recognition and equality between the races and sexes that took place in the decade and a half to follow. One of the most basic workplace rights is to be able to enjoy a nondiscriminatory work environment. However, due to the special nature of discrimination in the workplace this topic will be treated separately in the section below. In addition to a nondiscriminatory work environment an employee should be able to work free from harassment. The most common type of workplace harassment is sexual harassment which is a form of discrimination.

Other expected workplace rights are:

1. the right to privacy;
2. the right to fair wages;
3. the right to a safe work environment;
4. the right to be free from employer retaliation for protected activities;
5. the right to reasonable working hours and conditions.

Many of the rights employees have in the workplace are not only guaranteed by federal law (for example, workplace safety and the Occupational Safety and Health Act, and the Fair Labor Standards Act's regulation of work hours) but also by state laws regulating the workplace. Many states often have comparable companion state statutes that mirror federal legislation (for instance, state agencies regulating workplace safety or state equal employment commissions). Other rights, like the right to privacy, may have specific statutory protection—such as the Employee Polygraph Protection Act or drug testing laws[55]—but are also covered by common law principles. An employee will have a right to privacy in the workplace but this right is limited to the employee's private possessions and private mail. The right to privacy however is not absolute and the employer will have a right to monitor company e-mail accounts and telephone usage. Monitoring of phone calls is not

---

[54] Elise Gould and Will Kimball, *"Right-to-Work" States Still Have Lower Wages,* Economic Policy Institute, April 22, 2015, http://www.epi.org/publication/right-to-work-states-have-lower-wages/, retrieved July 27, 2017

[55] State laws may regulate the drug testing of employees in the workplace, for example § 40-44 of the Oklahoma Statutes or §§ 39-2-205 through 39-2-211, Montana Code Annotated. Federal employee mandatory drug testing is guided by the Drug-Free Workplace Act of 1988. Further, federal employers must follow the procedures set forth by the Substance Abuse and Mental Health Services Administration (SAMHSA).

permissible but if an employee has an employer issued cell phone used for work purposes the employer is entitled to monitor call minutes and data usage. In a 2010 case the U.S. Supreme Court ruled in favor of a public employer who disciplined an employee after discovering the use of a work pager for personal, sexually explicit messages to the employee's girlfriend. In *City of Ontario v. Quon* the municipal employer issued pagers to members of its police SWAT team so they could be in better communication with each other for work related activities.[56] The officers were allowed 25,000 characters per month in usage, anything over that would result in extra charges by the phone company. The police department's computer and internet use policy notified employees that their e-mail and internet activity could be monitored by the department. Although the policy did not specifically include text messages internal agency memorandums placed employees on notice that the policy extended to text messages. As a result of an audit of the pager bills resulting from excessive use by a number of officers, including Sgt. Quon, it was discovered that the married police supervisor was sending sexually explicit messages to his girlfriend through the department's pager while on job time. He was subsequently disciplined by the department. The eventual appeal to the U.S. Supreme Court centered on Quon's workplace privacy rights and the reasonableness of the employer's reading of his text messages. The Supreme Court ruled in favor of the employer by finding the review of the text messages to be a reasonable work-related search.

The *Quon* decision is limited in its scope and involved a public-sector employment relationship, however it did follow the general guideline for workplace administrative searches provided by the Supreme Court in *O'Connor v. Ortega*.[57] What *Quon* does illustrate is the extent to which an employee's expected privacy is not as complete in the work environment as might be expected. While public sector employees can resort to specific enumerated constitutional protections against government intrusion to remedy workplace privacy intrusions, private sector employees are more limited in their avenues of relief. Collective bargaining agreements in a unionized workplace or employment contracts and employee handbooks in nonunion settings guide private sector employee privacy expectations. Additionally, state and federal laws preempt employer invasion of employee privacy in certain areas. One of these areas is social media policy. In 2016 the Uniform Law Commission[58] adopted the *Employee and Student Online Privacy Protection Act*. Several states have adopted social media privacy laws which prevent employers from requiring job applicants or employees to disclose e-mail and social media account passwords to an employer or to allow an employer access to those accounts. There are presently 25 states with some form of legislation protecting employees from this type of privacy invasion. However, these laws do not prevent an employer from establishing a workplace social media policy to be followed by employees. Nor does it prevent an employer from monitoring employees in the workplace. If an employee is accessing a private e-mail or social media account through an employer's computer system, which is subject to monitoring, there is likely not going to be any privacy protection for the employee.[59]

---

[56] 560 U.S. 746 (2010)

[57] 480 U.S. 709 (1987): The Supreme Court found that in the context of an administrative search of a government employee's property conducted for legitimate work-related reasons there were different needs present than those involved in law enforcement, therefore it was not unreasonable to recognize an exception to the Fourth Amendment probable cause and warrant requirements in those areas related to work and generally within the employer's control.

[58] The National Conference of Commissioners on Uniform State Laws, established in 1892, is a non-profit organization aimed at encouraging uniformity of law throughout the 50 states by researching and drafting legislation for adoption by the different states.

[59] See, e.g., *Garrity v. John Hancock Mutual Life Insurance*, 2002 WL 974676 (D. Mass. 2002); *Smyth v. Pillsbury Co.*, 914 F. Supp. 97 (E.D. Pa., 1996)

FIGURE 13.1   Example of state social media privacy legislation

Rhode Island Employee Social Media Policy

§ 28-56-2 Social media password requests prohibited.

No employer shall:

(1) Require, coerce, or request an employee or applicant to disclose the password or any other means for accessing a personal social media account;

(2) Require, coerce, or request an employee or applicant to access a personal social media account in the presence of the employer or representative;

(3) Require or coerce an employee or applicant to divulge any personal social media account information, except when reasonably believed to be relevant to an investigation of allegations of employee misconduct or workplace-related violation of applicable laws and regulations and when not otherwise prohibited by law or constitution; provided that the information is accessed and used solely to the extent necessary for purposes of that investigation or a related proceeding.

§ 28-56-3 Social media access requests prohibited.

No employer shall compel an employee or applicant to add anyone, including the employer or their agent, to their list of contacts associated with a personal social media account or require, request, or cause an employee or applicant to alter settings that affect a third party's ability to view the contents of a personal social media account.

§ 28-56-4 Disciplinary actions prohibited.

No employer shall:

(1) Discharge, discipline, or otherwise penalize or threaten to discharge, discipline, or otherwise penalize any employee for an employee's refusal to disclose or provide access to any information specified in § 28-56-2, or for refusal to add the employer to his or her list of contacts associated with a personal social media account, or to alter the settings associated with a personal social media account, as specified in § 28-56-3; or

(2) Fail or refuse to hire any applicant as a result of the applicant's refusal to disclose or provide access to any information specified in § 28-56-2, or for refusal to add the employer or their agent to their list of contacts associated with a personal social media account, or to alter the settings associated with a personal social media account, as specified in § 28-56-3.

In addition to workplace privacy protections, a safe work environment, and freedom from retaliatory acts of the employer, an important employee right pertains to wages and working hours. The Fair Labor Standards Act (FLSA) sets minimum wages, work hours and overtime regulations for employees in the private and public sector. Most employees are covered by the FLSA but some are not due to statutory definitions in the FLSA. One of the most litigated areas of the FLSA is over what employees are considered "exempt" from overtime payments. While most employees are "nonexempt" and entitled to overtime pay according to the FLSA guidelines there are categories of employees who are in the "exempt" category and not entitled to overtime pay. An "exempt" employee is determined based upon a three-part test:

1. the salary level test wherein any employee paid less than $23,600.00 per year is considered "nonexempt";
2. the salary basis test wherein an employee is paid a guaranteed minimum amount of money he or she can expect for a work week for any amount of work completed;
3. the job duties test which looks at the type of work the employee performs and whether it falls within the "exempt" job category.

The employee has to meet all three requirements in order to be considered "exempt." Under the job duties test there are three separate categories of "exempt" job duties: executive, professional, and administrative. The FLSA outlines the criteria (see Figure 13.2) used to determine whether an employee fits into one of the "exempt" job categories. If an employee is "exempt" they have

FIGURE 13.2   FLSA Exempt Job Duties Categories

FLSA Exempt Job Duties		
Executive	**Professional**	**Administrative**
Regularly supervises two or more employees Management as primary position Genuine input into job status of other employees (hiring, firing, discipline)	Traditional "learned" professions Doctor, Lawyer, RN, Dentist, Clergy, Architect, Accountant Predominantly intellectual work requiring advanced schooling	Office or non-manual work directly related to management Primary component involves the exercise of independent judgment & discretion about matters of significance

virtually no rights under the FLSA's overtime rules other than to receive their full salary, while "nonexempt" employees are entitled to one-and-a-half times their regular rate of pay.

The following case of *Bright v. Houston Northwest Medical Center* involves an FLSA lawsuit over the payment of overtime for an employee's "on-call" status. This is a significant wage issue which depends upon a variety of factors for determining whether an employee is entitled to overtime payment. "On call" status for an employee is a period of off-duty time when the employee is waiting for their employer to contact them to perform a work related task. In reading the case consider the court's discussion regarding the "on-call" nature of the plaintiff's employment and whether it entitled him to overtime payments.

❖❖

Bright v. Houston Northwest Medical Center
934 F.2d 671 (5th Cir., 1991)

GARWOOD, Circuit Judge:

This is a former employee's suit for overtime compensation under section 7(a)(1) of the Fair Labor Standards Act (FLSA), 29 U.S.C. § 207(a)(1). The question presented is whether "on-call" time the employee spent at home, or at other locations of his choosing substantially removed from his employer's place of business, is to be included for purposes of section 7 as working time in instances where the employee was not actually "called." The district court granted the motion for summary judgment of the employer, defendant-appellee Houston Northwest Medical Center Survivor, Inc. (Northwest), ruling that this on-call time was not working time and dismissing the suit of the employee, plaintiff-appellant Frederick George Bright (Bright). A divided panel of this Court reversed and remanded. Disagreeing with the panel majority's contrary conclusion, this Court en banc now holds that the undisputed facts afford no basis for a finding that the employee's on-call time was working time for purposes of section 7. We accordingly affirm the district court's summary judgment for the employer.

I. FACTS AND PROCEEDINGS

Bright went to work for Northwest at its hospital in Houston in April 1981 as a biomedical equipment repair technician, and remained in that employment until late January 1983 when, for reasons wholly unrelated to any matters at issue here, he was in effect fired. Throughout his employment at Northwest, Bright worked a standard forty hour week at the hospital, from 8:00 a.m. to 4:30 p.m., with half an hour off for lunch, Monday through Friday, and he was paid an hourly wage. Overtime in this standard work week was compensated at time and a half rates, and it was understood that overtime work required advance approval by the department head, Jim Chatterton. When Bright started at the hospital, his immediate supervisor was Howard Culp, the senior biomedical equipment repair technician. Culp had the same work schedule as Bright. However, throughout his off-duty hours, Culp was required to wear an electronic paging device or "beeper" and to be "on call" to come to the hospital to make emergency repairs on biomedical equipment. Culp, as Bright knew, was not compensated for this "on-call" time (although Culp apparently was compensated when he was called). In February 1982 Culp resigned, and Bright succeeded him as the senior biomedical equipment repair technician and likewise succeeded Culp in wearing the beeper and being on call throughout all his off-duty time. Bright remained in that role throughout the balance of his employment at Northwest. The only period of time at issue in this lawsuit is that when Bright had the beeper, namely from February 1982 to the end of his employment in January 1983.

Bright was not compensated for his on-call time, and knew this was the arrangement with him as it had been with Culp. During the "on-call" time, if Bright were called, and came to the hospital, he was compensated by four hours compensatory time at his then regular hourly rate (which apparently was some $9 or $10 per hour) for each such call. This compensation was effected by Bright simply working that many less hours the following workday or days: for example, if Bright were called on a Monday evening, he might work in his regular work-shift only from 8:00 a.m. until noon on the following Tuesday, but would be paid for the entire eight hours on that day. There is no evidence that these calls on average (or, indeed, in any given instance) took as much as two hours and forty minutes (two-thirds of four hours) of Bright's time. This case does not involve any claim respecting entitlement to compensation (overtime or otherwise) for time that Bright actually spent pursuant to a call from Northwest received while he was on call.

It is undisputed that during the on-call time at issue Bright was not required to, and did not, remain at or about the hospital or any premises of or designated by his employer. He was free to go wherever and do whatever he wanted, subject *only* to the following three restrictions: (1) he must not be intoxicated or impaired to the degree that he could not work on medical equipment if called to the hospital, although total abstinence was not required (as it was during the daily workshift); (2) he must always be reachable by the beeper; (3) and he must be able to arrive at the hospital within, in Bright's words, "approximately twenty minutes" from the time he was reached on the beeper.

***

While the record does not reflect all of Bright's activities while on call, it is *undisputed* that the only restrictions imposed on him were the three above noted. It is also clear that while on call Bright did no work for Northwest—apart from being in the on-call status and what he did, and was fully and appropriately compensated for, pursuant to actually being called. Bright also testified on deposition that he was "called" on "average" two times during the working week (Monday through Friday) and "ordinarily two to three times" on the weekend.

***

II. DISCUSSION

At issue here is whether the time Bright spent on call, but uncalled on, is working time under section 7, which provides in relevant part as follows:

Except as otherwise provided in this section, no employer shall employ any of his employees . . . for a workweek longer than forty hours unless such employee receives compensation for his employment in excess of the hours above specified at a rate not less than one and one-half times the regular rate at which he is employed. 29 U.S.C. § 207(a)(1).

As the case was resolved below by granting Northwest's motion for summary judgment after ample time for discovery, and as Bright would have had the burden of proof on the dispositive issue at trial, we review the record to determine whether it contains sufficient summary judgment evidence to support a finding that Bright's on-call time, when he performed no active service for Northwest, was working time for purposes of section 7. *Anderson v. Liberty Lobby, Inc.*, 477 U.S. 242, 106 S.Ct. 2505, 2510–12, 91 L.Ed.2d 202 (1986); *Celotex Corp. v. Catrett*, 477 U.S. 317, 106 S.Ct. 2548, 2552–53, 91 L.Ed.2d 265 (1986). The relevant facts recited above are not genuinely disputed, and we conclude that the record reflects no genuine issue of material fact and contains no evidence sufficient to support a finding that Bright's on-call time at issue was working time. Accordingly, the district court did not err in granting Northwest's motion for summary judgment.

Bright urges, and the panel majority apparently agreed, that under the decisions in *Armour & Co. v. Wantock*, 323 U.S. 126, 65 S.Ct. 165, 89 L.Ed. 118 (1944) and *Skidmore v. Swift & Co.*, 323 U.S. 134, 65 S.Ct. 161, 89 L.Ed. 124 (1944), handed down the same day, the question whether such on-call time is working time is necessarily one of fact, thus precluding summary judgment or a directed verdict. This is not our reading of those decisions. Neither involved a summary judgment or a directed verdict or a discussion of the propriety of such a disposition. The thrust of the opinions in this respect was that whether waiting time was working time "is a question dependent upon all the circumstances of the case," *Armour* 65 S.Ct. at 168, as to which "[e]ach case must stand on its own facts", *Skidmore*, 65 S.Ct. at 164, for the Court could not lay down a single "legal formula to resolve cases so varied in their facts as are the many situations in which employment involves waiting time." *Id.* 65 S.Ct. at 163. But to state, as this language does, that the particular facts in each case are determinative, is not to say that where those discrete facts are found the resulting categorization as working or nonworking time is also necessarily always a factual rather than a legal question. Indeed, *Skidmore* expressly recognizes that "[f]acts may show that the employee was engaged to wait, or they may show that he waited to be engaged." *Id.* Obviously, the Court does not mean that the *same* set of facts may lead to different results, but rather that the different facts of discrete cases may produce different results.

Here, the undisputed facts show that the on-call time is not working time. In such a setting, we have not hesitated to so hold as a matter of law. See, e.g., *Halferty v. Pulse Drug Co.*, 864 F.2d 1185 (5th Cir.1989); *Brock v. El Paso Natural Gas Co.*, 826 F.2d 369, 374 (5th Cir.1987) ("'Stare decisis means that like facts will receive like treatment in a court of law.'"); *Rousseau v. Teledyne Movible Offshore, Inc.*, 805 F.2d 1245, 1247 & n. 1 (5th Cir.1986) (summary judgment as to offshore barges).

***

Armour and *Skidmore* clearly stand for the proposition that, in a proper setting, on-call time may be working time for purposes of section 7. But those decisions *also* plainly imply that that is *not* true of employer-required on-call time in *all* settings. In *Skidmore* the Court noted, with at least some degree of implied approval, the administrative interpretations that

[i]n some occupations . . . periods of inactivity are not properly counted as working time even though the employee is subject to call. Examples are an operator of a small telephone exchange where the switchboard is in her home and she ordinarily gets several hours of uninterrupted sleep each night; or a pumper of a stripper well or watchman of a lumber camp during the off season, who may be on duty twenty-four hours a day but ordinarily 'has a normal night's sleep, has ample time in which to eat his meals, and has a certain amount of time for relaxation and entirely private pursuits.' Exclusion of all such hours the Administrator thinks may be justified. Id. 65 S.Ct. at 163–64.

In *Armour* the plaintiffs were firemen who worked a regular 8:00 a.m. to 5:00 p.m. shift, and then were on call at the employer's premises from 5:00 p.m. until 8:00 a.m. of the following day, after which they had 24 wholly unrestricted hours, and then repeated the cycle. The Court observed that:

[t]he litigation concerns the time [5:00 p.m. to 8:00 a.m.] during which these men were required to be on the employer's premises, to some extent amenable to the employer's discipline, subject to call, but not engaged in any specific work. The Company provided cooking equipment, beds, radios, and facilities for cards and amusements with which the men slept, ate, or entertained themselves pretty much as they chose. They were not, however, at liberty to leave the premises except that, by permission of the watchman, they might go to a nearby restaurant for their evening meal. Id. 65 S.Ct. at 166.

Armour sustained the district court's determination, which had been affirmed by the Seventh Circuit, that all this time (apart from hours presumably devoted to sleeping or eating, a matter that the plaintiffs did not appeal) was working time. Bright's case is wholly different from *Armour* and *Skidmore* and similar cases in that Bright did not have to remain on or about his employer's place of business, or some location designated by his employer, but was free to be at his home or at any place or places he chose, without advising his employer, subject only to the restrictions that he be reachable by beeper, not be intoxicated, and be able to arrive at the hospital in "approximately" twenty minutes. During the period in issue he actually moved his home—as Northwest knew and approved—to a location seventeen miles and twenty-five or thirty minutes away from the hospital, as compared to the three miles (and some fifteen minutes) away that it had been when he started carrying his beeper. Bright was not only able to carry on his normal personal activities at his own home, but could also do normal shopping, eating at restaurants, and the like, as he chose.

To hold that Bright's on-call time was working time would be inconsistent with several of our own prior decisions, as well as those in other circuits, which have determined that considerably more restrictive on-call status did not result in work time.

In *Brock*, we held clearly erroneous and reversed and rendered a district court bench trial finding that "on call" time was compensable overtime. There, the employee claimants lived relatively near their employer's pumping stations where their regular workday was 7:30 a.m. to 4:00 p.m. However, during the nonworking hours of 4:00 p.m. to 7:30 a.m. every day, one employee was required to remain "on call"; this required the employee to remain at his home where he could hear an alarm; if it went off, he would go to the station to correct the problem. We noted that "[o]therwise, the on-call employee is free to eat, sleep, entertain guests, watch television, or engage in any other personal recreational activity, alone or with his family, as long as he is within hailing distance of the alarm and the station." *Id.* at 370. The employees were compensated for this time only in instances where they were actually called. We held that as a matter of law the on-call time was not work time for purposes of the FLSA.

In *Halferty*, we again held to be clearly erroneous the district court's finding that the on-call time was compensable overtime, and reversed and rendered judgment that it was not. There, the employee time in question was spent at home from 5:00 p.m. to 8:00 a.m. to be available for telephone calls as an ambulance dispatcher. We stated that in these cases "the critical issue . . . is whether the employee can use the time effectively for his or her own purposes." *Id.*, 864 F.2d at 1189. We held that as a matter of law the plaintiff there could use the time effectively for her own purposes and that she was hence not entitled to recover, stating:

The facts show that Halferty could visit friends, entertain guests, sleep, watch television, do laundry, and babysit. We, therefore, conclude that she could use the time for her own purposes and that she is not entitled to compensation for her idle time. . . . Id.

We noted that "[e]mployees who have received compensation for idle time generally have had almost no freedom at all." *Id.* at 1190. And, we cited and relied on, among other cases, *Norton v. Worthen Van Service, Inc.*, 839 F.2d 653 (10th Cir.1988), and *Pilkenton v. Appalachian Regional Hospitals, Inc.*, 336 F.Supp. 334 (W.D.Va.1971).

In *Norton*, the plaintiffs were van drivers who transported railroad crews at irregular and unpredictable intervals. During the disputed on-call time, "drivers must be near enough to the employer's premises to be able to respond to calls within fifteen to twenty minutes." 839 F.2d at 654. They were only compensated, however, in the event they were actually called. They argued "that the unpredictability of assignments and the short response time which they are allowed preclude their using this waiting period for their own purposes." *Id.* The district court judgment for the employer was affirmed, the Tenth Circuit noting that the "drivers spent their time between assignments at the homes of friends, at church, at laundromats, at restaurants, at pool halls, and at a local gymnasium" and that "a simple paging device, which the drivers are free to purchase and to use, would have allayed the necessity of remaining by a phone." *Id.* at 655–56.

In *Pilkenton*, the on-call employees had beepers and had to remain within an "approximately twenty minutes" drive from their employer's hospital during their on-call time. That time was held noncompensable (except for instances where they were called).

***

As noted, we have described "the critical issue" in cases of this kind as being "whether the employee can use the [on-call] time effectively for his or her own purposes." *Halferty*, 864 F.2d at 1189. This does not imply that the employee must have substantially the same flexibility or freedom as he would if not on call, else all or almost all on-call time would be working time, a proposition that the settled case law and the administrative guidelines clearly reject. Only in the very rarest of situations, if ever, would there be any point in an employee being on call if he could not be reached by his employer so as to shortly thereafter—generally at least a significant time before the next regular work shift could take care of the matter—be able to perform a needed service, usually at some particular location.

Within such accepted confines, Bright was clearly able to use his on-call time effectively for his own personal purposes. Indeed, it is evident that he was *much more* able to do so than the employees in the above discussed cases whose on-call time was held to be nonworking time. . . . Bright was not restricted to any one or a few fixed locations, but could go virtually anywhere within approximately twenty minutes of the hospital, and indeed he lived (and moved to) approximately seventeen miles and thirty minutes away from the hospital. Within that limit, anything was permissible, except excessive alcohol consumption . . . We have found no unreversed decision holding compensable on-call time that afforded even nearly as much freedom for personal use as did Bright's. Had the twenty to thirty minute "leash" been longer, Bright would, of course, have been able to do *more* things, but that does not mean that within the applicable restrictions he could not effectively use the on-call time wholly for his own private purposes. Millions of employees go for weeks at a time without traveling more than seventeen miles from their place of employment.

The panel majority did not disagree with our prior decisions. Rather, it placed crucial reliance on the fact that Bright throughout the nearly one year in issue never had any relief from his on-call status during his nonworking hours.

***

In essence, the panel majority inferentially conceded that for any given day or week of on-call time, Bright was as free to use the time for his own purposes as were the employees in the above-cited cases where the time was held nonworking. But the panel majority claims that a different result should apply here because Bright's arrangement lasted nearly a year.

We are aware of no authority that supports this theory, and we decline to adopt it . . . Further, the FLSA is structured on a workweek basis. Section 7, at issue here, requires time and a half pay "for a workweek longer than forty hours." What Bright was or was not free to do in the last week in September is wholly irrelevant to whether he worked any overtime in the first week of that month. As we said in *Halferty*, the issue "is whether the employee can use the time effectively for his or her own purposes," and that must be decided, under the statutory framework, on the basis of each workweek at the most.

We do not deny the obvious truth that the long continued aspect of Bright's on-call status made his job highly undesirable and arguably somewhat oppressive. Clearly, it would have been vastly more pleasant from Bright's point of view had he only been on call the first week of every month, for example. But the FLSA's overtime provisions are more narrowly focused than being simply directed at requiring extra compensation for oppressive or confining conditions of employment. A Texan working 8:30 p.m. to 3:00 a.m. six days a week (thirty-nine hours), fifty-two weeks a year, at a remote Alaska location has a most restrictive and oppressive job that as a practical matter prevents, *inter alia*, vacations, visiting relatives, and attending live operatic performances or major league sporting events, but it seems obvious that the FLSA overtime provisions provide no relief for those oppressive and confining conditions. Bright's job was oppressive and confining in many of the same ways, but it, too, did not involve more than forty hours work a week.

The district court properly granted summary judgment for Northwest, and that judgment is accordingly

Affirmed.

Questions Presented

1) How did the 5th circuit define "on call" time?
2) What was the basis for the court's denial of the plaintiff's lawsuit for compensation of his "on call" time?
3) How did the full court differ from its prior panel decision in the case?

❖❖

The conditions under which an employee will be considered to be "on-call" will vary according to the employer and the employment contract or collective bargaining agreement. The nature of the "on-call" conditions imposed upon an employee will have an impact in determining whether the employee is entitled to "on-call" compensation. "On-call" conditions are one of two categories: restricted and nonrestricted conditions. Restricted "on-call" conditions limit the employee from using the time-off for personal use. The criteria centers on the degree of control an employer has over an employee's time.[60] The U.S. Supreme Court first engaged the issue of "on-call' status in the 1944 cases *Skidmore v. Swift & Co.*[61] and *Armour & Co. v. Wantock.*[62] In both cases the Supreme Court found the "on-call" time that employees were required to maintain were compensable as overtime hours. However, as the Justice Robert Jackson noted in the *Skidmore* case, the factual circumstances of each case had to be considered when determining FLSA issues regarding "on-call" time.[63] Nonrestricted conditions in which the employee is free to utilize the time for his or her own purpose is not considered hours worked.[64]

IV. Discrimination in the Workplace

A. Discriminatory Practices

Employment discrimination occurs when an employer, supervisor, or co-worker treats an employee differently from other employees due to some attribute unconnected to work performance. This does not include bona fide differences based on education, work experience, or specialty in which an employee may be compensated more or hired at a higher level due to any one of these factors. Discrimination is generally based on impermissible employment treatment based on race, national origin, sex, genetic information, religion, physical disability, or age. These are federally protected classifications, though sexual orientation is also recognized by some state laws and individual federal statutes as a protected category. Marital status and political affiliation are also two categories under which employment discrimination claims have been filed.

Employment discrimination usually involves some bias or unlawful preference in hiring, promotion, retention, assignment, or termination. Discriminatory acts can also be the basis of retaliation and harassment claims. Title VII of the Civil Rights Act of 1964 provides the most common statutory protection against employment discrimination but there are other specific statutory protections, such as the Equal Pay Act and the Age Discrimination in Employment Act, which serve to protect certain classes of employees. Title VII of the Civil Rights Act originally only covered the categories of race, color, religion, sex, and national origin. Over the years other categories have been added to provide more comprehensive coverage. If a business has 15 or more employees then Title VII coverage will apply and aggrieved employees can seek enforcement through the federal Equal Employment Opportunity Commission (EEOC) which investigates and enforces Title VII

---

[60] See e.g., *Owens v. Local No. 169*, 971 F. 2d 347, 350 (9th Cir. 1992): "A determination of whether the on-call waiting time is spent predominantly for the employer's benefit depends on two considerations: (1) the parties' agreement, and (2) the degree to which the employee is free to engage in personal activities."

[61] 323 U.S. 134 (1944)

[62] 323 U.S. 126 (1944)

[63] See also, 29 C.F.R. § 785.14 General. Whether waiting time is time worked under the Act depends upon particular circumstances. The determination involves "scrutiny and construction of the agreements between particular parties, appraisal of their practical construction of the working agreement by conduct, consideration of the nature of the service, and its relation to the waiting time, and all of the circumstances. Facts may show that the employee was engaged to wait or they may show that he waited to be engaged." (*Skidmore v. Swift*, 323 U.S. 134 (1944)) Such questions "must be determined in accordance with common sense and the general concept of work or employment." (*Central Mo. Tel. Co. v. Conwell*, 170 F. 2d 641 (C.A. 8, 1948))

[64] See 29 C.F.R. § 785.17 On-call time. An employee who is required to remain on call on the employer's premises or so close thereto that he cannot use the time effectively for his own purposes is working while "on call." An employee who is not required to remain on the employer's premises but is merely required to leave word at his home or with company officials where he may be reached is not working while on call. (*Armour & Co. v. Wantock*, 323 U.S. 126 (1944); *Handler v. Thrasher*, 191 F. 2d 120 (C.A. 10, 1951); *Walling v. Bank of Waynesboro, Georgia*, 61 F. Supp. 384 (S.D. Ga. 1945))

claims. As an alternative most states have their own state agency equivalents to the EEOC which act as an ancillary and allow employees to file discrimination claims, copies of which, if applicable, will be filed with the EEOC. If a determination by either the EEOC or a state agency finds there is no probable cause to sustain a complaint of discrimination then an aggrieved employee can file a claim with a federal or state court. However, a condition precedent to the filing is a determination by the EEOC or state agency which will issue a right to sue letter upon its determination.

The EEOC lists the following types of prohibited discrimination it has the power to investigate and, if necessary, enforce the law against discrimination:[65]

- Age
- Disability
- Equal pay/Compensation
- Genetic information
- Harassment
- National origin
- Pregnancy
- Race/Color
- Religion
- Retaliation
- Sex
- Sexual harassment

Of the listed categories the one most recently added is discrimination based on genetic information. Title II of the Genetic Information and Nondiscrimination Act (GINA), signed into law by President George W. Bush on May 21, 2008 to take effect on November 21, 2009, prohibits genetic information discrimination in employment. Genetic information "*includes information about an individual's genetic tests and the genetic tests of an individual's family members, as well as information about the manifestation of a disease or disorder in an individual's family members (i.e. family medical history).*"[66] The law protects an employee from harassment, retaliation, or any type of discrimination based on their genetic information. This protects an employee from any disclosures made to an employer as a result of mandatory information which must be made available to employers under other federal laws like the Americans with Disabilities Act (ADA) and the Family Medical Leave Act (FMLA). GINA also requires the employer to keep genetic information about an employee confidential.

There are two types of general claims made regarding discriminatory practices—those that have a disparate impact and those that involve disparate treatment. Disparate impact occurs when an employer's actions in hiring, promoting, or firing employees have a statistically greater impact on one group than another. In a landmark 2009 employment law case, *Ricci v. DeStefano*, the U.S. Supreme Court found that the City of New Haven engaged in impermissible reverse discrimination when it discarded the test results of white firefighters on a promotion test because minority firefighters did not score well.[67] In *Ricci* the Supreme Court noted: "*Examinations like those administered by the City create legitimate expectations on the part of those who took the tests. As is the case with any promotion exam, some of the firefighters here invested substantial time,*

---

[65] U.S. Equal Employment Opportunity Commission, *Discrimination by Type*, https://www.eeoc.gov/laws/types/, retrieved July 28, 2017.

[66] Id.

[67] 557 U.S. 557 (2009)

money, and personal commitment in preparing for the tests. Employment tests can be an important part of a neutral selection system that safeguards against the very racial animosities Title VII was intended to prevent. Here, however, the firefighters saw their efforts invalidated by the City in sole reliance upon race-based statistics."[68] Disparate impact claims of discrimination are focused on discriminatory practices aimed at a group. Disparate treatment claims involve individual employees who claim that the employer treated them differently than similarly situated employees. The comparison to similarly situated employees is to those who do not share the attribute claimed by the complainant to be the basis of the discriminatory treatment. An example of a disparate treatment claim would be a female investigative reporter who, because of pregnancy, is alleging that she is not being assigned stories on the same basis as male reporters and nonpregnant female reporters due to her condition. Her treatment, she alleges, is different from other reporters based solely on her pregnancy and no other bona fide employment reasons. In such a case the complainant would have the initial burden of proof by a preponderance of the evidence that she was treated differently. The burden then shifts to the employer to provide a valid reason for its actions. Once the employer presents its case regarding its legitimate employment reason the burden shifts back to the employee to show the reason(s) were illegitimate or fraudulent.

The case of *Griggs v. Duke Power Company* is one of the first cases to deal with disparate impact in an employment case. It was a case that set the course 48 years later for the Supreme Court's decision in *Ricci v. DeStefano*. As you read the case consider the parallels between *Griggs* and *Ricci* and what they hold with regard to aptitude and achievement testing in the context of employment.

❖❖

Griggs v. Duke Power Co.
401 U.S. 424 (1971)

Mr. Chief Justice Burger delivered the opinion of the Court.

We granted the writ in this case to resolve the question whether an employer is prohibited by the Civil Rights Act of 1964, Title VII, from requiring a high school education or passing of a standardized general intelligence test as a condition of employment in or transfer to jobs when (a) neither standard is shown to be significantly related to successful job performance, (b) both requirements operate to disqualify Negroes at a substantially higher rate than white applicants, and (c) the jobs in question formerly had been filled only by white employees as part of a longstanding practice of giving preference to whites.

Congress provided, in Title VII of the Civil Rights Act of 1964, for class actions for enforcement of provisions of the Act, and this proceeding was brought by a group of incumbent Negro employees against Duke Power Company. All the petitioners are employed at the Company's Dan River Steam Station, a power generating facility located at Draper, North Carolina. At the time this action was instituted, the Company had 95 employees at the Dan River Station, 14 of whom were Negroes; 13 of these are petitioners here.

The District Court found that, prior to July 2, 1965, the effective date of the Civil Rights Act of 1964, the Company openly discriminated on the basis of race in the hiring and assigning of employees at its Dan River plant. The plant was organized into five operating departments: (1) Labor, (2) Coal Handling, (3) Operations, (4) Maintenance, and (5) Laboratory and Test. Negroes were

---

[68] Id at ___

employed only in the Labor Department, where the highest paying jobs paid less than the lowest paying jobs in the other four "operating" departments, in which only whites were employed. Promotions were normally made within each department on the basis of job seniority. Transferees into a department usually began in the lowest position.

In 1955, the Company instituted a policy of requiring a high school education for initial assignment to any department except Labor, and for transfer from the Coal Handling to any "inside" department (Operations, Maintenance, or Laboratory). When the Company abandoned its policy of restricting Negroes to the Labor Department in 1965, completion of high school also was made a prerequisite to transfer from Labor to any other department. From the time the high school requirement was instituted to the time of trial, however, white employees hired before the time of the high school education requirement continued to perform satisfactorily and achieve promotions in the "operating" departments. Findings on this score are not challenged.

The Company added a further requirement for new employees on July 2, 1965, the date on which Title VII became effective. To qualify for placement in any but the Labor Department, it became necessary to register satisfactory scores on two professionally prepared aptitude tests, as well as to have a high school education. Completion of high school alone continued to render employees eligible for transfer to the four desirable departments from which Negroes had been excluded if the incumbent had been employed prior to the time of the new requirement. In September, 1965, the Company began to permit incumbent employees who lacked a high school education to qualify for transfer from Labor or Coal Handling to an "inside" job by passing two tests—the Wonderlic Personnel Test, which purports to measure general intelligence, and the Bennett Mechanical Comprehension Test. Neither was directed or intended to measure the ability to learn to perform a particular job or category of jobs. The requisite scores used for both initial hiring and transfer approximated the national median for high school graduates.

The District Court had found that, while the Company previously followed a policy of overt racial discrimination in a period prior to the Act, such conduct had ceased. The District Court also concluded that Title VII was intended to be prospective only, and, consequently, the impact of prior inequities was beyond the reach of corrective action authorized by the Act.

The Court of Appeals was confronted with a question of first impression, as are we, concerning the meaning of Title VII. After careful analysis, a majority of that court concluded that a subjective test of the employer's intent should govern, particularly in a close case, and that, in this case, there was no showing of a discriminatory purpose in the adoption of the diploma and test requirements. On this basis, the Court of Appeals concluded there was no violation of the Act.

The Court of Appeals reversed the District Court in part, rejecting the holding that residual discrimination arising from prior employment practices was insulated from remedial action. The Court of Appeals noted, however, that the District Court was correct in its conclusion that there was no showing of a racial purpose or invidious intent in the adoption of the high school diploma requirement or general intelligence test, and that these standards had been applied fairly to whites and Negroes alike. It held that, in the absence of a discriminatory purpose, use of such requirements was permitted by the Act. In so doing, the Court of Appeals rejected the claim that, because these two requirements operated to render ineligible a markedly disproportionate number of Negroes, they were unlawful under Title VII unless shown to be job-related. We granted the writ on these claims. 399 U.S. 926.

The objective of Congress in the enactment of Title VII is plain from the language of the statute. It was to achieve equality of employment opportunities and remove barriers that have operated in the past to favor an identifiable group of white employees over other employees. Under the Act, practices, procedures, or tests neutral on their face, and even neutral in terms of intent, cannot be maintained if they operate to "freeze" the *status quo* of prior discriminatory employment practices.

The Court of Appeals' opinion, and the partial dissent, agreed that, on the record in the present case, "whites register far better on the Company's alternative requirements" than Negroes. 420 F.2d 1225, 1239 n. 6. This consequence would appear to be directly traceable to race. Basic intelligence must have the means of articulation to manifest itself fairly in a testing process. Because they are Negroes, petitioners have long received inferior education in segregated schools, and this Court expressly recognized these differences in *Gaston County v. United States*, 395 U.S. 285(1969). There, because of the inferior education received by Negroes in North Carolina, this Court barred the institution of a literacy test for voter registration on the ground that the test would abridge the right to vote indirectly on account of race. Congress did not intend by Title VII, however, to guarantee a job to every person regardless of qualifications. In short, the Act does not command that any person be hired simply because he was formerly the subject of discrimination, or because he is a member of a minority group. Discriminatory preference for any group, minority or majority, is precisely and only what Congress has proscribed. What is required by Congress is the removal of artificial, arbitrary, and unnecessary barriers to employment when the barriers operate invidiously to discriminate on the basis of racial or other impermissible classification.

Congress has now provided that tests or criteria for employment or promotion may not provide equality of opportunity merely in the sense of the fabled offer of milk to the stork and the fox. On the contrary, Congress has now required that the posture and condition of the job seeker be taken into account. It has—to resort again to the fable—provided that the vessel in which the milk is proffered be one all seekers can use. The Act proscribes not only overt discrimination, but also practices that are fair in form, but discriminatory in operation. The touchstone is business necessity. If an employment practice which operates to exclude Negroes cannot be shown to be related to job performance, the practice is prohibited.

On the record before us, neither the high school completion requirement nor the general intelligence test is shown to bear a demonstrable relationship to successful performance of the jobs for which it was used. Both were adopted, as the Court of Appeals noted, without meaningful study of their relationship to job performance ability. Rather, a vice-president of the Company testified, the requirements were instituted on the Company's judgment that they generally would improve the overall quality of the workforce.

The evidence, however, shows that employees who have not completed high school or taken the tests have continued to perform satisfactorily, and make progress in departments for which the high school and test criteria are now used. The promotion record of present employees who would not be able to meet the new criteria thus suggests the possibility that the requirements may not be needed even for the limited purpose of preserving the avowed policy of advancement within the Company. In the context of this case, it is unnecessary to reach the question whether testing requirements that take into account capability for the next succeeding position or related future promotion might be utilized upon a showing that such long-range requirements fulfill a genuine business need. In the present case, the Company has made no such showing.

The Court of Appeals held that the Company had adopted the diploma and test requirements without any "intention to discriminate against Negro employees." 420 F.2d at 1232. We do not suggest that either the District Court or the Court of Appeals erred in examining the employer's intent; but good intent or absence of discriminatory intent does not redeem employment procedures or testing mechanisms that operate as "built-in headwinds" for minority groups and are unrelated to measuring job capability.

The Company's lack of discriminatory intent is suggested by special efforts to help the undereducated employees through Company financing of two-thirds the cost of tuition for high school training. But Congress directed the thrust of the Act to the consequences of employment practices, not simply the motivation. More than that, Congress has placed on the employer the burden of showing that any given requirement must have a manifest relationship to the employment in question.

The facts of this case demonstrate the inadequacy of broad and general testing devices, as well as the infirmity of using diplomas or degrees as fixed measures of capability. History is filled with examples of men and women who rendered highly effective performance without the conventional badges of accomplishment in terms of certificates, diplomas, or degrees. Diplomas and tests are useful servants, but Congress has mandated the common sense proposition that they are not to become masters of reality.

The Company contends that its general intelligence tests are specifically permitted by § 703(h) of the Act. That section authorizes the use of "any professionally developed ability test" that is not "designed, intended *or used* to discriminate because of race. . . ." (Emphasis added.)

The Equal Employment Opportunity Commission, having enforcement responsibility, has issued guidelines interpreting § 703(h) to permit only the use of job-related tests. The administrative interpretation of the Act by the enforcing agency is entitled to great deference. See, e.g., *United States v. City of Chicago*, 400 U.S. 8 (1970); *Udall v. Tallman*, 380 U.S. 1 (1965); *Power Reactor Co. v. Electricians*, 367 U.S. 396 (1961). Since the Act and its legislative history support the Commission's construction, this affords good reason to treat the guidelines as expressing the will of Congress.

Section 703(h) was not contained in the House version of the Civil Rights Act, but was added in the Senate during extended debate. For a period, debate revolved around claims that the bill, as proposed, would prohibit all testing and force employers to hire unqualified persons simply because they were part of a group formerly subject to job discrimination. Proponents of Title VII sought throughout the debate to assure the critics that the Act would have no effect on job-related tests. Senators Case of New Jersey and Clark of Pennsylvania, co-managers of the bill on the Senate floor, issued a memorandum explaining that the proposed Title VII "expressly protects the employer's right to insist that any prospective applicant, Negro or white, *must meet the applicable job qualifications*. Indeed, the very purpose of title VII is to promote hiring on the basis of job qualifications, rather than on the basis of race or color." 110 Cong.Rec. 7247. (Emphasis added.) Despite these assurances, Senator Tower of Texas introduced an amendment authorizing "professionally developed ability tests." Proponents of Title VII opposed the amendment because, as written, it would permit an employer to give any test "whether it was a good test or not, so long as it was professionally designed. Discrimination could actually exist under the guise of compliance with the statute." 110 Cong.Rec. 13504 (remarks of Sen. Case).

The amendment was defeated, and, two days later, Senator Tower offered a substitute amendment which was adopted verbatim, and is now the testing provision of § 703(h). Speaking for the supporters of Title VII, Senator Humphrey, who had vigorously opposed the first amendment, endorsed the substitute amendment, stating:

"Senators on both sides of the aisle who were deeply interested in title VII have examined the text of this amendment, and have found it to be in accord with the intent and purpose of that title." 110 Cong.Rec. 13724. The amendment was then adopted. From the sum of the legislative history relevant in this case, the conclusion is inescapable that the EEOC's construction of § 703(h) to require that employment tests be job-related comports with congressional intent.

Nothing in the Act precludes the use of testing or measuring procedures; obviously they are useful. What Congress has forbidden is giving these devices and mechanisms controlling force unless they are demonstrably a reasonable measure of job performance. Congress has not commanded that the less qualified be preferred over the better qualified simply because of minority origins. Far from disparaging job qualifications as such, Congress has made such qualifications the controlling factor, so that race, religion, nationality, and sex become irrelevant. What Congress has commanded is that any tests used must measure the person for the job, and not the person in the abstract.

The judgment of the Court of Appeals is, as to that portion of the judgment appealed from, reversed.

Questions Presented

1) What was the basis for the discrimination claim in this case?
2) What was the correlation the Supreme Court was making between this case and its prior voter registration decision in *Gaston County v. United States*?
3) How did the Supreme Court interpret the meaning of § 703h of the Civil Rights Act of 1964 when it came to job qualifications testing?

❖❖❖

B. Discrimination Remedies

Discrimination in any form is unacceptable. As a practice discrimination not only hurts the employee but also has a negative impact upon the employer and its reputation. The various types of discriminatory practices outlined above can be addressed through federal and state laws specifically aimed at preventing and remedying discriminatory practices in the workplace. Depending on the type of case there are many different forms of remedies available to an employee who is aggrieved as a result of a discriminatory workplace practice. If an employee is fired for a discriminatory reason then the obvious remedy would be reinstatement along with backpay for lost wages. In such a case the reinstatement will include no loss of seniority and in addition to lost wages will also include health care benefits, lost overtime, pension contributions, sick leave and vacation time. If a potential hire is denied employment for proven discriminatory reasons then the remedy can include wages, credited seniority, and any other benefits otherwise entitled to if not for the illegal denial of employment. The aggrieved party, whether an incumbent or potential employee, has to prove an economic loss in order to obtain backpay. However, the economic loss is generally presumed when discrimination is proven and backpay is awarded.[69] The amount of backpay received will be reduced only by the amount of any interim payments from the employer or pay from alternative employment received by the aggrieved party during the period of economic loss.[70] An important prerequisite to obtaining backpay and benefits is that the aggrieved party attempt to mitigate damages by seeking other employment. The aggrieved party must use reasonable and diligent efforts to obtain other employment, this includes employment which is "substantially equivalent" to the prior employment.[71] A failure to use reasonable and diligent efforts will toll the employer's requirements to provide backpay.[72]

Other remedies available to an aggrieved employee are compensatory damages, punitive damages, attorney fees and court costs. The purpose of damages is to make the aggrieved employee whole—this

---

[69] See e.g., *Albemarle Paper Co. v. Moody*, 422 U.S. 405 (1975)

[70] See e.g., *Nord v. United States Steel Corp.*, 758 F.2d 1462 (11th Cir. 1985); *Chesser v. State of Illinois*, 895 F.2d 330 (7th Cir. 1990); *Whatley v. Skaggs Cos.*, 508 F.Supp. 302 (D.Colo. 1981)

[71] See e.g., *Ford Motor Co. v. EEOC*, 458 U.S. 219 (1982)

[72] Id.

is best summed up by the U.S. Equal Employment Opportunity Commission: "*Whenever discrimination is found, the goal of the law is to put the victim of discrimination in the same position (or nearly the same) that he or she would have been if the discrimination had never occurred.*"[73] While money damages are often the means of making the victim "whole" in reality they can never fully account for the pain, harm, distress, and loss realized as a result of unlawful discrimination. Yet, it remains the law's best available option for the victim seeking to remedy a discriminatory action by an employer.

Compensatory damages are those damages which actually seek to compensate the victim for the intangible effects of employment discrimination such as emotional distress, humiliation, mental anguish, loss of reputation. These are harder injuries to quantify and place a monetary worth upon but they represent the law's attempt to make the injured party whole for nonpecuniary damages. Compensatory damages are permitted in Title VII and Americans with Disabilities Act (ADA) claims. They are also available in civil rights claims against employers under 42 U.S.C. § 1981.[74] Compensatory damages are generally not awarded for Age Discrimination in Employment Act (ADEA) or Equal Pay Act cases. A majority of federal circuit courts of appeal have denied compensatory damages in ADEA actions.[75] In Equal Pay Act cases the type of relief awarded is guided by the Fair Labor Standards Act (FLSA) which limits it to unpaid wages plus unpaid overtime with liquidated damages set in the amount equal to the unpaid wages.[76] Injunctive relief is also available under the FLSA.[77] The courts have interpreted this as limiting the type of relief under the statute.

Punitive damages are awarded when an employer engages in discriminatory behavior with either malice or a reckless disregard for the rights of an employee. This type of damages award is used as a punishment to the offending employer as well as a deterrent against future discriminatory acts. It also serves as a deterrent to other employers. Because of the severity of punitive damages there are specific statutory guidelines as to when they can be awarded against an employer. Title VII and the ADEA allow for punitive damages as do claims under 42 U.S.C. § 1981. Punitive damages are awarded in addition to compensatory and other damages but they can also be awarded in the absence of any other damages recovery. While the goal of punitive damages is to punish and deter, the amount awarded cannot be "grossly excessive."[78] The U.S. Supreme Court has held that despite a "State's legitimate interest in punishing unlawful conduct and deterring its repletion" it rises to the level of a violation of the 14th Amendment Due Process Clause when it is not related to the extent of the interests to be protected.[79] Both punitive and compensatory damages are capped by statute for claims under Title VII and the ADEA. The caps are based on the size of the employer:

Employers with 15–100 employees = $50,000.00 limit

Employers with 101–200 employees = $100,000.00 limit

Employers with 201–500 employees = $200,000.00 limit

Employers with more than 500 employees = $300,000.00 limit[80]

---

[73] U.S. Equal Employment Opportunity Commission, *Remedies For Employment Discrimination*, https://www.eeoc.gov//employees/remedies.cfm, retrieved August 4, 2017.

[74] See e.g., *Johnson v. Railway Express Agency, Inc.*, 421 U.S. 454, 460 (1975): "*An individual who establishes a cause of action under § 1981 is entitled to both equitable and legal relief, including compensatory and, under certain circumstances, punitive damages.*"

[75] See, G. Terrell Davis, *Compensatory and Punitive Damages in Age Discrimination in Employment*, 32 U.Fla.L.Rev. 701 (1980).

[76] 29 U.S.C. § 216(b)

[77] 29 U.S.C. § 217

[78] *BMW of North America, Inc. v. Gore*, 517 U.S. 559, 568 (1996)

[79] Id.; see also, *Gertz v. Robert Welch, Inc.*, 418 U.S. 323, 350 (1974)

[80] 42 U.S.C. § 1981a(b)(3)

These monetary awards are limited to each aggrieved party in a single legal action, not to each claim of an aggrieved party in a single legal action.

Attorney fees and court costs are also available to a "prevailing party" under Title VII, the ADEA, and the Americans with Disabilities Act (ADA) for aggrieved individuals. A prevailing party is a litigant who is successful on any significant issue in a case resulting in a change in the legal relationship between the party and the defendant and achieves some of the benefit sought in originally bringing the lawsuit.[81] Court costs include filing fees, transcripts, and other costs not normally included in attorney's fees but necessary to the litigation. When awarding attorney's fees to a prevailing party courts will consider whether the fees are reasonable. In determining this the courts will look at several factors which include: the time and labor involved in the case; the complexity of the case; the experience, reputation and ability of the lawyer involved; the customary fee charged in the jurisdiction; and whether the fee was fixed or contingent.

SUMMARY

The path toward the recognition of employee rights in the United States has been long and arduous, yet today there exist a number of statutory protections for employees against arbitrary, capricious, and discriminatory employer actions. The history of employee rights in the workplace developed with industrialization in the United States and the transformation away from an agrarian economy. Recognition of employee rights gained increased momentum during the civil rights movement of the 1960s and 1970s, resulting in a present day range of recognized protections at the federal and state level. However, the extent of any right is determined by the status of the individual as an employee. If an individual is not an employee then they are an independent contractor and do not enjoy the same level of protection as an employee. An independent contractor though has a degree of autonomy that is not shared by an employee. The Internal Revenue Service uses a "Twenty-factor test" as a guideline for employers in determining whether someone is an employee. This distinction is important for the employer since taxes have to be withheld from employee paychecks, and employers are responsible for paying workers compensation and social security benefits for each employee. Independent contractors are responsible for their own tax withholdings.

Two main tests used by the courts to determine if someone is an employee are the "economic realities test"—which looks at the degree an individual is reliant upon an employer for wages and benefits—and the "right to control test"—which considers the degree that an employer can dictate the work activity of the employee. However, being identified as an employee does not necessarily confer job security. If an individual is an "at-will" employee they can be terminated at any time for any reason, short of an unlawful or discriminatory reason. At-will employment offers the least secure means of employment relationship. There are a few exceptions to the at-will doctrine but these exceptions, based generally on good faith and implied contract, are limited. A more secure form of employment relationship is "just-cause employment" requiring that an employer have a valid reason for terminating an employee. Under this form of employment relationship an employee is assured some type of process prior to termination. This can range from a progressive disciplinary scheme to a pre-termination hearing. Unionization provides employees with the most extensive

---

[81] *Texas State Teachers Ass'n v. Garland Independent School District*, 489 U.S. 782, 791–2 (1989)

type of workplace employment protections since many job protection rights are negotiated under the terms of a collective bargaining agreement. The right of employees to collectively organize in the workplace and bargain are protected under the National Labor Relations Act. Even though unionization in the workplace has decreased over the last few decades there are still strong union centers in the Northeast and West coast.

While there are many significant rights an employee can expect in the workplace—a safe working environment or the right to personal privacy—one of the most significant is the right to be free from unlawful discrimination. Discrimination based on a certain attribute of an individual which leads an employer to treat that individual or group of individuals sharing the attribute differently is illegal under federal and state laws. Discriminatory practices based on unequal treatment by an employer can lead to claims of either disparate impact or disparate treatment. In the former situation an employer's actions in hiring, promoting or firing has a statistically higher impact on a certain group than others. In the latter the employer's actions tend to treat an employee differently due to a certain attribute (for example: race, gender, religion) than other similarly situated employees who do not share the attribute. When there has been a case of proven discrimination in the workplace the law provides several remedies for the victim, but the most common is some form of monetary damages. The main purpose of money damages is to make the victim whole and place the victim in a place no worse than where they were prior to the unlawful discriminatory act. Money damages can include backpay and benefits, compensatory damages for nonpecuniary loss, and punitive damages meant as a punishment to the employer for its unlawful acts and as a deterrent against future unlawful acts. The type and amount of damages available will vary according to the type of discrimination and the specific limits set by the relevant statutes involved.

CHAPTER 14

BANKRUPTCY

LEARNING OUTCOMES

Upon completion of this chapter the student will be able to:

1 Explain and identify who is eligible to file for which kinds of bankruptcy.
2 Understand the purpose and mechanics of each kind of bankruptcy.
3 Explain and identify which types of debts are exempt from discharge in bankruptcy.
4 Explain and identify which types of assets are exempt from the bankruptcy estate.
5 Understand the priority of creditors in bankruptcy.

KEY TERMS

bankruptcy estate	exempt debt
bankruptcy trustee	individual debtor
business debtor	liquidation bankruptcy
Chapter 7	non-exempt assets
Chapter 11	non-exempt debt
Chapter 13	priority
commercial debtor	priority creditor
consumer debtor	rehabilitation bankruptcy
creditor	repayment plan
debtor	secured creditor
discharge	substantial abuse
exempt assets	unsecured creditor

I. Introduction

Bankruptcy is a legal procedure through which a debtor obtains financial relief from its creditors.[1] Essentially, a person or business entity that meets certain requirements (that will be discussed in this chapter) can apply to a bankruptcy court to discharge all or some of its debt. As the United States Supreme Court put it, the purpose of bankruptcy law is to "provide a procedure by which certain insolvent debtors can reorder their affairs, make peace with their creditors, and enjoy 'a new

---

[1] See Bankruptcy, Black's Law Dictionary (9th Ed, 2009).

opportunity in life and a clear field for future effort, unhampered by the pressure and discouragement of pre-existing debt.'"[2]

There are two main kinds of bankruptcy, liquidation and rehabilitation. In a liquidation bankruptcy, known as a "Chapter 7" or "straight" bankruptcy, all of a debtor's non-exempt debt is forgiven.[3] In a rehabilitation bankruptcy, a debtor is discharged only from some of the non-exempt debt it owes to creditors.[4] A bankruptcy can also be filed voluntarily by the debtor or involuntarily by the debtor's creditors.

This gives rise to the following questions:

1. Who is eligible to file for which kinds of bankruptcy?
2. What are the purposes and mechanics of each type of bankruptcy?
3. What debts are exempt from bankruptcy?
4. What assets are exempt from bankruptcy?
5. What creditors have priority in bankruptcy?

II. History and Governing Law

The United States Constitution gives Congress the right to make "uniform" laws regarding bankruptcy.[5] Congress passed and repealed a series of temporary bankruptcy laws beginning in 1800.[6] The first modern bankruptcy law, known as the "Nelson Act," was passed in 1898.[7]

> **U.S. Constitution Art. I, § 8, Cl. 4**
>
> "The Congress shall have Power to . . . establish . . . uniform Laws on the subject of Bankruptcies throughout the United States."

Currently, bankruptcy is governed by Title 11 of the United States Code. Much of the law currently governing bankruptcy was passed as part of the "Bankruptcy Abuse Prevention and Consumer Protection Act of 2005."[8]

Bankruptcy petitions are made to and heard by a special federal court that only hears bankruptcy cases.[9] Unlike most federal judges, however, a bankruptcy judge is not appointed to a lifelong term. A bankruptcy judge is only appointed for a term of 14 years. However, there are no limits on the number of terms that a bankruptcy judge can serve.[10] While federal courts administer bankruptcy cases, state law plays a major role in bankruptcy cases. It determines things like whether a creditor's lien is valid and the priority of payment for creditors. State law also determines what legal interests and rights a debtor has in property.[11] Though most states have enacted most of the Uniform Commercial Code, there are subtle differences in every state.

---

[2] *Grogan v. Garner*, 498 U.S. 279, 286 (1991) (quoting *Local Loan Co. v. Hunt*, 292 U. S. 234, 244 (1934)).

[3] See 11 U.S.C. §§ 524,727

[4] *See, e.g.*, 11 U.S.C. §§ 1127, 1322(a)(4);

[5] U.S. Const. Art. I, § 8, cl. 4

[6] 2 Stat. 19 (1800)

[7] 30 Stat. 544 (1898)

[8] 119 Stat. 23 (2005)

[9] *See* 28 U.S.C. § 127

[10] *See* 28 U.S.C § 128

[11] *Drye v. United States*, 528 U.S. 49, 58 (1999)

III. Bankruptcy Terminology and Parties

A. Parties to a Bankruptcy

There are three major players in every bankruptcy. The debtor is the person whose debts and assets are discharged and disposed of by the bankruptcy court. A debtor can be a natural person or a business entity (whether incorporated or not).[12] When the debts incurred by the debtor are primarily for personal, household, or family purposes, the debtor is known as a "consumer debtor."[13] All other debtors are considered "commercial debtors." Consumer debtors accounted for approximately 96% of bankruptcies in 2013.[14]

> ### Legal Definition
>
> **Consumer Debtor** – a debtor whose debts are primarily incurred for household, family, or personal purposes.

The next set of major players is the creditors. The creditors are the parties to whom the debtor owes money. There are two general types of creditors. There are secured creditors, which are creditors who have a security interest in at least some of the debtor's property. By contrast, an unsecured creditor is a creditor that does not have a security interest in any of the debtor's property.

Finally, a bankruptcy is often conducted by a trustee. The trustee is a person appointed by the bankruptcy court who, along with other duties, gathers all of the non-exempt assets of the debtor and distributes them to the creditors in the share required by law.[15]

B. Basic Mechanics of a Bankruptcy

When the debtor files a petition for bankruptcy, the debtor's assets and debts are essentially frozen in time at that moment. The debtor's eligible assets become known as the "bankruptcy estate." However, not all assets are eligible to become part of the bankruptcy estate. The assets not included in the bankruptcy estate are known as "exempt assets." The assets that are included in the bankruptcy estate are known as "non-exempt assets."

After the petition is filed, the trustee takes charge of the bankruptcy estate and uses it to satisfy as much of the creditor's claims as possible. Once this process is complete, the remaining debt is either discharged completely or reduced depending on the kind of bankruptcy filed. Some debt cannot be discharged or modified. This kind of debt is known as "exempt debt."

IV. Liquidation Bankruptcies ("Chapter 7")

Liquidation bankruptcies are frequently referred to as "Chapter 7" bankruptcies because they are brought under Chapter 7 of the bankruptcy code.[16] Chapter 7 bankruptcies are far more common than rehabilitation bankruptcies, accounting for about 62% of bankruptcies in the United States

---

[12] 28 U.S.C. § 101(41)

[13] 11 U.S.C. § 101(8)

[14] American Bankruptcy Institute, December 2016 Bankruptcy Statistics-State and District Filings, available at http://www.abi.org/newsroom/bankruptcy-statistics?page=1

[15] See 11 U.S.C. § 704

[16] The bankruptcy code is found in Title 11 of the United States Code

in 2016.[17] In a Chapter 7 bankruptcy, once the bankruptcy is filed, the debtor turns over all assets (except assets exempted by the bankruptcy code) to the trustee. The trustee then distributes all of the assets (including non-cash assets it sold) to the debtor's creditors in order of their priority under the bankruptcy code. After the property is distributed, the debtor receives a discharge of all remaining debt (except the debt exempted from discharge by the bankruptcy code). Essentially, the effect of a Chapter 7 bankruptcy is that the debtor no longer owes non-exempt creditors any money.

Legal Definition

Discharge – a release of a debtor's obligation to pay a creditor.

A. Voluntary vs. Involuntary Bankruptcy

A bankruptcy may be started either voluntarily by the debtor or involuntarily by some or all of the debtor's creditors. The vast majority of bankruptcy cases are brought voluntarily by the debtor. There are strict requirements that must be met for creditors to start a bankruptcy involuntarily. The requirements vary based on how many creditors a debtor has.

If a debtor has 12 or more creditors, at least 3 creditors must agree to bring the involuntary bankruptcy petition against the debtor.[18] The 3 creditors must also be owed at least a total of $15,775 between them.[19]

If a debtor has fewer than 12 creditors, there is no minimum number of creditors required to bring an involuntary bankruptcy petition.[20] The claims of the creditors filing simply must exceed $15,775 between them.[21]

B. Voluntarily Filing a Chapter 7 Bankruptcy

1. Who May File

A Chapter 7 bankruptcy can be voluntarily filed by almost anyone. It can be filed by virtually any person or business entity.[22] However, some entities are specifically prohibited from filing a Chapter 7 bankruptcy, including railroads, insurance companies, certain investment companies licensed by the Small Business Administration, and most banks and bank-like entities like credit unions.[23] Debtors must also undergo credit counseling no later than 6 months before filing a Chapter 7 bankruptcy petition.[24]

---

[17] American Bankruptcy Institute, Annual Business and Non-business Filings by Year (1980–2016), available at http://www.abi.org/newsroom/bankruptcy-statistics?page=1

[18] 11 U.S.C. § 303(b)

[19] See 11 U.S.C. § 303(b)(1). Under 11 U.S.C. § 104(a), the minimum dollar amount of claims that creditors must have to bring an involuntary bankruptcy increases with inflation. It was last adjusted in 2016.

[20] 11 U.S.C. § 303(b)

[21] See 11 U.S.C. § 303(b)(1). Under 11 U.S.C. § 104(a), the minimum dollar amount of claims that creditors must have to bring an involuntary bankruptcy increases with inflation. It was last adjusted in 2016.

[22] See 11 U.S.C. § 109(a)

[23] See 11 U.S.C. 109(b)

[24] 11 U.S.C. § 109(h)

2. What Must be in the Filing

When filing a petition for a Chapter 7 bankruptcy, the debtor must file a series of forms provided by the bankruptcy court. They include a list of assets and debts, a list of income and expenditures, a list of ongoing contracts and leases, a statement of financial affairs, a list of unsecured creditors, and a list of secured creditors.[25] The debtor must also file proof of all payments received from an employer within 60 days of the filing, which is usually provided in the form of the debtor's pay stubs[26] and the debtor's most recent federal tax return.[27]

All forms are due within 45 days after the filing of the bankruptcy petition.[28] A debtor's bankruptcy petition may be dismissed if all the forms are not filed as required by the court.[29]

3. Substantial Abuse

As the United States Supreme Court stated in *Grogan v. Garner*, bankruptcy is for the "honest but unfortunate debtor."[30] Not every debtor will be allowed to file for bankruptcy. Consider the following scenario.

Rob makes $12,000 a month. In January, he borrowed $10,000 from his friend Aileen and promised to pay her back at the rate of $500 per month until the loan was paid in full. His monthly expenses other than his debt to Aileen total $3,000 a month. Rob refuses to pay Aileen despite his promise to do so. He declares bankruptcy to try and avoid paying Aileen.

In the above case, Rob clearly has the means to pay Aileen. No court would allow him to avoid paying her simply because he attempted to file for bankruptcy. His filing would be considered a "substantial abuse" of the bankruptcy process.

A debtor may not file a Chapter 7 bankruptcy petition that is a substantial abuse of the bankruptcy system.[31] If the court finds that a debtor is engaging in substantial abuse, the court may either dismiss the Chapter 7 case entirely or convert the case into a rehabilitation bankruptcy (Chapter 11 or Chapter 13 bankruptcy).[32] The court can dismiss or convert a Chapter 7 bankruptcy on its own motion or on a motion made by the trustee or a creditor.[33]

a. Consumer Debtors Earning Less than the Median Income

Since 2005, courts have relied heavily on a means test to determine whether a consumer debtor's filing is substantially abusive. If a consumer debtor's income is below the median income of the state in which he or she resides, substantial abuse will not be presumed.[34] Income is calculated based on the average of the debtor's last 6 months of income prior to the filing.[35] If the consumer debtor's income is above the median income in the state in which he or she resides, the calculation becomes much more complicated.

---

[25] See 11 U.S.C. § 521; see *also* Fed. R. Bank. P. § 1007
[26] See 11 U.S.C. § 521(a)(1)(B)(iv); see *also* Fed. R. Bank P. § 1007(b)(1)(e)
[27] 11 U.S.C. § 521(e)(2)(A)(ii)
[28] See 11 U.S.C. § 521(i)
[29] See 11 U.S.C. § 521(i)
[30] *Grogan v. Garner*, 498 U.S. 279, 286-87 (1991).
[31] See 11 U.S.C. § 707(b)(1)
[32] 11 U.S.C. § 707(b)(1)
[33] 11 U.S.C. § 707(b)(1)
[34] See 11 U.S.C. § 707(b)(7)
[35] See 11 U.S.C. § 101(10A)

b. Consumer Debtors Earning More than the Median Income

For consumer debtors earning more than the median income, substantial abuse will be presumed by the court if the consumer debtor has sufficient disposable income to pay back creditors pursuant to a complicated formula. Essentially, the test determines disposable income by taking the consumer debtor's actual income over the last 6 months and subtracting expenses deemed necessary by IRS standards (food, clothing, etc.), any secured debt payments (most often car loan and mortgage loan payments), and certain other priority claims (which include child support and alimony).[36]

If the consumer debtor's disposable income is less than $7,700 for the next five years, substantial abuse will not be presumed.[37] If the consumer debtor's disposable income for the next five years is greater than $12,850, substantial abuse will be presumed.[38] If the consumer debtor's disposable income for the next five years is between $7,700 and $12,850, substantial abuse will be presumed only if the debtor can pay back 25% or more of the debtor's non-priority unsecured claims.[39] Non-priority unsecured claims, usually claims for credit card debt or personal loans, are essentially all the claims by creditors that were not subtracted from the debtor's current monthly income to determine disposable income.

c. When the Presumption of Abuse May Be Overcome

The means test only creates a presumption that substantial abuse occurs. The presumption may be overcome by the consumer debtor if the consumer debtor can show "special circumstances that justify additional expenses or adjustments of current monthly income for which there is no reasonable alternative."[40] Such special circumstances may include military deployment and major uninsured medical expenses.[41]

d. Substantial Abuse Can Be Found Even if a Consumer Debtor Passes the Means Test

Even if a consumer debtor passes the means test or earns less than the median income in his or her state of residence, the consumer debtor may still be found to be substantially abusing the bankruptcy process. For those consumer debtors, as well as for commercial debtors, the court may still make a finding of substantial abuse if it finds the debtor has filed the Chapter 7 petition with "bad faith . . . or the totality of the circumstances . . . of the debtor's financial situation demonstrates abuse."[42] If a consumer debtor earns less than the median income in the state in which he or she resides, a creditor cannot bring a motion to dismiss the consumer debtor's Chapter 7 petition or a motion to have the Chapter 7 petition converted to a rehabilitation bankruptcy, but the judge may bring such a motion.[43]

---

[36] See 11 U.S.C. § 707(b)(2).

[37] See 11 U.S.C. § 707(b)(2)(A)(i)(I). Pursuant to 11 U.S.C. § 104(a), this amount is adjusted every three years. It was last adjusted in 2016.

[38] See 11 U.S.C. § 707(b)(2)(A)(i)(II). Pursuant to 11 U.S.C. § 104(a), this amount is adjusted every three years. It was last adjusted in 2016.

[39] See 11 U.S.C. § 707(b)(2)(A)(i)(I). Pursuant to 11 U.S.C. § 104(a), this amount is adjusted every three years. It was last adjusted in 2016.

[40] 11 U.S.C. § 707(b)(2)(B)(i)

[41] 11 U.S.C. § 707(b)(2(B)(i)

[42] 11 U.S.C. § 707(b)(3)

[43] 11 U.S.C. § 707(b)(6)

Consider the following case.

❖❖❖

In re Hardigan
517 B.R. 374 (S.D. Ga. 2014)

J. RANDAL HALL, District Judge.

Suntrust Bank ("Appellant") appeals from the Bankruptcy Court's March 29, 2013 Order denying Appellant's and the United States Trustee's motions to convert Kenneth R. Hardigan's ("Appellee") Chapter 7 filing to a Chapter 11 or, in the alternative, to dismiss. Because the Bankruptcy Court did not err in refusing to convert the Chapter 7 case to one under Chapter 11 and did not err in applying the totality of the circumstances test when assessing abuse, this Court AFFIRMS the Bankruptcy Court's Order.

I. BACKGROUND

Appellee is a cardiologist residing in Savannah, Georgia. (Doc. no. 1-2 at 1, 19.) He filed his Chapter 7 petition for bankruptcy on March 7, 2012. (Doc. no. 1-8 at 1.) It is undisputed that his debts are primarily consumer in nature. (*Id.* at 3.) Appellant moved on May 23, 2012 to convert the case to a Chapter 11 or, in the alternative, to dismiss on the ground that Appellee's bankruptcy petition constituted an abuse of the Chapter 7 process. (Doc. no. 1-6.) In ruling on the motion, the Bankruptcy Court determined that no presumption of abuse based on the "means test" of 11 U.S.C. § 707(b)(2) existed. *In re Hardigan, 490 B.R. 437, 440 (Bankr. S.D.Ga.2013)*. Appellant alleged that given Appellee's ability to pay, his Chapter 7 petition constituted abuse based on the "totality of the circumstances" test set forth in 11 U.S.C. § 707(b)(3)(B). (Doc. no. 1-6 at 4-5.) The Bankruptcy Court held that based on a number of factors, Appellee's petition did not constitute abuse. *In re Hardigan, 490 B.R. at 459*. Additionally, the Bankruptcy Court declined to convert Appellee's petition to a Chapter 11 under 11 U.S.C. § 706(b). *Id.* at 446-47.

II. JURISDICTION AND STANDARD OF REVIEW

This Court has appellate jurisdiction pursuant to 28 U.S.C. § 158(a)(1) and Bankruptcy Rules 8001 et seq. On appeal, the Court reviews the Bankruptcy Court's factual findings for clear error, and its legal conclusions de novo. *In re Globe Mfg. Corp., 567 F.3d 1291, 1296 (11th Cir. 2009)*.

In determining whether Chapter 7 relief constitutes abuse under 11 U.S.C. § 707(b)(3), "bankruptcy courts have considerable discretion" and, when challenged, "[the district court] review[s] only for abuse of discretion." *In re Kulakowski, 735 F.3d 1296, 1298-99 (11th Cir.2013)*. A bankruptcy court abuses its discretion when it "applies the wrong principle of law or makes clearly erroneous findings of fact." *In re Piazza, 719 F.3d 1253, 1271 (11th Cir.2013)*.

III. DISCUSSION

This appeal presents two issues: (1) whether the Bankruptcy Court erred in denying Appellant's motion to dismiss under 11 U.S.C. § 707(b)(3)(B); and (2) whether the Bankruptcy Court erred in denying Appellant's motion to convert to a Chapter 11 under 11 U.S.C. § 706(b).

A. Dismissal Under 11 U.S.C. § 707(b)(3)(B)

On appeal, Appellant challenges the Bankruptcy Court's application of the "totality of the circumstances" test. The Court reviews this determination for an abuse of discretion. *See In re Kulakowski, 735 F.3d 1296, 1299 (11th Cir.2013)*.

The Bankruptcy Code provides for dismissal of a Chapter 7 case where "the granting of relief would be an abuse of the provisions of [the Code]." 11 U.S.C. § 707(b)(1). A presumption of abuse arises where the debtor fails the "means test," which is calculated by a statutory formula. 11 U.S.C. § 707(b)(2). Even where this presumption of abuse does not arise, however, the court may still find abuse by considering (1) whether the debtor filed the petition in bad faith; or (2) "the totality of the circumstances . . . of the debtor's financial situation . . . ." 11 U.S.C. § 707(b)(3)(A-B).

In the present case, the Bankruptcy Court found that Appellee's petition would not constitute abuse under the totality of the circumstances test. *In re Hardigan, 490 B.R. 437, 459 (Bankr.S.D.Ga.2013)*. In making its determination, the Bankruptcy Court relied on the following factors: (1) ability to repay a meaningful portion of debts; (2) whether the bankruptcy was caused by an unforeseen or sudden calamity; (3) eligibility for Chapter 11 or Chapter 13 relief; (4) the debtor's efforts to repay debts and negotiate with creditors; (5) the debtor's ability to provide a "meaningful" distribution in a Chapter 13 case; (6) ability to reduce the debtor's expenses without depriving the debtor of necessities; (7) the time period over which the debts were incurred; and (8) the stability of the debtor's income. *In re Hardigan, 490 B.R. 437, 447 (Bankr.S.D.Ga.2013)* (citing *In re Truax, 446 B.R. 638, 642 (Bankr. S.D.Ga.2010)*).

The Bankruptcy Court found that, although Appellee's ability to pay pointed toward abuse, other factors dictated a contrary result. Specifically, the Bankruptcy Court held Appellee's fresh start would be impaired by a Chapter 11 proceeding; the real estate market collapse constituted an unforeseeable calamity; Appellee's debts were incurred over years and not through a pre-bankruptcy "spending spree;" Appellee dealt fairly and honorably with creditors; and Appellee was not attempting to "game" the bankruptcy system. *Id.* at 451-57.

In challenging the Bankruptcy Court's application of this test, Appellant makes two claims. First, the Bankruptcy Court should have dismissed the case based on the ability to pay factor alone and, second, the Bankruptcy Court improperly relied on other factors not relevant to Appellee's ability to pay. (Doc. no. 14, "Appellant's Brief," at 14-21.)

As to the first contention, Appellant alleges that the "the ability to pay is the most important, and driving, factor in the totality of the circumstances analysis." (*Id.* at 16.) In so arguing, Appellant cites a number of cases where courts have found the ability to repay creditors sufficient, standing alone, to find abuse. *See, e.g., In re Lamanna, 153 F.3d 1, 4 (1st Cir.1998)* (holding that the "bankruptcy court may, but is not required to, find 'substantial abuse' if the debtor has an ability to repay, in light of all of the circumstances"); *In re Krohn, 886 F.2d 123, 126 (6th Cir. 1989)* (stating that the ability to repay debts "alone may be sufficient to warrant dismissal").

These cases, however, state that a bankruptcy court may permissibly rely solely on ability to pay. They do not dictate such a result. In fact, the court in *In re Lamanna* "reject[ed] any per se rules mandating dismissal for 'substantial abuse' whenever the debtor is able to repay his debt out of future disposable income, or forbidding dismissal on that basis alone." 153 F.3d at 4. Emphasizing that ability to pay is but one factor that can be utilized, the Eleventh Circuit declined to decide "whether a debtor's ability to pay his or her debts *can alone* be dispositive under the totality-of-the-circumstances test[,]" demonstrating that ability to pay is but *one* factor that *may* be considered. *In re Witcher, 702 F.3d 619, 623 (11th Cir. 2012)*(emphasis added).

In fact, many other courts have found that ability to pay, in and of itself, is insufficient to compel dismissal for abuse. *See, e.g., In re Lavin*, 424 B.R. 558, 563 (Bankr.M.D.Fla.2010) ("Congress could have required dismissal based solely on a debtor's 'ability to pay,' Instead, section 707(b)(3)(B) requires evaluation of the 'totality of the circumstances.' Thus, the UST must show something more than just the debtor's mathematical ability to pay."); *In re Rudmose*, No. 10-74514-WLH, 2010 WL 4882059, at *3 (Bankr.N.D.Ga. Nov. 8, 2010) (citing several cases for the proposition that "courts also generally hold that an ability to pay alone is not sufficient to justify dismissal of a case for abuse").

Appellant's second claim addresses the Bankruptcy Court's application of the other seven factors listed above. Specifically, Appellant alleges that the Bankruptcy Court "d[id] not provide sufficient reasons why any of the remaining factors — either separately or collectively — [were] relevant to [Appellee's] financial situation and outweigh his ability to repay a meaningful amount of his debts." (Appellant's Brief at 17.) While it is true the Bankruptcy Court addressed Appellee's fair and honorable dealings with his creditors, it also relied on a multitude of other factors that have bearing on the totality of Appellee's "financial situation," including his future financial prospects, the manner in which the debts were incurred, and the fact that Appellee sold or surrendered his real estate, reduced his unsecured debt, and will, following bankruptcy, retain little secured property. *In re Hardigan*, 490 B.R. 437, 455 (Bankr.S.D.Ga.2013).

Thus, based on a careful review of the Bankruptcy Court's Order and the parties' briefs, I cannot find that the Bankruptcy Court abused its discretion by refusing to find abuse of process based on ability to pay alone or by the other factors relied on in its analysis.

B. Conversion Under 11 U.S.C. § 706(b)

Appellant next challenges the Bankruptcy Court's failure to convert Appellee's case to a Chapter 11 under 11 U.S.C. § 706(b). As discussed above, the Court will review findings of fact for clear error and conclusions of law de novo. *In re Globe Mfg. Corp.*, 567 F.3d 1291, 1296 (11th Cir.2009).

Section 706(b) provides that, upon request of an interested party and after notice and a hearing, the court may convert a Chapter 7 case to a Chapter 11. 11 U.S.C. § 706(b). This section does not provide any additional requirements, instead leaving the decision to the "sound discretion of the court, based on what will most inure to the benefit of all parties in interest." S.Rep. No. 95-989, at 940 (1978), 1978 U.S.C.C.A.N. 5787, 5880; *see also In re Lobera*, 454 B.R. 824, 853 (Bankr.D.N.M.2011) ("[Section 706(b)] is not mandatory; the Court should use its discretion in any decision to convert.").

Courts have relied on various factors in determining whether a section 706(b) conversion would be appropriate: (1) the debtor's ability to repay debt; (2) the absence of immediate grounds for reconversion; (3) the likelihood of confirmation of a Chapter 11 plan; and (4) whether the parties in interest would benefit from conversion. *See In re Gordon*, 465 B.R. 683, 692-94 (Bankr.N.D.Ga.2012); *In re Schlehuber*, 489 B.R. 570 (8th Cir. BAP 2013) (relying on ability to pay and potential for confirmation).

The Bankruptcy Court, in its order, made the following findings of fact: Appellee had the ability to repay debts; the likelihood of confirmation of a Chapter 11 plan was "dubious" given the disputed claim between Appellee and a contractor; if the case continued under Chapter 7 all unsecured creditors could be paid within months; and conversion would not benefit all parties involved. *In re Hardigan*, 490 B.R. 437, 447, 451-53 (Bankr.S.D.Ga.2013).

Upon a careful review of the record, I find that the Bankruptcy Court's factual findings were not clearly erroneous. Accordingly, and applying the highly deferential standard of section 706(b) to those findings of fact, the Bankruptcy Court did not err in refusing to convert the case to Chapter 11.

CONCLUSION

As discussed above, the Court AFFIRMS the Bankruptcy Court's Order denying Appellant's motion to convert or dismiss. The Clerk shall terminate all deadlines and motions, and CLOSE this case.

Questions Presented

1) What factors did the court consider to determine whether there was "abuse" under the totality of the circumstances test?

2) What facts did the court consider to determine whether there was "abuse" under the totality of the circumstances test?

3) What factors and facts did the court consider to determine whether the petition should have been converted from a Chapter 7 petition to a Chapter 11 petition?

❖❖

C. Automatic Stay

When a bankruptcy petition is filed, a stay is automatically placed against virtually all of the debtor's creditors that prohibits the creditors from taking any action against the debtor.[44] In other words, most of the creditors can no longer pursue their claims against the debtor outside of the bankruptcy petition.

1. Actions the Automatic Stay Prohibits (General Rules)

The automatic stay prohibits creditors from taking almost any action outside of the bankruptcy petition. Though there are exceptions to the rule, the automatic stay is broad and powerful.

The automatic stay prohibits creditors from filing lawsuits to collect what they are owed by the debtor for actions that took place before the bankruptcy filing.[45] It also prohibits creditors from continuing lawsuits against debtors that were ongoing[46] and from enforcing judgments that were obtained before the bankruptcy petition was filed. It even prevents debtors themselves from appealing decisions made against them in litigation started by creditors.[47]

The automatic stay has a particular effect on secured creditors. Secured creditors[48] are prohibited from taking actions to create, attach, or perfect their security interests in collateral not already in their possession.[49] Secured creditors are also prohibited from attempting to repossess collateral even if they had the right to do so before the bankruptcy petition was filed.[50]

The automatic stay does not just apply to lawsuits and repossession. It prohibits creditors from doing anything outside of bankruptcy court to recover what they are owed, which means they cannot make debt collection calls or write demand letters.[51]

---

[44] 11 U.S.C. § 362(a)

[45] 11 U.S.C. § 362(a)(1)

[46] 11 U.S.C. § 362(a)(1)

[47] See, e.g., *TW Telecom Holdings, Inc. v. Carolina Internet Ltd.*, 661 F.3d 495, 497 (10th Cir. 2010) ("At least nine other circuit courts of appeals . . . have held that a bankruptcy filing automatically stays appellate proceedings where the debtor has filed an appeal from a judgment entered in a suit against the debtor.")

[48] See Chapter 11 for a more detailed discussion of Secured Transactions

[49] 11 U.S.C. § 361(a)(4)-(5)

[50] 11 U.S.C. § 361(a)(3)

[51] 11 U.S.C. § 362(a)(6)

2. Exceptions to the Automatic Stay

The automatic stay applies to the vast majority of creditors. There are, however, some important exceptions to the general rule. The automatic stay does not apply to actions for domestic obligations like child support and alimony.[52] It also does not apply to criminal proceedings,[53] lawsuits for actions taken by the debtor after the bankruptcy petition was filed,[54] and to certain actions taken by certain government agencies. For instance, it does not apply to a taxing authority attempting to collect property taxes[55] or to the Department of Housing and Urban Development's attempt to foreclose on a debtor's property.[56] It also does not prevent perfected creditors from taking actions to maintain their perfected creditor status like filing a UCC-1 financing statement continuation.[57]

3. Timing of the Automatic Stay

The automatic stay almost always goes into effect when the bankruptcy petition is filed.[58] However, if an individual debtor files a bankruptcy petition and had two or more bankruptcy petitions dismissed within the past year (not counting any cases that were converted from a Chapter 7 bankruptcy to a rehabilitation bankruptcy), the automatic stay will not go into effect at all.[59] The stay will only go into effect if the debtor can prove that the petition was filed in good faith.[60] There is a presumption that the petition was not filed in good faith if at least one of the petitions was dismissed because the debtor did not file the proper paperwork (unless the paperwork was not filed because of the debtor's attorney's negligence) or if there has not been a substantial change in the debtor's financial situation since the prior filings.[61]

The stay usually lasts throughout the duration of the petition.[62] However, the stay will only last 30 days if the debtor had a single petition for bankruptcy dismissed within the past year (not counting any cases that were converted from a Chapter 7 bankruptcy to a rehabilitation bankruptcy).[63] The stay can continue past 30 days if the debtor can prove that the petition was filed in good faith.[64] There is a presumption that the petition was not filed in good faith if the prior petition was dismissed because the debtor did not file the proper paperwork (unless the paperwork was not filed because of the debtor's attorney's negligence) or if there has not been a substantial change in the debtor's financial situation since the prior filings.[65]

Any creditor may also apply to have the stay lifted.[66] The creditor must have "good cause" to have the stay lifted. For example, a secured creditor has good cause to lift the stay when the

---

[52] 11 U.S.C. § 362(b)(2)

[53] 11 U.S.C. § 362(b)(1)

[54] See *Holland America Ins. Co. v. Succession of Roy*, 777 F. 2d 992, 996 (5th Cir. 1985) ("The [automatic] stay simply does not apply to post-bankruptcy events.")

[55] 11 U.S.C. § 362(b)18)

[56] 11 U.S.C. § 362(b)(8)

[57] 11 U.S.C. § 362(b)(3)

[58] 11 U.S.C. § 362(a)(1)

[59] 11 U.S.C. § 362(c)(4)(A)

[60] 11 U.S.C. § 362(c)(4)(B)

[61] 11 U.S.C. § 362(c)(4)(D)

[62] 11 U.S.C. § 362(c)(2)

[63] 11 U.S.C. § 362(c)(3)

[64] 11 U.S.C. § 362(c)(3)(B)

[65] 11 U.S.C. § 362(c)(3)(C)

[66] 11 U.S.C. § 362(d)

property in which it has a security interest is not adequately protected.[67] Essentially, if a bankruptcy petition was to harm the value of the secured party's collateral, the court may lift the stay as to that creditor and allow the creditor to take action to protect the value of its collateral, which could include actions like requiring the bankruptcy trustee to make payments to the injured creditor or provide additional collateral or replacement liens.[68]

D. The Bankruptcy Estate

The bankruptcy estate consists of all the debtor's non-exempt assets.[69] Non-exempt assets are assets that are not exempted from the bankruptcy estate. Exempt assets are assets that debtors are allowed to keep even though they filed for bankruptcy and that do not become part of the bankruptcy estate. In most Chapter 7 cases filed by consumer debtors, the exemptions cover almost everything the debtor owns.

1. Exempt Assets

FIGURE 14.1   Equation of a Bankruptcy Estate

Exempt assets are usually determined by state law.[70] The federal bankruptcy code lists assets that are exempted from the bankruptcy estate, but it allows individual states to replace those exemptions with a different set.[71] Most states have taken the federal government up on its offer and allow their citizens to only use state exemptions.[72] However, some states allow their citizens to choose between the federal exemptions and the state exemptions.[73] In states that allow the debtor to choose between state and federal exemptions, the debtor must choose either all the state or all the federal exemptions. The debtor cannot mix and match exemptions. The federal exemptions currently include the following:

a.   **Homestead Exception:** Up to **$23,675** in equity in the debtor or debtor's dependent's residence or burial plot. Any unused portion of this exemption may be used for any other property up to $11,850.

b.   **Motor Vehicle:** Up to **$3,775** in debtor's motor vehicle

c.   **Household Items:** Up to **$600 per item**, but not exceeding a **total of $12,265**, for personal items like household goods and furniture, clothes, appliances, books, animals, crops, or musical instruments.

---

[67] 11 U.S.C. § 362(d)(1)

[68] 11 U.S.C. § 361

[69] 11 U.S.C. § 541(a)

[70] See 11 U.S.C. § 522(b)(2); *Owen v. Owen*, 500 U.S. 301, 306 (1991) ("The Bankruptcy Code allows the States to define what property a debtor may exempt from the bankruptcy estate that will be distributed among his creditors.")

[71] See 11 U.S.C. § 522(b)(2); *Owen v. Owen*, 500 U.S. 301, 306 (1991) ("The Bankruptcy Code allows the States to define what property a debtor may exempt from the bankruptcy estate that will be distributed among his creditors.")

[72] See *In re Banner*, 394 BR 292, 299 (Bankr. D. Conn. 2008)

[73] See *In re Banner*, 394 BR 292, 299 (Bankr. D. Conn. 2008)

d. **Jewelry:** Up to **$1,600** in personal jewelry
e. **Residual Exception:** Up to a total of **$1,250** for any interest in any property not otherwise exempt
f. **Trade Items:** Up to **$2,375** for any tools or books used in the debtor's trade
g. **Life Insurance:** Any unmatured life insurance contract
h. **Health Aids:** Anything that aids in the debtor's health
i. **Welfare and Retirement Benefits:** Any social security, disability, unemployment, veteran's, alimony, child support, and certain retirement benefits.
j. **Personal Injury Lawsuit Proceeds:** Up to **$23,675** of proceeds from personal injury lawsuits.[74]

2. After-Acquired Property

The bankruptcy estate does not include most assets that the debtor gains an interest in after the bankruptcy petition is filed. For instance, all wages earned by the debtor after the petition is filed are not part of the bankruptcy estate. However, some property acquired after the bankruptcy petition is filed will become part of the bankruptcy estate. Any asset acquired after bankruptcy that is created by or arising from an asset already part of the bankruptcy estate becomes part of the bankruptcy estate as well. For instance, if a debtor owned a home before the bankruptcy that it rented to a tenant for $975 a month, that $975 a month would become part of the bankruptcy estate.

While this may seem like an easy line to draw, in practice, what after-acquired property becomes part of the estate can be difficult to determine. Consider the following case.

❖❖

In re Neidorf
534 B.R. 369 (B.A.P. 9th Cir. 2015)

JURY, Bankruptcy Judge.

Chapter 7 debtor Carrie Margaret Neidorf (Debtor) scheduled her real property (Residence) as an asset of her estate. There was no equity in the property. Postpetition, the lender obtained an unopposed relief from stay order and foreclosed on the property. Years after the foreclosure, but while her bankruptcy case was still open, Debtor received a postpetition payment in the amount of $31,250 (Foreclosure Payment). The payment was made to Debtor pursuant to a national settlement between banking regulators and certain financial institutions, including Bank of America (B of A). Debtor disclosed her receipt of the Foreclosure Payment to Robert A. MacKenzie, the chapter 7 trustee (Trustee). Trustee then filed a Motion to Compel Debtor to Turnover Estate Property (Turnover Motion), asserting that the Foreclosure Payment was property of the estate under § 541(a)(7). The bankruptcy court denied his motion, and this appeal followed. For the reasons discussed below, we AFFIRM.

I. FACTS

The underlying facts are undisputed. Debtor filed her chapter 7 petition on July 12, 2008. In Schedule A, Debtor listed her Residence located in Phoenix with a value of $350,000, subject to liens totaling $454,200. In Schedule C, Debtor claimed an exemption in the property for $150,000 under

---

[74] 11 U.S.C. § 522(d). Pursuant to 11 U.S.C. § 104, these amounts increase with inflation every three years. They were last adjusted in 2016.

Ariz. Rev. Stat. § 33-1101(A). In Schedule D, Debtor showed the property was encumbered by three liens, including a first position deed of trust in favor of Countrywide Home Loans, Inc. (Countrywide).

Countrywide obtained an unopposed order granting relief from the automatic stay with respect to the Residence on September 29, 2008. Countrywide's interest in the deed of trust was assigned to B of A sometime in 2008 as part of a merger/acquisition.

Debtor received a § 727 discharge on October 21, 2008. Debtor's Residence was sold at a foreclosure sale on July 14, 2009.

Trustee filed a Notice of Trustee's Final Report and Application for Compensation on November 14, 2013. The bankruptcy court entered an order approving payment for administrative fees and expenses on December 19, 2013, but the case was never closed.

Almost six years after her case was filed, Debtor disclosed to Trustee that she had received the Foreclosure Payment. On April 15, 2014, Trustee filed the Turnover Motion contending that the payment was property of the estate under § 541(a)(7).

At the May 13, 2014 hearing, the bankruptcy court took the matter under submission. On September 30, 2014, the bankruptcy court issued its findings of fact and conclusions of law and entered the order denying Trustee's Turnover Motion. Trustee timely appealed from that order.

II. JURISDICTION

The bankruptcy court had jurisdiction pursuant to 28 U.S.C. §§ 1334 and 157(b)(2)(E). We have jurisdiction under 28 U.S.C. § 158.

III. ISSUE

Did the bankruptcy court err by determining that the Foreclosure Payment was not property of Debtor's estate?

IV. STANDARDS OF REVIEW

Whether property is included in a bankruptcy estate is a question of law subject to de novo review. _Cisneros v. Kim (In re Kim)_, 257 B.R. 680, 684 (9th Cir. BAP 2000).

We may affirm the bankruptcy court's decision on any ground supported by the record. _Olsen v. Zerbetz (In re Olsen)_, 36 F.3d 71, 73 (9th Cir.1994).

V. DISCUSSION

Section 541(a)(7) makes property of the estate any interest in property that the estate (not the debtor) acquires after the petition date. "Congress enacted § 541(a)(7) to clarify its intention that § 541 be an all-embracing definition and to ensure that property interests created with or by property of the estate are themselves property of the estate." _TMT Procurement Corp. v. Vantage Drilling Co. (In re TMT Procurement Corp.)_, 764 F.3d 512, 524-25 (5th Cir.2014); H.R. REP. 95-595, 549, _reprinted_ in 1978 U.S.C.C.A.N. 5963, 6455 & 6523-24. Stated differently, for the after-acquired interest to be considered property of the estate under § 541(a)(7), the interest (1) must be created with or by property of the estate; (2) acquired in the estate's normal course of business; or (3) otherwise be traceable to or arise out of any prepetition interest included in the bankruptcy estate. _See Id._ at 525. The party seeking to include property in the estate bears the burden of showing that the item is property of the estate. _Seaver v. Klein-Swanson (In re Klein-Swanson)_, 488 B.R. 628, 633 (8th Cir. BAP 2013).

Here, Trustee has not shown how the bankruptcy estate acquired an interest in the postpetition Foreclosure Payment. The payment was neither created with or by property of the estate nor can it be said that the payment is traceable to or arose out of any prepetition interest included in the bankruptcy estate. The fact that Debtor's Residence became property of the estate, in and of itself, does not support the inclusion of the Foreclosure Payment as after-acquired property under § 541(a)(7). Rather, Debtor became entitled to the payment only as a result of qualifying events occurring after her bankruptcy filing.

Debtor's legal right to, or interest in, the Foreclosure Payment was as a "borrower," and did not arise until April 13, 2011, when B of A, acting through its Board of Directors, and the Comptroller of the Currency (Comptroller) entered into a consent order (2011 Consent Order). The Comptroller and B of A entered into an Amendment to the Consent Order dated February 28, 2013 (2013 ACO), which required B of A to make a $1,127,453.261 cash payment to a Qualified Settlement Fund (QSF). Under the 2013 ACO, only borrowers who had a pending or completed foreclosure on their primary residence any time from January 1, 2009, to December 31, 2010, were eligible to receive distributions from the QSF. In other words, it was the postpetition 2011 Consent Order and 2013 ACO which created the rights and remedies for the specified class of borrowers.

Seen in this light, that the estate had an interest in Debtor's Residence is not enough. Nowhere has Trustee shown how the estate obtained an interest in the Foreclosure Payment itself when the qualifying events giving rise to Debtor's legal rights to the payment all occurred postpetition and were held solely by the borrowers. *See Drewes v. Vote (In re Vote)*, 276 F.3d 1024 (8th Cir.2002). The payment is thus not an after-acquired interest of the estate. Therefore, we agree with the bankruptcy court's legal conclusion that the postpetition Foreclosure Payment received by Debtor was not property of her estate.

VI. CONCLUSION

Having found no error, we AFFIRM.

Questions Presented

1) How and when was the asset at issue acquired in this case?
2) Why was it not considered part of the bankruptcy estate?

❖❖❖

3. Assets of Business Entities in Personal Bankruptcies

Usually, a bankruptcy estate only includes assets owned by the entity filing for bankruptcy. Consider the following scenario. Matt is the sole member of an LLC called "Matt's Business, LLC." Matt files for Chapter 7 bankruptcy in his name but not the LLC's.[75]

In the above scenario, only the things personally owned by Matt will become part of the bankruptcy estate because Matt and his LLC are separate legal entities. Thus, the LLC's assets are not included in the bankruptcy estate. However, Matt's ownership interest in the LLC will become part of the bankruptcy estate, which means the Trustee could theoretically sell his business to someone else. This does not frequently occur because bankruptcy debtors' businesses usually have a negative net value and cannot be sold.

---

[75] See, e.g., *In re Desmond*, 316 B.R. 593 (Bankr. D.N.H. 2004).

For business entities that do not provide liability protection under state law, like partnerships and sole proprietorships, business assets can become part of the bankruptcy estate. In a partnership, for example, if one of the partners personally declares bankruptcy, that partner's portion of the partnership assets becomes part of the bankruptcy estate. This usually has little practical effect because the trustee only gains the rights the partner has in the assets, which is limited by the rights of the other partners. So, if the trustee were to attempt to sell partnership assets, the trustee would simply be outvoted by the other partners.

Conversely, if a partnership files for bankruptcy, the personal assets of the general partners can be reached by the bankruptcy trustee to pay the debts of the partnership.[76]

Assets belonging to another business entity are not always exempted from the bankruptcy estate however. Assets fraudulently transferred to avoid bankruptcy will be considered part of the estate. Consider the following case.

❖❖

In re Krause
637 F.3d 1160 (10th Cir. 2011)

GORSUCH, Circuit Judge.

Can a taxpayer avoid the IRS by moving money to a "diet cookie" company and then destroying records that might show the company to be a sham? Or by transferring assets to his "children's trusts" only to use the trusts to pay for his country club membership, buy cars, and fund his lifestyle? The answer, of course, is no. Why this is so takes a bit more explanation.

I

Gary Krause's feud with the IRS traces back decades. Beginning in the 1970s, Mr. Krause developed public housing projects and promoted tax-shelter partnerships. It didn't take long, however, before the IRS challenged his attempts to deduct a variety of claimed losses. As happens in these things, litigation soon broke out and proceeded to consume the better part of a decade. At the end of it all, the two sides reached a settlement in which Mr. Krause agreed that he owed taxes for 1975, 1978, 1979, 1980, 1981, 1982, 1983, and 1986, and the IRS calculated his liability at $3.5 million.

But as it turned out the settlement settled nothing. In 2005, Mr. Krause declared bankruptcy under Chapter 7, claiming that he had no meaningful assets and seeking a discharge of his federal tax liabilities. The IRS responded by initiating an adversarial proceeding in bankruptcy court. The agency sought a declaration that Mr. Krause's tax debts were not dischargeable in bankruptcy, that Mr. Krause had fraudulently conveyed various of his assets to other entities, and that the IRS's preexisting tax lien should attach to the assets held by those entities. Yet more litigation over these questions followed, but when the dust finally settled the bankruptcy court had decided two things.

First, the bankruptcy court held that two companies — Drake Enterprises and PHR, LLC — were the nominees or alter egos of Mr. Krause and that the IRS's tax lien attached to their assets. What these companies actually did and whether they enjoyed any existence independent of Mr. Krause was never quite clear. Drake Enterprises claimed to market a so-called "diet cookie." PHR appeared to do no more than hold title to the family residence. What was clear, however, was this. During discovery Mr. Krause intentionally erased computer hard drives containing the records

---

[76] See 11 U.S.C. § 723

of both companies. And in the process he violated court orders compelling production of the materials. For this misconduct and after an exhaustive three-day evidentiary hearing, the court entered a sanctions order declaring that it would treat PHR and Drake Enterprises as the "nominees or the alter ego[s] of Krause and . . . thus [the] property of [Mr. Krause's bankruptcy] estate and subject to turnover" to the IRS. Aplt's App. vol. 1, at 176.

Second, the bankruptcy court held that Mr. Krause had fraudulently conveyed certain assets to trusts nominally created for the benefit of his now-adult children, Drake and Rick Krause. Given this, the bankruptcy court held, the IRS tax lien attached to those assets as well. Unlike its holding with respect to Drake Enterprises and PHR, however, the bankruptcy court reached its conclusions about the trust assets on the merits and after a nine-day trial at which the court allowed Drake and Rick to intervene and participate along with their father.

After the bankruptcy court issued its final judgment, Drake and Rick, along with their father, appealed to the district court. The district court, however, affirmed the bankruptcy court's judgment, and it is this decision that Drake and Rick, now proceeding without their father, ask us to reconsider and reverse.

II

Turning to second things first, we begin with the bankruptcy court's judgment that assets Mr. Krause transferred to the children's trusts are subject to the IRS's lien under 26 U.S.C. § 6321. The scope of our review here is governed by that familiar formulation: we assess legal questions *de novo* but will reverse the bankruptcy court's factual findings only if they are proven to be clearly erroneous. See *In re Paul*, 534 F.3d 1303, 1310 (10th Cir.2008) (noting that although matters like this one reach us only "after an affirmance by the district court, we directly review the bankruptcy court's" decision). Because the facts found by the bankruptcy court in this case aren't meaningfully disputed, we proceed directly to our own analysis of the law's application to those facts.

On that score, § 6321 allows the IRS to satisfy a tax deficiency by attaching a lien on any "property" or "rights to property" belonging to the taxpayer. To determine whether a particular asset falls within the reach of a § 6321 lien, we and any court must engage in a two-part inquiry. First, we must ask what rights under state law, if any, the taxpayer has in the asset the IRS seeks to attach. This step is necessary at the outset because it is, after all, "state law [that] creates legal interests and rights" in things. *Drye v. United States*, 528 U.S. 49, 58, 120 S.Ct. 474, 145 L.Ed.2d 466 (1999) (internal quotation omitted). Second, now with a sense of what state legal entitlement the taxpayer enjoys in the asset at issue — with a sense of the bundle of rights state law gives him to the thing or *res* at issue — we must ask, under federal law, whether those "state-delineated rights qualify as 'property' or 'rights to property' within the compass of the federal tax lien legislation." *Id.* As the Supreme Court has explained the relationship between these two steps, it is "[s]tate law [that] creates legal interests and rights [and it is] [t]he federal revenue acts [that] designate what interests or rights, so created, shall be taxed." *Id.* (quoting *Morgan v. Commissioner*, 309 U.S. 78, 80, 60 S.Ct. 424, 84 L.Ed. 585 (1940)).

A

In Kansas, as in most states, a debtor cannot evade his creditors by fraudulently conveying his property to someone else. Such conveyances are, as a matter of state law, "deemed utterly void and of no effect." *See* K.S.A. § 33-102. Put differently, the transferor retains equitable ownership of the assets and those assets remain subject to attachment by his creditors. *See Gorham State Bank v.*

Sellens, 244 Kan. 688, 772 P.2d 793, 796 (1989) ("[A] debtor's property shall be liable for his debts, and he cannot avoid liability by a fraudulent transfer.") (internal quotation omitted). To determine whether a conveyance is fraudulent and so void as a matter of state law, Kansas law directs us to look for "six badges or indicia of fraud": "(1) a relationship between the grantor and grantee; (2) the grantee's knowledge of litigation against the grantor; (3) insolvency of the grantor; (4) a belief on the grantee's part that the contract was the grantor's last asset subject to a Kansas execution; (5) inadequacy of consideration; and (6) consummation of the transaction contrary to normal business procedures." *Koch Eng'g Co. v. Faulconer*, 239 Kan. 101, 716 P.2d 180, 184 (1986) (internal quotation omitted).

Mr. Krause wears these badges boldly. In setting up the "children's trusts," he transferred money first to his wife who, in turn, transferred them to the trusts, all for no consideration. Mr. Krause also transferred various insurance policies to the trusts, again for no consideration. Each of these transfers took place after Mr. Krause knew the IRS was conducting an audit of his taxes and after the IRS issued a notice disallowing certain of his claimed losses. And while Mr. Krause's brother, Richard, served as trustee for the children's trusts, both he and Mrs. Krause have admitted that Mr. Krause controlled the assets in question at all times. Indeed, Mr. Krause maintained no personal bank account after 2000 but instead used the children's trusts to pay for his country-club memberships, car loans, and other personal expenses. And Mr. Krause did all this without objection from Richard, who candidly described his philosophy toward the trusts as "stick your head in the sand and then you don't know what is going on." Aplt's App. vol. 1, at 300. In light of these remarkable and undisputed facts, badges of fraud all, it is plain that Mr. Krause remained the owner of the transferred assets; that the children's trusts held those assets simply as his nominees; and that those assets are subject to attachment by Mr. Krause's creditors under Kansas law. *See also* William D. Elliott, *Federal Tax Collections, Liens and Levies* 9.10[1] (2d ed. 2000) ("The subject of nominee liens refers to situations when taxpayer's property or rights to property is held in the name of another or transferred to another party.").

When the facts are bad, they say, argue the law. And with the facts so badly against them, that's exactly what Rick and Drake do here.

***

To reach the result we do, we need and do hold only that Kansas law recognizes fraudulent conveyance doctrine; that Mr. Krause fraudulently conveyed certain particular assets (cash and insurance policies) to the children's trusts; that the trusts held those particular assets as Mr. Krause's nominees; and that, for purposes of Kansas law, those assets still belonged to Mr. Krause and so were lawfully subject to attachment to satisfy his debts.

***

III

That still leaves us with the diet cookie company, the house holding corporation, Mr. Krause's destruction of their corporate records, and the bankruptcy court's sanctions order declaring both entities to be Mr. Krause's nominees or alter egos.

To the extent the brothers seek to challenge the court's order with respect to the cookie company, Drake Enterprises, we hold they lack standing. Long ago and for many years, the Bankruptcy Code permitted only a "person aggrieved" by a bankruptcy court order to challenge it on appeal.

Kane v. Johns-Manville Corp., 843 F.2d 636, 641-42 (2d Cir.1988); _In re DBSD N. Am., Inc._, 634 F.3d 79, 88-90 (2d Cir.2011). To qualify as a "person aggrieved," courts held, the putative appellant had to show that his rights or interests were "directly and adversely affected pecuniarily" by a bankruptcy court's order. _Kane_, 843 F.2d at 642. While the Code has since been amended many times and the "person aggrieved" phrase no longer appears, _see_ 28 U.S.C. § 158(d)(1); _id._ § 158(a)(1), many courts, including this one, have continued for decades to enforce the person aggrieved requirement as a matter of prudential standing. _See, e.g., Holmes v. Silver Wings Aviation, Inc._, 881 F.2d 939, 940 (10th Cir.1989); _In re El San Juan Hotel_, 809 F.2d 151, 154 (1st Cir.1987); _In re PWS Holding Corp._, 228 F.3d 224, 228 (3d Cir.2000); _In re LTV Steel Co., Inc._, 560 F.3d 449, 452 (6th Cir.2009); _Matter of Andreuccetti_, 975 F.2d 413, 416 (7th Cir.1992); _Matter of Fondiller_, 707 F.2d 441, 442-43 (9th Cir. 1983).

They have done so because, without such a requirement, bankruptcy litigation could easily "become mired in endless appeals brought by a myriad of parties who are indirectly affected by every bankruptcy court order." _Holmes_, 881 F.2d at 940 (internal quotation marks omitted). As the Second Circuit has explained:

Bankruptcy proceedings regularly involve numerous parties, each of whom might find it personally expedient to assert the rights of another party even though that other party is present in the proceedings and is capable of representing himself. Third-party standing is of special concern in the bankruptcy context where, as here, one constituency before the court seeks to disturb a plan of reorganization based on the rights of third parties who apparently favor the plan. In this context, the courts have been understandably skeptical of the litigant's motives and have often denied standing as to any claim that asserts only third-party rights.

Kane, 843 F.2d at 644.

Our case proves the problem. Those affected by the bankruptcy court's order — Mr. Krause and his wife — do not seek to appeal the sanction order. Only the sons Drake and Rick are before us, and neither they nor the trusts of which they claim to be the beneficiaries have _any_ interest in Drake Enterprises. In fact, even Drake and Rick's brief concedes that their father and mother were and are the sole shareholders of Drake Enterprises, just as the bankruptcy court found. Nor do Drake and Rick identify any other way in which they might be affected by an adverse decision against Drake Enterprises. Plainly, they lack prudential standing under our controlling precedent.

With respect to PHR, the story is slightly different. PHR is a limited liability company, and the trusts created for the benefit of Rick and Drake Krause are listed as members of that company. The government doesn't dispute that this is enough to afford them prudential standing to appeal the bankruptcy court's sanction order and, following the government's tack here, we will also assume without deciding that it is. Unlike certain other statutory or constitutional jurisdictional questions, the resolution of a sticky prudential standing question may be bypassed in favor of deciding the case on the merits when it's clear that the appellant will lose there anyway. _See Franchise Tax Bd. of Cal. v. Alcan Aluminium Ltd._, 493 U.S. 331, 336-38, 110 S.Ct. 661, 107 L.Ed.2d 696 (1990) (assuming without deciding question of shareholder standing because appellants lose on the merits); _Kennedy v. Allera_, 612 F.3d 261, 270 n. 3 (4th Cir.2010) (assuming without deciding prudential standing).

And that's exactly the case we have before us. The only merits argument Drake and Rick level against the bankruptcy court's sanction order is one we have already addressed and rejected. The brothers simply and again accuse the bankruptcy court of having defied Kansas law by engaging in reverse veil piercing to find PHR and Mr. Krause alter egos. As it happens, however, the sanctions order declared PHR to be the "nominee[] *or* the alter ego of Krause and are thus property of the estate and subject to turnover." Aplt's App. vol. 1, at 176 (emphasis added). So even assuming Drake and Rick are correct in surmising that Kansas is likely to prohibit reverse veil piercing, the bankruptcy court's order remains independently and separately justified under nominee theory. And, as we have already explained and so won't repeat at length here, nominee theory is analytically distinct from reverse veil piercing theory. To defeat the bankruptcy court's sanction order, Drake and Rick must knock out each of the legs on which it rests. Even assuming they might succeed in knocking out one, they make no effort to displace the other. So, it is that the bankruptcy's order necessarily remains standing, and the judgment in this case must be *Affirmed*.

Questions Presented

1) Why were the transfers considered null and void?
2) Why were the transfers to the trust considered fraudulent?
3) Is there anything the petitioner could have done to legitimize the transfers?

❖❖❖

E. The Trustee

The Trustee is an important person in a Chapter 7 bankruptcy. An interim trustee is first appointed when the bankruptcy petition is filed. The interim trustee becomes the permanent trustee if the creditors do not elect another trustee[77] at the creditors' meeting[78] required by statute. Any person may be a trustee, but the trustee is often appointed through the United States Trustee Program.

1. General Duties of the Trustee

A trustee's main duty is to "collect and reduce to money the property of the estate."[79] In order to accomplish this, the trustee is given other broad powers and specific duties as well. The trustee is tasked with investigating the debtor's financial affairs[80] and is accountable for all the debtor's property that he or she receives.[81] The trustee must also keep creditors updated on the status of the case when requested[82] and must provide certain information regarding the case to anyone to whom the debtor owes a domestic support obligation like alimony or child support.[83]

For individual debtors, the trustee is required to give the court an opinion as to whether the debtor is engaging in a substantial abuse of the bankruptcy process.[84] The trustee is also required to bring a motion to dismiss the case or convert it to a rehabilitation bankruptcy if the debtor earns more than the median income for the state in which he or she resides and fails the substantial abuse means test.[85]

---

[77] See 11 U.S.C. § 702
[78] See 11 U.S.C. § 341
[79] 11 U.S.C. § 701(a)(1)
[80] 11 U.S.C. § 701(a)(4)
[81] 11 U.S.C. § 701(a)(2)
[82] 11 U.S.C. § 701(a)(7)
[83] 11 U.S.C. § 701(c)
[84] 11 U.S.C. § 701(b)(1)
[85] 11 U.S.C. § 701(b)(2)

2. Strong-Arm Power

The bankruptcy code places the trustee in the position of a lien creditor as of the date of the bankruptcy filing.[86] This gives the trustee priority over certain creditors and the ability to avoid certain transfers of the debtor's property both before and after the filing of the petition. This is known as the "strong-arm" power. For instance, because the trustee is considered to have the powers of a lien creditor under the Uniform Commercial Code, which has been adopted in substantial form by every state, the trustee will have priority over unperfected secured creditors when it comes time to distribute the estate.[87]

The trustee has the power to set aside and avoid certain sales of the debtor's property made before or after the bankruptcy petition is filed as well as certain claims made by creditors.[88] This gives the trustee the power to avoid anything that is avoidable under state law by a lien creditor. For instance, if state law allows a fraudulent conveyance made within 4 years of the lienholder's lawsuit to be avoided, a trustee could avoid any fraudulent conveyance made with the debtor's property within 4 years of the filing of the petition.[89]

3. Other Avoidance Powers of the Trustee

A trustee has several specific avoidance powers. A trustee has the power to avoid any claim that the debtor could also avoid. For instance, if a creditor were to convince the debtor to enter into a contract under duress, the trustee could avoid the creditor's claim in bankruptcy because the debtor has a defense to enforcement.

The debtor may also avoid any fraudulent transfers of the debtor's property that take place within two years of the filing of the bankruptcy petition.[90] A transfer is fraudulent if it is made with the intent to "hinder, delay, or defraud" a creditor or in which the debtor received less than "reasonably equivalent value" for the transfer that resulted in the debtor's insolvency or inability to pay back debts.[91]

The trustee may also avoid certain transfers of the debtor's property known as "preferences." A preference is a transfer made to a creditor that gives that creditor more than it would have received as a result of the bankruptcy.[92] A trustee may avoid any preference that occurred within the 90 days before the bankruptcy petition was filed. If the preference was made to an "insider," the trustee can avoid it if it took place within a year before the bankruptcy petition was filed.[93] An insider is a person or business entity with whom the debtor has a sufficiently close relationship. For an individual debtor, this would include any relative, business partner, or corporation under the control of the debtor. For a business entity debtor, this would include any officer, employee, or owner of the business.[94]

---

[86] 11 U.S.C. § 544(a)

[87] Uniform Commercial Code § 9-102(a)(52)(C)

[88] 11 U.S.C. § 544(b)

[89] See, e.g., *In re Davis*, 138 B.R. 106 (Bankr. M.D. Fla. 1992)

[90] 11 U.S.C. § 548. This should not be confused with the "strong-arm" power. The strong-arm power gives the trustee the power to avoid any fraudulent transfer that can be avoided under state law, which is often a period longer than the two years allowed by this statute.

[91] 11 U.S.C. § 548(a)(1)

[92] 11 U.S.C. § 547(b)

[93] 11 U.S.C. § 547(b)(4)

[94] 11 U.S.C. § 101(31)

Preferences do not include a transfer of assets for new value,[95] a transfer in the ordinary course of business,[96] a transfer made by a consumer debtor of less than $600,[97] or a transfer made by a commercial debtor of less than $6,425.[98]

The trustee also has the power to avoid most transactions that occur after the petition is filed[99] and to avoid certain statutory liens. For instance, the trustee can avoid any lien that arose after the debtor became insolvent or filed bankruptcy and any lien for unpaid rent.[100]

F. Priority of Creditors

The most important question to any creditor is "How much will I get paid?" The bankruptcy code determines the answer by splitting creditors into types and classes. The two main types of creditors are secured creditors and unsecured creditors. Secured creditors are creditors who have a security interest in some or all of debtor's property. Unsecured creditors are those creditors who do not have a security interest in debtor's property. There is also an important subset of unsecured creditors called "priority creditors." These types of creditors are the unsecured creditors who have the highest priority.

Legal Definition

Priority Creditor – an unsecured creditor with a high priority of payment in bankruptcy.

---

1. Secured Creditors

A secured creditor has priority over unsecured creditors to the proceeds of the debt in which it has the security interest.[101] What will be done depends on whether the collateral becomes part of the bankruptcy estate. The collateral becomes part of the bankruptcy estate if the debtor's equity in the property is greater than the exemption allowed for that property. For instance, imagine if a debtor elects to use the federal exemptions in a state in which the federal exemptions are allowed. The debtor owes $3,000 on a secured loan for a car that is worth $10,000, giving the debtor $7,000 in equity. The federal exemption for automobile equity is only $3,775. Also assume that the debtor has no other exemptions available for the $3,225 of equity not covered by the automobile exemption.

In the above scenario, the trustee would take possession of the car and sell it because the debtor did not have enough exemptions to keep it out of the bankruptcy estate. The trustee would take the proceeds and pay the secured creditor and put all remaining proceeds minus the federal exemption amount into the bankruptcy estate to be distributed as required by law.

At the beginning of every case, the debtor must file a "statement of intent" with regard to what it wishes to do with the collateral subject to a security interest. If the debtor has no equity in the collateral or equity within the exemption amount, the debtor has three options.

---

[95] 11 U.S.C. § 547(c)(1)

[96] 11 U.S.C. § 547(c)(2)

[97] 11 U.S.C. § 547(c)(8)

[98] 11 U.S.C. § 547(c)(9). Under 11 U.S.C. § 104(a), this amount increases with inflation every three years. It was last adjusted in 2016.

[99] 11 U.S.C. § 549(a)

[100] 11 U.S.C. § 545

[101] For a discussion of which secured creditors have priority when multiple creditors have a security interest in the same property, see Chapter 11.

First, the debtor may reaffirm the debt and keep the collateral.[102] This means that the debtor can choose to continue making payments to the creditor after the bankruptcy but keep the collateral. If the debtor was behind on his or her payments before bankruptcy, the creditor can require the debtor to make his or her debt current before agreeing to a reaffirmation of debt. This has the advantage of allowing the debtor to keep the collateral but the disadvantage of keeping the debt from being discharged. After the reaffirmation agreement, if the debtor does not make payments under the reaffirmation agreement, the creditor can exercise its rights allowed by the reaffirmation agreement, which will usually include the ability to repossess the collateral and sue the debtor for payment.

Second, the debtor may choose to redeem the property by paying the creditor the fair market value of the property in a lump sum.[103] If this option is chosen, the debtor must pay the fair market value of the property, not the amount actually owed to the creditor. This has the advantage of not only allowing the debtor to keep the collateral but allowing the debtor to pay less than it otherwise would owe. The obvious disadvantage is that this is often not very practical. Very few debtors in bankruptcy have the money to pay a significant amount of money in a lump sum.

Finally, the debtor can choose to surrender the collateral to the secured creditor.[104] The secured creditor can accept the collateral in satisfaction of the debt or sell it and apply the proceeds towards its debt. If the debtor still owes money to the creditor after the sale, the creditor becomes an unsecured creditor as to the remainder of that debt.

2. Unsecured Creditors

Unsecured creditors are lower in priority than secured creditors. However, they are split into several classes of priority. Unsecured creditors are paid as a class, which means each class must be paid before the class next highest in priority can receive payment. If there is not enough money to pay a particular class, the class is paid in the same proportion. Some of the classes limit the claims to a particular dollar amount. If the claim is in excess of that dollar amount, any other amounts these claimants are owed are treated as claims by general creditors, which are the lowest creditors in priority. The classes of unsecured creditors are listed from the highest to the lowest priorities as follows:

a. Domestic support obligations like child support and alimony
b. Administrative costs like attorney's fees and the trustee's fees
c. In an involuntary case, a claim arising in the ordinary course of the debtor's business or financial affairs after the commencement of the case but before the appointment of a trustee
d. Wages, salary, and commissions earned within 180 days of the bankruptcy up to $12,850 per claimant
e. Amounts owed to employee benefit plans earned within 180 days of the bankruptcy up to $12,850 per claimant
f. Amounts owed to farmers from grain storage operations and to fisherman from fish storage and processing facilities up to $6,325.
g. Amounts paid as a rental or purchase deposit of property and amounts paid by a consumer for a service that was not provided up to $2,850.

---

[102] 11 U.S.C. § 521(a)(2)(A)
[103] 11 U.S.C. § 521(a)(2)(A)
[104] 11 U.S.C. § 521(a)(2)(A)

h. Certain kinds of taxes
i. Claims for personal injury or death resulting from the debtor operating a vehicle under the influence of alcohol or drugs
j. Claims by FDIC-regulated agency to maintain the capital of an FDIC-insured institution
k. General unsecured creditors (everyone else)[105]

FIGURE 14.2 Important Types of Creditors

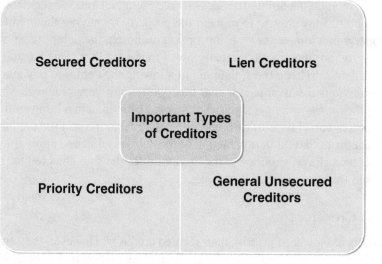

G. Discharge of Debt

The goal for every debtor is to have as much of its debt discharged as possible. However, not all debt is dischargeable in a Chapter 7 bankruptcy. Some kinds of debt are exempted from discharge, and the debtor remains liable for that debt even after the bankruptcy case is over. Consider the following case.

❖❖

In re Savage
311 B.R. 835 (B.A.P. 1st Cir. 2004)

HAINES, Bankruptcy Judge.

Educational Credit Management Corporation ("ECMC") appeals from an order of the United States Bankruptcy Court for the District of Massachusetts discharging all but $3,120 of the debtor's student loan obligations to ECMC under 11 U.S.C. § 523(a)(8). Because we conclude that the Debtor did not sustain her burden of establishing that excepting the debt from discharge would impose an undue hardship, we REVERSE the decision of the bankruptcy court.

JURISDICTION

A bankruptcy appellate panel may hear appeals from "final judgments, orders and decrees [pursuant to 28 U.S.C. §158(a)(1)] or with leave of the court, from interlocutory orders and decrees

---

[105] 11 U.S.C. § 507. Under 11 U.S.C. § 104, these amounts are adjusted every three years for inflation. They were last adjusted in 2016.

[pursuant to 28 U.S.C. § 158(a)(3)]." *Fleet Data Processing Corp. v. Branch (In re Bank of New England Corp.), 218 B.R. 643, 645 (1st Cir. BAP 1998)*. "A decision is final if it 'ends the litigation on the merits and leaves nothing for the court to do but execute the judgment.'" *Id.* at 646 (citations omitted). The bankruptcy court's order determining the dischargeability of the Debtor's student loan obligations is such a final order. *See id.* at 646-47; *see generally T I Fed. Credit Union v. DelBonis, 72 F.3d 921 (1st Cir. BAP 1995)*.

STANDARD OF REVIEW

We evaluate the bankruptcy court's findings of fact under the "clearly erroneous" standard and its conclusions of law *de novo*. *See Grella v. Salem Five Cent Savings Bank, 42 F.3d 26, 30 (1st Cir.1994)*; *see also Palmacci v. Umpierrez, 121 F.3d 781, 785 (1st Cir.1997)*. Several circuits have concluded that § 523(a)(8)'s "undue hardship" determination is a question of law that triggers *de novo* review. Neither the First Circuit nor this appellate panel has addressed the point. Here, both parties agree to *de novo* review of the bankruptcy court's undue hardship conclusion, so we will provide it without further inquiry. Of course, we will review the underlying factual findings for clear error.

BACKGROUND

On February 10, 2003, Brenda Savage filed a voluntary petition under Chapter 13 of the United States Bankruptcy Code. The case was subsequently converted to Chapter 7. Thereafter, Ms. Savage initiated an adversary proceeding seeking discharge of her student loan obligations to ECMC.

By the time of trial, Ms. Savage's student loan obligations, now owed to ECMC, consisted of five separate loans on which she owed $32,248.45 in total, including principal, interest and collection costs. Under amortization schedules running from fifteen to thirty years, Ms. Savage could repay all five loans with monthly payments ranging from $327.05 to $259.45. Under a federal program designed to assist student loan debtors (the William D. Ford Loan Consolidation Program), Ms. Savage could consolidate her loans and restructure her payments. Under the Ford Program option, her initial loan payments would be approximately $221 per month, subject to upward adjustments after two years.

Ms. Savage is a 41-year old single woman and is in good health. She attended college in the mid-1980's, but did not graduate. She resides with her fifteen year old son in an apartment, the cost of which is subsidized through the Section 8 housing plan. Her son attends private school at Boston Trinity Academy.

Ms. Savage has been employed by Blue Cross Blue Shield of Massachusetts since September 1999. At the time of trial, she worked an average of 37.5 hours per week, earning approximately $38,328.10 gross annually. According to her Schedule I, her monthly gross wages were $3,079.79. She also earned sundry employment benefits, including health insurance, dental insurance, life insurance, 401(k) plan, three weeks paid vacation and paid personal days. After deductions, her net monthly income was $1,850.12. In addition, she received monthly child support income of $180.60. Thus, Ms. Savage's total net monthly household income was approximately $2,030.72.

Ms. Savage's Schedule J, filed on March 10, 2003, listed monthly expenses of $1,725.74. Her amended Schedule J, filed December 8, 2003, listed expenses totaling $2138.44. The amended schedule itemized, among other things, $607 for rent, $221 for utilities, $76 for telephone, $23.99 for internet connection, $430 for food, $75 for clothing, $12.50 for laundry and dry cleaning, $23 for out of pocket medical expenses, $95.50 for transportation, $193.50 for charitable contributions, $43 for entertainment, $277.50 for her son's tuition at Boston Trinity Academy and $50 for her son's school books.

Employing a "totality of the circumstances" analysis to determine undue hardship, the bankruptcy court concluded ". . . it is reasonable that Ms. Savage pay $30 per week for two years, roughly, in order to satisfy a portion of the student loan debt." It entered judgment discharging all but $3,120 of the amount owing to ECMC.

DISCUSSION

I. Burden of Proof

Under § 523(a)(8), debtors are not permitted to discharge educational loans unless excepting the loans from discharge will impose an undue hardship on the debtor and the debtor's dependents. The creditor bears the initial burden of proving the debt exists and that the debt is of the type excepted from discharge under § 523(a)(8). *See Bloch v. Windham Prof'ls (In re Bloch), 257 B.R. 374, 377 (Bankr.D.Mass.2001)* (citations omitted). Once the threshold showing has been made, the burden shifts to the debtor to prove by a preponderance of the evidence that excepting the student loan debt from discharge will cause the debtor and her dependents "undue hardship." *See id.; see also Grogan v. Garner, 498 U.S. 279, 287, 111 S.Ct. 654, 112 L.Ed.2d 755 (1991)* (preponderance of the evidence standard for dischargeability complaints).

***

III. Undue Hardship: "Totality of the Circumstances"

Under "totality of the circumstances" analysis, a debtor seeking discharge of student loans must prove by a preponderance of evidence that (1) her past, present, and reasonably reliable future financial resources; (2) her and her dependents' reasonably necessary living expenses, and; (3) other relevant facts or circumstances unique to the case prevent her from paying the student loans in question while still maintaining a minimal standard of living, even when aided by a discharge of other pre-petition debts. *See Kopf, 245 B.R. at 739.*

A. *Past, Present and Reasonably Reliable Future Income*

The debtor must show not only that her current income is insufficient to pay her student loans, but also that her prospects for increasing her income in the future are too limited to afford her sufficient resources to repay the student loans and provide herself and her dependents with a minimal (but fair) standard of living. *See id.* at 745; *see also Burkhead v. United States (In re Burkhead), 304 B.R. 560, 566 (Bankr.D.Mass.2004); Bourque v. Educ. Credit Mgmt. Corp. (In re Bourque), 303 B.R. 548, 550 (Bankr.D.Mass. 2003)*.

Ms. Savage has not demonstrated that her current level of income and future prospects warrant discharge of her loans. Her present income may be insufficient to pay her student loans and still maintain precisely the standard of living she now has. But, as discussed below, we conclude it would enable her to repay the loans without undue hardship. Moreover, the record plainly establishes that her prospects for a steady increase in income over time are promising. She has been steadily employed at the same job and regularly receives annual raises. Nothing indicates change is in the wind. Moreover, Ms. Savage currently works 37½ hours a week, leaving time for some part-time work (or longer hours at her present job), a possibility that will become more and more practical as her son grows older.

B. *Reasonable Necessary Living Expenses.*

To prove undue hardship for purposes of § 523(a)(8), a debtor must show that her necessary and reasonable expenses leave her with too little to afford repayment. The bankruptcy court found Ms. Savage's expenses are "for the most part . . . extremely reasonable . . . This isn't an example of any lavish lifestyle by any means." App. at 197. Although we agree that Ms. Savage does not live lavishly, we disagree that her expenses demonstrate that repaying her student loans would burden her unduly.

As noted above, Ms. Savage's original Schedule J showed total monthly expenses of $1,725.74, leaving about $300 a month in "disposable income." Seven months later, she amended Schedule J, increasing, her monthly expenses to $2,138.44. The increase is attributable principally to private school expenses and church donations.

***

1. Private School Tuition

A necessary living expense is one the debtor could not cut from the budget and still maintain a minimal standard of living. *See In re Dolan*, 256 B.R. 230, 239 (Bankr.D.Mass.2000) (citing *Lohr v. Sallie Mae (In re Lohr)*, 252 B.R. 84, 88-89 (Bankr.E.D.Va.2000)). It is the debtor's burden to prove that expenses are reasonably necessary. *See In re Webb*, 262 B.R. 685 (Bankr.E.D.Tex.2001)

Private school tuition is not *generally* considered a reasonably necessary expense in bankruptcy cases even under the *more liberal* standard applied in the Chapter 13 confirmation context. We recently held so in a case where the proffered justification for the expense was, if anything, more substantial than that presented here. *See Watson v. Boyajian (In re Watson)*, 309 B.R. 652 (1st Cir. BAP 2004)(examining whether debtors' expenses were reasonable and necessary for purposes of § 1325); *see also Webb*, 262 B.R. at 690 (same); *Univest-Coppell Village, Ltd. v. Nelson*, 204 B.R. 497 (E.D.Tex.1996) (same). Although compelling circumstances may distinguish a given case, the authorities uniformly hold that a debtor's mere preference for private schooling is insufficient to qualify the attendant expense as necessary and reasonable.

Ms. Savage did not demonstrate a satisfactory reason why her son needs to attend private school at a monthly cost of $277.50 (plus $50 for books). When asked to explain why she did so, she testified:

> *There were a lot of fights, a lot of swearing, a lot of other things going on. I mean he would wake up every morning crying because he didn't want to go to school . . . So I had to find a school to put him in . . . where he was going to—I mean, he didn't do well that whole year. I had to keep going down to the school several times. He was just a mess the whole school year . . . So I had to find another school.*

App. at 172-73. Although we understand why Ms. Savage prefers that her son attend private school, she has not demonstrated that the public school system cannot adequately meet her son's educational needs. Her preference appears sincere, but that alone is not sufficient to sustain the bankruptcy court's implicit conclusion that foregoing this expense would constitute undue hardship within § 523(a)(8)'s meaning.

2. Other Expenses

Given the fact that at least $322.50 (private school tuition and books) in expense can be eliminated from Ms. Savage's budget without creating undue hardship, her student loans cannot be discharged under § 523(a)(8). It is worth noting, as well, that Ms. Savage's son will reach majority in just a few years, a consequence that will reduce her required expenses considerably. Moreover, we note that Ms. Savage's budget includes additional discretionary expenses that might, or might not, survive if they were scrutinized under the totality of circumstances test for undue hardship. Those expenses create issues we need not reach today, but their existence demonstrates that, with elimination of the private school expenses, Ms. Savage's budget remains sufficiently malleable to enable her to adjust to the necessity of repaying her student loans.

Church Donations. Ms. Savage makes monthly "tithes" to her church of approximately $193. Through the Religious Liberty and Charitable Donation Protection Act of 1998 (the "RLCDPA"), Congress amended several sections of the Bankruptcy Code to exclude "charitable contributions" totaling less than fifteen percent of the debtor's gross annual income from consideration by the bankruptcy courts for various purposes. *See* Pub.L. No. 105-183, 112 Stat. 517. For example, Congress amended § 1325 so that "charitable contributions" could not be considered "disposable income" by the bankruptcy court for plan confirmation purposes. Notably, though, § 523(a)(8) was not one of the Code sections amended by Congress. As a result, there is a split of authority as to whether Congress intended religious and charitable donations to be permissible expenses in determining undue hardship under § 523(a)(8). *Compare Lebovits v. Chase Manhattan Bank (In re Lebovits), 223 B.R. 265 (Bankr.E.D.N.Y.1998)* (tithing was permissible expense under § 523(a) (8)), and *Meling v. United States (In re Meling), 263 B.R. 275 (Bankr. N.D.Iowa 2001)* (monthly tithes of $100 were reasonable for purposes of § 523(a)(8)), with *Educational Credit Mgmt. Corp. v. McLeroy (In re McLeroy), 250 B.R. 872 (N.D.Tex.2000)* (finding that RLCDPA's provisions do not apply to § 523(a)(8)), and *Ritchie v. Northwest Educ. Loan Ass'n (In re Ritchie), 254 B.R. 913 (Bankr.D.Idaho 2000)* (religious tithing excluded from expenses in undue hardship analysis).

401(k) Contributions. Ms. Savage makes 401(k) contributions of approximately $42 per week. *See* App. at 189. Consistent with the generally prevailing view, the bankruptcy court considered those contributions as income from which Ms. Savage could pay some portion of her outstanding student loans without undue hardship. We need not address the issue here, but pause only to say that, as with other expenses considered in the totality of pertinent circumstances, courts would do well to analyze each debtor's particular situation carefully. The result may well differ with changes in a debtor's age, accumulated savings, proximity to retirement, and earnings and expense forecast. *See Peel v. SallieMae Servicing-Heal Loan (In re Peel), 240 B.R. 387, 392-93 (Bankr. N.D.Cal.1999)* (explaining why court should exercise discretion in assaying necessity of retirement savings); *see also In re Bell, 264 B.R. 512 (Bankr.S.D.Ill.2001)* (citing *In re Taylor, 243 F.3d 124, 129-30 (2d Cir.2001)*).

***

CONCLUSION

The bankruptcy court's order discharging all but $3,120 of the student loan obligations to ECMC is REVERSED and the matter is REMANDED for entry of judgment in ECMC's favor.

Questions Presented

1)   What standard did the court use to determine whether there was an undue hardship?
2)   What facts did the debtor try to argue constituted an undue hardship?
3)   What facts did the court rely on to determine whether there was an undue hardship?

The following kinds of debt are commonly exempt from discharge:

a. Back taxes incurred in the two years before the petition was filed
b. Claims for amounts owed that the debtor obtained by fraud
c. Claims arising from the purchase of luxury goods in excess of $675 from a single creditor within 90 days prior to the filing of the bankruptcy petition
d. Claims for cash advances from a credit card in excess of $950 obtained within 70 days of the filing of the bankruptcy petition
e. Claims by creditors who were not listed on the bankruptcy petition schedules
f. Claims for embezzlement, larceny, or fraud or misuse of funds while the debtor acted as a fiduciary
g. Domestic support obligations like child support and alimony and property settlements provided for by marital divorce and separation agreements
h. Claims for an injury caused willfully and maliciously by the debtor
i. Most government fines and penalties
j. Student loans
k. Claims for personal injury and death resulting from operating a motorized vehicle under the influence of drugs and alcohol
l. Loans taken against a retirement account[106]

In addition to the debts that are not dischargeable listed above, the bankruptcy court can deny a debtor a discharge of all debt if the debtor engages in certain kinds of misconduct before or during the bankruptcy proceeding. For instance, if the debtor destroys property of the bankruptcy estate intentionally[107] or conceals or destroys records,[108] the court can deny a discharge.

The court will also deny a discharge if the debtor has received a discharge in the previous eight years.[109]

V. Chapter 11 Bankruptcies

A "Chapter 11" bankruptcy is a type of rehabilitation bankruptcy and is the most common form of bankruptcy filed by businesses. It is commonly known as a "reorganization" bankruptcy. The purpose of a Chapter 11 bankruptcy is to reorganize the debtor's financial affairs so that its debts become more affordable. In a Chapter 11 bankruptcy, the debtor creates a plan to pay back part of its debt and is discharged from the rest.

A. Who Can File

Anyone who can file a Chapter 7 bankruptcy can also file a Chapter 11 bankruptcy. Railroads are also allowed to file.[110] While individuals can file Chapter 11 cases, the vast majority of Chapter 11 filings are commercial in nature.

---

[106] See 11 U.S.C. § 523
[107] 11 U.S.C. § 727(a)(2)
[108] 11 U.S.C. § 727(a)(3)
[109] 11 U.S.C. 727(a)(8)
[110] 11 U.S.C. § 109(d)

Like a Chapter 7 bankruptcy, the case can also be brought voluntarily by the debtor or against the debtor's wishes by its creditors. If a debtor has 12 or more creditors, at least 3 creditors must agree to bring the involuntary bankruptcy petition against the debtor.[111] The 3 creditors must also be owed at least a total of $15,775 between them.[112]

There is also an expedited Chapter 11 procedure for small business debtors. A small business debtor is a debtor who owns a business (other than one that primarily buys and sells real property) whose total amount of debt, both secured and unsecured, is less than $2,566.050. A debtor will not be eligible for the expedited process, however, if a committee of creditors is appointed unless the court determines that the committee is not active enough to provide effective oversight of the debtor.[113]

B. What Chapter 7 and Chapter 11 Have in Common

Chapter 7 and Chapter 11 bankruptcies have a lot in common. The automatic stay works in the same way in Chapter 7 and Chapter 11 cases.[114] Chapter 11 also prohibits the same actions by creditors that a Chapter 7 bankruptcy does and has the same exceptions to the stay that a Chapter 7 bankruptcy does.

The same documents also have to be filed by the debtor, including schedules of assets, creditors, and income. The same debts that are not dischargeable in a Chapter 7 case are also not dischargeable in a Chapter 11 case.

C. Differences between Chapter 7 and Chapter 11

Chapters 7 and 11 are different in important ways.

Unlike Chapter 7 bankruptcies, Chapter 11 bankruptcies are not means-tested. However, a court may still dismiss a Chapter 11 petition for the same reasons a Chapter 7 petition can dismissed, including substantial abuse. Chapter 11 cases can also be converted to Chapter 7 cases.

While individual debtors are allowed to exempt certain property from the bankruptcy estate even in a Chapter 11 case, commercial debtors are not allowed to exempt anything from the estate.[115] Because the vast majority of Chapter 11 cases are filed by businesses and the vast majority of Chapter 7 cases are filed by individuals, this is especially important. The purpose of Chapter 11 is to reorganize a debtor's finances so that it can continue to afford its debt. It is also designed to keep commercial debtors in business during bankruptcies. So, unlike in an individual Chapter 7 case, in a commercial Chapter 11 case, the debtor remains in possession of the property of the bankruptcy estate throughout the duration of the case.

Unlike in a Chapter 7 case, if an individual files under Chapter 11, the individual's property acquired after the petition is filed is considered part of the bankruptcy estate.[116]

Because the debtor remains in possession of the bankruptcy estate during a Chapter 11 bankruptcy, in most commercial Chapter 11 cases, a trustee is not appointed. The debtor assumes most of the duties and powers of the trustee.[117] In these cases, the debtor is referred to as the "debtor in possession."

---

[111] 11 U.S.C. § 303(b)

[112] See 11 U.S.C. § 303(b)(1). Under 11 U.S.C. § 104(a), the minimum dollar amount of claims that creditors must have to bring an involuntary bankruptcy increases with inflation. It was last adjusted in 2016.

[113] 11 U.S.C. § 101-51D

[114] See 11 U.S.C. § 362

[115] See 11 U.S.C. § 522(b)

[116] 11 U.S.C. § 1115(a)

[117] 11 U.S.C. § 1107(a)

The debtor in possession has the same strong-arm power to avoid certain liens that a trustee has in a Chapter 7 case.[118] The debtor in possession also has the same power to avoid fraudulent and preferential transfers as a trustee does in a Chapter 7 case.[119] A debtor may not be motivated to pursue recovering money from creditors it already paid, but it is required to do so under the bankruptcy code. Failure to do so may lead to the court appointing a trustee.

A discharge in Chapter 11 is also different than a discharge in a Chapter 7 case. In a Chapter 7 case, all of the debtor's remaining non-exempt debts are discharged. In a Chapter 11 case, non-exempt debt will remain after the case ends. Only the amounts not covered by the plan will be discharged. For individual debtors, a discharge will not even occur until after he or she completes payment under the reorganization plan.[120] For business debtors, discharge occurs when the plan is confirmed.[121]

D. Creditor's Committee

Shortly after the petition is filed by a Chapter 11 debtor, a committee of unsecured creditors is appointed by the court.[122] Other classes of creditors may form a committee if they make a request of the court to do so.[123] In small business cases, the court has the discretion to not appoint a committee at all if requested.[124] The Court cannot force a creditor to be on the committee.[125]

The function of the creditor's committee is to represent the interests of creditors in the class for which the committee is appointed. Orders are usually entered by the court only with consent of the creditor committees, but the court may make orders over their objections.

E. Reorganization Plan

The goal of Chapter 11 is to create a plan for the debtor to repay as much of its debt as it can. This plan is known as a "reorganization plan." The bankruptcy code strongly prefers that the debtor create its own reorganization plan. It gives the debtor a 120-day "exclusivity period" to file a plan. In the first 120 days following the filing of the petition, no party except the debtor is allowed to propose a plan to the court.[126] In small business cases, the exclusivity period is 180 days.[127] Following the exclusivity period, if an extension is not granted, any creditor can file a reorganization plan.[128]

The plan must contain a list of the classes and creditors, state how each class's claims will be treated, and show how the plan will be implemented.[129] All creditors in a particular class must be treated the same way, meaning all get paid in the same proportion (unless the impaired creditor consents).[130]

Once the plan is proposed, each class of creditors not paid in full votes on the plan. The plan will be accepted if a judge determines it is in the best interests of the creditors and more than half

---

[118] 11 U.S.C. § 544(a)
[119] 11 U.S.C. §§ 547, 548
[120] 11 U.S.C. § 1141(d)(5)
[121] 11 U.S.C. § 1141(a)
[122] 11 U.S.C. § 1102(a)(1)
[123] 11 U.S.C. § 1102(a)(2)
[124] 11 U.S.C. § 1102(a)(3)
[125] 11 U.S.C. § 1102(b)
[126] 11 U.S.C. § 1121(a)
[127] 11 U.S.C. § 1121(e)
[128] 11 U.S.C. § 1121(b)
[129] 11 U.S.C. § 1123(a)
[130] 11 U.S.C. § 1123(a)(4)

of the creditors in each half of the class vote to accept and those creditors represent at least 2/3 of the claims in that class.[131]

Even if classes of creditors reject a plan, the court may still choose to approve the plan so long as it does not unfairly discriminate against a class of creditors and the plan is fair and equitable.[132] This is known as a "cram down."

VI. Chapter 13 Bankruptcies

Chapter 13 bankruptcies are rehabilitation bankruptcies like Chapter 11 bankruptcies. However, while Chapter 11 is primarily for businesses, Chapter 13 is only for individual debtors. Business entities are not allowed to file under Chapter 13.[133]

Like a Chapter 11 bankruptcy, in a Chapter 13 bankruptcy, the debtor and creditors create a plan to pay back as much of the debt as the individual can. The rest is discharged. Commonly known as "wage-earner" bankruptcy, Chapter 13 is designed to rehabilitate the financial affairs of individuals that earn regular income.

A. Who May File

Only individuals who have (a) regular income, (b) unsecured debts less than $394,725, and (c) secured debts less than $1,184,200 may file under Chapter 13.[134] Unlike in Chapter 7 and Chapter 11 bankruptcies, creditors cannot bring a Chapter 13 case against a debtor involuntarily. The debtor must voluntarily bring the action.[135]

B. What Chapters 7, 11, and 13 Have in Common

Chapter 13 has a lot in common with Chapter 7 and Chapter 11. The automatic stay works in the same way that does in Chapter 7 and Chapter 11 cases.[136] It also prohibits the same actions by creditors that a Chapter 7 or Chapter 11 bankruptcy does and has the same exceptions to the stay that a Chapter 7 or Chapter 11 bankruptcy does. The only difference is that the stay does not take effect until a repayment plan is filed with the court. However, the plan must be filed within 14 days of the filing of the petition.

The same documents also have to be filed by the debtor, including schedules of assets, creditors, and income.

C. Differences between Chapter 11 and Chapter 13 Repayment Plans

Unlike a Chapter 11 plan, a Chapter 13 payment plan may only be offered by the debtor.[137] Further, unlike a Chapter 11 repayment plan, a Chapter 13 repayment plan is means-tested. If the debtor's income is below the median income in that state, the debtor will create a three-year repayment plan. If it is above the median income, the debtor will create a five-year repayment plan.[138]

---

[131] 11 U.S.C. § 1126(c)

[132] 11 U.S.C. § 1126(b)

[133] 11 U.S.C. § 109(e)

[134] 11 U.S.C. § 109(3). Under 11 U.S.C. U.S.C. § 104, these amounts are adjusted for inflation every three years. They were last updated in 2016.

[135] See 11 U.S.C. § 303

[136] See 11 U.S.C. § 362

[137] 11 U.S.C. § 1321

[138] 11 U.S.C. § 1325(d)

FIGURE 14.3   Priority Claims

Priority Claims
a. Domestic Support Obligations like child support and alimony
b. Administrative costs like attorney's fees and the trustee's fees
c. In an involuntary case, a claim arising in the ordinary course of the debtor's business or financial affairs after the commencement of the case but before the appointment of a trustee
d. Wages, salary, and commissions earned within 180 days of the bankruptcy up to $12,850 per claimant
e. Amounts owed to employee benefit plans earned within 180 days of the bankruptcy up to $12,850 per claimant
f. Amounts owed to farmers from grain storage operations and to fisherman from fish storage and processing facilities up to $6,325.
g. Amounts paid as a rental or purchase deposit of property and amounts paid by a consumer for a service that was not provided up to $2,850.
h. Certain kinds of taxes
i. Claims for personal injury or death resulting from the debtor operating a vehicle under the influence of alcohol or drugs
j. Claims by an FDIC-regulated agency to maintain the capital of an FDIC-insured institution

Unlike a Chapter 11 repayment plan, Chapter 13 plans are overseen and administered by a bankruptcy trustee. The debtor makes payments to the trustee. The trustee makes the payments to the creditors.[139] The debtor must begin payment under the plan even before the court confirms the plan.[140]

The debtor must also pay all priority claims in full as part of the plan.[141] Priority claims are the same for Chapter 13 bankruptcies as they are for Chapter 7 bankruptcies.[142] Like a Chapter 11 bankruptcy, all creditors within a particular class must be treated the same unless the impaired creditors consent.[143]

The debtor must also choose what to do with secured collateral in the plan except real property, which can be paid out over the terms of the original loan securing the collateral.[144] A plan will only be confirmed if each secured creditor agrees to accept the plan, the plan allows the secured party to keep its lien until paid in full or discharge occurs, or the debtor chooses to surrender the collateral.[145]

Unsecured creditors have less power than secured creditors. However, if an unsecured creditor or the trustee objects to the debtor's plan, the court can only confirm it if the value of property to be distributed by the trustee is equal to the amount owed to the objecting creditor or all of the debtor's disposable income is paid to creditors under the plan.[146]

D. Chapter 13 Bankruptcy Estate

Unlike in a Chapter 7 case, if an individual files under Chapter 13, the individual's property acquired after the petition is filed is considered part of the bankruptcy estate.[147] Everything else that is included in a Chapter 7 estate is included in a Chapter 13 estate.[148] Disposable income is determined in Chapter 13 in the same manner that it is determined under Chapter 7.[149]

---

[139] See 11 U.S.C. § 1322(a)

[140] 11 U.S.C. § 1326

[141] 11 U.S.C. § 1322(a)(2)

[142] 11 U.S.C. §§ 507, 1322(a)(2)

[143] 11 U.S.C. § 1322(a)(3)

[144] 11 U.S.C. § 1322(b)(2)

[145] 11 U.S.C. § 1325(a)(5)

[146] 11 U.S.C. § 1325(b)(1)

[147] 11 U.S.C. § 1396(a)

[148] 11 U.S.C. §§ 541, 1306

[149] 11 U.S.C. §§ 707(b), 1325(b)

Chapter 13 debtors may also exclude the same property from the bankruptcy estate that a Chapter 7 debtor may exclude.[150]

E. Chapter 13 Discharge

A Chapter 13 debtor is not discharged when the payment plan is approved. The debtor is not discharged until the payment plan has been completed.[151] The same kinds of debt that are not dischargeable under Chapter 7 are not dischargeable under Chapter 13.

FIGURE 14.4   Nondischargeable Debt

Nondischargeable Debt
a. Back taxes incurred in the two years before the petition was filed
b. Claims arising from the purchase of luxury goods in excess of $675 from a single creditor within 90 days prior to the filing of the bankruptcy petition
c. Claims for cash advances from a credit card in excess of $950 obtained within 70 days of the filing of the bankruptcy petition.
d. Claims by creditors who were not listed on the bankruptcy petition schedules
e. Claims for embezzlement, larceny, or fraud or misuse of funds while the debtor acted as a fiduciary
f. Domestic support obligations like child support and alimony and property settlements provided for by marital divorce and separation agreements
g. Claims for an injury caused willfully and maliciously by the debtor
h. Most government fines and penalties
i. Student loans
j. Claims for personal injury and death resulting from operating a motorized vehicle under the influence of drugs and alcohol
k. Loans taken against a retirement account

SUMMARY

Bankruptcy is meant for honest debtors that want to make their financial affairs manageable again. Chapter 7 bankruptcies are designed to liquidate all of a debtor's assets and debts and essentially provide a fresh start for the debtor. In most cases, all of the debtor's assets will be exempt from the bankruptcy estate and unable to be distributed to creditors, but the bankruptcy process has built in provisions to prevent abuse. For instance, fraudulent conveyances to other entities like the conveyances made in *In Re Krause*[152] will not be allowed, and the trustee has the power to avoid many kinds of pre-petition conveyances and liens.[153] Secured creditors must be especially careful to perfect their liens before bankruptcy to ensure that they survive the trustee's avoidance powers.

Chapter 11 bankruptcies are filed primarily by businesses. Unlike in a Chapter 7 filing, there is not usually a trustee and the debtor maintains possession of the bankruptcy estate throughout the filing. This is because Chapter 11 is designed to reorganize businesses and allow them to continue

---

[150] 11 U.S.C. §§ 541, 1306
[151] 11 U.S.C. § 1328(a)
[152] 637 F.3d 1160 (10th Cir. 2011)
[153] See, e.g., 11 U.S.C §§ 544, 547

running through and after bankruptcy. Instead of a discharge of all debt, the debtor makes payments over time under a plan that it can afford.

Chapter 13 bankruptcies are designed to rehabilitate the financial affairs of individuals who earn regular income and have a manageable amount of debt. It creates a way for those who earn too much money to qualify for Chapter 7 to create a feasible three or five year plan to repay their creditors and discharge unaffordable debts.

Bankruptcy provides a fresh start for debtors every day and ensures that creditors are paid as much of what they are owed as practicable.

Glossary

Acceptance (Contracts)   a voluntary act showing unequivocal assent (agreement) to an offer that is communicated to the offeree.

Acceptance (Secured Transactions)   promise of a drawee to pay an instrument when it becomes due.

Agent   a person acting on behalf of someone else.

Alienation   the term, as used in property law, refers to the transfer or conveyance of property from ownership of an individual to another. Property is generally termed to be freely alienable, i.e., subject to a transfer of ownership, although there can be a restraint on alienation, such as a provision in a real property deed restricting sale during the life of an individual. The term is primarily used with regard to the transfer of real property but it applies equally to personal property.

Arbitrary and capricious   a legal standard used to challenge administrative determinations that have no reasonable legal basis or without adequate consideration of the circumstances of the case.

Actual authority   an agent's authority, either express of implied, to bind the principal in accordance with principal's wishes.

Actual damages   damages that compensate an injured party for the direct losses stemming from a breach of contract.

Apparent authority   an agent's authority to bind a principal in contract to a third party despite lacking actual authority to do so; to exist, the principal must create the appearance that the agent has the authority necessary to bind the principal.

Area variance   the authorization of a zoning board of appeals for the use of land in a manner not allowed by the dimensional or physical specifications under the applicable zoning regulations.

Articles of Incorporation   a corporation's governing document filed with the state that sets out the number and classes of its shares as well as the name and duration of the corporation.

Assault   an intentional tort in which the tortfeasor intentionally places another in apprehension of an imminent battery.

Attachment   the process by which a security interest becomes enforceable.

Authority by estoppel   a doctrine prohibiting a principal from denying that an agent lacked authority when the principal knew of the third party's mistaken belief that the agent had authority or when the principal carelessly caused the appearance of the agent's authority to the third party; to invoke the doctrine, the third party must take a step in reliance on the purported agent's actions.

Automatic stay   in a bankruptcy case, an order that automatically goes into effect during the bankruptcy proceeding that prohibits the bankruptcy debtor's creditors from taking actions to enforce their claims against the bankruptcy debtor while the order is in effect.

Bailee   the person or entity to whom goods are delivered by a bailor for a specified purpose without the transfer of ownership.

Bailment   an agreement for the temporary placement of control or possession over personal property for a specific purpose as agreed to by the parties to the bailment agreement.

Bailor   the person or entity who entrusts the personal property to another, the bailee.

Bankruptcy estate   in a bankruptcy, all of the debtor's non-exempt property that the bankruptcy trustee can use to satisfy the debtor's obligations.

Bankruptcy trustee   in a bankruptcy, the person in charge of compiling and managing the debtor's bankruptcy estate.

Battery   an intentional tort in which the tortfeasor intentionally touches another person in a harmful or offensive way.

Bearer instrument   an instrument that is payable to anyone holding it.

***Beck* rights**   the right of a union member to opt out of paying the portion of union dues that go toward political activity.

Bill of particulars   this is a more detailed statement of a party's pleadings provided at the request of an opposing party; it is an amplification of the pleadings and with the verified complaint constitutes the core of a litigant's claim against the opposing party.

Binding authority   these are sources of law which a reviewing court must consider in reaching its decision in a case. Sources of binding authority includes higher court cases within the state, and relevant state statutes.

Board of directors   the group of persons who are vested with the management of a corporation, including the right to delegate the authority to manage to officers of the corporation.

Bylaws   a governing document setting forth a corporation's internal rules of governance.

Business debtor   in a bankruptcy, a debtor whose primary obligations are commercial in nature.

Cashier's check   an order to pay instrument in which both the drawer and drawee are a bank.

Cause in fact   in a negligence action, cause in fact is the requirement that Plaintiff's injuries would not have occurred but for the Defendant's conduct.

Certificate of deposit (CD)   a type of promise to pay promissory note in which a bank promises to pay back a fixed sum of money to a customer.

Chapter 7 bankruptcy   a type of bankruptcy in which all the debtor's non-exempt debts that remain after the bankruptcy estate is exhausted are discharged.

Chapter 11 bankruptcy   a type of bankruptcy, primarily used by business debtors, in which the debtor's non-exempt debts are reorganized under a payment plan and the non-exempt debt remaining after that payment plan is discharged.

Chapter 13 bankruptcy   a type of bankruptcy, which is only available to individuals that earn regular wages, in which the debtor's non-exempt debts are reorganized under a payment plan and the non-exempt debt remaining after that payment plan is discharged.

Chattel   the moveable or immoveable personal property of an individual exclusive of real estate.

Check   an order to pay instrument in which the drawee is a bank.

Checks and balances   in terms of a constitutional republic such as the United States it is a system of countermeasures between coordinate branches of government so that one branch cannot exceed its lawful authority or usurp power from another coordinate branch of government.

Closely-held corporation   a corporation that is managed by its shareholders and in which all of the shares are held by a small number of people.

Codicil   an addition or addendum to a will that alters, explains, revokes, or supplements the terms of the will without re-execution of the will; a codicil however, must meet the same formal requirements of a will.

Collateral   property that is pledged as security to pay a debt.

Commercial debtor   a debtor whose primarily incurred debt for business purposes.

Comparative negligence   a defense to negligence in which the Plaintiff's damages are reduced (or eliminated) proportionately to the degree to which Plaintiff contributed to his or her own injuries.

Consequential damages   reasonably foreseeable damages indirectly resulting from a breach of contract.

Consideration   anything of legally sufficient value exchanged for something else of legally sufficient value as part of the same bargain.

Consumer debtor   a debtor whose debts are primarily incurred for household, family, or personal purposes.

Contingent fee   a legal fee charged by an attorney for professional services only if the lawsuit is successful or favorably settled out of court.

Contract   a legally enforceable agreement between two or more parties.

Consumer goods   goods used primarily for personal or household use.

Contributory negligence   a defense to negligence that prohibits a Plaintiff from recovering damages if he or she contributed to his or her own injuries.

Conversion   an intentional interference with the personal property of another so severe that the tortfeasor must pay the entire fair market value of the personal property to the injured party.

Corporation   a business entity that exists only with the permission of the state, that is separate from its shareholders, that is managed by a board of directors, and that provides limited liability for its shareholders.

Counterclaim   a defendant's claim in opposition to the plaintiff's claim.

Covenant an agreement or undertaking for the performance of some action.

Cross-claim a claim made between co-defendants or co-plaintiffs in a case and that relates to the subject of the original claim or counterclaim.

Damages the amount of money a person is entitled to receive for a legally-recognized injury.

Debtor a person or business entity pledging collateral to pay a debt.

Defamation a cause of action allowing recovery for false statements made (either written or oral) that harm another's reputation.

Default judgment a judgment entered against a litigant who has either failed to comply with a court order or who has failed to appear in the litigation as scheduled.

Delegation of authority administrative agencies are permitted to act only within the grant of authority given to them by legislation. If Congress permissibly delegates authority to an agency to act in a certain area, then that agency cannot extend its authority on its own. Much discretion is given to agency action upon subsequent review by the courts but a clear violation of its delegated authority will be sanctioned by the courts.

Demand instrument an instrument payable at any time.

Deposition also, referred to as an examination before trial (or EBT) it is the stenographically recorded testimony of either a witness or a party to the litigation that is made out of court as part of the pre-trial discovery/disclosure process.

Detour an employee's insubstantial deviation from the principal's instructions while working within the scope of his or her employment.

Dictum these are ancillary or collateral remarks made by a judge in an opinion which has no binding authority in a case and cannot be cited as precedential authority in a subsequent case. It is judicial commentary made in a case as a suggestion or analogy or extended argument. The singular Latin form is dicta.

Discharge a release of a person's obligation to pay another.

Disclosed principal a principal whose identity and existence is known to the third party.

Dishonor refusal of the drawee to pay a properly presented instrument.

Dissolution the process by which a business entity ceases to exist.

Dividend corporate profits distributed to shareholders.

Draft an order to pay instrument.

Drawee in an order to pay instrument, the person who is ordered to pay the payee by the drawer.

Drawer in an order to pay instrument, the person ordering the drawee to pay the payee.

Due process a guarantee of fairness within a judicial system, or any governmental quasi-judicial body, such as an administrative tribunal, that ensures fair treatment through standardized procedures and clearly expressed laws or rules.

Ethics rules of right and wrong conduct governing personal or organizational behavior and conduct.

Equipment goods used to operate a business.

Exempt assets assets that do not become part of a bankruptcy estate.

Exempt debt debts that cannot be discharged by a bankruptcy court.

Exhaustion of remedies doctrine a requirement that prior to seeking relief in a state or federal court a litigant must pursue all available nonjudicial or administrative avenues of relief, otherwise a reviewing court will not hear the case.

False imprisonment the intentional and improper confinement of another to a limited area without consent.

Farm products goods like crops, livestock, and supplies used in or produced by a farming operation.

Federalism a system of government in which two levels of government control; in the United States there is the federal government which has limited, enumerated rights and the individual state governments that have more plenary powers to govern under their general police powers to ensure the health, safety and general welfare of state residents.

Frolic an employee's substantial deviation from the principal's instructions that takes the principal outside the scope of his or her employment.

General jurisdiction jurisdiction of a court to preside over a broad range of cases, including both criminal and civil, within the geographic area it is located.

General partner a partner who shares in the management of the partnership and who is liable for the partnership's losses.

General partnership a partnership in which all of the partners fully participate in the management of the partnership and in which all partners share the losses of the partnership.

Gift causa mortis from the Latin meaning "in contemplation of death' this refers to a gift made by a donor in the immediate anticipation of death.

Holder a person or entity in possession of a negotiable instrument who has the right to receive payment under it.

Holder in due course a holder of a completed instrument without irregularities that acquired the instrument in good faith for value without notice of its dishonor or of any other defenses to enforcement of the instrument.

Implied contract a legally enforceable agreement arising from the conduct between two parties, the relationship between the parties, or principles of equity.

In personam jurisdiction the power of a court to assert jurisdiction over an individual and personal rights; it is a broader assertion of jurisdiction than in rem.

In rem jurisdiction the power of a court to assert jurisdiction over property and determine an individual's rights to that property; it includes the authority to seize the property.

Incidental damages damages closely-associated with and closely-related to actual damages.

Individual debtor a debtor whose debts were primarily incurred for personal purposes.

Indorsee the person to whom an instrument is indorsed and delivered.

Indorsement a signature on a negotiable instrument intended to transfer ownership of the instrument to a new holder.

Indorser the person signing and delivering an instrument by indorsement.

Inherent authority the authority possessed by an agent because of the nature of its position as an agent.

Intangible collateral types of collateral that only exist because of their connection to intangible property.

Intentional infliction of emotional distress a cause of action against a person who intentionally causes another to suffer severe emotional distress by extreme and outrageous conduct.

Intentional torts the class of torts that requires the tortfeasor to intend the consequences of his or her actions.

Inter vivos gift from the Latin meaning "between the living" this refers to an irrevocable gift made by a donor during the normal course of life.

Interlocutory appeal this is an interim appeal taken to an appellate court to settle a question of law prior to trial. It does not result in a final decision in the case but merely decides an issue in the case that must be resolved so as not to cause irreparable harm in the prosecution of the case against the parties. It is a limited type of appeal that courts are reluctant to give so as to avoid what is termed "piece-meal" litigation.

Interrogatory a numbered list of written questions submitted to an opposing party as part of the formal disclosure/discovery process.

Inventory goods held by a business for sale.

Issuer the maker or drawer of an instrument.

Just cause in the employment context is a standard for employee dismissal for violating terms of an employment contract; it is generally based on some form of employee conduct that is incompatible with the employer's workplace expectations or for employee misconduct that is culpable, blameworthy, subject to censure, and can include intentional as well as negligent acts.

Last will and testament a legal document that outlines how a person wants their property distributed at death; it only takes legal effect upon the death of the person making the will (testator) and its execution requires by statute certain formalities, such as the presence of at least two witnesses, competency of the testator and a public declaration by the testator that the document is their last will and testament.

Lien a legal interest, usually created by a means other than contract, that is possessed in another's property to secure payment of a debt.

Lien creditor a creditor that has a lien on at least some of its debtor's property.

Limited jurisdiction jurisdiction of a court limited to a particular area of the law, such as probate matters, whose jurisdiction is set by statute.

Limited liability liability that is limited by law; for example, it is common for business owners of certain kinds of business entities to not be held personally responsible for the losses of their businesses.

Limited liability company (LLC) a hybrid business entity that exists only with the permission of the state, that is separate from its members, and that provides limited liability for its members; in a limited liability company, the members choose whether to be managed by the members or managed by a group of managers and whether to be taxed like a partnership or taxed like a corporation.

Limited liability limited partnership a limited partnership created by application to the state that grants limited liability to both the general partners and the limited partners.

Limited liability partnership (LLP) a partnership in which there are no limited partners that is created by application to the state and that grants limited liability to all partners.

Limited partner a partner in a limited partnership who does not participate in the management of the partnership and who is not liable for its losses.

Limited partnership a partnership in which at least one of the partners is a limited partner and at least one of the partners is a general partner.

Liquidation the process by which a dissolved business entity's assets are distributed.

Liquidation bankruptcy a bankruptcy in which all of the bankruptcy debtor's non-exempt debts that remain after the bankruptcy estate is exhausted are discharged.

Maker in a promise to pay instrument, the person promising to pay another.

Mandamus a judicial writ requiring a lower court or an individual, such as a public official, to perform a legal or statutory duty.

Member a person or business entity with an ownership interest in a limited liability company.

Minimum contacts these are the activities of a nonresident defendant, such as business activities, in a forum state that permit a plaintiff to assert a forum state's court's jurisdiction over that individual in a civil suit.

Misrepresentation a false or misleading statement inducing another to enter into a bargain; it can be both a defense to enforcement of a contract and give rise to a tort claim.

Moral relativism the idea that right and wrong are personalized values based on circumstances or cultural background; it does not view right and wrong as absolute values.

Mortgagee the lender in a mortgage backed financing of real estate.

Mortgagor the borrower in a mortgage backed financing of real estate.

Motion a litigant's written or oral application to the court requesting it to enter a requested ruling or order.

Negligence a tort requiring that the tortfeasor pay the damages caused by its breach of a duty owed to another.

Negotiation "a transfer of possession, whether voluntary or involuntary, of an instrument by a person other than the issuer to a person who thereby becomes its holder." UCC § 3-201(a).

Non-exempt assets assets that become part of the bankruptcy estate.

Non-exempt debt debts that can be discharged by a bankruptcy court.

Nonprofit corporation a corporation created for purposes other than to make profit.

Nonprofit unincorporated association an unincorporated entity whose purpose is something other than making a profit.

Offer a statement proposing a bargain to another to be accepted.

Officer a person vested with management responsibility by a corporation's board of directors.

Operating agreement   the document governing the management of a limited liability company.

Order instrument   a negotiable instrument payable only to the specific person or persons named by the instrument.

Order to pay   a negotiable instrument in which the drawer orders the drawee to pay the payee.

Organic statute   in administrative law this refers to the legislation creating a federal agency from which the agency's power derives. An example would be the National Labor Relations Act of 1935 which created the National Labor Relations Board to enforce the labor laws, and oversee private sector collective bargaining and unfair labor practices and union organizing.

Partially-disclosed principal   a principal whose existence, but not whose identity, is known to the third party.

Partner   a person or business entity who has an ownership interest in a partnership.

Partnership   a business entity in which two or more persons agree to run a for-profit business together as co-owners.

Partnership agreement   an agreement between a partnership's partners governing the management and organization of a partnership.

Pass through entity   a business entity that is not directly taxed as an entity but whose owners pay taxes on their individual earnings from the entity.

Payee   the person to whom payment is owed under an instrument.

Perfection   the process by which a secured party validates its security interest.

Personal defenses (Negotiable Instruments)   those defenses to which the rights of a holder in due course of an instrument are not subject.

Persuasive authority   these are sources of law, such as other court cases, law review articles, or legal treatises, which a court may consult or consider in deciding a case, however, the court will not rely on it in reaching its decision. Unlike binding authority these sources of law are merely advisory in nature to the court's decision-making process.

Preponderance of the evidence   the civil evidentiary standard and the lowest trial level burden of proof; it is evidence that tends to weigh in favor of one party over the other.

Presentment   when a holder of an instrument makes a timely demand to the drawee or maker of an instrument to pay or accept the instrument.

Presentment warranties   implied warranties made by those who transfer an instrument to the maker or drawee of an instrument.

Priority creditor   between creditors with competing interests, the creditor with the right to payment first.

Principal   someone who authorizes and allows another to act on his or her behalf.

Priority creditor   an unsecured creditor with a high priority of payment in bankruptcy.

Probate   the legal process by which the validity of a will is proven in court, usually a probate court or similar court of specialized jurisdiction, thereby allowing the distribution of property according to the directions in the will.

Procedural due process   ensures fairness in the process of a deprivation of a life, liberty or property right by the government by guaranteeing an individual the dual protections of notice and an opportunity to be heard.

Progressive discipline   an employee disciplinary structure that provides an increasing range of responses to employee misconduct based on the frequency, repetition, or severity of the employee acts or behavior; also may be referred to as corrective action procedures or performance improvement plans.

Promise to pay   a negotiable instrument in which the maker promises to pay the payee.

Promissory estoppel   the doctrine allowing enforcement of a promise made without consideration on which the promisee relied to his or her detriment.

Promissory note   a type of promise to pay negotiable instrument in which the maker promises to pay the payee a fixed sum of money on demand or by a particular date.

Proximate causation   in a negligence action, proximate cause is the requirement that the Plaintiff's injuries be a foreseeable result of Defendant's breach of duty.

Purchase-money security interest   a lender's security interest in goods bought with loan proceeds or a seller's security interest in goods sold to the debtor on credit.

Quasi in rem   a court's jurisdiction over an individual based on an interest in property located within the forum state.

Ratification (Agency)   a principal's affirmation of a contract made by an agent that lacked authority to bind the principal.

Ratification (Contracts)   the affirmation of a contract by a party to the contract that has the right to void the contract.

Rehabilitation bankruptcy   a type of bankruptcy in which a bankruptcy debtor's debts are reorganized by a payment plan and whatever non-exempt debts remain after that payment plan is completed are discharged.

Respondeat superior   a common law legal doctrine holding that master is responsible for the acts of his servant; this doctrine has subsequently been applied to the legal relationship between a principal and an agent, and in employment an employer is legally responsible for the acts of the employee.

Retainer   a client's authorization for a lawyer to act in a case; a fee paid to a lawyer to secure legal representation.

Secured creditor   a creditor that has a security interest in at least some of its debtor's property.

Secured party   a person who has a security interest in the debtor's collateral.

Secured transaction   a transaction in which a security interest is created to repay a debt or otherwise secure performance.

Security agreement   an agreement creating a security interest.

Security interest   an interest in property created to ensure payment of a debt.

Share   an ownership interest in a corporation.

Shareholder   a person or business entity with an ownership interest in a corporation.

Sole proprietorship   an unincorporated, for-profit business entity owned and managed by a single person.

Specific bequest   a gift to an individual made in a will of a specific item of property, for example, "I give and bequeath my baseball card collection to my son."

Standing   an individual's right to make a legal claim or seek enforcement of a legal claim of a duty or right.

Strict liability torts   a class of torts that imposes liability on the tortfeasor regardless of the tortfeasor's state of mind.

Substantial evidence   the legal standard of proof required in administrative trials for a party to prove its case. The standard is one of such relevant evidence that a reasonable person would accept as adequate to support a factual result; more than a mere scintilla of evidence.

Substantive due process   a requirement that legislation or administrative rules be clear and understandable to the average person and not contain any ambiguity or vagueness in their attempt to further a governmental need or objective.

Summary judgment   a court disposition on a claim that renders judgment on behalf of a party who makes a motion for relief when there is no genuine issue of material fact and the movant can be granted relief as a matter of law.

Tangible collateral   types of collateral that can be touched.

Third party   in agency law, the third party is the person or entity with whom the agent interacts with on behalf of the principal.

Time instrument   an instrument not payable until a specific time.

Tortfeasor   a person who commits a tort.

Trade acceptance   an order to pay instrument in which a seller of goods is both the payee and the drawer.

Transfer warranties   those warranties made by those who transfer an instrument to someone other than the maker or drawee of an instrument.

Trespass to chattel   an intentional, minor interference with the personal property of another.

Trespass to land   an intentional, unauthorized entry onto the land of another.

Unconscionability   a defense to the enforcement of a contract that is extremely unfair.

Undisclosed principal   a principal whose identity and existence is not known to the third party.

Unequivocal assent   the unambiguous and unqualified agreement of the offeree to the terns of the offer.

Universal defenses (Negotiable Instruments)   those defenses to which the rights of a holder in due course of an instrument are subject.

Unsecured creditor   a creditor that does not have a security interest in any of its debtor's property.

Use variance   the authorization of a zoning board of appeals for the use of land for a purpose which is prohibited by applicable zoning regulations.

Utilitarianism   a philosophical doctrine that conduct should be directed toward promoting the greatest possible good for the greatest number of people.

Variance   a municipal zoning board of appeal's exception that provides permission for property to be used in a manner not otherwise allowed by applicable zoning regulations.

Vested right or vested title   refers to an absolute ownership right in real property that is not subject to any contingencies to ownership. A person owning real estate in which another had a life estate would not have completely vested legal title until the death of the life estate owner. The term applies to any form of property ownership wherein a person has an absolute right to some present or future interest in property.

Void contract   a contract that can never be enforced.

Voidable contract   a contract that may be made void by one or more of the parties.

Voir dire   refers to either the process of an attorney's questioning of prospective jurors from a panel to see who is qualified and acceptable to serve on the jury, or to the preliminary examination to test the competence of an item of evidence or a witness.

Whistleblowing   public disclosure by an employee of a private corporation or government agency of fraud, corruption, illegal activity, or mismanagement.

Zoning   the legislative authority of a municipality, under its police power to regulate public health, safety and welfare, to divide itself geographically into specific areas (or zones) where certain land uses are either permitted or prohibited.

Index